William Wyler

William Wyler

The Life and Films of Hollywood's Most Celebrated Director

GABRIEL MILLER

UNIVERSITY PRESS OF KENTUCKY

Scholarly publisher for the Commonwealth,
serving Bellarmine University, Berea College, Centre College of Kentucky,
Eastern Kentucky University, The Filson Historical Society, Georgetown College,
Kentucky Historical Society, Kentucky State University, Morehead State University,
Murray State University, Northern Kentucky University, Transylvania University,
University of Kentucky, University of Louisville, and Western Kentucky University.
All rights reserved.

Editorial and Sales Offices: The University Press of Kentucky
663 South Limestone Street, Lexington, Kentucky 40508-4008
www.kentuckypress.com

All photos courtesy Jerry Ohlinger's Movie Material Store.

17 16 15 14 13   5 4 3 2 1

Library of Congress Cataloging-in-Publication Data

Miller, Gabriel, 1948-
  William Wyler : the life and films of Hollywood's most celebrated director /
Gabriel Miller.
     pages cm
  Includes bibliographical references and index.
  ISBN 978-0-8131-4209-8 (hardcover : alk. paper) —
  ISBN 978-0-8131-4210-4 (epub) — ISBN 978-0-8131-4211-1 (pdf)
  1. Wyler, William, 1902-1981. 2. Motion picture producers and directors—
United States—Biography. I. Title.
  PN1998.3.W95M55 2013
  791.43'0233'092—dc23
  [B]   2013010135

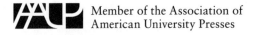
Member of the Association of
American University Presses

In memory of my father, Harold Miller,
and Kathy's mother, Patricia Fraser

Contents

Introduction

William Wyler liked to quip, "I could hardly call myself an auteur—although I'm one of the few American directors who can pronounce the word correctly." While he invariably said this in jest, the slight of being denied auteur status clearly rankled. Wyler saw his friends John Ford, Frank Capra, George Stevens, Billy Wilder, and John Huston celebrated by film scholars and historians as artists whose work exhibited distinctive styles and explored complex themes, while his was dismissed as mere craftsmanship, not worthy of extended scholarly attention.

Nonetheless, Wyler was celebrated early in his career by André Bazin, the father of *la politique des auteurs*, which defined directors as the primary auteurs of motion pictures—authors who "wrote with the camera." Believing that cinema and photography, unlike the traditional arts, are inherently realistic, Bazin maintained that film could probe for a deeper psychological complexity and that no other art form could examine life's ambiguities as effectively. He championed those directors who manipulated the medium the least, allowing all of life's mysteries and intricacies to remain intact on the screen.

In two articles published in *La Revue du Cinema* (1948), Bazin expresses admiration for Wyler's ability to extend and enhance film's predilection for realism, linking him with the Italian neorealists in his reverence for reality. According to Bazin, by utilizing depth-of-field cinematography, which brings all the planes of the image—foreground, background, and middle ground—into sharp focus and enables the director to cover a scene in a single take without resorting to editing, Wyler provides a vast array of information that allows spectators to formulate their own interpretations of what they see. Furthermore, Bazin finds the democratic equivalent of the spirit of the American spectator not only in Wyler's technique but also in the films' characters. He compares Wyler's mise-en-scène to the literary styles of André Gide and Roger Martin du Gard, which he categorizes as neutral and transparent, without any literary shadings or flourishes coming between the reader and the story.

Bazin's enthusiasm was matched in an article published the same year by Roger Leenhardt, who argues that after 1940 the tradition of classical Hollywood cinema—represented most purely by the films of John Ford—was replaced by a new tendency, heralded by Wyler, that prioritized "scene over image, decoupage over montage, story over drama, equilibrium over pace, character over symbol, modulation over effect."[1] For Leenhardt, as for Bazin, this aesthetic shift was heralded by similar stylistic changes in the novel.

When Bazin was preparing a collection of his essays for publication in book form in 1958, he revised his opinion of Wyler in a postscript, tempering his original enthusiasm because he felt that Wyler's films of the 1950s had not lived up to his earlier work. He maintained, however, that it was still possible to prefer the unique style of Wyler to the more spectacular cinema of Ford. Even in his early essays, however, Bazin may have inadvertently laid the groundwork for Wyler's future detractors. In discussing Wyler's body of work, Bazin notes that each film is different—that the form of *The Best Years of Our Lives*, for example, bears little resemblance to that of *The Letter*. Thereafter, because the auteurists felt that a director's worth was measured in consistent visual styles and personal preoccupations and themes, Wyler was dismissed because of his fondness for adapting the work of others and for tailoring his visual style to the needs of the screenplay. Unlike a John Ford or a René Clair, Wyler did not pursue a set of abiding themes that he revisited or expanded on, and this apparent lack of focus was anathema to the orthodox auteurists, who never forgave Wyler for the diversity of his films.

Andrew Sarris, the father of American auteurism, even utilized Bazin (mistakenly calling him a "French director") in his attack on Wyler by citing the title of Bazin's second article, "The Style without a Style," as a derogatory description. Writing that Wyler's career is "a cipher as far as personal direction is concerned," Sarris banished him to the purgatorial realm of "less than meets the eye" in his ranking of American directors.[2] Since Sarris's *The American Cinema* was published, others in that category—including Wyler's close friends John Huston and Billy Wilder—have seen their achievements reevaluated, while Wyler's reputation has remained in limbo. Nonetheless, writing for *Show* magazine in 1970, Sarris profiled

Wyler as his "Director of the Month," complimenting Wyler's "high polish professionalism" and referring to him as "the compleat angler of the most gripping camera angles." Sarris had praised *The Collector* when it was released in 1965, and the occasion for this laudatory piece was the release of what turned out to be Wyler's final film, *The Liberation of L. B. Jones*, which Sarris called "the most provocative brief for Black Power ever to come out of a Hollywood studio."[3]

If Sarris's negative judgments seem too extreme, Bazin's praise of Wyler's realism is also excessive. Deep focus does not really democratize the frame, nor does it extend our understanding and appreciation of the world any more than other cinematic styles do. Instead, in its own way, it too manipulates the spectator, though more subtly than montage does. Wyler's mise-en-scène is in no way neutral—he does not merely present material to the spectator to contemplate, assimilate, and then arrive at his or her own conclusion. Wyler's pictorial arrangements are often complex, but the director's purposes are always evident, and his compositions in depth clearly communicate his feelings and ideas.

One of the examples Bazin repeatedly cites in lauding Wyler's technique is the death scene of Horace Giddens in *The Little Foxes*, where the stricken man tries to climb the stairs to get his medicine while his estranged wife sits by, making no attempt to help him. Bazin considered Wyler's decision not to move the camera or cut to the dying husband stumbling up the stairs much more powerful than any technique to make the action more cinematic. Wyler does indeed keep his camera focused on Regina's face, but the viewer also sees Horace climbing the stairs in the background, although his ascent remains out of focus, which limits both the "realism" and the open-ended quality of the deep-focus technique. Wyler, in fact, had extensive conversations with Gregg Toland, his cinematographer, on how to best shoot the scene, but the truth is that his effective camera decision was already set out in Lillian Hellman's stage directions: "Regina has not moved during his climb up the stairs."

Also, as Wyler told his daughter, he had another, very practical reason for his decision:

Now there was another thing about this scene that nobody knows, aside from what we're talking about deep focus. Herbert Marshall, who played the man, has a wooden leg and cannot go up the stairs like he was supposed to. This is a kind of secret, a professional secret which I'm giving away here. If you ever see the picture again, he walks out of the scene and a double comes in the background and he starts going up the stairs, but he's so far in the background that you can't tell who he is. He starts going up the stairs and collapses in the middle. That's when she comes to him.[4]

Wyler, it seems, was trying less to penetrate the inner secrets of the real world than to provide cover for an actor with a disability. The scene, though still dramatically compelling, was more "reel" than real.

Bazin's other often-cited example is the "Chopsticks" scene from Wyler's masterpiece, *The Best Years of Our Lives*. Al Stephenson has asked Fred Derry to meet him at Butch's Bar, where he intends to tell the married Fred to break off his relationship with Al's daughter Peggy. Wyler shoots that scene in a traditional way, utilizing two-shots and shot–reverse shots to emphasize the tension between the two men. Agreeing that his relationship with Peggy might turn out badly for both of them, Fred goes to the front of the bar to call her and end it. Then Homer Parrish (whose hands were destroyed by an explosion and replaced with hooks) enters, greets Fred and Al, and moves over to the piano to play "Chopsticks" with his uncle, the bar's owner. As Homer and Butch play, Wyler shows us his three protagonists in one deep-focus shot: Homer sits in the front of the frame, happily showing off his dexterity; Fred is in the back, framed inside a phone booth as he breaks up with Peggy; and Al is in the center, feigning interest in Homer while thinking about Fred's call.

In his 1947 essay "No Magic Wand," Wyler explains his technique: "I can have action and reaction in the same shot, without having to cut back and forth from individual shots of characters. This makes for smooth continuity, an almost effortless flow of the screen, for much more interesting composition in each shot, and lets the spectator look from one to the other character at his own will, do his own cutting."[5] Of course, Wyler is being a bit disingenuous here: although we spectators do have the freedom to look at all the characters at once and take in a great deal of information, Wyler is nonetheless intervening by subtly manipulating our gaze. He does so by lighting the phone booth, which forces us to notice what Fred is doing, despite his distance from the camera, and by centering Al, which makes us aware of the intricacies of Fredric March's performance as he imperceptibly shifts his gaze during the sequence, seemingly following Homer's performance while repeatedly glancing in the direction of the phone booth. (Having the camera pick up such small but compelling performance gestures is a central element of Wyler's direction.) Meanwhile, by showing Al's concern and love for both his friends, Wyler visually establishes the brotherly connection between the men, whose military experience has tied them in ways that almost transcend the bonds of family.

Wyler's style, so admired by Bazin, emerged early. He was experimenting with it in his first sound films, *Hell's Heroes* (1930) and *A House Divided* (1931). Out of a number of notable examples in *Hell's Heroes*, one will suffice: As the three outlaws are returning to the covered wagon where the dying woman is about to give birth, Wyler positions "Wild Bill" at the center, where he is framed by the open end of the wagon's cover, with his two partners in the background. Bill is foregrounded because he will help the woman deliver her baby, while the other men form a community that will bring the baby to New Jerusalem. Wyler uses a modified deep focus here, but more important, he frames his characters in a significant compositional arrangement that minimizes cutting and maximizes his organization of characters in space.

One can see Wyler manipulating space again in *A House Divided*. In a scene that takes place shortly after mail-order bride Ruth arrives at the home of Seth Law, she prepares a meal for his grown son, Matt (Seth is out fishing and has not yet met his prospective bride). Wyler foregrounds Ruth in the frame, with Matt behind her, seated at the table; in the distance behind both of them is a window framing the sea. Ruth, a farm girl, has already admitted to Matt in the previous scene that she loves the water, and Wyler's framing indicates that Ruth's dream of living near the water will come true by marrying Matt, with whom she has already fallen in love, rather than his father. In a later scene, Seth meets Ruth for the first time and initially rejects her as a wife because she seems too frail for hard work. As she turns to leave, Wyler again frames his three characters in a long shot in which Seth is prominent in the front of the frame, Ruth stands in the rear at the door, and Matt is in the center. Symbolically, this composition anticipates the love triangle that will soon develop as Seth and Matt fight over Ruth.

When Wyler left Universal and signed with Samuel Goldwyn in 1936, he also began his association with Gregg Toland, who had worked his way up from being George Barnes's assistant and was at the time photographing most of Eddie Cantor's films and all of Anna Sten's. From 1934 to 1940, Toland was the most famous cinematographer in Hollywood, and his name is often linked with Wyler as well as Orson Welles. He certainly collaborated with Wyler and helped him develop his signature style. Wyler told Curtis Hanson, "He [Toland] and I would discuss a picture from beginning to end."[6]

Indeed, in their first film together, *These Three* (1936), deep focus is used minimally, but considerable attention is paid to the arrangement of characters in space, yielding suggestive compositions that direct the viewer's attention to multiple levels of information at once and invite complex assessments of what is happening. In one scene, Joe arrives at Karen and Martha's home/school to see his fiancée, Karen, but finds only Martha there. After they talk for a while, Joe falls asleep on the couch, and Martha, who also loves Joe, remains in the room and watches him. Wyler foregrounds Joe in the frame, while Martha sits in a chair near the fireplace in the background. The fire, which had been burning brightly when the scene began, has now almost gone out. Martha, at this point, realizes that she has lost Joe to her best friend.

One of Wyler's most significant works for Goldwyn, *Dodsworth* (1936), was made without Toland—Rudolph Maté was the cinematographer—but it also features some masterful staging. As he did in *These Three*, Wyler carefully positions the actors in space to indicate the complexity of their emotional and psychological relationships. The staging and composition in depth also open up the play's closed world cinematically, avoiding the look of confinement while at the same time retaining a respect for the text. In the scene where Fran and Sam argue, which culminates in Sam's decision to return to America alone, Wyler alternates between the estranged couple, each occupying the background of the frame in turn, reflecting the undercurrents of their conflict. He further accentuates the scene's dramatic impact by manipulating the play of shadow and light, again minimizing cutting. As in the examples lauded by Bazin, Wyler's mise-en-scène here is part social realism and part artistic calculation.

Stylistically, Wyler's breakthrough film is the undervalued *Dead End*

(1937), for which he again teamed up with Toland. Even though the film's action is limited to one set, Wyler manages to generate a great deal of movement through editing, but he also sets up an interaction between foreground and background that gives the illusion of various planes of action taking place simultaneously. With Toland's help, he is able to deepen the space of the set visually, thus breaking the confines of its theatrical origin. Wyler introduces this effect early on, as Baby Face Martin, a notorious gangster who has returned to his old neighborhood, talks with Dave, a childhood friend. Wyler foregrounds the two men, who are now antagonists, while also depicting life on the streets behind them—in the deep background of the frame, the viewer can even see a woman beating a rug on her fire escape. The camera creates a similar effect later when Wyler foregrounds the Dead End Kids by the dock, where they are framed by wood scaffolding, while visible in the distance is a new high-rise apartment building with a doorman and a wealthy-looking resident sitting on a bench. The layered composition, which brings the two classes together in the frame while separating them in space, offers the impression of a vibrant urban landscape.

In his study of the classic Hollywood film, David Bordwell highlights the scene in which Baby Face and his partner plot to kidnap the son of a wealthy tenant in the nearby high-rise. As the two gangsters sit talking in a restaurant near the window, Wyler shows a mother wheeling a baby carriage outside, framed by the window but somewhat out of focus. Bordwell notes that even though she is not the subject of the conversation, "the fact that she occupies frame center . . . gives her symbolic significance."[7] Later, when the kidnapping plan becomes problematic because of Baby Face's attempt to kill Dave, Wyler shows the two gangsters foregrounded by the pier but expressionistically barred by its shadows; once again, a woman wheels a baby carriage in the background—this time in focus.

Several interior scenes in *Wuthering Heights* (1939) display Wyler's mastery of composing in depth. As Heathcliff, returned from his travels, arrives to confront Cathy and her new husband in their elegant home, Wyler films his progress from the front door into the living area, where the Lintons are seated. He repeats this movement through space when Heathcliff leaves, emphasizing the stylish living space of the room while also highlighting the "space" that now separates Heathcliff from Cathy. Wyler's camera work manages to seem extravagant and controlled at the same time. When Heathcliff later attends a dance at the Lintons' home, Wyler begins the sequence by double-framing the initial view of the dance, which is seen through the doorway and then reflected in a mirror, thus constricting the space and suggesting that Cathy's choice of money and social status has compromised her. As he did in *Jezebel* the year before, Wyler utilizes the room's ornate columns to confine the guests, even as they seem to glide through space; he also cuts to a shot from behind the orchestra, taking in the whole room, the elaborate architecture, and the elegantly dressed partygoers.

A master at exploring repressed emotions, Wyler loved to employ the settings of spacious older homes, where he could exploit the linear effects of their staircases, columns, arches, and doorways to frame his shots. These formal houses, with their visually spacious but dramatically confined interiors, were perfect stages for Wyler to visualize human confrontation. They are used to impressive effect in *These Three, Jezebel, Wuthering Heights, The Little Foxes, The Heiress, Carrie, The Big Country, Ben-Hur,* and *The Collector.* Of all the structural features of these houses, Wyler was most fond of staircases, using them as loci for the emotional struggles that dominate his narratives. Although they rarely lead anywhere in particular, staircases often figure in his compositions as vertical planes on which characters can be arranged in commanding or authoritative positions—or in subordinate ones, with one character subjected to another's will.

In *The Little Foxes*, Horace waits for his wife at the top of the stairs. When she arrives, Wyler's camera seems to place Horace in a position of authority as he chastises Regina about her underhanded business dealings. But Regina climbs the stairs during the scene and confronts her husband at the top, seizing the power and demeaning him in the process. Later, when Horace is upstairs dying, Regina's brothers gather at the foot of the stairs to await news of his condition. Regina descends the staircase and speaks to them from one of the intermediate steps, demonstrating her power over them in the struggle for control of the family business. After Horace's death, Regina attempts to blackmail her brothers with her knowledge of their theft of her husband's bonds. During this conversation, Wyler shows Regina's daughter Alexandra, in deep focus, slowly descending the stairs as her mother did earlier. She overhears what Regina is saying, and the venality of her family becomes clear to her. At the end of the film, when

Alexandra breaks with her mother, Regina's position on the stairs seems diminished as Wyler magnifies her daughter's stinging rejection. Once Alexandra has gone, Regina mounts the stairs alone, and ironically, her ascent is now more that of a victim than a victor.

Wyler echoes this less than triumphant retreat upstairs in *The Heiress*. In the opening sequence, Catherine Sloper is seen descending the staircase, where she stops to greet the maid who is carrying the party dress Catherine will later be wearing when she meets Morris Townsend. Wyler catches her hopeful reflection as she pauses in front of a mirror. But in the film's final movement, after Catherine has exacted her revenge on Morris, she is seen climbing the stairs with a hardened expression—satisfied by her actions, but now doomed in Wyler's framing to life as a prisoner in her own house.

While Bazin's judgment that Wyler's deep focus "aims at perfect neutrality" is not accurate—in fact, it seems clear that the director deliberately organizes his frames to evoke specific responses—both Wyler's style and his attention to detail do support Bazin's assertion that Wyler is a realist. Among the numerous examples of his dedication to verisimilitude, a few stand out: the bill for the dresses and gowns worn in *Jezebel* came to $30,000, the furniture and props for the dinner scene were all period antiques, and the bar was a copy of the famous St. Louis Bar in New Orleans; for *The Little Foxes*, Wyler commissioned a research book with sections on cotton, agriculture, popular books of the time (1902), music, hotel prices, historical background, and so on; the arena for the chariot race in *Ben-Hur* covered more than eighteen acres, with 1,500-foot straightaways alongside a central *spina*, flanked by four statues standing 30 feet high; and for *The Heiress*, costume designer Edith Head went to a New York fashion institute to study women's fashion of the nineteenth century to ensure that every detail would be perfect. For *The Best Years of Our Lives*, as Wyler reported in a magazine piece: "We sent Myrna Loy and Teresa Wright, and young Cathy O'Donnell out to stores in company with our costume designer, Irene Sharaff, to buy the kind of clothes they would buy and wear in the lives they live on the screen. Not only that, but we asked them to wear them for a few weeks so that the clothes wouldn't look too new." In the same essay, he questions why rooms in Hollywood films "always seem about three times as big as they should be." He goes on: "To me a man should seem at home in his home. He should move with ease in a background which he is familiar. He should know where chairs are without looking for them. . . . This union of oneness with man and his background are seldom found on the screen. A home isn't a home unless people act at home. Certainly it isn't a home if it seems like a stage."[8]

Realism in film, however, goes only so far, and Wyler was too much of a showman not to understand that his plots needed heavy doses of melodrama if he was to entertain, move, and even instruct his audiences. He preferred properties that had been tested and proved successful in other forms, in part because they guaranteed a built-in audience, and in part because they delivered heavy doses of melodrama. All his films for Goldwyn, except *The Westerner*, were based on successful or famous literary properties. Of his three prewar loan-out films, *Jezebel* and *The Letter* were based on plays, while *Mrs. Miniver* grew out of a best-selling book. Those three works are primarily melodramatic, and *The Letter*, like *Wuthering Heights*, veers closer to expressionism than realism.

In this regard, it is important to note that Wyler was vitally interested in the mechanics and structure of storytelling; even though he never received screenplay credit on his films, he invariably made important contributions to the scripts. And, believing that writing and directing were interconnected, he tried to ensure that writers were always on the set. For his first sound film, *Hell's Heroes*, he conceived an ending so brutal that the producer insisted it be changed. On his next project, *A House Divided* (originally conceived as a silent film), he added almost a hundred scenes to the writer's revised script. He worked intimately with Lillian Hellman on the scripts she wrote for him (*These Three*, *Dead End*, and *The Little Foxes*), and he cowrote the minister's closing sermon for *Mrs. Miniver*, which was reprinted in numerous magazines.

One of the many projects Wyler worked on but was forced to abandon was *How Green Was My Valley*. It was eventually made into an Oscar-winning film by John Ford, but screenwriter Philip Dunne credits Wyler with coming up with the narrative device (limiting the story to Huw's childhood) that transformed the script. Also, after screenwriter Robert Sherwood decided to leave the closing scene of *The Best Years of Our Lives* to the director's imagination, it was Wyler who invented the aircraft graveyard scene that became one of the film's most affecting moments. Correspondence between Wyler and Ruth and Augustus Goetz shows that the director made important suggestions with regard to the script of *Carrie*. Wyler also hired Jessamyn West to adapt her story collection, *The Friendly Persuasion*, for the screen and then installed his brother Robert to help her; he still managed to make some important changes of his own to their script. He did the same on *The Collector*.

Intimately connected to Wyler's preoccupation with realism and story construction was his commitment to bringing out the very best in his actors—sometimes to the point of alienating them completely. His penchant for retakes made him the scourge of some actors, who ridiculed him as "ninety-take Wyler" or "forty-take Wyler" or "once more Wyler." His insistence on eliciting the best performance sometimes meant that he had an actor repeat the same gesture or hand motion until he felt it effectively revealed the character. For the famous scene in *Jezebel* when Julie Marsden arrives late to her own engagement party, Wyler instructed Bette Davis to hike up the train of her riding dress with her riding crop and hook it over her shoulder; he then exasperated Davis by making her go through the motion thirty-three times. As Davis commented years later, "No detail, however minor, escaped him." Although she claimed that "Wyler could make your life hell," she recognized that she had done her best work with him. And when she won her second Oscar for *Jezebel*, Davis acknowledged, "He made my performance. . . . It was all Willy."[9]

In an antiauteurist study entitled *The Genius of the System*, Thomas Schatz argues that the structure of the studio system made it impossible to isolate any individual as the singular creative force behind a film. Nevertheless, in his section on *Jezebel*, he singles out Wyler's direction for "bringing Julie Marston [sic] to life, shaping the viewer's conception of both character and story." He also points out that Wyler forced both Warner and Hal Wallis to recognize "how important Wyler's skills as a director were to the picture and Davis's performance." Schatz elaborates: "Through the calculated use of point-of-view shots, reaction shots, glance object cutting, and shot/reverse shot exchanges, Wyler orchestrated the viewer's identification with and sympathy for Julie, which were so essential if the story was to 'play.'"[10]

Wyler once remarked, "I want actors who can act. I can only direct actors—I can't teach them how to act." He recognized that "the director's most important function centers on the performance of the actors," and he considered getting the perfect shot secondary to capturing the best performance.[11] His obsession with detail—the perfect gesture, the subtle exchange—added depth, subtlety, and complexity to his already charged compositions. No director in history has guided actors to more Academy Award nominations (thirty-five) or more Academy Award–winning performances (thirteen). If Wyler himself could not always articulate what he wanted from an actor, Charles Laughton's definition of great acting would surely pass his test: "Great acting is like painting. In the great masters of fine art one can see and recognize the small gesture of a finger, the turn of a head, the vitriolic stare, the glazed eye, the pompous mouth, the back bending under a fearful load. In every swerve and stroke of a painter's brush, there is an abundance of life. . . . Not imitation—that is merely caricature—and any fool can be a mimic! But creation is a secret. The better—the truer—the creation, the more it will resemble a great painter's immortal work."[12]

Wyler was indeed committed to realism in décor, in performance, and in his preference for deep-focus shots. But David Thomson's insistence that he was merely "a reliable master of big projects," one who "never felt the need to ponder [his scripts] too deeply,"[13] is surely as overstated as Sarris's dismissal or Bazin's enthusiasm. Wyler's films, despite their diverse subject matter and multiple genres, display a remarkable thematic consistency. Much of his work mounts a quarrel with and an investigation of his adopted country—a personal inquiry that is reflected in the projects he chose to produce and direct and in the writers he worked with, many of whom were important literary figures of the day: Lillian Hellman, Sidney Kingsley, Sidney Howard, Elmer Rice, Robert Sherwood, Jessamyn West, Gore Vidal, Christopher Fry, and Jesse Hill Ford.

Wyler himself authored several published essays in which he articulated the responsibilities of the director-artist. In "Escape to Reality" he wrote: "I wondered why so few films and so few plays honestly reflect the conflicts of our times. Every age, every generation, every decade, every year, has some battle of mind, of emotion—some social cause that favors the time. Why does the screen seldom find these conflicts?"[14] Three years later, when accepting the One World Award for Motion Pictures, he defined what he meant by *morality*: "I mean the morality of civilized men, which is the morality of humanism, and the acceptance of the social morality it imposes. The dignity of men everywhere should be our great epic theme—the struggle of men to build their societies and to create the wonders of art, of ethics and of science."[15]

What these remarks indicate—and what is rarely discussed in connection with Wyler—is that his films clearly reflect a strong social and political vision. Sarris's judgment that Wyler's career "is inflating without expanding" is completely untrue.[16] From the early 1930s, Wyler was either planning or directing films that tackled issues such as capitalism, class structure, war and pacifism, and repressive politics, notably the House Un-American Activities Committee (HUAC). His choice of projects, though superficially diverse, reflects his abiding interest in important social issues and his quarrels with America.

Arguing Wyler's status as an auteur is largely irrelevant at this point in the evolution of film history, however. Any examination of production files from the studio era makes it plain that there was a varied division of labor and that every film was the product of many individual contributions. Scripts went through countless revisions and included scenes and dialogue by writers who were not acknowledged in the final credits. There were also some intense struggles between powerful producers and directors. While Schatz's claim that the auteur theory is "adolescent romanticism" may be a bit extreme, the notion of evaluating a classic Hollywood film solely as the product of an individual creative personality seems spurious. Of course, some powerful directors did manage to leave their mark on many of the films they worked on—Schatz cites John Ford, Howard Hawks, Frank Capra, and Alfred Hitchcock as directors "who had an unusual degree of authority and a certain style."[17] And, as I have argued here, Wyler, too, possessed a "certain style." He practically introduced depth of focus into the vocabulary of American cinema, and he, too, held an "unusual degree of authority," producing twelve of his films and wielding considerable control over many others.

Wyler grew up in the business by working with two powerful producers—his cousin Carl Laemmle, who founded Universal Pictures, and Samuel Goldwyn. He learned something about power and artistic control on one of his earliest jobs, as an assistant on *The Hunchback of Notre Dame* (1923). Laemmle's production chief was Irving Thalberg, who treated the picture like a prestige project, even constructing a replica of Notre Dame Cathedral on the studio's back lot. Then, dissatisfied with the look of the film, Thalberg insisted on retakes with larger crowd scenes, and he made other budgetary decisions without consulting either Laemmle or the New York office. The resulting rift with the studio head was an object lesson to Thalberg: he could not change the culture at Universal, and he left the studio shortly thereafter. Wyler would have his own troubles with Laemmle and his son, beginning with the studio's first sound film, *Hell's Heroes*, which he directed on location (see chapter 1). In 1932, Wyler and his friend John Huston looked into developing their own projects, which they pitched to the studio. None of them ever got to the production stage.

Wyler's most important association was with Samuel Goldwyn, for whom he worked after leaving Universal. Their contentious relationship began in 1936 and continued until after the war, culminating in Goldwyn's only Academy Award–winning film, *The Best Years of Our Lives*. Wyler chafed under the powerful producer's control, but he later admitted in an interview with his daughter, "He was the most important producer in my career because we made a series of pictures that were both critically and financially successful." He added, "We had fights, but the fights were not over money. They were over . . . matters of taste."[18] They also reflected the inevitable clashes between two determined individuals who were each striving for a kind of perfection—Goldwyn pursued quality properties, and most of the films Wyler made for him were based on successful plays, but Wyler's own meticulousness often got in the way of Goldwyn's need to maintain something resembling a bottom line.

Still, the two had enormous respect for each other, and as Scott Berg observed, they had other things in common: "A rapport developed between the two men, partly because of their near-equal inability to express themselves. Deeper than that, after years of working almost exclusively with Gentile directors, Goldwyn had found a fellow European Jew with similar artistic aspirations."[19] If Goldwyn provided Wyler with the materials that released his genius, the director certainly gave Samuel Goldwyn Productions a measure of cachet it had not enjoyed before. Five of the films Wyler directed for Goldwyn were nominated for Best Picture Oscars. Berg wrote that Wyler's first film for Goldwyn, *These Three*, "gathered notices the likes of which Goldwyn had not received before. In language more thoughtful than the usual Hollywood superlatives, they treated the film with artistic respect, especially the demanding English critics."[20]

In fact, the legendary "Goldwyn touch" should more properly be called the "Wyler touch." All of Goldwyn's best films were directed by Wyler, and after his departure in 1946, most of the producer's subsequent films were undistinguished. As Danny Mandell, who edited a number of Wyler's films and countless others for Goldwyn, remarked, "I never knew what the Goldwyn touch was. I think it was something a Goldwyn publicist made up." Wyler himself was more direct: "I don't recall his contributing anything other than buying good material and talent. It was all an attempt to make a name for himself as an artist. But as far as being creative, he was a zero."[21] Wyler was surely being overly harsh, for he did admire Goldwyn's respect for talent and his desire to hire the best people, especially writers. But Wyler was protective of his legacy to the end. In 1980, the year before he died, he exclaimed to Berg, "Tell me, which pictures have the 'Goldwyn touch' that I didn't direct?"[22]

Nearly all of Wyler's prewar films for Goldwyn engage with social issues. His first film for Goldwyn, *These Three* (1936), examines the destructive force of lies and evil intent. Many American films released that year were still dealing with the Depression, even though the economy was finally on the upswing. But Wyler's film—unsurprisingly, considering his European roots—focuses instead on the impending storm abroad. *Dead End* (1937) is based on an agitprop play of the same name by Sidney Kingsley. Here, Wyler exposes the debilitating effects of slum life as a breeding ground for gangs, gangsters, the breakup of families, and prostitution. As a Depression film, it also deals with unemployment, the violence visited on strikers demanding better wages, and the damaging divide between the wealthy and the poor. *The Little Foxes* (1941), his second Lillian Hellman adaptation in five years, further demonstrates how rampant capitalism and industrialism can destroy a family, ravage a community, and rape the land.

Wyler, like many of his colleagues and friends in the film industry, was fully committed to the American war effort, both prior to U.S. engagement and during combat. He directed one of the most acclaimed documentaries of the war, *Memphis Belle* (1944), which is the only film ever reviewed on the front page of the *New York Times*. Some years after the war, in a letter to Y. Frank Freeman, production chief at Paramount, he explained his personal engagement: "As a foreign-born American I was perhaps more alarmed from the beginning by the threat of Nazism than the average American."[23]

Born into a Jewish family in Mulhouse, France, Wyler was twelve years old when World War I began. His birthplace was fought over by the French and German armies, and Wyler told his biographer about spending the night in the cellar and emerging in the morning to learn whether he was French or German.[24] The Germans occupied the town until the end of the war, when it was taken over by the French. Interestingly, Mulhouse was also the birthplace of Alfred Dreyfus, the Jewish military officer accused of treason for being pro-German. Members of the Dreyfus family were still living in Mulhouse when Wyler was a boy, and the lessons of the "Dreyfus affair," which consumed France for over a decade and served as an index of French anti-Semitism, were not lost on him. In fact, Wyler's files indicate that he actively tried to rescue relatives in Europe before and during the Second World War and succeeded in saving a member of the Dreyfus family.

Before America's entry into World War II, Wyler accepted an assignment at MGM to make *Mrs. Miniver* (1942), which he always referred to, proudly, as a propaganda film. He started work on the film when the United States was still technically neutral, thus making the story's interventionist bent potentially controversial; then he upped the ante by significantly altering a scene in which Mrs. Miniver encounters a downed Nazi pilot on her property. In a late script version, the pilot is presented sympathetically, as a young man who reminds Mrs. Miniver of her son, who recently joined the British Air Force; she cleans his wounds and offers him tea. But Wyler scrapped all this sentimental harmony and turned the pilot, in his words, into a "typical little Nazi son-of-a-bitch" who threatens Mrs. Miniver and predicts, "We will come. We will bomb your cities, like Barcelona, Warschau, Navik, Rotterdam. Rotterdam we destroy in two hours." Louis B. Mayer, fearful of offending his foreign audiences, wanted the scene to remain as written, but Wyler held his ground. Then, when Pearl Harbor was bombed, Mayer relented, and Wyler's version prevailed. He further sharpened the film's message by coauthoring a new speech to be given by the vicar in the partially bombed-out church, calling the fight against the Nazis "the people's war." By this time, the vicar was addressing American audiences as well, and the speech was so effective that it was printed in many publications, including *Time* and *Look*.

As early as 1941, Wyler had tried to join the war effort personally, volunteering for the Army Signal Corps, but he was turned down. When he finally received his commission as a major in the Army Air Force in 1942, his orders were to produce films about the Eighth Air Force, designed to boost morale. *Memphis Belle* (1944) deals with the crew of a Flying Fortress from the Eighth Air Force on its last mission, and *Thunderbolt* (1945) chronicles how the face of Italy was changed from the air. In an essay titled "Flying over Germany," Wyler wrote about the spirit of community aboard a plane, which became a living testimonial to his notion of humanism: "You're inclined to worship the skipper once he's brought you back safely and look on all other men on board as brothers. They depend on each other. They save each other's lives every day."[25]

The chasm between that ideal and the reality of the postwar experience became one of the central themes of Wyler's masterpiece, *The Best Years of Our Lives* (1946). That film reflects Wyler's own feelings as a war veteran and, as such, is his most personal film. The narrative follows three returning servicemen who encounter problems while trying to reintegrate themselves into society, and it explores some of the same issues of the postwar culture that were laid bare in Arthur Miller's *All My Sons*, which opened on Broadway a year later. When Wyler's character Al Stephenson remarks, "Last year it was kill Japs, and this year it's make money," he is sounding the disillusionment of countless citizen-soldiers. The film raises other vital issues as well: unemployment, strikes, and volatile labor conditions; the specter of another war—when "none of us will have to worry because we'll be blown to bits the first day"—versus American isolationism; and the ongoing trend of small businesses being taken over by conglomerates and chains.

Best Years won Wyler his second Oscar and marked the end of his association with Goldwyn. In July 1945, he entered into an ambitious venture with Frank Capra and Samuel Briskin to found Liberty Films, an independent film company designed to "allow each individual complete freedom to pursue his own creative bent and retain his artistic integrity." This enterprise—which was soon joined by George Stevens—grew out of these directors' war experiences, which changed the way they thought about film and its relevance to society. In his essay on Wyler, Bazin quotes the director's comment on *Best Years*: "Without this experience, I could not have made my movie the way I did. We had learned to better comprehend the world

. . . I know that George Stevens isn't the same since he saw the bodies at Dachau. We were forced to see that Hollywood hardly reflected the world or the time we lived in."[26]

Liberty Films released only one film, Capra's *It's a Wonderful Life* (1946), before cash-flow problems forced a sale to Paramount, which signed Wyler to a five-picture deal and guaranteed him artistic independence. Although he soon learned that the studio would insist on project and budget approval, thus compromising his independence, Wyler's choice of projects reflected his engagement with postwar issues. Like the post-Dachau films of Stevens, Wyler's postwar films projected a much darker vision than his prewar work.

To be sure, Wyler's work throughout his career invariably tilted toward the somber and grim aspects of life. His first two sound films, *Hell's Heroes* (1930) and *A House Divided* (1931), reflect a bleak worldview veering toward despair. The earlier film was the third version of Peter B. Kyne's popular western retelling of the Gospel according to Matthew, *The Three Godfathers* (1913). Unlike those other cinematic adaptations, Wyler's version, which Kyne detested, pointedly lacks any mitigating layer of sentimental Christian allegory. His protagonist, though ultimately redeemed by sacrificing his own life while delivering an orphaned infant to safety, is portrayed as a hard, selfish man who, along with his fellow bandits, traverses a desert wasteland. In some early examples of deep focus, Wyler emphasizes the empty, hostile quality of the terrain, even instructing his cameraman to make the landscape "look horrible."

Like *Hell's Heroes*, his next project opens and closes with images of death. Although its locale is a fishing village, the action of *A House Divided* takes place primarily inside the home of Seth Law, whose destructive Oedipal relationship with his son is exacerbated when the father's young mail-order bride falls in love with the son instead. Utilizing the indoor scenes that would become a hallmark of his later work, Wyler emphasizes the tyranny of confined space, vertical lines, and staircases as he drags—literally, in Seth's case—his conflicted characters through an emotional catharsis. The final scene, uniting the young lovers, echoes the safe deliverance of the baby at the conclusion of the earlier film, but both "happy endings" come at the expense of the death of the "fathers," thus capping off the depiction of a world so bleak and closed off that the audience feels no real emotional release.

Wyler's films for Goldwyn often reflect the split between the producer's penchant for happy endings and the director's desire for resolutions that include at least some ambiguity. In *Dodsworth* (1936), the final image of Fran screaming above the din of the crowd, "He's going ashore! He's going ashore!" after her husband decides to leave her is one of the most devastating moments in all of Wyler's work. By almost losing sight of the abandoned woman among the passengers milling about on the ocean liner's deck, the director visually seals her desolation. The Sidney Howard play on which the film is based ends on that note, but the film ends with Sam Dodsworth's return to Edith Cortwright—a contrived depiction of happiness that feels intrusive after the dramatic power of the earlier image.

Wyler provides a variation on that image of desperation in *Come and Get It*, released the same year as *Dodsworth*. This film, which Wyler took over from Howard Hawks at Goldwyn's insistence, ends with Lotta Bostrom leaving Barney Glasgow to run off with the man she loves, his son Richard. Like Fran Dodsworth, Barney has failed to recognize that it is too late to save this discordant relationship—in his case, because he is old and cannot give the younger woman what she wants. Wyler ends the film with Barney calling his guests to dinner by grimly ringing the same triangle he once used as a young lumberjack. Barney's face is framed in the triangle, clearly indicating that he is now trapped by the acknowledgment that his youth is over and his earlier decision to marry for money rather than love has blighted his life.

A similar visual strategy is employed in *The Little Foxes* (1941), Wyler's film version of Lillian Hellman's play. As she had in her first collaboration with Wyler—on *These Three*, based on her first hit play *The Children's Hour*—the playwright suggested substantive revisions to her work. Her major change was to add a love interest for Regina Giddens's daughter Alexandra (Zan), in order to enlarge and humanize the character. Whereas Zan's forceful repudiation of her mother's values concludes the play, Hellman's screenplay ends with the actual departure of the daughter and her lover as they run off together, presented from Regina's point of view. Wyler cuts to a final shot of Regina's face, which is framed by the bars of the window. As she watches the young couple leave, her face becomes engulfed in darkness, a final judgment on the life she has led.

The corrupting effects of money, explored in the turn-of-the-century setting of *Little Foxes*, was a theme Wyler returned to in the postwar *Best*

Years of Our Lives, with its critical reflections on banking, the rise of chain stores, and hometown businessmen's failure to accommodate returning soldiers. His first film for Paramount, *The Heiress* (1949), though set in 1850s New York, picks up on this theme. Once again choosing to adapt a successful play—this one based on Henry James's *Washington Square*—Wyler delivers a claustrophobic film whose action delves into the dark forces of money and revenge. Catherine Sloper, the heiress of the title, is a shy, plain woman who will be worth "thirty thousand a year" upon the death of her father, a prominent doctor. That money comes between Catherine and her father when she falls in love with a fortune hunter, Morris Townsend. Catherine eventually learns that Morris's affections are indeed motivated by greed and that her father has no more feeling for her than her mercenary suitor does. All the relationships in the film are poisoned and then destroyed by money.

Carrie (1952) was a logical successor to *The Heiress* because its central character, Carrie Meeber, is, like Morris Townsend, motivated by a powerful desire for the security and pleasure that money can buy. Carrie's quest for these advantages no doubt interested Wyler because it allowed him to focus his artistry on social issues prevalent in American society. Her struggle for upward mobility is paralleled by the story of George Hurstwood, who gives up a successful career, as well as a fine home and family, to marry Carrie. His fall from grace seems to mock the romantic aspirations of characters like Catherine Sloper and Barney Glasgow, for in the Darwinian America of this film, love is a mere sideshow.

Carrie's script contains a number of scenes that powerfully portray the underside of the American dream, but some of them did not make the final cut because the studio deleted them while Wyler was in Italy making *Roman Holiday.* (One scene, which takes place in a homeless shelter, was restored in the DVD version released in 2005.) Both *The Heiress* and *Carrie* end with a death image: the final shot of Catherine Sloper is of a woman who has chosen death in life, while Wyler ends the later film with Hurstwood's fall rather than Carrie's rise. The released film merely shows Hurstwood manipulating the burners of the stove in Carrie's dressing room, a foreshadowing of his suicide that was more directly represented in Wyler's version. *Carrie*, in the director's words, "showed America in an unflattering light."[27] It was too uncompromising for its time.

The abusive actions of the House Un-American Activities Committee affected Wyler's personal life as well as his professional one. When that committee began issuing subpoenas in 1947, he joined John Huston and Philip Dunne in founding the Committee for the First Amendment (CFA), whose stated aim was to defend individual constitutional rights and decry any attempt "to throttle freedom of expression." The CFA chartered a plane that flew many high-profile stars to the hearings as a show of support, but the hostile behavior of the group known as the Hollywood Ten divided the CFA, and some members drifted away. Others were pressured by the studios and their agents to renounce their support of the Hollywood Ten. Even Wyler was forced to resign from the group, which was in tatters, and the CFA soon disbanded.

Two of Wyler's projects in the wake of the HUAC hearings reflect his attitude toward the committee's actions. *Detective Story* (1951), his second partnering with playwright Sidney Kingsley (the first was *Dead End* in 1937), concerns a troubled protagonist—a police officer with intolerant views and a tendency to bend the law to enforce his own judgments. Writing about the play years later, Kingsley described this character's motives as follows: "He wants to achieve efficiency by taking the law into his own hands by making people abide by the right as he sees it."[28] The parallel to the HUAC and the imposition of its will on artists and intellectuals was not lost on Wyler, who completed the film in record time.

Wyler left for Italy to direct *Roman Holiday* in large part to escape the poisonous political atmosphere, though it hounded him even there. That film, a comedy made on location, is open and vibrant—a far cry from the cramped and conflicted *Detective Story*. Yet even that project, which hardly seems political at all, was tinged by the blacklist, for the original story was penned by Dalton Trumbo, one of the Hollywood Ten. (Trumbo's name did not appear on the film when it was released; Ian McLellan Hunter fronted for him and received an Oscar.)[29]

Wyler's last film for Paramount reflects the somber and sour mood that overwhelmed him when he returned to America. He asked the studio to buy the rights to Joseph Hayes's best-selling book *The Desperate Hours* (which was also dramatized for the stage). Like *Detective Story*, it is an indoor film that tells the story of three escaped convicts who terrorize a suburban family, holding them hostage inside their own home. Reflecting the anxiety and paranoia of 1950s America—which Wyler feared was threatening the traditions of individual liberty—*The Desperate Hours* became a parable, warning against the use of force as a mechanism for social control.

Wyler's preoccupation with the issues raised by the war and the HUAC era continued after he left Paramount, resulting in a series of films questioning the limits of pacifism and individual conscience. Between 1956 and 1959, he made *Friendly Persuasion*, *The Big Country*, and *Ben-Hur*, each of which deals with these questions in different ways.

What intrigued Wyler about Jessamyn West's series of interrelated stories about a Quaker farm family in mid-nineteenth-century Indiana was the quandary of a committed pacifist when personally confronted with the prospect of violence. When he first met with West, who would coauthor the screenplay for *Friendly Persuasion*, Wyler told her that he was no Quaker—his experiences in the war had convinced him that evil had to be resisted with violence. Wyler wanted to confront this issue more forcefully than West had done in her book, but his film version ultimately suffers from a failure of nerve. Jess, the father, is shown to be a man of principle; in Wyler's words, "He was honest about his doubts, he was the reasoning man. He was the best Quaker of all."[30] Jess is certainly the most sympathetic character in the film, but the scene in which he is tempted to resort to violence but resists lacks any real drama or conviction, and Wyler never follows up to show how the battle experience affects Jess's son. Unlike *Mrs. Miniver*, *Friendly Persuasion* ends with an almost comical return to normalcy—never having explored the war's impact on the Quaker family or the community it represents. Despite the darker and more dramatic ambitions of Wyler's final shooting script, the released film dodges the questions Wyler wanted to raise.

In *The Big Country*, Wyler utilizes the western genre to tell the story of an eastern hero who comes out west to marry the woman he loves. A peaceful man in a violent country, he refuses to be lured into the feud that consumes his fiancée's father or to be goaded into fistfights by the local bullies. Wyler thus tries to invert the classic western formula by substituting a pacifist hero, a man who does not carry a gun and refuses to use one, even when pushed into a duel with the son of the enemy. Nonetheless, the film concludes with a violent confrontation between the two feuding landowners, which Wyler films partially in a heroic style in an apparent effort to compensate for the anticlimax of the younger men's indecisive meeting. By trying to have it both ways, he hopelessly compromises the film's message.

Both these "pacifist" films seem to confirm that Wyler himself was not a pacifist. Two world wars had taught him that human nature is dark, flawed, and at times inexplicably evil, and there is no way to deal with it other than through violent confrontation. In both films, Wyler indeed demonstrates that he is "no Quaker."

He explores this issue most effectively in *Ben-Hur*, a film about political tyranny, betrayal, and, once again, the limits of pacifism. Judah Ben-Hur, a prince of Judea, is opposed to the tyranny of the Roman occupation but also preaches nonviolence in an effort to prevent armed conflict. He turns violent, however, when his childhood friend Messala betrays him, arrests his family, and condemns him to the life of a galley slave. Ben-Hur shows strength of character by saving the commander of his ship during a battle, but his hatred of Messala indirectly leads to his enemy's death during the famous chariot race scene. The story's pacifist message is made plain at the end, when Judah hears an account of Christ's Sermon on the Mount from his beloved, Esther. The film ends with him climbing the staircase of the family home to greet his mother and sister, who have been cured of their leprosy as Christ died on the cross. This conclusion raises some questions, however, for Wyler was not a religious man, and the sections of the film devoted to Christian themes are far less compelling than the relationships between the central characters. The Christ story is included as a concession to the source novel, and Wyler's resorting to it as a kind of deus ex machina reveals his frustration with the pacifist theme.

While the protagonists of all three films are clearly men of principle and sympathetic characters, they are also flawed messengers in worlds that are based on violence, dissension, and hatred. Perhaps because of his experiences with the HUAC, Wyler saw himself in those men—well-intentioned, committed, and humanistic, but still susceptible to compromise.

Ben-Hur also deals with the subject of betrayal. When Messala asks Judah to give him the names of rebels and troublemakers, Judah retorts, "Would I retain your friendship if I became an informer?" Messala replies, "To tell me the names of criminals is hardly informing." Judah defends his refusal to name names by stating that these individuals are not criminals but "patriots." Clearly, the unsettling experience of the HUAC era was still on Wyler's mind when he made this epic film, which he followed with a remake of *The Children's Hour*, another parable about the HUAC. Politics and principles remained at the center of his films of this period, and in giving Judah those lines, Wyler was still defending his persecuted colleagues.

Wyler made four more films before retiring in 1970. The two most interesting are *The Collector* (1965) and *The Liberation of L. B. Jones* (1970), both of which reflect his increasingly dark view of human possibility and, despite the earlier film's English setting, the blighted American social landscape. *The Collector*, surely Wyler's most pessimistic film to date, presents a rebuttal to the quasi-religious ending of *Ben-Hur*. Unlike that sprawling epic, this film returns to the claustrophobic interior settings of Wyler's youth as he tells the story of a disturbed young man who kidnaps and imprisons a young woman in a dungeon. At the end of the film, Wyler makes an interesting change to the plot of the John Fowles novel on which it is based, as if forcing the audience to remember his earlier work. Struggling to escape, Miranda hits her captor with a shovel, drawing blood. Although she then has an opportunity to finish him off and escape, she does not follow through. Her revulsion against violence links her to earlier Wyler protagonists, but her failure to match her captor's cruelty seals her doom.

Wyler's final film is just as bleak. The "liberation" promised in the title is, in fact, the death of that character. His story anchors an unremittingly grim exposé of race relations in America—a dramatic counterpoint to the success of contemporary films emphasizing racial harmony, such as *In the Heat of the Night*, which was also written by *Jones* scenarist Stirling Silliphant, and *Guess Who's Coming to Dinner*. In fact, Wyler sets up his audience for a potentially uplifting liberal morality tale and then undercuts that expectation at every turn. The film's main character, a lawyer who is also the town's leading citizen, initially appears to be a man whose humane instincts will win out; instead, he is revealed to be corrupt and unethical. His liberal-minded nephew, who has come south to join his uncle's law firm, is impotent and unable to effect change; at the end, he merely leaves town, having accomplished nothing. A black man who has come to town to exact revenge on the policeman who beat him when he was younger decides to renounce violence, only to change his mind and kill the lawman after the death of Jones. Released in the aftermath of the assassinations of Robert

Kennedy and Martin Luther King, and as the Vietnam War was still raging, *The Liberation of L. B. Jones* offered no solace to the American public. It was Wyler's last word as a filmmaker.

Wyler's career as a director spanned forty-five years, beginning with a series of two-reel westerns in the 1920s. He went on to make successful films in a variety of genres, including social dramas, melodramas, comedies, documentaries, epics, and, at the end of his career, a musical, *Funny Girl*. He grew up with the film industry. Having started at Universal, he cut his teeth on numerous silent westerns, then directed that studio's first all-sound movie shot outside the studio (*Hell's Heroes*). He also directed the first black-and-white film in Vista-Vision (*The Desperate Hours*) and one of the first in Technorama or widescreen (*The Big Country*).

Considered a preeminent director by his peers, he was nominated as Best Director twelve times by the Motion Picture Academy and won three times. (He was also nominated three times as a producer.) His films won 38 Oscars out of a total 127 nominations. His actors earned thirteen Oscars, having been nominated for thirty-five. These are all record numbers—no other director has come close. In 1965, the Academy gave Wyler its Irving G. Thalberg Memorial Award for motion picture achievement. He won the New York Film Critics Award and the French Victoire Award three times each. He was nominated for the Directors' Guild Award six times, winning it once, and in 1966, he received its D. W. Griffith Award for distinguished achievement in motion picture direction. In addition, he won the Cannes Film Festival's Golden Palme for *Friendly Persuasion*, and in 1976, he became the fourth recipient of the American Film Institute's Life Achievement Award, joining fellow directors John Ford and Orson Welles.

Individual directors heaped praise on him as well. Billy Wilder considered the opening scenes of *The Best Years of Our Lives* to be the most moving he had ever seen. Sergei Eisenstein loved *The Little Foxes* and, according to Lillian Hellman, showed it numerous times at parties; he told her that for the shaving scene alone, Wyler "deserved motion picture fame for the rest of his life."[31] Japanese director Kamisaburo Yoshimura studied Wyler's *Wuthering Heights*, which he viewed during the war, and thereafter declared Wyler his favorite foreign director, echoing his countrymen Mizoguchi and Ozu.[32] Wyler is also admired by Curtis Hanson, who did a two-part interview with Wyler when he was the editor of *Cinema* (1967), as well as Steven Spielberg. Bette Davis considered him the best director she ever worked for, and Charlton Heston included him among the finest directors in film history. (Both won Oscars under Wyler's direction.) Lillian Hellman termed him simply "the greatest of all American directors."

In 1966, Henri Langlois, director of the Cinémathèque Française, launched a retrospective to celebrate Wyler's place in film history. Referring to the deep-focus technique, Langlois noted that Wyler's new style, created in the late 1930s, had influenced filmmakers on four continents. He declared that critics were mistaken when they credited that style to Orson Welles, who, he said, "was still groping and being influenced by Wyler." Langlois went on to say: "Wyler's strength lies in having gone all the way in analyzing the most delicate and impressionistic of human feelings and to have put his art and his science of directing actors at the service of a new concept. The concept was to allow him to go beyond naturalism and without betraying truth or simplicity in acting, give performances with the intense strength which the masters of the German silent cinema had reached, but without resorting to their artifices and their symbolism."[33] Wyler himself sounded a similar note when he said, "A movie should not be an advertisement. Drama lies in the subtle complexities of life—in the greys, not the blacks and whites."[34]

This study traces the development of Wyler's "complexities" by examining the evolution of his cinematic style and his engagement with the American social scene. Attention is also paid to the production histories of many of his most ambitious projects, in an effort to show how they progressed and changed, finally emerging as the finished films we enjoy today. It is my hope that Wyler will emerge in these pages not as a mere craftsman but as a significant artist who expressed his ideas and convictions through his films, many of which serve as a testament to a creative talent and a dedicated humanist who was fully engaged by and with his times.

1

Discovering a Vocation and a Style

The Shakedown (1929), *The Love Trap* (1929),
Hell's Heroes (1930), *A House Divided* (1931)

William Wyler grew up with the movies. He came to America from Mulhouse (Mulhausen), Alsace-Lorraine, in 1920 at the invitation of his mother's first cousin, Carl Laemmle, who was the founder and head of Universal Studios. Laemmle's young cousin would soon eclipse his fame in the industry that would come to dominate American culture.

Laemmle himself had arrived in his adopted country in 1884, joining his older brother in Oshkosh, Wisconsin, where he became a branch manager for a successful midwestern clothier. When he was thirty-nine, Laemmle moved to Chicago, seeking to become his own boss. A chance stroll past a movie theater on State Street aroused his curiosity, and he paid the ten cents admission to watch the film being shown there. Three weeks later, he owned his own nickelodeon. That was in 1906. Within a decade, Laemmle would have a chain of movie theaters throughout the Midwest. By 1910, he had become a film producer and had founded Independent Moving Pictures, which later became Universal Pictures. Laemmle also introduced the star system to Hollywood when he lured Mary Pickford away from the Biograph Company by offering her more money and prominent billing. Prior to that innovation, actors' names were not revealed to the moviegoing public.

Laemmle vacationed in Europe every summer, and when Wyler's mother, Melanie, learned that her famous cousin would be traveling through Switzerland, she wrote to Carl about her son. He responded by inviting them to meet him at a hotel in Zurich. Laemmle offered the young man a job at Universal's New York office that paid $25 a week, from which $5 would be deducted until the cost of the transatlantic trip on the *Aquitania* had been reimbursed. Known for bringing ambitious young men to America,

Laemmle already had more than a dozen relatives on his payroll. Indeed, his penchant for nepotism was legendary, even prompting an Ogden Nash couplet: "Uncle Carl Laemmle / has a large faemmle." Many years later, however, critic Charles Affron would note, "Wyler's career is an excellent argument for nepotism."[1]

William Wyler turned out to be an ambitious kid. Within a year, he asked to be transferred to California, and by 1922, just two years after arriving in America, he was working, in his words, as a "gofer" on *The Hunchback of Notre Dame* starring Lon Chaney (some sources list him as an assistant director). By 1925, shortly after his twenty-third birthday, he was directing his first two-reel western, making him the youngest director on the Universal lot. That first "mustang" two-reeler (twenty-four minutes long) was *Crook Buster*. Over the next two years, he directed twenty-one mustang films and also worked on MGM's *Ben-Hur* (1925). On that film, he was one of sixty assistant directors assigned to control the chariot race scene, for which the studio had hired thousands of extras and built a Circus Maximus. In 1926, Wyler graduated to his first five-reeler, *Lazy Lightning*, a "blue streak" western. He would direct five more through 1927.

The first film to offer intimations of what would become Wyler's distinctive mise-en-scène was *The Shakedown* (1929), which was released in both silent and sound versions and cost around $50,000 to make. Wyler's brother Robert discovered the story. He had spent the previous two years at Universal learning the business and preparing to become a producer, and he also had a hand in writing the script, along with Charles A. Logue and Clarence Marks. Robert would be associated with a number of his brother's films in the future, but his contributions to *The Shakedown* were uncredited.

The story concerns a crooked boxer, Dave Hall (James Murray), who is involved in a shakedown ring that travels from town to town, where the bosses arrange fixed fights and encourage the locals to bet on the outcome. After establishing his identity in one town and provoking a fight with Battling Rolf, a professional fighter, Dave, who has become the local favorite, loses the fight, and the townspeople who have bet on him lose their money. Dave then moves on to establish himself in another town and set up another shakedown. Most of the film takes place in Boonton, where Dave works in the oil fields; there, he falls in love with a waitress, Marjorie (Barbara Kent), and adopts an orphan, Clem (Jack Hanlon), whose life he saved. Dave is beginning to feel at home there. When his associates come to town to set up his fight with Rolf, he wants to run away, but Clem convinces him to stay, fight, and redeem himself. Dave wins the fight and presumably will settle down with Marjorie and Clem.

The Shakedown is an early example of Wyler's artistry in evoking the American way of life, introducing, in embryonic form, what would become his signature combination of social observation and an entertaining story that appeals to the audience. As an early example of the gangster narrative (which would become a seminal genre just two years later), The Shakedown still resembles many silent films featuring gangster protagonists, in that its generic signs are basically unformed and sublimated to the melodramatic elements of the story. The emphasis here is on redemption—that of a corrupted hero rehabilitated by a saintly heroine and (for good measure) an engaging orphan—rather than the traditional gangster's dramatic fall from prominence and belated moment of bitter recognition.

The film opens in a bar with a pool table—a locale that would soon become iconic in gangster films. Some of Wyler's most impressive camera work follows, as he introduces Boonton, an oil town. He first shows Dave working on an oil well, where he is framed by its wooden scaffolding; in the background, a long line of wells dominates the landscape. Then, in a virtuoso sequence, Wyler situates his camera below the well while Dave, mounted on a pulley, is hauled up to the top. When the scene shifts to the café where Marjorie works, Wyler gives the frame a double perspective, combining the cozy interior of the hometown eatery with the wells looming in the background—a fusion of the old, rural America and the booming economic energy of the new.

Here, Wyler introduces a tension that will be developed with more complexity in his mature work, characterizing the twentieth century as a site of conflict involving the individual's relation to the emerging industrialized society—particularly the opposition between traditional social forms (the café and the incipient family unit) and the gangster figure, who represents the fragmentation of tradition and the potential for anarchy created by new patterns of consumption and the corresponding emergence of new and more liberating lifestyles.[2] As noted earlier, Wyler at this point still sublimates this thematic culture clash to the exigencies of the melodramatic plot, concentrating on Dave's evolving relationships with Clem and Marjorie and his decision to quit the shakedown gang.

The Shakedown also contains some early examples of Wyler's staging strategies, the most interesting of which is his use of deep focus early in the film. The story opens in a saloon, where Dave wins a pool game. The gang organizer then puts Dave's winnings under a napkin and challenges anyone to try to take them as Dave stands on the napkin. This is Battling Rolf's cue to join the sting. Wyler places Rolf in the foreground of the frame, where he is seated at the bar, while Dave seems to disappear in the rear amid a group of patrons who nearly blot him out. Further in the distance, the buildings of the town are visible through a doorway. The crowd disperses, but Wyler maintains his composition in depth by continuing to focus on Rolf in the foreground, while Dave is framed against the exterior setting. The director seems to be indicating that his protagonist is not a bad man and has the potential to move into the townspeople's world and embrace their traditional values.

Universal loved the film. The internal reports on *The Shakedown* called it "Another Willie Wyler Winner." Another raved, "Mr. Wyler comes through 100%." A third seemed to predict where the young director was heading: "Willy Wyler's direction should be highly recommended. He is developing like a million dollars and his picture shows a sense of realism and pace and endows every little incident in it with charm and entertainment value."[3] The studio's enthusiasm, however, was not reflected in the film's reviews; most critics found it bland and a bit saccharine.

In the spring of 1929, Wyler agreed to direct a bedroom comedy, *The Love Trap*, starring Laura La Plante, one of Universal's biggest stars. The film's budget exceeded that of *The Shakedown* by some $25,000, and it had a longer shooting schedule. Although the plot falters, especially at the end, Wyler manages to demonstrate, very early in his career, the capacity to move almost effortlessly from genre to genre. In *The Love Trap*, he does best in the darker sections that dominate the first part of the film, exploring the often dangerous, desperate world of the single woman, whose plight in this case is exacerbated by the loss of her job and her home. Wyler is ruthless in exposing the divide between the classes, which, despite the "happy ending," is never really breached.

The story follows the fortunes of Evelyn Todd (La Plante), a recently fired chorus girl who is invited by a friend to go to a party thrown by a wealthy bachelor, Guy Emory (Robert Ellis), where she can make $50.[4] Although Evelyn is presented as a sympathetic character, she knowingly puts herself in a risky situation by attending this party. Her theatrical background and her access to women who know their way around the party circuit invest her with a backstory that is more risqué than that of the comic heroines who would dominate 1930s social comedies. Evelyn gets herself into a sexually compromising position but manages to extricate herself and leaves the party, only to find that she is homeless and her furniture has been thrown out on the street. Evelyn, we soon learn, is a virginal young woman who is only trying to get along as best she can. She is picked up by the wealthy Paul Harrington (Neil Hamilton), who is being driven home in a cab. In a lame bit of comic business, he arranges to have three additional cabs pick up her furniture, and all the drivers head south. The two fall in love and get married shortly after this meeting, but trouble begins when Evelyn is rejected by Paul's mother and sister. Complicating the situation is Paul's uncle, Judge Harrington (Norman Trevor), who met Evelyn at Guy Emory's party and considers her unfit for his nephew. The judge tries to buy her off, but in an awkward comic sequence that dominates the last part of the film, Evelyn maneuvers the judge into a compromising situation, exposes him to Paul, and saves her marriage.

The first part of the film shows Wyler's strengths as a director and as a social observer. The early scenes at Guy Emory's party anticipate the techniques he will use to depict high society in *Dodsworth*, *Jezebel*, *The Heiress*, and *Carrie*. As he did in *The Shakedown*, Wyler continues to explore the framing strategies that will distinguish his mature work.

After Evelyn is fired from the chorus line, she returns to the dressing room and stares into the mirror while her friend, sitting to her left, tells her about Emory's party and the chance to earn $50 "just for looking pretty." Evelyn is thus framed within a frame as she decides whether to negotiate the dangerous party scene, anticipating the way Wyler later frames Fran Dodsworth, Julie Marsden, and Carrie Meeber as they decide whether to embark on equally treacherous courses. Evelyn is, of course, part of a comic universe, and her likely fate is not as dire as that of the others, but because Wyler does not stage the party in a comic style, he is freer to explore the scene in ways that are more suited to his temperament.

When she is first seen at the party, Evelyn is part of a crowd around the bar, where she tries to prove that she is an experienced drinker. Wyler squeezes her in the frame with a group of guests, as he later does with Fran Dodsworth when her husband finally decides to leave her. Evelyn is introduced to Judge Harrington, whom her friend describes as having "blue blood and green bucks." Evelyn's attempts to flirt with the judge are so awkward that her friend sends her away, pointing her in Guy Emory's direction, while the friend takes on the judge herself. Guy immediately gives Evelyn $50, and Wyler cuts away to the friend putting her own money in her stocking. Obviously, Evelyn has placed herself in a compromising position, and Wyler is giving his audience a glimpse into the darker and seamier side of high society. In an attempt to get Evelyn upstairs, Guy spills a drink on her dress, which gives Wyler a chance to employ the expressive imagery of a staircase for the first time. He uses it here to achieve tension by shifting among the spatial structures inherent in the set—the downstairs public area of the party and Guy's private space upstairs. It also allows him to visually fill the frame vertically and in depth.

Guy leads Evelyn upstairs, and while she is in the bedroom taking off her wet dress, Wyler cuts to Guy on the landing in a modified low-angle shot that emphasizes his unsavory desire as he looks down on the dancers below. Guy then surprises Evelyn by walking in on her while she is in her slip. Wyler again captures the action in a mirrored shot, matching the one in the dance hall, but this time including Guy. As the scene in Guy's bedroom plays out, Wyler's fondness for vertical lines and in-depth framing is apparent: he frames Evelyn between the bed curtains, a prisoner of Guy's lust, and then frames Guy himself in the window as he airs out the wet dress. When he lets it drop to the street below, Wyler's camera seeks out Evelyn in the rear, where she is again framed by the bed curtains. Sensing danger, she flirts with Guy and beckons to him, but then punches him and flees the house. Her resourcefulness in making this escape anticipates her ability to manipulate Judge Harrington in the film's final sequence.

Wyler again uses the staircase, but this time for comic purposes, in the first scene of Evelyn and Paul after their marriage. Returning home, Paul finds Evelyn waiting on the staircase landing, where she assumes Guy's position from the earlier scene. In a comic variation on that scene, however, Paul climbs onto a desk to greet her on the stairs and takes her hand. Paul's mother and sister soon arrive to meet his bride, and Paul is seen greeting them in the living room. Wyler then cuts to Evelyn in the bedroom, where she is getting ready to meet her new family. That room, with the bed in the background, is now her safe haven—Wyler's pictorial repetition brings the two sequences together, emphasizing the contrast between them.

Next, Evelyn tries to make a grand entrance by descending the stair-case, but she slips and falls on her bottom. This inauspicious debut antici-pates her failure to impress Paul's family, who look down on her lack of social standing. Here, Wyler anticipates his staging of the confrontation in *These Three*, as Martha and Karen try to defend themselves against the ac-cusations of Mary Tilford. When Paul's family members distance themselves from Evelyn, Wyler isolates her in the frame. He cuts liberally throughout the scene, using shot–reverse shots and compositions that seclude Evelyn while the Harrington women, soon joined by the judge, join forces against her. Wyler will repeat this strategy seven years later, visually isolating his heroines in *These Three* as the forces of repression gather against them.

The Love Trap was made in both a silent version and a 25 percent sound version. The latter features a musical score and synchronized sound in the final sequences, including the overly long confrontation between Ev-elyn and the judge. Because of the actors' evident difficulty in making the transition to sound, what is supposed to be a comic sequence seems even more melodramatic, which, unfortunately, magnifies Wyler's struggle to keep the scene light and comic.

Following the completion of *The Love Trap*, Wyler was asked to shoot some special scenes of La Plante in Spanish for a film exposition in Barce-lona. Then Carl Laemmle Jr. (known as Junior), who was now the general manager of his father's studio, asked Wyler to direct an installment of *The Cohens and the Kellys in Scotland*, which he refused to do because he did not like the story. This was just the first of many times that Wyler stood up to a producer when he disliked the material he was offered. In a letter to his parents, he was already displaying the temperament of an artist: "I probably would be considered of the large army of ingrates who got their starts with Carl Laemmle and then left him. But I don't want to sacrifice my future for the past."[5]

Wyler's refusal to listen to Junior almost cost him his next project, *Hell's Heroes*—a film that would display Wyler's considerable gifts and allow him to impose his own vision on the material. Fortunately, Junior decided to sublimate his anger for the good of a project he had great confidence in. Recognizing that Wyler had brought a touch of class to both *The Shakedown* and *The Love Trap*, he decided to assign *The Cohens and the Kellys* to William Craft and let Wyler direct *Hell's Heroes*. It would not be the last time the director's intransigence netted him superior material.

Hell's Heroes was a coup for Wyler, since it was to be Universal's first all-sound film and would require considerable outdoor location filming. Wyler later recalled the complications involved in making the film:

> It was made under tremendous difficulties because the camera had to be muffled in the padded booth with a soundproof window in front and a padded door in the back. Of course, George Robinson, the cameraman, was stuffed into the booth with the camera. Since the story had the men fleeing or trying to reach salvation, I couldn't very well have them stop all the time to declaim.
>
> They *were* fugitives and had to move even when they spoke. So, we had to devise *moving* shots with dialogue. That meant putting the padded boxes on rails. Just imagine a dozen guys pushing this padded shack on rails in Death Valley in August in absolute silence. Microphones were concealed in cactus and sagebrush every ten feet or so.[6]

The film was based on a novel, *The Three Godfathers* (1913), by Peter B. Kyne, a writer of popular fiction whose work appeared regularly in magazines such as *Collier's*, the *Saturday Evening Post*, and *Sunset*. The novel, a retelling of the Gospel according to Matthew set on the nineteenth-century American frontier, had already been filmed twice before in silent versions—in 1916 by Edward J. Le Saint (starring Harry Carey) and in 1919 by Wyler's friend John Ford as *Marked Men* (also starring Carey). It would be remade twice after Wyler's version—by Richard Boleslawski in 1936 (starring Chester Morris, Walter Brennan, and Lewis Stone) and by Ford again in 1948, in Technicolor, as *Three Godfathers* (starring John Wayne, Pedro Armendariz, and Harry Carey Jr.; Carey Sr. had died a year earlier). Later in their careers, Ford would often joke that it was now Wyler's turn to remake *The Three Godfathers*.

Kyne's novel begins with four outlaws holding up a bank in Arizona. As they flee, one is killed and another, Tom Gibbons, is wounded. The three survivors manage to make it to California, and after resting, they decide their best course is to head for a water hole known as Terrapin Tanks. But when they reach their destination, they discover that the water hole is dry. Then they find a woman in a wagon (with no horses) who is about to give birth. A baby boy is born in the evening, and before she dies, the mother names the child after the three men, asking them to be her baby's godfathers and to save him. Bob Sangster, the leader, agrees to her request, and all three men commit themselves to the well-being of the child. Having lost their horses, they must walk through the desert, taking turns carrying the child. Gibbons, because of his wound, is the first to die. Wild Bill Kearny dies soon after of thirst and madness, but not before telling Sangster how to get to New Jerusalem, the closest town. Sangster reaches the town on Christmas Day, thirsty, bloody, raving, and clutching the child to his breast. He hears music coming from a saloon, hands the baby to a woman, and collapses.

Wyler's film, unlike the book and Ford's famous remake (his original does not survive), lacks sentimentality. Wyler wanted the film to be realistic, rooted in the sweltering desert locales. The screenplay, by Tom Reed, considerably darkens Kyne's story. Unlike the original and the other film versions (notably Ford's), Wyler's film begins and ends in New Jerusalem—the site of the bank robbery. Sangster knows that returning there means sure death because during the course of the robbery they killed a teller, who turns out to be the baby's father, in an ironic twist that is unique to Wyler's version. The Sangster of *Hell's Heroes* is a gruff, selfish character, unlike either his counterpart in the book or the almost saintly Robert Hightower (Wayne) of Ford's film. And whereas the novel's Sangster is the first to agree to the dying mother's request, Wyler's Sangster is the last; the others practically have to force him to do so. Initially, he even refuses to share the milk they find in the wagon with the baby; he wants to drink it himself.

In both the novel and Wyler's version, Sangster dies after reaching New Jerusalem. In the final version of Wyler's film, but not in novel, he deliberately drinks poisoned water so that he can walk the last mile; then he dies on a church doorstep. In Ford's version, however, Hightower lives, and his heroism saves him from hanging. He is sentenced to one year in jail, and the film makes it clear that after he serves his time, he will return to help raise the boy, who has been adopted by the sheriff and his wife.

Wyler's original ending was more brutal than the one in the released film:

> The surging, angry crowd has surrounded Bickford [Charles Bickford, the actor playing Sangster].
> A dance-hall girl snatches away the child from the dazed bandit. The crowd knocks him down, ties him. A rope is thrown around him and a horseman begins to drag him through the street. The Sheriff rushes up, claims Bickford in the name of the law. He picks up the fallen man, promises to hang him.
> We see the bandit's face—inhumanely gruesome, nightmarish. The Sheriff shakes him. No sign of life. He slaps his face again. With his finger he pries open the bandit's eye and we see the dead, glazed white. The Sheriff announces him dead. Ugh![7]

The supervisor Junior had hired to oversee Wyler thought the director's commitment to realism had ruined the film. He wrote to Junior that the ending was "the most gruesome scene we have ever seen on film and . . . will give audiences nightmares for weeks." Junior obviously agreed even before he saw the ending, for he wrote to Wyler: "It looks from this report that you have evidently butchered a great picture."[8]

Wyler filmed *Hell's Heroes* on location in the Mojave Desert and the Panamint Valley in August because he wanted the sweltering conditions to emphasize the realism of the setting and the extreme predicament of the three outlaws. Indeed, the desert functions as a force of nature, a brutal stage on which a tale of redemption is played out. Wyler strips Kyne's story of its religious symbolism, concentrating instead on man alone in an indifferent universe where he is forced to work out his own fate. Though less grand and less visually spectacular than Ford's Monument Valley setting, the desert here becomes a typical Wylerian enclosed world in which the sum of one's life is determined solely by the efficacy of action. The birth of the baby in this setting not only functions as a symbol of life but also becomes emblematic of man's capacity for endurance and moral regeneration.

The film opens with a breathtaking composition: a desert landscape framed by a grotesque, bent cactus-like tree. Its interesting shape foreshadows the opening in the covered wagon's canvas top that will later frame the mother. Next, in an extreme long shot, we see three riders moving toward the camera. Coming closer, they discover a sign for New Jerusalem that is accompanied by a hangman's noose—an unusual double image associated with death and salvation. Barbwire Gibbons (Raymond Hatton), who will be the first to die, sacrificing himself for the group and for the child, is framed by the noose. The first view of New Jerusalem reveals an isolated, ramshackle town that occupies only one side of a street and is surrounded by the infinite space of the desert. Wyler nearly duplicates this scene when Jim McKay arrives in San Rafael at the beginning of *The Big Country* (1958).

A fourth member of the group is already in town, staking it out. After the bank robbery, one of the four outlaws is killed, shot by the minister—one detail (among others) by which Wyler undercuts the religious themes of the story. The three who escape soon find themselves trapped in a dust storm that causes them to lose their horses and forces them to take shelter by digging a hole and covering it with burlap. Wyler cuts to the next day with a lyrical shot of a circling buzzard, which, despite its gruesome implication, has a haunting beauty.[9] The juxtaposition of the buzzard and the men's emergence from their hole in the ground offers another double image of death and potential resurrection.

The shots that follow show the three men, in shadow, walking across an immense landscape that is blank, bleak, and empty—except for a sign warning of poisoned water, topped by the skeletal head of a steer. When the men reach Terrapin Wells, they discover that the well has been dynamited and the water is gone. There is, however, a covered wagon, and Sangster goes to investigate. His first sight of the woman inside is a point-of-view shot through the sight of his rifle. There is nothing compassionate about his reaction, as he hides his discovery from his friends, hoping to have the woman to himself. But when Kearny (Fred Kohler) sees her, he immediately realizes that she is sick and pregnant. In both shots, the woman is framed by the curved lines of the wagon's arch. In Ford's film, that composition suggests a cathedral arch before which the men stand in awe, hats in hand, as they look inside, but Wyler's framing is devoid of any such inspirational feeling, as are the initial reactions of the men. Sangster's reaction, in fact, seems utterly bestial.

One of Wyler's subsequent shots of the wagon is again suggestive of his emerging style. As Sangster and Gibbons wait for Kearny on a hill, Wyler shoots the wagon in deep focus, with rock formations in the background. The effect is poetic, indicating that the men's salvation is within reach if they can overcome their selfishness and move beyond it to get to New Jerusalem again. The men eventually agree to be the baby's godfathers, although they baptize him in dirt instead of water. In this version, the baby is named after his father, Frank Edwards, who was killed by the godfathers earlier in the film. Wyler's film contains no scene like the one in Ford's showing the burial of the mother.

Wyler handles the deaths of Gibbons and Kearny with restraint. Gibbons, who has been weakened by his wound, decides that he can struggle no longer, delaying the others. He lies down at the foot of a tree and tells them to go on, refusing the offer of water. Then, in the best deep-focus composition in the film, Wyler shows Sangster and Kearny moving away in the front of the frame, while Gibbons and a tree shaped like a cross are seen in the background. We hear a shot but do not see Gibbons die, as the men walk toward the camera. Kearny's death is handled with utter simplicity: after bidding good night to Sangster in front of the campfire, he feeds the baby for the last time, and when Sangster wakes up the next morning, Kearny is gone, leaving behind only a note.

The film's final moments are beautifully crafted. Left alone, Sangster is initially angry at the baby and threatens to leave him behind. He can't, however, and after feeding the baby the last of the water, he sets off for New Jerusalem with the child in his arms. At one point, Wyler films that desperate journey in one long tracking shot, showing not the trudging man but, at first, straight footprints, then a crease along the track, which is soon revealed to be made by his trailing rifle, which Sangster drags for a while and then abandons. We then see more footprints, his hat, more footprints, and a handkerchief. At last, following a very high-angle shot looking down on Sangster as he staggers forward, carrying the baby, Wyler cuts to an expressionistic point-of-view shot of the hangman's noose, blurred and out of focus, as Sangster collapses by the poisoned well. Before that, however, he lets his final bag of gold scatter in the sand—implying, perhaps, that he has discovered a different treasure. He decides to drink the poisoned water, knowing that it is his only hope of traveling the final mile or so into New Jerusalem.

When he finally reaches the town, the inhabitants are gathered in church, singing "Silent Night" and celebrating Christmas. Wyler cuts to a long shot of Sangster walking up the street, back to the interior of the church, then back again to Sangster, tracking him slowly as he staggers toward the church. Wyler films Sangster framed through the windows of the bank as he moves past it. Finally making it into the church, he dies with his godson in his arms, surrounded by the congregants. Without any fanfare, Bob Sangster, the most selfish of the three godfathers, is thus redeemed through his sacrifice—as the other two have already been redeemed by giving up their lives to ensure the baby's deliverance.

Peter Kyne hated Wyler's grim version of his sentimental, religious story. In a letter to screenwriter Tom Reed, he proclaimed, "Frankly, I think your Mr. Wyler murdered our beautiful story. . . . It was dreadfully directed and dreadfully played by that leading man. . . . I don't care how much money the picture makes, my conscience will not let me cheer for the atrocious murder of one of the few works of art I have ever turned out."[10]

The film did indeed make money, grossing $18,000 during its first week in New York. It also did well in other parts of the country and in Europe. Most important, it established Wyler as an important director. Universal offered him a new contract at $750 per week; this was supposed to jump to $1,000 the following year, but because economic conditions at the studio were bad in 1932, Wyler was ultimately forced to compromise on his salary, which leveled out at $850 per week.

Seeking another quality property to direct after *Hell's Heroes*, Wyler tried to interest Junior in *The Road Back*, the sequel to the studio's highly successful adaptation of *All Quiet on the Western Front*, but Junior was hesitant to commit. Finally, Robert Wyler found the story that would become his brother's next film. *A House Divided* was adapted from Olive Eden's magazine story "Heart and Hand" (the original title for the film as well) by John Clymer (*The Love Trap*) and Dale Van Every, with some additional dialogue by John Huston. Most likely inspired by Eugene O'Neill's

Desire under the Elms, it is the story of a middle-aged fisherman, Seth Law, who sends for a mail-order bride after his wife's death. He is expecting a sturdy, hardworking woman named Ada, but the petite and pretty Ruth Evans arrives instead, because Ada has already married. Initially, Seth rejects Ruth as being too frail, but during their first dinner together, he decides to marry her after all. The marriage worsens the already tense relationship between Seth and his son Matt, who hates both his father and the fisherman's life that has been imposed on him. When Matt tries to protect Ruth from his father, the two men fight, and Seth is seriously injured in a fall from the staircase. During his lengthy recuperation, Ruth and Matt fall in love. Suspecting that his wife loves his son, Seth crawls upstairs one night and challenges Matt to a fight. Ruth, terrified, runs to the pier and hides on a boat. Refusing to strike his father, Matt goes to find Ruth, only to discover that a storm has dislodged the boat from the pier, and Ruth has been carried out to sea. Father and son head out to save Ruth, catching up to her just as her boat is approaching some dangerous rocks. Seth ties a rope around himself, providing a lifeline for Matt to reach Ruth. As the young couple reach the safety of the shore, they discover that Seth's boat has capsized, and he has drowned. The film ends with Matt and Ruth looking out to sea.

The film stars Walter Huston, who gives a complex and sympathetic performance as the gruff, unsympathetic Seth. In this early sound film, Huston has no difficulty transitioning to the new medium. Matt is played by Kent Douglass, and Ruth by Helen Chandler, who was also the love interest of Bela Lugosi in *Dracula* that same year. During production, Wyler again taxed Junior's patience, as the film ran ten days over schedule and $53,000 over budget, bringing its total cost to $284,000.

Wyler also had problems with the script, which was originally written as a silent film. Just before filming began, Jack Clymer was asked to transform the script into a talkie, which he managed to accomplish in two and a half weeks, although Wyler was left with a script that had plenty of gaps. As a result, he improvised a great deal on the set, ultimately adding almost 100 scenes to the 332 in Clymer's script. Junior blamed Wyler for the overruns, ranting, "You do not have to shoot every scene from three different angles. Confine yourself to the shots necessary to cover the action."[11] Less than a week later, he admonished Wyler again: "For your information, permission for retakes must be given by me and I don't want this to ever happen again."[12]

Unlike *Hell's Heroes*, which is almost wholly an outdoor film, *A House Divided* emphasizes confined indoor settings and shifting spatial relationships between characters and sets, providing multiple examples of the director's emerging preference for composition in depth. As in *Hell's Heroes*, where—much to Kyne's displeasure—Wyler largely eliminated the story's religious and sentimental overtones, his visual arrangements here enforce an emotional distance from a story that is at heart melodramatic.

This film, too, opens with a shot of nature—this time featuring the sea, the mountains, and the coastline between them. In the middle distance, a rowboat has just settled on the beach. Soon we see some men, including Seth Law, untying a coffin from the boat. (Always deliberate in his visual details, Wyler ends the film with a corresponding image of Seth tying himself to a rowboat to save his wife and son—an act that leads to his death, the boat becoming his coffin.) Seth, his son Matt, and others then proceed toward a cemetery. Like its predecessor, this film begins with a scene of death, although here it is literal rather than symbolic. During the procession, Wyler cuts to another in-depth long shot, casting the diminished figures in shadow even as they are dwarfed by the mountains and the sea. As the minister concludes the service and the mourners file away, Wyler draws attention to the sound of the earth hitting the coffin, and this mundane detail further undercuts the sentimentality of the scene, while adding to Matt's grief and pain over the death of his mother. Seth, a hard man, is unaffected by the funeral. Like O'Neill's Ephraim Cabot (also played by Walter Huston in the Broadway premiere of *Desire under the Elms*), he has a cold, indifferent nature. Later, after taking his emotional son to a bar and forcing him to drink, Seth fights with Matt, knocks him out, and carries him home.

On the day Ruth arrives, Seth refuses to meet her, so Matt does so instead. Wyler's handling of their meeting is an introduction to his mature style: the sequence opens with a shot of the sitting room, featuring a staircase that will figure prominently in the rest of the film. Matt dashes down the stairs to answer the door and is startled to see Ruth, who is framed in the doorway. Most of their ensuing dialogue is filmed in two-shots; Wyler cuts away to Ruth only twice, and Matt never appears in the frame alone. This minimal cutting preserves the sense of their coming together—something that is never established in the scenes between father and son. Matt then shows her around, and Ruth takes to the water immediately, declaring, "I always knew I'd love the ocean." The scene ends with them standing by the water; it then dissolves to a high-angle shot of the front of Seth's boat as it enters the harbor, dominating the space as if to mock Ruth's dreams.

Returning home after a day of fishing and meeting Ruth for the first time, Seth immediately rejects her as a wife. In the frames that make up this sequence, Wyler maintains his earlier strategy of fixing his attention on Matt and Ruth in two-shots, with minimal cutting. Seth, in contrast, is usually pictured alone. When he belatedly decides to propose during dinner, Ruth seems ambivalent, and while she is drying the dishes with Matt, Wyler returns to his two-shot framing. Seth then enters, framed by the doorway in deep focus, and announces that the marriage will be celebrated that very night. Matt leaves to make the arrangements, and Seth moves to the front of the frame, taking Matt's place beside Ruth. All this significant movement is conveyed in a single take without a cut—clearly presaging Wyler's mature style and demonstrating that as early as 1931, he was experimenting with the technique of filming significant action in segments whose duration and staging exceeded the reach of the standard shot.

When Seth and Ruth return home after the wedding, Wyler shoots them at opposite ends of the room, emphasizing the distance between them. Seth walks slowly toward her, while Ruth, her back to him, looks toward the window; she begs to get out of the marriage, but Seth insists that all will be well. The mood becomes further strained when Matt enters and Wyler cuts to a triangular three-shot with Matt in the center—another type of framing he will come to favor when emphasizing the inherent tension in a given situation. Seth sends Ruth upstairs. Matt then stands at the foot of the staircase, pleading with his father to give Ruth time, but Seth tells his son to leave and says that perhaps Ruth will give him a real son. Seth then ascends the stairs, and Wyler cuts to a frontal shot of him that practically fills the frame—a composition he will use again in *The Heiress*. When Matt tries to stop him, a fight ensues on the landing, and Seth falls to the ground floor, unconscious. (As in *The Little Foxes*, Wyler uses the staircase here as an area where the characters negotiate power.) Unlike the scene in the bar after the funeral, Matt defeats his father this time, and Wyler emphasizes this power shift in the last shot of the sequence by framing Seth's face in the space between the staircase railings.

In the final confrontational sequence, a storm rages outside as Seth, lying in a bed downstairs, asks Ruth to massage his legs. While she does so, Seth tries to woo her, showing great tenderness and sensitivity—here, Huston demonstrates his range by making the character sympathetic and multidimensional. However, this compassionate moment is interrupted by Matt, and Wyler cuts to another triangular shot with the son in the middle. Soon Matt and Ruth ascend the stairs, leaving Seth (still not fully recovered from his fall) on his downstairs bed. In a low-angle shot, Seth watches as Matt, now framed by the railings, bids goodnight to Ruth—the son has clearly triumphed. Wyler builds sexual tension in this sequence as he cuts between the principals, with the sounds of the storm in the background—a scene the writers clearly lifted from *Desire under the Elms*, when Eben declares his love for Abbie. As Seth writhes on his bed, Ruth paces the room upstairs, her pent-up anxiety symbolized by the pelting rain against the window that frames her. These shots are intercut with images of Matt, who is also pacing and also goes to the window, opening it and letting the rain wash over his face—an expressive shot that Wyler would repeat in *Wuthering Heights*.

As Ruth finally enters Matt's room, Wyler cuts to the scene downstairs. In a shot composed in depth, with the railing in the foreground and Seth sitting up in the background, he initiates the final confrontation between father and son. Seth slinks toward the staircase like some primordial sea creature that emerged from the ocean at the beginning of time. As he clutches the railings, his face is framed by them, expressing both his desire and his hatred of the son and rival who has reduced him to this state of bestial impotence. He struggles up the stairs, catches the lovers together, and vows to kill Matt. Matt refuses to fight his crippled father, but there is a scuffle; Matt falls down the stairs but recovers and goes after Ruth, who has fled into the storm.

Wyler concludes the film with father and son trying to rescue Ruth, and Seth dying in the process. Like *Hell's Heroes*, this film ends with the death of its most compelling character. The final image is a brief shot of Matt and Ruth looking out to sea. Although there are a few other characters in the film, and the fishing village is depicted effectively, Wyler makes this tragic story convincing through his obsessive concentration on the three principals. Nothing matters beyond their struggle in an enclosed space, which allows him to experiment with the framings that would invest the story with visual and geometric tension. Throughout his career as a director, Wyler would thrive in the studio setting with properties, often originating on the stage, that were limited and confining, thus pushing him to experiment further with depth-of-field staging, which tested the limits of the shot's visual richness.

2

Coming into His Own

Counsellor-at-Law (1933)

The experience of directing *A House Divided* whetted Wyler's appetite for more serious projects. That desire was also fueled by John Huston, with whom Wyler formed a lifelong friendship. (Huston once commented that he considered Wyler his best friend in the industry.) Huston, who had lived among the poor in Mexico, convinced Wyler to try a socially conscious film. Hoping to develop a story about the millions of Americans who had been dispossessed and left jobless by the Depression, the two men decided to live among the poor and the homeless to find material for their film. "To know what it was to be a bum, we both took ten cents with us, went downtown in old clothes. . . . We got a lousy free dinner in a mission after we listened to a spiel and signed statements to the effect that we had come to Christ. Then we spent the night in a flophouse. Ten cents it cost."[1]

That experience produced no script, but Huston and Wyler did collaborate on a screenplay based on a property called "Steel," which Universal had owned for some time. After reading their script, Carl Laemmle Jr. was interested in producing the film, but the project was eventually shelved. The pair was not idle for long, however. Universal had bought the rights to Oliver La Farge's 1929 Pulitzer Prize–winning novel *Laughing Boy*. Working on that script would occupy Wyler and Huston for much of 1932.

Laughing Boy focuses on the clash between mainstream American culture and that of the Native American peoples of the Southwest. La Farge, who was also an anthropologist, utilized material from his frequent archaeological and sociological expeditions to the region. His novel deals with poverty and the spiritual alienation of Native Americans, as well as prostitution and racism.

Wyler believed that he could turn this story into an epic film foregrounded by a compelling love story, even though Laughing Boy's love interest, Slim Girl, works for a time as a prostitute for white men. By way of research, Wyler and Huston made multiple trips to Arizona, where they camped out with the Navajo. They also traveled to Oklahoma City and Lawrence, Kansas, to watch sacred dances and confer with medicine men on the reservations of the Hopi, Comanche, Crow, and Blackfoot. In his autobiography, Huston wrote of sitting "all day long in a Hogan watching a sand painting being made."[2]

Wyler was also in contact with La Farge, who helped by authenticating the details of the script. In a letter written in 1932, Wyler asks him for more color sketches of gods and goddesses and for sketches he can use "for costuming for any or all characters at different stages of the story." He even asks for pictures of blankets "at different stages of weaving."[3]

The project was eventually shelved by Universal, primarily because of problems related to casting the leads. Huston had proposed making the film with real Indians—Mexicans or American Indians—"but even Willy thought that was too wild a notion."[4] In a letter to La Farge, Wyler did not specify why the studio had halted production, merely reporting that the film was "indefinitely shelved or postponed." He went on to write, "I have tried, although unsuccessfully, to interest another studio in the purchase of the book and script, which I understand Universal is willing to sell, and I hope to be able to accomplish this—if not now perhaps later this year, because I don't think *Laughing Boy* should remain unproduced."[5] Universal eventually sold the rights to Metro as a vehicle for Ramon Novarro, but Huston dismissed the film as "wretched and vulgar."[6]

Wyler and Huston next worked on a script based on Daniel Ahearn's story "The Wild Boys of the Road." Like the original, their script, titled "Forgotten Boy," was about children who had run away from home during the Depression because their parents could not support them. Many of them rode the rails, crossing state lines. In some states, officials refused to allow these children to get off the trains, and when a dozen of them died from starvation and thirst in a Texas boxcar, it caused a national scandal. Wyler and Huston traveled around California, talking to brakemen, hobos, and kids. Wyler also had a reader from the studio search for stories in the *Los Angeles Herald Examiner* about children caught committing crimes, and he attended night sessions of juvenile court.

Huston recalled the script's final scene, involving two boys who had tried to rob a pawnshop: "One of them had been seriously wounded—dying—and the other held a menacing crowd at bay with a gun in his hand. Standing over his dying friend, he shouted to the crowd, 'You killed him!' The camera then came around so the kid was pointing the gun into the audience, with the accusation, 'You killed him!'"[7] The film was never made because, according to Huston, as it was being prepared for production, Franklin Delano Roosevelt's new administration promptly put these runaways to work in the reforestation program of the Civilian Conservation Corps.

In 1932, Wyler directed a film for Universal, *Tom Brown of Culver*, about a rebellious boy attending a military academy and his relationships with various friends. Although this material had already been filmed, and the protagonist's character type was based on the nineteenth-century British story "Tom Brown's School Days," Wyler researched the project with the same thoroughness he had devoted to the two unrealized scripts co-written with Huston. While spending two weeks living in a barracks at a military school, he heard that upperclassmen terrorized the freshmen and wanted to witness this practice firsthand. "So one day I got a couple of older boys to hide me in a closet," he recalled, and he watched as naked plebes got "slapped around for no reason."[8] He included such a scene in the film, but the superintendent of the school, who had final script approval, insisted that it be removed. Nonetheless, Wyler was proud that he had filmed the project on location—a rarity in those days.

Tom Brown of Culver is a pedestrian effort. Wyler gives the film a light touch, emphasizing the camaraderie among Tom and his friends. The more serious subplot—in which Tom discovers that his father, a decorated war hero supposedly killed in action, is really alive—is handled melodramatically. The father ultimately admits that he was really a deserter and runs away again, but Tom finds him and prevents him from committing suicide. Tom then resolves to leave school and stay with his father. As he prepares to do so, however, the father joyously informs his son that he has been exonerated and his Medal of Honor reinstated. The film concludes with Tom proudly pinning the medal on his father and then returning to Culver to complete his studies.

Wyler left Universal briefly in January 1933 because of the studio's failure to make good on its agreement to let his brother Robert direct a film. Wyler was distraught over his desertion of the studio because he felt he owed an enormous debt to Carl Laemmle. Although Laemmle was no longer involved in the day-to-day operation of the studio—which had been taken over by his son—Wyler wrote a heartfelt letter to his old mentor, declaring, "Even though I will no longer be connected with Universal I do not regard my indebtedness to you as being at an end. I will never be able to repay you for your many kindnesses."[9]

Despite his increased stature in the industry, Wyler was unable to find work. (He even tried to sell the script of *Laughing Boy* to Paramount when he heard that Universal was willing to unload it.) Frustrated and confused, he returned to Universal a month later, signing a one-picture, $8,000 deal to direct *Her First Mate*, the third in a series of four comedies starring ZaSu Pitts and her husband, Slim Summerville. Based on a Broadway play called *Salt Water*, it is a tired film that is not very funny and quite devoid of comic energy. Speaking to his biographer about this sorry project years later, Wyler made the best of it: "There were little pieces of business that were sort of advanced for their time. The wife claims she's pregnant, then her husband discovers she is not but still uses the stratagem."[10]

Wyler, however, was just biding his time. *Her First Mate* marked the end of his apprentice period, and soon thereafter he signed a new contract with Universal for $1,125 a week. His next assignment was Pulitzer Prize–winning playwright Elmer Rice's *Counsellor-at-Law*. With that film, Wyler would declare himself one of Hollywood's major directors and initiate an extraordinarily rich and productive phase of his career.

Wyler's association with Rice is a fascinating example of the coming together of two artists whose careers have been perceived in similar ways, although today, Wyler is the more famous of the two. Both men were of German origin. Wyler was born in Mulhouse, France, but the town was under German control at the time, and his mother's family was German-Jewish. When he started to attain success in motion pictures, he changed his name from Willy to the more formal William, which he thought would look more imposing on the screen. Rice, ten years older than Wyler, was born in America to German-Jewish parents. Like a true American, he rejected his ancestral past and proclaimed that his identity began with his grandparents' arrival in America. This New World sensibility also motivated his name change from Elmer Leopold Reisenstein: "I saw no reason for hanging on to a foreign-looking name with which I had no associations or emotional ties."[11]

Both men started out in the business world. Wyler was sent to business school in Switzerland to prepare to take over his father's haberdashery, while Rice started as a claims clerk and later put himself through law school. He then rejected both business and the law to become a writer. Likewise, Wyler felt himself unsuited for business and his father's way of life and moved to America to work for his cousin Carl Laemmle in the movies. The most important similarity between the two, however, was their artistic versatility. Rice became an accomplished playwright who successfully utilized a variety of forms. Unlike many of his contemporaries, he seemed equally at home with such divergent styles as expressionism, naturalism, melodrama, and farce. Similarly, Wyler has confounded critics because of his determination to try everything. Not settling for any particular genre, he achieved equal success with intimate character studies, epics, musicals, social films, and melodramas.

Rice was a critic of the Broadway theater, and his concerns seem applicable to Wyler's work in Hollywood as well. Writing in the 1930s, he questioned whether American drama as represented on Broadway could claim to be serious art or whether economic exigencies rendered it merely commercial and thus subliterary. This conflict of art and commerce has been cited numerous times in the decades since, and it has often been used by critics to undercut Hollywood directors. That Rice raised this question is interesting in itself, since his own career is marked by startling inconsistency. Like his literary idols Ibsen and Shaw, Rice wanted to write socially significant drama, and some of his work is still performed and anthologized today, particularly *The Adding Machine* and *Street Scene*, but also the lesser-known *The Subway* and *We the People*. However, like other American playwrights, Rice also craved Broadway hits, turning out dross such as *Cock Robin* and *The Grand Tour*. The artist and critic who hectored the commercial theater was also addicted to it.

Rice's first play, *On Trial* (1914), was an enormous success. The playwright successfully exploited the rarely used flashback technique to tell the story of the rape of an innocent girl who is on trial for murder. The search for the real murderer moves the trial plot forward, while the story of her rape is told in flashback. The play was such a sensation that during the second intermission on opening night, George M. Cohan offered Rice $30,000 for the rights to the play, but Rice, suspecting a prank, turned him down. Although he eventually made $100,000 from *On Trial*, Rice dismissed his work as nothing more than "a gimmick." And as a student of playwrights such as Shakespeare, Galsworthy, and Shaw, he wrote, "I could not understand all of this acclaim."[12]

Street Scene (1929), which anticipates the structure of *Counsellor-at-Law*, is a useful guide to Rice's strengths and weaknesses as a playwright. Like the later play, it interweaves a number of plots and introduces a large cast of characters. Most of the incidents are short, building interest and anticipation; Rice shows himself to be adept at altering mood and tempo. He also introduces an array of ethnic types representing melting-pot New York, although by modern standards, most of these characters seem rather broad and stereotypical. It is interesting, since Rice was Jewish, that no character is as unattractive as the Jewish socialist Abraham Kaplan, who is described as "hook nosed with horn rimmed spectacles." Kaplan's accent is exaggerated, as Rice seems to relish stretching out every syllable and word. Also, although Rice empathized with socialism, his was an idealistic rather than a practical position; he never joined the party and did not care for political squabbles. Nor does he shy away from revealing the anti-Semitism of the other characters. Kaplan is regularly referred to as a "kike" by others, and some of the neighbors are appalled by the relationship between Kaplan's son, Sam, and the Irishwoman Shirley Maurrant. Even Sam's sister tells Shirley that she disapproves of intermarriage. *Street Scene* is tinged with politics and social commentary, but every time Rice raises an important issue, he quickly diffuses the controversy by resorting to melodrama. The play itself revolves around a melodramatic plot involving Anna Maurrant's love affair, which is discovered by her husband, who then murders his wife and her lover. The issues of poverty, the failure of capitalism, anti-Semitism, and violence are all blurred by the mechanics of the plot and the cartoonish nature of some of the characters, few of whom experience any moments of introspection.

These same weaknesses would also plague *Counsellor-at-Law*, which opened two years after *Street Scene* and shared its interest in presenting a variety of ethnic characters. Unlike its predecessor, this play takes place indoors rather than outside a tenement building. Reflecting Rice's experience as a lawyer, *Counsellor* unfolds in the law offices of Simon and Tedesco, utilizing the firm's waiting room to showcase the variety of social and ethnic types who pass through the office. Rice also throws in references to the Depression, including mention of a businessman jumping off a roof and of a communist agitator who is beaten by the police.

Unlike *Street Scene*—which, as the title implies, is about the interplay of characters in a New York City neighborhood—*Counsellor-at-Law* focuses on a bona fide protagonist: George Simon, a high-powered Jewish lawyer. The plot is fueled by his relationships with his high-society WASP wife, his Italian American partner, and the various clients, rich and poor, who come to see him. But as a social drama, the play remains superficial. Rice portrays Simon as a heroic figure who rises above his immigrant origins to become one of New York's most powerful lawyers. He overcharges the rich to get them out of their foolish scrapes but dispenses free legal advice to the poor, especially people from his old neighborhood. He is married to a socially prominent woman whom he blindly worships but who is condescending to him. Her children from her first marriage actively despise him and refuse to consider him their father. Through this relationship, Rice introduces anti-Semitism more obliquely than he did in *Street Scene*, implying here that Simon's wife and her children reject him because of his Jewishness. This implication becomes more explicit in the depiction of Simon's mother as a caricature of the doting Jewish mother who regularly visits her successful son at his office. The scene between Simon's wife and his mother is one of Rice's best as he highlights their social and ethnic differences and the wife's dismissive and barely tolerant attitude toward her mother-in-law.

Again, however, Rice fails to develop or examine his observations about these ethnic and social divides. Although Simon is depicted as savvy and sharp, he remains oddly obtuse when it comes to his wife. She refuses to support him when he is threatened with disbarment over an impropriety in an old case—discovered by a rival blue-blood lawyer who also resents his Jewishness. She elects instead to go on a cruise with a lover from her own social circle. The play concludes as Simon attempts to jump out the office window but is saved at the last minute by his devoted secretary who not-so-secretly loves him. Once again, a serious issue is undercut by a melodramatic conclusion.

Rice handles the issue of the communist sympathizer in the same way.

Harry Becker, the son of a friend from the old neighborhood, has been beaten and then arrested for making speeches on the street. When Simon confronts him, Becker accuses the lawyer of being "a traitor to his class." He goes on to say, "How did you get where you are? . . . By betraying your own class. . . . By climbing on the backs of the working class. . . . Getting in right with crooked bourgeois politicians and pimping for corporations."[13] Simon clearly feels there is some truth in Becker's remarks, but all he can do is threaten to hit him. Rice resolves the scene with an interruption, and the issue is not raised again, as Becker later dies of his injuries.

Counsellor-at-Law ultimately does not succeed as a social play because Rice's progressive instincts yield to those of the commercial showman. The spectacle of Simon's world, the potential scandal, the love story, and the excitement of the multiple stories that crowd the play take precedence over any serious consideration of the issues introduced in the plot. Once again, Rice proves to be a remarkable storyteller with a keen ability to juggle multiple plotlines and a talent for evoking character types with broad strokes. George Simon is a potentially compelling and dynamic character, but he, like the play itself, lacks the depth and complexity to generate significant drama. Dancing around the important questions raised, Rice's melodramatic approach so deeply implicates his protagonist in the corrupt, cynical world around him that the play ultimately glorifies that world, rendering it as an exciting, pulsating locale.

Counsellor was a Broadway success. It did so well, in fact, that a road company production opened in Chicago while the play was still running in New York; it also played in Los Angeles and San Francisco. Universal paid the rather exorbitant sum of $150,000 for the rights to that play and to Rice's *The Left Bank*. The deal included Rice's services as screenwriter.

The studio wanted Paul Muni, who had played Simon on Broadway, to reprise the role in the film, but he refused; Muni wanted to avoid being typecast as a Jew. Instead, he would make his film debut playing Tony Camonte in *Scarface*. Samuel Goldwyn, who would soon hire Wyler to direct for his company, famously remarked, "You can't have a Jew playing a Jew; it wouldn't work on screen."[14] Other actors considered for the part were Edward G. Robinson, Otto Kruger (who starred in the Chicago production), William Powell, and Warner Baxter. The name at the top of the studio's list was John Barrymore—seemingly an odd choice to play a

Jewish lawyer from the ghetto—but the younger Laemmle wanted him, despite his hefty fee of $25,000 a week and his reputation for heavy drinking. Even Rice was "delighted to hear that Barrymore is in the cast."[15] Thirty years later, however, Rice confessed in his autobiography that he "had doubts about his rightness for the part; moreover, he was definitely on the decline."[16]

Viewing the chance to direct an actor of Barrymore's stature as a great opportunity, Wyler did not object either. Barrymore was also pleased to be working with Wyler. When they met, the actor put his arm around the director, declaring, "You and I are going to get along fine, you know. Don't worry about all that temperamental stuff you've heard about the Barrymores. It all comes from my sister and she's full of shit."[17] Moreover, Barrymore assured Wyler that he was happy to work with him, explaining, "Because you're Jewish you'll be able to help me a great deal with the character."[18]

Hoping to get an early start on the screenplay, Universal sent Wyler to Mexico City to meet with Rice, who was vacationing there with his family. Because the trip would take three days by train, Wyler flew from Juarez on the first Mexican airline; he was the only passenger. And when the plane was forced to land in Leon because of bad weather in Mexico City, he found himself stranded there for three days: "Well, there I was stuck in a crummy hotel full of cockroaches in this town where no one spoke English."[19] Roaming around the airport, and anxious to get to his destination, Wyler spotted a Mexican worker with bandaged eyes who needed to get to the capital for surgery. He persuaded the pilot that they had to leave immediately or the worker's blindness would be on his conscience. When he finally arrived in Mexico City, however, Rice informed him that he would not discuss business while on vacation, so Wyler spent a few days sightseeing by himself.

Because Rice wanted to fill out the cast with actors from the New York production, Wyler tested a number of them but ended up using only four in the film. For the part of Harry Becker, the communist agitator, he chose Vincent Sherman, who had played the role in the Chicago production and later became a noted film director himself (*The Hard Way*, *Mr. Skeffington*). Two other future directors, Bobby Gordon and Richard Quine, also had bit parts. But Wyler opted to cast Hollywood actors for the important

supporting roles: Bebe Daniels as Simon's loyal secretary, and Doris Kenyon as his wife. He had some trouble casting Roy Darwin, Mrs. Simon's
lover. The studio wanted Sidney Blackmer, but Wyler was "strongly opposed," explaining in a memo to Laemmle: "casting a man without sex
appeal or distinct personality of any kind in the part of Roy Darwin will
prove greater harm than you may realize."[20] Wyler got his way, and Melvyn
Douglas got the part.

The shooting schedule was set for twenty days. Having signed Barrymore for just two weeks at $25,000 a week, the studio instructed Wyler to
shoot all the scenes with Barrymore as quickly as possible and not to stop
for close-ups of anyone else—those bits could be done later. "It was mad,"
Wyler later noted. "In every scene, I shot only Barrymore, skipping close-
ups of anybody talking to him for later. It's a terrible way to make a picture."[21] As it turned out, even with this feverish method, the picture took
three and a half weeks to complete, largely because of Barrymore's inability
to remember his lines.

The actor complained that his part "was longer than the Old Testament,"[22] and the lines had to be delivered at lightning speed. A studio log
noted at least four substantial delays, some lasting half a day, because of
"Mr. Barrymore not knowing his lines."[23] Vincent Sherman told Jan Herman (Wyler's biographer) that his roommate John Qualen, who had a small
part in the film, had been delayed for a dinner appointment because Wyler had to do fifty-six takes of a scene with Barrymore. These memory
lapses got so bad that Barrymore's lines sometimes had to be printed on
cue cards that were held up by a script girl riding on a dolly. Wyler noted,
"Sometimes we had to write on the walls for him or on a piece of the ceiling."[24] Sherman also reported that Barrymore's face looked so puffy that
the makeup department had to tape up his jowls with fish skins before he
could go in front of the camera.[25]

Throughout this struggle with the aging actor, Wyler was getting
memos from Laemmle telling him to keep up the pace, as well as constant
threats that he would be fired if the film was not finished on time. Wyler
responded by employing rough tactics on the set, particularly with the supporting players. Freda Rosenblatt, Wyler's assistant, reported, "Willy wore
everyone down on the set. . . . The actors were ready to kill him."[26]

Barrymore tried to impress Wyler with his Jewish gestures. While preparing for an early scene in which Simon is at his desk, talking on the phone, Barrymore asked Wyler if he had any suggestions. "No," said Wyler. "Pick up the phone and talk." Though Barrymore played the scene well, he added an odd gesture when he picked up the phone, which, he explained to Wyler, was meant to be Jewish. Wyler replied that Simon was a modern, successful man who would pick up the phone like everyone else. Barrymore was unhappy at this correction, and he had to be reined in on other occasions when Wyler thought he was being too ethnic.[27]

Counsellor-at-Law was the first important American play that Wyler transferred to the screen. (There would be twelve more such adaptations—counting his two versions of *The Children's Hour*. One could argue, of course, that none of these plays has stood the test of time—only *The Little Foxes* has had important revivals—but in their day, both the plays and the playwrights were important figures on the American cultural landscape.) This film (and many of the adaptations that followed) shows that Wyler had few peers when it came to faithfully transferring a play to the screen without artificially opening it up and introducing exterior scenes. His preferred approach was to exploit cinematic space primarily through editing and fluid camera work. For instance, all the action in Rice's play takes place over a week's time, either in the law firm's waiting room or in George Simon's office, and Wyler showed his independent streak by resisting the demands of Laemmle and studio manager Henry Henigson that he expand this limited space. Instead, he maintains the interior structure but adds several other locales to Rice's two settings: the building's lobby, where individuals get on and off the elevators, and the offices of John Tedesco, Simon's secretary Regina (Rexy) Gordon, and Herbert Weinberg, a young attorney. Wyler's camera moves rapidly through these various spaces, matching the frenetic pace of the protagonist's typical workday. "I wanted to retain the construction of the play and at the same time have movement," Wyler explained. "It was only an illusion; we never left the lawyer's offices."[28] This is not completely true, as the action does move out into the lobby on numerous occasions, but as Wyler observed, "No critic ever wrote that it was just a photographed stage play. I avoided that feeling by using several offices . . . or by having the actors walk or move around at certain moments."[29]

The film opens with its only exterior shot, a low-angle view of the Empire State Building. The camera slowly moves up the structure, emphasizing its grandeur as a monument to American ingenuity and enterprise. *Counsellor-at-Law* was released in 1933, at the nadir of the Great Depression. More than 5,000 banks had closed, and the nation's industry and agriculture were in shambles. No one was predicting a return to prosperity. But Franklin Roosevelt had been inaugurated nine months before the release of Wyler's film, and his ideas for reviving the American economy were beginning to take hold during its preparation and filming. Like the opening shot, the film reflects Wyler's optimism about the direction of the new administration, which was marked by a commitment to balance. In the words of historian Richard H. Pells, "The New Dealers were especially disturbed by the *chaos* of private capitalism; in their view, American life needed a greater sense of order and control if the nation was to survive the depression." They also wanted to promote harmony among all social classes without destroying the free-enterprise system. "They believed that government, business, and labor should all subordinate their internal differences to the common welfare."[30] Wyler uses Rice's protagonist to illustrate some of the tensions and difficulties inherent in achieving that kind of political and social transition.

After the exterior shot of the building, Wyler cuts to the elevator, from which a mailman emerges on Simon's floor. The camera pauses on the office door and then follows the mailman into the waiting room, where it pauses again at the switchboard, which is buzzing with activity. Surveying the waiting room, Wyler immediately establishes the ethnic flavor of the firm's clients. Two men who wait for Mr. Tedesco converse in Italian. The arrival of Mrs. Chapman (Mayo Methot) to see Mr. Simon creates a flurry. Her recent acquittal in a notorious murder case is revealed as Wyler cuts away to a newspaper photograph of her behind bars. She is obviously a wealthy celebrity client—the kind that gravitates to Simon, who is clearly the star of the firm and whose entrance is anticipated by everyone.

While Mrs. Chapman is accepting the congratulations of the staff and is being gawked at by the other clients, Wyler keeps Mrs. Becker (Malka Kornstein) in focus at the rear of the frame. The audience will learn later that she is from Simon's old neighborhood and that her son has been arrested as a communist agitator. Her modest presence attests to her outsider status; she quietly observes Mrs. Chapman's celebrity but is clearly not part of that world. This distinction is underscored when Mrs. Chapman, looking around for a seat, refuses to share the couch where Mrs. Becker sits, selecting another seat instead. During the course of this rapidly cut sequence, Wyler introduces Mr. McFadden, a working-class Irishman and a former client who now works for Simon. The audience also gets glimpses of Weinberg's office, Tedesco's office (his back is to the camera), and Rexy's office. Simon's office, which we see before he enters, is grand, spacious, and modern, with a view of the New York skyline. As Rexy enters to put some papers on Simon's desk, Wyler moves his camera away from her to magnify the space. Then he cuts away to watch as Simon finally arrives through his private entrance from the lobby. The important business of the day can now begin.

Wyler's strategy is to introduce various classes and ethnic types either in separate frames or in deep focus because this diverse clientele represents the new and emerging America. George Simon, who embodies American power and capitalist enterprise, but who also arrived in steerage not so long ago, is the one figure who can potentially bring this disparate group together. Perhaps his combination of business acumen and working-class compassion will be the tonic that can restore America's luster.

This more deliberately social and political emphasis may be Wyler's way of compensating for the casting of John Barrymore as a Jewish immigrant. As discussed earlier, Rice softened the anti-Semitic aspects of his play by not developing their implications. The play, however, had a distinctly Jewish actor in the lead; the film does not. This difference becomes problematic in the film during Lena Simon's visits to her son's office. Clara Langsner plays her as an exaggerated version of the doting Jewish mother, and her performance seems even more overplayed today because overuse has made the Jewish mother syndrome a cliché. Her scenes with Barrymore verge on the ludicrous, as do those in which Simon's stepchildren show disdain for his "Jewishness" and then happily go off to lunch with their mother's lover, Roy Darwin (Melvyn Douglas, who looks no more ethnic than Barrymore).

Nevertheless, the film's defects are outweighed by its considerable strengths. Despite Barrymore's inept "Jewishness," he delivers one of his best performances for the screen. Pauline Kael wrote that it "revealed his measure as an actor."[31] Margot Peters summed up Barrymore's experience on the film and his contribution to it: "Jack's fast, abrasive, angry, and very moving performance reflects the harassment he suffered while filming it even as it testifies to the histrionic powers of an almost finished actor."[32]

Barrymore's George Simon is best seen as a character caught between the simple values he learned as a poor kid growing up in humble circumstances and the pressures of realizing and inhabiting his brilliant success. He embodies the typical American success story, with its attendant anxiety and heartbreak. As a lawyer, George veers between representing wealthy clients in high-profile cases for exorbitant fees and dispensing free legal advice to the poor. He is a sympathetic character in both the stage and film versions, despite some underhanded dealings, such as taking advantage of insider stock tips to make a quick profit for himself and his partner. Such opportunism is tempered, however, by his generosity: he gives money to Mrs. Becker to buy groceries, bails her son out of jail, and then pays for his funeral.

The plot revolves around two central stories. George discovers that he is in danger of disbarment because a rival lawyer, Francis Clark Baird, has discovered that years earlier George went along with a client's perjured testimony. George did so only because he hoped his client, Breitstein, could be rehabilitated, but he gets no sympathy from his wife, Cora, who worries how a scandal will affect her social life. She is also annoyed by her husband's associations with lower-class characters and implores him to act more like a "gentleman." George's attempts to save his career and his marriage form the focal points of the plot. His career is saved thanks to McFadden's underhanded discovery that Baird is having an affair, but his joy is short-lived when he learns that his wife is leaving for Europe with Roy Darwin. Devastated, he is about to jump out his office window when he is stopped by Rexy, who is secretly in love with him. Then the phone rings, bringing news of a new wealthy client in desperate need of his help. Reinvigorated by the prospect of work, he leaves with Rexy to meet his new client.

The audience, no doubt, feels that George's blackmailing of Baird is justified and that he is better off without his society wife and her awful children. A potential union with the compassionate, working-class Rexy (who also gets along with his mother) seems designed to put George in better touch with his true nature and create a more enduring partnership. George, the ending implies, will maintain the lucrative side of his practice, while his relationship with Rexy will solidify his commitment to the working class and the disadvantaged. Roosevelt's vision of a more inclusive America has a chance to succeed.

Wyler shared with other American artists a sense of optimism in the midst of doom: the system was collapsing, but out of the rubble, maybe something better could be built. Wyler had seen his own childhood collapse amid the devastation of World War I, and now, a mere decade after arriving in America, he saw its vaunted system careening out of human control. But the 1930s gave rise to a new cultural radicalism in America, as many came to believe that they could affect their own future. Committing oneself to a cause, regardless of its philosophy, became a form of salvation.

The attitudes and ideologies that were taking root in the 1930s had their basis in the criticisms of American capitalism arising in the previous decade. The breakdown of the country's industrial network was, for artists and intellectuals, a symptom of a more significant problem. The Depression confirmed their belief that competition and acquisitiveness were eroding the country's social foundation. America was losing or had already lost a sense of cohesiveness and community. James Rorty observed in 1932 that the United States "has everything needed for comfortable survival except a definition of human life."[33] Wyler's George Simon is a man who must put aside his preoccupation with "making it" in order to see what a meaningful human life can be.

Wyler's visual strategy for developing this theme can be traced in a few key scenes. Early in the film, Simon is visited in his office by his wife and his mother. The sequence opens in the lobby, where Roy Darwin is waiting for an elevator and Cora Simon emerges from one. They talk about one of George's high-profile cases—the Crayfield divorce—which Darwin has asked him to drop because it would embarrass the socially prominent Mrs. Crayfield. Then Darwin invites Cora to join him for lunch, and she accepts. The banter is comfortable and casual, and Wyler films them standing face-to-face in two-shots.

Next Wyler cuts to the switchboard, then to Cora in Rexy's office, where she is making calls to arrange the details of an upcoming cruise. Wyler cuts again to the outer office as George's mother Lena enters and sits on the couch without identifying herself. While she waits, Mrs. Simon is greeted by McFadden, a friend from the old neighborhood, who tells her that George has given him a job at the firm. Mrs. Simon beams when she hears about her son's good deeds. Wyler also films this scene in two-shots, but here the characters sit close to each other on the couch; their relationship is tender and affectionate. This framing is repeated when Peter Malone—

like McFadden, distinctly ethnic—enters and sits with Mrs. Simon on the couch, holding her hand and talking about her son. Again, the voluble, convivial nature of these unpretentious characters is emphasized. When George appears, he embraces his mother and kisses her affectionately, further emphasizing the close bond he shares with these common people.

As George walks his mother into his office, they are framed by the blinds and the partition of Rexy's office, where Cora is making her phone calls. The class bonds that separate Cora from mother and son are thus rendered visually. In George's office, Mrs. Simon sits on the couch close to George, who is munching on chocolates, and she chides him about spoiling his appetite. Here, as in the waiting-room scene, the framing connotes a connection between these characters, their closeness suggesting affection and love. When Lena brings up the subject of George's dissolute brother who has just passed a bad check, he gets up, paces the office, and yells at his mother, refusing her pleas for help. Despite their disagreement, what Wyler evokes in this exchange is the characters' ability to express themselves passionately and fervently.

Cora and Mrs. Simon then meet briefly in the office. The mood is formal and cold as the two women stand face-to-face; then Cora lights a cigarette. Here Wyler uses some shot–reverse shots—abrupt cuts that he does not employ in any other scenes featuring George's mother. In parting, Mrs. Simon formally shakes Cora's hand and wishes her a pleasant trip. Cora stays to intervene on behalf of Mrs. Crayfield. The ensuing scene in which Cora asks George for a favor lacks any of the intimacy or passion of his mother's plea on behalf of his brother. George and Cora are presented in a two-shot, but rather than sitting close together, George sits on the edge of his desk and Cora sits in a chair. Their speech is even and formal. When Cora declares that she wished George "practiced law like a gentleman," he moves away from her toward a window, no longer facing his wife. Cora's reference to her husband's lower-class origins obviously stings—to her, apparently, he is no better than his brother, a petty criminal. Still, he decides to accede to her request and drops the Crayfield case, much to Rexy's disgust. (Wyler cuts to a close-up of her face as George tells her to draw up the papers.) George then asks Cora if he now rates a kiss, and Wyler quickly cuts away from them as the sequence ends.

Wyler emphasizes these points in another paired sequence, this time featuring Cora Simon's children and Harry Becker, the communist agitator. Cora arrives at the office and leaves her children seated in the waiting room, where Harry also sits with his mother. The children are condescending to the workers in the office, and their attitude is not lost on Harry. At one point, when young Richard asks one of the staff to fetch him a magazine, Wyler cuts to Harry's back and then to the children's point of view as he looms over them in a low-angle shot. The children are clearly frightened.

That sequence is interrupted by a shot of Cora waiting in George's office. Wyler places her in a long shot, dwarfed by the office's space. He will replicate that shot with one of George after Cora leaves, and again at the end of the film when he realizes that his marriage is falling apart. George enters and confides to Cora that he is facing disbarment; she is only marginally interested. Again, Wyler films their exchange in a two-shot, and again, they do not touch. Their exchange is formal and cold. Cora's only concern is being involved in a scandal, and George is clearly crushed by her indifference when she insists on leaving for Europe without him.

After she leaves, Harry Becker is ushered in. As their confrontation begins, George is getting his shoes shined, and his back is to Harry. During their exchange, Wyler uses two-shots featuring Harry's blurred, slightly out-of-focus face in the front of the frame, with an in-focus George lecturing him. Harry rejects George's help and says he is not grateful that George bailed him out of jail. His reference to the police as "Cossacks" gets George's goat—he refuses to accept the comparison between America and Russia. When Harry accuses him of being on the wrong side of the class war, George launches into a speech of his own. Wyler moves the camera in on him, isolating him in the frame as he speaks of his origins: "Do you think I don't know what it is to sweat and to freeze and to go hungry? . . . Don't you come around me with any of your half-baked Communist bull and expect me to fall for it."

Wyler's framing seems to give George the upper hand until he cuts to Harry, who rises, towering over the seated George, and accuses him of being "a traitor to his class" and "getting in right with crooked politicians and crooked corporations that feed on the blood and sweat of the workers." George takes all this sitting down, but when Harry calls Cora a "kept parasite," he rises up to face him. Harry keeps going, however, calling Cora's children "pampered brats." During this exchange, Harry faces the camera, while George stands with his back to it. When Harry spits on the floor and leaves, George remains facing away from the camera. He has been defeated, and he knows it. Later, when he realizes that Cora has betrayed him, all Harry's accusations will be confirmed.

Counsellor-at-Law is an assured film, expertly made and beautifully acted. It features rapid cutting as Wyler matches his film's style to the fast pace of the play. He employs some expressive camera movements and framings to accentuate the social and political aspects of the play he has chosen to forefront. Although *Counsellor* does not display the hallmark of Wyler's mature style, which emphasizes staging scenes in depth during extended dialogue scenes and thus eliminating the need to cut back and forth, it is a model of his ability to use editing, with some in-depth stagings, to bring a stage piece vividly to life on the screen.

After filming, Wyler had difficulty with the censors. Near the end of the play, after Rexy's intervention to prevent George's suicide, there is a call from Theodore Wingdale, president of the American Steel Company. Rexy asks George if he wants to speak with Wingdale, and he replies, "Tell him to go to hell." This line was deemed unacceptable. Wyler argued that the line was necessary because it was funny—"not because of the humor of the particular line, but because with the deletion of the climax the picture remains unrelieved and we eliminate the only bit of comedy relief in the ending of the picture."[34] Wyler lost that battle: the line was changed to "Tell him to go to the devil."

The film opened on December 7 at Radio City Music Hall. The critics loved it, and it turned into a commercial success as well. Rice, who did not like Hollywood, was delighted with the film. In a telegram to Wyler he wrote, "The picture is excellent in all its details and you have every reason to be proud of the fine job you have done. I am sure that your work will receive general recognition."[35]

Wyler, however, was not entirely happy with the "recognition." Although the Los Angeles press praised his direction, the New York press generally avoided naming the director in its reviews. This rankled, given that Wyler's name was included in many of the film's advertisements. Wyler knew he was coming into his own as a director of importance, and he wanted industry members to be aware of his work as well.

3

First-Class Pictures

These Three (1936)

Wyler's last film for Universal, the studio that had nurtured him for fifteen years, was *The Good Fairy*, released in 1935. That same year, after returning from his honeymoon with Margaret Sullavan, he made his first freelance film for producer Jesse Lasky at Twentieth Century–Fox. That film, *The Gay Deception*, starring Francis Lederer and Frances Dee, was the first Wyler film to earn an Oscar nomination (for Best Original Story). More significant than the nomination, however, was that the film brought Wyler to the attention of Samuel Goldwyn.

In 1935, Goldwyn's fortunes were waning. Of his recent films, only a few Eddie Cantor pictures had done well critically or commercially, and he was looking for a new actress to change the fortunes of his studio. He wanted someone like Bette Davis, who had won that year's Best Actress Oscar, or Katharine Hepburn, who had won the previous year. Joel McCrea, one of Goldwyn's contract actors, had been trying to promote his wife, Frances Dee, as this potential star for months. Frustrated by Goldwyn's lack of interest, McCrea brought a print of *The Gay Deception* to the studio and ran it for Goldwyn. His boss was delighted and charmed by the film, but he had no interest in Frances Dee. Instead, he turned to McCrea and asked, "Who directed this?" "A funny little guy named Wyler" was the reply.[1]

Leland Hayward, who was Wyler's agent (and who would soon marry Margaret Sullavan after her divorce from Wyler), reported that Goldwyn needed a director for a property he had recently purchased and wanted to meet Wyler. "He couldn't have been more charming," Wyler remembered of that meeting, "but I thought he had lost his mind. He told me he wanted to make 'The Children's Hour.'"[2] Lillian Hellman's first play had caused a sensation when it opened in November 1934, in part because of its lesbian theme. Wyler could not believe that the Production Code Administration

(PCA) would allow a film version to be made. In fact, in a letter to Goldwyn following a discussion of the project, PCA head Joseph Breen confirmed that Goldwyn could not "use the title 'The Children's Hour'" and
could "make no reference directly or indirectly in either advertising or exploitation of the picture . . . to the stage play 'The Children's Hour.'" In addition, Goldwyn was instructed "to remove from your finished production
all possible suggestions of Lesbianism."[3]

Years later, Hellman recalled that she had been able to sell Goldwyn
the screen rights by persuading his story editor, Merritt Hulburd, that the
play's deeper implications transcended lesbianism. "It's not about lesbians.
It's about the power of a lie. I happened to pick what I thought was a very
strong lie."[4] Goldwyn would become the only bidder for the screen rights,
offering $40,000 and eventually paying $50,000. And once Goldwyn had
explained Hellman's reasoning to him, Wyler jumped at the opportunity to
direct it, noting that "Sam Goldwyn's name stood for something, for quality. I had been making second-class pictures, and Goldwyn was making
first-class pictures, so it was a good step for me."[5]

Within months of each other, Wyler and Hellman both signed three-
year contracts with Goldwyn. Wyler's contract gave him a first-year salary
of $88,000, paid out over forty months. Goldwyn paid him $2,500 a week
for the first fourteen weeks to direct *These Three*, and $2,083 a week for
the next fourteen weeks. Hellman's three-year contract guaranteed her ten
weeks' salary a year, at $2,500 a week. Both contracts allowed the prin-
cipals to be loaned out to other studios if their schedules did not conflict
with Goldwyn's production plans. There was also a provision for "suspension and extension," meaning that if either one turned down a project that
was not to his or her liking, the time that would have been devoted to that
assignment would be added on to the contract. Wyler was often suspended.
As he explained, "I always chose the best material he had. I refused to do
things I didn't like. . . . When I refused I was suspended and extended."[6] So
his three-year contract ended up running for five years.

In the spring of 1933, as he was finishing *The Thin Man*, Dashiell
Hammett had come across a collection of British court cases compiled by
William Roughead under the title *Bad Companions* (1931). Hammett was
particularly taken by the chapter "Closed Doors, or The Great Drumsheugh
Case," which took place in 1810 and involved Jane Cumming, a student at

a Scottish girls' school called Drumshuegh Gardens. Jane had informed her grandmother, Dame Helen Cumming Gordon, that two of her teachers (who had also founded the school) had displayed "inordinate affection" in front of their students. Dame Helen used her influence to have all the students removed from the school within forty-eight hours. The teachers sued for libel, but despite what was clearly false testimony, the jury found in favor of Dame Helen. Although the teachers later appealed and won, the case was never fairly resolved, and after eleven years, they settled for around £1,400 each; the school never reopened. Hammett thought the story might make a good play and considered writing it himself, but he eventually concluded it would be more suitable for Hellman and offered it to her.

Hellman was fascinated by the concepts of malice and evil, which figure prominently in a number of her works, including *The Little Foxes* (which Wyler would film five years later). Clearly concerned with the destructive effects of lies and the implications of unprovoked malice, "The Great Drumshuegh Case" proved irresistible to her. Doris Falk writes that in her manuscript notes for the play, Hellman compared Mary Tilford (her version of Jane Cumming) to Shakespeare's Iago as the exemplar of "motiveless malignancy." According to Hellman, the only difference between Mary and *Othello*'s villain is Mary's fear of the possible consequences of her actions.[7]

Hellman retains many plot points from the legal case in her play. Mary Tilford, a student at a New England girls' school, falsely accuses her teachers, Karen Wright and Martha Dobie, of lesbianism. Mary, like her real-life counterpart, has an influential grandmother, Mrs. Tilford, who uses her influence to have all the children removed from the school. Martha, like her model, has an aunt, Lily Mortar, an actress who lives at the school and teaches there. As in the British trial, a fabricated keyhole is introduced as evidence, and true to the original, the teachers sue for libel and lose. Hellman, however, makes some crucial changes. In *The Children's Hour*, Mrs. Tilford eventually discovers the truth and tries to make amends, but she arrives just moments too late to prevent either Karen's loss of her fiancé or Martha's suicide.

The playwright also adds a surprise revelation at the end: before shooting herself, Martha admits that there is some truth to Mary's accusation—she does harbor erotic feelings for Karen, and the incident has forced her to confront aspects of her nature she had previously suppressed. In his biography of Hellman, Carl Rollyson points out that in the first draft of the play, Hellman labeled Martha an "unconscious lesbian."[8] Martha's startling confession may be an attempt on Hellman's part to push the play toward tragedy, but as a belated ironic recognition, it doesn't quite work. The main action of the play turns on Mary's role as an agent of evil, and Hellman concentrates on the injustice of her accusation rather than the reasons behind it.

Indeed, the major criticisms of Hellman's dramatic adaptation involved Martha's last-minute declaration. Both Brooks Atkinson and Eric Bentley thought the play should have ended with the pistol shot signaling Martha's suicide, with no messy confession to dilute its impact. In his review of the original production, Atkinson wrote in the *New York Times*, "When two people are defeated by the malignance of an aroused public opinion, leave them the dignity of their hatred and despair."[9]

To ensure a focus on Mary's evil, Hellman made another important departure from her source material. In Roughead's book, Jane Cumming is described as the bastard child of an aristocrat's liaison with a black woman, and Roughead ascribes Jane's motives to her illegitimacy—she is determined to wreak revenge on those who have punished her for breaking the rules. Hellman eliminates this complication, in large part to make Mary, in William Wright's words, "a symbol of pristine evil."[10]

Other than Clifford Odets, whom she preceded on Broadway by three months, Hellman was arguably the most acclaimed new playwright of the 1930s. *The Children's Hour* ran for 691 performances—a total that Odets never even approached, and one that would be bettered by only six other plays in the entire decade. *The Children's Hour* exhibits many of the strengths and weaknesses common to Hellman's plays, which are reliably well constructed, tight, vivid, and lively. However, because of her habit of prioritizing the establishment of clear moral points over the development of characters and relationships, she regularly encounters problems in creating truly memorable characters. In her introduction to *Six Plays*, Hellman rationalizes this flaw, declaring, "I am a moral writer, often too moral a writer, and I cannot avoid it seems, that last summing up."[11]

The play's success was largely due to Hellman's ability to weave liberal social attitudes into a suspenseful plot. There was also the taboo but titillating subject of lesbianism, although it is difficult to say how much this shock factor contributed to the play's success. In 1927, Edouard Bourdet's *The Captive*, which deals with lesbianism more directly, had been shut down by the courts after a police raid. The same year, Mae West's *The Drag*, about male homosexuality, was closed by its producers out of town rather than face the inevitable police action. Presumably, *The Children's Hour* was allowed to run because lesbianism was not its central issue.

The play in large part belongs to Mary, whose malignancy blights the lives of all those around her. Her lies lead to the closing of the school, the death of Martha, the dissolution of Karen and Joe's engagement, and the humiliation and spiritual dissipation of her grandmother, who shares in Mary's guilt. Mrs. Tilford is portrayed as a self-righteous yet gullible woman (she instantly believes her granddaughter's lies) and a gossip. In addition to the lives of three innocent people, her willing participation in character assassination ultimately destroys an entire society, just as a similar malignancy would do almost two decades later in Arthur Miller's *The Crucible*. Hellman displays her distrust of liberalism when Joe and Karen come to learn that reason is useless when confronted by a force like Mary. Rollyson explains: "Because he cannot take the radical view—that a lie is just that, a false insupportable assertion—[Joe] is doomed to half-believing in the lie he would try to persuade Mary to reject. Hellman's plays imply that the liberal mentality goes only half-way toward opposing evil."[12]

The Children's Hour opens with a student reading from the "quality of mercy" speech from *The Merchant of Venice*. In fact, mercy is what is missing in the world of the play—apparently, Hellman felt that society should be reminded of this lack in the midst of the Depression, when suffering by the weak and exploitation by the powerful seemed likely to be alleviated only by significant political reform. At the end of the play, Karen is left alone: her best friend is dead, her fiancé is gone, her school is an empty shell. But when Mrs. Tilford attempts to make amends, Karen is able to accept the older woman's apology and her offer of friendship. Such mercy is "not strained"—it comes as a blessing. Her gesture ends the play on a note of muted triumph, as Mary and her evil have been pushed to the background and Karen takes steps toward building a new life. By breaking free of the oppressive, if misguided, power represented by Mrs. Tilford, Hellman implies, the young can overcome entrenched, conservative forces that threaten their prospects for the future. This somewhat upbeat mood was reflected in the politics of the period. President Roosevelt's New Deal came out squarely for the young in its establishment of the Civilian Conservation Corps and the National Youth Administration, which created jobs for unemployed young people.

Hellman worked on one screenplay for Goldwyn before starting on her adaptation of *The Children's Hour*. That film was *The Dark Angel* (1935) for director Sidney Franklin, whom Hellman came to despise when she learned that he consulted his card-playing buddies on how to revise her script. She was teamed with British playwright Mordaunt Sharp—who, in an interesting coincidence, had shocked Broadway in 1933 with his play *The Green Bay Tree*, featuring a homosexual theme. *The Dark Angel* was also adapted from a play; it had been filmed by Goldwyn as a silent in 1925, with a script by Frances Marion. Hellman claimed that she never read the original play by Guy Bolton but worked directly from Marion's script.

Hellman's work on *The Dark Angel* is interesting, in that it sheds light on how she restructured *The Children's Hour* into the film *These Three*. After writing the play, she was still preoccupied by its triangular structure, involving two protagonists who were college friends and a male lead who is the fiancé of one of them. Hellman's film version of *The Dark Angel* focuses on similar themes of love and friendship. The characters Gerald Shannon (Herbert Marshall), Alan Trent (Fredric March), and Kitty Vane (Merle Oberon) are childhood friends; the Vanes and the Shannons are neighbors, and Trent and Shannon are cousins. In a prologue, Hellman introduces them as children enjoying a picnic in the decade before World War I. A gust of wind—prefiguring the winds of war that will force them apart—scatters their food. The subsequent plot of the film is less important than its anticipation of the writer's adaptation of her own play, including an attempt, later abandoned, to include a prologue introducing Karen and Martha as children.

Hellman was aware that she would have to revise her play for the movies—Breen's memo had been very specific, and she was prepared to abide by it. Breen's stipulation that Goldwyn's film must not reference the stage play in any way was accomplished by changing its title to *These Three*. Though believing that the film deserved a life of its own, Hellman worked to ensure that the thematic integrity of her play—the power of a lie—was retained.

Later, she rejected the notion that Hollywood was a "dead end for serious writers," declaring, "I wouldn't have written movies if I thought that."[13]

Hellman's drafts went through a variety of permutations. The earliest prose treatment in the Goldwyn files is undated but was probably done in early August 1935. In it, Hellman creates an entirely new backstory for Karen and Martha to open the film, apparently having decided that, unlike the play (which opens with Mrs. Mortar teaching in the school), the film should focus immediately on the two friends. This early version of the story begins in England, where Karen's family, the Wrights, are landed gentry and Martha Dobie is a distant cousin. When Martha's father dies unexpectedly, leaving her only £100, she is taken in by the Wrights, who raise the two girls like sisters. World War I intervenes, and Karen's father dies, "a wreck from the war"; her mother dies shortly thereafter from grief. Mrs. Mortar—the black sheep of the family because she is an actress—becomes their chaperone. Karen and Martha conclude that they are best equipped to start a school and decide to do so in America, where they feel their English ancestry will convey a certain prestige. Once in America, Karen meets Dr. Joseph Cardin at a garden party; they fall in love and decide to marry. The school, however, is not doing very well, so Joe recommends that they visit Mrs. Tilford, who decides to send her granddaughter Mary to the school and then persuades others to send their children as well. One evening, Joe is called to the school to attend to a student suffering from pneumonia; he spends the night with the dying girl, who is being treated in Martha's room. While Karen lingers in the room with the dead girl, Mary sees Joe put his arm around Martha's shoulder as they emerge from the room. Mary fakes a heart attack and returns to her grandmother's house, where she accuses Karen and Martha of killing students and charges that Joe is having an affair with Martha. From there, the treatment follows the plot of Hellman's play until the end, at which point Martha patches things up with Karen and Joe and returns to England.

Why Hellman wanted to embellish the story in this way is not clear. None of the other treatments or drafts utilizes these details, including the two women's English beginnings. Perhaps, in an attempt to placate Breen, Hellman was trying to truly distance the film from the play. However, she obviously decided that this treatment pushed the story too far into the past, because the next treatment, dated August 21, 1935, opens in Karen and

Martha's college dormitory room, where graduation gowns are being delivered amidst great excitement about the day ahead. It is established that
Karen has inherited an old farmhouse, and the two young women decide
to start a school there. When Karen and Martha arrive at the house, they
meet Joe Cardin, who is tearing shingles off the roof to get rid of the bees
that have nested there. This homely introduction of Joe was retained for the
film, but other details were dropped in a treatment dated five days later, including that Joe and Karen had been childhood friends, that Joe is related
to Mrs. Tilford, and Joe's proposal to Karen in the garden of Mrs. Tilford's
estate (in the finished film, it occurs at a town fair). The treatment ends
with Mrs. Tilford telling Martha and Karen that she has made a public
apology for defaming their character and handing them a check as a gesture of restitution. The script ends with Martha on a ship alone and Joe and
Karen getting back together.

In the August 26 treatment, as in the earlier draft, Mary's lie is un-
masked when Rosalie's mother finds the bracelet her daughter had stolen
from a classmate—Mary had been using this theft to force Rosalie to cor-
roborate her lie about Martha and Karen. Martha decides that she must
bring Karen and Joe back together, but she knows she cannot stay with
them. Joe and Karen decide to pick up the pieces together, but somewhere
else—"any place in the world."[14]

Hellman and Wyler became close friends during this period, and their
friendship lasted throughout their lives. Describing Wyler as "the greatest
American director," Hellman carefully detailed her praise: "He had a wonderful pictorial sense—he knew how to pack so much into a shot that I felt
I could leave certain things unsaid, knowing Willy would show them. We
had to become friends, because we were the only two people in the Goldwyn asylum who weren't completely loony."[15] She also commented, "Willy
left you alone. He said things like, 'Don't bother about the shots. Just do
the dialogue. Don't tell me where to put the camera.' And I thought, this is
heaven."[16]

By the time Wyler was hired to direct the film, Goldwyn had already
cast the three main characters: Miriam Hopkins (Martha), Merle Oberon (Karen), and Joel McCrea (Joe). Wyler chose Bonita Granville to play
Mary, and she remembered the experience fondly: "[Wyler] had infinite
patience and never once raised his voice. Without putting it into specific

terms, I realize now that each day he was teaching me something important—the technique of how to move, how to build to a climax, how important it is to listen to a scene—but most of all he taught me that integrity was absolutely vital to acting."[17]

Wyler was not thrilled with the rest of the cast, however. He would have preferred Leslie Howard for the role of Joe, and McCrea was not pleased that Wyler put him through so many takes. Oberon resented Wyler's attention to Granville and complained to McCrea that the child actress was stealing the picture. Hopkins had a reputation for being a difficult actress with a bad temper.

These problems with the actors were more than offset by Wyler's introduction to cinematographer Gregg Toland, who would become one of his most important collaborators—they worked together on all of Wyler's films with Goldwyn except *Dodsworth*. Toland was just as meticulous as Wyler, and as a result, their relationship got off to a rocky start. Wyler recalled, "I was in the habit of saying, 'Put the camera here with a forty-millimeter lens, move it this way, pan over here, do this.' Well, he was not used to that. . . . I considered it part of my job. You don't do that with a man like Gregg Toland."[18]

In Toland, Wyler recognized a kindred spirit. They both valued a style that emphasized depth-of-focus photography, which enabled realism and fluidity in the storytelling. For a special section devoted to Toland in *Sequence*, Wyler commented on this style: "Because of it, I have been able to stage scenes in depth, keeping two or more people on the screen at the same time during extended dialogue scenes, and eliminating the need for cutting back and forth from one to the other. This makes for greater flow and continuity, intensifies dramatic situations, holds the audience's attention more compellingly and, of course, in addition makes for more exciting composition by adding the illusion of the third dimension, depth, to the two-dimensional screen." He elaborated: "Most photography in Hollywood is 'soft' and diffused, using less light and a larger lens opening. This photography is a handmaiden of the star system, and is designed to make the stars as young, beautiful and glamorous as possible. Toland's style, on the other hand, was an attempt to achieve *reality or truthfulness* on film."[19]

This is the philosophy André Bazin drew on when formulating his theories of cinematic realism and his assessment of the contributions of Orson

Welles and William Wyler. These directors, according to Bazin, followed a tradition established by precursors such as Robert Flaherty and Erich Von Stroheim, who were more interested in "revealing" reality than adding to it. Depth of focus became one of the high points in the evolution of film because it brought the spectator "into a relation with the image closer to that which he enjoys with reality." It also required a "more active mental attitude on the part of the spectator and a more positive contribution on his part to the action in progress."[20]

Wyler also noted that he and Toland discussed each film "from beginning to end." Like the direction, the style of the photography varied, depending on the subject. "In *These Three*," Wyler explained, "we were dealing with little girl things. What was good was rather simple, attractive photography."[21]

As Hellman and Wyler worked on the project and filming progressed, the nation's economy was beginning to turn around; business was expanding, and New Deal programs were working. Radical politics—the exploration of alternatives to a failed capitalist system—was still popular, however, with artists and intellectuals. As part of a group of New York intellectuals working in Hollywood, Hellman was friendly with other writers such as Dorothy Parker, Donald Ogden Stewart, and Ring Lardner Jr., who were politically active and were becoming increasing vocal about the rise of fascist governments in Europe. Around this time, Benito Mussolini annexed Abyssinia, forcing Emperor Haile Selassie to flee, and then formed an alliance with Germany; Adolf Hitler remilitarized the Rhineland and forged alliances with Russia and Japan; and General Francisco Franco initiated a civil war against the elected Popular Front government in Spain. Structuring *The Children's Hour* (her first play) according to the conventions of melodrama, which presented society as a battleground between good and evil, Hellman trusted that audiences in 1934 would have no difficulty seeing a connection between Mary Tilford and her grandmother and the rise of totalitarian governments in Germany, Spain, and Italy. In this play, as well as in subsequent works, Hellman locates her plots in realistic settings and populates them with bold, stark, and compelling characters whose schemes and struggles imply that the war between good and evil is the central dilemma of the times.

In Hollywood, Hellman and her fellow screenwriters were also up in arms over MGM's shelving of Sinclair Lewis's *It Can't Happen Here*, the story of the rise of a dictator in the United States. The studio had bought the rights to the novel when it was still in typescript and hired Sidney Howard, who had adapted *Arrowsmith* for Goldwyn in 1931 and would go on to adapt *Dodsworth* for Goldwyn and Wyler in 1936, to prepare a script. The first news releases announced that Will Hays, head of the Motion Picture Producers and Distributors Association of America, had stopped the film, fearing international problems and the wrath of the Republican Party, but the Hays office denied banning the film. MGM announced that the project had been shelved because it was too expensive, and Goldwyn maintained that the film was canceled because of casting difficulties. Howard claimed to have seen a lengthy memo from Joseph Breen noting "dangerous material" in the script and suggesting drastic revisions. In any case, the film's cancellation was heartily approved by both Germany and Italy; the German Film Chamber called Lewis "a full blooded Communist." Lewis's biographer, Mark Schorer, concludes that the studio's motive for shelving the film was probably "less political than economic. Not only would this film have been banned in Germany and Italy and other foreign markets, but probably all Metro films would henceforth have been kept out of Germany and Italy."[22]

It was in this volatile atmosphere that Wyler embarked on his first film with Goldwyn, based on Hellman's controversial play. Wyler, of course, was an interested observer of the situation in Europe, having arrived in the United States just fifteen years earlier. He had established his liberal credentials while filming *Counsellor-at-Law*, and even the light comedy *The Gay Deception* offered both a gently satiric portrayal of the wealthy and a warm, affectionate look at the working class. The latter, typical of the decade's screwball comedies, concludes with the marriage of a prince from a fictitious country and a secretary who dared to dream of spending as much as $19 for a hat. Wyler's friendship with Hellman, however, now sharpened and focused his political views and also made him more confident when he insisted on the artistic integrity of his projects and stood up for his own creative ideas.

The changes Hellman and Wyler made in transferring her play to the screen are substantive; in many ways, they constitute an improvement over the original. While the script was being prepared, a number of titles were suggested or briefly adopted, including "The Lie." In a memo to Goldwyn, though, Merritt Hulburd indicated that he preferred "A Lie Is Told" and also suggested "Word of Honor."

Hellman's script begins with the delivery of graduation gowns around campus. There are shots of the Glee Club singing and girls calling out to the delivery boy from their windows, complaining that he is late. There is a cut to Karen and Martha's rooms, where we see Martha packing her trunk and Karen tutoring a student. From this cozy dorm scene, the camera moves to the college president delivering a speech to the graduates; then to Martha's aunt, Lily Mortar, telling another parent about the sacrifices she has made for her niece; and finally to Karen and Martha lounging on the campus green and talking about their future.

Feeling that this section was still too long, Wyler cut it considerably to make the completed film's opening move along quickly. Shots of the graduates standing in two uniform rows with the precision of a military drill immediately evoke a sense of the societal conformity that will be rocked by the ensuing scandal. That image—echoed later in a shot of the jury as the judge renders the verdict in the libel trial—captures the mind-set of fascist societies and deftly implies that America itself might share it. The opening shot is held long enough to accommodate the last words of the president's speech, at which point Wyler cuts to Karen and Martha, separating them from the crowd. They are seen as a unit, isolated from the rest of their classmates, until Martha's Aunt Lily (Catherine Doucet) intrudes. Karen wants to distance herself from Lily, but Martha holds on to her, and they deal with Lily together. In these scenes, the director visually establishes the bond between the two women and the entrance of a third party who causes a disturbance, foreshadowing the fate that awaits them. Although here Lily seems to be a harmless, self-centered actress, she is later revealed to have a cruel and sadistic streak when it comes to her niece, and she will play a significant role in Martha's undoing.

In the next scene, back in their dorm room, Karen suggests that Martha join her in converting her grandmother's farmhouse into a school. Here, the action is presented in either two-shots or shot–reverse shots. Rollyson describes this scene as "a kind of proposal," although he rejects the notion of any sexual attraction between the two women.[23] Both John Baxter and Bernard F. Dick, however, suggest that Wyler is able to subvert the Breen office's ultimatum by having Hopkins act as if her character, Martha, is in love with Karen.[24] But the film does not support this theory, especially when Wyler shoots most of the "proposal" as a shot–reverse shot that isolates the two friends in separate frames rather than presenting them together. What is indisputable is that the film focuses on Karen and Martha rather than on Mary Tilford.

The opening sequence is thus indicative of the predominant style of *These Three*, which proceeds in a fluid, elegant, and compact manner, much like *The Gay Deception*. Wyler's first collaboration with Gregg Toland is not distinguished by the deep-focus compositions they would later employ, although there are hints of that technique in some scenes. Instead, in this early work, Wyler points Toland's camera work toward suggestive compositions to bring out the film's themes. Wyler makes strides in framing his characters more effectively in relation to each other, thus eliminating some cutting back and forth, but this film utilizes more cuts and close-ups than his other Goldwyn films.

The preamble material, including the introduction of the young man who will complete the central trio, takes up roughly one-third of the film. (The play's opening scene, in which Peggy [the film's Helen] reads from *The Merchant of Venice*, does not occur until half an hour into the film.) After leaving college, Karen and Martha arrive in Lancet, where they find the farmhouse in ruins. While looking the place over, Karen peers through a broken window and sees a mouse—this is Wyler's first use of a shot framed by a window, a motif that will become a metaphor of entrapment. Discouraged by the condition of the house, the two young women consider abandoning their plans when suddenly the sound and then the spectacle of shingles being thrown off the roof attract their attention. This interruption is followed by the appearance of a man in beekeeper's gear and a swarm of bees around his head; he is Joe Cardin, a neighbor and a doctor at the local hospital. He climbs down, introduces himself, and offers to share his lunch. Karen and Martha are hesitant at first but then warm up to him. Their conversation as they sit in the yard is genial and friendly, and Wyler films it with minimal cutting, including all three in the frame to indicate that those two have now become "these three."

The scene's outdoor setting, like Karen and Martha's taxi ride to the farm, is presented as idyllic. Throughout much of the film, Wyler invests the natural world with a beauty and grace that is conspicuously missing from the formalized social structure that dominates. Like much of Wyler's work, *These Three* is primarily an indoor film, and as such, it introduces Wyler's preoccupation with images of constriction and claustrophobia. This emphasis makes the outdoor scenes in the film all the more startling.

The idyllic mood is further developed as Joe delivers some lumber to the house, which the three are now repairing. Joe drives while Karen lies on her back on the logs, gazing up at the trees and sky as Alfred Newman's romantic music, first heard during the taxi ride, is reprised. (Joe will soon propose to Karen under a tree.) The drive is interrupted by their meeting with Mrs. Tilford (Alma Kruger) and Mary (Granville), who are being chauffeured home. As Joe greets Mrs. Tilford, whom he knows, the shot is framed through her car window—as is her introduction to Karen. Here again, by confining the characters in a tight, constricting frame, Wyler foreshadows the threat Mrs. Tilford and Mary pose to Joe and Karen's romance and to the bucolic time they are sharing. The introduction of Mary is also significant: Wyler's shot lines up Karen (whose head is in the foreground), Mrs. Tilford, and Mary, who is seated beside her grandmother but slightly out of focus. Mrs. Tilford remarks that she knew Karen's grandmother and would like to enroll Mary in the new school. When Mary erupts in a temper tantrum, the scene concludes with inside-outside shots that frame first Mrs. Tilford, then Karen and Joe in the car's window. Karen's excitement at the prospect of obtaining her first pupil is reinforced when Joe tells her that the community follows Mrs. Tilford "like lambs," but the phrase offers an ominous suggestion, reinforced by the window framing, of how easily Mrs. Tilford will later be able to destroy Karen and Joe. As the lovers drive away, Wyler's camera pulls back to emphasize the natural setting as it envelops Joe's car.

After the proposal scene, the indoor world takes over. The idyll is officially broken in the next scene by the arrival of Lily Mortar, who volunteers her services at the school. As Lily approaches the house (her image framed by a window), Martha's horrified reaction is shared by the audience and the camera. Then, as Lily is speaking to Martha, Wyler employs a modified deep-focus shot to show Karen and Joe descending the staircase, slightly out of focus. Wyler holds this shot for just a moment before cutting to a shot of Karen with Joe behind her, as Lily looks up at them from the foot of the stairs. In this triangular shot, Joe's raised position indicates that he has displaced Lily in Karen and Martha's life.

Over the course of his career, Wyler would become a master at expressing repressed emotional states through visual indexes such as the staircase, used here as an important thematic signpost. Numerous key emotional confrontations in Wyler's films take place on staircases, which he uses to make the characters seem either more or less dominant, depending on the perspective. He utilizes them to great effect in his next Hellman adaptation, *The Little Foxes*.

After Lily's arrival, the school officially opens. Thereafter, the film follows the basic plot of the play, with some modifications in dialogue to accommodate the substitution of an apparent love triangle for the play's lesbian relationship. The character of Mary in *The Children's Hour* is an Iago-like villain who loves to read Théophile Gautier's novel *Mademoiselle de Maupin*, about a transvestite heroine, from which she supposedly learns enough about aberrant sex to make her lie believable. In the film, she becomes bent on revenge after being exposed as a liar in three separate instances: for cheating on a Latin translation, for claiming to have picked a bouquet of flowers for Lily when in fact she had retrieved them from the garbage, and for faking a heart attack. So when Joe inadvertently spends the night in Martha's room, Mary exaggerates this innocent incident into a scandalous lie, which provokes her grandmother to exert her influence to have all the girls removed from the school.

The scene depicting Joe's overnight stay in Martha's room is one of Wyler's most elegant and effective sequences. Following his proposal to Karen and her acceptance as they stand under a tree—the outdoor setting underscoring the romantic quality of their attachment—Wyler's camera next moves to Martha alone in her room, where she is preparing to paint a table. When Joe arrives at the school, looking for Karen, Wyler frames him in the door and then double-frames him through a pane of glass from an interior door, again foreshadowing his entanglement in the scandal that will soon ensue. Joe calls out for Karen, but Martha, standing at the top of the stairs, tells him to quiet down (so as not to wake the sleeping girls). Here, the staircase becomes a place where Martha faces her own emotions, the space between her and Joe signifying an unbridgeable emotional gulf. Joe enters her room, and the divide is accentuated as he lies down on the couch and Martha resumes painting the table. As she talks about her childhood, which she spent following her aunt Lily from show to show, Wyler moves his camera away from Joe and toward Martha, pausing for a medium close-up of her face, framed by the table legs, as she concludes, "I was so alone."

While she is talking, Joe falls asleep, and Martha looks longingly at him. She then goes to sit in a chair, with the fireplace lit significantly behind her. Martha watches Joe as Wyler's camera pans slowly to the right, revealing the snow outside the window—thus visually evoking the fire and ice that are emblematic of these two characters' relationship. Next, there is a dissolve as the camera reverses direction. Time has passed, but Martha is still watching Joe, who wakes abruptly and knocks over a glass of milk. A quick cut shows Mary being awakened by the sound; she then sneaks into the hallway and witnesses Joe's departure, as Martha begins to pick up the pieces of broken glass. The noise also wakens Lily, who enters the room and reminds Martha that Joe and Karen will be marrying in the spring. Depressed over losing both her friend and Joe, Martha starts to cry, as Mary continues to spy from the shadows. The cut to Mary deepens the connection between her malevolence and the fate of the three principals. Wyler's layered mise-en-scène and strategic editing thus manage to convey Martha's loneliness, her feelings of abandonment, and Mary's evil intentions more effectively than Hellman had been able to do in the play.

It is after this scene that Wyler cuts to the "quality of mercy" speech that opens the play but serves here as a herald for Mary's entrance bearing the flowers that will be her undoing. Mary, of course, is the antithesis of mercy, as Karen tries to show the girl after catching her lies. Mary rejects Karen's admonitions and is punished. Angry and bitter about her punishment, she runs away from school and then tells her grandmother the lie that will upend all their lives. The sequence in which Mary informs her grandmother that Martha is having an affair with Joe concludes with Mary at the top of the stairs and Mrs. Tilford below, having been persuaded by the lie. The power has now shifted to Mary, who seems to be in control of events.

The confrontation between Mrs. Tilford and the victims of Mary's lie is another display of Wyler's emerging style. Again, there are minor modifications of the play, such as when Joe announces that "three people" (instead of two) are coming before her "with their lives spread on the table."

Martha, Karen, and Joe enter together and appear posed, shot from a low angle to emphasize their moral stature and the rightness of their position. Wyler repeats this grouping a number of times during the scene, even staging some of the dialogue sequences with all four (including Mrs. Tilford) in the frame without cuts. However, most of the sequence proceeds traditionally, with a cut to each member of the trio as he or she emerges to make a statement and then retreats back to the group.

Wyler next repeats the grouping of the three in the courtroom scene, where they face a jury that is filmed as if its members were a single unit—uniform and intolerant of difference. This image echoes the impression created in the graduation scene, with its visual evocation of a society that marches in step. At the end of the trial, when the jury finds against the three, the onlookers break into applause, as if confirming the societal acceptance of Mary's lie.

The dialogue that opens act 3 of *The Children's Hour* is some of Hellman's best writing. As the two women exchange words that are bare, static, and brutal, the playwright indicates that their previous vitality has been drained and life has lost its meaning. They seem to occupy the sterile world depicted by the absurdist playwrights twenty years later:

MARTHA: It's cold here.
KAREN: Yes.
MARTHA: What time is it?
KAREN: I don't know. What's the difference?[25]

In filming this sequence, Wyler finds a visual equivalent for the stark dialogue. The scene opens with a view of the school's exterior. The yard is full of leaves, the atmosphere overcast and desolate, making the place look even more forbidding than it did when Karen and Martha first saw it in its run-down condition. At that point, they were viewing it in the light of day; now, it appears dark and hopeless. The camera finds the two women seated before a fireplace, speechless, and then pulls back, framing them in the window as the rain begins to fall.

In both the play and the film, Karen sends Joe away. The play's Karen simply feels that they need some time apart, while the film's Karen still has doubts about Joe and Martha. When Karen admits to her friend that she had suspicions about Joe even before Mary's lie, Martha clutches her hand in sympathy, a gesture that is repeated from the first part of the film and a trope that Wyler will employ again at key emotional moments in later films. Finally, in this film's last staircase scene, Martha admits to loving Joe as Karen climbs the stairs—it is a symbolic movement that Wyler will repeat at the end of *Jezebel*, when Amy leaves Julie at the bottom of the staircase, effectively granting her permission to care for Preston. At this confessional moment in *These Three*, Martha is left standing at the foot of the stairs, looking up as Karen ascends, seemingly having renounced her love—as Catherine Sloper will do at the end of *The Heiress*.

As in the play, the film's action is partially resolved by the recovery of the stolen bracelet. In the play, a remorseful Mrs. Tilford calls on Karen to apologize for her actions, but in the film, Martha goes to Mrs. Tilford and asks her to call on Karen and encourage her to go back to Joe. In a later scene, Karen finds Joe in a coffeehouse in Vienna, where they embrace and kiss, to the delight of the patrons.

This ending was undoubtedly a last-minute contrivance. Hellman had offered a version of this conclusion in her October 8 screenplay, but that scene ends with Karen staring through the window of a Viennese bakery and then laughing before running up the steps of the nearby hospital. The November 23 version merely notes at the end, "Tag end to follow." This notation is preceded by Martha's farewell instructions to Karen: "Go back to Joe—wherever he is. Tell him that you believe him now. I'm going to leave you Karen. . . . I'll be all right now. I'm sure of that. Very sure."[26] Goldwyn, who liked happy endings, may have insisted on the Viennese finale to assure the audience of the couple's reunion, but its actual provenance is not clear.

Like the endings of *Come and Get It* and *Dead End*, this one seems oddly muted. Martha has been set adrift—although her actions in the aftermath of the crisis are presented as noble and selfless, she is left alone, her future unclear. The trio celebrated in the film's title has been dispersed by malevolence and mistrust. The film's conclusion, nonetheless, is clearly more hopeful than that of the play, where Martha commits suicide and Karen, having sent Joe away, is left alone. In the play, the three friends have been reduced to one.

Despite its "happy ending," the film presages the political import of the gathering storm in Europe better than Hellman's play manages to do.

And Wyler's remake in 1962, with the play's original title intact, would be even more telling in the aftermath of the HUAC hearings and the blacklist. Audiences would come away from both these cinematic versions sobered by the dramatic evidence of damage done by the self-righteousness, selfishness, and blindness of seemingly good people.

These Three received superb reviews—the best of both Goldwyn's and Wyler's careers up to that point. The film made Wyler an important director, and Goldwyn would henceforth trust him with some of his most important projects. Graham Greene, then a film critic for the *Spectator*, wrote: "After ten minutes or so of the usual screen sentiment, quaintness and exaggeration, one began to watch with incredulous pleasure nothing less than life. . . . Never before has childhood been presented so convincingly on the screen, with an authenticity guaranteed by one's own memories."[27] David Selznick called *These Three* "a superb picture certain of great success."[28] Jesse Lasky wrote in a telegram, "Nothing that has happened recently has thrilled me as much as preview of your last picture . . . stop . . . Your direction is human[,] fine[,] and distinguished and this picture will put you right at the top."[29] Lasky was right—Wyler was now one of Hollywood's major directors.

4

The Wyler Touch

Dodsworth (1936)

In *Counsellor-at-Law*, Wyler deals with the cultural divide in Depression-era America while touching on the need for community and a concern for what constitutes a meaningful life. In adapting Lillian Hellman's *The Children's Hour*, he focuses on Hellman's thematic study of how evil can unmoor and destroy a group, especially when individuals lack the moral backbone to stand up to it. In *Dodsworth*, Wyler translates another important literary property: Sidney Howard's successful dramatic adaptation of Nobel Prize–winning novelist Sinclair Lewis's work of the same name. While that novel deals, in part, with the Jamesian motifs of the American abroad and the resulting clash of cultures—a subject that would naturally interest Wyler, a European immigrant—it is also the study of a marriage and of the essential American character. These key issues, lightly touched on in *Counsellor*, receive fuller treatment here.

Dodsworth, like much of Lewis's major fiction, asks what it means to be an American—a question that *Counsellor*'s George Simon confronts as well. In Elmer Rice's work, however, we never gain insight into Simon's thought process, and this lack undercuts the play's claim to complexity. Unlike Lewis's more celebrated works *Babbitt* and *Main Street*—both satires that focus on the smug provincialism of small-town American life—*Dodsworth* explores a wider subject. Here, protagonist Sam Dodsworth moves from small-town Zenith through a variety of European locales where he encounters a larger world and new ideas. Thus investing his tale with an international theme, Lewis downplays the satire and concentrates on a comparative analysis of American and European character, not endorsing either as a cultural standard but trying to isolate what is most valuable in each. In the end, *Dodsworth* offers a sympathetic view of American values—Lewis admires his countrymen's naturalness, idealism, and even their business sense and vision. Sam Dodsworth may have some of the small-town "hick" in him, but he also possesses the wisdom to judge what is good and bad in the foreign world he encounters and to use what he learns there as a means to grow. Ultimately, he is not intimidated by European culture, and he refuses to be stymied by those who attempt to belittle him. Lewis celebrates Sam's emerging confidence and sense of self.

Sam Dodsworth is introduced as a captain of industry, a wealthy automobile manufacturer and inventor who has made important contributions to the industry. He believes in "the Republican Party, high tariffs, and as long as they did not annoy him personally, in prohibition and the Episcopal Church." Lewis takes pains to distance this protagonist from Babbitt: "To define what Sam Dodsworth was at fifty, it is easiest to state what he was not. He was none of the things which most Europeans and many Americans expect in a leader of American industry. He was not a Babbitt, not a Rotarian, not an Elk, not a deacon. He rarely shouted, never slapped people on the back, and he had attended only six baseball games since 1900. He knew, and thoroughly, the Babbitts and baseball fans, but only in business."[1] Portrayed as an amiable, energetic, and honest man, he is not crude like many of his associates. He enjoys and appreciates culture, but not people who are pretentious about it. He even looks forward to his European vacation as an opportunity to learn something about the world and about himself.

In this novel, published before the stock market crashed, Lewis presents Dodsworth as a capitalist hero. In so doing, he champions American progress, enterprise, and advancement, but he also indicates that he sees some danger signs. Dodsworth sells his Revelation Automobile Company to the Unit Automotive Company, which will absorb it and turn Sam's high-quality cars into cheaper, mass-produced models. The president of Unit, Alec Kynance, prefers assembly lines to European architecture and is more interested in balance sheets and bottom lines than in the quality and excellence of his product. And through him, Lewis raises important questions about the future of American industry as it passes from the hands of true pioneers such as Dodsworth. Will America continue, like Dodsworth, to strive for excellence, or will it settle into the mass-produced mediocrity represented by Kynance? Will America achieve the kind of civilization that will be the envy of Europe, or will it slip into decadence?

Sam Dodsworth approaches his foray abroad with the awe typical of a child of nature confronting civilization. Soon, however, he begins to respond to the European locale and enjoys exploring it on his own. In Paris, while visiting Notre Dame, he reflects on his own search for meaning beyond the sphere of his wife's shallow, pretentious friends: "He saw life as something greater and more exciting than food or sleep. He felt that he was no longer merely a peddler of motor cars; he felt that he could adventure into this Past about him—and possibly adventure into the far more elusive Present. He saw, unhappily that the . . . existence into which Fran had led him was not the realization of the 'great life' for which he had yearned, but its very negation."[2] Dodsworth is forced to ponder what America is—its strengths and weaknesses—and as a result, he matures and grows. When he returns home for a short visit without his wife, Fran, he sees his homeland differently. New York, which now appears noisy, aimless, and petty, triggers a negative reaction, and when he gets to Zenith, he sees his friends through new eyes as well: "He saw slowly, that none of his prosperous industrialized friends in Zenith were very much interested in anything whatever. They had cultivated caution until they had lost the power to be interested. . . . The things over which they were most exclamatory—money, golf, drinking— . . . these diversions were to the lords of Zenith not pleasures but ways of keeping so busy that they would not admit how bored they were, how empty their ambitions."[3]

Lewis's capitalist hero does not despair over these things. He still revels in American inventiveness and energy, and he sees that, unlike Europe, America still has a frontier of limitless possibilities. During the course of his trip, he even plans a new industrial enterprise: the development of garden suburbs and dwellings that will evolve into the best in America. In Dodsworth's eyes, America is the future, while Europe is mired in the past. In Richard Lingeman's words, "What Dodsworth finds in his quest is not only a healing of his psychological troubles but his sense of identity, of acceptance of who he is, including his fundamental Americanness."[4]

Fran Dodsworth is the opposite of her husband. She thinks of herself as cultured because she visited Europe before she was married. Regarding her husband and her own country as uncultured, she becomes a parody of the European sophistication she so admires—all surface glitter and charm, but incapable of truly understanding her new surroundings. If Europe renews

Sam's sense of self, it becomes the instrument of Fran's destruction. Linge-man labels Fran a "lonely, narcissistic child who can't help herself."[5] Sam accepts this shortcoming in his wife and strives to overlook her flirtations and affairs until he can take no more. As Sam understands, Fran is afraid of growing old and is attempting to use Europe as her fountain of youth. Like Gatsby, she will discover that she cannot turn back the clock or stop time in its course.

But Fran is by no means an empty person. Her frustration with her life as an industrialist's wife in Zenith strikes a chord with the reader and with Lewis. She tells Sam, correctly, that she has been a dutiful wife, a devoted mother, and a citizen of her community, but now she wants more. Having exhausted everything Zenith has to offer, she is desperate for a new experience. "Any real woman, she argues, is quite willing . . . to give up her own chances of fame for her husband, providing he is doing something she can admire. . . . But she isn't willing to give up all her own capabilities for the ideal of industrial America."[6] Some of Lewis's critics have called Fran a deficient character because the novelist allows his distaste for the narcis-sism of his own first wife, Grace Livingstone Hegger, to overwhelm the character. But it is important to recognize that Fran exhibits the qualities that Lewis admired in Grace as well: her personal flair and her independent spirit. It is this side of Fran that Wyler tries, without success, to make more prominent in his film version.

The novel is full of trenchant observations and beautifully realized scenes. When they are presented effectively, as in the scene with Kynance, Lewis's penchant for social observation hits its mark. Unfortunately, as a number of the novel's critics have pointed out, Lewis is too close to his pro-tagonist to give the novel the objectivity it strives for. Too many characters are introduced merely to present their opinions in a mechanical way, and some seem no more than sounding boards for Dodsworth. Lewis also rush-es through his descriptions of Europe, presenting cities as though he were writing a guidebook rather than a novel. The most serious problem is that many potentially dramatic scenes are either summarized or unrealized, and this flaw is corrected in some scenes of Sidney Howard's dramatization.

Howard, like Rice, was a Pulitzer Prize–winning playwright (*They Knew What They Wanted* [1925]). He convinced Samuel Goldwyn that he could make an effective screenplay out of Lewis's 1925 Pulitzer Prize–

winning novel *Arrowsmith*. The eventual film, which was directed by John Ford and starred a miscast Ronald Colman and Helen Hayes, was a critical success that did not do well at the box office. While working on that project, however, Howard recommended that Goldwyn buy the screen rights to *Dodsworth*, which were available for $20,000. When Goldwyn refused, Howard dramatized the novel for the stage—with some last-minute assistance from Lewis, who also contributed an essay, "The Art of Dramatization," to the published version. The play opened to critical acclaim in 1934, with Walter Huston in the title role. Goldwyn then decided to buy the film rights, although the price had jumped to $160,000. When Howard reminded him that he could have owned the rights three years earlier for a fraction of the cost, Goldwyn quipped, "This way, I buy a successful play. Before, it was just a novel."[7]

Dodsworth became the longest-running production of Walter Huston's career, playing to capacity crowds at the Shubert Theatre for 1,238 performances. Fay Bainter, who had just completed her first film role in *This Side of Heaven* (and who would win an Oscar under Wyler's direction in *Jezebel*), played Fran Dodsworth. Huston's wife, Nan Sunderland, played Edith Cortwright, with whom Dodsworth falls in love at the end. Huston thought the play worked because audiences could identify with both Sam and Fran. As he explained, "Everybody knows Sam Dodsworth and his wife. We recognize them among our friends and neighbors—the earnest, plodding chap who has devoted himself to business so unrelentingly that he has forgotten all about play and romance, and his pathetic wife, bored with the mere spending of money, who craves the things that quicken and color life before the fires of youth are gone forever."[8] After the Broadway run, the play toured a variety of American cities, concluding in Cincinnati in March 1936 to effusive reviews. By that time, Sunderland had replaced Bainter, who had become ill, in the role of Fran.

In his introduction to the published play, Howard writes about the difficulties of adapting a great novel for the screen and the stage. He concedes that he was unable to realize the scope of the novel—"a panorama of two Americans in Europe"—because the economics of theatrical production prohibit the use of too many settings. What he came up with instead was "a marital journey's end in dramatic form" that was "very much less than the panorama called 'Dodsworth,'" but "a good thing for any play to be."[9]

Despite Howard's dissatisfaction with his work, he solved some of the novel's problems and found ways to dramatize key scenes that Lewis had merely summarized. To his credit, Lewis understood the need to alter the novel. Understanding that many of the book's speeches sounded "lousy" on the stage, he encouraged Howard to cut or alter them. In his introduction, Howard reports that when Lewis had finished revising the script, "there was scarcely a line of the book left."[10]

Howard made two crucial changes: introducing Mrs. Cortwright much earlier in the play—in scene 3, aboard the ocean liner to England—and dramatizing Fran's affair with the financier Arnold Israel, which is told in letters in the novel. (Goldwyn, predictably, stripped that character of his Jewishness and renamed him Iselin.) Howard also added several scenes: one in a villa, where Israel presses his desire for an affair with Fran; a later scene in which Sam confronts Fran and Israel about their affair; and another depicting Fran's meeting with her German lover's mother (Maria Ouspenskaya in both the play and the film), who breaks up their engagement. In fact, Howard dramatizes almost all the scenes that Lewis had either summarized or merely hinted at.

In his introduction, Howard also discusses "dramatizing by equivalent," a technique that he learned when adapting *Arrowsmith*. By this phrase he means compressing into one scene what the novelist has developed over multiple scenes and many pages. His example is the scene in which Dodsworth returns to Zenith alone and must readjust to his house, which is now occupied by his daughter and son-in-law. Howard's scene is comic at its core: Dodsworth cannot open his liquor cabinet because his son-in-law has the key, his daughter has turned his humidor into a planter, and he cannot use his desk because a jigsaw puzzle is spread out all over it. In the novel, Lewis offers multiple incidents to convey Sam's displacement: his class reunion at Yale, an awkward talk with his son, and an outing with his daughter during which he realizes she no longer needs him. The kind of effective compression produced by Howard's single unified sequence both tightens and focuses Lewis's story.

Howard also writes of a scene he invented between Dodsworth and his successor at the auto plant, describing it as funny and moving and the "truest scene in the play." During rehearsals, however, he saw that it did not work. The satire on American business was so broad that it made Dodsworth's own past seem trivial and futile, lessening the audience's sympathy for him.

This process of streamlining and condensing produced a number of important thematic and character changes. Because the novel offers both a dissection of an American couple's confrontation with Europe and an anatomy of their marriage, Lewis has Sam spend a great deal of time thinking about his Americanism, discussing it, and defending it. His protagonist often feels insecure about his sophistication and intellect, so he defers to his wife, but over the course of the novel, we see him grow in confidence, while Fran is exposed as shallow and childish. Howard's Dodsworth, in contrast, is less introspective and more confident from the outset. He seldom feels the need to justify his Americanness, and he seems more easygoing, more perceptive, and stronger.

The play uses the European locales mostly as settings for Fran's three love interests: Clyde Lockert in England, Arnold Israel in France, and Kurt von Obersdorf in Germany. Its focus remains on the Dodsworths' marriage rather than the cultural theme, dwelling on the contrast between Fran's refusal to age gracefully and her husband's easy acceptance of getting older and moving on in life. (Wyler's camera later exploits this aspect of the play with marvelous precision, demonstrating how each affair's disastrous conclusion reiterates Fran's failure to learn from experience.)

In putting together the creative team for the film version, Samuel Goldwyn retained Sidney Howard to adapt his stage play for the screen, and the film closely follows the play rather than reverting to an adaptation of the novel. There is evidence in Wyler's papers that a rough, undated draft was prepared by Hans Kraly, but there is no other information about his participation. Jerome Chodorov also worked on an early version. Goldwyn originally wanted Gregory La Cava (*My Man Godfrey*, *Stage Door*) to direct, but he was so impressed by Wyler's work on *These Three*—and by the glowing reviews that film received—that he opted for Wyler instead.

Walter Huston was virtually guaranteed the title role because, under the terms of his Broadway contract, if he were not offered the film role, he would be entitled to 10 percent of the fee for the film rights. In place of Fay Bainter, Goldwyn chose Ruth Chatterton, a two-time Oscar nominee, for the role of Fran. The crucial role of Edith Cortwright was up for negotiation—Geraldine Fitzgerald and Mary Astor were being considered, but Nan Sunderland wanted the part. When Wyler came to see the play during its final run in Cincinnati, Sunderland thought she might be out of the running for Edith but did not know that the role of Fran had already been cast.[11] She was devastated when she did not get either part. Goldwyn wanted Rosalind Russell or Dolores Costello (who had recently divorced John Barrymore) to play Edith. Wyler liked the idea of Costello but felt that Russell's "personality is not striking enough . . . as you know Mrs. Cortwright's should be."[12] The part finally went to Mary Astor.

Wyler liked Sidney Howard's script, but he "wanted to loosen it up a little more."[13] He went to New York to work with the playwright, and together they devised a number of new scenes that were in neither the novel nor the stage play. None of these additions, however, made it to the screen. Howard was pleasantly surprised by Wyler's ear for dialogue and his feel for character and script structure.

In his "Notes for a Treatment," Howard cites the "danger that on the screen *Dodsworth* may seem a hard story." Worried that his play "begins too bleakly," he wanted to start with Sam's youth to give the film "nostalgia and character background." He explains, "I want the mature Dodsworth to enter the picture as a man whose whole life has been automobiles, so that there may be no doubt of what he is given up when Fran lures him abroad."[14]

An early version of the script by H. C. Potter opens with a scene on a country road. Fran and Sam are driving along in an early model of his car, which breaks down. At this point, Sam (still unidentified in the script) gets under the car to fix it while Fran waits. Finally, she accepts a buggy ride, unbeknownst to Sam, who is still under the car. Once it is finally towed away, the camera cuts to a barn with a sign reading, "DODSWORTH MOTOR COMPANY. SAMUEL DODSWORTH, FOUNDER AND PRESIDENT."[15]

Believing that Fran was presented as "a bitch at the outset," Wyler felt strongly that her character needed to be softened and presented more sympathetically.[16] Howard agreed—in fact, he had already expressed this idea in his notes: "Important point for Fran—and this never satisfied me in the play—to establish a case for her as a woman who has done her job, even though her husband, along sound American lines, has too often thought more of his business than his wife. This is important because Fran will never convince an audience if she is presented merely as a demon of vanity and social ambition."[17]

In his play, Howard emphasizes Fran's fear of growing old, and Ruth Chatterton decided to make that insight the spine of her characterization. Mary Astor wrote in her autobiography that Chatterton was trying to hold on to her own youth at the time, so she identified with the character.[18] This reading of Fran's character, however, generated heated and nasty fights on the set between Wyler and Chatterton. "It was like pulling teeth with her," Wyler said. "She played Fran like a heavy, and we had momentous fights every day. She was very haughty. She had been a big star."[19]

Chatterton despised Wyler. Her agent had tried to smooth things over beforehand, writing to the director, "I beg you to have a talk with Miss Chatterton before you start shooting. Please put her mind at ease. Needless my telling you how miserable she's been surely through no fault of yours as she has terrific respect for you. Therefore I think if you could have understanding that she will give you [a] great performance."[20] Unfortunately, nothing worked. Wyler wanted a more nuanced performance, which Chatterton refused to give. Astor wrote, "She disagreed with his direction of every scene, and he was stubborn and smiling, and it drove her to furious outbursts."[21]

David Niven, who played Lockert, also disliked Wyler, describing the director as a "Jekyll and Hyde character" and "a sonofabitch to work with." He added that Wyler could be "kind of fun and cozy" off the set, but "he became a fiend the moment his bottom touched down in his director's chair."[22] Wyler commented that Niven "was sort of a playboy around town. He and Merle [Oberon] had a romance. But he fit the part in *Dodsworth*. He played himself."[23] Wyler and Niven would continue to have difficulties three years later on *Wuthering Heights*.

Mary Astor had no problems with Wyler. "We got in step very quickly. He was meticulous and picky, and he had a sharp tongue, sometimes sarcastic and impatient. . . . But he knew somehow that sharp criticism bottled me up completely. Nothing would come out. He could use spurs but not a whip."[24]

Wyler also got along well with Walter Huston, with whom he had worked on *A House Divided*. Wyler said of Huston, "He was not an actor you had to hold down. If anything, he was underacting. He was first-class."[25] In a 1971 interview, Wyler recalled that Huston "had played the part on stage and was letter-perfect in the film. No acting ruses, no acting devices, just the convincing power that comes from complete understanding of the role."[26]

During filming, Mary Astor became embroiled in a scandal that eventually grew into a national sensation—even generating a headline in the *New York Times* on August 11, 1936. A sexually liberated woman, Astor had had her first affair when she was seventeen with then forty-one-year-old John Barrymore. Later, while married to Kenneth Hawks (brother of director Howard Hawks), she had an affair that resulted in a pregnancy and abortion. After Hawks's death in a plane crash, she married Hollywood gynecologist Franklyn Thorpe, with whom she had a daughter, Marilyn. During this marriage, she had an affair with playwright George S. Kaufman, who was in Hollywood in 1935 writing *A Night at the Opera* for the Marx Brothers. When Kaufman moved on to Palm Springs, where he collaborated with Moss Hart on *Merrily We Roll Along*, the affair continued. Astor agreed to a divorce and surrendered custody of their daughter to Thorpe in 1935, but a year later, she changed her mind and brought suit against Thorpe to set aside the divorce, obtain an annulment, and gain custody of the child, along with money and property. Thorpe countersued and tried to get Astor's diary, which chronicled her sexual history, admitted into evidence. When this legal gambit failed, he leaked portions of it to the press instead. Photographers set up camp outside the United Artists studio where *Dodsworth* was being shot and at Astor's home. The judge suspended the trial for a week so that Astor could finish filming, and Goldwyn had a dressing room turned into a suite with a kitchen so that she could live there and would not have to leave the studio.

With pressure mounting, Goldwyn called a meeting that was attended by Jack Warner, Irving Thalberg, Jesse Lasky, Harry Cohen, A. H. Giannini, Louis B. Mayer, and their advisers, as well as by Astor and her lawyer. The producers felt that Astor was making a mistake in going to trial, which would give the industry a bad name. Astor's lawyer insisted that they were going forward as planned. When asked if he was going to invoke the morality clause in the actress's contract, Goldwyn replied, "A woman fighting for her child? This is good." He stood behind Astor.[27] The judge found in Astor's favor, awarding her temporary custody.

The America of 1936 was not the same country Sinclair Lewis had contemplated in 1928–1929 when he was writing and publishing his novel.

That earlier America had not yet spiraled into economic depression or been rocked by the wave of radical political movements advocating communist or socialist revolution. Lewis may have been sharply critical of the capitalist underpinnings of his country, but the temper of his novel is basically conservative, and it still depicts American vitality as the hope for Western progress. By 1936, however, the economic issues that had dominated the intellectual conversation for the first half of the decade began to give way to apprehension about the worsening situation in Europe. Liberals concluded that Nazism posed the gravest threat to Russia and the West, so the political debate shifted from the conflict between capitalism and socialism to the need to defend democracy against the fascism taking hold of Europe.

The film's Sam Dodsworth is an idealized American whose virtues are magnified by Huston's performance, highlighting the character's charm, patience, intellectual curiosity, and devotion to his wife. His openness and folksy humor stand in contrast to the snobbish, selfish Europeans and to his shallow, childish wife. The film's Dodsworth is not a polemical thinker like his fictional counterpart. In chapter 23 of the novel, for example, Dodsworth engages in a debate with Professor Braut on the differences between Americans and Europeans. Braut holds that whereas a culture is measured by the number of great men it produces, America advocates the average achievement of the many. Dodsworth agrees with this concept but argues that the Europeans have mistakenly classified Americans as money-grubbers, gangsters, and rustics. He insists that Europeans are no less materialistic than Americans, that his countrymen do reflect on themselves and their culture, and that this self-examination is evidenced in their desire to grow and mature. These characteristics are simply embodied in the film's protagonist without the need for such didactic exchanges.

In the film, Wyler does not belabor Dodsworth's significance as an idealized type. Dodsworth's most profound antagonist is not a dangerous villain or demagogue but Dodsworth himself, as he fights to overcome his loneliness and examine his untested notions about his country and its culture. The dissolution of his marriage is also presented as a test of his loyalty and of his ability to harness his inner resources and conquer his doubts. The film's Dodsworth also displays the trait that Sinclair Lewis found most attractive in his character—a vitality that the Old World cannot match and that eventually enables him to rise above his uncertainties and emerge triumphant. It is this quality that Wyler, the European émigré, also implies will empower the American democratic spirit to triumph over the threats of fascism then threatening to overwhelm Europe.

Both the novel and the play exploit settings in multiple European capitals and resorts, but location shooting on that scale was out of the question in the 1930s. Instead, Wyler sent cameramen to London, Paris, Vienna, Montreux, and Naples for background shots. "I gave them detailed instructions, of course, and the sets were built so there would be props in the foreground and back projection of matching locations."[28] Because he wanted to diminish the sense of a travelogue that permeates parts of the novel, however, many of the atmospheric shots of places that figure in the book did not make it to the film. The ones that did make it—parts of Paris, Lake Geneva, and the bay of Naples—play crucial roles.

As it is both a studio film and, like *Counsellor-at-Law* and *These Three*, an adaptation of a play, most of *Dodsworth* relies on interior locations, some of them duplicating Jo Mielziner's sets for the play. The opening of the film, for example, nearly echoes the first scene of the play: "Through the vast, square-paned window of his private office, Samuel Dodsworth . . . can look out over the roofs and chimneys of his plant at the skyscrapers of Zenith."[29] But Wyler soon demonstrates his ability to transform and deepen the play's action in cinematic terms. Unlike *Counsellor*, in which he tries to obliterate stage space by means of rapid editing, *Dodsworth* exhibits a sophisticated sense of various modes of cinematic expression. Here, Wyler explores theme through compositions in space, restricting and constricting space and using mirrors to create symbolic spaces. He also structures much of the film by cutting between Fran's escapades and Sam's isolation, thus keeping the narrative focus on the Dodsworth marriage and Sam's "education." Early in the film, while sailing for Europe on board the *Queen Mary*, Sam confides to Edith Cortwright that he's making this trip to "get a perspective on the U.S.A." and "to get to know myself at the same time." This dual quest becomes Wyler's focus as well.

Wyler establishes this theme of exploration from the opening moments when Sam, his back to the camera, looks out his office window. Stretching out before him is the empire he has built. To the left are the words "Dodsworth" (seen clearly) and "Motor Company" receding in perspective along a factory building where smoke billows from a chimney. From this formal portrait of a solitary industrial tycoon contemplating his creation, the camera slowly zooms in on its subject to the strains of "Auld Lang Syne" and then pans to the left, where a newspaper headline announces that Dodsworth Motors has been sold. The table on which the newspaper lies also holds a framed photograph of Fran Dodsworth in shadow. These images reflect the twin poles of Sam's life—his business and his wife—and as soon becomes apparent, he has sacrificed one to make the other happy. A shadow crosses the paper, and Wyler dissolves to Sam, his back still to the camera, moving through a crowd of workers bidding him good-bye. This is Lewis's ideal industrialist: a man who has achieved excellence, brought benefits to an emerging civilization, yet retained his humanity in the process. The final dissolve—to Sam in his car—emphasizes this aspect of his character. We see him face-front for the first time, pushed to the left as Wyler devotes the center of the frame to a view, through the car's rear window, of the factory chimneys receding and then, in a quick cut, to a full view of them. Sam Dodsworth is clearly being identified with America's industrial progress. The shot in the car signals that his divorce from this life will not bring him the happiness he expects from retirement.

Sam's car pulls up to a mansion that is every bit as impressive as Julie Marsden's estate in New Orleans. Like Julie, Sam is greeted by his butler, but he does not command his own space as Julie does. Instead, Wyler cuts to Fran, who is clearly in charge on the domestic front, and when she greets her husband, he dejectedly announces that the company has been sold and twenty years of his life are now over. Fran walks Sam into the study, encouraging him not to be "too mournful." They talk about their future and their upcoming trip to Europe, and then Fran recedes to the background of the frame as she prepares a drink for him. When Sam declares, "I'm just as keen on this trip as you are, Fran. I'm rarin' to go! I've always wanted to see London and Paris," Wyler cuts to Sam at a modified low angle, accentuating his self-assurance and purpose.

As Fran announces her high expectations for their journey—"[I want more] than a trip out of this . . . I want a new life!"—Wyler makes her prominent in the frame, while Sam's back is to the camera. It is here that the film script makes an important change in dialogue from the play, adding Fran's argument that they have done their job, brought up their child and married her off, and been dedicated citizens. Fran feels that they have earned a new start. In Howard's play, Fran talks not about parenting but of her desire to sell the house and be free of Zenith altogether. By legitimizing her place in the frame and making her rationale more sympathetic, Wyler is trying to humanize Fran, which Howard neglects to do in his play. Unfortunately, Chatterton's cold performance works against Wyler's attempt, and the sympathetic perspective is not sustained throughout the film.

The film eliminates the Dodsworths' time in London, dramatizing Fran's flirtation with Lockert on board the *Queen Mary* instead. Here, Wyler introduces a visual narrative strategy that he employs throughout the remainder of the film. Sam is shown mostly alone—on deck admiring the view, looking at nautical maps with the ship's officers, or sighting Bishop's Light, which signals their imminent arrival in London. Fran, in contrast, is pictured enjoying the ship's social life—dancing in the ballroom and imagining a sophisticated romance. The film also introduces Edith Cortwright on the ship, where Sam meets her while taking one of his solitary evening walks on deck. As they exchange pleasantries, she surmises that what Sam is looking for in Europe is "the education of an American."

On the *Queen Mary*, this "education" consists largely of observing Fran in the throes of her first flirtation. After Sam's introduction to Edith, Wyler dissolves to a scene of Fran and Lockert in the Dodsworths' stateroom. Fran is seen combing her hair in the mirror, her face framed within a frame. She is denigrating Sam's bourgeois attitude, but Wyler's framing device comments on her own naïveté, which will soon be exposed. After fixing her hair, Fran moves toward Lockert, who is preparing drinks at the left. Most of the frame is devoted to a view of the ocean through the window, which serves as a reminder of Sam's space and also of Fran's dangerous indulgence in freedom without knowledge. They both cross to the window, where Fran tells Lockert that Sam "has all the old-fashioned virtues except jealousy." The camera then cuts from the stateroom to the bar, where Sam continues his talk with Edith. Fran's private flirtation is thus contrasted with Sam's more public and proper social encounter. Sam tells Edith that traveling is not bad, but he might not like it for an extended period. He adds, "For a steady thing, give me America. For Americans, that is." Edith then tells him that "drifting is not so pleasant as it looks"—surely an indirect comment on Fran's ambitions.

The scene then shifts back to the Dodsworths' stateroom, where Lockert kisses Fran and she reacts with annoyance that the flirtation has gone too far. Again, Wyler shifts this confrontation to the left of the frame, with the ocean view in the center. He then dramatizes their breakup in a series of shot–reverse shots, whereas earlier they were framed together. Lockert insults Fran by pointing out that she is unsuited to the role she is trying to play: "You think you're a woman of the world. You're nothing of the sort. And I'm awfully afraid you never will be." As he finishes, Sam enters, forming one of Wyler's many triangular framings.

After Lockert departs, leaving the Dodsworths alone, Fran starts weeping and lies facedown on her bed. Sam, dominating the frame, then echoes Lockert's put-down, telling Fran that they are out of their depth and that Fran's behavior "makes us look like the hicks we are"—which only infuriates her further. Her sudden announcement that she wants to skip London and go directly to Paris precipitates the couple's first fight, during which Wyler again shifts to shot–reverse shot framing. As Fran flirts with Sam in an attempt to get her way, Wyler concludes the scene with another mirrored framing, imprisoning Fran in the foreground with Sam in profile behind her. The tight composition, featuring figures divided in space and turned in different directions, strongly hints that their marriage is doomed.

This suggestion is reinforced in the Paris section, where Fran, undaunted by her previous experience, takes up with Arnold Iselin (Paul Lukas), a sophisticated banker. They meet at a club, and Wyler again cuts between Sam, sitting alone at an outdoor café, and his wife, hobnobbing with her new beau.

After attending a party, the Dodsworths return to their hotel suite, where they argue again over their travel plans. This scene demonstrates Wyler's realistic visual approach at its most assured; he maintains the integrity of space by integrating movement and image while carefully orchestrating the balance between moving and fixed shots. His use of space masks the scene's stage origins by emphasizing long shots and shots in depth with minimal cutting. The scene begins in the sitting room, where Sam is unbuttoning Fran's gown. He suggests that they have had enough of Paris and should start thinking about going home. Meanwhile, he walks toward the bedroom, leaving Fran visible in background; the open bedroom door cuts the frame in the middle, seeming to enclose each of them in a separate space. As Sam continues to talk about the other cities he wants to see before returning home, he sits on the bed, still foregrounded in the frame, and begins to undress. Fran follows him, and they both undress and get into their pajamas—a display of intimacy that was highly unusual for a mainstream Hollywood film. The scene even continues into the bathroom, as Sam fetches Fran's face cream. As she applies the cream and he removes his shirt, the effects of aging are clearly apparent, even as the couple's antagonism is magnified.

Fran, intent on pursuing her relationship with Iselin, does not want to leave Paris. She rejects Sam's plans, and Wyler finally cuts to Fran as she suggests that Sam go home without her. As their argument builds, Wyler maintains the spatial integrity of the scene by having the estranged couple speak from different sides of the room. Sam demeans Fran's friends, contending, "Do you think the real thing in Paris would hang out with a couple of hicks like us?" He adds, "I'm just an ordinary American businessman and I married the daughter of a Zenith brewer." Wyler cuts to Fran's face, covered with cream, thus highlighting her chagrin at the truth of this statement.

Insisting again that they go their separate ways, Fran moves to the rear of the frame, leaving Sam in the foreground. But when she argues that she has been a good wife and deserves her fling because Sam is "rushing at old age," the camera centers on her. Wyler again seems to be trying to elicit some sympathy for the character, but the momentum quickly shifts as Sam walks back to the sitting room, his shadow preceding him into the dark room. As he goes to check the ship's departure schedule, he is, once again, front and center, while Fran remains in the background, framed by the bedroom doors.

Fran's flirtation with Iselin then continues in Montreux, while Sam returns home to discover that his daughter is settled and no longer needs his financial assistance. Iselin's wooing of Fran, set on the balcony of a villa overlooking mountains and a lake, partially echoes the scene with Lockert on the ship. As Fran and her paramour are shown sitting at a table, she at frame left and he on the right, their positions parallel those of Sam and his daughter in the car in the previous scene. Fran receives a letter from Sam and she moves to the rear of the frame to read it, while Iselin remains seated in the foreground—thereby duplicating the dominant separate framing of Sam and Fran in their Paris hotel room. Fran is dressed, ironically, in a white chiffon gown with a white headband, looking rather like a Roman vestal virgin. When she finishes the letter, she walks toward Iselin, complaining that reading about life in Zenith has spoiled her fun. As she expresses her unhappiness, Wyler again switches to a shot–reverse shot until the two are together in the frame. Claiming that he is "making love to her," Iselin moves closer and declares, "If your husband saved for you some of the love he's lavished on carburetors, my dear, innocent Fran. . . ." Fran's back is to the camera as she hears this remark, but she abruptly turns around and defends her husband, asserting that he does love her. "And whatever Sam lacks," she concludes, "I've always been able to trust him." For the moment, dressed in white and romantically lit, Fran again appears to be a sympathetic figure. Iselin replies that he lives in the present and that the letter is the past. When Fran claims that the letter is the future too, Iselin replies, "Then let's get rid of both past and future." Wyler's careful editing and staging—including Rudolph Maté's suggestive lighting, which plays effectively off Chatterton's gown—add to the seductive, romantic quality of the scene.

The play's equivalent scene is wordier, requiring Iselin (Israel in the play) to deliver a long speech about how people in love should give of themselves to each other and to promise, finally, that he will remain faithful "as long as the thing may last." Playwright Howard thus emphasizes the rather dissolute morals of this European roué. Wyler, however, plays it like a love scene: as Fran grapples with her own fading morals and debates whether to give herself over to the moment, Iselin solves her dilemma by setting the letter on fire, holding it for a moment while it flickers. He then lets it go, and the breeze wafts it across the terrace—a stunning cinematic image that announces the consummation of their affair and, by implication, the end of the Dodsworths' marriage. This suggestive image also alludes to the illusory nature of dreams and of Fran's foolish attempt to turn back time, as reflected in her virginal costume and her desire to escape the past and the future.

Mary Astor wrote that Wyler spent an entire afternoon shooting the burning letter's symbolic progress: "He wanted it to go slowly for a way, then stop, and then flutter along a little farther."[30] Wyler's perfectionism is not wasted here, as he pulls off an effect that beautifully encapsulates one of the film's most insistent themes.

Suspecting his wife's involvement with Iselin, Sam returns to Paris to confront the situation. As the Dodsworths travel from the train station to the hotel, Wyler reverses Sam's position in the car in the two earlier framings—Dodsworth's drive home after selling his company, and the ride with his daughter during his recent return home—placing Fran at the left and Sam to the right. Visually, Sam has been displaced.

Back in their suite, Sam is again placed at the center of the frame, while Fran's back is to the camera. Unbeknownst to Fran, Sam has summoned Iselin, and the subsequent confrontation is one of Wyler's most effective compositions. When Iselin arrives, Wyler frames him in a curtained entrance, emphasizing the theatrical air of the proceedings as choreographed by Sam. Iselin enters the room in the center of the frame, while Sam is in the upper left and Fran's back is to the right—the three figures forming a triangle. As the confrontation continues, Wyler lines the three actors up so that Fran and her lover are looking away from the camera, their position corresponding in profile to an antique bust (representing the Old World) located between them. As Sam continues to direct and dominate the proceedings, he moves to center frame, with Fran at left and Iselin at right. When Sam remarks, "the old triangle stuff," the group again suggests a visual triangle. At length, Iselin leaves, and Fran is defeated. She apologizes to Sam, as she did earlier on the ship. But as the ensuing action—the film's final movement—shows, she has learned nothing.

Fran's last romantic adventure takes place in Vienna, where she agrees to marry Kurt von Obersdorf (Gregory Gaye), a nobleman with a title but no money who is considerably younger than Fran. They go out for an evening of dancing (Wyler is one of the violinists in the orchestra), and their solo waltz anticipates Julie and Preston's famous dance at the Olympus Ball in *Jezebel*. All eyes are on the pair, and although the spectators approve of the exhibition in this case, it spells the end of Fran's marriage. As he does in *Jezebel*, Wyler sometimes frames the dance from behind the orchestra.

Later, in the Dodsworths' suite, Fran's image is again reflected in a mirror as she goes to check on Sam. And when Kurt proposes, exclaiming, "Why are you not free!" Wyler repeats the mirrored framing of Fran, her back to the camera. She then turns toward the camera, and the camera frames both lovers in the mirror. As Kurt is about to leave, they kiss passionately; this is the first time she has been shown willingly kissing another man. Then, as Fran retires to her bedroom, the camera lingers in the sitting room, centering on Sam's door and silently invoking his presence.

Later that evening, Sam and Fran fight again, and she informs him that she wants a divorce so she can marry Kurt. Sam tells Fran they need to go home where they belong, but Wyler's composition indicates that he will lose the argument: Fran is seen facing the camera, her partially open door cutting the frame in half. Defeated, Sam agrees to stay in Europe until the divorce is finalized.

Fran's meeting with Kurt's mother (Maria Ouspenskaya) completes her humiliation. The baroness frankly declares her disapproval; as a Catholic, she will not countenance her son's marriage to a divorced woman. The unkindest cut to Fran, however, comes when she is told that she is too old to give Kurt an heir. Like the earlier confrontation with Iselin, this meeting is staged as a triangle, with Kurt standing between the two seated women, and this positioning gives the proceedings an ominous feel. Wyler edits the face-off between the two women primarily as a shot–reverse shot, concentrating on the baroness's necklace, a crucifix that alternately goes bright and dark, and on the flower between Fran's breasts, signifying her hope, which is clearly out of sync with the snow falling in the background.

Fran's defeat is contrasted with Sam's reunion with Edith Cortwright in Milan. She invites him to stay at her villa, where he regains his enthusiasm for life. He even decides to start a new business, initiating an airline route between Moscow and Seattle. This promising love affair is interrupted, however, when Fran calls to tell Sam that she has dropped the divorce. Sam feels obligated to go back to Fran, despite Edith's pleas for him to stay. He meets his wife on the ship, but as it is about to sail, he is so appalled by her selfishness that he leaves abruptly, telling Fran that "love has to stop somewhere short of suicide." Realizing that her husband has left her, she wails, "He's going ashore!" and the scream, punctuated by the ship's whistle, dramatically captures her sense of abandonment and desperation. The film's final moments show Sam returning to Edith on a small boat; he waves to her as Edith's joyful face fills the screen. This explicit denouement revises the ending of the play, whose curtain falls on Fran's piercing cry. Wyler and Howard have given the film a "Hollywood" ending, focusing on Sam's release rather than Fran's despair.

In Sam Dodsworth, Wyler and Howard affirm their faith in the basic dignity of the American character. Despite his wealth and success, Sam represents the average American as a reasonable, decent, and tolerant human being. He is open to new ideas, observant of his changing environment, and able to see through Fran's shallow friends. His commitment to growth, experimentation, and progress makes him a more vibrant figure than the antiquated Europeans, who are seen as mere devotees of what is old and comfortable. Sam's embrace of "education" allows him to triumph in the end. It is this spirit that the American in Wyler wanted to embrace as well—the underlying strength that would allow the United States to withstand the emerging threat of fascism in Europe.

The film would also be an artistic triumph for Wyler, a clear demonstration of the realistic style that would mark his best work. *Dodsworth* shows its director in full command of the spatial design that is the hallmark of his most significant social films. It is important to note that Wyler made this film without Gregg Toland, who was then working on *Come and Get It* with Howard Hawks. Rudolph Maté did the camera work in his absence. Although based on a play, *Dodsworth* rarely displays its stage origins; the expansive interior sets allow Wyler's camera to explore the space so effectively that the viewer becomes immersed in the realism of the characters' world. Even the rear-screen projections of European locales are melded effectively into the outdoor sequences, maintaining the realistic feel.

Wyler's purposeful use of space allows his characters to express themselves at any given moment both in relationship to their environment and with respect to the other characters they interact with. Rather than requiring his actors to indulge in extended psychological musings, he articulates the emotional tensions between them by means of spatial structures that encapsulate a scene's meaning. Beginning with *Counsellor-at-Law*, he demonstrates an ability to remain essentially faithful to a dramatic text while freeing it from its stage origins by letting the camera capture nuances—of character, emotion, and space—that are simply unavailable to a playwright.

Dodsworth previewed at the Warner Brothers Hollywood Theater for a select group of invited guests and then opened a week later, on September 23, 1936, at the Rivoli Theatre in New York. Sinclair Lewis loved the film. He sent an effusive telegram to Goldwyn: "I do not see how a better motion picture could have been made from the play and the novel than you have made Stop I am so delighted with it that I don't need the feebleness of adjectives to express my pleasure."³¹ The critics also loved the film, honoring Walter Huston with the New York Film Critics Award for his performance; he also received an Oscar nomination. Wyler himself received his first Oscar nomination, among seven nominations for the film overall.

Nonetheless, *Dodsworth* won only one Oscar (for art decoration) and did tepid box-office business. Goldwyn claimed, "I lost my shirt. I'm not saying it wasn't a fine picture. It was a great picture, but nobody wanted to see it. In droves." Then he complained that the film had failed because "it didn't have attractive people in it."³² Believing that audiences did not want to see a film about middle-aged people, he thought for years about remaking it with Clark Gable. Conversely, Goldwyn would also declare that *Dodsworth* was "one of the biggest hits I ever had. It made a fortune."³³

In the early 1970s, the Los Angeles County Museum of Art rediscovered *Dodsworth*, naming it one of the fifty great American films selected for a retrospective. It is now recognized as an important work, certainly one of the key films of the 1930s.

5

A Concoction

Come and Get It (1936)

While Wyler was shooting *Dodsworth*, Howard Hawks was filming *Come and Get It* for Goldwyn one sound stage away. Meanwhile, the studio head himself was recovering from intestinal surgery in New York. Upon his return to Hollywood, and against doctor's orders, Goldwyn demanded to see the footage of both films. He was upset by all the excess footage Wyler had shot for *Dodsworth* but delighted by the quality of the film. Hawks's work, however, nearly sent him back to the hospital. He wrote to Edna Ferber, author of the novel on which the film was based, "After I saw what [Hawks] had filmed, I suffered a relapse for a full two weeks, it upset me so."[1] Hawks recollected, "He saw what I had shot, and it was a shock to him. He bought a story, and he didn't get it."[2]

Goldwyn became further enraged when he confronted Hawks and learned the director's ideas about the film's central focus. According to Hawks, "He told me a director shouldn't write, and I wasn't very polite with my answer."[3] Goldwyn was devoted to the prominent writers he courted and adamant that the integrity of their work be respected. He was appalled by what Hawks was doing to Ferber's novel: turning it into a Hawksian buddy movie about two guys and a girl. What was supposed to be the story of a lame girl who tries to entertain a group of loggers with her songs but gets hooted at was being changed into the story of a "lusty wench."[4] When Hawks announced that he was quitting, Goldwyn replied that was fine, because Hawks was fired.

Faced with the task of restoring a prestige property he felt was ruined, Goldwyn needed to find a director he could trust to rework and complete the project. He decided on Wyler, who was then putting the finishing touches on *Dodsworth*. Having been ordered back to bed, Goldwyn summoned Wyler to his home—it was Wyler's first invitation to the producer's residence.

But when Goldwyn announced that he greatly admired *Dodsworth* and wanted Wyler to finish *Come and Get It*, the director protested, stating that he was still editing *Dodsworth*. Goldwyn told him that that project could wait, and besides, Wyler was not a film editor. Wyler countered, "I can't just walk into another picture like that. It's Howard Hawks's picture." Goldwyn told him that Hawks had been fired, at which point Wyler simply refused the assignment.[5] Wyler remembered, "He carried on like a madman about me having to do this, that I was legally obligated to do it and that he'd ruin my career if I refused. He got so furious that Frances Goldwyn took a flyswatter and beat it over his legs on the bed and I ran out of the room."[6] Later, Wyler had his lawyer review his contract and learned that Goldwyn was right—there was nothing he could do but accept the job or be suspended. Also suspecting that "if he was getting somebody else to finish the Hawks picture, he'd get somebody else to finish mine,"[7] Wyler started working on *Come and Get It* in August 1936.

Wyler inherited the film with Hawks's actors already in place. Goldwyn had wanted Spencer Tracy for the role of Barney Glasgow, but Louis B. Mayer refused to loan him out, so the part went to Edward Arnold. Walter Brennan, slight and thin, was cast as Swan Bostrom, Barney's best friend, even though Ferber described the character as the "strongest man in the North woods." Joel McCrea, fresh from *These Three*, was cast as Barney's son, Richard, and Mady Christians got the role of Lotta's aunt Karie. For the crucial double role of Lotta, Goldwyn wanted Miriam Hopkins, but Hawks had convinced him that she was not suitable. Shortly thereafter, and with considerable publicity, Goldwyn announced that Virginia Bruce had been given the coveted role. Hawks, however, had other ideas. While viewing rushes from a Bing Crosby vehicle, *Rhythm on the Range*, he had noticed Frances Farmer, a young actress whose blonde hair, blue eyes, and sturdy physique made her perfect to play a girl from the Wisconsin woods. After having her read for him—ostensibly for a smaller part—Hawks offered her the lead and then proceeded to spend countless hours nurturing his new protégée. Because of this casting decision, the character of Lotta Morgan shifted from a lame, reserved girl into a lusty, sexy barroom singer. The emotionally fragile Farmer would have a difficult time adjusting to Wyler, who was both more demanding than Hawks on the set and annoyed at having to be there in the first place. She described acting for Wyler as "the nearest thing to slavery," while Wyler quipped, "The nicest thing I can say about Frances Farmer is that she is unbearable."[8]

The extent of Wyler's contribution to the finished film is a matter of some controversy. According to Jan Herman, Wyler himself claimed credit for around 50 percent.[9] Daniel Mandell, a frequent Wyler collaborator (although he did not edit this film), contends that Wyler did "more than half."[10] In his biography of Goldwyn, Arthur Marx writes that Wyler "reshot the last half . . . at an additional cost of $900,000."[11] Hawks's biographer, Todd McCarthy, states that Wyler was responsible for only the film's last half hour, which is supported by Scott Berg; however, McCarthy asserts that Wyler worked on the film for about a month (August 19–September 19), while Berg claims he did so for only two weeks.[12] At another point, McCarthy states that Hawks shot for "forty-two of the seventy days *Come and Get It* was in production."[13] The Goldwyn files support McCarthy's dates, as well as his contention that Hawks worked on the film longer than Wyler did, but they do not necessarily prove that the completed film was more Hawks's work than Wyler's. In a telegram to Wyler dated October 29, 1936—more than a month after shooting was completed—Eddie Curtiss, the film's editor, indicates that the final product contained more of Wyler's footage than Hawks's. He apportions the total footage of 8,945 feet as follows: 4,506 to Hawks, which includes 473 by Richard Rosson; 4,205 to Wyler; and 234 for titles.[14] Rosson directed the second-unit footage, filmed primarily in Idaho, which included shots of falling trees, tree trunks sliding down flumes, logging camps, dynamiting ice, and lumber being sent downriver. Wyler considered these scenes among the best in the completed film. Once Rosson's footage and the titles are subtracted from the total, Curtiss's numbers indicate that Hawks directed 4,033 feet of completed film and Wyler 4,205, thus supporting the conclusion that Wyler was responsible for about half the film.

As completed, *Come and Get It* is thematically closer to Wyler's work than to Hawks's. It echoes the subjects and themes Wyler explored during the previous decade—notably, the strained relations between husband and wife (*Counsellor-at-Law*, *Dodsworth*), triangular relationships (*These Three*, *Dodsworth*, *Counsellor-at-Law*), the folly of attempting to recapture one's youth, and the emotional cost of sacrificing love for ambition. In his essay on Hawks, Andrew Sarris concludes that "the pathos of the unat-

otut exceht

tained woman sacrificed upon the altar of excessive ambition . . . seems to be more Wyler's speed, but the brawling sequences on the road to power do have a distinctly Hawksian flavor."[15]

The film's content is an integral part of the controversy over directorial credit as well. After the film was completed, Goldwyn wrote a letter of apology and explanation to Edna Ferber, blaming his illness for preventing him from overseeing the project more closely and emphasizing that he wanted to do justice to her book. He goes on, "I found that Hawks had filmed a completely different story from what you had written. . . . I decided to try to get as much of your story onto the screen as I possibly could, under the conditions. I threw away most of what Hawks had photographed, put William Wyler onto the picture and spent a good two months rephotographing it, trying to get what I thought would come as near to your book as possible."[16]

In a reply written four days later, Ferber expresses her admiration and gratitude to Goldwyn for the "courage, sagacity, and power of decision which you showed in throwing out the finished Hawks picture and undertaking the gigantic task of what amounted to a new picture. Few producers would have done this."[17] Both parties seem guilty of overstatement, since Wyler did not spend two months on the film, nor did Goldwyn make what amounted to a "new picture."

Just three days earlier, however, before receiving Goldwyn's letter of apology, Ferber had been singing a different tune. In a telegram dated October 28, she makes it clear that her novel's central subject is "the destruction of forests and rivers by the wholesale robber barons of the day . . . for now we know that the droughts and floods and dust storms of our time are the result of the Barney Glasgows of fifty years ago."[18] This is certainly a prescient observation, and although the novel occasionally preaches these ideas, it places far more emphasis on the multigenerational saga of a powerful family—in fact, Ferber seems to find much to admire in Barney Glasgow. The ecological argument remains peripheral to the film, which focuses more closely on the themes of lost love and fathers and sons.

Ferber's novel covers four generations of the Glasgow family. When it opens in 1907, Barney Glasgow is already one of the wealthiest men in Wisconsin and one of the preeminent business tycoons in the country. Theodore Roosevelt may be trying to break the trusts, but Barney is not concerned, for he is a man of limitless confidence in himself, his methods, and his success: "Gover'ment my foot! I'm the gover'ment when it comes to my own business. . . . I'll cut my timber and fix my rates and ship my logs as I see fit. Always have. Always will."[19] The novel then goes back in time to the early days of lumbering and papermaking in Wisconsin, when Barney was a boy and worked as a lumberjack in the camps where his mother was a cook. Astute and ambitious, young Barney catches the eye of his boss, Jed Hewitt, and after making some successful deals and investments, he marries Hewitt's daughter, Emma. Ferber then traces the history of the family from 1907 through the expansion of the war years, the economic boom of the 1920s, the stock market crash and subsequent Depression, and into the present (the book was published in 1935), at which point the family has lost much of its power and wealth.

Despite Ferber's claims to Goldwyn, the novel is not primarily a conservationist's exposé of the destruction of the land by robber barons. True, she does deplore the ravaging of the land and Glasgow's insensitivity toward the natural resources he is exploiting, but Ferber is not an effective muckraker. A passage early in the novel describing the residents of Butte des Morts, Barney's hometown, is representative of her efforts: "They never dreamed of resenting these houses or the millions they represented; or the raping of the forests, the harnessing of the rivers, the manipulation of the railroads, the razing of the hills. Over the lovely little town hung the acrid smell of acids, pricking the nostrils, and the fumes of sulphur and ammonia in the great digesters were the incense offered up on the funeral pyres of the vanquished trees. This miasma Butte des Morts inhaled with rapture."[20]

Late in the novel, Tom Melendys, a lumberjack's son who has become a college professor, writes a book entitled *The Rape of American Forests*; he then becomes a surrogate father to Barney's grandchildren and raises their political consciousness. However, these developments seem to materialize out of nowhere in the narrative, and the character of Tom remains more a concept than a believable creation. By the time he appears, after Barney's death, the novel has already run out of steam, and Ferber seems unable to create any new characters to command the reader's interest. The last third of the novel reads rather like a forced historical overview, as Ferber seems more interested in surveying the first thirty years of the new century than in creating convincing characters and situations.

Like many writers who center their tales on business tycoons, Ferber evidently admires her protagonist. Despite their sins, captains of industry like Barney Glasgow, with their pioneering, creative spirits, make more compelling characters than their more sensitive offspring. Like Eugene O'Neill, Theodore Dreiser, and Frank Norris, Ferber understands that entrepreneurial energy and ruthlessness are captivating:

> They conducted their business over black cigars, whisky and bawdy stories. . . . They saw what they wanted and grabbed it, as all their lives they had done. Their enemies walked the plank. Most of them, in early life had labored with their hands. They were at ease with the workmen of their own generation and even the younger ones; friendly, hearty in their talk with them. . . . Bernie [Barney's son], on the other hand, regarded them as though they were something you had to placate, not because you liked them but because it was politic and economic to keep them contented and good-natured, like performing animals in a cage.[21]

Despite her reservations about Barney, one senses that Ferber prefers him to his son. (Although he alludes to different circumstances, Sinclair Lewis foresaw a similar diminution in the generation of automotive tycoons that replaced Dodsworth, with its attention to the bottom line and its disregard for the product's integrity.) Ferber's fascination with and grudging admiration for the patriarch of her fictional dynasty are apparent in the vibrancy of her narrative as well. Once Barney dies, she seems to lose interest in his descendants, undercutting the reader's involvement in the rest of the story.

Come and Get It follows the standard American business novel formula by focusing on the catastrophe of success. Barney, despite his money and power, is unhappy in a marriage that was motivated by ambition rather than love. He becomes acutely aware of the emptiness of that bargain when, in his fifties, he meets Lotta, the granddaughter of his best friend, Swan Bostrom. As a young lumberjack, Barney had known her grandmother, a saloon singer. (The film suggests that he harbored some feelings for her, which he sacrificed to marry the boss's daughter instead. Ferber does not dwell on this theme of romantic loss in her novel, but she does parallel Barney's story with that of his daughter Evie, who gives up the man she loves—a laborer in her father's factory—to marry someone from her own social circle.) Barney now attempts to compensate for his unhappiness by bestowing on Swan, his daughter Karie, and her daughter Lotta all the advantages they desire. Lotta is a young woman who instinctively knows her own worth and is aware of her extraordinary beauty, and she allows Barney to shower her with gifts, rationalizing that he is doing so out of regard for her grandfather. In fact, she has set her sights on Barney's son, Bernie, the heir to his father's business. Barney is so besotted with Lotta that he does not recognize her true ambition, and he plans to divorce his wife and marry her himself: "I've got my life to live and I'm going to take a few million dollars right in my old pants pocket and live it by God, with the most beautiful woman in the world."[22]

Events come to a head at the Glasgows' annual lawn party, where Barney catches Bernie and Lotta in an embrace. The two men fight, and Lotta tries to break them up. When Bernie shouts, "Lotta and I are going to get married," Barney counters, "[She] belongs to me." Lotta protests, saying, "I wouldn't have him touch me. Why would I! I wouldn't have anything to do with an old man like him."[23] This scornful rejection deflates Barney, who tells them both to get out of his house and announces to his wife that he is going to disinherit their son. Before he can carry out his threat, however, Barney, Emma, and their daughter Evie are all killed in a boating accident. Bernie ends up inheriting the family fortune and marries Lotta.

The film remains faithful to the spirit of the novel by focusing on Barney's unrequited love for Lotta—though she is now Bostrom's daughter rather than his granddaughter. The screenwriters are more effective than Ferber in establishing Barney's attraction to Lotta's mother (grandmother in the novel), also named Lotta (Morgan); in the novel, their meeting is brief and is quickly followed by her marriage to Swan and her violent death. The film also portrays in some detail the courtship of the younger Lotta by Richard (the novel's Bernie), which Ferber does not narrate at all. And the screenwriters further extend the romantic contours of the plot by having Evie abandon Orvie, her fiancé, and declare her intention to marry Tony Schwerke, a laborer in her father's plant who is also in partnership with Richard in the manufacture of a new product—the paper cup.

The film concludes with the confrontation between Richard and Barney over Lotta, but the ending is handled differently than in the novel. As

Ben Hecht and Charles MacArthur would do three years later in *Wuthering Heights*, the screenwriters conclude the film version of Ferber's novel by simply dispensing with the stories of Barney's descendants and even with his own death—none of the screenplays in either the Goldwyn or the Wyler collection goes beyond Barney's own story. (The first-draft screenplay ended with the dedication of a park in Barney's honor and the unveiling of a bust of him, but this conceit was quickly dropped.) Apparently, utilizing the coda to Ferber's novel was never an option for any of the screenwriters.

The first part of the film seems to belong to Hawks, whom Robin Wood credits for "the splendidly shot and cut documentary on lumberjacking, the camaraderie which Barney Glasgow loses when he gains financial success and social position, [and] above all, the saloon fight in which Barney, Swan and Lotta vanquish opposition by hurling tin trays."[24] Wood is wrong about the lumberjacking sequence (Hawks assigned Rosson to film those scenes) but right about the rest. The film opens with the lumberjacks gathering around the dinner table after a long day. Barney makes a speech, complaining that the men are not cutting enough lumber and will have to increase their productivity. He then gets into a fistfight with two of the men. This is a typical Hawksian situation: a group of men engaged in a dangerous profession and the valorizing of male camaraderie.

The reshaping of the character of Lotta Morgan was no doubt due to Hawks, who tailored the role for Frances Farmer. A minor character in the novel, she is described as only a mediocre singer with a limp (because one leg is shorter than the other). In the film, she is beautiful and lusty and an accomplished singer. Wyler also changed Lotta's song. In Ferber's novel, she sings a loggers' drinking song with the refrain "Heigh ho! Drink round brave boys,"[25] but in the film, her musical number is the traditional folk ballad "Aura Lee," which extols an idealized, romantic love: "Aura Lee! Aura Lee! Maid of golden hair / Sunshine came along with thee, and swallows in the air." The song embodies Barney's reaction to the singer—instantly smitten, he announces that a saloon is no place for her and offers her train fare to return home. When she refuses his money, he courts her and declares his love. Barney soon abandons Lotta, however, when Hewitt sends him a telegram inviting Barney to his home and reminding him that his daughter Emma is waiting. Barney asks Swan (who also loves Lotta) to tell her good-bye for him, and Swan ends up marrying her instead. This highlighting of the romantic love theme, followed by Barney's unwilling-ness to face Lotta, establishes his ruthless ambition with a dramatic flair that far exceeds the novel's spare narration.

Barney's willingness to pursue financial success rather than romantic love further undercuts the Hawksian preoccupation with professionalism for its own sake. The character's hardheartedness in love suggests that, rather than being an integral part of a fraternal group, Barney may be merely using his position within the group to exploit his men, which would be antithetical to the Hawksian code. The early scripts by Jane Murfin—she replaced Edward Chodorov (who also worked on *Dodsworth*) when Ferber objected to his changes to her novel—do not establish Barney's love for Lotta Morgan. There, Lotta seems to love Barney, but he thinks Swan would make her a better husband, and Lotta seems equally fond of Swan, which is not the case in the finished film. Murfin's scripts also suggest that Lotta understands that Barney's priority is making money, and his un-willingness to pretend to have a romantic interest in her makes him more sympathetic.

It is possible that Wyler reworked some of the opening sequences to make the loss of romantic love a central theme and to give Lotta's love for Barney more emphasis than is evident in either the novel or Hawks's con-ception. Such an intention also seems to be signaled by the use of "Aura Lee" in the film's introductory title sequence. Wyler may have wanted to darken Barney's character and expose the brutality of a system that pro-duces men like him—a theme that is closer to Wyler's concerns during this period than to Hawks's. According to Scott Berg, Hawks shifted the focus of the plot in the direction of a "buddy movie, the story of two friends and a girl."[26] Wyler, then, seems to have readjusted that focus, telling the tale of a tycoon's quest to recapture the past by courting the daughter of his abandoned love.

Although the film opens in 1884 with a statement about men who "hacked and tore and gauged and schemed and took and took and nev-er replaced," neither director paid much attention to Ferber's ecology theme. Nor is there any sustained effort to develop the rapacity-of-business theme. When the film's narrative shifts to Barney as a wealthy man with two grown children, there is a scene at the breakfast table (lifted from the novel) in which Barney's son, Richard, talks about Theodore Roosevelt's plans to intervene to curb the abuses of big business—which Barney naturally opposes. The reference to Roosevelt's trust-busting efforts would not have been lost on audiences in 1936, who were familiar with Franklin Roosevelt's reform movement toward responsible and progressive capitalism. Nevertheless, these incipient themes of the male group ethos, Barney's ruthless business practices, and the preservation of natural resources all promptly disappear from the film, which devotes its energy instead to the story of Barney's love for the younger Lotta and the rivalry with his son for her affections.

Barney first encounters this young woman when he visits Swan at Iron Ridge. She is working as a waitress at the local restaurant, and when she comes over to his table, the "Aura Lee" theme is heard. She looks just like her mother, and Barney, entranced, evidently sees in her the happiness that has so far eluded him. (Earlier, at Swan's house, when asked if he is happy, Barney hesitates before answering with a tentative yes.) We soon learn, however, that this Lotta has a touch of Barney in her. In a scene with her aunt Karie (not her mother, as in the novel), she acknowledges that she is aware of Barney's interest and suggests that she will use it to her advantage. This frank acknowledgment of her ambition immediately undercuts Lotta's potential as a romantic ideal, and it places Barney in a position much like that of Fran Dodsworth, who is out of her depth in European society but blinded by its surface brilliance and sophistication. Captivated by Lotta's youth and beauty, Barney cannot see her American need to "come and get it." And like Fran, he will fail to recognize that he is too old for his romantic fantasy until he is forcefully confronted by the reality of it—Fran's rebuke by Baroness von Obersdorf will be echoed in Lotta's harsh rejection of Barney late in the film.

The film, meanwhile, faithfully follows the plot of the novel, underscoring Barney's infatuation as he takes Karie, Swan, and Lotta to Chicago and installs them in a cottage near his house. He employs Swan and Karie at his factory and sends Lotta to business school. The film's narrative then breaks from the novel, showing Richard falling for Lotta and courting her in scenes that include a charming and suggestive episode in which he helps her make candy. This scene is generally credited to Hawks, though the strengthening of Richard's role—and, by extension, the screen prominence of Joel McCrea, who was given star billing—is most likely Wyler's doing.

The film also develops an interesting connection between Barney's relationship with Lotta and that with his daughter Evie. Evie, like Lotta,
calls her father Barney, while her mother refers to him as Mr. Glasgow.
The candy-making scene between Richard and Lotta is closely followed by
one in which Evie, who is playing with a string toy, tells her father that she
is breaking off her engagement to the wealthy Orvie and intends to marry
Tony Schwerke. Unlike her father—and unlike her character in the novel,
who goes ahead with the marriage to Orvie—the film's Evie will marry for
love. And like her brother, she will marry someone who is beneath her socially. This mixing of classes, offering the potential of upward mobility and
the promise of a revitalized and more beneficent capitalism, gives *Come
and Get It* an optimistic feel that no doubt contributed to its success with
audiences.

During the confessional scene, Evie warns her father against his involvement with Lotta, although she claims to understand his unhappiness
and his desire for romantic love. But Barney, fearing that his son will outdo
him, proposes to Lotta soon afterward. His advances are interrupted by
the arrival of Karie with some homemade candy, but Barney tells Lotta
that they will speak further at the company lawn party—thus leading to
the confrontation that concludes the film.

The party sequence has all the visual hallmarks of a Wyler film. The
scene opens with Barney and his family greeting guests. Before the Bostroms
arrive, Richard brings Lotta into the house, where he proposes to her in an
elegantly shot sequence in which the two are profiled in front of a window,
the white curtains highlighting the black hat that occasionally shadows
part of Lotta's face. The lighting by Rudolph Maté, who took over from
Gregg Toland when Wyler became director, is soft, and the shadows give
the scene a painterly feel. The proposal scene is interrupted, however, when
Wyler cuts to Barney hurrying through the large dining room, looking for
Richard. Here, Wyler's fondness for emphasizing space is reminiscent of
his treatment of Mrs. Tilford's home and the Dodsworths'. Barney's search
leads him upstairs (another Wyler staircase), where he must confront his
real self—the man he is, rather than the one he left behind decades earlier.

When Barney opens the door at the top of the stairs, the camera offers the most stunning shot in the film as it finds Lotta and Richard over
Barney's shoulder, framed by the door and the curtains, the shadows prac-

tically hiding Lotta's face. Barney confronts his son, slaps him twice, and dares him to fight. Then he punches Richard, who falls. When Richard gets up, the two men clinch, and Richard tells his father that he and Lotta are in love and plan to marry. Infuriated, Barney is about to restart the fight when Lotta cautions Richard not to hurt his father, who is an old man. This remark stops Barney in his tracks and defeats him. Again, the moment directly parallels that in which Kurt's mother reminds Fran of her age in *Dodsworth*.

Robin Wood and others have argued that this scene is Hawksian because it anticipates the confrontation between Tom Dunson (John Wayne) and his adopted son, Matthew Garth (Montgomery Clift), in *Red River*. Wood writes, "At the crisis, father and son begin to fight. The girl intervenes, and her presence is responsible for bringing the father to his senses, making him realize his love for his son, and leading him to accept the young people's marriage."[27] Wood's comparison, however, does not take into account the differing circumstances and motivations of the aging fathers who are resisting their sons' maturity. Tom Dunson's fury is driven by his consuming need to sell cattle—as he explains to Matt and Groot (Walter Brennan), he is broke. In *Come and Get It*, however, Barney's jealousy is motivated by emotional need—he will never be able to accept his son's marriage.

After the confrontation with Richard, Barney begins to descend the staircase. At the same time, his wife heads up the stairs, looking for him. Wyler foregrounds Barney in shadow, while Emma is sharply lit in the background. As they descend together, Barney tells her that he has thrown Richard out of the house because he is marrying "that girl." Emma, who is aware of Barney's infatuation, is relieved to learn that her husband is not leaving her. Simply remarking that "perhaps even you can't have everything you want," she then urges Barney to call in the guests for dinner.

Walking over to the triangle he once used to summon his crew to meals when he was a lumberjack, Barney admits to Swan that he is a foolish old man. As he begins to ring the triangle, Wyler frames his face in it, as if forcing Barney to accept his diminished condition. Wyler then cuts to Richard and Lotta as they move through the crowd and away from the house, and then back to Barney's face, still framed in the triangle, reflecting pain and anguish as he calls "Come and get it" more forcefully—almost hysterically.

The tight framing and his anguished expression suggest that Barney has finally acknowledged that his life, sacrificed on the altar of money and success, has been wasted. Like Fran Dodsworth, he is made to recognize his errors in judgment at the film's conclusion.

Wyler's final scene in *Come and Get It* is markedly different from Hawks's conclusion to *Red River*. Hawks's scene, for one thing, is much more violent: when Tom confronts Matt, he shoots at him five times, trying to force his son to draw his gun, and when this fails, he starts punching Matt until the younger man finally fights back. The struggle is eventually broken up by Tess (Joanne Dru), who reminds them that they really love each other. Father and son acknowledge their love, and the film ends with Tom making Matt his partner at the ranch and changing the brand to signify a union that, until that moment, had been unspoken. Hawks was criticized for substituting a more conventional happy ending for the traditional one originally planned for his film, which would have had Tom, the flawed tragic figure, dying at the end but recognizing his failings before he dies and leaving Matt free to live his life.

Wyler's vision is more unsparing, but after all the script modifications and then the change in directors, *Come and Get It* is neither well developed nor focused enough to qualify as tragedy. Unlike Tom Dunson, Barney Glasgow is left at the end without his son or Lotta. He still has the wife he never loved and a business empire that no longer fulfills his needs. The differences in temperament between the two directors are as marked as their styles, but in *Come and Get It*, Wyler has the last word.

When filming was finally finished, Wyler and Goldwyn had another fight. Goldwyn wanted to drop Hawks's name altogether and give Wyler sole credit as director. Wyler adamantly refused, insisting not only that Hawks's name be retained in the film's credits but that his own be omitted. Goldwyn finally compromised, and both names appear in the credits. Wyler won a victory of sorts, however, in that Hawks's name appears first. Wyler never considered *Come and Get It* one of his films and rarely discussed it.

Despite its considerable problems, *Come and Get It* fared just as well with the critics as *Dodsworth* had. The *New York Times* opened its review by praising Goldwyn and pronouncing the film "as fine in its way as those earlier Goldwyn successes of this year, 'These Three' and 'Dodsworth.' It has the same richness of production, the same excellence of performance, the same shrewdness of direction."[28] In a letter to Wyler, Jimmy Townsend of Myron Selznick's office wrote that William Wellman, who had attended the premiere, said "he would be proud to have his name on the picture" and went on to call it "the current rave in Hollywood."[29] This assessment turned out to be accurate: despite its escalated costs, *Come and Get It* outperformed *Dodsworth* at the box office.

6

The Street Where They Live

Dead End (1937)

After *Come and Get It*, Goldwyn decided to assign his star director to another prestige property, *Dead End*. Wyler and Goldwyn had seen the play together in March 1936 (it had opened in October of the previous year), when Wyler was working with Sidney Howard on the *Dodsworth* script. Once Goldwyn had purchased the rights, Wyler would see it for a second time in September with noted playwright Clifford Odets, who was apparently being considered to write the screenplay. After the show, Wyler sent his boss a telegram: "Odets and I saw Dead End for second time tonight both feel we could make outstanding picture."[1]

Dead End was the second hit for playwright Sidney Kingsley, whose first play, *Men in White* (1933), had won the Pulitzer Prize. It then became the Group Theatre's first commercial success, running for 357 performances on Broadway; it had a substantial run in London as well. *Dead End* would prove to be an even bigger success, with 684 performances—an extraordinary run for a serious play.

Kingsley's early success as a playwright was due in part to some fortunate production choices. Much of the success of *Men in White* was due to Lee Strasberg's brilliant direction. Intuiting that the central strength of Kingsley's play was its detailed portrait of hospital life, Strasberg centered on the pictorial qualities of the work, culminating in a breathtaking scene of an operation: Bright white lights focused on the operating table, flooding the area and causing the doctors' gowns and the sheet over the patient to stand out against the blue walls. When the doctor said "Scalpel," another light made the blade glint as it was lowered toward the body. Producer Cheryl Crawford recalled that this effect was "as painful as the scalpel making the incision."[2]

The staging and the spectacular effects distracted audiences—but not critics—from Kingsley's shortcomings as a playwright, which included a tendency to create one-dimensional, representative characters and cumbersome dialogue that drained those characters of any capacity for self-reflection or genuine emotion. Kingsley's plays, however, remain notable for their sense of optimism and their faith in progress, the future, and the human spirit. *Men in White* is a tribute to the medical profession and to the doctors who sacrifice their personal happiness for the improvement of medical care. Kingsley dedicated the play to "the men in medicine who dedicate themselves, with quiet heroism, to man," thus aligning it with the optimism of New Deal America and assuring the play's popularity.[3]

Dead End would also be distinguished by a spectacular set, designed by Norman Bel Geddes, that stunned audiences with its depiction of an entire neighborhood. A narrow tenement street ran down one side of the stage, while the other featured a new apartment building for the wealthy. Another street dead-ended at New York's East River; the pier's pylons and rotting timbers were extended over the edge of the stage and into the orchestra pit, which doubled as the river. Bel Geddes even recorded the sounds of the streets, the river beating against the pier, the foghorns in the harbor, and the splash of water when the tenement kids jumped into the river to swim—the actors actually jumped into a net in the orchestra pit below, while a stagehand threw some water up onto the stage to make it appear that the pit was filled with water.[4]

Like much of his work, Kingsley's second play is a didactic piece that remains firmly rooted in the social activism that was prominent in much of the literature and theater of the 1930s. This work, too, revolves around social issues, presenting characters who typify either a condition or a social position. *Dead End* is a naturalist drama, focusing on the environment's role in shaping character and on the tendency, in a society that allows wealth and poverty to exist side by side, to foster and encourage crime. The play's epigraph is from Thomas Paine: "The contrast of affluence and wretchedness is like dead and living bodies chained together." Despite its shortcomings, Kingsley's presentation of a reality so stark and so uncompromising ultimately forced his society to confront those problems. Eleanor Roosevelt came to see the play three times and arranged its command performance at the White House. President Franklin Roosevelt subsequently appointed a slum study commission. *Dead End* was also the inspiration for

Congress's passage of the Wagner housing bill, providing financial assistance to the states to eliminate unsafe and unsanitary housing conditions.

At the center of the play is a gang of teenagers who congregate on the streets and swim in the filthy East River. (The neighborhood is the East Fifties, near what is now Sutton Place.) They play cards, fight with other gangs, and roast potatoes in garbage cans. But the coarse vitality of this street culture is being impinged on by the presence of new high-rise luxury apartments, whose residents view these kids as hoodlums. The lives of the teenagers are interlaced with several other story lines. One involves a young, idealistic, but out-of-work architect named Gimpty, who grew up in the neighborhood and sympathizes with the boys' plight. He loves a young woman named Kay, who lives in the new luxury apartment building, and he idealizes her, in part because she seems unreachable. He is also friendly with Drina, the older sister of a gang member who is raising her brother and is active with her union.

One day, Baby Face Martin—a childhood friend of Gimpty, but now a notorious killer wanted by the FBI—returns to the neighborhood. In Kingsley's didactic scheme, Martin represents the worst-case scenario of what the slums can produce, and he functions as an obvious contrast to Gimpty's humanistic social ideals. The play's two emotional high points are Martin's reunions—first with his mother, and then with his former sweetheart, Francey. His mother spurns him, recoiling from his presence. When he offers her money, she slaps and curses him. The scene with Francey offers another of the play's stark contrasts. Here, Martin recoils when he discovers that she has become a prostitute and is suffering from a venereal disease. Francey not only accepts his money but asks for more.

The final plot strand involves the neighborhood gang, focusing particularly on Tommy, Drina's brother. In another of the play's contrasts, the gang members' lives are paralleled with that of Philip Griswold, a pampered child who lives in the high-rise apartment with his well-connected parents and a nanny. In one scene, some of the boys beat up Philip and steal his watch. When Philip's father catches Tommy, he locks him in a stranglehold, retrieves the watch, and calls the police. While struggling to free himself, Tommy manages to cut Mr. Griswold with a knife and escapes. Griswold is not seriously hurt but insists that the police catch Tommy and arrest him.

These two plots converge as Gimpty informs the FBI of Martin's whereabouts; a gunfight ensues, and Martin is killed. Likewise, another gang member, Spit, informs on Tommy, who eventually gives himself up. Griswold insists on pressing charges, but Gimpty pleads for Tommy, claiming that reform school will only make him a hardened criminal like Martin. Griswold refuses to relent, and Tommy is taken away by the police. The play ends with Gimpty's promise to Drina that he will use the reward money for informing on Martin to hire the best lawyer possible for Tommy. Gimpty and Drina leave together as the curtain falls.

Goldwyn was interested in the rights to the play from the very beginning. Merritt Hulburd wrote to Goldwyn on November 8, 1935, a little more than a week after *Dead End* opened, and informed him that a common stock company called Dead End Inc. owned 50 percent of the film rights. Hulburd advised, "While there is [a] definite element of risk from a business standpoint in this deal, we feel that since we are solely interested in acquiring rights to this play, it is a worthwhile undertaking."[5] Two weeks later, Hulburd notified Goldwyn that someone had offered "substantially in excess of $100,000" for the rights to *Dead End*. He believed David Selznick had bid $150,000 for the play and warned that Goldwyn would have to top that offer.[6] The next day, Goldwyn closed the deal for $165,000. "That was the great thing about Goldwyn," Wyler said. "If there was some great material and he wanted it, he would just buy it, just like that."[7] Wyler had reason to be excited. On the night Wyler saw the play with Goldwyn, the producer hired him to direct the film—it would be Wyler's third assignment directing a prestige property. After they reached an agreement, Goldwyn put down a $25,000 good-faith deposit and left for Europe.

Goldwyn wanted Sidney Howard, who had just scripted *Dodsworth*, to adapt *Dead End* as well. Hulburd wrote to Howard in September 1936, saying that he needed him to start at once. Howard, however, was busy working on *Gone with the Wind*, so Goldwyn turned to Lillian Hellman, whom he cajoled by writing, "Believe me, I do not think there is anyone who can write 'Dead End' as well as you can."[8] At the time Hellman, was busy completing a social play of her own called *Days to Come*; in adapting Kingsley's play, she would manage to insert some of her ideas about labor and unions.

For the role of Drina, which was made more prominent in the film,

Goldwyn insisted on Sylvia Sidney, who was under contract to Walter Wanger. Sidney had already starred as an oppressed working girl in Josef Von Sternberg's *An American Tragedy* and in King Vidor's film of Elmer Rice's *Street Scene*, which *Dead End* resembled in some details. (Wyler telegrammed Goldwyn that Margaret Sullavan, whom he would soon divorce, would be a good choice for the role if Sidney was unavailable; as it turned out, Sidney got the role.) Joel McCrea was once again chosen to co-star as Dave Connell—Gimpty's new name for the film. This revised character would lose his limp and, instead of informing on Baby Face Martin, would hunt him down and shoot him himself.

For the role of Baby Face, Goldwyn wanted James Cagney, who had just won a case against Warner Brothers breaking his long-term contract. Reeves Espy, a Goldwyn executive, advised his boss that even though Warner Brothers was appealing the decision, there was no reason that Cagney could not be approached. He warned Goldwyn, however, that becoming embroiled in a Warner-Cagney fight was not advisable. The part was next offered to George Raft, who turned it down because he thought the character too vicious. Finally, the role went to Humphrey Bogart, who had recently won acclaim on Broadway as the gangster Duke Mantee in Robert Sherwood's *The Petrified Forest*, a role he reprised in the film version. Marjorie Main reprised her stage role as Martin's mother, and Claire Trevor was cast as Francey.

Goldwyn wanted to cast the street kids from among the usual group of Hollywood child actors, but Kingsley, with Wyler's help, convinced him that this would be a mistake, and the actors from the original stage production were hired. Kingsley explained, "I had spent many months working with these kids, and they were as close to the real thing as he could find; and although they had individual problems, they were gifted and precisely the characters—nobody could play them as well."[9] Indeed, Leo Gorcey, Huntz Hall, Gabriel Dell, Bernard Punsley, Bobby Jordan, and Billy Halop did so well that they were dubbed "The Dead End Kids" and went on to sign contracts with Warner Brothers, which made a series of films about their exploits.

Wyler wanted to shoot the film in New York to capture the authenticity that Kingsley had tried to achieve in the play. Goldwyn, however, disliked location shooting because it meant he had less control over his directors.

So he hired Richard Day, who had just won an Oscar for the set design on *Dodsworth*, to build an elaborate set duplicating a ghetto street with shops and seedy apartments and even the balcony of a luxury apartment; one end of the sound stage was excavated and filled with water to stand in for the East River. The result was much like the stage set, only on a grander scale—it cost Goldwyn around $100,000. It was the talk of Hollywood, although Wyler hated it and found it "phony": "It was very fashionable in those days to build in the studio even when the real thing was standing somewhere. That was one battle I lost."[10]

Despite all the effort and expense he had put into duplicating a slum, Goldwyn wanted it to be clean. Wyler would litter the set each morning to make it look authentic, but Goldwyn was horrified and insisted that Wyler clean up the street. When Wyler refused, the producer picked up the debris himself and threw it away. "Goldwyn didn't like dirt," Wyler recalled. "Everything in his movies had to be clean."[11] Even the soundtrack was free of city noises. As Scott Berg notes, Goldwyn's "pictures had a distinctive look about them—a feel that was always tasteful, even in an East Side slum."[12] Goldwyn's desire for fastidiousness was reinforced by Joseph Breen, who wrote, "We would like to recommend in passing, that you be less emphatic, throughout in the photographing of this script in showing the contrast between conditions of the poor in tenements and those of the rich in apartment houses."[13] The filmmakers should refrain from showing "the presence of filth or smelling garbage cans, or garbage floating in the river, into which the boys jump or swim." Breen felt that such details would "give offense."[14]

Wyler compensates by creating his most expressionistic film. Although much of *Dead End* takes place outdoors, the film has an interior feel. It is composed of numerous vertical shots, diagonal angles, and frames within frames, thus embracing within its mise-en-scène Kingsley's notion that environment can trap individuals and crush them. On the stage, Bel Geddes's set made the audience feel as if they were watching the activity of a real New York street. Wyler, in turn, emphasizes the artificiality of his film set, taking Kingsley's stark patterning of character and situation for his stylistic blueprint. He imprisons his characters in space and relentlessly manipulates them there. The film is intricately structured, featuring shaded close-ups, elaborate setups, and quick vignettes.

Wyler's vision was aided by important modifications in Hellman's ad-

aptation of Kingsley's play, taking into account the suggestions of both
Goldwyn and Breen. Hellman's emphasis on stark character opposition
(as exemplified in *The Children's Hour*) rather than internal conflict made
Kingsley's characters easy to shape. However, she made some significant
alterations in the characters. As indicated earlier, Gimpty is renamed Dave
and, as portrayed by Joel McCrea, is more heroic than his stage model.
No longer a cripple—Kingsley's awkward symbolism had to go—the film's
Dave is able to transcend his environment. Hellman's Dave is not ravaged
by slum life; he is an active, crusading, romantic hero, and McCrea's rugged good looks only enhance that image. The speeches Kingsley gives to
Gimpty—such as when he calls New York "the biggest tombstone in the
world," and his lecture on evolution, wherein he declares that the "God
planted in men's hearts takes away their reason and their sense of beauty"[15]
—are eliminated. Dave is not a philosopher; he is a doer. Kingsley himself
seemed to endorse this change. In an undated telegram to Goldwyn, he
wrote, "In order to give him character I agree with Miss Hellman stop He
must act decisively and courageously on own strength."[16]

Hellman also makes Drina a more important character. This change
was largely determined by the casting of Sylvia Sidney, who was a star.
Drina becomes a more active figure, a labor advocate who is beaten by the
police while on a picket line. In making this change, Hellman was no doubt
influenced by her own play *Days to Come*, set in an Ohio factory where the
workers strike, pitting a strike organizer against a factory owner. In Kingsley's play, Drina makes her first appearance more than ten pages after the
opening, when she helps a new boy who was just cockalized (humiliated by
having his pants pulled down) by the gang. In the film, she is introduced
in her apartment, where she is seen ironing and explaining to her brother
Tommy why they need to get out of the slums and why she is on strike. Her
dual status as a surrogate mother and an activist is immediately established.

In building up Drina, Hellman diminishes the role of Kay (Wendy Barrie) and makes her less sympathetic. The play's Kay occasionally leaves her
luxury apartment to spend time with Gimpty in his slum apartment, but in
the film, she is so appalled by the filth and cockroaches in Dave's building
that she flees. In Kingsley's play, Kay's rich boyfriend's yacht and its place
on the river are associated with Gatsby-like visions of romance and yearn-
ing for Gimpty and the slum children—something they can see but can nev-

er hope to attain. This allusive imagery is mostly dropped in the film and replaced by more concrete situations, such as when Dave sees Kay standing out on the balcony, looking far away and unattainable.

In the play, Gimpty's pairing off with Drina at the end seems almost happenstance, a resigned consequence of Kay's decision to go on a cruise with her wealthy boyfriend. In the film, however, Dave only temporarily loses sight of Drina because of his infatuation with the glamorous Kay. Hellman makes it clear that Dave and Drina are naturally united by their social conscience and desire for a better world. Whereas Dave tells Kay late in the film that they are too different to have a future together, in the play, Gimpty practically begs Kay to stay with him.

The character of Baby Face Martin is also altered by Hellman. In the play, Martin is a gangster who exemplifies Kingsley's thesis that slum life breeds criminals. Gimpty emphasizes this point after Martin's death, while also evoking a measure of sympathy for his childhood friend: "Yeah . . . Martin was a killer, he was bad, he deserved to die, true! But I knew him when we were kids. He had a lot of fine stuff. He was strong. He had courage. He was a born leader. He even had a sense of fair play. But living in the streets kept making him bad."[17]

The film's Martin is also a gangster and a criminal, and he has a sympathetic side as well. In Hellman's script and in Wyler's presentation, he becomes another of the director's dreamers—a man who, like Barney Glasgow and Samuel Dodsworth, wants to recover something of the past. He returns to his old neighborhood to see his mother and his former girlfriend. Confused and nostalgic, he seems to be in search of the boy he once was, hoping to discover where he went wrong. When he is rejected by his mother and then shattered by the realization of what Francey has become, Wyler and Hellman create parallel scenes in which Martin sits in a restaurant, brooding about what he has just experienced and trying to make sense of it. Baby Face thus becomes the embodiment of the 1930s gangster who is literally "dead-ended." He tries to justify himself to Dave by bragging, like a traditional movie gangster, about his custom-made shirts and tailored suits—thus identifying himself with the wealthy who are taking over the neighborhood. Both the gangster and the rich (and, by extension, Kay) threaten to destroy the familial society of the streets by their excess and their idleness. Martin, however, seems to sense that his time is up;

his words sound hollow, and even he knows it. A gangster who seems disgusted by his own success, he is alone (except for a lone sidekick), looking for something he has lost. He is a sad figure, not grand or outsized like the screen gangsters seen earlier in the decade.

In the play, Martin demeans Gimpty in front of the street kids, at one point even stepping on his crippled foot. Kingsley thus gives Gimpty a motivation for informing on Martin, who is later cornered and shot down by the FBI. The film's Dave, however, suffers no indignities from Martin. It is only when Martin tries to kill Dave after he interrupts a kidnapping plan that Dave retaliates, pursuing his old friend across tenement roofs and shooting him as he clings desperately to a fire escape. Martin's "fall," however, is pathetic. He is shot by an architect, not by the FBI, and he dies in the place that produced him. The world he thought he had escaped claims him in the end.

According to Carl Rollyson, Hellman's refusal to make Dave an informer is prophetic of the stand she would take in *Scoundrel Time*. Even at the beginning of *Dead End*, a member of a rival gang wears the scar of a "squealer"—a cut that Tommy is about to inflict on Spit, when he is stopped by Dave. Rollyson writes: "It would never be right to inform in any circumstances—this is the logic of Hellman's absolutist code. There must be a decisive split between right and wrong; evil must be external to the hero, not a part of him."[18]

Kingsley's play is a naturalistic document intended to demonstrate that economic inequity breeds crime. Hellman's screenplay is less didactic and a bit less grim, emphasizing character at the expense of dogma by turning Kingsley's Gimpty into a Joel McCrea–type hero and Drina into a working-class heroine. Even Hellman's prologue—slyly remarking that "every street in New York ends in a river"—seems more descriptive than Kingsley's call-to-arms quotation from Paine. She goes on to explain that, in their desire for homes with river views, the rich moved eastward until they reached a dead end, and their apartments "looked down on the windows of tenements." Hellman's prologue introduces a story; Kingsley's is closer to agitprop.

Wyler's camera, however, manipulates space to emphasize the confinement of the slum environment. Wyler and cinematographer Gregg Toland turn *Dead End* into a story of entrapment in which the characters are repeatedly boxed into claustrophobic, heavily shaded places. Visually, it is

Wyler's darkest and most brooding work, and the mood is compounded by the depiction of Baby Face Martin. Unlike the gangster figures of the early 1930s, whose rise from their immigrant status to lives of glamour and riches made them emblematic of the success ethic, this film's gangster is consumed by remorse. In his second inaugural address in 1937, Roosevelt promised to undermine "old admiration of worldly success as such" and to be intolerant of "the abuse of power by those who betray for profit the elementary decencies of life."[19] The New Deal's replacement of rugged individualism with social responsibility and activism made the traditional gangster figure obsolete; instead, the representatives of law and order became heroic figures in the movies. Like his real-life namesake, "Baby Face" Nelson, *Dead End*'s Baby Face Martin is hunted by the FBI and, in the play, is gunned down by FBI agents.

Bogart's Martin is an extension of his role as Duke Mantee in *The Petrified Forest*, a character he originated for the stage in 1934 and reprised in the 1936 film version, reviving his flagging screen career. *The Petrified Forest* is an allegorical play in which Sherwood brings the gangster face-to-face with an itinerant poet and philosopher, Alan Squire, in an isolated gas station–luncheonette in the eastern Arizona desert. The poet first recognizes Mantee as "the last great apostle of rugged individualism." Indeed, to Gramp Maple, Duke is the very spirit of America: "He ain't a gangster; he's a real old-time desperado. Gangsters is foreign. He's an American." But modern America, according to Sherwood, has no use for either the poet or the gangster, and Squire eventually tells Mantee, "You're obsolete Duke, just like me."[20] Organized crime has made the lone gangster outmoded, and the burgeoning industrialized America has no place for poets. In Sherwood's play, they both go to the old frontier to die.

Kingsley's Baby Face Martin returns to New York from the Midwest (St. Louis)—thus reversing the mythic American journey—to revisit the neighborhood that shaped him. Unlike Mantee, who is described as shabby, stooped, and almost animal-like, Martin has a surgically reconstructed face and expensive clothes. This makeover does not effectively disguise him, though, because he is immediately recognized by Dave. Most important, this aging gangster is nostalgic, hoping to rediscover who he once was, and he yearns to reconnect with his mother and his first love. As he explains to his sidekick, Hunk, in a line that was written for the film, "I'm getting sick of what I can pay for." Like Wyler's restructured and reimagined Barney Glasgow, who returns to the woods looking for his lost self, Martin makes the same journey with the same destructive results. Martin, like the prototypical screen gangster, is killed, while Barney belatedly realizes that he has ruined his own life. The gangster and the businessman suffer similar fates.

The film opens with an unbroken crane shot scanning the New York City skyline and then descending across an apartment house window, tenement roofs, the street of a slum neighborhood, and the entrance to a new luxury apartment, finally coming to rest with a low-angle shot of a policeman dwarfed by the size of the building and the sight of a tugboat moving down the river. Within the next eight minutes, Wyler introduces all the principal characters. The Dead End Kids are fooling around, awaiting the arrival of their leader, Tommy, who is impatiently waiting for his sister, Drina, to finish ironing his shirt. As she completes her task, Drina explains to Tommy that she is on strike to earn better wages so that they can escape this neighborhood. Next, we see Philip Griswold breakfasting on the terrace of a luxury apartment, surreptitiously pouring his milk into a plant.

After Tommy leaves, Drina speaks to Dave's mother, Mrs. Connell, through a barred window; Mrs. Connell is framed by the bars of the fire escape. They mention that Dave had been looking for Drina the previous night, but she was late coming home from a strike meeting. Drina comments that Dave used to wait for her, "but now . . ." She stops, and Wyler cuts to a balcony in the new building showing Kay looking out, framed by the leafy branches of a tree. It is a lovely, visual cut that establishes both Drina's entrapment in the slum and the sense that Kay's world, despite its proximity, is far away. Whether Dave (whom we have not met yet) could ever attain such a dream is brought into question. The film will force both Drina and Dave to face choices—hers, whether to leave the neighborhood to find a better life for herself and Tommy; his, whether to abandon Drina and the poor people he grew up with to enter the world of the idle rich.

Dave is an architect—his profession is a metaphor for his potential to create a new, just society—but he cannot find work and is forced to do menial labor. He is first seen painting the window of a local restaurant, where Drina stops to talk with him about the strike. While fixing her shoe, she notices that Dave is distracted by the sight of Kay on her balcony; frustrated by his lack of attention, she leaves.

When Wyler introduces Martin and his associate Hunk, their clothes make them look out of place in the neighborhood. Dave immediately recognizes Martin, and they talk. When Dave says that he envies Martin for getting away from the neighborhood, the gangster responds, "Yeah, far away." His words echo the free-floating image of Kay on her balcony, but coming from Martin, they imply that money may not be the answer to escaping the slums. He confirms this suspicion when, after laughing at Dave for going to college for six years only to be forced to live off "handouts," Martin shows off his shirt and his $150 suit but then wistfully remarks, "Sometimes I get the jitters and sometimes I get a terrific yen to stay put." Turning away from Dave, he looks up the street to where his mother lives and then toward the river, his face partially hidden, clearly longing for something he cannot quite articulate. Martin's body language points toward love, not money, as the essence of fulfillment; it is the reason he has come home. This is the truth that Dave will rediscover when he turns away from Kay and remembers his love for Drina.

Wyler places the two scenes between Dave and Kay near the water to give them a romantic feel—similar to his use of the ocean at the end of *A House Divided*—unlike the dirty water of the East River where the boys swim. Kay admits to liking another man and reveals that she is thinking about going away with him. She says she was "hard up" when she and the other man met and is "tired of being hard up." Like Barney Glasgow, she is willing to marry for money and security. She admits to Dave that her suitor wants to marry her, and she is tempted because she is "frightened of being poor again." Dave agrees that poverty is terrible but asks her to wait until he hears about a potential job. In the play, Kay arranges Gimpty's job interview; the more forceful Dave of the film gets the interview on his own. And yet, in the play, Gimpty lectures Kay that "not to look forward to love . . . God that's not living at all!" The film's Dave is less aggressive because, like Kay, he is unsure of their relationship.

Wyler's staging of these scenes is interesting as well. In Dave's meeting with Martin (which precedes the scene with Kay), Martin sits on a rail, which places him above Dave. In the next scene, Kay leans against a wall while Dave sits, placing her higher than Dave. In both cases, the higher positions connote economic advantage, but Wyler is using this spatial indicator ironically, for in both scenes, Dave occupies the moral high ground.

Dave's outdoor scenes with Kay are contrasts to a similar encounter with Drina. She is shown crocheting under a wooden structure, where it is dark and shadowed. Drina tells Dave about a rich man she met on the subway who took her out to dinner and has a house in the country; she admits that she is tempted to run away with him. (Drina, significantly, meets her dream man on the subway, an apt image of constricted city life, whereas Kay's man has a yacht.) Dave, in turn, declares that he would like to give her those things, but Drina quickly admits that it is just a fantasy—presumably, like Dave's dreams of Kay. Unlike Kay, Drina has no real chance of escaping unless, perhaps, she is rescued by Dave. Through much of this speech, Wyler films Sylvia Sidney in beautifully key-lit close-ups, emphasizing her haunted yet lovely face. Surely Dave notices what the camera sees.

One of the most skillfully realized sequences in the film is the scene in which Kay visits Dave's apartment. This episode created by Hellman (it does not appear in the play) gains power from the skillful way in which Wyler and Toland develop its implications. Hellman considered various possibilities for the sequence: in her earliest treatment (dated April 7, 1937), she invented a series of scenes in which Dave's mother plans a party for Kay, where she will use her special teacups, previously reserved only for visits by the priest. But this party sequence was discarded entirely, and Mrs. Connell appears in only one scene with Drina, early in the film. The sequence that remains is mostly silent. Informed by a neighbor that he has a visitor, Dave rushes back to his building. Wyler then cuts to Kay ascending a staircase, where she is framed by the bars of the stairs and the reflected shadows, which crisscross on the wall behind her. As she starts to climb a second staircase, she looks to her side, and in a tunneled view, the center of the frame reveals a dingy hallway with a child playing on the floor. As she makes her way upward, she stands aside for a man carrying a garbage can downstairs. She looks to her side and sees another overflowing garbage can with a cockroach crawling on top. She is horrified and turns away, rubbing her hand on a filthy part of the banister. As she backs away, looking up and debating whether to continue her ascent, there is a cut to a modified deep-focus composition: we see Kay, her back to the camera in the front of the frame, and Dave at the foot of the stairs, framed by a doorway, looking up at her. The setting and the space between them effectively communicate that this pair can never be together, even suggesting that Dave's infatuation is preventing him from realizing his true self. As Kay rushes down the stairs to escape, Dave hides in the shadows, with a hallway to his left darkly lit and at a tilted angle—an expressionist visualization of his despair. The sequence concludes with Kay running down the street and disappearing into her more comfortable and comforting world.

That decisive sequence is followed shortly by the reunion of Martin and his mother, which provides another of the film's high points. The dialogue remains essentially true to the play, but Wyler films the scene indoors rather than outside. The action begins outdoors, however, with a shot of Martin prominent in the front of the frame as he watches his mother walk toward her building in the distance. Wyler then cuts to Martin's face, which resembles that of an expectant Hollywood lover as he rushes toward her. The scene in the hallway where they meet is dark and shadowed; again, it takes place on a staircase, with the mother standing above her son. Through most of the scene, the faces of both actors are shadowed or in profile. Mrs. Martin rejects her son, slapping him and finally telling him to "die and leave us alone." She then wearily climbs the stairs as the camera looks up at her. As is usually the case in Wyler's films, these stairs do not lead anywhere in particular; they are used to explicate moments of confrontation and recognition. Martin lingers at the foot of the stairs, staring briefly after his mother before leaving and entering Pascalgi's restaurant.

In the play, the scene concludes with Martin offering his mother money, which she rejects. Martin then asks her if she is going to call the cops. She replies, "They'll get you soon enough," but he assures her that they won't get Baby Face Martin. The film dispenses with this entire exchange; Wyler instead follows a dejected Martin into the restaurant, where Hunk tries to cheer him up by putting on some music. Martin tells him to turn it off—he is clearly miserable, and Wyler keeps the camera on Bogart's disconsolate face. When Hunk says that Martin should have slugged his mother, Martin angrily tells him to leave. Whereas Kingsley's Martin ends the scene with an expression of hubris, flaunting his stature in front of his mother, the film's gangster is humiliated and in despair.

The parallel scene is Martin's reunion with Francey. Prior to this meeting, Martin remarks to Hunk that he wishes he had a place where he could sit in the same chair every day. His desire for a stable life is interrupted by Francey's arrival, which is depicted like Mrs. Martin's: again, we see

Martin in the front of the frame, with Francey walking toward him from the rear. In this outdoor scene, the characters meet in the light, but Martin quickly moves Francey into an alley. The reunion is then shot mostly in close-up, with their faces close together and in profile, or in medium close-up with the same configuration. They recall their plan, made ten years earlier, to get married, and Martin insists that he has come back to marry her now. Francey cries that it is all a dream; she waited for him, but it has been too long. Pushing him away, she yells, "I'm sick, can't you see it!" and Wyler cuts to her face as she moves into the light, showing the ravages of her life as a prostitute.

Next there is a cut to Martin—the first shot–reverse shot of the sequence—who is still in the dark as the camera moves closer. Wyler cuts back to Francey and then returns to Martin, who is once again disillusioned by the reception he has received. His dream of turning back time has been crushed by the reality of the world he tried to escape. He yells out, "Why couldn't you get a job?" She replies, "They don't grow on trees." He asks, "Why didn't ya starve first?" and her retort—"Why didn't you?"— stops him cold. Her final question, "What did ya expect?" elicits only a dejected, "I don't know." Francey accepts Martin's money, but he refuses to give her either the extra $20 she asks for or a farewell kiss. He thus ultimately rejects her, much as his mother rejected him, and this time he ascends some stone steps, repeating his mother's upward movement, as he once more escapes to Pascalgi's, his hopes shattered.

As Martin sits down in the restaurant, Wyler films him through the window, trapping him and sealing his doom. Hunk commiserates with his boss, telling him that he should never have come back and offering the old gangster's credo—"Never go back, always go forward." (This is another addition by Hellman.) Martin has reached the end of the line. Having lost what he came for, he decides to kidnap Philip Griswold and at least get "some dough."

Dave too is in despair; he is bothered by Tommy's use of a knife on Mr. Griswold and by Kay's reaction to the squalor of his apartment building. He runs into Drina, who is once again seen in shadow, moving under the wooden structure of the docks. She is looking for her brother, who is hiding from the police, and commiserates with Dave over Tommy's fate. Dave blames the neighborhood, saying that the kids don't have a chance growing up in such a place—it makes them fight and makes them tough. Drina argues that Dave wasn't hardened by his environment; he responds that he was a fool to believe he could do something to rebuild the neighborhood, and he shares his feelings about Kay's reaction to his building, which upsets Drina: "You always talked about that. How you were going to tear this place down and all the other places like it. You were going to build a better world where people could live decent. Now you want them down so she won't see them." Throughout this speech, Wyler focuses on Drina's face, which is softly lit and free of shadows as she makes her impassioned plea for communal values and social action. It is another moment that is unique to the film, serving to build up Drina's character and her relationship with Dave. Although it clearly reflects Hellman's own socialist bent, this scene was probably also influenced by Robert Wyler's notes on improving the screenplay. He felt that the switching of Dave's affections to Drina at the end of the film happened too quickly: "In order to make this believable, it is essential to show that Drina is in love with Dave but that Dave has brotherly affection for her."[21] A number of scenes in the film are designed to reinforce this idea, but this confrontation is a culminating moment that makes Dave realize that Drina really loves him and that he, perhaps, has always loved her as well. It also reignites his social conscience, which has been rendered temporarily dormant by his infatuation with Kay.

Drina is then shown running up the stairs to her apartment, where she is again framed by the bars of the staircase. This final section of the film, beginning with the sequence just described, shows Wyler at his most expressionistic. Drina's despair over her brother's situation is now magnified by her sense that she has lost Dave. When Drina finally finds Tommy, she tells him that they will run away together—she has nothing to stay for. Then, when she hears Dave calling to her, Wyler cuts to Dave's face, framed by his window. Drina ignores him, pulling down her window shade, and Wyler cuts to her face, which is half in the light, half shadowed. This is one of the film's most expressive moments, suggesting that she is torn between her love for Dave and her need to protect her brother.

Wyler cuts back to Dave, who is once more double-framed by his window and by the fire escape bars. He looks down and sees, in a high-angle shot, Martin's men walking along the docks—they too are framed by bars and distinctly shadowed. In yet another sequence that is original to the film, Martin, Hunk, and a third man meet by the dock to plot the kidnapping of Philip Griswold. At one point, Wyler pushes the three to the side of the screen, where they are seemingly dwarfed by the high-rise apartment building looming over them. Dave, who knows about their plan, sneaks up on Martin and Hunk and tells them to leave, or he will call the cops. When he turns his back, Martin hurls a knife into him, and Hunk throws him off the pier and into the river.

Having survived the knifing, Dave is seen pulling himself out of the river. There is a cut to a policeman running his club along a gate—this image of approaching authority anticipates the action in *Jezebel*, when Preston runs his cane along the balustrade of Julie's staircase. In both instances, the sound is a sign of imminent catastrophe. Wyler films Martin's attempt to escape by isolating him and confining him in various spaces. Martin is first surprised by Dave, who knocks him down, but he gets away as Dave and Hunk struggle for the latter's gun. Martin then runs into an abandoned warehouse, which is completely dark except for a filter of light coming through an open door. Again, there is an ascent of a staircase, and Martin ends up on the roof of the building, with Dave in pursuit as they shoot at each other. Wyler cuts to an image of Martin from below, the frame dominated by fire escapes on the right. Like the classic gangster, Martin is now "on top" yet fatally trapped. He grabs at the bars of the fire escape but is shot by Dave; he cannot hold on and falls to the ground. Martin's death—a short, unexciting scene in the play—becomes, in Wyler's hands, a cinematic tour de force that anticipates the techniques he would use to build dramatic tension in the Olympus Ball sequence of his next film, *Jezebel*.

The film winds down quickly following this climactic showdown. Dave, after being checked by a doctor, ascends the alley and looks up at Kay's building, a grim expression on his face. Martin's diamond ring and his cash are removed by the police—a veiled comment about the futility of Dave's dream of escaping with Kay. Wyler then cuts to Tommy, whose face is barred by shadows as he learns that the police are still after him. He, too, climbs to the top of the pier and looks down on his friends, hoping to discover who "ratted him out." When he learns that it was Spit, Tommy comes up with a plan to catch him.

This sequence is contrasted with Dave's farewell to Kay, who is presented almost literally as an emissary from another world—she is adorned in a white stole and a white floor-length gown. Wyler first films them from above, echoing the angle he used moments earlier to show Drina looking for Tommy. The repeated effect links both stories: Drina will lose Tommy, and Dave will lose Kay. In another scene by the water, Dave tells Kay that he does not belong in her world and releases her to join her wealthy lover. Tommy then gives himself up, but only after Dave has stopped him from cutting Spit's face with a knife to mark him as a squealer.

The film concludes with Tommy being taken away by the police and Dave promising Drina that he will use his reward money to hire a good lawyer for the boy. Drina retorts that he should use it to escape the slum, but Dave assures her that he now understands that escape is not what he wants. Drina looks at him lovingly and takes his hand as they walk toward Tommy. One of Hellman's drafts had the film end there, but the revised ending echoes that of the play. The street kids are roasting potatoes over a fire in a garbage can, and the police force them to put it out. As the smoke from the fire rises, Wyler follows the kids as they sing, "If I had the wings of an angel, over the prison walls I would fly—Straight to the arms of my mother." The street gang walks together, again framed by the wooden supports of the pier, into the darkness. The visuals provide an ironic counterpoint to the hope expressed by the song and the tentative good feeling generated by Dave's reconciliation with Drina and his offer to help Tommy. Again, Wyler undercuts a potentially satisfying conclusion by underscoring it with shades of ambiguity.

Dead End reflects the sense of cautious optimism generated by the prospect of Roosevelt's second term, which was soon tempered by the bombing of Guernica, the escalating political turmoil in Europe, and another economic downturn at home a few months after the president's second inauguration. In the month the film was released—August 1937—Japan attacked Shanghai, starting a war with China. The ambivalent mood of Wyler's film was also being reflected in *Lost Horizon*, a film that celebrates a society devoid of conflict—the alternative proposed by James Hilton's novel for a world on the verge of chaos. *Lost Horizon* begins in revolutionary China, a society engulfed by the struggles of the poor, as depicted in Irving Thalberg's *The Good Earth*, released the same year. *Dead End* eclipsed both films at the box office, garnering excellent reviews and critical praise for Wyler. It received four Oscar nominations, including one for Best Picture, but Wyler was not nominated, and the film did not win any awards.

7

Gone with the Plague

Jezebel (1938)

In the summer of 1937, Hal Wallis, production head at Warner Brothers, decided that he wanted Wyler to direct *Jezebel*, an antebellum story set in New Orleans. The film would capitalize on the craze generated by David O. Selznick's national search for an actress to play Scarlett O'Hara in *Gone with the Wind*.

Jezebel was Bette Davis's consolation prize for missing out on the plum role of Scarlett. Jack Warner had held the first option on Margaret Mitchell's best seller, but he passed on it because of his legal battles with Davis. She had left the studio in a dispute over the inferior roles she had been given after winning her first Oscar for *Dangerous* in 1935. After sailing for England to avoid being served with legal papers by Warner's lawyers, Davis signed with an Anglo-Italian producer to make films in Europe. Warner Brothers then served her with an injunction prohibiting her from offering her services anywhere, and the two sides prepared for a court battle. Jack Warner came to London with William Randolph Hearst, whose newspapers depicted Davis as an ungrateful, spoiled child. Eventually, Warner won a three-year injunction, and Davis was forced to return to the studio. In an effort to placate his star, Jack Warner relieved Davis of the obligation to pay the studio's share of the court costs and gave her a series of prestige pictures, culminating in *Jezebel*.

Originally a Broadway play that was both a critical and a commercial failure, *Jezebel* closed early in 1934 after only thirty-two performances. But Wyler, who had seen the show when he still worked for Universal, recommended it as a potential film project: "I believe that *Jezebel* contains an excellent foundation for a picture. It's a very dramatic love story. . . . The weaknesses of the play can be overcome in a picture through the addition of many incidents and sequences only suggested and talked about. A good deal of action can be added. The atmosphere and costumes lend themselves to beauty in production."[1]

By then, Wyler was developing both a taste for projects about the American social scene and an understanding of how stage properties could be translated effectively to the screen. He had already sublimated his own conflicts about America's lure for the immigrant in his work on *Counsellor-at-Law* for Universal. *Jezebel*, with its melodramatic explorations of racism and the potential effects of industrialism on the American landscape in the second half of the nineteenth century, naturally piqued Wyler's interest, and he could clearly envision how to strengthen the underdeveloped play.

On stage, the role of headstrong, spoiled socialite Julie Kendrick was played by Miriam Hopkins, who had taken over the part when Tallulah Bankhead became ill during rehearsals. Despite the play's failure and the protagonist's unsympathetic nature, Bette Davis thought this property would be an ideal vehicle for her, and she spent more than a year trying to persuade Jack Warner to buy the rights.

Walter MacEwen, Hal Wallis's executive assistant, read the play for Warner Brothers and expressed his reservations in a 1935 memo. Reiterating the critics' verdict—that the play was "not very good"—he went on to say, "The trouble is that there really is no one in the play to pull for, to offset the bitchiness of the leading part." MacEwen added, "While Bette Davis receives acclaim for tasty supporting roles, I doubt if a picture built solely around her in an unsympathetic part would be so well liked." Like Wyler, however, he felt that the play could be improved by giving the character of Julie a "slant" that would make her more "acceptable to audiences." MacEwen suggested that Julie could start out as "a spoiled little vixen," which could be justified by her upbringing, and then undergo "regeneration through suffering," which would make her "a wiser and more palatable person after the final shot."[2] This suggestion would be incorporated into subsequent revisions of the screenplay.

Warner bought the rights two years later, although Edmund Goulding (Wallis's original choice as director) echoed MacEwen's concerns. In a lengthy memo to Wallis, he commented that although Davis would likely distinguish herself in the role, audiences would have a difficult time identifying with the character. The studio, however, was determined to cash in on the *Gone with the Wind* craze and went ahead with the film.

Jezebel was filmed during one of the delays in the making of *Gone with the Wind*, and the Warners took pleasure in their opportunistic gambit. Selznick, however, tried to bully Jack Warner into thinking that *Jezebel* would be "damned as an imitation by the millions of readers, and lovers, of *Gone with the Wind*." He specifically mentioned the dinner scene in *Jezebel*, where the men discuss the differences between the North and the South and the imminent war, leading to Preston's declaration that the North will win because of its superior machinery. When Selznick charged that the scene "is lifted practically bodily out of *Gone with the Wind*," Warner responded nonchalantly, pointing out that the dinner scene was taken directly from Owen Davis's play. He sent Selznick a copy of the scene and thanked him for his "splendid interest."[3]

Jezebel would be Davis's first film with an important director. The production budget was around $800,000, but the film ended up costing more than $1 million because Wyler went twenty-eight days over the forty-eight allotted for filming. Warner had borrowed Wyler from Goldwyn, stipulating that he would be paid $75,000 for twelve weeks beginning on or about September 6, 1937; if his services were required beyond that time, he would be paid $1,041.66 per day.[4]

As noted earlier, Wallis originally considered hiring Edmund Goulding, who was considered an important director at Warner Brothers, to direct the film, and Goulding wrote a preliminary report on the project. But Lou Edelman, a production supervisor and producer at Warner, felt that Goulding was not up to the job. In a memo, Edelman complained that Goulding did not grasp the shadings of Julie's character, and he called the director's ideas about the film old-fashioned and conventional. Edelman wrote that *Jezebel* was trying "to tell the story of a bitch," whereas Goulding's story was "not about a Jezebel but about any violent woman."[5] Wallis obviously agreed, and he decided to borrow Wyler from Samuel Goldwyn. Goulding was assigned to direct *The Dawn Patrol* with Errol Flynn instead, and a year later he would direct Bette Davis in one of her greatest triumphs, *Dark Victory*.

Wyler came to the studio with a reputation for being exacting and difficult—obsessive about details and fond of ordering multiple takes for scenes. His autocratic behavior had already incurred the wrath of Ruth Chatterton, Miriam Hopkins, and Sylvia Sidney. Humphrey Bogart, who had just finished shooting *Dead End* with Wyler, joked with Davis that she wouldn't last two weeks.

At first, Davis was put off when she heard that Wyler would be directing. She had never forgotten an unpleasant encounter with him in 1930 when she had tested for *A House Divided*. The wardrobe department had dressed her in a low-cut dress that showed too much cleavage, and Wyler is reputed to have "whispered" loud enough for Davis to hear, "What do you think about these dames who show their tits and think they can get a job."[6] Davis was humiliated. But now that she was in a position of power, she looked forward to exacting her revenge. Davis later recalled: "In a state of elation I went to his office at Warner Brothers for my first interview with him. . . . I sat down and immediately told him that he had tested me at Universal many years ago. He did not remember. I told him what he had said. . . . There was a long pause, and Mr. Wyler said, 'I am a much nicer person now!' They say revenge is sweet. I found it to be futile that day."[7]

In Wyler, Davis would discover her ideal director. Like her, he was a perfectionist who knew exactly what he wanted. Wyler's other leading ladies often found him to be temperamental, rude, and even abusive, and he would retake a scene as many as forty times. Unlike some of her predecessors, however, Davis reveled in the Wyler "touch." In her autobiography she wrote, "I became such a champion of his talent—and still am—that one would have thought I was his highly paid press agent. It was he who helped me realize my full potential as an actress. I met my match in this exceptionally creative and talented director."[8] Davis would give three of her finest performances under Wyler's direction; she won her second Academy Award for *Jezebel* and then went on to star in *The Letter* (1940) and *The Little Foxes* (1941).

In a note to his play, which was written as a vehicle for Tallulah Bankhead, Owen Davis states that he "wants to combine the technique of modern playwriting with the glamour of the old theater."[9] But there is very little of the modern in *Jezebel*. Davis lifts Eugene O'Neill's device of using two giant live oaks to dominate the stage and represent the color and romance of the Deep South. This stale, simplistic symbolism is typical of the play as a whole, which presents a series of two-dimensional characters struggling through a story of sin and redemption.

The play's Julie is surnamed Kendrick, as is Preston (known as Pres),

her fiancé and cousin. (Her name is changed to Marsden in the film, his to
Dillard.) Early in the play, she exclaims, "We Kendricks have always married with our own kin . . . so what's bad in us just naturally keeps on getting
worse."[10] The reason for the couple's breakup is not convincingly presented, as Julie merely reports that she wore a red dress instead of the white one
Pres preferred. Hurt by his rejection, she vows never to wear white again
and ends their engagement. The scene in which Julie decides to repent and
then meets Pres's new wife also lacks drama, emotion, or tension. Davis
tries on occasion to inject some social commentary into the play, but these
attempts come off like afterthoughts and do not contribute to its texture.

Wyler knew he would need a strong screenplay to realize his concept of
the film. Early in 1937, Wallis commissioned a script from Robert Buckner,
who delivered a first draft on April 30. Although Buckner's script makes
some substantial changes, it does not overcome the weaknesses of the original. In his introductory note, Buckner writes that New Orleans should be
the factor that makes this story "less static, less familiar." As "the most
truly southern [city] in spirit and history," he feels that New Orleans has
been neglected as a film locale. Buckner invents a scene in which Julie goes
to a cockfight while looking for one her servants. Pres objects to her going,
follows her there, and notes the "true wildness of her character, the un-
governed element of latent cruelty and sadistic passion" as she watches the
cockfight. When he reproves her, she slaps him across the face, which leads
to their breakup and to Julie's subsequent trip to Paris and New York, the
highlights of which are depicted in the script, including a scene in which
she kisses a French officer at a dance. When Julie returns to New Orleans,
ready to reclaim Pres, she learns that he has married. That scene, like the
one in the play, has no real dramatic effect—Amy, Pres's wife, is not even
present. Later, professing that he still loves her, Pres takes Julie in his arms
and kisses her. This scene is witnessed by Buck Cantrell and Amy. When
Pres apologizes to Amy, Julie slaps him again, and Buck challenges Pres to
a duel. Julie is remorseful about her part in this episode and tries to stop
the duel. She confesses her love to Pres, who admits that he still loves her,
too. He tells Julie that Amy knows the truth, "that between you and I there
is something too strong for any of us to forget—something she could never
share—it's there—it always has been, and it always will be." They declare
their enduring love for each other as the film ends.[11]

Buckner's screenplay was deemed unsatisfactory, so the studio hired Clements Ripley to fashion a script. Ripley's treatment, submitted on July 14, was not much better. The Olympus Ball sequence, the finished film's centerpiece, is not included. In a scene similar to Buckner's version, Julie goes out on the town with Buck Cantrell, who gets into a fight and kills someone. When Julie returns home, Pres is waiting for her and insists that they go to the ball. She refuses, they fight, and Julie slaps Pres. He leaves, and Julie goes to Paris and New York. In Ripley's version, when Julie learns of Pres's engagement to Amy, she attempts, unsuccessfully, to seduce Pres, then abruptly announces her engagement to Buck. The film concludes with a duel between Pres and Buck; Pres shoots in the air and is mortally wounded by Buck's return shot. When Amy (who has since married Pres), goes to see her dying husband, she realizes that he still loves Julie. The script ends with Julie going to Pres as Amy leaves, refusing to stay with a man who loves another woman.

Warner then assigned the project to Abem Finkel, who had recently written the Ku Klux Klan exposé *Black Legion* and *Marked Woman* for Bette Davis. He added many of the scenes found in the completed version of *Jezebel*, including Davis's striking entrance in her riding habit. The revised treatment, coauthored by Finkel and Ripley, is dated September 4. A month later, at Wyler's request, Wallis approved the addition of John Huston to the writing team to work on the last half of the script. In a memo to Henry Blanke, the associate producer, dated October 28, 1937, Wallis wrote, Wyler "maintains that Huston knows exactly his feelings and thoughts about the script, and his views on the last half of it. He explains that he himself cannot devote the time to consult with the writers, and that Huston will be a sort of go-between operating between the writers, and you, and himself."[12] Huston was hired after filming had already started, and his contribution consisted of punching up some of the dialogue, especially in the two dinner scenes; strengthening the character of Julie; and improving what Wyler thought were implausible sections at the end of the script.

Much of the supporting cast came from Warner Brothers' able company of actors. George Brent, who was cast as Buck Cantrell, was considered one of the studio's top leading men; he appeared in countless films as either the first or second male lead, including eleven films with Bette Davis. Brent was an undistinguished actor, but actresses adored him. Davis had an affair with him in 1934; that same year, he was requested by both Greta Garbo for *The Painted Veil* and Myrna Loy for *Stamboul Quest*. Davis remarked that Brent had an excitement he rarely transferred to the screen. In *Jezebel*, however, Wyler coaxed him into giving one of his better performances.

Fay Bainter, playing Julie's Aunt Belle, went on to win a Best Supporting Actress Oscar. Davis, who unselfishly appreciated the work of other cast members, commented, "Her performance in *Jezebel* was an enormous contributing factor to the believability of the picture as a whole and to my performance in particular. Julie would never have been as great a success for me without her."[13]

Other actors of note were Donald Crisp as Dr. Livingston, Richard Cromwell as Ted Dillard (Pres's brother), and Spring Byington as Mrs. Kendrick. Anita Louise was the original choice to play Amy, Pres's New York wife, but she was a flamboyant blonde who did not look the part of a proper, demure wife. Margaret Lindsay, who had appeared with Davis in *Dangerous*, was cast instead.

Henry Fonda was a last-minute choice to play Preston Dillard. Wallis had originally toyed with the idea of casting an unknown actor, Jeffrey Lind (later known as Jeffrey Lynn), who was appearing on stage in Chicago.[14] He also considered Franchot Tone. Fonda, who was still a year away from the roles that would make him an A-list star, was known as a paradigm of honesty and sincerity. Davis, who had appeared with him the year before in *That Certain Woman*, directed by Edmund Goulding, liked Fonda and was pleased when he was cast opposite her.

Fonda's contract stipulated that he could leave the production by December 17 to be in New York for the birth of his child. However, Wyler's excessive retakes and Davis's illness, followed by an outbreak of pimples on her face, resulted in delays. Fonda had to leave before the film was wrapped, so Davis filmed her close-ups out of sequence with her director. She recounted, "All those close-ups of me showing my love for Hank were shot after he had finished his scenes and left the lot. It was Willy—off camera—I was looking at!"[15] By that time, Davis did not have to draw on her acting skills: she had fallen in love with her director and was having an affair with him. Shortly after finishing the film, she learned she was pregnant. Years later, Davis admitted, "Looking back, I should have married Willy after my divorce . . . and taken the chance that it would work out. . . .

After four husbands, I know that he was the love of my life. But I was scared silly."[16] Wyler, for his part, was not in love with Davis, and after his tempestuous, short-lived marriage to Margaret Sullavan, he did not relish the idea of marrying another successful actress.

Jezebel is a film about social conventions and values and an individual's ambivalent attitude toward them. It also examines, as do all of Wyler's best social films, the role of individual action amid the pressures of historical forces and cataclysmic public events. Even though playwright Owen Davis was not a southern writer, he was aware of the literary tradition he was working in, and although he could not come to grips with some of the serious issues introduced in his play, he paid lip service to them. A central aspect of this tradition is the legend of the South—the myth of a community and a charmed way of life. The Civil War threatened to destroy this way of life, which only made it more fiercely cherished and more vital to the aesthetic form the legend would eventually assume. This legend of the antebellum South would, of course, become the controlling subject of *Gone with the Wind*. Wyler's *Jezebel* is a more nuanced and complex work than either Davis's play or the legendary film based on Mitchell's novel.

Jezebel's stature as a film is also a testament to Bette Davis, who gave a career-changing performance—one that altered her status at Warner Brothers and made her that studio's undisputed female star for the next decade. Davis's collaboration with Wyler is considered one of the great director-star pairings in Hollywood history. Though brief, it was intense, grueling, and sometimes agonizing. Wyler was known to brood endlessly over scenes and was prone to insomnia, worrying that his mistakes as a director would be preserved on film. He empathized with Davis and understood her mania for perfection and her attention to detail. Davis told a Hollywood reporter, approvingly, that when Wyler "can't get a scene exactly as he wants it, he almost loses his mind."[17] For his part, Wyler did not consider Davis a difficult actress: "I think one of the reasons we got on so well is that both of us wanted the same results, and Miss Davis, she's a hard worker, same as I was, and very demanding, most of all from herself. She was tireless."[18]

When they met, both were already successful. Wyler had gained a reputation as an important director, and one with a special affinity for actors. Since 1936, five actors in his films had received Academy Award nominations, and Walter Brennan had won a Best Supporting Actor Oscar for

Come and Get It. The fact that Warner Brothers requested Wyler for *Jezebel* was a testament to the prestige he had gained in his profession. Davis had already appeared in thirty-five films, receiving top billing in eleven of them, and she had won an Oscar two years earlier.

According to Vincent Sherman, who would direct Davis in *Mr. Skeffington* (1944), "In the pictures she did at Warners prior to *Jezebel*, Bette had tremendous energy and a striking personality, but I don't think she was a terribly good actress. It was Willy Wyler who taught her something about films and film acting that she hadn't realized before: that the most effective moments in a film were the silent moments."[19] Charles Affron notes, "The director [Wyler] seems to have taught the actress that finding her place in the frame is the basis of her screen being."[20]

As noted earlier, the screenwriters had improved on Owen Davis's play and strengthened the character of Julie. Wyler and his leading lady, however, went further; under his direction, she learned the value of small gestures and movement within the frame, which became an integral part of her characterization. Wyler's trademark techniques—deep-focus photography, long takes, and staging within a scene—which he refined over the years, add depth and dimension to *Jezebel*. Although Wyler's work has often been criticized for his detached, classical style, this style often plays against the melodrama of the source material by adding emotional and psychological depth. Wyler's camera collaborates with the actress, a notable example being when Pres breaks off his engagement with Julie. Her face and eyes follow him as he leaves, making camera movement unnecessary. This is what Bazin means when, in dissecting Wyler's "styleless style," he notes the importance of the looks characters give one another: "These always constitute with Wyler the foundation of the *mise-en-scene*. The viewer has only to follow these looks as if they were pointed index fingers in order to understand exactly the director's intentions."[21] As Affron notes in his study of Davis's acting, "The space of *Jezebel* radiates from Davis no matter where she is in the frame."[22]

The film is beautifully structured, as Wyler builds its design around recurring and parallel sequences: the New Orleans street shots that frame the film; two formal dinners; two parties in Julie's honor; her appearance at the Olympus Ball in a red dress, paralleled by her appearance at Halcyon in a white dress; and three sequences at the Long Bar at the St. Louis Hotel. Within the formality of the structure, Wyler creates virtuoso sequences.

Jezebel, like much of Wyler's best early work, is primarily an indoor film. This interior focus is due, in part, to Wyler's preference for transferring stage plays to the screen, but also to his penchant for closed-in, claustrophobic settings. Within these settings, Wyler is able to explore the actors' shifting relationships to one another and to the spatial limitations of the frame, the décor, and the camera. Prior to making *Jezebel*, he had already cut his teeth on three important dramas, dissecting the disintegration of a marriage in *Dodsworth*, the effects of rumor on relationships in *These Three*, and urban decay in *Dead End*. Despite *Dead End*'s outdoor locations, Wyler uses geometrical patterning and a studio-built set to create the feel of confined interior space.

Jezebel opens in 1852 New Orleans, with the camera tracking down a busy city street. While the front of the frame features vendors selling masks and other holiday merchandise, the movement of the camera is matched in the rear of the frame by a horse-drawn carriage rolling down the street and, behind the carriage, a formally dressed gentleman walking in the direction of the camera. Wyler's first cut replicates the movement of the anonymous carriage with a close-up of another carriage—moving in the opposite direction—which lets off Buck Cantrell (George Brent) and Ted Dillard (Richard Cromwell) in front of the St. Louis Hotel. The two men descend a winding staircase to the hotel's Long Bar, which is full of upper-class gentlemen conversing and drinking. The liveliness of the bar scene matches the spirited buying and selling outside. The mood throughout is festive and buoyant.

The field of focus is not as expansive once the action moves indoors. After following Buck and Ted down the stairs, Wyler's camera, instead of taking in the rather spacious bar, shifts to medium-close shots of groups of men huddled together and talking at the bar, as if to contrast the gaiety of the season with a social system in decline. Cantrell, whose character is emblematic of a society that is out of touch with the coming of industrialism and a potential civil war, challenges another patron, De Lautruc, to a duel for mentioning the name of Julie Marsden, who is engaged to Ted's brother Preston. Uttering the name of a lady in a bar is not permissible, according to the prevalent social code. By implication, the scene also introduces us to Julie, the film's protagonist, who has, according to De Lautrec, just jilted Cantrell to become engaged to Pres. The film then shifts to the family mansion, where Julie is once again the subject of conversation because she is late to her own engagement party.

What Wyler and his writers have done here is to create a sense of suspense and anticipation in the mind of the audience, focusing on a heroine who has yet to be seen. The effect is comparable to Ibsen's strategy in introducing Hedda Gabler and Strindberg's in introducing Miss Julie—both of whom Wyler's protagonist resembles in several important respects. Each of these headstrong women lacks what Richard Gilman calls a "principle of coherence" out of which flows self-esteem.[23] Each is psychologically and spiritually divided, thus reflecting the ongoing changes in their respective societies. And each will willingly destroy herself when confronted with the truth of who she is.

Julie's initial appearance is indeed memorable: she makes a noisy arrival on horseback in the cobblestone entryway, sitting sidesaddle, wearing a long riding habit, and carrying a crop in her hand. She barks to her young slave Ti Bat (Stymie Beard), who struggles to control the horse: "Don't stand there with your eyes bulging out like that. He knows you're scared." Like Miss Julie's mongrel dog, which represents her mixed parentage, the horse is emblematic of this Julie's restless, hard-to-control spirit. The riding crop also echoes Strindberg's play, where Miss Julie is first mentioned when the servants gossip about how she forced her fiancé to jump over her riding crop like a trained dog. The film's Julie mistakenly thinks she can control her fiancé as well. Both women must learn that there are limits to their arrogance.

The arrival scene concludes with an inspired piece of business devised by Wyler. He wanted Davis to hike up the train of her dress with the riding crop and hook it over her shoulder as she strides into the house. Wyler asked Davis to practice this gesture until it became second nature to her, and she thought she had perfected it. Wyler, however, disagreed, and after twelve takes, he was still dissatisfied.

"What do you want me to do differently?" she asked him.

"I'll know it when I see it." Wyler replied.

Thirty-three takes later, Wyler finally said, "Okay, that's fine," and called an end to the day's filming.[24]

Furious, Davis demanded to see the takes—only to learn that Wyler was right: what she thought she had done the same way looked different each time. The early takes seemed practiced and artificial. The later ones looked more natural, but because she was feeling irritable and tired, she seemed vibrant and excitable—which was precisely what Wyler wanted and the scene demanded.[25]

After Julie's spectacular entrance, the camera follows her through the crowd of guests, registering her evident intention to shock them by wearing her riding habit to the party. (The scene clearly prefigures the celebrated sequence at the Olympus Ball, when she wears a red dress instead of the socially acceptable white.) Wyler orchestrates this entrance with characteristic exactness, carefully situating Davis within the frame. As Julie enters the house, she faces the camera and strides forward through the doorway and a curtained archway; then she pauses, framed by columns, to hand her riding crop to the slave, Uncle Cato (Lew Payton). She pauses again, seemingly contained under the stairway, as she hands her gloves to Uncle Cato and tells her maid that she has no time to change. Then, her riding habit flowing behind her, she moves forward and pauses again in the entranceway to the ballroom, the camera at her back. This is the fourth interior framing of the sequence, by which Wyler indicates that Julie is trapped even though she seems so free. In addition to slowing down the pace, these pauses create a subtle rhythm that gives Davis a chance to suggest through gesture Julie's more vulnerable side; these moments allow her to gain the momentum she clearly needs before facing her guests.

Entering the ballroom, she remarks, "Terribly sorry to be late. I had trouble with the colt." As she speaks, she moves her body from side to side and opens up her fingers. Barbara Leaming points out, "The opening of her fingers timed to coincide with her second sentence may seem a small piece of business, especially since it all takes place so quickly . . . but it is precisely with such subtle effects that Bette and her director create the vivid portrait of Julie Marsden."[26] Wyler had Davis and the cast repeat this entrance sequence nine times before he felt satisfied that the timing was exactly right.

Julie is a split and vacillating individual. She represents and embraces the "Old South" but is also a rebellious individual who must assert herself against those aspects of her world that are holding her back. The film's production notes describe her as a "product of her environment" and one who "typifies it." In fact, "she IS the deep south, beautiful, exotic, alluring, lavish and also savage and deadly dangerous. She moves by instinct rather than reason. . . . Her chief traits are absolute ruthlessness of purpose, and an intellectual honesty."[27] In the notes to his treatment, Clements Ripley wrote, "The only way to stop Julie would be to kill her."[28] It is an observation that applies to Ibsen's Hedda Gabler and to Strindberg's Miss Julie as well, for all three heroines are honest enough with themselves to finally embrace death rather than live with the consequences of their impetuous decisions.

Throughout much of the film, Wyler's camera allows Julie to seemingly dominate space, while also trapping and confining her within the boundaries it has established. This ironic effect becomes apparent when she insists to her aunt that she can lure Pres away from his meeting within the male stronghold of Dillard and Sons Investments. Aunt Belle (Fay Bainter) warns her not to go to the bank, but Julie ignores her, intent on proving that she can train Pres to do her bidding. Unlike the shot of Julie entering her home late for her own party, where she dominates the expansive scene despite being framed by the entryway, Wyler now captures her, from a distance, through the bars of a bank teller's station. She is not only dwarfed by the composition but visually trapped within it—implying that Julie's first overt effort to trample on societal conventions will fail, as will her subsequent attempts. After this framing, Wyler allows her to stride all the way across the bank lobby before she is stopped at the door of the meeting room. Julie's confidence in her power is seemingly shared by the camera, but the earlier framing undercuts this confidence and even magnifies her failure when Pres tells her he cannot accompany her to the dressmaker. Julie is defeated, but she will not show it.

Wyler then doubles this scene in a comic way in the dressmaker's shop. Seated on a stool, Julie is trapped within a hoopskirt frame while trying on a white crinoline dress, and Wyler focuses on the image of her back in a mirror, creating a frame within a frame. Uncomfortable in the white dress and determined to exasperate Pres, she demands that it be removed so that she can try on a red dress. With her underwear caught in the hoopskirt frame and exposed in the mirror as well, she flaunts herself in the red dress, which her aunt declares to be a "vulgar" outfit suitable for an "infamous Vickers woman," as opposed to the traditional, virginal white gowns worn by unmarried women in polite society. Julie, in a show of defiance, objects: "This is 1852 . . . not the Dark Ages. Girls don't have to simp around in white just because they're not married." She claims to be emancipated, but the framing implies just the opposite.

Wyler repeats some of these patterns when he features Pres. After his meeting at the bank, Pres decides to confront Julie at her home. When he enters the Bogardus mansion, the home of Julie's guardians, he is framed in the doorway, just as Julie was when she arrived late for her party. Like Julie, he hands his riding crop to Uncle Cato. When Julie refuses to come downstairs to greet Pres, he grabs a walking stick, intending to discipline her with it. Upstairs, Wyler's camera follows him as he strides across the hallway, just as it followed Julie across the bank's lobby. Here, Wyler foregrounds the balusters, which Pres clicks with the stick as he moves toward her room. This image presages the futility of his plans—he will be unable to bend Julie to his will, just as she was unable to convince him to leave his meeting.

Julie refuses to open her door, teasing Pres while he repeatedly knocks with his stick. As in the scene at the dressmaker's shop, Julie's amused expression is triple-framed in three mirrors as she is being made up—again indicating that her rebellion will not free her from the constraints of a rigid society. (Her profiled, haughty expression in the middle mirror will be repeated in the Olympus Ball sequence, where she receives her comeuppance.) Here, her victory over Pres—she charms him into kissing her, his stick leaning impotently in the doorway—is only a temporary one. When he leaves, Pres warns her not to wear the red dress to the Olympus Ball.

Julie's visit to Dillard and Sons is preceded by a scene in the bank's boardroom, where Pres is participating in a business conference. Like Julie, he is shown to be out of step with the attitudes of his associates. In the meeting, Pres expresses his belief that the expanding northern railroad lines and freight shipments are bypassing the South, but many of the board members see no reason to invest in the railroads, insisting that sticking with the commerce on the Mississippi River is good enough. Pres's grasp of the changing times neatly mirrors Julie's attitude toward acceptable behavior for women—in both cases, society is dead set against change.

In the same scene, Dr. Livingston, who is also a member of the bank's board, warns about the impending yellow fever epidemic and the need to prepare for it. The board turns a blind eye to this warning as well. Yellow fever, like the idea of war, thus becomes a symbol of the South's self-delusion and its inability to face the future. Unlike *Gone with the Wind, Jezebel* does not sentimentalize the South, for Wyler shows, early on, the willful blindness of its social and business leaders. By the end of the film, New Orleans is a city ravaged by disease—a premonition of the coming war, which will literally and figuratively destroy the region in the decades ahead.

The character who most directly represents the Old South is Buck Cantrell; indeed, in Owen Davis's play, he functions more as a symbol than a character. The film, however, gives Buck some added dimension and stature, showing that he is impulsive, quick to challenge others, and ready to stand up for traditional values. As he remarks at one point, "I like my convictions undiluted, same as I do my bourbon." Nonetheless, he manages to exhibit a dawning awareness of the limitations of his own values and those of his society. Buck is first presented in a more sympathetic light after Julie and Pres quarrel over her dress. She sends Buck a note inviting him to pick her up the following evening, and when he arrives, she views him from above, framed by a window. Buck is seen going to the door from a high angle (one of Wyler's favorite shots), here suggesting another of Julie's misguided notions—that she can control him. Wyler's framing also foreshadows Buck's death, although, in the scene that follows, Buck will have the last word. He admires Julie's red dress, sarcastically asking, "Are you all dressed up for a hog killing?" When he realizes that she wants him to escort her to the ball to arouse Pres's jealousy, he declines, explaining that southern manners will not allow it: "It's just they got rules and they go by 'em, same as you and I." Rebuffed, Julie turns to go inside, and Wyler emphasizes her shadow on the door, presaging not only Buck's death but also Julie's and Pres's, and the demise of the world they represent. Buck's most poignant moment comes when he is manipulated by Julie into defending her honor and his own, for Buck knows he has been betrayed. His final words to Julie before he dies—"I guess there's a lot I don't understand"— assume a much wider context than just his impending doom. Finally recognizing the shortcomings of his culture, Buck's words suggest that his view is more closely aligned with Pres's than it was earlier in the film.

The centerpiece of the film is the Olympus Ball, one of Wyler's most memorable accomplishments. The sequence begins with a view of the dais and the king and queen of the ball. The camera then cranes back to take in the dancers on the floor, the scene dominated by a chandelier. The camera movements and the editing emphasize the formality of the event, an elegant reminder of the rule-bound society Buck chastised Julie about moments earlier. Wyler's camera movements are smooth, expressive, and graceful, providing a prelude to the arrival of Pres and Julie, whose audacious appearance immediately upsets the harmony of the scene. Wyler signals this disruption by utilizing more editing as the couple appears to pass through a gauntlet of disapproving expressions while others either look away or turn to avoid them. Davis acts with her eyes, which dart back and forth and flutter up and down as she is shunned by her social group. No longer indulged as the brilliant sensation she was at her own party, she is now treated as a spectacle, an outcast from the society she has offended. Humiliated and embarrassed, she asks Pres to take her home, but he refuses, insisting that they stay and dance.

Wyler then turns their dance into a study in the use of space. Julie's individualism is tested against the expanse of the ballroom, and her confidence breaks down, all the other dancers having retreated to the edges of the frame. Julie's hauteur is dwarfed by the empty space of the ballroom floor; her red dress—which fills the screen twice, as Wyler cuts to it in close-up—emphasizes the enormity of her arrogance and her lack of judgment. A series of close-ups further reflect Julie's embarrassment and her inner struggle as she pleads with Pres to leave.

As the scene shifts to Julie's home, where Pres is saying good-bye, Wyler partially veils Julie's face in shadow; the lighting that accentuated her earlier close-ups is now dimmed. Julie slaps Pres, who pauses, says good-bye again, and walks to his carriage. Wyler then cuts to Julie, whose face and eyes, again in close-up, follow him as he leaves. We hear the carriage departing but see only Julie, whose eyes become a substitute for the camera. Davis's expression registers the completion of Julie's humiliation. As she turns to go into the house, Wyler's camera looks down on her as it did earlier on Buck. Inside, Julie climbs the stairs with the camera, but her ascent is slowed by her inability to convince herself that Pres will return to her. The first half of the film thus ends with Julie symbolically falling as she rises, and Wyler diminishes her space even as she attempts, through an act of will, to dominate it.

The second part of the film takes place one year later. Pres has broken off his engagement to Julie and is working in the North. The yellow fever epidemic is ravaging the city, and Julie and her family are advised by Dr. Livingston to move to their countryside plantation, Halcyon, to escape the disease. The doctor also commiserates with Aunt Belle over Julie's melancholy and her secluded lifestyle since Pres's departure. Julie's mood is lifted, however, when she is told that Pres is returning to New Orleans on account of the yellow fever outbreak. Certain that they will be reconciled, she plans a homecoming party for him at Halcyon, where she envisions asking his forgiveness.

When Pres appears, he introduces his northern wife, Amy (Margaret Lindsay), to a stunned but gracious Aunt Belle, who excuses herself and anxiously goes to look for Julie. The film's second great set piece opens as Julie appears behind Pres in a stunning white dress. In what is arguably the most superbly acted scene of Davis's career, she seems determined but subdued while apologizing to Pres, who simply exclaims, "You're lovely." Wyler shoots Julie over Pres's shoulder but not from his point of view, as if only the camera can frame and contain the overwhelming effect of her beauty. As Julie kneels in surrender at Pres's feet, the dress puddles around her, both accentuating her beauty and leaving her rooted to the floor, as she was earlier in the dressmaker's fitting room. Her image fills the frame as she begs his forgiveness and asks him to love her as she loves him. At that moment, Amy appears, and Pres walks away to introduce her to Julie as his wife. Wyler's close-ups of Julie as she attempts to regain her composure and absorb the news display a delicacy previously unrealized in Davis's acting.

The film's most important political scene follows, depicting the first formal dinner at Halcyon. The sequence is visually elegant and beautifully realized, reflecting the money and care that went into the production, including the magnificent clothing worn by the guests, the dinnerware on the table, the silver decanters, the crystal goblets, and the candelabras. The publicity for the film proudly proclaimed that the furniture and other properties were all antiques and that the four coal-oil lamps used in one scene were worth $1,000. Bette Davis offered some candlesticks and other heirlooms from her own family to decorate the set.

The scene opens with a high-angle shot, the camera hovering over the table to take in all the guests and the servants. The conversation begins with the claim that "William Lloyd Garrison is a fanatic!" and as this assertion is being discussed, Wyler's camera maintains its distance while showing the slaves who are fanning the diners and serving them. Wyler then cuts among the various guests while keeping his attention on Julie, Buck, and Pres. Julie is openly flirting with Buck, hoping to arouse Pres and incite an argument about politics, but Pres is not cooperating. Buck declares, "Cotton is king. Folks are bound to ship cotton downriver. So how can New Orleans keep from being the greatest city in America?" Pres counters, "In a war of commerce the North must win." He goes on to shock the other guests by predicting, "It'll be a victory of machines over unskilled slave labor." During Pres's remarks, Wyler pointedly includes Uncle Cato in the frame, either showing him pouring drinks or allowing his hand to enter the shot.

Pres resists Buck's attempts to challenge him, concluding their argument by saying, "I think you know I'm no abolitionist. I believe the tide has turned against us. But I'll swim against the tide just as far as you will, Cantrell. . . . Naturally, we claim the right to the customs we were born to, even some of us who question the value of those customs." It doesn't take long for Buck to come around to Pres's point of view. Shortly after being challenged to a duel by Pres's brother Ted (who has been provoked by Julie), Buck echoes the suggestion that the customs that impel him to fight may be outdated. Even Julie, while trying to talk Buck out of the duel, calls his code "stupid"—a thing for "fools." Wyler's principals all understand or come to understand that they are caught in history's vise.

The film winds down quickly after the altercation at dinner. Summoned to the city to help with the yellow fever epidemic, which is now taking a heavy toll, Pres will soon become a victim himself. After Buck's death in the duel, Julie is chastened to learn that Buck knew what she had done and said so before he died. General Bogardus admonishes Julie and refuses to continue as her guardian, while Aunt Belle calls her "a Jezebel." Determined to change, Julie vows to return to Pres's side in the now quarantined city. Accompanied by her servant Gros Bat (Eddie Anderson), she travels in a rowboat through misty swamps, under cover of night, to reach New Orleans.

The film's climax pits Julie against Amy, who has also arrived to attend to her husband. As men come to evacuate Pres to Lazarette Island, where the sick are quarantined, Julie begs Amy for a chance to prove herself worthy of Pres and make herself "clean again" by accompanying him to the island, where they both will surely die. Amy at first refuses, insisting that she must go with her husband, but Julie convincingly pleads her case, declaring that she is stronger and better suited for the arduous task ahead. Humbled, Julie finally comes to terms with her own faults and is made stronger by the chance to redeem herself, to throw off the stigma of being a "Jezebel" and prove her love for Pres.

Wyler films this scene by moving Davis among various planes of action. Julie first confronts Amy at the foot of the stairs, but much of their conversation takes place on the staircase itself, with Amy above Julie as the latter debases herself. Wyler's shots of Davis are anything but starlike; her hair is pinned back, and she is plain looking. The exchange between the two women is conveyed primarily in two shots, but when Amy ultimately yields, Wyler again focuses his camera on Julie, who now appears even plainer yet beatific, even heroic. It is not a glamorous close-up, but the intense expression on her face makes it one of the most moving shots of the film.

The film closes with Julie riding alongside Pres on a wagon that is carting the sick to their certain death on Lazarette Island. In stark contrast to the stylish carriage that opened the film, moving through the vibrant streets of the crowded marketplace, this rough wagon rumbles down a dark street lit with flames, and a final profile shot focuses on Julie, whose look, in Affron's words, "matches the blaze of the bonfire."[29]

8

Home on the Moors and the Range

Wuthering Heights (1939), *The Westerner* (1940),
The Letter (1940)

Wyler's next important film about America was *The Westerner*, which was completed in 1939 but, due to a variety of postproduction problems, not released until September 1940. Before taking on that project, however, he made another film for Goldwyn—*Wuthering Heights*—that turned out to be one of his most honored and well-known works. Indeed, the New York Film Critics named it the best film of 1939 over *Gone with the Wind*, and it received eight Oscar nominations, including one for Wyler's direction. Stylistically and thematically, *Wuthering Heights* is an important film, as it reflects Wyler's deepening exploration of expressionist filmmaking techniques and represents his fullest treatment of the theme of idealized love. The portrayal of the character Catherine Earnshaw is dramatically related to that of *Jezebel*'s Julie Marsden, and it anticipates Wyler's treatment of Catherine Sloper in *The Heiress* (1949).

Goldwyn and Wyler's route to *Wuthering Heights* was a circuitous one. Ben Hecht and Charles MacArthur had decided to adapt Emily Brontë's classic novel on speculation in 1936. In refashioning the novel's complex plot for the screen, they eliminated its second half to focus on the romance between Cathy, the daughter of Mr. Earnshaw, and Heathcliff, an orphan that Earnshaw had brought home from Liverpool. Eliminating many of the secondary characters and telescoping the time frame of the book, the screenwriters concentrated exclusively on the twisted, passionate love of the two principals. The script made the studio rounds before independent producer Walter Wanger bought it for two of his stars, Sylvia Sidney and Charles Boyer. But before making that picture, Wanger wanted the pair to appear in *Algiers*, with Sidney supporting newcomer Hedy Lamarr. Already studying a Yorkshire accent for her role in *Wuthering Heights*, Sidney refused, which made Wanger so angry that he decided not to reward her with the part of Cathy. However, his second choice for the role, Katharine Hepburn, was considered box-office poison at the time, so he lost interest in the project.

Hecht and MacArthur then offered the script to Goldwyn, but the producer had his doubts. The flashback structure of the screenplay confused him, and he thought the lovers were too unattractive—the heroine irresponsible, the hero too filled with hate—to appeal to audiences. Goldwyn sent the script to Wyler for his opinion. Wyler loved it and recommended that Goldwyn buy it, but to ensure that he did so, Wyler showed the script to Bette Davis, who had just won the Oscar for *Jezebel* and was anxious to work with Wyler again. Davis then showed the script to Jack Warner and asked him to buy it for her. When Goldwyn heard about this possibility, he immediately purchased the script. However, knowing that Warner would not loan him his biggest star, he asked Wyler if he thought Merle Oberon could play the part. Wyler said she could, and the deal was set.

Wuthering Heights has been examined by critics primarily as an example of a film adaptation of a classic novel,[1] but it can be regarded, alternatively, as another of the director's meditations on how the forces of society conspire to destroy the individual. One can fight back, as do Karen, Martha, and Joe in *These Three*; Sam Dodsworth; Drina and, ultimately, Dave in *Dead End*; and Julie Marsden. Or one can give in, as do Mrs. Tilford, Fran Dodsworth, and Buck Cantrell. This film's Catherine Earnshaw, unlike her fictional counterpart (who marries Linton in order to help Heathcliff), suppresses her individualistic emotional attachment to the orphan and yields to the more comfortable and orderly ways of genteel society. Belatedly, she realizes her mistake, but she is ruined anyway. In fact, she wills her own destruction. What excited Wyler about the script for *Wuthering Heights* was the opportunity to explore his themes of idealized love and the individual's struggle with society in a bold new way. This was why he urged Goldwyn to buy it. When Michael Anderegg writes that the film is more an expression "of Goldwyn's showmanship" than of "the director's developing dramatic and stylistic interests,"[2] he fails to recognize the political and social dimensions of Wyler's artistic vision.

Stylistically, *Wuthering Heights* is quite different from Wyler's other films made inside or outside the Goldwyn studios during the 1930s. Less emphasis is placed on realism, more on the symbolic and pictorial qualities of the image. *Wuthering Heights* actually works best as an imaginative rendition of an ideal, for within its insular perspective, the outside world—the larger society that Catherine is drawn to and then abruptly rejects—finally ceases to exist. A handful of supporting players have tangential roles, but all the film's energy is concentrated in its obsessive focus on the two lovers' tempestuous and destructive passions.

This is also Wyler's most self-conscious film, making the viewer very much aware of the camera and the artifice of the cinema. Wyler always worked closely with cinematographer Gregg Toland in planning the visual design of a project. Of this film, Douglas Slocombe writes, "Toland recognized the essential romanticism of the Brontë novel and decided to go all out for romantic pictorial effect, with heavy diffusion, soft candle-light, long warm shadows and chilly swirling mists."[3] Anticipating *Citizen Kane* in the use of low ceilings to create confined spatial effects, Toland and Wyler also use candlelight to create atmospheric, expressionist compositions, and Wyler has his camera move and probe more than ever before. In a sense, the camera announces itself so often that it becomes another presence in the film.

Richard Griffith, in his monograph on Goldwyn, offers the most insightful comment on the symbolic artistry of *Wuthering Heights*:

> The setting of the film was not the moors of Yorkshire but a wilderness of the imagination. To have reproduced on the screen any large expanse of landscape would have been to chain the story and its characters to the actual. Instead, Toland and Wyler devised a close-in camerawork which, in every shot, seemed to show only a small part of the whole scene, in which roads, crags, housetops, and human figures were revealed in outlines against dense grays and blacks. Thus was created a chiaroscuro country of the mind in which the passionate Brontë figures can come credibly alive.[4]

The film opens in a snowstorm that looks fake, as Wyler takes no pains to hide the artifice. The man traipsing through the storm (Lockwood, played by Miles Mander) moves like a stage actor, and the camera adopts his point of view as he happens upon a house that is backlit to make it ap-

pear haunted. (Both Anderegg and Harrington point out that the opening
has the feel of a horror film.[5]) This contrived effect is reinforced by a written prologue that describes the house as "bleak and desolate" and warns
that only a lost stranger would "have dared to knock on the door." When
Lockwood enters this forbidding place, he is attacked by dogs, but they
are soon called off, leaving him to take in the house, which is in disrepair.
From Lockwood's point of view, the camera then locates a series of strange
faces—the two servants, Joseph and Ellen Dean (Leo G. Carroll and Flora
Robson), to the right; Heathcliff (Laurence Olivier), standing by the fire
in the center; and his wife, whose face peers from around a chair to his
left. Heathcliff's face is in shadow, while Lockwood's is brightly lit. Since
the camera has adopted Lockwood's point of view—and thus conditioned
ours—we fear for him. This dramatically gothic opening sequence sets the
tone for what follows.

Lockwood is granted permission to spend the night at the house, and
Joseph shows him to a bedroom, the bridal chamber, which has not been
used in years. Again, the room appears stark, filthy, and depressing, as both
the low ceiling and the light from Joseph's candle increase its haunted effect. Once Lockwood falls asleep, Wyler cuts to a banging shutter, and the
camera seems to shift its point of view to Cathy's spirit as her theme music
is heard and the camera dollies from the window around to Lockwood lying on the bed, framed by the bedpost. It settles on him until he awakes and
goes toward the window, where he stares out. Wyler cuts to a close-up of
his face in the windowpane as he hears Cathy's voice calling out, "Let me
in! Let me in! I'm lost on the moor." Wyler makes sure that the audience
shares Lockwood's experience: we hear what he hears, and his vision is not
presented as a hallucination. Heathcliff accepts Lockwood's story as well,
rushing out into the storm to find Cathy.

Lockwood is understandably curious about this midnight intrigue, so
Ellen Dean, with her face backlit by the firelight, begins to tell the story in
flashback. The camera pulls away from her as the story moves into the past.
With this narrative turn comes a change in lighting: the dark, forbidding
house is now bathed in light both inside and out. In many of the following flashback sequences, Wyler communicates effectively with the camera,
while the dialogue, which is often clunky and stilted, feels obtrusive.

The most noteworthy childhood images of Cathy and Heathcliff are the outdoor scenes when they escape to Pennistone Crag, which they imagine is a castle where they are king and queen. In contrast to the almost exclusively indoor settings of Wyler's other Goldwyn films, these scenes have a vitality and freedom that is exhilarating, such as when the two children are shown racing their horses through the moors toward their "castle" in long shots. The camera participates in these moments by emphasizing the liberating spaciousness of nature and its opposition to the constraints of the social world, later exemplified by Heathcliff's demotion to the status of a stable boy and by the genteel lifestyle of the Earnshaws' neighbors the Lintons.

In this regard, Wyler uses two scenes at Pennistone Crag as contrasts to incidents that follow. In the first scene, Heathcliff and Cathy are shown as children, anointing the spot as the site of their kingdom, divorced from the rest of the world. This idyllic moment is followed by the death of Mr. Earnshaw, one of Wyler's most striking compositions. Again, a single flaming candle dominates the center as the children, with their backs to the camera, are framed by the entrance to another part of the room; the low ceiling and the door frame seem to squeeze them into a tight space—a direct contrast to the expansive landscape of the previous scene. The lighting is mostly dark as they face the staircase where Dr. Kenneth (Donald Crisp) descends to inform them of their father's death.

The next pairing shows them as older: Heathcliff, who is now a stable boy, sees Cathy running toward the crag through a window, which will serve as a connecting leitmotif for the sequence. He joins her at their "castle," but when they hear the sounds of the Lintons' party, Cathy insists that they go and look in on it because she wants "dancing and singing in a pretty world." This marks the end of their idyll, announced visually by the first window view, indicating that Cathy will be torn between her desire for society and the need to stay true to her essential self. In the evening darkness, they jump over a wall and make their way to the Lintons' house to peer inside at a brightly lit room—a vision framed by the window. Cathy and Heathcliff, in contrast, are lit by low-key lights, suggesting their gloomier life at Wuthering Heights. The Lintons' guests are elegantly dressed and dancing, while the plainly dressed couple stands in shadow outside. As they stare at the bright spectacle, the camera pans with their gaze, showing that Cathy, at least, is dazzled by what she sees. When the dogs alert the guests to the intruders and then attack them, Wyler contrasts the formal attire of the Lintons and their guests, which seems oddly extravagant outdoors, with the more natural appearance of Cathy and Heathcliff. Once they enter the house, however, to attend to Cathy's wounded ankle, it is the young couple who appears out of place in the glare of the lighted room.

When Cathy returns to Wuthering Heights after an extended recuperation at the Linton home, she quarrels with Edgar Linton (David Niven), who is now in love with her, over his unkind and demeaning remarks about Heathcliff. She runs upstairs, sees herself in the mirror dressed up like a Linton, and proceeds to rip off her dress. This willful reaction against the elegant costume in her framed reflection offers a variation on the scene in *Jezebel* when Julie, mirrored from behind, is trying on ball dresses at the dressmaker's and rejects the traditional white gown in favor of the red one that will destroy her relationship with Pres. Here, realizing that an engagement to Edgar will ruin her, Cathy sheds her finery and runs to meet Heathcliff at their "castle." This vacillation between orderly respectability and her untamed love for Heathcliff will continue for the rest of the film.

These contrary impulses explode in the scene where Cathy tells Ellen that Edgar has proposed to her. When she talks about Edgar's virtues, she is seated, but when Ellen asks her about Heathcliff, she becomes agitated and moves about, commanding the camera's attention. After she accuses Heathcliff of having "sunk so low," Wyler cuts to the kitchen, where Heathcliff had been hiding, and a flash of lightning illuminates the spot where he once stood, making it his surrogate. Then, as Cathy realizes that she "is" Heathcliff, the storm erupts again, and the lightning illuminates her. This melodramatic mise-en-scène is excessive but in keeping with the rest of the film.

Cathy finally does marry Edgar, and as their home life is introduced by Ellen's narration, Wyler repeats his camera movements and framing from the earlier scene when Cathy and Heathcliff peered into the Lintons' home for the first time. Again, it is dark, and Wyler's camera moves through a lighted window, which at first frames Cathy doing needlepoint. (Her activity anticipates that of another Cathy—Catherine Sloper—whose needlepoint is also a substitute for sublimated passions.) She is sewing an angel, a representative of the heavenly world in which she does not belong (as she told Ellen earlier). Heathcliff enters in a long shot, striding across the length of the room. Now returned from America, he is a gentleman and has bought Wuthering Heights. The scene concludes as it began, with Wyler's camera reversing direction to exit through the window as a storm rages in the dark.

The final moments of the film, as Heathcliff takes the dying Cathy in his arms so that she can see the moors from the windowed doorway to the balcony, summarize—as Harrington points out—all the windowed images in the film:[6] the banging window shutter in the opening sequence, Lockwood reaching his hand through the window and feeling Cathy's spirit, Heathcliff shoving his hands through a window after Cathy goes off with Edgar, the two camera movements through the window into the Linton house, and Cathy crying "I *am* Heathcliff," with the windows behind her. All these carefully composed scenes are contrived to represent the emotional turmoil raging within the characters, as well as demarcating the boundaries between nature and society, between the world of experience and that of the imagination.

These same conflicts were explored by Wyler in different ways in earlier films. *Counsellor-at-Law*'s George Simon is torn between his immigrant past (his true self) and the "real American" he wants to become. *These Three*'s Karen and Martha expect to live peacefully and happily in the insular world of their own creation until an evil harbored within their walls destroys it. Dodsworth is torn between his love for his wife, which is destroying who he is, and his growing need to declare his independence and restore his sense of self. Julie Marsden chafes at being bound by social rules but realizes too late that she has lost her chance at happiness by prioritizing her independent spirit. Barney Glasgow, like Catherine, ruins his life by choosing society and success over love.

Wuthering Heights is Wyler's most self-consciously experimental film. Its weaknesses derive from Merle Oberon's failure to bring alive the earthier aspects of Cathy—much of her performance seems forced—and from Olivier's struggle with dialogue that is overly literary and announces its theme too often. Olivier credited Wyler with teaching him how to act for the camera, but much of his performance remains theatrical and contrived—as if he were trying to compensate for Oberon's lack of vitality in the emotional scenes. Wyler, however, manages to offset these shortcomings with his camera work, realizing the spirit of the novel with his technical and visual virtuosity. In *Wuthering Heights*, he consolidates and articulates his themes in dramatic cinematic terms, heralding his status as an auteur.

There is a postscript to this story. The film, as conceived, ends with Heathcliff's death. After hearing Lockwood's tale of hearing and seeing a woman at the window of the bridal chamber, Heathcliff rushes into the storm to Pennistone Crag, where he freezes to death. The published screenplay ends with the following description: "It [the camera] dissolves to HEATHCLIFF lying at the CRAG, his flesh frosted in death, and this sight dissolves to a series of views of the moors as CATHY and HEATHCLIFF beheld them in the springs, summers and winters of their youth, ending with TWO BIRDS hovering over the 'CASTLE,' then flying away into the winter sky."[7]

Wyler is not wholly sympathetic to any of his characters who try to turn back the clock or make time stand still—both Fran Dodsworth and Barney Glasgow are ultimately defeated. Catherine Earnshaw also makes a tragic mistake, which she recognizes and pays for, while Heathcliff is so obsessed by his need for revenge that he destroys others. This couple's wild and destructive passions exploded Hollywood's standard template for romantic movies (as did *Dodsworth* by focusing on a middle-aged couple). *Variety* put it best: "*Wuthering Heights* in theme, characters, plot and setting possesses not one familiar attribute for which studio scenario departments search zealously through thousands of manuscripts, plays, novels, and synopses. It violates all the accepted rules of successful film stories. Its leading characters are something less than sympathetic—they are psychopathic exhibits."[8]

This rebellious quality was precisely what initially attracted Wyler, who gravitated toward stories and characters that veered from the norm. The film's original ending was consistent with Wyler's view of characters who are either unable or unwilling to mature or who make wrong choices. (Judge Roy Bean in *The Westerner* meets a similar fate.) Goldwyn, however—motivated in part by a disastrous preview held two weeks after the last retakes were completed—insisted on a "happier" ending. The audience response cards from that showing were among the worst Goldwyn had ever read.[9] The audience found the film hard to follow and the final image off-putting. Goldwyn asked Flora Robson, who was still in Hollywood, to read several speeches designed to tie episodes of the film together. He also wanted Wyler to create the illusion of a happy ending by showing the star-crossed couple's spirits walking off into the mist and snow together. Wyler recalled, "He didn't want to look at a corpse at the fadeout. So he asked me to make a shot of them walking hand in hand through the clouds to show that they were together in heaven. I told him there was no way I would shoot it."[10] Despite Wyler's refusal to violate the spirit of his film, Goldwyn was undeterred. He asked Henry Potter to film the closing image of Olivier's and Oberon's doubles from the back. Wyler always maintained that the resulting image was horrible, but the audience loved it. With Goldwyn's corrections, the second preview was a great success.

Wyler's first western since *Hell's Heroes* in 1930, *The Westerner* is, naturally, an outdoor film. By 1939, when it was made, the genre was reemerging in John Ford's *Stagecoach* and Cecil B. DeMille's *Union Pacific*. *The Westerner* was released in 1940, a year that also featured Fritz Lang's *The Return of Jesse James*, Michael Curtiz's *Virginia City*, and Henry King's *Jesse James*. The return of the western was a sign that the Depression was waning, for the genre reflected a sense of optimism that celebrated America's founding myth. The Roosevelt administration fostered this buoyancy through the National Recovery Administration's and Works Progress Administration's support for artists, the writing of state guidebooks, and other initiatives of the Federal Writers' Project. Unlike the gangster film, which had ushered in the decade, the western suggested that America's story was moving forward.

   The Westerner exhibits many western themes and motifs that had been introduced in literature and echoed in earlier films but would become mainstreamed as these films matured and deepened in the 1940s and 1950s. Wyler's film is notable, however, for its reshuffling of these standard themes, presenting them in unusual ways. In their survey of the western genre, George Fenin and William Everson describe *The Westerner* as "one of the most outstanding films of the period" but also as "strange, moody, and unevenly paced."[11] All these judgments are true. Wyler and his writers—Jo Swerling, Niven Busch, and Stuart N. Lake—take on a variety of themes: the solitary hero/drifter and his relationship to the land, wilderness versus civilization, homesteaders versus cattlemen, and the impact of the law (represented by the historical figure of Judge Roy Bean) on an emerging town. Wyler also tosses in another historical character, Lillie Langtry, as an idealized woman with whom Bean is infatuated—thus introducing an aspect of his character that complicates our reaction to him. Also, the relationship between the hero, Cole Hardin (Gary Cooper), and Bean (Walter Brennan) clearly interests Wyler more than Hardin's evolving romance with Jane-Ellen Mathews (Doris Davenport), the outspoken daughter of a homesteader who opposes Bean and his idea of frontier justice.

Goldwyn intended *The Westerner* to be a quickie project, rushing it into production partly to take advantage of the popularity of *Stagecoach* and partly because, owing to his ongoing distribution battle with United Artists, he needed a success. As studio head, he hoped the combination of his star director and his star contract player, Gary Cooper, would turn the property into a moneymaker.

Goldwyn bought a story and treatment (dated May 12, 1939) from Stuart N. Lake, which was tentatively titled *Vinegarroon*, after the town where Bean had settled and set up his court. Niven Busch said of the treatment, "There was really only a slim tracing of story and no character for Cooper at all."[12] In actuality, Lake's story was well fleshed out and detailed—although much of it was eventually jettisoned—and it featured a substantial role for Cooper. However, Goldwyn faced some legal haggling over the rights to the story of Roy Bean. Darryl F. Zanuck wrote to him in July and claimed that he owned the rights to a book, *The Law West of the Pecos* by Everett Lloyd, and had been "dickering with MGM who wanted to buy it for Wallace Beery. . . . I have an entire script on the subject and I have a considerable amount invested in it." Zanuck informed Goldwyn that Lake knew of the story and had asked several times to work on it, and then he made an offer: "If you are actually going ahead with the picture, I will be perfectly willing to sell you the rights that we own for exactly what they stand us."[13]

Goldwyn immediately contacted Lake, complaining that he should not have accepted his money if he knew that Zanuck was working on the same story. Lake sent Goldwyn a detailed reply, pointing out that the first copyright recorded on the Roy Bean saga was a story he had published in the *Saturday Evening Post* on February 7, 1931. Lake further stated that Zanuck had contacted him about using this story as a vehicle for Will Rogers in March 1931, but Rogers had expressed no interest. In addition, Lake noted that Zanuck had filed his intent to make *The Law West of the Pecos* with the Hays office in 1933 and that Lloyd's book had been published and copyrighted in May 1931, three months after his own story had appeared in the *Post*.[14]

The issue must have been resolved in Goldwyn's favor, because in August he told Zanuck that he could not loan him Walter Brennan for *The Grapes of Wrath* because the actor was working on "the Judge Roy Bean story."[15] Meanwhile, Goldwyn also learned that his favorite screenwriter, Lillian Hellman, was "very disappointed in *Vinegarroon*" and "not interested in the Judge Bean character."[16] Oliver La Farge was also consulted, but he thought the story made Bean too comic and trivial a figure. La Farge believed that Bean was a man with a vision who knew that outlaws needed to be expelled from the Pecos territory and law established before the coming of the railroad. He wrote, "Some distinction clings to him for all his roughness."[17]

Lake's original story provides an elaborate backstory for protagonist Steve Randall, who becomes Cole Hardin in the film. Randall is a glamorous figure who lives on Fifth Avenue in New York City in the 1880s and is the son of a senator who played a pivotal role in ousting Boss Tweed. Steve himself is more of a sportsman and a ladies' man. When we meet him, he is courting Lydia Lyndow, the "Damask Rose," a ballerina from Europe who is one of the most famous beauties in the history of the theater and is currently on a tour of America. Steve meets Lydia when her carriage is hijacked as she rides through Central Park; he slows down the horses and takes control of the carriage. (This incident is used in later drafts of the script to introduce Lillie Langtry.)

This eastern story alternates with what is happening out west, until the two narrative strands finally merge. Lake writes that the territory west of the Pecos River harbors many criminals, including some from the East who have taken refuge there to avoid extradition. One of these men is Dapper Dan McClosky, a fugitive from Boss Tweed who was sent there by Randall's father. Now head of a western gang, he prospers by turning stolen goods into cash. Roy Bean is the law in Vinegarroon, as well as a saloon owner who is anxious to take advantage of whatever new business will be generated once the railroad comes through. He, too, is in love with Lydia Lyndow, even though she is "as unattainable as the stars." Also introduced is Blanche Colton, an "authentic young woman of the frontier" who runs the local eating-house with her mother.

As the story progresses, Steve is framed for murder by Dan McClosky's brother. Not wanting to disgrace his father, he escapes from New York and heads to the territory west of the Pecos. There, he is accused of stealing a horse and is brought before Judge Bean, whose courtroom/bar is decorated with pictures of Lydia Lyndow. Having read about Steve and Lydia in the paper, however, Bean suspends his sentence. Steve begins to work for Bean, bringing criminals to justice. Meanwhile, back in New York, a friend of Steve's has informed Lydia that Steve is innocent of the murder charge that caused him to flee.

When the railroad comes to Vinegarroon, Bean leaves Steve in charge when he goes to attend a performance that Lydia is giving on her tour of the West. This substitution lays the groundwork for the evolving love story between Steve and Blanche Colton, who will tend to him when he is wounded in an attack by the McClosky gang. When Bean returns, he renames the town Lydia and his bar the Damask Rose.

Lydia decides to visit the town that is now named for her and offers to give a performance there. She tries to resurrect her relationship with Steve, asking him to return to New York with her and promising to marry him when her tour is over. Steve refuses, telling her that he has obligations to Bean and the town.

McClosky uses Lydia's concert as a cover to attack the town again. Blanche protects Lydia during the battle, during which Bean is shot. After McClosky surrenders, Bean orders Steve to hang the man and then dies while he stares at Lydia for the last time. At Bean's funeral, Steve informs Lydia that he belongs in the West, remarking, "This country burns its own brand," and stating, "I never thought I could come to love such an unlovely land." Recognizing that Steve has transferred his affections to Blanche as well, Lydia bids them farewell, and the last scene is of Steve and Blanche holding hands as they walk up the road.

Lake's revised treatment makes some important changes. Steve is still forced to leave New York because of a trumped-up murder charge, but not before expressing an interest in going out west, where his father owns a ranch. He tells his father that he is sick of New York and wants to "help make a new country, rather than try to make over an old one."[18] Bart McClosky is still the villain, but in this second version, he sells Steve a stolen horse, hoping that Bean will hang him. One of McClosky's hired guns, whom Steve eventually kills, is named Cole Hardin—which would become the name of the hero in the finished film. Here, it is Hardin's shooting that gets Steve arrested in neighboring Jacktown, where McClosky runs things, and with the help of some deputies, he escapes a plot to kill him. In this version, Bean is the protector of Blanche and her mother, whose ranch was destroyed when rustlers killed Blanche's father. At the end of this treatment, Bean makes Steve his successor. Texas Rangers, who have been sent to make Bean a real judge, appoint Steve instead, who stipulates that he wants McClosky and his associates sent back to New York. The treatment concludes with Steve proposing to Blanche.

In August, Dudley Nichols and Jo Swerling were brought in to reshape the story. By this time, their script was titled "Cooper Story." Their revisions bring the story closer to that of the finished film. It opens in Bean's court, where a horse thief is being sentenced to hang. He turns out be Gary Cooper, whose character's name is not mentioned until the end of the script. Cooper hands Bean his watch, which contains a picture of Lillie Langtry (formerly Lydia Lyndow), and this stops Bean in his tracks. Cole Hardin then enters the bar. He works for McClosky—the rivalry between McClosky and Bean is still retained at this point but would eventually be dropped. According to Swerling and Nichols, McClosky represents "legal law," which he has corrupted, while Bean represents "gun law," devised out of necessity. The Cooper character recognizes Hardin as the man who sold him the stolen horse and demands his $100 back, but Hardin answers with an insult, whereupon Cooper punches him in the jaw, knocks him out, and takes back his money. When Hardin recovers, he pulls his gun on the unarmed Cooper, but Ella (who will become Jane-Ellen) shoots it away. Cooper tells Ella that he wants to go farther west, where there are no women, and buy a ranch there. Bean suggests that he go with Ella instead; she has a ranch but no stock since her father was killed by rustlers, most likely headed by McClosky. There follows a series of exciting cinematic action scenes, including one in which Cooper happens on Hardin and others herding stolen cattle. Flicking away a match, Cooper starts a fire that causes a stampede. Cooper then rounds up the cattle and drives them to Vinegarroon. After McClosky arrests Cooper in Jacktown, Bean organizes a posse to rescue him; a battle ensues, and Bean is wounded and captured. Meanwhile, Cooper has captured McClosky, and a prisoner exchange is arranged, over Bean's objections.

Lillie Langtry gives a performance in Vinegarroon. She meets Cooper backstage, and we learn that they knew each other in the East—Lake's backstory, however, has been eliminated. Lillie asks Cooper to join her for the rest of her tour and then return east with her. During the concert, Mc-Closky's men attack, and Bean is wounded again. Belatedly learning that he has been appointed a district judge, he makes it his first and last order of business to reverse his ruling on Bingham Smith (Cooper's name); then he dies, surrounded by Cooper, Lillie, and Ella. Lillie, who has intuited that "Bingo" is in love with Ella, leaves to resume her tour.

Niven Busch replaced Dudley Nichols and, in a revision titled "Saddle Tramp," produced a story that most closely resembles the finished film. Cooper's character is now named Cole Hardin, and the entire eastern backstory, along with his relationship with Lillie Langtry, has been dropped. Bean's relationship with Cole is brought to the fore, leaving the evolving love story between Cole and Jane-Ellen in the background. The writers included a humorous note in this script: as Bean is presiding over a greased pig contest (cut from the film), the directions read, "It is obviously impossible to describe in detail the progress of the contest, since not even Mr. Wyler can tell a greased pig what to do."[19] Busch also adds the final shoot-out at the Davis Opera House, where Bean buys all the tickets to Lillie's show and must confront Cole, who has been deputized to arrest him.

The changes in the final script were no doubt motivated by a memo from Edwin Knopf, a story editor for Goldwyn. He criticized Swerling, who, he advised, should be taken off the project for splitting the action between Jacktown and Vinegarroon. Knopf thought the film should take place entirely in Vinegarroon and its environs, stating, "It would tighten up the arena in which the play is performed and give you a concentration of action . . . [but] most importantly, it would emphasize the battle of Cooper versus Bean which to me is the essence of the drama."[20] Knopf's suggestions were echoed by Jock Lawrence, Goldwyn's head of publicity, who emphasized that the second most important element was the love story involving Cole Hardin and the girl; the major story line, however, was the relationship between Cole and Roy Bean.[21]

Realizing that the starring role belonged to Bean (Walter Brennan), Cooper wired Goldwyn that he did not approve of the material. "It looked like his [Brennan's] picture," Cooper wrote. "A cowboy ultimately rode in and exchanged a few shots to the detriment of the judge, but that struck me as being incidental. I couldn't see that it needed Gary Cooper in the part."[22] Goldwyn, complaining that that "Goddamned Cooper is trying to kill me," fired back a telegram: "While I appreciate the sincerity of your solicitude about the story I am sure that you must realize that the responsibility for the selection of stories is always mine and I have never had any desire to shift this responsibility to you or anyone else."[23]

Over the next couple of weeks, Goldwyn assured Cooper that his part was being revised and expanded and that if he did not report to work, he would be sued for all expenses incurred on the film to date, amounting to $400,000. Cooper reported for work, but not before sending Goldwyn a strongly worded letter: "After careful and reasonable consideration I regret to advise you that the character Cole Hardin is still inadequate and unsatisfactory for me, in my opinion as is the story." He went on to say that the script's weaknesses violated the spirit of their working agreement: "Like you, I have a position to uphold. My professional standing has been jeopardized from the beginning." He concluded by writing, "The force and your strategy in throwing the blame on me is unprecedented. . . . I bow to your threats since normal reasoning and friendly relations mean little, if anything to you."[24] Goldwyn tried to placate his star, writing that he did not think "there is any justification for such feelings on your part." He insisted that he had done everything he could to make Cooper happy and assured him that they could work together again, even mentioning three projects he was developing for Cooper: "Seventh Cavalry," "Hans Christian Andersen," and "Arrowsmith."[25]

The film was budgeted for $1 million and filmed on location outside Tucson, where Goldwyn got the governor of Arizona to proclaim the location site Goldwyn City, Arizona—a publicity stunt that made headlines in the *Hollywood Reporter*.[26] Goldwyn even built a replica of the Fort Grand Opera House, where Lillie Langtry once made an appearance. For the range war between the cattlemen and the homesteaders, local cowboys rounded up 7,000 head of cattle, the largest herd ever put onscreen up to that time.

Wyler wanted to cast his new bride—Margaret "Talli" Tallichet, whom he married in 1938—as Jane-Ellen Mathews, but Goldwyn would not hear of it. He wanted to use an unknown actress, Doris Davenport, whom Goldwyn thought was marvelous in a recent screen test Wyler had done. Though Wyler considered her sweet but untalented, he yielded to Goldwyn's demands. Davenport made no impression in the role, and she never appeared in another film.

The shoot was not easy. Wyler's assistant, Freda Rosenblatt, recalled, "We'd get up at six in the morning and drive eight miles out of town to the set. There would be snow and ice on the ground. By ten the sun would come out and we'd bake. We'd shoot till sundown. . . . Lots of times Willy would want a rewrite for the next day. The crew, including Willy didn't get much sleep."[27]

Wyler finished filming *The Westerner* in November but did not complete postproduction work until January. One difficulty was Goldwyn's desire to print the film in a sepia tint, to which Wyler vigorously objected. He felt that sepia "tends to destroy realism which we are striving for in this picture." He went on to point out that sepia gets tiresome after three or four reels and that it had ruined *Of Mice and Men*.[28] Wyler was still arguing against the use of this technique as late as August, when he conceded that sepia might make the outdoor scenes more attractive but would ruin the realistic effect in the interior scenes.

Sepia printing was still an issue as late as August in part because Goldwyn had delayed the picture by asking Alfred Newman to redo Dmitri Tiomkin's score. The question of the music had been raised April, when Tiomkin urged Goldwyn not to be swayed by "some jealous hirelings about the merit of my score."[29] But Goldwyn was clearly dissatisfied, and he insisted that the picture be rescored. *The Westerner* was finally released in September 1940, just two months before *The Letter*, which Wyler had begun filming for Warner Brothers in May.

The Westerner is an unusual, uneven, eccentric film. It has some of the elements that have come to be associated with classic westerns—particularly the subject of territorial expansion and the struggles between settler-landowners, who wanted to fence off their claims, and cattlemen, who wanted to keep the ranges open. In some important respects, it follows the pattern of what Richard Slotkin calls the "historical romance." These films, Slotkin notes, are "relentlessly progressive: in their reading of history, celebrating all persons, tendencies, and crises that yield . . . more civilized forms of society."[30] Yet the film's center is what might be called the love story between Judge Roy Bean, a crude, hard-drinking tyrant who represents "the law west of the Pecos" in the wide-open, anarchic 1880s, and Cole Hardin, a laconic drifter who gets dragged into Bean's court on the charge of stealing a horse. Their relationship seems like the prototype for that between Judah Ben-Hur and Messala, which Wyler would direct twenty years later. The bond between the two is also the basis for a great deal of humor—despite the film's lofty thematic aims, the characters talk more than they act, and *The Westerner* is among the funniest westerns of the period. Indeed, Wyler was attracted primarily by the comic elements: "There was subtle comedy in there. It gave me the opportunity to do some improvising in the scenes between Cooper and Brennan,"[31] which are the high points of the film.

The film opens, as do other historical films of the period, with a rolling title. The time frame is after the Civil War, the setting of many classic westerns. The title sequence also heralds a time of renewal: "After the Civil War, America in the throes of rebirth set its face West where the land was free." The title then sets the stage for the conflict between the cattlemen and Judge Roy Bean, "who took the law into his own hands" but "left his impress on the history of Texas"—a "tribute to his greatness." In the conflict between the small farmer and the more powerful cattleman who is represented by Judge Bean, there may be an allusion to the Depression era's Dust Bowl conflict between small farmers and banks.

The discrepancy between Bean's historical status and his portrayal in the film is one of the principal problems. Goldwyn, who wanted the film to be endorsed by some of Texas's prominent politicians, was sensitive to the need to depict the local hero in a favorable light. The opening title was no doubt added later, along with the map of Texas at the end, to gain their approval. These additions obviously satisfied the Texans, who allowed Goldwyn to premiere the film in Fort Worth and hold a parade down its main street.

The presentation of Bean was also a bone of contention among the film's contributors and studio executives. Oliver La Farge, the Pulitzer Prize–winning author and western historian who was hired to advise on the script, felt that it would be a mistake to turn Bean into a comic figure and poke fun at his court. In fact, he wrote in his notes on the script, "As the original script correctly states, he never forgot his family's long tradition of service in the cause of justice. His court is irregular, rough, frontier, informal, but it must not be comic, and above all it must not give the impression that justice frequently miscarried in it."[32] But one of the first scenes in the film shows Bean condemning a homesteader to hang for mistakenly shooting a steer, and as depicted by Wyler, Bean's court is a place where justice is regularly "miscarried."

In his notes on the Swerling-Busch script, Jock Lawrence echoes La Farge. He comments that Bean came as a pioneer to a lawless country: "No law officer or judge has dared come into this territory. Bean believes Texas' future lies in cattle. He has *had* to take law into his own hands to put some order into this lawless country."[33] Lawrence believed that Hardin had to be torn between the validity of Bean's argument and that of the settlers, but the film never portrays this conflict as effectively as it should. Wyler's Bean is too comic and too indifferent to human life for an audience to sympathize with his pioneer values.[34] Later in the film, Cole makes the case for Bean's values even better than Bean does. Bean's point of view is that he and his kind are responsible for transforming the wilderness into an economically viable open range. He argues for rugged individualism and the right to profit. Unfortunately, he cannot see beyond his own historical moment.[35]

This societal conflict is largely relegated to the background during the first half of the film; it comes to the fore in the second part only when the comedy disappears and the struggle between the cattlemen and the homesteaders turns violent. The film's main focus is three interlocking "love stories": the evolving bond between Hardin and Bean; Hardin's love for Jane-Ellen Mathews, which draws him into the conflict between Bean's cattlemen and the homesteaders; and Bean's love for Lillie Langtry, a woman he worships but has never met and whose pictures adorn his bar and his bedroom.

Bean's adoration of Langtry is based on fact, and the real Bean did indeed see the real Langtry once—during an American tour in the spring of 1888 (the year the film is set), when Bean, dressed in his Prince Albert suit, bought a front-row seat for her appearance in San Antonio. The film, however, plays with the facts. In the movie, Bean sees Lillie during an American tour in the town of Fort Davis, where he buys out the house and is the only one in the audience, dressed in his Confederate Army uniform, complete with sword. He later changes the name of his town from Vinegar-roon to Langtry. In fact, the historical Bean did preside over Vinegarroon in 1882, but he followed the railroad to the town of Langtry later. The judge claimed that he named the town after the girl of his dreams, but the railroad claimed it was named after one of its own officers.

Bean's infatuation with Langtry fits in with Wyler's other studies of men obsessed with women they cannot truly possess. Bean, however, goes beyond Wyler's other protagonists, falling in love, like Pygmalion, with an image, a dream of beauty and womanhood he can only imagine. His absurd obsession is manifested by her pictures plastered all over his walls and in the comic episodes as he attempts to get the lock of her hair that Cole tricks him into believing he has. It is because of Lillie that Bean develops his relationship with Cole, who claims to know her in an elaborate ruse to save himself from hanging. (In earlier drafts of the script, of course, he actually does know her.) Wyler's amusing portrait of Bean's "love" sometimes serves to take the edge off his abuse of the law. Bean's love of Lillie and of Cole humanizes him and complicates our reaction to his behavior, but Bean's world is a masculine one without real women—Wyler depicts the cattlemen as a male enclave of drinkers, gamblers, and killers. Bean's form of justice may have been a necessary step in the evolution of the West, but it must now make way for a society that includes families and schools. His infatuation with Lillie is perhaps a subconscious recognition of that need.[36]

Bean's fixation on a romantic ideal is also equated with death, for hanging alongside Lillie's pictures is his sword from the Civil War. An officer who fought in the battle of Chickamauga, he still clings to the myth of the Old South. As noted earlier, when he rides to Fort Davis to see Lillie, he wears his Confederate uniform and his sword, suggesting that he is victimized by nostalgia and illusion, trapped in the past and unable to face the future of a state and a nation he once helped nurture. In the film's final act, Cole shoots Bean in the theater, and he gets to see Lillie just before he dies. As he looks at her, her image fades to black in an instant. Illusion must give way to reality—the theater is both a perfect setting for Bean's illusory world and the appropriate place for him to die. Just as the past must give way to the future, men like Bean must yield to the progressive social forces represented by Cole.

The film's first image is of a lone rider, in shadow, on the open range.

He is Cole Hardin, the "westerner" of the title who will help transform the wilderness into a garden. The gray, dark tinges in the sky give the film a twilight look, which Toland maintains through much of the outdoor shooting. He manipulates light and dark into shadings that visually place *The Westerner* in a transitional moment in American history. The evolution of the West was not pretty, and this western is not full of imposing, picturesque vistas. The outdoor scenes take place in dusty, empty, and largely uninviting landscapes that are more Depression-era Dust Bowl than grand, mythic frontier.

In the opening shots, Wyler's lone rider is followed by pictures of wagon trains of settlers heading west in the hope of finding free land where they can farm and raise their families. The director then cuts to shots of enormous herds of cattle being driven across the land. When their path is impeded by barbed wire, the cattlemen cut it. When the cattle roam onto the cornfields of the homesteaders, a gunfight ensues. When a farmer mistakenly shoots a steer, he is seized.

Wyler cuts to Vinegarroon, a ramshackle town with dirt roads that is dominated by Bean's bar/courtroom and a couple of other equally nondescript shacks. This is clearly an emerging town, but it has no restaurant, no hotel, and not even a sheriff. Bean, the town's leading citizen, is the sole interpreter of the law. Wyler's camera does not suggest that the town has any life other than what transpires in Bean's court. The only other establishment he lets us glimpse is that of the dentist/embalmer, whom Bean keeps busy because his "rulings" invariably involve hanging. Indeed, the town of Vinegarroon is mostly presented as the interior of Bean's establishment—as if Wyler has grown uncomfortable with anything but indoor settings.

Wyler cuts from the capture of the steer-killing farmer to a series of exterior shots of Bean's courthouse/bar as we hear his voice pronouncing the verdict for committing the worst crime west of the Pecos: "shooting a steer." The condemned man is then seen in a medium shot with a noose around his neck—the juxtaposition is jarring. The prisoner pleads for mercy, claiming that he shot the steer by accident. The first view of Bean is also a medium shot, isolating him in the frame; he blames the prisoner for not being able to shoot straight, prays for his soul, and then kicks the horse out from under him. There is a cut to the prisoner's silhouette as he dangles from the noose and then another of Bean fingering the dead man's money—confiscating the property of the dead accounts for a substantial part of his income.

This painful image is juxtaposed with a shot of the embalmer/dentist abandoning a patient so that he can go and collect the new body. He changes the sign on his door to "Funeral/Back Later" as he hurriedly leaves. Having broken the darkly ironic mood of the hanging with this brief comic moment, Wyler follows up with a cut to the townsfolk gathered to drink at Bean's bar, where the judge toasts Lillie Langtry as "the fairest flower that ever bloomed." This association between Bean's "dream," which remains linked to the past, and the notion of a blooming flower—a symbol of the future of the West—is his blind spot and will ultimately doom him. (In fact, when the real Lillie finally visited Langtry, Texas, in 1903, Bean was already dead from the effects of drinking.) The man he has just hanged is a harbinger of what will turn the wilderness into a garden, and the irony of this thematic concurrence is enforced when Wyler cuts from Bean's toast to the arrival of the undertaker's hearse.

This highly problematic introduction of Bean is followed by the entrance of Cole Hardin, who is led into Vinegarroon on his horse, with his hands tied behind his back. We first see him framed by the rope used to hang the homesteader (Wyler repeats this image from *Hell's Heroes*); here, it forms a triangle, echoing the image that concludes *Come and Get It*. Cole is led into Bean's court and accused of stealing the horse he was riding, which belongs to Chickenfoot, an officer of the court. Bean calls his court into session by placing a Bible on the bar and a gun on the Bible, a composition that is emblematic of his form of justice. Informed that the penalty for horse theft is hanging, Cole is asked how he pleads, and he answers, "Innocent." The horse is then brought into court, and when Chickenfoot asks the horse if it belongs to him, the horse nods its head up and down, and Bean rules that the horse does indeed belong to Chickenfoot. Cole does not dispute that fact but claims that he bought the horse from someone else. Wyler films these proceedings in tight group shots, making the small room seem even smaller.

Cole's trial is interrupted by Jane-Ellen Mathews, who stands up to Bean, disputes his credentials as a judge, and mocks his notion of justice. Admiring her moxie, Bean declares that if not for Lillie, he would marry

Jane-Ellen. Cole can see that he is in trouble, and Cooper plays him as a shrewd, calculating charmer. When the jury retires to consider the verdict with a bottle of the judge's "rub of the brush," Wyler repeats his undertaker/dentist joke—the sign on the room is changed from "Table Stakes" to "Jury Room." The humor of this action, in conjunction with the heroic persona of Gary Cooper, who shows no fear, is an indication that nothing serious is going to happen to Cole. Having noticed the pictures of Lillie on the wall, Cole begins to rhapsodize about her beauty. He claims to know her and asserts that he owns a lock of her hair. The jury then returns a guilty verdict, but Bean suspends the sentence in the hope of getting that lock of hair from Cole. Meanwhile, the actual horse thief enters the bar, Cole recognizes him, and they fight; eventually, Cole knocks him out and takes the $60 he paid for the horse from the fallen man's pocket. When the thief recovers and pulls a gun, Bean shoots him. This exchange becomes the basis of the two protagonists' friendship.

Cole Hardin is not a typical western hero. There is no indication that he is proficient with a gun, and he shows no propensity toward violence. (In that regard, he anticipates Jim McKay in *The Big Country*.) His survival skills seem to consist of caution and thoughtfulness and the ability to match wits with the sly, manipulative Roy Bean. When he finally shoots it out with Bean at the Fort Davis Opera House, he prevails not because of any superior skill with a gun but mostly because of luck. Cole is, in Robert Warshow's words, "a man of leisure."[37] When he is questioned by Bean, he admits to being "from nowhere in particular" and having no specific destination, although he later confesses that he wants to go to California. He is essentially a saddle bum, a man without a home or a family. His spur-of-the-moment decision to work for the Mathews family is apparently based not on the need for money but on his attraction to Jane-Ellen and his instinctive sympathy for the homesteaders' cause.

The growth of the relationship between Cole and Bean dominates the first part of the film. After the shooting of the real horse thief, Cole and Bean spend the rest of the day trying to outdrink each other. Wyler shows them sleeping together the next morning, Bean's arm around Cole, introducing a brief note of homoeroticism.[38] When he awakes, Cole washes up and tries to check his appearance in a mirror covered with pictures of

Lillie. Cole's vanity—he repeats this gesture several times—coupled with the plentiful evidence of Bean's obsession, makes for more comedy. When Cole rides out of town, however, he again passes the hanging noose and then a graveyard. Those images are juxtaposed with that of Bean standing at the bar with the pictures of Lillie behind him, again linking the looming death motif with Bean's seemingly comic fixation. Then, suddenly remembering Cole's claim to have a lock of Lillie's hair, Bean rides after him, eventually knocking them both off their horses. The shot of Bean and Cole crawling in the dirt while the judge reminds his friend of his promise to deliver the lock of hair is one of the film's comic high points.

The second plot involves Cole's romance with Jane-Ellen, the daughter of one of the homesteaders, and his growing involvement in their cause. His arrival at the Mathews house is given a comic touch as well. It is night, and Toland utilizes firelight that flickers light and shadows on the wall of the house, projecting an element of beauty onto what is otherwise a drab setting. Jane-Ellen tells her father about the stranger she met earlier that day, who she thinks was certainly hanged. "I kept on seeing his face all day," she says. Then, as she carries a lighted match to a lantern, she sees Cole's eyes through the window. She is startled, but the coincidence is funny.[39] Cole walks in and says he has stopped by to thank her for her help earlier in the day. More comic business follows, as her father urges Jane-Ellen to play up to Cole and romance him. (Mathews actually has a practical reason for wanting his daughter to ensnare this fellow, since most of his farmhands have been frightened away by Bean's men, and Mathews needs help harvesting the corn.)

Some of the homesteaders want to ride into Vinegarroon to lynch Bean. Getting wind of their plan, Cole rides ahead to warn the judge; then he succeeds in disarming the farmers and tries to negotiate a truce. First, he presents the cattlemen's viewpoint—namely, that the cattlemen had the land first, and the homesteaders often cultivated the land for only a year before their crops failed: "So the homesteaders moved out and the thistle and gypsum moved in. The land was no good for men or cattle." Bean interrupts at this point, agrees with Cole, and throws the homesteaders out of the bar. Cole, however, continues the argument with Bean, insisting that the homesteaders "have a right to defend their homesteads. . . . When you make war

on them, you make war on their women and children too." He urges Bean
to be a "real judge for all the people."

Traditionally in westerns, the new moral order (or the rule of law) is
dependent on the violent intervention of the western hero. But Wyler's film
veers away from the traditional formula—its hero is not portrayed as a
violent man or even a gunman. (In early drafts, Cole is an easterner who
doesn't even know how to use a gun; in a later version, he is taught to shoot
by Jane-Ellen!) *The Westerner* is, furthermore, the first important western
to use the homesteader versus cattleman plot (which famously figures in
Shane and, much later, in *Heaven's Gate*), and Cole's defense of the homesteaders introduces a concept that would become a standard motif of the
genre. Women would come to represent the Christian moral order of civilization, their presence in the western landscape denoting a decisive step
forward from the male rule of violence that is clearly depicted here by the
cattlemen and the "rulin's" of Bean's court.

When Cole finally guns down this defender of the old order at the end
of the film, it is because Bean has broken his word to him. Following Cole's
presentation of the homesteaders' case, Bean is less interested in that argument than in securing the lock of Lillie's hair that Cole claims to possess.
Cole offers to give it to him if Bean and his men will remove all the stray
cattle from the homesteaders' land, and Bean agrees to do so. Cole, however, has to come up with a lock of hair, so he tricks Jane-Ellen into letting him cut off a lock of hers. Bean rounds up the cattle and gets what he
thinks is Lillie's hair in return.

The homesteaders celebrate their harvest with festivities, including a
dance, where an American flag is seen in the corner. Here, Wyler offers
some of his most evocative images of nature and the transformation of the
wilderness. He shows the settlers kneeling before the cornfields and being led in prayer by Caliphet Mathews (Jane-Ellen's father), whose voice is
heard as Wyler cuts to various views of the fields and the land bathed in the
beauty of Toland's black-and-white–streaked sky. Mathews intones, "The
land that was desolate has become like a garden."

Wyler cuts away to Cole and Jane-Ellen. She is showing him what she
considers the most beautiful parcel of the land in the area—a perfect place
for a home. Cole seems more receptive to the notion of a home than he
was earlier, even telling Jane-Ellen how to build one. As they kiss, how-

ever, Wyler cuts to a fire in the distance. The homesteaders' dream is being destroyed; Mathews will soon be killed and his home destroyed. Wyler's quick cuts showing the devastation of the land are as effective as the earlier pastoral views. Shocked and hurt, Cole confronts Bean and forces him to admit that he is responsible for the fire. Cole promises to stop him and goes to Fort Davis to have himself deputized. In the meantime, Bean has changed the name of Vinegarroon to Langtry—a place for cattlemen. His announcement is greeted by gunfire, not prayer.

The final showdown, as noted earlier, takes place in the theater where Lillie is set to perform. Bean has bought all the tickets, and he is the only one in the audience. Before the curtain rises, Wyler's camera cranes up, isolating Bean in the theater. The illusory world he is anticipating is then shattered when he sees Cole onstage instead of Lillie. A gun battle ensues, and Bean is wounded. In a last gesture of friendship, Cole helps him backstage to meet Lillie, who appears like a vision to him in a tiara and a white dress. All he can say is, "I'm pleased to meet ya," as the vision fades and he dies.

In the background of this affecting scene is heard "Do You Remember Sweet Betsy from Pike"—a traditional mid-nineteenth-century song by an unknown composer detailing the travails of a man and his sweetheart. Betsy and Ike cross the country and the desert, suffering multiple hardships. Finally reaching their destination, they attend a dance, where Ike asks Betsy, "You're an angel, but where are your wings?" They marry, but Ike soon becomes jealous and wants a divorce, and Betsy is happy to see him leave. The song celebrates a love that endures many hardships but ultimately fails. Bean, in contrast, is allowed to die happy, holding on to his illusion of Lillie, but his town for cattlemen will be trampled by historical necessity. The film's closing scene shows Cole and Jane-Ellen in their home, presumably married, as they watch a wagonload of settlers returning to the land. A map of Texas is displayed prominently on their wall, and the final image is a field of wheat in full bloom.

The Westerner is an unbalanced film whose numerous script revisions never arrived at a clear conception of the Cole Hardin character. Over the course of multiple revisions, his past was eliminated and few character lines were filled in. Cooper was right to object to playing such a slight character, although he managed to give a fine, strong performance. Bean, in contrast, is a superbly realized character, and Brennan played him to the hilt. Although the judge is in most respects a despicable character, Brennan made him likable. Even when he deceives Cole and burns out the homesteaders, the actor brings such poignancy to Bean's dying moments—the way he tucks his hand into his uniform, the bravery he wants to show Lillie, the look of adoration in his eyes—that the audience sympathizes with him at the end. (Contrast this performance with his Pa Clanton in *My Darling Clementine*, a wholly evil man who elicits no sympathy.) The imbalance in the relationship between the two male leads is matched by the film's failure to realize the character of Jane-Ellen, which is not helped by Doris Davenport's overly aggressive performance, or to persuasively present the homesteaders' viewpoint.

In consequence, the film really belongs to Judge Roy Bean, and this muddles it thematically. Wyler softens this man's murderous, antisocial side by focusing on his affection for Cole and his outsized obsession with Lillie. But Bean's desire for power is pathological, and his desire for Lillie should be more effectively implicated in his madness; that his obsession is presented comically and even indulgently undercuts the film's social message, which should be carried by Cole and Jane-Ellen. The heroine's struggles against what Bean represents and her determination to save and work her land are meant to symbolize the triumph of civilization and American progress, but both her marriage to Cole and the western movement of the wagons offer no more than lip service to these ideals. The film makes a stronger case for Cole's love for Bean.

Wyler's direction is also patchy. Despite the fact that he cut his teeth on westerns, he seems more comfortable indoors than out. The scenes inside Bean's courthouse are effectively staged and handled, but many of the outdoor sequences—especially the fights and the scenes of the homesteaders riding toward Vinegarroon with Cole in pursuit—look clumsy, and the editing is awkward. Wyler commented that he was attracted to the interplay between Bean and Cole, and frankly, he seems to have been bored by other aspects of the story.

Nonetheless, the film was given a spectacular send-off. The premiere in Fort Worth was tied to a charity show hosted by Bob Hope. A rodeo-style parade through town was attended by Wyler and his wife Talli, Gary Cooper, and other Hollywood celebrities. More than 300,000 people lined the streets to watch the festivities. The film earned Stuart Lake an Oscar nomination for his original story, and Walter Brennan won as Best Supporting Actor, even though his was the starring performance.

The Westerner was bookended by Wyler's two most stylized films, *Wuthering Heights* and *The Letter*. The latter was also released in 1940 and, like *Jezebel*, was made for Warner Brothers. *The Letter* also reunited Wyler with Better Davis, who gave another outstanding performance and earned her second Oscar nomination under Wyler's guidance. It was Wyler's fifth film in five years to earn a Best Picture nomination, and it was the third time in five years that he was nominated as Best Director.

The Letter, like most of Wyler's recent efforts, was adapted from a play. This one, by W. Somerset Maugham, had opened in London in 1927 starring Gladys Cooper and on Broadway in 1929 with Katharine Cornell. (Also in 1929, Paramount released a film version starring Jeanne Eagels, with Reginald Owen and Herbert Marshall.) The play is about Leslie Crosbie, the wife of an English plantation manager in Malaysia who murders her secret lover out of anger and jealousy and then uses her social position to hide the truth and claim self-defense. In filming this dark tale, Wyler again examines the themes of unfulfilled passion, social hypocrisy and compromise, and sexual tension. *The Letter* covers much the same ground as *Wuthering Heights*, but with more sophisticated and polished pictorial flourishes. Wyler sidesteps Maugham's broad psychological portraits, substituting atmospheric and exotic visual compositions.

The film's central image, which recurs at various key moments in the film, is a full moon. It first appears at the beginning, when Leslie shoots six bullets into her lover. Screenwriter Howard Koch told Jan Herman that Wyler felt something was missing from the script: "An image. Something to unify the story that isn't there now." Koch suggested using the moon, which was already part of the opening, to represent "the woman's suppressed guilt behind the façade of her protested innocence."[40] The image undoubtedly meant even more than that to Wyler, which is why Koch's suggestion seized his imagination.

Leslie Crosbie, like Catherine Earnshaw and other Wyler protagonists, is stifled by a society that cannot contain her passions. She feels trapped in her marriage to a sweet but dull businessman (an Edgar Linton–like char-

acter) who loves her but can never satisfy the deeper yearnings and unfulfilled aspirations the moon represents. Romantic poets often employed the
moon as a symbol of poetic reverie and heightened imaginative consciousness. William Wordsworth's "A Night Piece," for instance, offers a poetic
example of the moon providing a glimpse of the infinite:

> He looks up—the clouds are split
> Asunder—and above his head he sees
> The clear Moon, and the glory of the heavens.
> There in the black-blue vault she sails along,
> Followed by multitudes of stars.

Wyler and cameraman Tony Gaudio strive to capture this image in their
portraits of the moon, featuring every detail the poet describes (except the
stars). The photography is so evocative that one can even see the blue.

Wyler extends the symbolic qualities of this image even further. Using lowered blinds on the windows, Wyler casts the moonlight on Leslie as
though, in Koch's words, he is "printing prison stripes on her dress"[41]—suggesting both her imprisonment within herself and her guilt over the murder.
Mimicking techniques from German Expressionism, Wyler's dramatic ap-
plication of this shadowed effect from the blinds anticipates their use in film
noir, where they became a stylistic hallmark. Also, although the film feels
as if it takes place almost entirely at night, Wyler carefully alternates light
and dark spaces to illuminate the dual aspects of his heroine's personality.
Charles Affron notes, "The audience of *The Letter* is caught in a visual inquiry, its characters in a moral and legal one. The clash between the image's
clarity and the situation's ambiguity is rendered by Davis and Wyler."[42]

Wyler also effectively uses Leslie's lace-making as a device to embody
her frustration at having to restrain her sexual desires and passions to
maintain her social position as the wife of a planter. (Both Catherine Earnshaw and Catherine Sloper are shown embroidering in the same way, and
for the same reasons.) The film's final image is of Leslie's lace fluttering in
the breeze in her room as the moonlight streams through the slats, illumi-
nating the floor beside it. The eerie effect of this image is anticipated in a
scene in which Leslie meets her murdered lover's Eurasian widow (Gale
Sondergaard) in a darkly lit establishment in the Chinese section of the

city. Wyler emphasizes its Byzantine alleyways and air of mystery, and Leslie attempts to disguise herself by wearing a lace head covering, which the widow asks her to remove. In one of the scenes in that sequence, Leslie's head, covered by the lace shawl, is shown in three-quarter profile against a latticed, lighted window.

The opening tracking shot of the film is justifiably famous, as Wyler's camera slips past some sleeping natives, past the Crosbie house, and up the front porch. Suddenly, a shot is heard, a cockatoo in the foreground flies off, and a man stumbles out of the house onto the porch. A woman exits the house and shoots at him with a handgun. She then fires four more times as the camera tracks to her face, revealing a cold, hard expression that veers toward contempt. This sequence, opening with a shot of the moon and without any dialogue, fully captures the world of Maugham's play. Wyler's skill at manipulating space—this time, within what seems like a single shot (it is actually two)—effectively introduces the multiple worlds of the film and its various planes of meaning. (This sequence was Wyler's invention; it has no basis in the script, which begins with shots of Malay boys working the rubber trees and the sound of axes.)

Wyler would repeat the effect at the end of the film, whose closing scenes produced a certain amount of controversy between Bette Davis and the director. Leslie's final confrontation with her husband, Robert (Herbert Marshall, who had played the lover Hammond in the 1929 version), begins when he enters their bedroom. The shadows from the blinds cross him, prefiguring the end of their marriage, and Leslie confesses, "With all my heart, I still love the man I killed." She is telling her husband that she can no longer endure their marriage and that murdering Hammond has not killed her desire for him. Davis said, "I couldn't conceive of any woman looking into her husband's eyes and admitting such a thing. I felt it would come out of her unbeknownst to herself, and therefore she would not be looking at him."[43] Wyler disagreed: "If she turns away from him, she just lessens the impact, and she's ashamed to admit it. But if she says it to him in a desperate moment of honesty and self-flagellation, then, it seemed to me, it hits him twice as hard and it's a terrible confession to make. You can't say that looking away."[44] Davis walked off the set but eventually relented: "I did it his way. It played validly, heaven knows, but to this day I think my way was the right way. I lost, but I lost to an artist."[45]

After this confrontation, Leslie walks toward the back door, whose windows are covered by blinds. Opening the door, she faces a lush outdoor world filled with exotic plants—the contrast is startling. As Leslie walks through this garden area, preceded by her shadow, she sees the moon go behind the clouds, and the screen goes dark. She continues until she comes face-to-face with Mrs. Hammond, flanked by a male companion; he holds Leslie while the widow stabs her. As they attempt to walk away, they are stopped by two policemen. The moon comes out as Wyler's camera pans to Leslie's body and cranes up a wall into the Crosbie house, where, from a distance, party guests are seen dancing, framed in the doorway. The camera then pans to Leslie's room, settling on her lace and the final shot of the moon.

Wyler's expressionist ending thus emphasizes Leslie's retreat into her world of romance and fantasy, which can be realized only in death—another of the moon's meanings. Ultimately, the only way for Leslie to achieve her desires, which transcend the world she lives in, is to leave that world. Wyler's constricted image of the party and the shot of Leslie's abandoned lace seem to have the final word until he cuts to the moon one last time.

Wyler's original conception of the final sequence was more poetic. Koch remembered: "The way Wyler directed it, the actual stabbing was left to the audience's imagination. As she walked out into the garden toward the avenging knife, a slight wind brushed her white scarf. The ghostly figure seemed to dissolve into the moonlight as though her dead lover had reclaimed her."[46]

Wyler was forced to add the more prosaic killing of Leslie and the arrest of Mrs. Hammond and her accomplice to satisfy the Breen office. When Warner Brothers first considered buying the film rights in 1938, the Breen office rejected the story because it presented "adultery without compensating moral values" and an unpunished murder brought about by a perversion of justice.[47] Wyler noted that everyone had to be punished: "Even the Eurasian widow somehow had to be punished. We had to put in two cops to apprehend her. That was silly but we had to do it."[48] Although *The Letter*'s conclusion is compromised by this mundane pantomime of justice, it is interesting that both films Wyler made for Warner Brothers end on dark and brutal notes. Without Goldwyn and his insistence on happy endings, Wyler could shape his material in a way that more closely reflected his vision.

9

Bette Davis and the South Redux

The Little Foxes (1941)

Goldwyn's studio was virtually shut down by the summer of 1940 as a result of a lawsuit over distribution rights with United Artists. The only film he had in development was an adaptation of Lillian Hellman's play *The Little Foxes*, which he would refer to for most of his life as "The Three Little Foxes." He had purchased the rights to the hit play in 1939, despite warnings from one employee that it "deals with terribly greedy unpleasant people."[1] His story editor, Edwin Knopf, reiterated that judgment and added that the story was "too caustic for films."[2] Goldwyn reportedly snapped back, "I don't give a damn how much it costs. Buy it."[3]

Wyler expected that he would be directing *The Little Foxes* when Goldwyn resumed production. In the meantime, he was loaned out again, this time to Twentieth Century–Fox, whose production head, Darryl F. Zanuck, had long admired Wyler. Zanuck wanted to make another prestige property as a follow-up to John Ford's successful film adaptation of John Steinbeck's *The Grapes of Wrath*. Because Ford was busy with another project, Zanuck chose Wyler to direct the film version of Richard Llewellyn's *How Green Was My Valley*, for which he had paid the astounding sum of $300,000.

Zanuck commissioned a script from Ernest Pascal and then asked Philip Dunne (*Stanley and Livingstone*, *Johnny Apollo*) to rewrite it. In his autobiography, Dunne characterizes the script as "long, turgid, and ugly."[4] When he wrote to Zanuck and asked why he had bought the rights in the first place, Zanuck sent him a copy of the novel, which Dunne found to be full of "warmth, love, nobility, and earthy humor."[5] It tells the story of Welsh coal miners whose valley is destroyed by industrial pollution, but above all, it is about a proud, self-reliant family that is divided over the right to strike. Dunne enthusiastically accepted the assignment but told

Zanuck that because the novel had so much worthwhile material, he would have trouble cutting it to a manageable size. *Gone with the Wind*, at four hours long, was then the largest grossing film in the country, so Zanuck gave Dunne the go-ahead to write a four-hour film.

When Zanuck received Dunne's script, he pronounced it "twice too long." Wyler came on board shortly thereafter, and his first job was to help Dunne make cuts. Dunne was thrilled to have Wyler as a collaborator (they had been friends since Wyler's marriage to Margaret Sullavan). Dunne's political bent was decidedly left wing, and he considered Wyler a fellow liberal and progressive who would be sympathetic to his pro-union approach to the story. In 1940, a union's right to organize was still a hotly contested issue in the United States. Screenwriters like Dunne were fighting for recognition of the Screen Writers' Guild, to which Zanuck was opposed. Dunne refused to write an anti-union script, but he knew Zanuck would never approve a militantly pro-union one. He wrote, "I proposed a sort of compromise: let the preacher . . . who in the earlier version was a fire-eating socialist, decide the family dispute by coming down firmly in favor of the union, but with the proviso that the young unionists accept full responsibility for their actions."[6]

Wyler persuaded Zanuck to pay for a two-week trip to a mountain resort, where he and Dunne worked on revising the script. They succeeded in cutting parts of it, but in the process, they added two pages for every one they cut. By the time they returned to Los Angeles, the script was even longer than before. In the meantime, casting had begun, and a Welsh mining village was being built in the Malibu hills. Dunne and Wyler spent ten more weeks working on the script. Dunne remembered, "I would shout in aggravation, 'What is wrong with the god damn scene?' And he would merely say, 'You could do it better'—and eventually I always could."[7]

The major problem the scriptwriters faced was trying to tell the entire life story of the protagonist, Huw, as he looked back on his childhood. The solution came when Wyler discovered a new child actor who had recently arrived in America. A certain Mrs. McDowall had contacted an agent to represent her son, Roddy. The boy was sent to MGM to test for *The Yearling* but was not right for that part, so he was sent to Fox to test for *How Green Was My Valley*. The casting director was reluctant to show McDowall's test to Wyler, however, claiming that the boy was "bowlegged and walleyed. He has a gap in his teeth, and he's ugly."[8] Wyler insisted on seeing the test anyway and knew immediately that he had found his Huw. McDowall's casting clarified the story arc in Wyler's mind. Believing that McDowall was a captivating enough actor to carry the film, he decided that Huw need not grow up—the film would deal with only the first half of the novel. (Similar abridgments had been made in the film versions of *Come and Get It* and *Wuthering Heights*.) This solution pleased both Dunne and Zanuck, as the latter was growing weary with all the delays.

Wyler's contract with Fox was for only fourteen weeks, and time was already running short. If he could not get an extension from Goldwyn, filming might have to be postponed. Wyler's difficulties were solved, however, when Fox's New York office pulled the plug on the film. Dunne blamed the studio heads, not Zanuck, for the film's temporary suspension. He wrote that they "hated the script, hated the absence of real starring roles, hated Willy's reputation as an extravagant director, predicted disaster for the entire project, and refused to put up the money for it."[9] Some months later, John Ford agreed to direct the film and bring it in for $1 million. On those terms, the New York office was willing to green-light the film.

Wyler always regretted not making *How Green Was My Valley*. In many respects, the film was his; he had worked on the script and the sets and had done much of the casting, including discovering Roddy McDowall, which he was always proud of. The film also represented his liberal political views and dealt with the kinds of social themes that interested him. Ironically, Wyler would lose out to Ford as Best Director at the 1941 Academy Awards, and in the Best Picture category, *How Green Was My Valley* won over both *The Little Foxes* and *Citizen Kane*.

Once his involvement with *How Green Was My Valley* ended, Wyler returned to Goldwyn to direct *The Little Foxes*. Hellman was having trouble turning her play into a film, and by January 1941, she still did not have a satisfactory script. Since she was in New York revising her newest play, *Watch on the Rhine*, and had no time to work on further revisions, she recommended to Goldwyn three people she trusted to produce a script that would not tamper with the basic structure and plot of her play: her former husband, Arthur Kober (to whom the play is dedicated); her close friend Dorothy Parker; and Parker's husband, Alan Campbell. Goldwyn hired all three.

Hellman had started work on the screenplay in 1939, the year the play opened on Broadway. The play's title, suggested by Dorothy Parker, comes from the Song of Solomon (2:15): "Take us the foxes, the little foxes, that spoil the vines, for our vines have tender grapes." The foxes who are destroying the land of the South are represented by the Hubbards, the family at the center of the play. The play's action takes place in the spring of 1900 in a small town in the Deep South. Industry is beginning to rise in the South, and the region's entrepreneurs are trying to compete with New England and other locales. The role of the Industrial Revolution in shaping America provides both setting and theme for a number of Wyler films, including *Dodsworth*, *Come and Get It*, and *The Westerner* (in its original conception, *The Westerner* dealt with the coming of the railroad). Industrialization also forms the backdrop of *How Green Was My Valley*, and Preston Dillard speaks of it in *Jezebel* as a challenge the South must come to grips with if it is to compete with the North. As in *The Children's Hour*, however, Hellman is less interested in analyzing this social background than in showing how the values inculcated by this system affect the interactions of the family.

The story concerns Regina Giddens and her brothers Oscar and Ben Hubbard, who are planning to build a cotton factory in partnership with Chicago businessman William Marshall. Regina's husband, Horace, who is being treated for a heart ailment at Johns Hopkins, is also involved in the deal and is supposed to put up a third of the money. When the brothers pressure Regina to turn over the funds, she sends her daughter, Alexandra (Zan), to Baltimore to bring her father home. Meanwhile, she bargains with her brothers for a larger share of the business. Ben wants this to come out of Oscar's share, and when Oscar objects, Ben assures him that he will get the money back when Zan marries Oscar's son Leo.

When Horace comes home, he refuses to give Regina the money. So the brothers conspire, behind Regina's back, to have Leo, who works in Horace's bank, steal Horace's railroad bonds from his safe-deposit box, which they will then use as collateral for the loan from Marshall. Horace discovers the theft but prevents Regina from gaining the upper hand in this sibling intrigue by telling her that he will claim he lent her brothers the bonds. Then, in his will, he will leave Regina only the bonds, and the rest of his estate will go to Zan. Regina taunts Horace, causing him to have a heart attack, and she lets him die by refusing to help him get his medicine. She then confronts her brothers about the theft and blackmails them into giving her the lion's share of the business. She apparently wins, but by the end of the play, Zan voices her suspicions about her father's death, and Ben realizes that Regina is vulnerable. Zan tells her mother that she is leaving, and Regina is seen ascending the stairs alone at the end of the play.

The Little Foxes is generally considered to be Hellman's finest play. It is certainly her most often revived work. It is also her last work produced in the 1930s, the decade that shaped her politics, and it offers her most focused dissection of the historical roots and internal forces behind the failure of capitalism. However, the play is not as tendentious as it sounds. It is filled with Hellman's best theatrical writing and populated by characters who are funny, ironic, sad, and aware of their own personas. Like *The Children's Hour*, it leans toward melodrama, but like any great work, it finally transcends category—particularly in Hellman's refusal to tie things together at the end of the play. She deliberately leaves the "solution" of the family crisis to the imagination of her audience.

The Hubbards are a rapacious and materialistic family whose members view even the most elemental family bonds as commodities that can be manipulated and used as tools for negotiation, blackmail, or even murder. Every family relationship has its price or value. Regina is willing to consider marrying off her daughter to her nephew Leo if it will help grease the business deal she has negotiated with her brothers. Oscar and Ben are complicit in encouraging Leo to steal his uncle Horace's bonds and thus seal their arrangement with Marshall. Regina is even willing to sit idly by and watch her husband die when she finds out that Horace intends to significantly cut her inheritance in his soon-to-be-revised will.

The modus operandi of the Hubbards is self-interest. The play's central conflict is not so much how this noxious family will destroy the weaker and more decent people around them but which of them will outfox the others. Each family member is continually trying to take advantage of the others, and Hellman constructs the play largely around a series of situations in which one or more of the siblings attempt to outmaneuver another— whether it is Regina versus Ben (the wiliest ones), Ben versus Oscar, Oscar versus Regina, or the two brothers versus their sister.

Hellman also borrows a major thematic element from Chekhov: the societal transition from an agrarian culture, with its decorous, mannered lifestyle, to a more modern industrial-technological milieu whose ways are coarse, materialistic, and ruthless. During their dinner with Marshall, Ben differentiates the Hubbards from the "aristocrats," who "have not kept together and have not kept what belonged to them." He goes on to say that the aristocrat "can adapt himself to nothing," while people like the Hubbards "have learned the new ways and learned how to make them pay."[10] Like Chekhov, Hellman portrays the aristocrats, whom the "foxes" will trample, sympathetically. Horace Giddens, for one, refuses to invest in the cotton mill. In act 2, he tells Regina he will not participate in the exploitation of workers, which will be an inevitable by-product of this development, nor will he countenance the social misery that will surely be its legacy. Hellman's pro-union sympathies obviously come into play here in her exposure of the Hubbards' venality; one of their central arguments in favor of building a mill in the South is the absence of unions and the consequent ability to exploit cheap labor. But Horace's values—and Hellman's—have no place in the Hubbards' Darwinian world. They insist that they must heed the call of progress, or the region will die. The land and its values must be raped, like Chekhov's cherry orchard, if modernity is to be respected.

Birdie, Oscar's wife, is another leftover aristocrat who has no place in the present. She is the heiress of Lionnet, an elegant cotton plantation that was unable to survive the war; the Hubbards have ravaged it further. Birdie lives in the past and loves music, a passion she shares with her niece Alexandra. During the dinner with Marshall, she is anxious to show him her Wagner autograph but is stopped and silenced by her husband. Her education is wasted, providing no defense against her son Leo or her husband. Music, breeding, and culture are superfluous in Hellman's New South, as Birdie recognizes in a central moment in act 3: "My family was good and the cotton in Lionnet's fields was better. Ben Hubbard wanted the cotton and Oscar Hubbard married it for him. . . . Everybody knew what he married me for. Everybody but me. Stupid, stupid me."[11] Defeated and ignored, Birdie now chooses to lose herself in nostalgia and drink. Her saving grace is that she recognizes the emptiness of her withdrawal and warns Zan not to become like her.

Hellman, however, withholds unqualified sympathy for Horace and Birdie. In that thematically important scene in act 3 when Birdie speaks of the past, the black servant Addie, who functions as one of the moral voices of the play, says, "Well, there are people who eat the earth and eat all the people on it like in the Bible with the locusts. Then there are the people who stand around and watch them eat it. Sometimes, I think it ain't right to stand and watch them do it."[12] Hellman's attitude toward weak, well-intentioned people like Horace who stand by and watch is similar to that reserved for the bystanders in *The Children's Hour*: someone who lets himself be exploited is just as guilty as those who exploit him. One must fight, but as Ben observes, the aristocrats lack the spirit to fight, so their ancestral lands are ripe for the taking.

Alexandra is the one member of the family who observes and listens. She is close to her mother but also loves her father and her aunt Birdie. She is aware of the financial machinations going on around her, but she is also a participant at the table when her father and aunt talk about the past. On a political level, Zan undergoes a conversion at the end. She absorbs what Addie and her father say, but she is also aware that her family has designs on her freedom, expecting to play her as a pawn in the Hubbards' power struggle. Her mother, after all, has entertained the possibility of a marriage between Zan and Leo as a way to keep all the profits from the cotton mill in the family. At the end of the play, Hellman also has Zan overhear some of her mother's threats to Ben, leading her to suspect that Regina may be implicated in her father's death.

At the end of the play, Alexandra takes Addie's warning to heart, announcing to her mother that she will not watch passively as her family devours the earth. She proclaims that she will fight as hard as she can "some place where people don't just stand around and watch." When Regina soothingly concedes that Zan has spirit and invites her to come talk with her and sleep in her room, Zan archly replies, "Are you afraid, Mama?" Without answering, Regina exits, and the curtain falls.

The play thus ends on a note of ambiguity. Zan, like Ibsen's Nora, has not been active or decisive during much of the play, and Hellman toys with her audience's expectation of closure—which a well-made drama like *The Little Foxes* naturally invites. Because there is no strong opposition to Regina's triumph over her brothers and no revelation of her complicity in Horace's death, Hellman leaves the audience with an unsettling sense of transition. Zan is moving toward a future that is uncertain at best. Regina has seemingly triumphed over her brothers, having won the lion's share of the money. She has succeeded in a man's world but sacrificed her motherhood in the process, and she, too, is left in an uncertain state. In all likelihood, Hellman wanted her audience to ponder these uncertainties. She raises provocative issues but adamantly refuses to provide easy answers.

In adapting her play for the screen, Hellman realized that she needed to make some basic changes. Goldwyn thought movie audiences would have trouble relating to a conniving character like Regina Giddens, so he asked the playwright to add some conventional elements to the story while magnifying its dramatic power—specifically, enlarging the role of Alexandra. In an undated letter to Goldwyn (probably written in March 1940), Hellman agreed: "I believe with you that Alexandra should be more important to the story; I knew that was true when I was writing the play. . . . I saw the addition in terms of the plantation Lionnet—perhaps the manager of the plantation could be a young man: a bright, aware, young man who sees in the Hubbards the dangerous rise of people who are constantly ready to sacrifice anything for their own profit. It might be through him, through her love for him that Alexandra rebels against her family."[13] Hellman felt that adding a love interest for Alexandra would enlarge and humanize the story and might also serve to elucidate the ending, which she had avoided in the play. Eventually, this plantation manager would turn into David Hewitt, a writer for the local newspaper.

The addition of the love story bothered some of Goldwyn's story editors, however. Reeves Espy wrote that it "lessened the drama and impact of the play."[14] Edwin Knopf, in a more detailed analysis of the script, wrote that Hellman had made a structural error by starting the story from Zan's point of view and then reverting to the structure of the play. He suggested that the ending be strengthened: "We get little more from Zan at the end than the fact that she *understands*. Having understood, she *does nothing about anything*. I therefore think it is of major importance to our story that both Zan and David be incorporated into the final action. Just how I am not prepared to say."[15] In a memo to Goldwyn, Jock Lawrence objected that "the cruelty and strength of Regina has been dissipated through the change of point-of-view to the daughter." He suggested that to compensate for that loss of narrative energy, "David needs to be given more guts and importance."[16]

Wyler generally endorsed Hellman's changes, writing:

I was delighted during the reading of the script. I believe the main difficulty—in fact the only serious difficulty that confronted us with the play has been solved because Lillian was able to find, and add, the delightful character of David, who, together with Alexandra make up a romance of the most delightful kind—a romance of two charming, kind, attractive and normal people and I feel that now the presence of David and Alexandra, although he does not enter into the plot of the story, together they contrast the somewhat abnormal characters of the story. . . . I think on the whole, it is a great script of the play because it tells the story of that play effectively and contains that which I believe we all agree is necessary to the picture—mainly a love interest for the daughter. . . . I think the fact that the boy is not only high-minded, but his constant teasing attempt at educating Alexandra into a different direction from her family, is an excellent note in his character.[17]

Hellman was still turning out revisions in January 1941 when she recommended Kober, Parker, and Campbell to polish the script. She explained, "The script doesn't need actual rewriting. It needs cutting in places and perhaps expanding in others, in general someone able to put some of the scenes so that they come through the camera's eyes rather than through the theater's eyes. And that is all I honestly believe it needs."[18] Goldwyn also urged that the film should take place in the spring or early summer rather than in the winter, "as the play was"—in fact, he was mistaken, as the play takes place in the spring. He thought that seasonal setting would "give it a much more romantic flavor and also give us the opportunity to play scenes like Lionnet."[19]

Goldwyn and Wyler both wanted Bette Davis for the role of Regina Giddens, even though she was under contract to Warner Brothers. While they were working together on *The Letter*, Wyler had told Davis that he thought the role of Regina was perfect for her, but after reading an early draft of the screenplay, Davis was hesitant, feeling that Regina was off-screen too much. Warner's biggest star wanted to be center stage at all times. Wyler, however, insisted that her acting skill had reached such a level that she could carry a film like *The Little Foxes*. Davis, who was still under Wyler's spell, agreed to do the film.

Goldwyn, however, had to persuade Jack Warner to loan Bette Davis to him. His initial requests were denied, despite the fact that Warner owed Goldwyn a whopping $425,000 in gambling debts. Warner Brothers had also undertaken Jesse Lasky's pet project of filming *Sergeant York*, and all agreed that the ideal star for that film was Gary Cooper, who was under contract to Goldwyn. The two executives finally agreed to swap Cooper for Davis, with Warner paying Davis's salary and Goldwyn paying Cooper's. It was the only time Warner Brothers loaned out Davis between 1937 and 1949, when her contract expired.[20] The final financial deal between the two rivals was that each star would receive $150,000. However, according to Davis, Goldwyn ended up paying her $385,000 for the film; on top of that, "Mr. Warner on my steely request gave me Warner's share of the deal."[21] Usually, the star received the difference between the loan-out fee and the amount the studio was paying the star, but Davis seems to have kept it all.[22]

Goldwyn wanted a fresh face for the role of Alexandra, and Hellman's revisions had made the part an attractive role for launching a career. While in New York, Goldwyn went to see Clarence Day's play *Life with Father*, in which Teresa Wright was making her stage debut. He recalled: "Miss Wright was seated at her dressing table when I was introduced, and looked for all the world like a little girl experimenting with her mother's cosmetics. I had discovered in her from the first sight, you might say, an unaffected genuineness and appeal."[23] Goldwyn offered her a contract on the spot.

The role of Horace Giddens, Regina's husband, went to Herbert Marshall, who had also played Davis's husband in *The Letter*. Goldwyn wanted Miriam Hopkins, who was under contract to him, for Birdie, but Wyler vetoed that choice on the grounds that she "lacks sweetness and weakness."[24] He wanted Lillian Gish, who was unable to get out of her contract for *Life with Father*, so he settled for Patricia Collinge, who had originated the role on Broadway. The rest of the Hubbards also came from the original cast: Charles Dingle (Ben), Carl Benton Reid (Oscar), and Dan Duryea (Leo). Wyler tried to get Ethel Waters for Addie but was unsuccessful; the character was played by Jessie Grayson.

Davis and Wyler encountered even more difficulties on *The Little Foxes* than they had in making *The Letter*. On the earlier film, they had fought over how Davis should play the climactic scene between husband and wife; now they violently disagreed on the basic interpretation of the character. Goldwyn had recommended that Davis go to see Tallulah Bankhead perform the role in Cleveland, and Davis felt that Bankhead portrayed Regina as a cold, greedy, conniving, and evil woman—an interpretation that made sense to her. Wyler, however, wanted a more shaded portrayal of Regina as both funny and charming as well: "I wanted her to play it much lighter. This woman was supposed not just to be evil, but to have great charm, humor, and sex. She had some terribly funny lines. That was what our arguments were about."[25] This argument, ironically, was a repeat of the disagreement he had had with Ruth Chatterton on *Dodsworth*.[26]

The argument over the interpretation of the character went deeper, however. Wyler insisted that Davis's performance "be simple and dignified and not resort to a lot of gestures and accentuated speech and tricks that are just plain bad."[27] In an interview he gave in 1941, after extensive press coverage of their disputes, Wyler said, "Boy did it irritate me to read that I was making her copy Tallulah! That wasn't true. I was just making her play Regina Giddens and not Bette Davis when the camera started. She was inordinately frightened of the charge of mimicry."[28] Nonetheless, Wyler's wife told Barbara Leaming, "As I remember, he wanted Bette to have more of the quality that Tallulah Bankhead had had on the stage: a quality of lustiness and sexuality. Tallulah had played it as if she were really enjoying herself! That's the kind of performance he wanted to get from Bette."[29]

Davis's feuds with Wyler were exacerbated by the weather. Southern California was experiencing an abnormally hot spring, and temperatures exceeded 100 degrees on the Goldwyn sound stages. Davis "wore a corset laced so firmly that it required two wardrobe ladies to pull the cords," which "compelled her to breathe with her ribs rather than with the full diaphragm."[30] Wyler was also fighting with Davis over her makeup. Convinced that she looked too young to play a woman of forty-one with a seventeen-year-old daughter, Davis whitened her face with calcimine to give the appearance of a powdered southern lady. As a result, she looked so pale that Gregg Toland had to do extensive tests to balance her lighting with that of the rest of the actors. Wyler thought the makeup made her look like a clown and demanded that she take it off. Davis refused, and the fighting escalated.

Finally, two weeks after shooting started, Davis walked off the set and went to Laguna Beach, where she had rented a house. "I was a nervous wreck," she said. "My favorite and most admired director was fighting me every inch of the way. I just didn't want to continue."[31] Goldwyn implored her to return to the set, but she adamantly refused. He then allowed her to take some time off, from May 12 to 21. Since *The Little Foxes* was an ensemble piece, Wyler was able to shoot around her during that period. Rumors abounded in the press, and there was speculation that Davis was ill or pregnant. There were also rumors that she was going to be replaced by either Miriam Hopkins or Katharine Hepburn. Even Hellman wrote to Davis, offering encouragement:

> I am bewildered that you are having so much trouble with Regina.
> . . . I never meant Regina to be a violent woman or a fiery woman:
> it is obvious that a woman of the violence that Tallulah showed
> would never have stayed with Horace or with the town. . . . I was
> very pleased when you agreed to do the picture, and only because
> I thought it was the kind of casting that was right for the play. You
> will be better as Regina than Bankhead ever could have been. . . . I
> have great faith in Willy as a director and a great faith in his abil-
> ity to project character.[32]

Bette Davis finally returned to the set on June 2, but she refused to accede to Wyler's demands, and he was forced to accept her interpretation of the role. They never worked together again.

His concessions to Davis notwithstanding, *The Little Foxes* is one of Wyler's supreme achievements. He again demonstrates a profound understanding of the differences between theater and film, particularly how the director's creative mise-en-scène can more effectively communicate the play's meaning. Although Hellman's screenplay adds outdoor scenes, which open up the play in conventional ways, the film's greatness is achieved primarily through Wyler's ability to create visual compositions and exploit space, particularly closed-in space within the Giddens house. According to André Bazin, "There is a hundred times more cinema, and better cinema at that, in one fixed shot in *The Little Foxes* or *Macbeth* [Orson Welles] than in all the exterior traveling shots, in all the natural settings, in all the geographical exoticism, in all the shots of the reverse side of the set, by means of which up to now the screen has ingeniously attempted to make us forget the stage."[33] In his study of Bette Davis, Charles Affron notes, "Obsessively bound together in space by this director, the 'little foxes' find their dreadful intimacy contained in a movie camera." He goes on to say, "*The Little Foxes* is a film of duets, trios, quartets, and small ensembles, which fully exploits an enviably collaborative cast."[34] Michael Anderegg perceptively calls the film a "realization" of Hellman's play rather than merely an adaptation.[35] In "realizing" his film, Wyler not only utilizes character configurations but also reworks some of his favorite devices—staircases, mirrors, and windows—to create visual meaning. He also collaborated closely with Toland, fresh from *Citizen Kane*, to create some effective deep-focus compositions.

The film begins with the passage from the Song of Solomon on which the title is based. This passage is also spoken by Horace during the wine and cake party shared by the good people (Zan, Birdie, David, and Addie) later in the film. These lines are not spoken in the play, but the filmmakers felt the need to explain the passage to the movie audience: "Little foxes have lived in all times, in all places. This family happened to live in the deep South in 1900."

This literary stage setting is followed by a cinematic sequence of outdoor scenes, invented for the film by Hellman, that precede the dinner party that opens the play. We are given a glimpse of the town the Hubbards live in as the day begins. A wagon loaded with cotton, with a black farmhand lying on top of it, moves up a country road. This image was probably Wyler's idea, as it does not appear in any of Hellman's drafts but duplicates the shot in *These Three* in which Karen lies on top of the lumber that Joe is hauling. We see more action as Addie and Zan ride in a buggy past the various scenes that make up the town. This introductory sequence matches Wyler's strategy in the opening of *Jezebel*, where he presents New Orleans by following individuals walking down the street. Here, the audience is given glimpses of cotton being unloaded at the Hubbards' warehouse and of clothes being washed in a tub. The buggy stops in town, where Zan greets David, and we see the food loaded in back of the buggy, which will be prepared for that evening's dinner party. This encounter, added by the scenarist, establishes Zan and David's relationship, which is teasing and playful but full of mutual affection. Wyler connects all these scenes with wipes and dissolves that emphasize the pastoral, slow, friendly nature of the town, which will soon be threatened by the cotton mill the Hubbards plan to build.[36]

The buggy then pulls up to the Hubbard house, and Wyler introduces some of the family members—Birdie and Ben—as they stick their heads out the windows. Regina, arranging her hair, is seen framed by a veranda. Instead of wipes, Wyler cuts between the Hubbards, accentuating the feeling that the rhythm of life here is harder and sharper than it is in town. These characters are boxed and confined—a motif Wyler will more fully exploit when his camera moves inside the house itself, where the major power struggles are acted out. Now, however, amid the outdoor rhythms of the opening, a more jarring visual note is introduced as we meet three separate characters, each in his or her own box.[37] The outdoor preamble then continues with shots of Oscar and Ben, first viewed by David through his window, as they are walking to town on their way to work. This sequence is followed by a single shot of Ben walking from his house to town, which is also viewed by David through his window. David thus makes the first political observation in the film when he tells his mother about the proposed cotton mill and notes that workers in the town are paid the lowest wages in the country. Hellman and Wyler's pro-union sympathies are first expressed here. This series of scenes takes up the first ten minutes of the film and, like the opening sequences Hellman devised for *These Three*, they are not in the play.

The dinner party for businessman William Marshall, which opens the play, follows these brief introductory character sketches in the film. Wyler spends some time with the characters seated around the elegant dinner table, as he did in *Jezebel*. In the play, all the conversations with Marshall take place after dinner in the living room; Wyler, however, divides the action between the two spaces. When Ben contradicts Marshall's assumption that the Hubbards are aristocrats—declaring that they are in trade—Wyler cuts to his first mirrored shot. Ben is still foregrounded in the frame, with Birdie on his right, but behind him, the mirror reflects Regina standing behind Ben, with Marshall in the center and Zan on the right. The framing of Regina here echoes her initial presentation on the balcony and anticipates her framing in the film's final shot. Unlike Ben, Regina plans to take her place in sophisticated society in Chicago, Marshall's hometown. The framing shot, however, undercuts her aspirations, which, significantly, also include Zan, whom she wants to take with her but will lose in the end.

When the dinner breaks up, the camera lingers for a few moments on Birdie and then cuts to the living room, where the evening continues. Regina is centered on the couch, with Marshall to her left and Ben to her right. Soon Birdie and then Zan play the piano for their guest, and Wyler's camera discreetly captures the Hubbards' idiosyncratic gestures as they listen. This sequence is followed by a scene created for the film: in the kitchen, Addie instructs the other servants to feed some children who are waiting outside. "Feed the hungry," she says. Enveloping the living room scene with shots of Birdie and Addie, who are humane and charitable people, puts the Hubbards' callous business machinations in context.

Once Marshall leaves and Regina, Ben, and Oscar are reveling in their triumph, Wyler has Regina walk to a window that is curtained with lace and illuminated by a lamp. She speaks of moving to Chicago with Zan and leaving her brothers. Alone in the frame, in a medium shot with the light and lace behind her, she dominates both her space and the frame—her moment of supreme confidence is realized forcefully by Wyler's mise-en-scène. The siblings then gather to discuss Regina and Horace's unpaid share of the money owed to Marshall. Again, Wyler situates Regina on the couch in the center of the frame, with Ben to the right and Oscar in front, his back to the camera. The most interesting aspect of this shot is that, in deep focus, Wyler also frames Birdie in a chair behind Regina (a reversal of the mirrored shot at dinner). Birdie does not participate in the conversation, but her presence reminds us of a worldview not shared by the siblings. Also included in the shot and behind Birdie is the staircase where Horace (the absent subject of this conversation) will die, while his wife sits on the very same couch.

To facilitate the deal with Marshall, Regina decides to send Zan to Baltimore to fetch her father. When Addie objects that Zan is not old enough to make the trip alone, it is suggested that Zan is old enough to get married. Oscar prods Leo into talk of marriage, and Wyler cuts to Regina as she looks in the mirror. She is obviously thinking about her own failed marriage, also undertaken at a young age. Regina's back is to the camera, and her face is caught in the mirror's reflection—another box, and a frame within a frame. Like many Wyler protagonists, Regina sees that her youth is gone and her life has been thrown away because she married a man she detests. A similar moment occurs just before Horace returns home. The servants are readying his room when Regina picks up a picture. She studies it wistfully and then looks in the mirror. Her reflection, this time at a canted angle, shows an aged, sour, and bitter face. Wyler then cuts to the picture, which shows a beautiful and youthful Regina, her hair in ringlets. By contrast, the mirror's reflection reveals her evolution into a true Hubbard/fox.

The sequence concludes with Wyler's first staircase shots. Regina is first shown on the second floor, lording it over Oscar because she has just negotiated part of his share of the business deal for herself. This scene is followed by one in which Birdie hysterically tells Zan that she cannot marry her son Leo. Oscar overhears Birdie and slaps her. When Birdie cries out, Zan runs from her room to the top of the balcony to check on her aunt. She looks down on Birdie, who seems like a small, isolated, pathetic figure, while Zan is filmed from a low angle and dominates her aunt. Wyler's mise-en-scène suggests that Zan will not suffer Birdie's fate; she will not be crushed by the Hubbards but will prevail over them.

Wyler repeats the mirror-reflection motif to spectacular effect in a scene in which both Oscar and Leo are shaving. Leo tells his father about Horace's bonds, kept in the safe-deposit box at the bank where he works. This exchange takes place in Regina's living room in the play, but the screenplay sets the scene in Oscar's bedroom, where the set-up is solely Wyler's creation. Sergei Eisenstein once commented to Lillian Hellman that he often showed *The Little Foxes* at private parties and particularly admired the shaving scene, for which Wyler "deserved motion picture fame for the rest of his life."[38] Oscar and Leo are shown standing back to back but speaking to each other through their respective mirrors. We see Oscar reflected in the larger mirror, while Leo's face appears in a small, round shaving mirror as well as in the larger one. The staging unmasks the deviousness and hypocrisy of the family, as both father and son feel like they are getting away with something if they do not look directly at the other. The director, however, is choreographing and exposing their images even as they are manipulating each other.

The shaving scene is followed by one in which father and son stick their heads out their separate windows—more boxes—to see Horace's buggy arriving. Inside the house, Regina sits in front of a mirror, creaming her face (a variation on the shaving cream) in anticipation of her husband's return.

All the foxes are getting ready to pounce, but Wyler's mise-en-scène has trapped them just as they are planning to trap Horace and one another. Charles Higham and Joel Greenberg criticize Wyler's style in the film as "cold and mechanical,"[39] but in sequences such as this, the director's style seems both bold and theatrical as he exposes, traps, and reveals his characters to the audience.

Wyler varies this effect one more time in a tour-de-force shot after Horace settles in his room and is greeted by Regina. They talk and quarrel for a few moments, and then Regina gets up and looks out the window; there is a cut to the arrival of Ben and Oscar, who are framed by a section of the veranda. As Regina looks down at them, they appear small and insignificant. Wyler next cuts back to Regina, who is framed by the window, but on the right side of the screen, framed by another small windowpane, is the seated Horace, looking frail and trapped. None of these men seem to have a chance when subjected to Regina's gaze.

After Horace refuses to join the brothers' business scheme, Ben and Oscar go downstairs and plot with Leo to steal the bonds. Wyler films their conference in a medium three-shot. Their bodies fill the frame as if they are trapped within it. When Ben announces to Regina that they have the money and do not need her contribution, Regina has already descended the stairs and is on his level. Ben preens for the camera as he exits, a theatrical gesture that is lost to Regina but on display for the audience. The director lets him enjoy his moment, although the earlier framing suggests that it won't last long.

The scene between Ben and Regina is witnessed by Horace, who stands at the top of the stairs—the one moment when he seems more powerful than his wife. He tells her, "There must be better ways of getting rich than building sweat shops and pounding the bones of the town. . . . You'll wreck the town, you and your brothers. You'll wreck the country." This speech, which defines the moral center of the film, is overheard by Alexandra, who also hears her mother tell Horace, "I hope you die. I hope you die soon." At this point, Wyler centers Regina in the frame, highlighting her evil power, while Horace turns his back to her and seems to fade into insignificance, which is the fate of his kind. The scene ends with Alexandra clutching at her father, whose face slowly dissolves into Leo's reflection in the Planters Bank sign. The foxes will indeed inherit the earth.

Next comes the one tender moment in both the play and the film, as the positive characters gather for the one and only time they are seen together. (In the film, David is included in this group.) The sequence begins with a shot of the staircase; its emptiness indicates that this stage of power has been temporarily abandoned. There is a cut to Birdie playing the piano— an image of the humanism being destroyed by the Hubbards—along with a deep-focus image of Horace sitting in the garden, his body lined up with Birdie's and framed by a full-length windowed doorway. When Wyler cuts to the outdoors, he fills the scene with pastoral images (a stylistic hallmark) of Birdie showing Horace some flowers picked at Lionnet and then a scene of Alexandra in a tree picking apples. At the wine party that follows, Birdie reminisces about the first time she met Oscar Hubbard and recalls her mother's comment that the Hubbards cheated colored people out of their money. Addie responds with her searing statement about "people who eats up the whole earth and all the people in it . . . and people who stands around and watch them do it." Horace then recites the line from the Song of Solomon that gives the play its title as he dominates the frame, with Alexandra and Addie lined up behind him. Horace is, of course, one of the bystanders; Alexandra will be the one who absorbs her father's humanism but follows Addie's call to action. As the scene continues, Birdie admits she does not like her own son and comes to the realization that Oscar married her for Lionnet's cotton. She begins to sob as Alexandra leads her away. Wyler concludes the sequence with another meaningful dissolve from Horace's face to Leo at his station at the bank, his face framed by the teller's bars.

The most famous scene in both the film and the play depicts Horace's heart attack and Regina's reaction to it. Bazin analyzes this scene in detail as a supreme example of deep focus: Regina's immobile face is seen in the front of the frame, while Horace struggles up the stairs to fetch his medicine in the background. Prior to that moment, Regina, wearing a black veil over a hat with a large feather, is pictured within a curtained entrance— she seems ready for the kill. Again, Wyler emphasizes the Hubbards' theatrical nature and how much they enjoy being on display. The framing, however, indicates that the director is very much in control of the action. Horace, who is seated like a spectator, tries to take the upper hand, telling Regina that he knows Leo stole the bonds but will take no action against his nephew. Instead, he will consider the bonds a loan and intends to leave them to Regina in his will; Alexandra will inherit everything else. When Regina seems incredulous about the missing bonds, he insists that she look in the safe-deposit box. When she does, Wyler frames her face in the lid of the box. Horace seems to be in control, but not for long.

Regina retaliates by destroying what is left of Horace's pride, telling him that she has always found him repellent and has used a variety of excuses to avoid having sex with him. She says she married him in the hope that he would give her the world, but he turned out to be only a "small-town clerk." Regina is thus revealed as another Wyler protagonist who has married for money, only to be bitterly disappointed. As Regina speaks, Wyler repeats the earlier framing of her walking to the window. It is now raining outside—always an ominous sign in a Wyler film.[40] However, unlike the scene after the dinner party for Marshall, the front of the frame is now shared by Horace's stricken face. Regina moves to the couch at the center of the frame and reclines, as if she enjoys humiliating her husband. In the play, she boasts of cheating on him to retaliate for his dalliance with "fancy women," but this accusation is omitted in the film, both because it would compromise the audience's sympathy for Horace and, more important, because it would have offended the Breen office.

At this point, Horace suffers a heart attack and, while trying to reach his medicine, knocks the bottle to the floor. Regina remains immobile, her look dispassionate and hard. She has assumed the role of spectator—though one whose gaze dominates the action. This scene is often praised for its effective use of deep focus, in that it exposes two planes of action at once: Regina's fixed expression, and Horace in the background, struggling up the stairs to secure another bottle of medicine. The scene, however, belongs to Regina, whose *in*action remains the focal point, while our view of Horace is blurred. Wyler downplayed the deep-focus aspect of the scene, however, explaining its strategy in purely utilitarian terms: "Now there was another thing about this scene that nobody knows, aside from what we're talking about, deep focus. Herbert Marshall . . . has a wooden leg and cannot go up the stairs like he was supposed to. This is a kind of secret . . . a professional secret which I'm giving away here. If you ever see the picture again, he walks out of the scene and a double comes in the background and he starts going up the stairs but he's so far in the background that you can't tell who he is."[41]

Wyler effectively employs deep focus again, shortly after this scene. After Horace's death, Regina once again has power over her brothers. Seated in the front of the frame, she dictates her terms to Ben, who is behind the couch and centered, and to Leo and Oscar in the rear, framed by curtains—helpless players in the struggle between Regina and her more powerful brother. Regina wants 75 percent of the business, and she threatens all of them with jail if they do not cooperate. Meanwhile, Alexandra is seen descending the stairs in deep focus. Regina, undaunted by what her daughter has heard, finishes her threat and dismisses the men.

The film ends as the play does, with Alexandra rejecting her mother. Wyler films this pivotal moment as Regina ascends the stairs and Alexandra remains at the foot. Alexandra declares that she will not stand by and watch her mother and her kind "eat the earth." Regina asks her daughter to spend the night with her, but before she does so, Wyler has her look at the door of Horace's room, and the camera lingers on it. It is a poignant moment that emphasizes Regina's loneliness and fear—a cinematic gesture that expands and enlarges on the literary text. Alexandra refuses and offers a veiled challenge: "Are you afraid, Mama?" These lines conclude the play but not the film, which shows Alexandra leaving the house as Regina struggles to maintain her composure. She manages to assume the steely expression she wore during Horace's death scene, but there is a slight crack now. Wyler then cuts to a curtained window, behind which is a shadow. The curtains open to reveal Regina's face, framed by the bars of the window, as she watches Alexandra and David leave together. Her face becomes engulfed in darkness as the film ends.

Wyler's cinematic ending is a significant improvement over the one in Hellman's script, which has Alexandra telling David that she is going away to learn to stand on her own and fight. She assures Addie, who wants to go with her, that she remembers a song Addie taught her: "You got to live a life of service. You got to live it by yo'sef." She then asks David if he loves her and if he will wait for her. David replies, "Whenever it is, I'll be waiting for you." Hellman's ending thus focuses on Alexandra's conversion. It is very much the upbeat conclusion of a political play in which a character rejects the corrupt politics of the present and vows to reform both herself and the world (just as Tom Joad does at the end of John Ford's *The Grapes of Wrath*, released a year earlier). Instead, Wyler ends with the image of

Regina isolated, alone, and defeated—as he did with Barney in *Come and Get It* and as he might have with Fran screaming in *Dodsworth*. Regina is yet another Wyler character who has sacrificed everything for material gain and ended up with nothing.

The Little Foxes finished filming on July 3, 1941, ten days after its projected June 23 wrap date. Its total cost was somewhat over $1 million. The shoot was exhausting for both Wyler and Davis, who fought regularly. Wyler told a reporter for the *New York World Telegram*, "I'm not knocking Bette for she is a great actress, but I am relieved the picture is done. Maybe she is just as relieved."[42] Davis later told Whitney Stine: "To be happy to have a film with Wyler as the director finished was indeed heartbreak for me. He has never asked me to be in [another] one of his films in all these years. I have few ambitions left—one is to do one more film with Willie before I end my career."[43] They corresponded on and off about the possibility of doing another project together, and in 1947, Davis contacted Wyler about directing her in *Hedda Gabler*, but nothing came of it.

Hellman's attitude was curiously ambivalent. When she first saw the film, shortly before its release, she wrote to the Kobers that it was a "fine picture as pictures go but it should have been better and I think Willy did a bad job."[44] Implying that he was frightened of being labeled melodramatic, she complained to Wyler himself that the film did "not hit hard enough," was "choppy in the beginning," and jumped around too much.[45] She backpedaled in her letter to the Kobers, however, describing Wyler's direction as superior to anything she had seen for some time. Forty years later, she must have softened even further, for she told Austin Pendleton, who was directing a Broadway revival of *The Little Foxes* with Elizabeth Taylor: "The one that came closest to what I intended was Willie Wyler's film."[46]

10

War Films

Mrs. Miniver (1942), *Memphis Belle* (1944),
Thunderbolt (1945)

In 1941, MGM, the biggest and most glamorous studio in Hollywood, borrowed Wyler to work with producer Sidney Franklin—and, by extension, Louis B. Mayer—on an adaptation of *Mrs. Miniver.* The film would be based on a series of loosely connected stories by Jan Struther that had originally appeared in the *London Times* and were later published as a book in 1939. The stories present an idealized portrait of an upper-class, though not aristocratic, English family enjoying the communal world and family life to which their affluence entitles them. The Miniver stories gain drama and some poignancy from allusions to the impending war, which threatens their way of life.

Sidney Franklin had enjoyed a successful career as a director for Irving Thalberg (*The Good Earth*); after Thalberg's death, Franklin became a producer and was noted for his elegance and taste. His other notable directorial efforts include *The Dark Angel* (Lillian Hellman's first screenwriting credit, and the vehicle for an Oscar-nominated performance by Merle Oberon), Noël Coward's *Private Lives*, and *The Guardsman* (starring Alfred Lunt and Lynn Fontanne). Wyler was still directing *The Little Foxes* when Franklin started courting him for this project. Wyler jumped at the chance to work with Franklin. During a lunch meeting, Franklin insisted on reading Wyler the script, and before he was halfway through, Wyler had agreed to direct the film.

The script for *Mrs. Miniver* utilized very few incidents from the book. The screenwriters—Arthur Wimperis, James Hilton, George Froeschel, and Claudine West—kept a few plot details but essentially refashioned the book's episodic structure into a well-crafted, unified story that focuses on the war. The script actually began where the book left off, in September

1939, just as England declares war on Germany. The screenwriters added the central subplot of Lady Beldon and the rose-growing contest with the local stationmaster, Mr. Ballard, which adds an element of social commentary on British class conflict and shows how the war started the process of bringing the classes together. (The coming together of the classes also makes the Minivers' world seem more American.) The romance between Lady Beldon's granddaughter, Carol, and Vin Miniver was also added. Most important, the entire Miniver saga was transformed into a propaganda piece in support of America's joining the European conflict.

Wyler began shooting *Mrs. Miniver* in November 1941, when the United States was still technically neutral, even though Roosevelt, in his "Four Freedoms" speech in January, had stated: "Every realist knows that the democratic way of life is at this moment being directly assailed in every part of the world."[1] Wyler had always been an ardent supporter of FDR and was vehemently anti-Nazi. More than a decade later, while being investigated by the HUAC, he explained his politics in a draft letter prepared for Y. Frank Freeman, production chief at Paramount: "My interest in any organizations of a political nature began during the Roosevelt Era here and the rise of Nazism abroad. . . . As a foreign-born American I was perhaps more alarmed from the beginning by the threat of Nazism than the average American. As one who had spent his childhood in a country constantly fought over, Alsace-Lorraine, and its people divided into two nationalist groups, I understood that extreme nationalism always leads to loss of freedom for the people."[2] At the end of his life, he stated categorically, "I was a war monger. I was concerned about Americans being isolationists. *Mrs. Miniver* obviously was a propaganda film."[3]

MGM, the studio with the most stars and the most money, was originally gun-shy about producing films that smacked of controversy. As the war in Europe escalated, however, and more European markets were closed to American films, some filmmakers began to insert pro-war sentiments into their work. As early as 1939—and in spite of objections from the Breen office—Warner Brothers released *Confessions of a Nazi Spy*, which exposed pro-Nazi organizations in America. That same year, fellow émigré Fred Zinnemann, whom Wyler had employed as a consultant for *These Three* and was now working in MGM's shorts department, made a one-reel film for its Crime Does Not Pay series about espionage in the United States. In 1940, Alfred Hitchcock made *Foreign Correspondent*, which closes with a speech delivered by Joel McCrea (playing an American correspondent in London reporting on the Blitz) that probably served as a model for the concluding speech in *Mrs. Miniver*, written in part by Wyler. (Hitchcock would continue his cinematic war against the Nazis with *Saboteur*, released the same year as Wyler's film.) Also in 1940, Charlie Chaplin satirized Hitler in *The Great Dictator*, which culminated in a speech urging people everywhere to unite and fight for freedom.

In the summer of 1941, these films and others prompted two isolationist U.S. senators, Gerald P. Nye of North Dakota and Bennett Champ Clark of Missouri, to launch an investigation into propaganda disseminated by Hollywood films. This inquiry was tied to a probe of the allegedly monopolistic practices of the eight major studios, whose vertical integration allowed them to exhibit their films in their own theaters.[4] Harry Warner, Darryl Zanuck, and attorney Wendell Willkie defended the studios against these charges. Nye was a popular figure with the fascist-friendly America-First Committee, and his racist and anti-Semitic ranting against the foreigners who ran Hollywood—a place he described as swarming "with refugees and British actors"[5]—eventually caused the press to condemn him in print. The senators were discredited both by their antiforeigner views and by their ignorance of the films they condemned. When Clark was asked to back up his claims against Warner Brothers by producing evidence from the films, he proclaimed: "No, I have not seen any of them. I am not going to see any of them."[6] The bombing of Pearl Harbor on December 7, 1941, effectively ended the investigation.

While these debates were raging in the Senate, the Office of War Information (OWI) was trying to get the Hollywood studios to release films that emphasized America's connection to England and its other allies. Lowell Mellett, chief of the OWI's Bureau of Motion Pictures, said at a gathering of film producers, "We would like to see pictures that dramatize the underlying causes of the war and the reason why we fight. Unless the public understands these, the war may be meaningless."[7] Roosevelt's secret meeting with Winston Churchill off the coast of Newfoundland, where the Atlantic Charter was issued, cemented the partnership between the two countries even before the United States entered the war. Many Americans, however, viewed England as a class-ridden society that was not truly democratic.

According to Clayton R. Koppes and Gregory D. Black, "Though the British upper classes fascinated Americans, they also produced an opposite reaction. Roosevelt thought Britain's trouble was 'too much Eton and Oxford.'"[8] Hollywood's delight in presenting films about the British aristocracy and their imperialist policies would have to be tempered in favor of stories that accentuated their democratic spirit.[9] Although *Mrs. Miniver* was made before the OWI achieved much influence in Hollywood, it celebrates the connection between the two countries that the U.S. government wanted the film industry to showcase.

Wyler always envisioned *Mrs. Miniver* as a serious propaganda film. In 1942, he told Hedda Hopper, "People say we should be making escapist pictures today. I say 'Why? This is the [*sic*] hell of a time to escape from reality! We're in an all-out war—a people's war—it's the time to face it. Let's make propaganda pictures, but make them good.'"[10] Wyler's trademark perfectionism, however, grated on the nerves of a variety of individuals, particularly the film's star, Greer Garson, and set designer Cedric Gibbons. As a result, producer Franklin had to work hard to keep everyone on an even keel. In his quest for realism, Wyler wanted to make the film at the Denham Studio in London, but the war prevented it. Instead, he was forced to film at Culver City, where the sets, designed in MGM's lavish style, created a "chocolate box world of rose strewn villages, landed gentry and old family retainers."[11] Wyler despised the set.

Wyler even quarreled with Louis B. Mayer over one of the film's most famous scenes—when Mrs. Miniver encounters a downed Nazi pilot. In a late script version,[12] the German is depicted rather sympathetically, suggesting that he reminds Mrs. Miniver of her son Vin, who recently volunteered for the British Air Force. She spends time cleaning and dressing his wounds; speaks to him about his duties, hoping to get a better understanding of Vin's military life; and even offers him tea. Wyler, who thought the sympathy for the Nazi was carried too far, refused to film the scene as written and as Mayer wanted. Wyler declared: "Mr. Mayer, if I had several Germans in the picture, I wouldn't mind having one who was a decent young fellow. But I've only got one German. And if I make this picture, this one German is going to be a typical little Nazi son-of-a-bitch. He's not going to be a friendly little pilot but one of Goering's monsters."[13] Mayer, who did not want to offend his foreign audience—particularly his German audience—finally relented. And once Pearl Harbor happened, the incident was forgotten.

Wyler also made some key emendations to the script. For instance, he cut a prologue that opens in an old-fashioned upper-class London club. As an English gentleman is about to depart, he asks the score of a cricket game and banters with a stockbroker about investing in aircraft, since the price is going up. He leaves and is then seen entering his apartment, where his secretary is waiting. He tells her that he has had a moment of inspiration, asks not to be disturbed, and starts dictating in German, which then changes to English. What follows is a radio broadcast. In the original concept, this character's broadcasts were intended to be cut into the film at various points, interrupting the action. Wyler retains only one of these broadcasts, which is heard at a pub until one of the patrons quickly turns off the radio. The original character is arrogant and reprehensible, and although Wyler clearly had no qualms about presenting Germans this way, he obviously considered this device dramatically inept; he preferred to present his material in ways that emerged more effectively from the story.[14]

The early script's opening broadcast offers the following diatribe: "In this report I shall deal with the class that is most accurately representative of any nation—the Middle Class. The Middle Class was once the bulwark of England's greatness—but today, moved by a frantic urge to ape the luxury and ostentation of the class above them, they have no aim in life save the preservation of their own material security. . . . Self indulgent, comfort-loving, materialistic, the Middle Class of England, in its decadence, will offer little resistance to the world domination of a master race."[15] Although Wyler was interested in propaganda, this was just the kind of clumsy, overstated writing he wanted to avoid. He begins the film, instead, with a written prologue that offers a testament to the values of the English people, who are described as a "happy, careless people who work and play, rear their children . . . soon to be fighting desperately for their way of life and for life itself." Wyler wanted to put his audience in an inclusive mood, and he chose to do so by Americanizing the Minivers into an English version of MGM's Hardy family.

The original script contained further references to the materialism of the middle class, much of which Wyler eliminated. Instead, he has the aristocratic Lady Beldon (Dame May Whitty) deliver lines about the unfortunate blurring of class differences in an offhand, humorous way that makes the point but softens the impact. Wyler's film emphasizes that the English want the same things Americans do—to work hard, to live comfortably and in peace, and to enjoy their prosperity, which occasionally means buying nice things like new hats and cars.

Arthur Wimperis helped Wyler inject more realism into the script. Because of his experiences as an air-raid warden and a river patrolman, he was able to lend some authenticity to parts of the film. He also contributed details to the depiction of Belham, the fictional town where the Minivers live, giving it some of the attributes of his own hometown. Wimperis placed Belham on the banks of the Thames so that he could incorporate the story of Clem and the Battle of Dunkirk, which he had learned about from friends. British playwright R. C. Sheriff was later hired to write the bomb-shelter scene.[16]

Wyler's reputation initially discouraged actor Walter Pidgeon, who remarked, "I heard so many tales about William Wyler that I decided not to do it."[17] Eddie Mannix, an executive at MGM, finally talked him into taking the part of Clem Miniver. Greer Garson was not MGM's first choice to play Mrs. Miniver. Norma Shearer had already turned down the role. Shearer, too, had initially been put off by the prospect of working with Wyler, and he confirmed her misgivings. When she suggested that in order to play the mother of a twenty-year-old son she would have to be aged, Wyler undiplomatically told her that she looked just right for the part. He later apologized, explaining that the character was ageless and the role should be played by someone as young and attractive as possible.

On the first day of shooting, Garson tried to defuse any tension by presenting the autocratic Wyler with a pair of black velvet gloves, which he wore the entire day. But over time, Wyler's method of reshooting scenes angered and frustrated her, and their relationship deteriorated. He once asked her to light Walter Pidgeon's cigarette so many times in one scene that she became ill from inhaling too much smoke. Bette Davis, however, assured Garson that if she were patient, she would give the performance of her career under Wyler's direction. Garson eventually acknowledged that Wyler was indeed a master director, and like Davis, she won an Oscar under his guidance. During one emotional scene, she recollected, "Willy came over to me and said, 'The tears in your eyes. That was very good. But you let them spill over one second too soon. Now if you get the tears again, I want you to hold them there. And then I want you to let that tear run down your cheek.'" Garson did as she was told, and when the camera moved in on her again, "the tear obligingly and obediently rode out and down my cheek."[18]

Wyler fought with Mayer over the part of Carol Beldon. Mayer wanted to use one of the young actresses on the lot, but the director insisted on Teresa Wright, whom he had introduced in *The Little Foxes.* Wyler told Hedda Hopper that "Teresa has the quality for this particular part," and he promised MGM, "If you give me Teresa, I'll take any young man you've got on the lot for the juvenile."[19] He chose Richard Ney from the studio's cadre of youthful actors to play Vin Miniver, and Wright went on to win an Oscar for her acting in the film.

Mrs. Miniver offers the most idealized portrait of marriage presented by Wyler since he started working for Goldwyn in 1936. The first part of the film is closer to the idyllic, fairy-tale world of *The Good Fairy* and *The Gay Deception* than to anything Wyler directed after 1935, but it turns dark in the second half, which is dominated by destruction and death. *Mrs. Miniver* also feels more insistently claustrophobic and looks darker than those earlier works, as Wyler utilizes more nighttime settings.

The first part of the film presents a stylized portrait of a picture-postcard English town where neighbors live in harmony, and the Minivers are a portrait of domestic bliss. Early on, there are discreet references to the war in Europe, but this looming danger does little to upset the daily life of Belham. Clem Miniver is a prosperous architect, and his devoted wife, Kay, is the adoring mother of Vin, a student at Oxford, and two younger children. The opening of the film shows Mrs. Miniver shopping for a hat and feeling guilty about her extravagance, only to learn later that her husband bought a new car that same day. While returning home from the city with her purchase, she encounters the vicar, who has just indulged his own passion by buying a box of cigars. On the train, they are joined by Lady Beldon, Belham's dominant figure, who complains about the crowds and laments that, these days, "Everyone is trying to be better than their betters. . . . No wonder Germany is arming." Her remark is funny, but it sounds an ominous note.

The centerpiece of the film is the annual flower show. Mr. Ballard (Henry Travers), the stationmaster, has the audacity to enter his rose against

Lady Beldon's, which wins every year. Early in the film, when Mrs. Miniver returns from her shopping trip, Ballard persuades her to come see his rose, which is on display in his office. He shyly asks if he can name the rose for her, because "you've always had time to stop and have a word with me—and I always waited for you to come home, and you remind me of the flowerer." The flower-show competition represents the British class system, whose strictures seem to be cheerfully accepted in the film but whose disintegration Wyler clearly endorses. Lady Beldon's eventual gracious acceptance of the superiority of Ballard's rose, in effect, Americanizes her, as it symbolizes the recognition that class structure is a thing of the past. By that time, she has also accepted Vin Miniver as a suitable fiancé for her granddaughter, Carol. Indeed, this section of the film has all the elements of a story by Wyler's friend Frank Capra.

The centrality of the rose as an emblem of England itself is also supported by Ballard's retort to a friend, who claims that if war comes, there will be no flower show. The stationmaster replies, "You might as well say good-bye to England. There will always be roses." Wyler has shown his penchant for evocative natural images before (in *These Three*, *Come and Get It*, and *The Little Foxes*), and he will later utilize this motif most effectively in *Friendly Persuasion*, a pacifist film made after the war. Here, the rose serves as a symbol not only of England but also of a world that will be effectively destroyed by the war. Despite the fairy-tale images and Wyler's pro-war sentiments, the film contains hints of his characteristic doubts about the world's direction after the war. This sense of foreboding would be confirmed by the dark tone of many of his postwar films and the elegiac tone (first seen here) of others, such as *Friendly Persuasion*, *The Big Country*, and *Funny Girl*.

Wyler's careful manipulation of this symbolism is evident in the scene in which Ballard invites Mrs. Miniver to look at his rose. They walk into his office, where the rose stands in a vase on a ledge with a mirror behind it. Wyler employs his characteristic frame-within-a-frame composition, momentarily focusing on Ballard's reflection in the mirror as he walks toward the rose. The stationmaster then signals Mrs. Miniver to approach the rose. She gazes at it with admiration, pronouncing it the loveliest rose she has ever seen. Then, as she moves forward to smell it, Wyler catches Ballard in the mirror again and—in a typically suggestive composition—shows Mrs.

Miniver smelling the rose while she seems to be staring at Ballard's face in the mirror. Ballard will win the rose competition, but a short time later, he will be killed in the Blitz. Wyler thus embodies both the ideal of rural England and its imminent destruction in one shot. On viewing the film a second time, one cannot help but see both Ballard's triumph and his death in that single image.

Wyler makes a similar visual point shortly thereafter. In the bell tower, Ballard and his friend are ringing the bells as they engage in a dialogue about the potential wartime cancellation of the flower show. After Ballard retorts, "There will always be roses," Wyler cuts to a sarcophagus in the church before showing the parishioners streaming in for the Sunday service. This cut offers another indication that although the war will not destroy the spirit of the English, it will demolish their way of life. The death image is then repeated during the service. Wyler first shows the Minivers lined up in their pew and then cuts to the Beldons, with Lady Beldon closest to the camera and Carol to her left, lined up with another sarcophagus in an alcove beside her. Moments later, the vicar informs the congregation that the prime minister has just announced that the country is at war. During his remarks, Wyler cuts twice to the Beldon pew and includes the sarcophagus in the composition; the second time, in a more extended shot, it actually dominates the frame, almost dwarfing the women. In the forefront of the frame, the Beldon name, on a gold plate attached to the door of their pew, is lined up with the top of the figure on the sarcophagus, whose hands are held in a gesture of prayer. Again, the cut and the framing foretell the end of a class structure, as well as the death of Carol Beldon.

The most effective sequence of the second part of the film shows the Minivers in an air-raid shelter as the Germans bomb their town. The narrative strategy of the entire film forces the audience to experience this episode through the Minivers' point of view, and Wyler's tight framing and use of low angles magnify the claustrophobic feel, practically imprisoning both the characters and the audience in the frame as they hear but do not see the destruction taking place outside. The scene becomes a bit heavy-handed when Mrs. Miniver reads a passage from *Alice in Wonderland* during the bombing, but Wyler recovers his artistic balance when the door of the shelter bursts open and the smoke from the bombs permeates the door frame behind the huddled family.[20]

This scene is followed by a sequence in which the Minivers greet Vin at the train station. This time, instead of returning home from college, he is returning from his honeymoon with Carol. Upon the couple's arrival, we see the destruction caused by the bombing—much of the Miniver home has been destroyed. This scene is followed by the flower show, where Lady Beldon demonstrates her democratic spirit by overturning the judge's decision and awarding first prize to Mr. Ballard. This sequence is the emotional high point of the film and, in all likelihood, is the precursor to the county fair scene in *Friendly Persuasion*, where another idyllic communal event is overshadowed by the outbreak of war. Characteristically, Wyler follows this scene with the death of Carol Beldon.

Carol's death comes as she is driving back to the Miniver house with Kay after the flower show. During the drive, which takes place at night, Wyler films the two women as if they are trapped in the car; the tight construction recalls the air-raid shelter scene, although this time, both women can see the destruction through the car window. They watch as a downed airplane bursts into flames and fear it might be Vin's. During the aerial battle, Carol is hit by a stray bullet from a plane and dies shortly after reaching the Miniver house. Wyler memorializes Carol's death by cutting from a shot of Kay holding Carol's body and sobbing to a shot of an empty staircase—an iconic image in Wyler's work and the setting for numerous moments of emotion and conflict. Although the staircase motif does not figure prominently in this film, it is the scene of one of its most joyous moments when Vin, home on leave, bounds up the stairs and stands grinning between his mother and his new bride. Now, however, it is bare and desolate. Only the clock that Clem is always adjusting bears witness to the tragedy—its time now literally "out of joint."

The final scene takes place in the church, which, like the Miniver home, has been partially destroyed in the bombing. The vicar eulogizes those villagers whose lives were lost, including Mr. Ballard and Carol Beldon. He then turns to the congregation. In the final draft of the script, his speech is brief: "The homes of many of us have been destroyed, the lives of young and old have been taken, yet we gather here, those of us who have been spared, to worship God as our ancestors for a thousand years have worshipped him under this roof . . . a damaged roof, but one through which the sun now shines as it never did before."[21] He then reads Psalm 91, and the congregation rises to sing a hymn, "Our God Our Help in Ages Past," as the film ends. Wyler, however, was dissatisfied with the speech and with Henry Wilcoxon's portrayal of the vicar, so he rewrote the speech to make it more rousing and patriotic. In the film version, the vicar tells his congregation to take the devastation of the Blitz as a test of their national will. The new speech goes in part:

> Surely you must have asked yourselves this question. Why, in all conscience, should these be the ones to suffer? Children, old people, a young girl at the height of her loveliness? Why these? Are these our soldiers? Are these our fighters? Why should they be sacrificed?. . .
>
> Because this is not only a war of soldiers in uniform, it is a war of the people—of all the people—and it must be fought, not only on the battlefield, but in the cities and in the villages, in the factories and on the farms, in the home and in the heart of every man, woman and child who loves freedom! . . .
>
> Fight it, then! Fight it with all that is in us! And may God defend the right.

Churchill was so taken with the film that he described it as "propaganda worth a hundred battleships."[22] After a private screening at the White House, Roosevelt ordered MGM to release it across the country immediately. The president was so impressed with the vicar's speech that he asked to have it broadcast over the Voice of America in Europe, translated into several languages, and air-dropped as leaflets over German-occupied territory.[23] It was also reprinted in numerous publications, including *Time* and *Look*.

Mrs. Miniver was Wyler's greatest financial success. It became not only the top-grossing film of 1942 but also one of the biggest moneymakers in ten years—second only to *Gone with the Wind*. The film won six Oscars, including Best Director for Wyler. It was his first win in four nominations since 1936. When his name was announced, however, Wyler was already overseas, serving his country (like Vin Miniver) in the U.S. Air Force. His wife, Talli, accepted the Oscar for him.

Wyler did not finish *Mrs. Miniver* until February, and he was already anxious to join the war effort. In December 1941, he had applied for a temporary appointment to the U.S. Army and assignment to the Signal Corps, but he learned in March 1942 that "there is no vacancy at present in the Signal Corps to which you could be assigned if appointed."[24] He was confused and frustrated by this news, as a number of his colleagues, including John Ford, Frank Capra, and Darryl Zanuck, had already received military commissions. Wyler then appealed to Lieutenant Colonel Richard Schlosberg, head of the army's Photographic Division, who had recruited him some months earlier. Wyler told Schlosberg that he would be flying to Washington with Zanuck, who had received a lieutenant colonel's commission and was assigned to supervise training films. What Wyler did not know was that Schlosberg disliked Hollywood types in general and had no use for Zanuck in particular. Frank Capra had also been trying to secure a commission for Wyler and had recently received a major's commission himself. Schlosberg transferred Capra out of the Photographic Division and assigned him to Special Services, where he would supervise films designed to boost military morale. In his autobiography, Capra wrote that Schlosberg told him, "One Darryl Zanuck around here is enough."[25]

The delays were grating on Wyler. A possible solution presented itself through Samuel Goldwyn, who received a message from Roosevelt that America needed a film about Russia, which was being threatened that winter by Hitler's army. In her memoir *An Unfinished Woman*, Lillian Hellman wrote, "The Russian news was very bad that winter of 1942, but all of America was moved and bewildered by the courage of a people who had been presented to two generations of Americans as passive slaves."[26] Goldwyn wired Mellett at the OWI to say that he would produce a documentary about the Russian people and release it commercially. Wyler and Hellman were asked to prepare a film, and both were excited about the project. They both went to Washington, along with cinematographer Gregg Toland, to meet with the Soviet ambassador, Maxim Litinov, who told them that making such a film would be impossible without the cooperation of the Russian government, which, given the current situation, was unlikely. The next day, however, Foreign Secretary Vyacheslav Molotov approved the idea. Hellman and Wyler returned to New York the next day and met Goldwyn at the Waldorf Towers. The producer agreed that Wyler and Hellman should travel to Russia to see what sites could be photographed. It was also made clear that many of the resources needed to make the film—planes, cameras, crew—would be supplied by the Russians. Hellman described the meeting as "pleasant," recalling that "the three of us were, for a change, in complete accord on all details."[27]

The goodwill was soon shattered, however, when the issue of salaries arose. Wyler asked Goldwyn to pay his salary to his wife in monthly installments while he was in Russia. Goldwyn's face changed color, and Hellman tried to break the tension by saying that she wanted her salary paid in two installments—"half on the day we started photography, half on the day I arrived home, even if I came back in a coffin." But Goldwyn exploded, accusing Wyler and Hellman of lacking political convictions and being unpatriotic for expecting to be paid for their work on this film. Wyler shot back, "This picture is being made for commercial release, and you intend to profit on it as you profit on any other movie. The Russians, as a matter of fact, are giving you a free ride." Hellman added that the entire argument was "nonsense" and that they should certainly be paid for their work. Goldwyn was incredulous: "You call it nonsense to take money away from your government?"[28] Wyler and Hellman finally left, quite sure that they would be compensated, and this impression was confirmed when Goldwyn called and admitted that Wyler was right. The arguments, however, stalled the project.[29]

Some months later, Wyler heard from Capra, who wanted Wyler to make a film for his Why We Fight series. Wyler chose to make *The Negro Soldier* and asked Hellman to write the script. In April, Capra sent him a telegram: "When can you leave for picture we discussed Hellman agreeable."[30] On the back of Capra's telegram, Wyler noted, "Tried to reach you by phone. Am dubbing and scoring picture [*Mrs. Miniver*] for final preview end of next week which I would like to attend. Can leave by plane Sunday April 19th. If very urgent will of course leave sooner."[31] Two weeks later, Wyler telegrammed Capra: "Arriving Monday morning ready to work. Will call you upon arrival. Please don't forget hotel reservations."[32] Capra told him that he would be attached to Special Services as a civilian "expert consultant" at a salary of $10 a day.[33] While these discussions were taking place, Hellman wired Wyler that she had asked Goldwyn to finance the film, and he was willing to do so. She had also asked Paul Robeson to appear in it. Her plans fell though, however, when Wyler opted for two other writers, Marc Connelly (*The Green Pastures*) and Carlton Moss, a black actor-writer who had worked with Orson Welles at the Federal Theater in Harlem.

After some delays, Wyler received orders that he would be traveling to Kansas City, Fort Riley, New Orleans, Alexandria, Camp Claiborne, Montgomery, Tuskegee, Fort Benning, and Fort Bragg to gather background information.[34] Wyler was put off by the South, however, where Moss could not stay in the same hotels or ride in the same railway cars as Wyler and Connelly.[35] At Tuskegee, George Washington Carver refused to see Wyler, although he agreed to speak with Connelly. Discouraged, Wyler began to lose interest in the project. He wanted to participate more actively in the war effort, and an opportunity soon came his way.

In June, screenwriter Sy Bartlett took Wyler to a party at the home of Major General Carl A. Spaatz. Spaatz had been ordered to organize the Eighth Air Force for combat, and his unit would be based in England. Wyler introduced himself to Spaatz and convinced the general that his efforts should be recorded on film. Spaatz, who was no doubt aware that *Mrs. Miniver* had just opened to great acclaim, agreed and turned Wyler over to his chief of staff, Brigadier General Claude E. Duncan. Wyler reported to Duncan's office at Bolling Field, where he was assigned the rank of major and subjected to a physical examination. He was found to be "22 pounds over ideal weight for age and height. But . . . recommended for General Military Service with waiver for weight and waiver for insufficient number of teeth."[36] On June 13, he received orders to proceed by military airplane or rail to Wright Field, Ohio, on temporary duty in connection with air force technical matters. He was accompanied by First Lieutenant Jerome Chodorov (who had worked on the script of *Dodsworth*).[37] Wyler's creative team also included cameraman William Clothier, an aerial photographer who had worked on *Wings* for William Wellman; cameraman William Skall, who had been recommended by an air force officer; and Harold Tannenbaum, a sound man at RKO who had served in the navy during World War I.

Wyler received orders to fly to London on July 23, with a stopover in New York, along with Chodorov, to purchase sound and motion picture equipment. Upon arriving in London, Wyler had difficulty finding a flat, so he decided to stay in a room at the Claridge Hotel, which was also home to a number of British film executives, including Alexander Korda. The hotel was conveniently located, only a short walk to both General Spaatz's headquarters and Wyler's office. His orders were to "organize and operate the activities of the Eighth Air Force Technical Training Film Unit," produce films for "public morale and education," and record "events of historic value."[38]

He quickly outlined five projects that interested him and began his research. Those five original projects were *Nine Lives*, the story of a bombing mission and the crew of one ship; *Phyllis Was a Fortress*, based on the experiences of Lieutenant Paine and the crew of a B-17 on a bombing mission to Meaulte, in occupied France, on October 3, 1942; *R.A.F.-A.A.F.*, about the cooperation between the air forces of Great Britain and the United States; *Ferry Command*, about ships that delivered bombs; and *The First Americans*, about several members of the Eagle Squadron, who were the first Americans to fight in the war. Two of these projects contained the basic form of *Memphis Belle*, the first film Wyler would direct for the air force and one of the most acclaimed American war documentaries.

The story of the British and American air forces occupied most of Wyler's attention in the spring of 1943. He sent a detailed memo to the commanding general of the Eighth Air Force and enclosed a first draft of a story written by lieutenants Terrence Rattigan and Richard Sherman, "both prominent playwrights in civilian life." The story concerned four airmen—two Americans and two Brits—and "intends to dramatize the following facts: a. The striking force of combined air power and the importance of this theater of war. b. The comradeship of British and American airmen. c. The harmony and cooperation that exists between the two Air Forces."[39] In the same memo, Wyler requested that Thornton Wilder, who was attached to the commanding general of the Army Air Forces, be assigned temporarily to the Eighth Air Force so that he could write a shooting script. He also requested that Lieutenant James Stewart be brought in to play one of the characters. The commander of the Eighth Air Force was very interested in the film and approved it the same day.

Back in September 1942, however, Wyler was still trying to beg, borrow, or steal equipment. That month, he met John Ford, who had two camera crews. Sick with envy, he managed to borrow some equipment from Ford. In early November, Wyler requested that he and his officers be put on flying status. To capture the real experience of the air war, he felt he needed to be aboard a plane on an actual bombing mission. His oft-repeated commitment to realism was articulated in a 1943 memo: "It is intended that the approach to these themes and the telling of the story be very realistic and represent a true picture of the life of combat crews."[40] Major General Ira B. Eaker agreed that Wyler needed to go on missions so that his films could "portray the U.S. Army Air Force carrying the air war to the enemy." He went on to say, echoing Wyler's sentiments, "These films are conceived as documentary motion pictures exploiting the human element as contrasted to factual newsreel material."[41] To achieve flying status, Wyler and his officers had to undergo gunnery training at Bovington, and the required approval did not come through until February 1943.

Meanwhile, on November 3, 1942, Wyler's plans sustained a serious blow when he learned that all his equipment had been lost in transit while en route from Wright Field, Ohio. He would have to make do with forty handheld 16mm cameras obtained in London, and the finished film would have to be blown up later to 35mm.

In December, Beirne Lay was assigned to help Wyler negotiate the military bureaucracy by taking over the unit's logistical operations. Lay was a graduate of Yale and the author of the novel (and subsequent screenplay) *I Wanted Wings*. After the war, he wrote (with Sy Bartlett) *Twelve O'clock High* and *Strategic Air Command*. Lay recognized that Wyler was an artist and should be allowed creative freedom. One of Lay's earliest decisions was to transfer Chodorov back to the United States. Chodorov wrote his own request to be "relieved from his present temporary assignment," stating that the change was "for the good of the service."[42] According to Lay, Wyler wanted all the combat footage to be shot during actual combat, and Chodorov argued about the need for so much authenticity.

Wyler and his crew finally attended gunnery school, where they also took courses in aircraft recognition. Learning these skills was difficult and, for Wyler, life threatening. The *New York Times* reported on February 4 that he "narrowly escaped serious injury when a 50-mm aerial cannon with which he was training exploded near his face."[43] This experience did not deter Wyler from going on his first bombing mission with the Ninety-First Bomb Group stationed at Bassingbourn. He reported on February 26 for

his briefing and learned that the primary target would be the harbor facilities at Bremen, with the naval base at Wilhelmshaven as a secondary target.
Wyler was assigned to a B-17 called the *Jersey Bounce*, piloted by Captain
Robert C. Morgan. This was not Morgan's usual plane. Normally, he piloted the *Memphis Belle*, another B-17 that had been grounded for repairs
after sustaining damage during a bombing mission over the submarine facilities at Saint-Nazaire.

Wyler's first mission resulted in only 250 feet of film, "the quality of
which is doubtful," he stated.[44] Wyler, however, found the experience exhilarating: "Aerial warfare takes place in altitudes where the oil in your
camera freezes, where you have to wear oxygen masks or die, where you
can't move around too much and keep conscious. . . . These and other conditions are far removed from the comforts of Stage 18 in Burbank or Culver
City. This is life at its fullest. With these experiences I could make a dozen
Mrs. Minivers—only much better."[45]

A week after this bombing mission, Wyler learned that he had won his
first Oscar, for *Mrs. Miniver*. He was treated to a celebratory dinner by a
variety of British and American officers but felt somewhat embarrassed:
"Here I made this film and I didn't know what I was doing." He had refused to attend a London screening of the film arranged by top military officials, and when he was finally pressured into attending, he found himself
crying along with the rest of the audience at the end. His reaction: "Christ,
what a tearjerker!"[46]

While in London, Wyler encountered Laurence Olivier and Vivien
Leigh. Leigh invited him to see her perform in a revival of Shaw's *The Doctor's Dilemma*, and Olivier asked Wyler to direct him in a planned film
version of Shakespeare's *Henry V*. Wyler turned him down, claiming, "I'm
not a Shakespearian," and admitting that he was more interested in working on his war documentary. Olivier, of course, went on to star in the film
and direct it himself.

Wyler's second mission took place six weeks after the first. This time,
he joined Morgan and his crew on the *Memphis Belle*, which was to bomb
U-boat bases along the Atlantic coast in occupied France, 300 miles away.
The planes were ordered to climb as quickly as possible and accomplish
their mission before being spotted by German planes. The accelerated
climb, coupled with the weight of the bombs they were carrying, damaged

some of the planes, and they were forced to turn back. The *Memphis Belle* was one of those that never reached its target at Lorient.

Also on the mission was Wyler's sound man, Harold Tannenbaum, who was assigned to take pictures from a B-24 Liberator bomber. When his plane was shot down while returning from Brest, he was first declared missing in action and later confirmed dead. The loss of his colleague devastated Wyler. He wrote a heartfelt letter of condolence to Tannenbaum's widow: "I thought 'Here is a man who knows what he's fighting for'—and he was fighting hard. No one had to tell him why. We both went to war for the same reasons—and we knew our reasons."[47]

Wyler's third bombing mission, again on the *Memphis Belle*, consisted of another attempt over Lorient. After his fourth mission, on another B-17 nicknamed *Our Gang*, Wyler felt he had enough footage to assemble a film. In his essay "Flying over Germany," published in the summer of 1943, he wrote about his experiences:

> There are many difficulties of aerial combat photography. There aren't many openings for a camera. You're cluttered up with a 'chute, oxygen equipment, a Mae West heavy flying suit, gloves, camera. You try to squeeze yourself into a small space under a machine gun. About that time the glass you are trying to see through gets fogged up or your camera freezes. Then when you're all set to shoot forward, the principal action takes place astern. You focus, your exposures vary from one side to another, into the sun and out of it. Hot cartridges are coming down your neck. You can't move around too much because you're on oxygen and you may pass out.[48]

He also sang the praises of the men: "They're not only wonderful at their jobs and veterans after they've been over a few times, they're the most alert, most alive, and most stimulating group of young men I've ever met."[49] It was this spirit, among other things, that Wyler wanted to capture in the documentary he was now calling "25 Missions"— the number of missions Eighth Air Force bomber crews had to complete before being shipped home. The *Memphis Belle* was closing in on that number, and the story of its final trip was to be the focal point of Wyler's story.

Before Wyler could begin assembling the film, the footage needed to be blown up from 16mm to 35mm, which had to be done in the United States. Before putting in for his leave, however, Wyler learned that King George and Queen Elizabeth were scheduled to tour Bassingbourn as a morale booster; knowing that this would make a perfect coda for his story, he arranged for them to inspect the *Memphis Belle*.

Four days after the royal visit, Wyler flew his fifth mission (not on the *Belle*); this qualified him for an air medal, which he received on June 7. On June 28, in a letter to Robert Lovett, assistant secretary of war for air, he indicated that he was leaving for the States and noted, "In sixty days I hope to be able to show you the finished picture which will be in the form of a documentary short subject on the 8th Air Force activities in general and Captain Robert Morgan and the crew of the B-17 'Memphis Belle' in particular."[50]

Upon returning to California, Wyler set up his offices at the Hal Roach studios—now dubbed "Fort Roach"—in Culver City. He would be able to cut, edit, and dub the film there, but he had to wait until he received his 35mm print from the Technicolor Company. By the end of August, Wyler reported that "due to unavoidable technical difficulties and uncontrollable delays by Technicolor Company," he would be unable to complete the film on schedule and requested "an additional month to finish the job."[51]

Meanwhile, the *Memphis Belle*'s crew had returned to the States in June and been welcomed as heroes. Captain Morgan was touring the country, putting on demonstrations of acrobatic flying to raise money for war bonds. The crew was traveling across the country as well, being feted with parades and others honors.

Although his film had originally been planned as a two-reel feature documentary, Wyler now believed that it should be expanded. He expressed his enthusiasm in a cable to Beirne Lay in the summer of 1943: "Possibilities of this project far greater than previously anticipated and of greater and more immediate benefit than RAF-AAF feature project due to complete authenticity and fact that Morgan and crew of Memphis Belle have become national heroes. Expect finished film will run four to five reels."[52] He also requested that the crew of the *Belle* be sent to Culver City so he could record (in sound and color) their "spectacular civic and military reception and their message to war workers for end of picture."[53] It is unclear whether such footage was ever assembled; none of it appears in the released film.

Wyler brought back 19,000 feet of color film, all of it silent. He needed some dialogue and also a new script. As late as November, he wrote to Tex McCrary, a radio personality who was working for General Eaker, "that the picture was pretty much SNAFU."[54] The problem was still the length. The personnel assigned to cut the film, whose primary responsibility was producing training films, had been told to make it two reels or less. Wyler's critique of their methodology provides an important insight into his obsession with realism and his predilection for the details in camera shots and in actors' gestures that contribute to achieving the perfect look: "They cut out what they considered unessential. But it has been my experience that the so-called unessentials are often what make the essentials—*essentials*." In addition, "the commentary had been greatly changed and was read, for the greater part, like a radio announcer at a football game."[55] Wyler needed more time to expand the film and rewrite the dialogue, and he had to fly back to England to make his case in person, but it worked. Eaker granted Wyler an extension. He then returned to Culver City to make a longer film and hired Lester Koenig to rewrite the script.

Koenig had a variety of partially written and completed drafts to digest. Wyler's papers include two uncredited scripts; one is undated, and the other, comprising only fifteen pages and titled "Eighth Air Force," is dated August 6, 1943.[56] The first, which is handwritten, contains lengthy sections of prose narration that follow the crew from the briefing room to the preparation for takeoff, the actual takeoff, the ride into enemy territory, the dropping of the bombs, the race to avoid the flak fired by German planes, and the party after their safe return home. The opening narration reads in part: "This film is not about how the bombs got here, nor how the planes were built and flown over, nor how the men were trained and brought here. We're just going to try to indicate what it takes in ships and men, fields and guts, to take the bombs out of the bomb-dump and drop them on a specific place—somewhere in Germany—also to bring back the men and ships who do the job—so they can do it again—and again—until the enemy has had enough."[57] The dated script utilizes the verse-like form that Koenig would hone and stylize in his final draft. This version has more dialogue, as the crew members talk about their experiences and their familial feelings for one another, and it specifies the location of the mission (Saint-Nazaire). The final script focuses on the mission to Wilhelmshaven.

These two versions may have been written by Maxwell Anderson, whose name appears on two prose drafts that bear some resemblance to the scripts in terms of language and use of incidents. Anderson's credited drafts are titled "Skeleton Commentary for Documentary Film in Colour Featuring Captain Morgan and the Crew of 'Memphis Belle.'" Koenig would utilize many of the details and continuity from Anderson's treatment, which begins, "This is a bomb dump," and concludes with a repetition and a coda, "This is a bomb dump. And this is an air photo of Vegesack (a third location) after our boys delivered the bomb." Anderson, however, had envisioned a short film; Koenig, whose script was for five reels (forty-one minutes), was able to provide more detail and nuance. Koenig's script was written in poeticized prose, producing a cadenced, staccato rhythm. The difference between Anderson's flat reportage and Koenig's metrical narration is striking:

> And this is the crew of the Memphis Belle.
> 324th Squadron, 91st Heavy Bombardment Group.
> Just one plane and one crew
> In one squadron.
> In one group.
> Of one wing.
> Of one air force.
> Out of fifteen United States Army Air Forces.[58]

Although the film is technically a documentary, Koenig's narration occasionally moves away from the descriptive and factual into more abstract, conceptual language, such as when the bombers increase their altitude on the way to their targets:

> You look out at the strange world beyond—
> Reflections in plexiglass.
> Like nothing you ever saw before.
> Outside of a dream.
> Higher and higher

Into the lifeless stratosphere
Until the exhaust of engines,
Mixing with the cold thin air,
condenses and
streams the heavens with vapor trails.[59]

In recommending Koenig for a Legion of Merit Award, Wyler noted that his "superlative commentary and the ideas expressed in it" were largely responsible for the success of the film.[60]

Koenig completed the script on November 18, 1943—the same date the animation work was completed. The dubbing was finished on December 23. A number of different titles were suggested after "25 Missions" was dropped, including "Germany through a Bombsight," "Round Trip to Wilhelmshaven," "25,000 Feet over Germany," and "To Wilhelmshaven and Back." The nickname of Captain Morgan's B-17, *Memphis Belle*, was finally chosen.

The film's opening depicts the crews of a variety of Flying Fortresses and other bombers as they prepare for and take off on a bombing mission over Wilhelmshaven, Germany. Wyler turns this panoramic vision into a personal, human story by focusing on the crew of the *Memphis Belle*, who will be flying their twenty-fifth mission for the U.S. Eighth Air Force. Regulations require that airmen who successfully complete twenty-five missions be returned to the United States to train other aircrews for service in the European theater. The entire base is aware of the mission's importance to the *Belle*'s crew, and this air of expectancy gives the film a certain suspense and poignancy. The story of the bombing run is framed by opening and closing segments on the ground, thus establishing a cadence for the air sequences, which were photographed by Wyler (uncredited), William Clothier, and Harold Tannenbaum.

The film opens with a jarring juxtaposition. A series of quick shots of the English countryside—cows grazing in a field, a farmhouse, a church, and the church cemetery—is followed by the booming, baritone voice of the narrator (Eugene Kern), intoning, "This is a battlefront." We then see shots of bomber planes in wheat fields and, in one instance, nestled in the foreground with a church in the background. By projecting these incongruous images, Wyler immediately establishes the desecration of the pastoral world he so meticulously detailed in the first part of *Mrs. Miniver.*[61] He repeats the effect when the planes are about to take off, again intercutting shots of the countryside—now shorter in duration—with rapid cuts from bomber to bomber or to different parts of the plane, including an extreme close-up of the nose. This montage of disparate images is accompanied by a repetition and variation of the narration:

> This is a battlefront.
> Like no other in this or any other war.
> No monster armies.
> No booming cannon.
> Only the roaring engine sound
> Of the bombers pounding through
> The quiet English countryside.
> This is an air front!

The film then follows the routine of preparing for a bombing mission. Wyler spends time focusing on the bombs themselves, offering close-ups of some of the unwieldy explosives and the "hauling job" as they are loaded onto the planes. (Here, the film almost has the feel of an antiwar document.) Next, the crews are briefed, they board the planes, and the planes take off. These procedural scenes, however, are interrupted by an animated sequence—a technique that Wyler would use more extensively in *Thunderbolt*—showing how the raid is organized and detailing the routes of the various planes. We then see the planes flying higher in the sky, the formation of ice on the windows, and the crews' resort to oxygen masks.

The depiction of the bombing raid itself—during which the planes have to dodge bursts of flak—and the point-of-view shots—looking outside the planes as they approach their targets and offering views of other planes and the positions of machine guns—are remarkable. Because of the authenticity of shots like these, *Memphis Belle* is among the best documentaries of the war. Equally absorbing is the sequence taken inside the *Belle* as the crewmen fight off German planes on the way back to base. Here, Wyler dubs in dialogue between crew members over their interphones as they track enemy planes, followed by the sound of machine guns. There is even a shot of a stricken American plane, billowing with smoke as it falls from the sky.

Wyler then cuts from the aerial action to the crews on the ground, who are "sweating it out" as they wait for the planes to return. He shows them playing games, such as matching pennies, and then their growing suspense as they anxiously search the sky. Karel Reisz writes that in these sequences, the "full psychological tension is brought home with remarkable power." He also notes that in the aftermath of the landing, which includes shots of exhausted airmen—one even kneels to kiss the ground—Wyler achieves a "spontaneous, unaffected realism which is to be found nowhere else in his work."[62] The film concludes with the crew of the *Belle* being welcomed back after their final mission, followed by a visit from the king and queen, who honor and decorate them.

Memphis Belle was an enormous success. When Wyler showed it to Roosevelt at the White House, the president's eyes filled with tears and he told Wyler, "This has to be shown right away, everywhere."[63] Over the next few days, Wyler screened the film numerous times, showing it to Secretary of War Henry L. Stimson; to Army Chief of Staff George C. Marshall; and to the head of military espionage, Colonel "Wild Bill" Donovan. Bosley Crowther's review in the *New York Times* was printed on the front page— the first time in the newspaper's history that a film review was deemed worthy of such prominence.[64]

The film was also a financial success for Paramount, which released it nationally. In a confidential memo to Wyler, Darryl Zanuck noted that the film was a hit "because it is primarily entertainment." He went on to say, "If the War Department is going to release films to the general public, and I'm sure they are, then a constructive lesson should be learned from MEM- PHIS BELLE. Documentaries will only be played by exhibitors and enjoyed by the public if they contain *entertainment*. You cannot ask the public to pay good money to receive a lecture no matter how vital the lecture happens to be."[65]

Zanuck also wanted Wyler to direct the film version of Moss Hart's popular stage play *Winged Victory*, which was intended to do for the Air Corps what Irving Berlin's *This Is the Army* was doing for the infantry. It also bore some similarities to *Memphis Belle*. Like Wyler's film, the play's title refers to the name of an actual plane flying combat missions, and the story follows the fortunes of three cadets from different parts of the country through their Air Corps training to an island in a combat zone in the

South Pacific. Wyler, however, decided to pass on the project. He wired Hart in Beverly Hills, "Finally saw 'Winged Victory' last night. It is a magnificent show and you can all be proud of such a wonderful job and a really great contribution. I too am proud that you asked me to direct the picture. . . . As for me, I want to make more documentary films along the lines of the one you saw and am presently making efforts to follow this impulse."[66] Two days later, he wired Zanuck: "I know you will make a great picture of Winged Victory and I just want to wish you good luck on it. Someday let us do a real bang up job together and not just stop to scare each other. If the first two times didn't take maybe the third time will."[67]

Wyler's next assignment for the military was to tell the story of the P-47 Thunderbolt fighter-bombers of the Twelfth Air Force, focusing on the Fifty-Seventh Fighter Group stationed at the Alto air base on Corsica. In a memo, Edward Munson Jr., the acting chief of army pictorial services, reported that Wyler "is proceeding to the Mediterranean Theater on orders from General Arnold and General Baker to make a film on air cooperation with ground and naval forces."[68] Once again, Wyler asked Lester Koenig to write the script, and he also invited John Sturges, a lieutenant in the air force and the future director of *Bad Day at Black Rock*, *The Magnificent Seven*, and *The Great Escape*, to be his codirector. Sturges had worked as an editor for David Selznick and had already edited dozens of air force training films. Wyler was enthusiastic about the project, declaring in a memo that "the Mediterranean Theatre of Operations affords splendid opportunities for making an excellent motion picture portraying the work of the Tactical Air Force."[69]

Thunderbolt's subject was the use of tactical airpower in support of ground troops. The Thunderbolt fighter-bombers had been engaged in the war since 1942 and were considered, along with the German Focke Wulf 190, the most durable and substantial aircraft, capable of taking more punishment than other planes. The documentary was to show how Allied strafing and bombing of German railroad lines and bridges behind the front broke the stalemate that had been holding up the advance of the U.S. Fifth and British Eighth Armies. Those land forces had been stymied for five months at Cassino, a mountainous area and a vital target on the German-held Gustav Line. The Allies' Operation Strangle, designed to cut off all shipping to the front, was Wyler's subject.

The Thunderbolts were already equipped with cameras to verify reports of downed enemy planes. Whenever a pilot began firing, a camera attached to the trigger began filming the targets. Wyler and his crew installed additional cameras on the planes' tails, under the wings, and in the cockpits, and connected them to Start and Stop buttons on the control panels. The pilots who agreed to these installations (some did not) became camera operators in addition to their other duties.

Because the Thunderbolt's design accommodated only a single pilot, Wyler was unable to go along on any missions, as he had done when filming *Memphis Belle*. Forced to entrust the aerial filming to the pilots, Wyler felt compelled to accumulate as much ground footage as possible. Within days of his landing at Caserta, Wyler commandeered a jeep and followed the infantry into Rome for that city's liberation. Working as his own cameraman, he captured the jubilant mood as the city was freed from fascist rule. Wyler went to Mussolini's balcony, where he filmed a civilian scraping a Nazi sign off a wall, and he also attended the pope's first press conference with Allied journalists and photographers at the Vatican. (The papal press conference did not appear in the film.) Wyler then spent the next few months driving around Italy: "He traveled north from Rome following a zigzag path toward the front in central Italy. He filmed bomb damage where Thunderbolts had destroyed bridges and railroads in the battle against Field Marshal Kesserling's forces."[70]

To get additional footage of Thunderbolts in the air, Wyler convinced General Eaker to assign a North American B-25 to the camera unit. Through the B-25's doors and windows, cameras could be pointed in almost any direction. Wyler went along on these flights, but because of the deafening noise on the plane (from the engine and the wind), he had some trouble communicating with his cameramen (one in the back and one below). Nonetheless, he managed to get some extraordinary footage.

By the end of September, Wyler felt he had at least enough film for a rough cut. He and Sturges flew back to London, where they spent about a month editing the film and blowing up usable footage to 35mm. In October, Wyler came down with flulike symptoms and stayed at the Claridge Hotel to recuperate. He wrote to a friend, "I'm not sure whether it is the English weather, or whether I'm getting too darned old for this war."[71] Wyler liked the footage they had prepared, so he sent Koenig and Sturges to Hollywood to do some further editing and to write the narration. Wyler stayed behind because he did not want to miss the fall of Berlin. He obtained orders to proceed to Paris, where Colonel George Stevens was filming for the Sixth Army; Stevens would soon record the liberation of a number of concentration camps and would take some of the first pictures of the horrors perpetrated there. Stevens loaned Wyler a driver—Leicester Hemingway (Ernest's brother)—and he saw a great deal of the European front. Wyler even managed to return to his hometown, Mulhouse, where, to his delight, he discovered that his father's store was still standing. The caretaker had saved Wyler's share of the profits, which she proudly presented to him. Upon his return to General Spaatz's headquarters, Wyler learned that the *Hollywood Reporter* had reported him missing in action. He frantically wired his wife to reassure her of his safety. Talli, however, had been on a trip to Mexico and was unaware of the news.

In an attempt to get more "atmosphere shots," as he called them, Wyler went up one last time in the B-25. But when the plane landed at Grossetto, he could not hear and had trouble walking straight. He was examined and sent home, temporarily deaf. After months of testing at various air force hospitals in the East, he recovered some hearing in his left ear. The eventual diagnosis was that the nerve had been damaged and there was no cure. Although his hearing remained impaired, Wyler was able to make some adjustments to compensate. He would plug himself into his sound man's microphones, listening to scenes through a set of headphones: "This way, instead of hearing the scene from behind the camera, you hear it as it happens on the soundtrack."[72] For the rest of his life, Wyler would receive $60 a month from the U.S. government as compensation for his hearing loss.

Thunderbolt shares similarities in narrative structure and theme with *Memphis Belle* but lacks its force and its cumulative emotional effect. Koenig's script was less poetic and more descriptive than the one he contributed to the earlier film. Too often, the narration merely duplicates what we are seeing on the screen, and when Wyler's images are striking and arresting—such as the scenes of the planes strafing German railroad cars and tracks—it seems intrusive. The central difference, of course, is that *Thunderbolt* lacks a personal drama, whereas *Belle* is structured around the suspense of the "final mission" and the communal values shared by the crew—a group the audience has followed throughout the film. The later work lacks this unifying thread of a group dynamic, and although some members of the unit are introduced early on, they all disappear, with the exception of Gil Wyman, the leader. Koenig inadvertently highlights the problem in his notes for an early treatment: "The treatment indicates a rather full documentary coverage of the way a Tactical Air Force works. There is no really personal story as there was in Memphis Belle."[73]

Koenig tries to compensate for this lack of a personal element by inserting multiple sequences of the crew on Corsica, either preparing for flight or relaxing. And while some of these moments are endearing or comic, they provide little more than additional documentary-style information. In the first sequence, we see soldiers brushing their teeth, washing out their helmets, and combing their hair; in another, they are swimming, waterskiing, playing with puppies, and reading. In his initial notes on the squadron's briefing, Koenig writes, "Keeping in mind the tension we want to build for the morning mission, we follow the pilots through their typical routine."[74] Unfortunately, the film never builds any tension, either in that sequence or elsewhere.

Koenig attempts to duplicate his blank-verse narration, but again, instead of heightening the mood with poetic and abstract effects, the verse is merely informational. In his revised treatment, he writes:

> There are two main divisions of air power.
> Strategic—heavy bombers and
> Their fighter escort destroy
> Enemy productions at long range.
> Hammer the heart of the war effort.
> Tactical—when we meet the enemy on the ground—
> mediums and fighter bombers prevent his
> moving supplies and reinforcements to the front.
> Destroy his transport. His communications.
> Cut his troops from the rear.[75]

The film does contain some of Wyler's most extraordinary flying sequences, particularly the shots of the squadron flying from Corsica to Italy. The camera follows the planes' upward movements as they separate from one another and climb toward 10,000 to 12,000 feet. The pilots' point-of-view shots of the land below, juxtaposing images of farm animals and potential targets, followed by the bombing of bridges or roads and, in particular, the point-of-view shots of strafing as the planes fly low to the ground, are electrifying and breathtaking.

There is too little of this firsthand excitement, however. Instead, the film details how the war effort in Italy changed in 1944. The two narrators, Eugene Kern and Lloyd Bridges, describe how the military brass decided that the most effective way to break the long stalemate at Anzio was to bomb the Germans behind their lines and thus deprive them of food, fuel, and reinforcements. They then proceeded to use their airpower to blow up train tracks, bridges, and roads.

The end of the war forestalled the need to obtain a commercial release for the film. Suddenly, there was not much enthusiasm for it, even in the air force. Wyler wrote numerous letters trying to drum up interest in the film, and in a letter to Francis Harmon, he expressed his frustration: "My personal disappointment over this is of no consequence, but the disappointment of all the Army Air Forces . . . is I believe something to be considered. . . . I think the picture of their vital contribution to the war effort deserves a better place than a shelf in the Pentagon building, particularly since no one quarrels with the quality of the picture."[76] In a later letter to Harmon, he suggested that a studio such as Republic—which has "not been burdened heavily with the distribution of Government films during the war"—might be willing to take it on. Wyler added, "I don't want to leave any stone unturned in an effort to bring the picture to the people who have paid for it."[77]

Wyler maintained that a variety of conditions beyond his control contributed to the delay in producing a finished film. The main problem was his reliance on the automatic cameras installed in the planes—"for months we were unable to know the results, and the ratio of usable film was less than 1%." Another difficulty was the need to transform 16mm prints into 35mm Technicolor prints, which was "entirely in the hands of Technicolor."[78] The company's technicians took their time with the process. And, of course, the war ended sooner than anyone expected.

Wyler arranged a screening of *Thunderbolt* for the Hollywood trade press in October 1945 and tried to get the War Department involved. Unfortunately, distributors were now indifferent to war documentaries, and Wyler failed to drum up any interest. Finally, in 1947, Monogram decided to release *Thunderbolt*. The studio agreed to keep 75 percent of the profits and turn over 25 percent to the U.S. Treasury. Monogram also decided to donate 25 percent of its profits to the Army Air Force Aid Society. In an effort to increase the film's box-office potential, Jimmy Stewart agreed to donate his services and provide a short introduction to the film. But even his remarks acknowledged that the events portrayed were now "ancient history."

11

The Way Home

The Best Years of Our Lives (1946)

When Wyler returned from Europe after the war, his feelings about his life and profession had changed. He told Hermine Isaacs, "No one could go through that experience and come out the same. You couldn't live among war-torn civilians, among airmen flying missions and ground crews waiting for their return without learning about people and how they function as individuals."[1] Twenty years later, he elaborated, "The war had been an escape into reality. In the war it didn't matter how much money you earned. The only thing that mattered were human relationships. . . . Only relationships with people who might be dead tomorrow were important."[2]

He still owed Goldwyn one more film. One planned feature was a life story of Dwight D. Eisenhower, a project Goldwyn had been negotiating for months. Robert Sherwood was working on a screenplay, and there were tentative plans that he and Wyler would go to Germany and spend some time with the general. Wyler, however, was not enthusiastic about the project. He also turned down *The Bishop's Wife*, based on Robert Nathan's 1928 best seller, which Goldwyn wanted for David Niven. What sparked his interest, instead, was a project that Goldwyn had shelved: *Glory for Me* by MacKinlay Kantor.

The producer had originally commissioned the project in 1944, when, on his wife's recommendation, he read a *Time* magazine article entitled "The Way Home," about marines who were having difficulty readjusting to life after the war.[3] Kantor, who would go on to win a Pulitzer Prize for his Civil War novel *Andersonville* (1955), had flown missions with the Eighth Air Force and the Royal Air Force as a correspondent. He signed an agreement with Goldwyn in September 1944 to come to California to discuss a story idea suitable for a film tentatively called "Home Again"—a variation on the *Time* article title. Kantor later signed a contract to write a fictional

239

adaptation of approximately 100 pages. He was to be paid $12,500, of which he received $5,000 in advance. The story was to be delivered in ten weeks.

Kantor then spent several months touring hospitals and studying the problems of discharged patients before, inexplicably, turning in a novel in verse that ran close to 300 pages. Goldwyn found the blank verse incomprehensible and wanted to shelve the project, but he agreed to let Kantor work on a treatment. When Wyler expressed interest in the project, Goldwyn tried to talk him out of it. "He thought it was nothing—ten thousand wasted," Wyler recalled.[4] But Wyler liked Kantor's story precisely because it was about ordinary soldiers, unlike the Eisenhower project, which focused on leadership at the top. More important, it resonated with Wyler on a personal level: "I knew these people, shared a good many of their experiences."[5]

Wyler brought Kantor's material to Robert Sherwood, who was working on the Eisenhower project and had three Pulitzer Prizes for drama to his credit (*Abe Lincoln in Illinois*, *Idiot's Delight*, *There Shall Be No Night*), as well as a number of impressive screenwriting credits (*Rebecca*, *The Scarlet Pimpernel*, *The Divorce of Lady X*). (In fact, he would go on to write *The Bishop's Wife* for Goldwyn in 1947.) In addition, he had served as a speechwriter for President Roosevelt and headed the Office of War Information. Sherwood, too, preferred Kantor's story, and the two of them convinced Goldwyn to go ahead with the project.

Despite his enthusiasm for Kantor's book, Sherwood ultimately decided he did not want to work on the film. In a memo to Goldwyn, story editor Pat Duggan summarized Sherwood's feelings: He was writing a play of his own (*The Rugged Path*) at the time, and he had reservations about adapting Kantor's story. He disagreed with its underlying criticism of civilians and with the basic implication that all returning soldiers were maladjusted. Nonetheless, he believed the book was going to be successful (it was scheduled for publication), and he did not want to be responsible for doing "a typical Hollywood trick of softening a good property." Sherwood preferred to do an original story, for which he would charge $125,000.[6] Goldwyn decided to wait until Sherwood had completed his play, hoping he might see the project in a different light. Instead, Sherwood wrote to Goldwyn on August 27, urging him to abandon the film:

I have been thinking a great deal about "Glory for Me" and I have come to the conclusion that in all fairness, I should recommend to you that we drop it. This is entirely due to the conviction that by next Spring or next Fall, this subject will be terribly out of date. . . . Willy Wyler said one thing that impressed me tremendously when the three of us were talking in Hollywood a month ago: this picture could prevent a lot of heartaches and even tragedies among servicemen who were confronting demobilization and returning to civilian life. However, the sudden end of the Japanese war has changed all that because, by the time the picture is released, the demobilization process will have been completed in many millions of cases.[7]

Goldwyn telegrammed Sherwood a week later: "I have more faith in it now than I had six months ago because I feel the subject matter will be even more timely a year from now than it is today. As you said, there will be several million men coming home next year . . . and to release a picture at that time presenting their problems seems to me to be hitting it right on the head."[8]

Sherwood was obviously convinced—he agreed to write a screenplay as soon as his play had opened. In November, Goldwyn reported that he had received forty pages of Sherwood's first draft and noted, "I am very anxious that Wyler and you people read it so that we can begin to line up some of the cast. . . . The plan as it now stands is to have the first draft ready by the first week in December."[9]

Kantor's story follows three men who, after being discharged from the service, return to their midwestern hometown—Boone City, which was modeled after Cincinnati but named for the Boone River in Iowa, near where Kantor grew up. The novel's central character is Fred Derry, an Eighth Air Force bombardier who was a soda jerk in a drugstore before the war and lived on the wrong side of the tracks with his alcoholic father and his stepmother. While in training, he married Marie, a woman he had known only briefly, and after a few days of marriage, he was shipped overseas and eventually became a decorated war hero. On his first night home, Fred finds Marie making love to another man and gives her the money to get a divorce. Al Stephenson, Harvard class of 1924, is a middle-aged man

who was an infantry sergeant. He returns home to his wife and two grown
children and to his job as assistant vice president of the Cornbelt Trust and
Savings. Al soon grows uncomfortable with his job, finding himself torn
over reconciling business ethics with the social conscience he developed as
a soldier. Kantor also supplies Al and Fred with stream-of-consciousness–
style flashbacks that complicate the forward movement of the story. The
third character is Homer Wermels, a seaman second class, who was engaged to the girl next door when he left. He returns from the war a spastic, unable to control his movements, and he fears that his fiancée, Wilma,
will marry him out of pity. Discovering that drinking allows him to control his movements more effectively, Homer is on the verge of becoming an
alcoholic.

Sherwood and his wife arrived in Los Angeles in December 1945 and
were put up at the Goldwyns' home while the playwright grappled with
the screenplay. One evening, feeling blocked and unable to come up with a
dramatic arc that would unite the various strands of the story, Sherwood
announced that he was giving up and returning east. But he changed his
mind, convinced himself to try one more time, and unlocked the key to his
script. Sherwood decided that the central plotline would be the emerging
love story of Fred Derry and Peggy Stephenson, Al's daughter. Whereas in
Kantor's novel and treatment, Fred discovers his wife's infidelity as soon as
he comes home, Sherwood's script has Fred trying to pick up the pieces of
his life with Marie but discovering that they were never really in love. In the
meantime, he meets Peggy, and a relationship begins to blossom. Sherwood
knew he would have to amplify Peggy's role in the story so that "Fred could
meet the girl, lose the girl, then get the girl."[10] He also used the bar owned
by Homer's uncle Butch as a central location where many of the story's dramatic events take place.

Sherwood, with input from Wyler, made other important changes to
Kantor's novel and the film outlines he had submitted in December 1944.
The most significant change was to the character of Homer Wermels, now
renamed Homer Parrish. Wyler told the New York Times, "I realized such
a character would never ring true; that no actor, no matter how great his
talent, could play a spastic with conviction."[11] At one point, he even considered cutting the character out of the story. Then, at a war bond rally to
raise funds for disabled veterans, Wyler saw a documentary entitled *Di-*

ary of a Sergeant, which told the story of Harold Russell, a sergeant in the paratroopers who had lost both hands when a dynamite charge exploded prematurely during maneuvers in North Carolina. The film chronicled Russell's life as he was outfitted with prosthetic hooks and learned to master those devices—as, in Wyler's words, he "rose above his physical limitations" and became "a great object lesson."[12]

With an eye toward casting him in the film, Wyler decided to have Russell flown out to Hollywood for an interview. When a Goldwyn executive called him, Russell thought it was a joke. Since being released from Walter Reed Hospital, he had toured for some bond rallies before going home to Cambridge, Massachusetts, to work at a local YMCA. After interviewing Russell, Sherwood endorsed the idea of making Homer an amputee, and he supported Wyler's decision to cast Russell in the role. Wyler noted, "No matter how good a performance an actor gave of a man without hands, an audience could assure itself by saying, 'It's only a movie.' With Russell playing Homer, no such assurance was possible."[13]

The resolution of the other characters' stories also involved some important changes. In the book, Al, disgusted with his bank's attitude toward veterans, quits his job and goes into business with another ex-GI to "grow things" and raise flowers. Homer becomes an alcoholic and attempts suicide but fails. He finally becomes convinced of Wilma's love, and as the novel ends, Wilma is studying medical texts in an effort to help him. Fred, frustrated over his inability to find meaningful work, attempts to rob Al's bank, but Al stops him. Fred is rescued by Peggy's love and decides to go back to school on the GI Bill and enter into a business partnership with the drugstore owner.

True to his commitment to realism, Wyler felt (and Sherwood agreed) that solutions to the men's problems should not reflect the dramatic reversals of fortune that might be expected of characters in movies. Sherwood held, for example, that Al Stephenson should not simply quit his job at the bank and go into something else. Millions of real-life veterans would not have the luxury of such an option—most of them would have to persevere and try to change their institutions from within. In the film, therefore, Al stays at the bank, declaring to the president that he will fight for more liberal loan policies for veterans.

Homer's story also has a more effective resolution. In the film, Homer tries to avoid Wilma not because he doesn't love her but because he feels it wouldn't be fair to marry her. To address this sensitive personal issue directly, Sherwood devised a scene in which Homer takes Wilma to his bedroom one night and shows her how difficult it is for him to undress. Wyler later managed to direct the scene without violating the Production Code.

The arc of Fred's story was also revised. Sherwood wanted Fred's experience to demonstrate that returning veterans needed to be realistic and not expect preferential treatment because of their military service. It is Fred's responsibility to find a new job and learn it with the same dedication he applied to his service as a bomber pilot. When he decides to take a job as a laborer in the construction business, the implication is that Fred's fortunes will grow with this burgeoning industry, since more Americans will want houses as the postwar economy continues to grow.

Many of the script problems had been ironed out by the middle of 1946, and Sherwood turned in his final draft on April 9. By then, the project's title had been changed, but agreeing on a new one had been difficult; Goldwyn even did audience tests to gauge responses to such options as "When Daylight Comes," "Three Roads Home," and "No More Bugles." Eventually, however, Sherwood decided to borrow a phrase that Fred uses in a speech to Peggy: dejected over his prospects, he laments that "the best years of my life have been spent"—an idea she rejects. *Glory for Me* thus became *The Best Years of Our Lives*.

Casting the film presented few problems, as Goldwyn wanted to use many of his young contract players to fill the roles. Dana Andrews, who had had a small role in *The Westerner*, would play Fred Derry; Virginia Mayo was cast as his wife Marie; and Cathy O'Donnell, who would later marry Robert Wyler, made her screen debut as Wilma (she also appeared in her brother-in-law's *Detective Story* and *Ben-Hur*). Goldwyn originally wanted Farley Granger for Homer, but Wyler decided to cast Harold Russell. Teresa Wright, who had costarred in *The Little Foxes* and *Mrs. Miniver*, would play Peggy Stephenson. Goldwyn wanted Fred MacMurray and Olivia de Havilland to play Al and Milly, but neither considered the parts important enough, so Leland Hayward suggested two of his clients, Fredric March and Myrna Loy. Goldwyn doubted that Loy, who was still a major star, would accept such a small part, but to his surprise, after a dinner at his home, she accepted without much prodding and received top billing.

The United States emerged from World War II with its industrial strength and political influence undiminished. The sense of possibility in what Henry Luce famously called "the American Century" is reflected in the film. There is, however, a sense of wariness and foreboding in *Best Years* as well, reflecting both the nation's sadness following the death of Franklin Roosevelt and the growing labor unrest that soon gripped the country. There were strikes at Ford and General Motors, there was a housing shortage, and the economy was in the midst of an inflationary spiral. And worse, it was becoming apparent that the war's end had not brought peace abroad—the alliance with the Soviet Union had unraveled even before Roosevelt's death, there was an impending civil war in China between the Nationalists and the Communists, the collapse of Japan brought political chaos to that country, and Greece and North Korea were being pressured by the Soviet Union.

The most frightening postwar issue, however, was the advent of atomic energy. America was still reeling from the devastation caused by the dropping of the atomic bomb on Japan. Everyone understood that the world had changed for the worse, but few were willing to deal with the troubling implications of the new order that was likely to take its place. In *Best Years*, on his first night home, Al's teenage son asks him about the Hiroshima bombing, which Al seems to know little about—certainly not as much as his son knows. It is clear, however, that Al is disturbed by what the postwar world looks and feels like. The price of victory weighs on him.

Best Years focuses, in part, on how returning soldiers would be assimilated into the workforce and, most pointedly, whether there would be jobs waiting for them. When asked about "rehabilitation" at the start of the film, Fred responds, "All I want is a good job." Given that the United States had so recently endured a depression, questions about what would happen to the economy at the end of the war—and the employment boom associated with it—were real and frightening. Wilma's father warns Homer, "Hard times are coming, boy"—reflecting many Americans' anxiety about the economic repercussions of closing factories that had manufactured products for the war effort. President Truman's "Full Employment Act" was designed to alleviate these fears, but they persisted nonetheless. There was also widespread suspicion that returning soldiers would take jobs away from workers, a misgiving articulated in Wyler's film.

In addition, many soldiers had been traumatized by their wartime experiences. In their study of American films released in 1945–1946, Charles Affron and Jona Mirella Affron note that "nearly half of the 1.6 million servicemen and women demobilized through November 30, 1945 suffered some degree of impairment."[14] This pervasive legacy is reflected in Wyler's film by Fred's nightmares, Al's alcoholism, and Homer's struggles with not only physical wounds but psychological ones as well. *The Blue Dahlia*, which was released the same year as *Best Years*, deals with the subject of postwar trauma in its treatment of the characters Buzz (William Bendix), who experiences fits of violence as a result of an explosion, and Johnny (Alan Ladd), who, like Fred, discovers that his wife has been unfaithful. Another contemporary film, *Till the End of Time*, follows the same structure as *Best Years*, detailing the stories of returning soldiers: Cliff (Guy Madison) is restless and cannot hold a job until, like the men in Wyler's film, he is healed by the love of his girlfriend (Dorothy McGuire); meanwhile, his two buddies struggle with their disabilities—Perry (Bill Williams) has lost both legs, and Bill (Robert Mitchum) has a metal plate in his head.

The Best Years of Our Lives is an example of a great film loosely adapted from a crude, formulaic source. Whereas Kantor's novel is written in blank verse with few of the merits of poetry, Wyler's version actually offers a more novelistic treatment—it is firmly grounded in the details of everyday life, which makes it richer, denser, and more vivid. The film's overall achievement is the result of the creative fusion of Sherwood's writing, Gregg Toland's photography, and Wyler's framing and mise-en-scène, coupled with a near-perfect articulation of the script by his actors. (Indeed, Wyler's ability to bring out the best in his actors reaches its apotheosis in *Best Years*.) Because the film reflects many of Wyler's own experiences, he was able to infuse it with a level of realism he had not achieved before—heightened, in this case, by harnessing his pictorial eye to the contours of Sherwood's script. As he told Hermine Isaacs, "A picture of reality alone is nothing. It is dull. Only when reality has been molded into a dramatic pattern can it hold an audience."[15] In the end, Wyler was able to combine this expressive patterning with Toland's vivid pictures—which, according to James Agee, reminded him "of the photographs of Walker Evans"[16]—to achieve his most perfect compositions.

The film, like the novel, is structured around the difficulties encountered by the three returning servicemen as they strive to pick up their lives after the war. Each of these protagonists is etched as a believable individual, but as a group, they are representative of the experiences of all servicemen as they tried to readjust. They come from different branches of the service: Al was a sergeant in the army, Fred a bombardier in the air corps, and Homer a sailor. Each also embodies a different social status: Al, the upper middle class; Homer, the middle class; and Fred, the lower class. Even though Fred is from the other side of the tracks, he was an officer, the highest ranked of the three. The film's structure is more fluid than that of the novel, however, because of Sherwood's changes—making the courtship of Fred and Peggy more central to the story and using Butch Engle's bar as a regular meeting place for the three men.

Best Years begins at Welburn Air Terminal, where we are immediately introduced to Fred Derry (Dana Andrews), who is trying to get a flight to Boone City. In the first of the film's deep-focus compositions, Fred is placed in the middle of a scene that differs widely from the close-knit corps of soldiers he fought with—here, he is just one of many, a position analogous to what he will find in the indifferent world he is about to officially enter. At the commercial airline desk, he is told that there will be a considerable wait and that he should try the ATC (Air Transport Command) desk instead. Standing next to Fred is a businessman in a suit, who gets his flight and happily pays for his excess baggage. The two-shot at first seems unimportant, but this man's weight, accented by his large cigar, and his smug expression mark him as the first of a number of self-satisfied, crass businessmen who will be juxtaposed to the returning servicemen throughout the film. By contrast, the soldier standing next to Fred at ATC is friendly and personable. Like Fred—and unlike the businessman—he is having trouble getting where he wants to go.

Wyler introduces his other protagonists with a degree of economy that becomes typical of the film. The name of Homer Parrish (Harold Russell) is called along with Fred's when a flight to Boone City becomes available. Homer's prostheses are presented without any dramatic flair: when, like Fred, he is asked to sign a boarding form, he grips the pen in his hook without any problem. The two then join Al Stephenson (Fredric March), who is already on the plane. As Homer tells his new friends about the accident that cost him his hands, Wyler films the scene in a tight three-shot in a single take, without emphasizing Homer over the other two. The implication is that while Homer's wounds are the most dramatic and overt, all three suffer from emotional wounds that will unite them throughout the film. The constriction of space, a common Wyler preoccupation, also emphasizes their shared dilemma.[17]

Shots of the soldiers are then intercut with shots of the American landscape and two shots of the horizon. The second is more poignant, as Fred and Al talk about their marriages: Al reveals that he has been married for twenty years, while Fred's prewar marital experience was less than twenty days. This second horizon shot is Wyler's reminder (like the bucolic shots recalling happier days in earlier films) that these men's lives as returning citizens and their dreams for the future (rehabilitation) will be difficult to reconcile. The shot is repeated a third time with Homer alone: the camera stays on Homer's face in close-up for about fifteen seconds after he looks at the horizon, his dream of marrying Wilma seemingly a distant memory.

There is a swift transition to the three men in the back of a cab—again in a tight three-shot—as Wyler cuts from them to a series of evocative traveling shots of Boone City. Then, in a rare display of artful composition, Wyler's camera seemingly imprisons the men in the car's rearview mirror, reaffirming their separation from the world (both new and old) they are joining. When they pull up to Homer's house, Wyler repeats the shot twice, reaffirming visually that what Homer is about to experience will be shared by Fred and Al.

The scene in which Homer is greeted by his family is justifiably famous—even Billy Wilder claimed that it made him cry. The camera views Homer through the screen door of his house as he stands before it. Seeing him, his sister runs next door to tell Wilma (Cathy O'Donnell), and the camera pans with her, temporarily leaving Homer. His parents' greeting is framed through the window of the cab, seemingly from the point of view of Fred and Al—this is Wyler's second use of a frame within a frame to enclose his characters in space. The meeting between Homer and Wilma, who is first seen from the porch of her house, roughly anticipates the Al-Milly reunion a few moments later. Wilma stares at Homer as Wyler cuts to a close-up of her beaming, loving face. She runs into his arms and hugs him, but he remains stiff, not returning her affection. Wyler then cuts to Homer's face, again reflecting the fear and ambivalence seen in the extended close-up on the plane, but the following cut to Wilma's face, still full of joy, suggests that perhaps Homer's "horizon" will be realized after all, though not without struggle and hardship.

Al lives in a fancy apartment building, complete with a concierge to announce visitors' arrival and an elevator man. Wyler, whose comfortable, successful prewar lifestyle most closely resembled that of Al, based the Stephensons' reunion on his own with Talli:

> It happened when I returned home from the war and my wife met me in New York. It was at the Plaza Hotel. . . . I went to the hotel and looked for her, got the room number and went up to whatever floor it was, and I looked around for a while, couldn't find her. Finally, I saw her at the end of a hallway, a long hallway, and it was just a little unusual. We had to run to each other. So, I thought I would repeat it, do the same thing. . . . It's no great invention, but it made the scene very effective.[18]

The Stephensons' reunion scene also emphasizes space. Al enters the apartment and signals his two children to keep quiet. Wyler then cuts to Milly (Myrna Loy), who is in the kitchen. She asks twice who rang the doorbell, and when she gets no answer, she suddenly realizes that her husband is home. She turns, looks out into the hallway, and sees Al. They move slowly toward each other, then embrace and kiss. Wyler keeps them in the middle distance as viewed by the children, allowing them some privacy from the audience until he cuts to a close-up. This couple's warm embrace contrasts with that of Wilma and Homer, but Wyler's decision to keep them at a distance from the camera conveys that they, too, have adjustments to make.

Fred's homecoming illustrates his different socioeconomic status. He lives in a shantytown in a shack that he can barely fit into. He is met by his stepmother, whom he calls Hortense (Gladys George), and shakes hands with his father (Roman Bohnen), who must put aside his bottle to greet his son. Fred's father is obviously overcome with emotion, but in the Derry home, there is little of the familial warmth that characterizes the Parrishes and the Stephensons. Unlike the other two families, the Derrys clearly cannot offer Fred much support. Troubled that his wife, Marie, is not at home, Fred is told that she has moved out and now works in a nightclub, and he hurries out to find her.[19]

On their first day home, all three men find themselves at Butch's, the
bar owned by Homer's uncle. Fred goes there because he cannot find his
wife, Homer because he finds his family's concern overbearing, and Al because he cannot seem to adjust to being with his wife and kids. Wyler and
Sherwood use Butch's as a haven for the men, who meet there often. It is
one of the film's accomplishments that their frequent resort to this locale
never seems forced or manipulated.

The difficulties of "rehabilitation" occupy the main narrative thrust of
the film. Al is welcomed back to the bank by Mr. Milton and given a pro-
motion, but he finds himself unable to resume his old business outlook. He
says to Milly, "Last year it was kill Japs; now it's make money." In an earlier version of the script, Al complains to Fred about the bank: "Cobwebs.
Oh—you can't see them. But they're here."[20] In another version, he tells
Milly that he wants to quit his job; in another, he complains about having
to fight for approval of every loan he makes and refers to his fellow bankers as zombies.

Al's attitude anticipates that of Chris Keller in Arthur Miller's *All My
Sons*, which opened on Broadway in January 1947, just a few months after
Wyler's film. Talking about his own postwar adjustment, Chris says, "And
then I came home and it was incredible. I . . . there was no meaning in it
here; the whole thing to them was a kind of a—bus accident. Like when I
went to work with Dad, and that rat race again. . . . Because nobody was
changed at all."[21]

Wyler effectively illustrates that sense of disillusionment in the film.
Businessmen and banking executives are presented negatively. Al's boss,
Mr. Milton, looks very much like the businessman who boarded the plane
ahead of Fred in the opening scene—he is pompous and large in his double-
breasted suit. As he lights Al a Cuban cigar (another link to that businessman at the airport), Milton complains about economic uncertainty and
taxes. He is confident, however, that there will be a recovery. Wyler emphasizes Milton's large chest in the front of the frame as he squeezes Al between Milton and the wood-paneled wall.

That scene is preceded by Fred's return to Bullard's Drugstore, which
has been taken over by the Midway chain. Here, Wyler pictures the sleek
new bastion of American consumerism that seems to belie Milton's sour
evaluation of the economy. Wyler's deep-focus shots take in counters of

perfume, toys, and cosmetics. Hanging from the ceiling are countless signs advertising prices and sales, counterpointed by the din of cash registers, chatter, and children firing cap pistols. The manager, Mr. Thorpe, looks down on the store from a windowed office above the ruckus; he tells Fred that his experience as a pilot does not qualify him for a job. Sherwood pointedly uses modern business lingo, having Thorpe ask Fred whether, during the war, he had any experience in "procurement."

The drugstore scene visually parallels various scenes involving Fred, Peggy, Al, and Milly in nightclubs, which are also crowded—as if the modern world, let alone Wyler's frame, cannot contain all the people. It is small wonder that the returning veterans cannot fit in: there is barely room for anyone else. As the drugstore's assistant manager (who once worked under Fred), comments, "Nobody's job is safe with all these servicemen crowding in." Fred, like so many veterans, is now seen as an inconvenience, and an unqualified one at that.

Al gets in trouble for approving a loan to a veteran who wants to buy a farm but lacks collateral. At a banquet to honor his military service, Al gets drunk because of his growing dissatisfaction with the bank's insensitive policies and, in his acceptance speech, bitterly and sarcastically insists that the bank is "alive, generous, and human" and that its loan policies are a sign of belief in "the future of this country." Wyler films Al at the front of a banquet table from a medium-far distance. He seems alone and isolated, as what he is about to say will require courage; here, his frankness is abetted by alcohol, which lends the scene a comic touch. His speech is a somewhat toned-down version of an earlier rendition by Sherwood that made Al sound more like Tom Joad: "Am I my brother's keeper? Who is my brother? I'll tell you who he is. He is anyone who is sick—anyone who is broke—anyone who is in danger. You all remember about the Good Samaritan?"[22]

As if to support Al's endorsement of the bank, Wyler cuts to a high-angle shot of a crowded dance floor at a nightclub where Peggy and her date have joined Fred and Marie for a night out. Peggy has arranged this get-together because she is in love with Fred and wants to find out if he still loves his wife. In a scene in front of a mirror in the ladies' room, Marie drools over money and encourages Peggy to marry Woody (her date) because he is rich—she claims that love will come if a man has money. Wyler films the women along with their reflections—Marie wearing black, and

Peggy in white. Marie is loud and crass, Peggy demure and ladylike. Wyler wrote of the two women's allegorical significance: "Marie . . . stands for the kind of fellow Fred Derry was, prior to his going into the Armed Forces. Ignorant, insular, and selfish. . . . On the other hand, Peggy . . . is knowing, aware of the larger world about her, interested in problems beyond her own."[23] Wyler emphasizes this contrast visually. At first, we see and hear Marie, who is filmed in front of the mirror along with her reflection. All we see of Peggy is her reflection as she begins to grasp the degree of Marie's selfishness and materialism. As Peggy listens, Marie turns toward her, and Wyler shows Peggy looking somber and solemn as she is reflected in the mirror. Caught with her in the frame is the image of the black restroom attendant—Peggy's worldview, apparently, takes in others. Peggy, less concerned than Marie about Fred's salary, has faith in his character and his ability to grow along with the nation.[24]

Homer's story is handled with delicacy and restraint. Having introduced Homer's proficiency with his prostheses early in the film, Wyler relegates this subject—potentially charged with emotion—to only a secondary concern in Homer's relationship with Wilma. Harold Russell, who was expert in the use of his hooks, delivers a believable and affecting performance, contributing greatly to the effectiveness of Homer's story. Homer never feels sorry for himself, and neither does the audience. Homer, however, has a hard time dealing with his family; they all try entirely too hard to please him and pretend that he does not have a disability. Wyler's depiction of Homer's first night at home, when the Parrishes entertain Wilma's family and serve lemonade, neatly illustrates the director's handling of domestic scenes. As Wilma's father speaks about the poor economy, Wyler centers Homer in a tight frame, as if he is on display; with the exception of a few brief cuts to other family members, he maintains this basic composition throughout the scene. While Homer answers banal questions and everyone tries to make him feel comfortable, Wyler's tight framing emphasizes the feeling of being hemmed in by both families. When Homer finally escapes to Butch's bar, the audience experiences his relief as well.

Wyler handles Homer's difficulties with his hooks in two bedroom scenes, both combining disability issues with domestic ones. In the first scene, as Homer's father helps him undress for bed, the emphasis is placed on Homer's dependence and helplessness. Throughout this scene, Wyler focuses on Homer's face; we do not see what the father does or the actual removal of the hooks. Homer's brooding, serious expression recalls both the long close-up on the plane and the cut to his face when Wilma first hugs him. Later in the film, Homer asks Wilma to come to his bedroom and watch him get ready for bed. That scene was crucial because, as Wyler explained, "We wanted to have a scene in which Homer tells Wilma the reason he has been avoiding her is not that he doesn't love her, but that he doesn't feel it fair to her to marry her." The difficulty in doing a bedroom scene was to avoid violating the Production Code. Wyler continued: "There were delicate problems in bringing a boy and a girl to a bedroom at night, with the boy getting into his pajama top, revealing his leather harness, which enables him to work his hooks, and finally taking the harness off. We solved the problems without the slightest suggestion of indelicacy, and without presenting Homer's hooks in a shocking or horrifying manner. As a matter of fact, we felt we could do quite the opposite and make it a moving and tender love scene."[25]

The scene is indeed tender and moving. The sequence begins with Homer walking home. He stops and looks toward Wilma's house and sees her through a window, her figure made a bit hazy by the white lace curtain. Wyler cuts again to Homer's face, emphasizing his realization that she is his "horizon," and the bedroom scene quickly follows this revelation. By the time this scene takes place, Homer has become more adept in getting himself ready for bed. Wyler films much of the scene in a medium two-shot as Homer demonstrates the process of taking his hooks off and wiggling into his pajama top. The camera focuses closely on Wilma's reaction: she is unfazed by what she sees and declares her love for Homer. As she tucks him into bed, we see Wilma's picture by the lamp. Before Wilma's arrival, while Homer is alone in the room, Wyler films him looking at pictures of himself playing basketball and football in high school; now the focus is on Wilma. After she turns off the light and leaves, Wyler cuts to Homer's face again, this time in shadow, as a tear falls to his cheek. He has accepted Wilma's love and is ready to move on.

In many respects, Fred Derry is the film's central character. He is the first person the camera focuses on, and his story directly intersects the narratives of the other two. By the end of the film, it is clear that Fred will marry Al's daughter Peggy, and in the concluding scene, Fred is the best man at Homer's wedding. Before being drafted and going to war, Fred was a soda jerk at the drugstore, of an age to start thinking about choosing a career, getting married, and putting down roots. The war interrupted those plans, however, and in the speeded-up, hectic life of a conscripted soldier, Fred hastily married a cocktail waitress who looked like a Hollywood pin-up girl; she, in turn, fell for a man in uniform. After the war, it is apparent that they are unsuited for each other. Fred has matured; the attractions of a superficial blonde no longer interest him. It is clear that Marie has been unfaithful to him, and when Fred later finds her with another man, he asks her to leave. Marie's inability to love Fred once he is out of uniform symbolizes her inability to make the transition to a more adult and lasting relationship. Peggy Stephenson, in contrast, is the kind of woman who, Richard Griffith notes, Fred can reach only "after a long struggle."[26] Fred's story thus implies that one of the tragedies of war is the blighting of lives by the loss of all those years—"the best years"—and that one needs to rediscover and reclaim them, if possible.

Kantor's novel and earlier versions of the script gave Fred a more elaborate backstory, indicating that while in Europe, he had an affair with an English society woman. Part of Fred's maturation process was his exposure to European society, a rather heady experience for a boy from the wrong side of the tracks. Sherwood and Wyler eliminated this problematic history in order to make Fred a more wholesome character. In the film, he remains patient with Marie, even as it becomes increasingly clear that she does not love him. (It is left to Peggy's date in the nightclub scene to point out that Fred and Marie "can't stand each other.") Fred finally walks out only when he discovers her with another man.

The released film also spends less time on Fred's job search. Whereas earlier versions show his increasing frustration as he is turned down for a variety of jobs, the released film includes only a brief scene of Fred reading the want ads while on line at an unemployment office; any actual job hunting goes on behind the scenes. Instead, we are made aware of Marie's frustration over Fred's lack of money, and we learn that he finally settles on a job back at the drugstore for $32 a week.

In an earlier version, Fred—long after separating from Marie—tells Peggy that it is wrong of him to continue seeing her because he cannot give her the material comforts she has come to expect. His despair becomes apparent as he exclaims, "It's the lack of something in me—the feeling that I'm not going anywhere—that maybe it would have been better if I had gone down in flames over Berlin."[27] In a later draft, he is offered a job in Alaska but he must travel to Seattle to claim it. He decides to take the job and tells Peggy that he is leaving, but then he declares, "I don't care what the job is—or how long it lasts. I've shot the best years of my life already." Peggy is livid and calls Fred's remarks "disgusting." She replies, "If you had any sense—any guts—you'd know that the best years of our lives are still ahead of us." As she drives away, Fred's face "breaks into a broad, slow grin." He realizes that she loves him and decides to stay.[28]

Fred's story concludes with a sequence that was Wyler's invention. Sherwood's final script has Derry leaving town discouraged and defeated, unable to find a job, about to be divorced from his wife,[29] and having broken off his relationship with Peggy. He goes to the airport to hitch a ride on an army plane to anywhere. While waiting, he wanders over to an enormous military scrap heap composed of rows and rows of dismantled bombers. (Wyler discovered this evocative site in Ontario, California, and used it as the location for the scene.) Sherwood's script has Derry climb into an abandoned B-17 and then simply defaults to the director: "here Mr. Wyler will have to invent something cinematic."[30]

At first, Wyler was concerned about inventing something without Sherwood's assistance. He telegrammed the writer on June 6:

> I want to make one last effort to sell you the idea of coming here for a few days in order that you may see the film we have shot so far. I sincerely believe that you will agree that the picture creates a great amount of expectancy and that after seeing it you will have considerably less difficulty in writing something that will meet this expectancy. Naturally I will do everything I can with the scene in the B-17 but frankly I am terribly worried that the last part of the picture may be a let down. . . . Sorry to sound a little desperate but perhaps we here are not completely clear on all your ideas.[31]

Despite these qualms, Wyler eventually invented one of the film's best sequences:

> We did nothing in the interior of the B-17 except show Fred Derry seated and staring out through the dusty Plexiglas. Then we went

to a long exterior shot of the plane, in which we could see the engine nacelles, stripped of engines and propellers. We panned from
nacelle to nacelle, as though there really were engines in them, and
the engines were starting up for takeoff. Then we made another
long shot, on a dolly, and also head on. We started moving our
dolly in toward the nose of the B-17, through which we could see
Fred seated at the bombardier's post. This shot created the illusion of the plane coming toward the camera, as if for takeoff. To
these shots we planned to add sound effects of engines starting
and then let the musical score suggest flight. We then cut inside to
a shot of Fred's back, and as we moved in, we saw his hand reach
for the bomb release. We continued moving until we reached an
effective close-up of Fred, framed against the Plexiglas nose of the
bomber."[32]

To amplify the illusion that Fred is reliving his war experiences, Sherwood
wrote a scene in which Fred's father reads his son's citation for the Distinguished Flying Cross to Hortense, thus supplying Wyler with an ironic
counterpoint to Fred's current situation.

The filthy Plexiglas window also offers an ironic reminder of the three
soldiers looking out the window of the plane as they return home, with
views of rolling fields, sports stadiums, and highways. As Fred relives the
takeoff of the B-17, Wyler offers an extended close-up of his agonized,
sweating face, followed by a cut to the back of his head. We then see Fred
from the front, his eyes closed as if in reverie, through a fogged and filthy
window. It is one of the most beautiful and suggestive shots in the film. Wyler employs mirror shots liberally throughout, but here, Fred is almost cut
off from view, seemingly invisible to the country he has served.

Prior to this scene in the scrap heap, Fred returns home from looking
for a job and finds Marie entertaining another man. Before Fred arrives,
Wyler places Marie in front of a mirror as she tells her lover, Cliff, that her
husband cannot find work because he is not very bright. This dismissive attitude echoes her words to Peggy in the nightclub scene, where she is also
framed in a mirror, putting on makeup. When Fred arrives and confronts
Cliff, the two men are standing near a photograph of Fred in uniform with
Marie—again, as in the scene in Homer's bedroom, Wyler uses photos

from the past as markers of where his characters once were versus where they are now. As Cliff leaves, Wyler catches his back in the mirror—suggesting, perhaps, that Cliff's rehabilitation will consist of a series of affairs with women like Marie. Fred, however, will move on. Following his reverie in the hollowed airplane, he is offered a job as a laborer; the pay is low, but the job might lead to a future in the construction business. Fred's story is resolved not by his finding a good job but "by a change in his attitude to a realistic appraisal of himself in relation to the time in which he lives."[33]

The film concludes at the Parrish home, where Homer and Wilma are to be married. The setting promises a traditional happy ending, yet Wyler structures it to imply that the future for all his protagonists will be difficult, that their "rehabilitation" is not yet complete. The Parrish home is crowded and cramped, with barely enough space for the guests. Wyler's frame thus recalls the crowded nightclubs, the Midway drugstore, and the Parrish living room on Homer's first night home. When the three friends meet on the porch, we are reminded that Al continues to have a drinking problem, that the relationship between Fred and Al is strained, and that Fred has moved back in with his parents.

The wedding ceremony is famous for its deep-focus compositions. As the minister is reading the vows, the camera encompasses not only Homer and Wilma but also Fred, Milly, and Peggy. Milly's presence in this framing reminds us that the Stephensons' marriage may be entering a rough phase due to Al's drinking and his unhappiness at work. Peggy, of course, is still in love with Fred, who is standing up for Homer. At one point, Wyler departs radically from the expected two-character scenario: just as Wilma is repeating her vows, he cuts away from the couple to focus on Fred and Peggy; then, during the conclusion of the ceremony, he juxtaposes Homer, Wilma, and Fred with Peggy, who stands in the distance—thus dividing the audience's attention between the two couples. This inclusive framing persists through the moment when the bride and groom kiss: as family and friends gather around Homer and Wilma, Wyler keeps Fred and Peggy in the frame and then focuses exclusively on them as Fred indirectly declares his love and they kiss, as if they, too, are united in this marriage tableau.

The Best Years of Our Lives was Wyler's last film with Gregg Toland, and it remains one of the noted cinematographer's singular achievements. As always, the two worked closely together, and Wyler decided "to try for as much simple realism as possible." He went on to explain, "We had a clear-cut understanding that we would avoid glamour close-ups, and soft diffused backgrounds."[34] There were no abnormal camera angles, such as those Toland devised for Orson Welles, and, as Douglas Slocombe notes, "no forced perspectives."[35] Deep focus was utilized as a primary visual strategy, though it remained unobtrusive. According to Slocombe, "When a figure is placed near the camera and action simultaneously takes place in the background, it seems so natural to see both planes in focus, that one doesn't worry about it."[36]

It has become commonplace to cite one shot in the bar scene—also described by André Bazin in his famous essay on Wyler[37]—in which Toland captures action on three planes: in the foreground, Homer and Butch (Hoagy Carmichael) are playing "Chopsticks" on the piano; far in the background on screen left, Fred is in a phone booth, ending his relationship with Peggy; in the middle distance, but closer to screen right, Al watches Homer play piano and glances behind him to look at Fred. As Bazin points out, two separate actions are being presented simultaneously: the lesser action of Homer showing Al how he can play the piano, which occupies the foreground of the frame and dominates the soundtrack, and the more important action of Fred breaking up with Peggy in the background, which happens silently. The viewer, Bazin notes, takes the place of Al—thus experiencing the dramatic tension of having his attention divided between two fields of engagement. Michael Anderegg elaborates on this point by observing that Wyler, as he has for much of the film, is framing his three protagonists in the same frame, but now, instead of grouping them together, he places them on different planes, with "Fred in particular, isolated in the background."[38] This technique of spatial division within a single composition emphasizes the tensions that have developed between the characters.

Bazin makes two other important points in his essay. He notes that Wyler tries to eliminate any stylistic flourishes, thus prioritizing the dramatic structure and the acting. This restraint also allows Wyler to do one of the things he does best: allowing facial and body gestures full play in the scene. The realism of the acting in this film—most notably, that of Fredric March—is unmatched in any of Wyler's work. Wyler himself noted, "I can have action and reaction in the same shot without having to cut back and forth from individual cuts of characters. This makes for smooth continuity, an almost effortless flow of the scene, for much more interesting composition in each shot, and lets the spectator look from one to the other character at his own will, do his own cutting."[39] Bazin also differentiates between Toland's deep-focus work with Welles and with Wyler. Whereas Welles's deep-focus scenes are designed to "provoke and torture the audience," Wyler merely wants viewers to see everything there is and to choose what they want to focus on. "It's an act of dramatic loyalty toward the spectator, an attempt at dramatic honesty."[40]

The filming ended on August 9, after four months. Wyler had almost 400,000 feet of film, at a cost of $2.1 million. Shortly after shooting ended, editor Danny Mandell had a rough cut of around 16,000 feet (almost three hours) to show. The picture was previewed before an audience in Long Beach on October 17. They loved it, and Goldwyn was delighted with the film. He decided against further cuts, even though a picture of that length would be difficult to distribute.

Goldwyn initially wanted to release the film in 1947, but Wyler convinced him to move up the opening to qualify for that year's Academy Awards. It opened on November 21 at the Astor Theater in Times Square and on Christmas Day at the Beverly Theater in Beverly Hills. The New York Film Critics named it Best Movie of the Year on December 30, and in January it was nominated for eight Academy Awards, including Best Picture and Best Director. The Oscar ceremonies were broadcast nationally for the first time that year, and *The Best Years of Our Lives* won Samuel Goldwyn his first and only Academy Award. Wyler won for Best Director and received the statue from his friend Billy Wilder, who called *Best Years* "the best-directed film I've ever seen in my life." It also won awards for Fredric March, Harold Russell (who received a second special Oscar "for bringing hope and courage to his fellow veterans"), Robert Sherwood, Danny Mandell, and Hugo Friedhofer for his musical score.

Sadly, despite the film's enormous success, Wyler's professional association with Goldwyn—always fitful—was irreparably harmed when the producer reneged on his promise to finally grant him the screen credit "A William Wyler Production." *Best Years* was Wyler's first film for Goldwyn in which the director's name came last in the credits—a significant upgrade—but Wyler was angry and decided to end his association with Goldwyn. The situation got worse when Wyler discovered that Goldwyn had withheld royalties from him. He was reluctant to sue Goldwyn because he still retained a certain fondness for the man, but Wyler finally had no choice and took the producer to court in 1958, alleging that the net profits from the film from 1947 to 1951 had been understated by $2 million.

Goldwyn was also being attacked by the project's first writer, MacKinlay Kantor. After publicly praising the film and claiming pride in his association with it, Kantor did an about-face and complained to the press that Goldwyn had changed his title and many of the plot developments in his original story. Goldwyn lashed out against Kantor, noting that he had paid the writer $12,500 for a fifty-page treatment and declaring, "There's nothing wrong with Kantor that wouldn't drive a psychiatrist crazy." Goldwyn added that he had generously allowed Kantor to keep the publishing profits and concluded, "Kantor is a plain liar. I couldn't use his screenplay because it wasn't any good. As a matter of fact, the book was bad, too. You can quote me on that."[41]

As Wyler's suit against Goldwyn dragged on, he remained reluctant to be nasty to his former boss. In a letter to his lawyer, he cautioned, "Please avoid saying anything that sounds insulting to Goldwyn. . . . P.S. But since we *are* suing, let's *win!*"[42] By the time the suit was filed, *Best Years* had earned an additional $5 million. The two men finally settled out of court in 1962, when Wyler agreed to a payment of $80,000.

12

The American Scene I

The Heiress (1949)

One of Wyler's postwar ventures was an ambitious partnership with Frank Capra and Samuel Briskin (a former vice president in charge of production at RKO and Columbia) to run Liberty Films, an independent film company that would allow him to be his own boss. Capra announced the formation of the company in January 1945 and incorporated Liberty Films on April 10, with himself as president and major stockholder. Wyler joined the company in July.

Early on, Capra had asked Leo McCarey to participate in this venture, but McCarey, whose film *Going My Way* had won an Oscar in 1944, declined. At the same time, United Artists decided to pass on a deal to distribute Liberty's films—"a stark indication of how much Capra's status in Hollywood had eroded during his wartime absence from commercial production."[1] Needing another important director to strengthen his bargaining power with distributors, Capra offered a partnership to Wyler, who was also unsure of his future. This deal offered Wyler the opportunity he wanted—to be free of Goldwyn. Wyler told Axel Madsen, "I guess he believed I'd never leave him; he had sort of a father complex. . . . He offered his projects to me first, but I was engaged elsewhere and I didn't want to go back to the old Goldwyn days."[2]

Capra insisted on keeping a controlling interest but was "willing to offer his potential partner an equal voice in major company decisions such as story purchases and casting; creative autonomy during production, as long as the film remained within its budget; control of postproduction; and possessive credit" (that is, the director's name above the title—a distinction Goldwyn had never given Wyler).[3] Once Wyler became part of the group, Capra was able to reach an agreement with RKO to release nine films. He was also busily recruiting other directors. He was turned down by John

Huston, and George Stevens put him off until he returned home from the war. When Stevens finally decided to join, on New Year's Day 1946, the partnership was complete. With Stevens on board, RKO modified its agreement to require three films from each director and stipulated that each of the Liberty Films partners would fulfill this obligation by 1951.

In an interview for *Film Daily* in 1946, Wyler capitalized on his new freedom, urging a freer hand for directors. He asserted that it was contrary to a director's interests to capitulate to studio demands by accepting weak scripts. This kind of arrangement does "the industry no good, and it only dries up whatever creative talent the director possesses."[4] Because Wyler was still completing *Best Years* for Goldwyn, the early trade ads for Liberty Films did not announce any projects for him, but they did trumpet forthcoming films from Capra (*It's a Wonderful Life*) and Stevens (*One Big Happy Family*). They also announced that Capra would direct *No Other Man*, from the novel by Alfred Noyes, and *Friendly Persuasion*, from the novel by Jessamyn West—a project that would eventually be directed by Wyler instead, and for another studio. Also advertised was an original romantic comedy directed by Stevens, tentatively titled "It Must Be Love."

In their promotional booklet, the partners stated the company's philosophy: "Described simply, the company comprises an experienced group of top-ranking picture makers banded together to give fullest advantage of unified production facilities and executive management, at the same time permitting each individual complete freedom to pursue his own creative bent and retain his artistic integrity, to the end of more worthwhile entertainment."[5]

While Wyler's *Best Years* was enjoying enormous success (for Goldwyn), Capra's *It's a Wonderful Life* went $1 million over budget and ended up costing close to $4 million. It also struggled at the box office, eventually losing more than $400,000. RKO rushed it into release to qualify for the Academy Awards, and although it received five nominations, including Best Picture and Best Director, it lost to Wyler's runaway favorite. *Best Years* was the top-grossing film of 1946, with rentals of $11.3 million—a figure surpassed at the time only by *Gone with the Wind*.

Only a month into the release of *It's a Wonderful Life*, Capra started talking about unloading Liberty Films. The main problem was cash flow. With his film looking like a box-office flop, and Wyler and Stevens not yet engaged in their initial projects, Capra felt he had to act quickly to mini-mize their losses. He thought it would be wise to sell the company and sal-vage whatever assets they could. Capra was also tired of being independent. In 1971 he told Richard Schickel, "It was the most gentlemanly way of go-ing broke, and the fastest way, anybody ever thought of. We didn't have enough capital, so we decided to sell Liberty Films, which was a very, very, hopeless thing to do."[6] Wyler was willing to stick with Liberty, but he knew this was Capra's decision. Stevens objected to such a precipitous decision until he learned that another independent company he had been consider-ing was also for sale.

Paramount and MGM made offers for Liberty, which still owned the rights to *The Friendly Persuasion* and *No Other Man* and, even more im-portant, the services of the three directors. Paramount, which wanted to make "prestige" films, offered the four partners (including Briskin) a block of stock worth slightly more than $3 million. The deal was negotiated for Liberty by Jules Stein, the head of MCA, and a tentative agreement was reached with Paramount on April 14, 1947. The actual deal was closed on May 16. Wyler's share amounted to $750,000; he also agreed to make five films for Paramount at a flat fee of $150,000 per picture. Wyler told Mad-sen, "They assured us we would have the same independence as before, which didn't turn out to be true. We all had to have their approval of sub-ject and budget."[7]

Paramount's story department owned a variety of properties that Wyler considered interesting, including two of Theodore Dreiser's classic novels: *An American Tragedy* and *Sister Carrie*. Dreiser had wanted Sergei Eisen-stein to direct *An American Tragedy*, but Eisenstein abandoned the idea. A year later, in 1931, Adolph Zukor gave the project to Josef von Sternberg, whose film so angered Dreiser that he took Paramount to court—and lost. Stevens would eventually turn the novel into the Academy Award–winning *A Place in the Sun* (1951). In 1940, when Dreiser's reputation was at its na-dir, his agent managed to sell *Sister Carrie* to Paramount for $40,000, but no one could write a satisfactory screenplay. Wyler would eventually tackle it, but first he was considering *Twelve O'Clock High*, a story about the psychological pressures endured by American fliers during the war, which was being written by his former air force buddies Sy Bartlett and Beirne Lay. The studio turned down that idea. And later, while he was making

The Heiress, Wyler worked with Michael Wilson on a script for Thomas Wolfe's *Look Homeward, Angel*, but he was taken off that project as well. Wyler sent an angry memo to the studio: "This is the second time I wanted very much to make a picture and spent a great deal of time and energy on it, only to have the project turned down."[8]

While Wyler was nursing his wounds, he got a call from Olivia de Havilland. She had just returned from New York, where she had seen the play *The Heiress*. She felt the role of Catherine Sloper would be perfect for her, and she was certain she could help Wyler convince Paramount to buy the film rights. De Havilland was an independent-minded actress who liked to pick her own roles. After suing Warner Brothers to get out of her contract and winning a landmark suit in 1944, she had resumed her career at Paramount in 1946 and won an Oscar for *To Each His Own*. Now, Anatole Litvak, a friend of Wyler's, had just finished directing her in *The Snake Pit*, which was generating considerable buzz.

Wyler went to New York to see the play in January 1948, four months after it opened. Adapted by Ruth and Augustus Goetz from Henry James's novella *Washington Square*, *The Heiress* (earlier titles were "The Doctor's Daughter" and "Washington Square") was a hit on Broadway. The play was produced and directed by Jed Harris and starred Wendy Hiller as Catherine, Basil Rathbone as her father, and Peter Cookson as her suitor. (In London, the play was later staged by John Gielgud, with Peggy Ashcroft alternating in the title role with Wendy Hiller, and Ralph Richardson as the father.) The action is set in nineteenth-century New York City and centers on Catherine Sloper, the plain and socially awkward daughter of a prominent physician. When Catherine falls in love with the charming but questionable Morris Townsend, her domineering father threatens to disinherit her if she marries him. The power struggle that ensues teaches Catherine that her father does not truly love her, and neither does Morris. Wyler, who had already directed a period piece in *Jezebel*, was fascinated primarily by the psychological tensions and the struggle between family members, which links this film thematically with *The Little Foxes*.

After seeing the play, Wyler immediately contacted the playwrights' agent to arrange a meeting. Ruth Goetz recalled that event for Wyler's biographer, Jan Herman: "We came down from the country and met him at the Pierre Hotel. He wanted to know all about James's original story, and what

A reptilian fisherman (Walter Huston) comes between his mail-order bride (Helen Chandler) and his son (Kent Douglass), who wants to take her from him, in *A House Divided* (1931).

John Barrymore greets his "Yiddishe mama" (Clara Langsner) in
Counsellor-at-Law (1933).

The young members of a love triangle (Joel McCrea, Merle Oberon, Miriam Hopkins) gather around the patron who ruins them (Alma Kruger) in *These Three* (1936).

A similar triangular configuration in Wyler's remake of *The Children's Hour* (1961) features James Garner, Audrey Hepburn, Shirley MacLaine, and Fay Bainter (back to the camera).

Sam Dodsworth (Walter Huston) and his wife, Fran (Ruth Chatterton), are American innocents whose marriage breaks apart on a European vacation in *Dodsworth* (1936).

(*Above*) Wyler maximizes space with his use of depth-of-field shots on the set for *Dead End* (1937). (*Below*) A group shot from *Dead End* puts the characters on different planes, featuring "Baby Face" Martin (Humphrey Bogart) and the Dead End Kids.

(Above) Julie Marsden (Bette Davis), escorted by her fiancé, Preston Dillard (Henry Fonda), scandalizes southern society in her red dress in *Jezebel* (1938). *(Below)* Julie tries on a conventional white dress before rejecting it; Wyler traps her within the mirror's frame.

Heathcliff (Laurence Olivier) and Cathy (Merle Oberon) enjoy freedom in their natural habitat in *Wuthering Heights* (1939).

Judge Roy Bean (Walter Brennan), the sole patron at Lillie Langtry's concert, is surprised by his executioner and friend Cole Hardin (Gary Cooper) in a tightly framed "unwestern" space in *The Westerner* (1940).

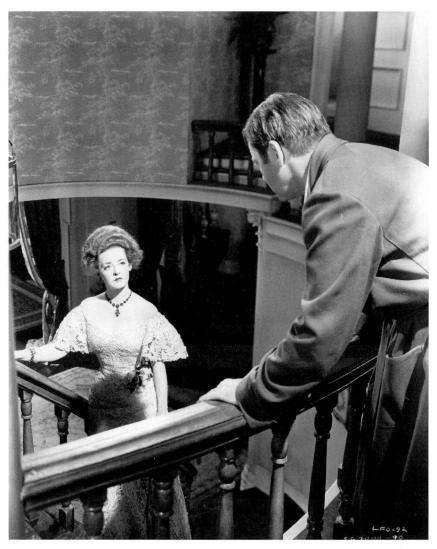

Horace Giddens (Herbert Marshall) thinks he has the upper hand in a confrontation with his wife, Regina (Bette Davis), in one of the many staircase scenes in *The Little Foxes* (1941).

Mrs. Miniver (Greer Garson) ministers to an injured Nazi pilot (Helmut Dantine) in *Mrs. Miniver* (1942).

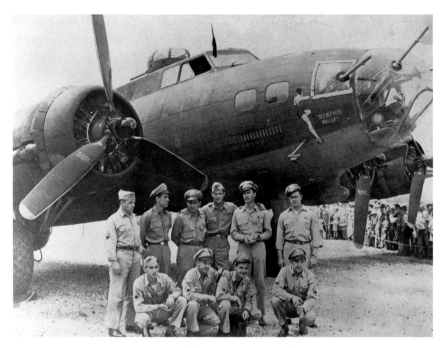

(*Above*) The crew of the *Memphis Belle*, with their fighter plane in the background, were the subject of Wyler's acclaimed 1944 documentary. (*Below*) Fred Derry (Dana Andrews), a decorated fighter pilot, is dwarfed by all the junked planes he surveys in *The Best Years of Our Lives* (1946).

Morris Townsend (Montgomery Clift) courts Catherine Sloper (Olivia de Havilland) at a dance in *The Heiress* (1949).

In one of Wyler's many elegant dinner scenes, Morris tries to convince Catherine's father (Ralph Richardson) that he will make a "suitable son-in-law."

Fascistic police detective James McLeod (Kirk Douglas) confronts an armed criminal (Joseph Wiseman) in Wyler's HUAC parable, *Detective Story* (1951).

Carrie (Jennifer Jones) attempts to return money to Hurstwood (Laurence Olivier) in *Carrie* (1952).

Another Wyler staircase shot built on multiple planes of action: this one features Mary Murphy, Martha Scott, and Humphrey Bogart in the foreground, with Fredric March at the top of the stairs, in *The Desperate Hours* (1955).

Josh Birdwell (Anthony Perkins) decides to go against his Quaker principles and defy his mother (Dorothy McGuire) by fighting in the Civil War in *Friendly Persuasion* (1956). His father (Gary Cooper) is pushed to the side of the frame.

Uncredited screenwriter Gore Vidal sought to inject a homoerotic element in the relationship between Messala (Stephen Boyd) and Judah Ben-Hur (Charlton Heston) in *Ben-Hur*.

Wyler's camera emphasizes the grandeur and scope of the chariot race
scene from *Ben-Hur* (1959).

A composition in depth evokes the creepy isolation of a victim (Samantha Eggar) and her victimizer (Terence Stamp) in a cave-like room in *The Collector* (1965).

(Above) A white southern policeman (Anthony Zerbe) beats his African American mistress (Lola Falana) in Wyler's uncompromising study of racism, *The Liberation of L. B. Jones* (1970). *(Below)* Wyler dines with leading lady Bette Davis circa 1937, when they were romantically involved during the filming of *Jezebel*.

A publicity shot of a young William Wyler.

we changed and what we had supplied. I'm always amused when people say we simply took everything from the original. It's not true. The James story doesn't have the jilt in it. We also found the key to the story: the cruel fact that Catherine is a child her father didn't love. It was brutal stuff, and nobody had put that in the theater before." Goetz remembered that they discussed the play for three hours, "and by the time we left him that day, we knew he wanted us. I thought he was first-rate."[9]

A few days later, Paramount made an offer that the Goetzes thought was too low; they wanted a percentage of the gross, which Paramount refused to consider. The studio eventually raised the offer to $250,000 for the rights and a salary of $10,000 per week to write the screenplay, and the playwrights accepted those terms. The film was to be shot entirely on the studio lot, but production head Barney Balaban, in an effort to ensure a high-quality production, approved a budget of $2.5 million. Now that Wyler was serving as his own producer, he hired his brother Robert and Lester Koenig as associate producers.

Wyler assembled a superb cast. In addition to de Havilland, he managed to lure Ralph Richardson to Hollywood—and was later delighted to discover that Richardson shared his affection for motorcycles. He also signed Miriam Hopkins (costar of *These Three*) for the role of Lavinia Penniman, Catherine's aunt. For Morris Townsend, who is portrayed as a rake in the stage version, Wyler initially wanted Errol Flynn, hoping to capitalize on that actor's reputation as a ladies' man—Flynn had famously costarred with de Havilland in *Robin Hood* and eight other films for Warner Brothers. But when he learned that Flynn had no interest in the role, Wyler was actually relieved because he had decided to soften the character by making his motives more ambiguous. He decided to cast Montgomery Clift, who was then enjoying critical acclaim for his debut film performance in Fred Zinnemann's *The Search* and had just completed *Red River* for Howard Hawks.[10]

When Augustus Goetz first met Clift, the actor was wearing a torn jacket, jeans, and a T-shirt. "He looked like a bum, and I thought, how could he ever play the suave, elegant Townsend?" But when Clift showed up in costume and makeup, Goetz was flabbergasted: "The transformation was startling. He was the most fashionable youth I ever saw."[11] Clift himself looked forward to meeting Wyler, whose films he admired, but was cowed by the director's reputation. Wyler recalled that on the first day of shooting, "Monty came to me on the set and said quietly, 'If you ever bawl me out, don't do it in front of the crew.'"[12] Wyler assured the actor that he would not, although he would later be livid about Clift's insistence on bringing his acting coach to the set and his need to consult with her regularly.

The actors did not get along well on the set. Clift especially did not like de Havilland and considered her an inferior actress: "She memorizes her lines at night and comes to work waiting for the director to tell her what to do. You can't get by with that in the theater; and you don't have to in the movies. Her performance is being totally shaped by Wyler." He also felt that Hopkins was stealing scenes and Wyler was doing nothing to stop her. As for Richardson, Clift was intimidated by him. "Can't that man make any mistakes?" he groaned after Richardson repeated a take for the thirtieth time in the same polished manner.[13]

Clift was right about Wyler's attention to de Havilland. Ruth Goetz remembered: "She got a lot of attention from Willy because he knew she didn't really have the ass to swing it. She was no heavyweight. Tola [Anatole Litvak] had gotten a good performance out of her in *The Snake Pit*. That was really her only serious picture. Willy believed he could get a good performance too, if he kept at her."[14]

It may seem unusual for a prominent director to follow a film that tackles contemporary problems with a period piece set in the mid-nineteenth century. Such eclecticism certainly contributes to Wyler's reputation as a craftsman in the service of the project rather than an auteur forging his own vision. This impression is strengthened by the fact that, after moving to Paramount, Wyler was also his own producer and had some control over which projects he chose. Wyler admitted that he preferred adaptations of successful plays because they offered excellent stories and scripts and had built-in name recognition: "If you have a successful play, you have a lot to work with already. You know that you have an audience for it. If it is a well constructed play, you have a beginning, middle and an end."[15]

This rationale is an oversimplification, however, because it belies Wyler's attraction to certain kinds of material. *The Heiress* shares the tightly structured melodramatic plot in *Counsellor-at-Law*, *These Three*, *Dead End*, and *The Little Foxes*. Like the Hellman plays, *The Heiress* deals with revenge and presents a heroine who learns that she must adapt to a man's world by becoming a cold and calculating person, as she discovers both her father and her fiancé to be. One of Wyler's frustrations with *The Little Foxes* was that he wanted Regina to be a warmer, more sympathetic, and more rounded figure, but Bette Davis refused to soften the character. As his own producer, however, he could give different shadings to his characters, making the two male protagonists, Dr. Sloper and Morris Townsend, more compassionate and ambivalent than they were in either James's novel or the Goetzes' play. And in fashioning his heroine, he was able to portray the evolution of her sensibility in a male-dominated social system with a precision he had been unable to achieve in *The Little Foxes*.

The film also reflects the grim postwar mood Wyler so carefully articulates in *Best Years*. Though Catherine Sloper cannot be strictly classified as a noir heroine, her personal trajectory is most decidedly tinged by that genre. In many postwar noir films, the protagonists return from the war to find their wives or sweethearts dead or unfaithful, and society as a whole is presented as dark and corrupt. In *The Heiress*, Catherine goes from believing in her patriarchal social world to rejecting it outright. The film's final images of Catherine closing herself off from her world—recalling Lavinia Mannon's locking herself up in her family's house at the end of Eugene O'Neill's *Mourning Becomes Electra*—are among the darkest in all of Wyler's work.

Wyler's film is a more faithful realization of the Goetzes' play than of James's novel. In adapting the book for the stage, the playwrights made some fundamental decisions about emphasis and character development—indeed, they note in the published version of the play that their work is "suggested" by James's novel, a clear sign that they have taken liberties. (This partial disclaimer is repeated in the film's credits as well.)[16] James uses an omniscient narrator to tell the story of Catherine's courtship by Morris and her relationship with her father. This detached, ironic voice offers the reader multiple perspectives in measuring the heroine's sensibility and her maturation. The narrator gives almost equal weight to Catherine's growth and Dr. Sloper's views of human behavior and society. James, writing amid the fallout from the American Civil War, was examining the conflict between the primacy of reason, as embodied in Dr. Sloper's rigid philosophy, and a democratic society that values practical choice. Although the democratic lifestyle can be messy and murky, the potential that exists in democratic choice can be exhilarating. In forging a middle ground between her father's and her suitor's attempts to victimize her, the novel's Catherine achieves a muted triumph. She moves from a limited understanding of society to a more mature one, a shift not seen in any of the other important characters in the story.

In adapting Catherine's story, however, the dramatists shift from an emphasis on psychological complexity and consciousness—a focus on how others see and interpret Catherine—to a sympathetic study of her transformation into a woman who is finally able to challenge her father and her fiancé. In the novel, Catherine is a private person who hides her feelings; her most observable trait is her passivity. In presenting her as a dramatic heroine, however, both the play and the film have to demonstrate more forcefully how Dr. Sloper's ironic wit and cruelty affect his daughter and force her to change. In doing so, the dramatists of both stage and screen convert the narrative irony of James's story into a melodrama of revenge in which a mistreated heroine dispenses justice to those who have hurt her.

Both play and film also focus attention on the power of money, as Catherine becomes a pawn in the conflict between emotional and economic realities. The title change accentuates Catherine's status as the potential beneficiary of a considerable income ($30,000 a year). Her position as a financial commodity is commented on by her father and her two aunts, and it looms as the one asset that Morris prizes above all else. On another level, however, both dramatic versions also explore the extent to which Catherine is heir to her father's cold, incisive intelligence and icy heart. This aspect of her personality becomes apparent when she turns the tables on him in the second half of the play.

The Goetzes had to impose some important alterations in plot development and structure to make the story effective as drama. The first, as mentioned earlier, was to sharpen the conflict between Catherine and her father. Also, because of Wyler's insistence that Morris's motivations be more ambiguous (necessitated in part by the casting of Montgomery Clift), the Goetzes' created two effective scenes that diverge significantly from James's text. In the novel, Morris breaks off the engagement in a fumbling, awkward way by alluding to his plans in a conversation with Catherine and then following up with a letter that formally ends their relationship. In the play and the film, however, the couple plan to elope on the night Catherine returns from Europe with her father, but Morris fails to show up. The dramatic effects on Catherine are considerable: she understands that Morris, like her father, does not love her. Her final illusion that she is worth loving has been destroyed.

In the second inserted scene, which ends both the play and the film, the story comes full circle as Catherine gets her revenge. Whereas the couple's final meeting in the novel is a subdued scene in which Catherine calmly explains to Morris that she has no desire to marry him, the dramatic versions show Morris coming back some years later and asking Catherine—a wealthy woman, since her father's death—to elope with him at last. She seems to agree, but when he returns to pick her up, she bolts the door against him and ignores his repeated knocking.

The effectiveness of this second invented scene is related to another crucial alteration made by the Goetzes. James's novel takes place over twenty years, while the film's time frame is roughly three or four years. Thus, when the film's Morris returns from California, he is still young, and his appearance has not radically changed. (Clift now sports a mustache but still looks very much the same as he did at the beginning of the film.) Her suitor's relatively youthful appearance heightens the dramatic impact of Catherine's decision to reject and humiliate him. In contrast, the novel's Morris is in his mid-forties, and Catherine has become an "admirable old maid" who takes little satisfaction in rejecting him two decades after their original breakup.

The most significant difference between Wyler's film and the novel, as mentioned earlier, is that Catherine not only recognizes her father's contempt, Morris's hypocrisy, and her aunt's complicity but also acts on that knowledge with savage force, playing out her revenge against all concerned. Catherine's metamorphosis also affects the emotional balance of the story—as she grows harder and colder, some of the audience's sympathy shifts toward Dr. Sloper and Morris. In gradually acquiring the strength and purpose to stand up for herself, Catherine becomes more like those she now despises, and this evolution mitigates her eventual triumph.

In this sense, Catherine Sloper's "triumph" is more ambiguous than that of Regina Giddens in *The Little Foxes*, who prevails in a man's world by outfoxing her brothers, who are as venal and duplicitous as she is. Regina, however, is surrounded by sympathetic characters. She is responsible for the death of her husband, Horace, who is presented as a humanist, unalterably opposed to the plan of his wife and her brothers to strangle the community for profit; she alienates her daughter, Alexandra, and her sister-in-law as well. At the end, Wyler's camera captures Regina alone, framed in one of his characteristic shots by a window, looking down at Alexandra and her fiancé as they leave her behind. In *The Heiress*, however, despite being awkward and dull, Catherine is presented as authentic and kind, a devoted daughter and niece. Her virtues stand out in contrast to the grasping, limited people around her, whose main concern is money. By then having Catherine become more like them, Wyler leaves us in a dark and unattractive world.[17]

Wyler's technique and mise-en-scène again concentrate on the characters' relationships and the shifting moods of the story. The film opens with a close-up on Catherine's embroidery frame, which depicts various views of the front of her home on Washington Square; these views then dissolve into an outdoor scene showing the home and the street re-created to look like New York in the 1850s. In contrast, the Goetzes' script dated June 7, 1948, opens with a series of lithographs depicting New York in the 1850s.[18] While this strategy communicates similar information about the era and setting of the story, the use of the heroine's embroidery is more effective; it immediately emphasizes the opposition between Catherine's "art" and the reality of street life, thus anticipating the film's concluding scene when she shuts herself up in her house, renouncing participation in the world around her. The opening credit sequence also indicates that the film is concerned with the characters' relationships within the confines of the home (the focus of most of Wyler's play adaptations), not their engagement with the wider world outside.

In an interview to promote the film, Wyler defended his philosophy of using space with integrity and intelligence: "Just because movies move, some people think they have to move all the time. A love scene, for instance, that would normally be played in a drawing room is played in a moving carriage or at the racetracks, merely to keep things in motion. But when you wrench a scene from its appropriate setting, you only succeed in distracting the audience."[19] Most of the film takes place in various rooms of the house—with one notable exception and two minor ones. One central scene takes place at a dance at the home of Catherine's cousin, where she meets Morris. The other two are brief: a scene in a Paris café during Catherine's unhappy European trip with her father, and a later one in the park outside her house, when she refuses to go to her father's deathbed.

Catherine is introduced as she hurries down the stairs toward a servant who is coming up with a package that has just been delivered, containing the dress Catherine is to wear to the dance. She is briefly seen in a mirror in a shot that captures her predicament—not only anticipating her fate, like the opening shots of the embroidery, but also revealing her subordinate position in the household. The impression of entrapment is reinforced when she is caught in the frame of her father's office window as she continues her descent; he occupies the front of the frame, giving orders to another household servant. The stairs function (as they do in *Jezebel* and *The Little Foxes*) as locations for power and dominance; mirrors and window frames (as usual in Wyler's films) are their opposite, outlining images of restriction and powerlessness. Catherine is next seen buying fish from a fishmonger to make her father one of his favorite dishes, but Dr. Sloper's dismissive response is that, next time, she should "let the man carry it for you."

The dance itself has no equivalent in the play (there, Morris meets Catherine while visiting the Slopers with his cousin). The festive scene is visually interesting, and it serves to extend the pacing and rhythm of the play, where the young couple seem to fall in love all too quickly. The film's tempo is more effective, as it makes their courtship seem lengthier and more realistic. Morris's introduction is dramatic, initiating Wyler's visual strategy of situating the young man in the frame to suggest his aggressive intentions. Catherine sees him before we do, and her face reflects the intensity of her reaction. Before his face appears, he is shown from the back as he walks across the frame, momentarily blocking our view of Catherine and her aunt. Morris then takes the place of Aunt Penniman beside Catherine, sharing her screen space as he, too, attempts to dominate her. During the dance, Wyler films them both in medium two-shots; they seem to be the only two people at the party, and Catherine appears happy and relaxed. This effect contrasts strongly to her first scene with her father, when she models her new party dress for him. There, the composition is formal and strained, emphasizing the considerable space between them, with Aunt Penniman in the middle.

In the following scene, as Morris comes courting at the Sloper home for the third time that week, Wyler's framing is similar, but with subtle differences. Morris arrives to find that Catherine is not home, so he must pass the time with Aunt Penniman. When Catherine comes in, he immediately goes to the hallway to greet her, and once they are alone in the drawing room, he moves in very close to her. Catherine tries to walk away from him—even bending backward to reduce their proximity—but Morris persists in invading her space. At one point, she manages to move into a separate frame, but Morris soon occupies that as well. Then, as he walks to the piano to play the French love song he learned in Paris, Wyler suddenly emphasizes the space between them. Morris sits at the piano while Catherine sits at a distance, allowing the viewer to take in the beauty and elegance of the rooms. As Morris plays and sings, "The joy of love lasts but a short time but the pain of love lasts your whole life," Wyler cuts between them for the first time with shot–reverse shot sequences. On that line, the camera lingers on Catherine's face.

Wyler also places significant objects in his composed shots. After Morris proposes and then leaves, Catherine is shown framed by the doorway and reflected again in a mirror, along with a lighted lamp that will be used in subsequent scenes. When she informs her father of her engagement, he moves toward a similar lamp to get a cigar. We then see Catherine happily ascending the stairs with the same joy and alacrity she showed when descending them at the beginning of the film. This time, however, her shadow and the shadows from the stairwell reflect ominously on the wall behind her. This hint of foreboding is followed by a wide-angled shot of Dr. Sloper's face—in the front of the frame and lined up with Catherine's latest embroidery—looking worn and concerned.

With Montgomery Clift playing Morris, Wyler accomplishes one of his most dramatic shifts from James's—as well as the Goetzes'—version of the story. In the novel, there is no doubt that Dr. Sloper is right about Catherine's suitor, but when Mrs. Montgomery (Morris's sister) warns the doctor, "Don't let her marry him," Sloper's satisfaction in being right is mitigated by James's suggestion that Sloper's rightness is not always a good thing. In the play, Mrs. Montgomery does not state her opposition so baldly, but she insinuates it by saying, "If you are opposed to the marriage, then as a father you must find a kinder way of stopping it." Mrs. Montgomery also indicates that she is more concerned about protecting Catherine than Morris. The playwrights even provide a scene between Morris and Aunt

Penniman—it was cut for the film—where he admits his fear that Catherine will be disinherited and states his dissatisfaction at being guaranteed only $10,000 a year: "On ten, ma'am, you live like your neighbor. . . . But thirty is something to look forward to."[20] In the film, the tenor of Dr. Sloper's interview with Mrs. Montgomery is less ominous. She refuses to censure her brother, and when pushed to say something negative about him, she merely says, "I have to go." Then, as Dr. Sloper sees her to the door, Wyler catches him in the mirror—the only time in the film—implying his own judgment of Catherine's father.

Wyler enforces the ambiguity of Morris's character by invariably letting him share the frame with others. Only in Morris's strained scenes with Dr. Sloper does the director occasionally resort to the shot–reverse shot. Clift portrays Morris as a likable, charming character, and his very contemporary (and very American) style of acting effectively clashes with Richardson's more classical English style, which makes Morris's American "innocence" seem vulnerable and ingratiating. His evident charm also makes Catherine seem less foolish than she does in either the novel or the play. There is a moment at the end of the party sequence when, as Morris bids good night to Catherine, Wyler's camera stays on the young man in a medium close-up. He looks handsome and hopeful, but Wyler invests the shot with an undertone of mystery and ambiguity by lingering on him so long. This element of mystery endures until the sequence that ends the first part of the film.

Morris's jilting of Catherine is one of the high points of the film both dramatically and stylistically, again demonstrating Wyler's ability to convert a well-developed and structured scene from the stage into a great moment on film. Prior to that sequence, Morris and Catherine meet in the rain (always an ominous sign in a Wyler film) to discuss their elopement. The scene concludes with Catherine telling Morris that they should not expect anything from her father and that she wants nothing from him. Back at home, her departure scene begins as Catherine carries her bags down the stairs, along with a lighted lamp. She is dressed in black, and the room is in shadows. Despite the funereal atmosphere, Catherine is excited—she opens a window, letting in the air and looking out expectantly. Obviously, she feels free—she is about to start a new life.

Next, the lighting seems to change for a moment, and Catherine sits by the round lamp, checking her bag. Reflected in the mirror next to her, the shadows on the stairway undulate as her aunt descends—the sequence looks like something out of a horror film. Aunt Penniman is dressed in light-colored nightclothes, which contrast with Catherine's black coat. Catherine explains to her aunt that she is eloping, and they wait for Morris together. She then informs her aunt of her estrangement from her father, declaring that she will never see him again. When Aunt Penniman asks if she has told Morris that she will be disinherited, Catherine says yes. Her aunt replies, "Oh, you didn't! You shouldn't!" At that moment, they hear the sound of a carriage and Catherine rushes out, framed by the doorway, but it isn't Morris.

Wyler stages the next sequence formally, emphasizing its pictorial and geometric style. Catherine is seen in profile, seated by a column in the sitting room and parallel to her aunt, who is seated near the lamp by the window. Catherine, though anticipating her wedding, is dressed in black, like a widow; her aunt is in white. The color reversal highlights Catherine's betrayal. Both women sit still, a shadow between them. When Catherine finally asks why she shouldn't have told Morris about the money, Aunt Penniman replies, "Oh, dear girl, why were you not a little more clever?" Her aunt's words imply what Catherine must now recognize—that the male-dominated social world is governed by money and power. Aunt Penniman herself has learned to survive in the constricted space she inhabits—after all, she lives in the house at her brother's invitation. Catherine protests that Morris still could have expected $10,000 a year, exclaiming, "It is a great deal of money!" But her aunt replies, "Not when one has expected thirty." The mise-en-scène of the two women sitting in similar positions unites them. Having learned her painful lesson, Catherine starts to cry, and her aunt closes the doors, as if shielding her from the audience. There is a cut as the camera surveys the hallway, then Catherine emerges with her suitcases. Wyler's camera follows her as she trudges wearily up the stairs, bearing the burdens of her luggage and her new knowledge.

The final half hour of the film reverses the positions of Catherine and her father. Shortly after we see Catherine ascending the stairs, Wyler cuts to Dr. Sloper descending the stairs in the morning. He is clearly weak, his steps uncertain. This is the first time in the film that Dr. Sloper is shown on the staircase, his downward progress symbolizing his loss of power. There is a cut to Catherine embroidering—according to her father, it is her only talent—and again she is reflected in a mirror in profile. The camera holds this shot longer than usual: Catherine's face is grim and determined, and the static framing suggests that she may be stronger than her father now, but rather than liberating her, this newly acquired knowledge and power have imprisoned her. When Aunt Penniman comes in, she has now assumed the black cloak that Catherine was wearing the night before.

The following scene opens with Dr. Sloper in his study, performing a self-examination. The room, in contrast to its appearance in the first part of the film, is now dark, and the curtains are drawn. Apparently having determined that he will die soon, the doctor gives Maria, the house keeper, and Catherine instructions to prepare his sick room, whereupon Maria begins to cry, but Catherine shows no emotion. Dr. Sloper then learns from Catherine that she will not be leaving home after all. This scene takes place in front of a lighted window. Sloper hopes that Catherine has broken off the engagement, and she uses Morris's abandonment to turn the tables on her father, undercutting him with her words as effectively as he did her, earlier. She taunts him by exposing his contempt for her: "You have cheated me. You thought that any handsome, clever man would be as bored by me as you were. . . . It was not love that made you protect me. It was contempt." She goes on to say, "I don't know that Morris would have hurt me or starved me for affection more than you did."[21] When Catherine taunts him further, offering to help him rewrite his will when he threatens to change it, Wyler composes the scene by placing Sloper at the front of the frame, emphasizing his pain and grief. Catherine then moves to his side, repeating the two-shot pattern of her early scenes with Morris—only now, the framing emphasizes her cruelty. At this point, the audience's sympathy shifts to Dr. Sloper. Whereas in James's novel, Sloper takes satisfaction in being right about Morris's motives, Wyler's character takes no such pleasure, and the humiliation inflicted by his child feels unnecessarily cruel. He exits with dignity through the same doors that Aunt Penniman closed for Catherine, and we see him for the last time outlined by the door frame as he climbs the stairs toward his death.

The scene dealing with Dr. Sloper's death is Wyler's final sequence outside the house. The camera finds Catherine, in profile, seated on a park bench, looking stern. Maria emerges from the house, announcing that her

father is asking for her. Again in profile—the positioning recalls her place-
ment at her embroidery frame after she is jilted—Catherine tells Maria that
she will not see him. (In the novel, she tends to her father until he dies, and
there is no such scene in the play.) In the film, Catherine's refusal to react
to her father's impending death recalls Regina's coldhearted forbearance in
The Little Foxes, when she lets Horace die as he tries to climb the stairs to
get his medicine. In that scene, Wyler focuses on Regina's determined and
emotionless face. Here, in another deep-focus sequence, Catherine remains
seated on the bench while, in the rear of the frame, Maria turns from the
doorway of the house to see if her mistress has changed her mind. Catherine sits, unmoved.

Her final meeting with Morris begins with the estranged couple facing each other in profile, much like the early scenes between daughter and
father. When Catherine finally invites Morris to sit, he faces her while she
looks steadily toward the camera, working at her embroidery. Unlike in
the early scenes of his courtship, Morris now finds himself unable to penetrate her space. Nonetheless, Catherine agrees to marry him that night, and
Morris leaves to pack. Closing the curtains and returning to her embroidery, Catherine remarks to her aunt, her voice dripping with hatred: "He's
grown greedier with the years. The first time he only wanted my money,
now he wants my love too." Later, when Morris calls for her, Catherine
is shown again in profile, surrounded by her embroidery frame and the
round, lighted lamp. She instructs Maria to bolt the door, and at the sound
of the bolt being drawn, Catherine cuts the thread on her embroidery, signaling that she is finished. Again in profile, she picks up the lamp and ascends the stairs as Morris pounds on the door, calling her name. Catherine
is now wearing white, as if signaling that, by cutting herself off from her
lone suitor, she is finally wed to a life divorced from everyone.

The Heiress opened at Radio City Music Hall after Paramount ran
a series of high-toned ads celebrating Wyler and the film—one ad trum-
peting, "The Greatness of 'The Heiress' Is the Paramount Achievement of
William Wyler." The film did well in New York and received excellent reviews. Bosley Crowther of the *New York Times* commented, "Not many
film producers are able to do the sort of thing that William Wyler has done
with 'The Heiress,' the mordant stage play of two seasons back. For Mr.
Wyler has taken this drama, which is essentially of the drawing-room and

particularly of an era of stilted manners and rigid attitudes, and has made it into a motion picture that crackles with allusive life and fire in its tender and agonized telling of an extraordinary characterful tale."[22] The film later had another prestige opening at the Carthay Circle Theatre in Hollywood.

Outside of New York, however, the film did not do so well, although it eventually earned a profit. Wyler was disappointed. He told *Variety*, "I expected it to make a lot of money. It cost too much. It should have been done cheaper. But then it wouldn't have been the same picture. As it was, I didn't go over the estimated budget by more than sixty to seventy thousand dollars."[23] Years later, Wyler reflected that perhaps he had made Morris too sympathetic: "He's got to be convincing to her or she looked like a fool. And he was so convincing that when it turned out that he was after her money it was such a disappointment. . . . That the audience was so disappointed, you know not getting a happy ending to this beautiful couple. . . . I went too far this way . . . I don't know what happened."[24] Still, *The Heiress* garnered eight Academy Award nominations, including for Best Picture and Best Director. It eventually received four Oscars: a Best Actress win for Olivia de Havilland (her second), one for Aaron Copland's score, and awards for costume design and art direction.

The Heiress ranks among Wyler's singular achievements, and it remains one of the best examples (along with *The Little Foxes*) of how to adapt a play to the screen. Like all his great work, this film shows off Wyler's ability to create "action" out of internal struggles and crises. In service to that aim, he masterfully orchestrates his actors within restricted space and skillfully utilizes mundane objects such as lamps, clothing, doors, and windows to great visual and symbolic effect. He creates powerful dramatic moments by means of formal staging and long, expressive takes, especially in the scene of Catherine's abandonment by Morris. Indeed, this sequence ranks among Wyler's highest achievements, along with the Olympus Ball in *Jezebel*, the death of Horace in *The Little Foxes*, Baby Face Martin's meeting with Francey in *Dead End*, and others in which rich dramatic tension is created through gestures, subtle acting moments, and careful attention to composition. *The Heiress* is a worthy successor to *The Best Years of Our Lives*—despite the differing eras and social strata portrayed, both films explore the dehumanizing effects of money on human relationships.

13

The American Scene II

Carrie (1952)

Carrie, Wyler's film of Theodore Dreiser's 1900 novel *Sister Carrie*, is in theme and outlook a logical successor to *The Heiress*. There is a moment early in Dreiser's novel when eighteen-year-old Carrie Meeber, a poor girl from a small town, is escorted to a posh Chicago restaurant by Charles Drouet, a salesman and "masher" she has met on the train. Carrie is dazzled by the selection of food, the clothing of the patrons, and the décor— much as Morris Townsend is overwhelmed by the Slopers' richly appointed Washington Square home. "She felt a little out of place but the great room soothed her and the view of the well-dressed throng outside seemed a splendid thing. Ah, what was it not to have money! What a thing it was to come here and dine!"[1] *Sister Carrie*, which was condemned and then almost suppressed by its publisher because its central characters defy conventional morality, appeared only twenty years after *Washington Square*. And though the worlds of James and Dreiser are far apart, both share an interest in their characters' preoccupation with money and position. Like Morris Townsend, Carrie Meeber is motivated by a powerful desire for security, money, and pleasure. Wyler was no doubt attracted to the property because, like many of his earlier projects, it focused on social problems that were still prevalent in American society.

Wyler first expressed interest in *Sister Carrie* in 1947, when he asked Lillian Hellman if she would be interested in writing a screenplay based on the novel. She was enthusiastic about undertaking the adaptation, but other projects intervened, and she began to lose interest. At one point, Robert Wyler suggested Julius and Phillip Epstein as possible screenwriters, and in 1949 Wyler asked for Hellman's help in interesting Arthur Miller in the project, but Miller was too busy with other work. Hellman also suggested Norman Mailer, whose first novel, *The Naked and the Dead*, had made him the newest literary sensation, but Wyler preferred to work with an older writer and a dramatist rather than a novelist.[2] Finally, he decided to rehire Ruth and Augustus Goetz—signing them up before *The Heiress* even opened—and he had a treatment in hand by the end of May 1949.

By the end of that year, Wyler was sufficiently satisfied with the script to begin looking for a cast. Hoping to engage Laurence Olivier to play Hurstwood, he cabled his brother Robert in London and had him deliver a copy of the script to the actor. Since starring in *Wuthering Heights* for Wyler in 1939, Olivier had become a considerable presence in films—his screen version of *Hamlet* won him an Oscar for Best Actor in 1948, as well as a Best Director nomination, and the film was named Best Picture. He had recently been named director of the St. James Theatre in London, where he was preparing to direct and star in Christopher Fry's *Venus Observed*. He cabled Wyler his regrets, citing his commitment to the play, which would be one of the hits of the London season. Wyler, however, refused to take no for an answer and offered to change his schedule to accommodate the actor. Paramount even had Dreiser's widow, Helen, write to Olivier, calling him "the greatest dramatic intellect of his time" and praising his film versions of *Henry V* and *Hamlet*.[3] When Vivien Leigh was offered the lead in *A Streetcar Named Desire*, Olivier, not wanting to be separated from his wife, accepted Wyler's offer to come to Hollywood. He was paid $125,000 for the role, and Paramount agreed to pay him an additional $1,000 a week to cover the costs of, among other things, a chauffeur, a car, and a maid.

For Carrie, Wyler wanted Elizabeth Taylor. She was eighteen—the right age for the role—and she possessed the arresting beauty that would justify the character's appeal. Taylor had just completed George Stevens's *A Place in the Sun* (an adaptation of Dreiser's *An American Tragedy*), opposite Montgomery Clift. Wyler asked Olivier to meet her and convince her to take the role. But MGM, which owned Taylor's contract, would not release her. While working on the script with the Goetzes in 1949, Wyler had sent a copy to David O. Selznick, seeking his input, and thereupon found himself inundated with memos, both before and after the film. Above all, Selznick wanted the role of Carrie for his wife, Jennifer Jones. He felt that playing opposite Olivier would enhance her prestige and that working with Wyler would enlarge her sense of craft. When he learned that Wyler had already offered the role to Taylor and that Paramount was then in negotiations with Ava Gardner, he fired off an angry memo to the director: "I must now ask you to consider that Jennifer is not available. . . . I do not wish further to demean [her] or her great standing as a star by what I am forced to regard as the type of double dealing which has made me so fed up with Hollywood."[4] Wyler apologized, assuring Selznick that no deal had been made with anyone. Selznick then reconsidered his position, and Jones was signed to star in *Carrie* by the end of June.

At first, Olivier was pleased to be working with Jones, but he soon grew impatient with her. In a letter to Vivien Leigh, he vented his frustrations: "No soul, like we always said about them, dumb animals with human brains."[5] Olivier, however, received Wyler's full attention. He made sure that his star was met in New York by the Goetzes, who gave him a tour of the Bowery so that Olivier could see how real derelicts lived, which the director thought would serve the actor well when they filmed the final scenes. Olivier was also concerned about having the right dialect and cabled Wyler from London: "Feel strongly my natural way of speaking quite wrong for Hurstwood who was probably born in Chicago. . . . Please be kind and line up a man you can trust to check my accent and intonations so I can feel in tune and happy about this."[6] Wyler secured him a coach, and Olivier also made use of Spencer Tracy, who was from the Midwest.

Olivier steeped himself in the role. Elia Kazan recalled "watching Larry go through the pantomime of offering a visitor a chair. He'd try it this way then that, looking at the guest, then at the chair, doing it with a host's flourish, doing it with a graceless gesture, then thrusting it brusquely forward—more like Hurstwood that way?"[7] When he came to the sequences in which Hurstwood is starving and begging for money, the actor starved himself. He wrote to Leigh, "I don't feel at all hungry—just as if I'm dying. It's very good for Hurstwood right now."[8]

Wyler had managed another casting coup when he signed Eddie Albert for his first dramatic role as Drouet. But early on, Wyler encountered a vexing problem with Ruth Warrick as Mrs. Hurstwood. He had chosen her over Geraldine Fitzgerald and Miriam Hopkins but was not happy with her performance. He fired Warrick after a few days and replaced her with Hopkins, who had just played Aunt Lavinia in *The Heiress*. Hopkins succeeded in embodying the cold, heartless Mrs. Hurstwood with the same expertise she had shown in playing the romantic, eccentric aunt in the earlier film.

Once shooting started, Wyler encountered a major problem with Jennifer Jones, who announced that she was pregnant—a fact that became more obvious as filming progressed. Wyler was irritated, but he tried not to show it. Although he attempted to talk her out of strapping herself into the corsets required for the period costumes, she insisted on wearing them. Jones eventually lost the baby, but her pregnancy was largely responsible for the many close-ups of her face in the film—which was unusual in Wyler's work and was noted by some critics.

Wyler knew that *Sister Carrie* had a troubled history in Hollywood. Joseph Breen, who enforced the film industry's Production Code, had rejected treatments of Dreiser's novel numerous times beginning in 1937, when Warner Brothers expressed interest in filming it, and a year later when Columbia Pictures sent him a film treatment. Breen considered Carrie an immoral woman who goes unpunished, and he found Hurstwood's suicide "morally objectionable" and "bad theatre."[9]

Wyler took on the Production Code, pronouncing it "old-fashioned." He also called for "men of courage" in Hollywood to take on significant material that had so far been avoided: "We need men of courage in high places who will not be intimidated and coerced into making only 'safe' pictures—pictures devoid of any ideas whatsoever. . . . The best pictures are made by thinking people who are vitally interested in politics or anything else that has public significance. Our people should be familiar with what is going on in the world unless all they want to make are fairy tales."[10] As filming of *Carrie* was about to begin, he told a reporter, "There will be censorship troubles, of course, but that's because of the terrible yardstick applied by the industry."[11] Dreiser's novel appealed to Wyler because of the director's own feelings about poverty and social justice and the novelist's compelling descriptions of poverty amid the flowering of big business and the triumph of capitalism.[12]

As indicated in a letter he wrote to the Goetzes,[13] both Wyler and his screenwriters were familiar with the adaptation of *Sister Carrie* that Clifford Odets had written for RKO in 1944. As he often did, Odets had reconceived Dreiser's story, establishing Carrie as a determined and ambitious woman in the first sequences. His script opens with the death of Carrie's mother, who is described as the family's breadwinner, while Mr. Meeber is presented as a shiftless, lazy man. (Odets's plays are full of strong mothers and weak fathers.) Before Carrie leaves for Chicago, her mother's former employer (a man of means) proposes marriage, but she refuses. Carrie seems determined to move to the city and make something of herself.

Odets also places more emphasis on Carrie's relationship with her sister's family and her courtship by Drouet. Most important, her interest in the theater is established early on, and Odets gives her an important speech in which she articulates her theory of a more realistic style of acting (Carrie as a forerunner of the Group Theatre?) than the heavily theatrical style she has observed at shows attended with Drouet. One of Odets's most audacious changes is transforming Moy, one of the owners of Fitzgerald and Moy's, the bar/restaurant that Hurstwood manages, into a central figure in the story. Here, he becomes Julia Hurstwood's father as well. Moy admires (and pities) his son-in-law and despises his daughter—in her, he sees the reincarnation of her cold and heartless mother. Nevertheless, he helps his daughter get out of her marriage when, after hiring a detective to follow Hurstwood, he learns of his son-in-law's evolving relationship with Carrie. Despite fulfilling his fatherly obligation to his daughter, Moy is generous to Hurstwood, whom he considers integral to his business and largely responsible for its success. After Hurstwood steals the money and runs off with Carrie, Moy allows him to pay it back in installments and later offers him a partnership in the business if he agrees to leave Carrie. Because Odets's Hurstwood is better at finding jobs than his counterpart in Wyler's film, his decline seems more precipitous. He decides to leave Carrie to allow her to realize her ambitions, which she does by becoming a successful actress. Odets's script ends with Hurstwood killing himself by running into a burning building while Carrie is being courted by Ames, a writer. His death is thus balanced by her success and a blossoming relationship with someone her own age.[14]

The Goetzes scrapped most of Odets's ideas and moved closer to the details of Dreiser's novel. What they retained, however, is the mutual devotion displayed by Hurstwood and Carrie. Odets understood that the film's characters needed to elicit the audience's sympathies in ways that the novel's did not. Dreiser's narrative is not really a love story, even though many of the events recounted resemble a tale of passion and romance. Carrie feels a certain affection for both Drouet and Hurstwood, but her heart never rules her self-interest. In fact, Dreiser's Carrie seems incompletely developed as a character. She simply falls under the sway of superhuman forces, while Hurstwood is the one who exhibits passion. When first introduced, he is at the summit of his career. Well liked and highly regarded, he socializes with the rich and powerful. He has everything to lose by becoming involved with Carrie, especially considering that she is drawn to his wealth and prestige and is not motivated by romance or love. Odets's characters are stronger and more determined, as well as warm and passionate. In his version, Carrie and Hurstwood risk a great deal for each other, and their love endures through the difficulties they experience.

The Goetzes' treatment contains summaries of many scenes that never made it into the final film.[15] In a letter to Wyler, the screenwriters acknowledge that the treatment is too long (at fifty-two pages), but they note that writing it was a valuable exercise: "From your point of view, this is probably far too long but from ours, it has turned out to be a very useful thing to have done. It has given us the basis for every dramatizable point in the continuity."[16] Their treatment spends some time developing Carrie's interest in the theater, and it includes Carrie's debut at an amateur theatrical production at the Elks' Lodge that is attended by Drouet and Hurstwood, a central scene in the novel. Virtually all these scenes were cut from the final script, however. Most important, the treatment devotes significant attention to Hurstwood's decline—including numerous scenes of his rejection for a variety of jobs, as well as his work as a strikebreaker—thus emphasizing his story at the expense of Carrie's.

This imbalance has also been noted in criticism of the novel, where Dreiser certainly depicts Hurstwood's fall in long, detailed sequences that underscore the contrasting fates of the two main characters. Both are struggling to survive in a precarious, materialistic world, and while Hurstwood fails to move ahead, Carrie remains focused on success. As good fortune continues to elude him in New York, Hurstwood increasingly looks back on his lost prosperity and his life in Chicago, now forfeited in the vain pursuit of love. His descent offers a lesson in the fate of a dreamer whose hopes have been destroyed—in this respect, Hurstwood's story is a more extreme version of Catherine Sloper's. In stark contrast, Carrie's story, both in Dreiser's novel and, to a lesser extent, in the Goetzes' treatment, provides an object lesson in success. Hers, however, is not the typical American success story, for Carrie triumphs despite her questionable virtue. There is no correlation in Dreiser's world between social morality and material success.

Wyler, who always supervised the evolution of his scripts, was concerned about the amount of attention focused on Hurstwood in the second half of the treatment. In a detailed letter to the Goetzes, he itemized his suggestions for tightening the dramatic structure: "In the second part of the story, after the marriage in New York [in this scene, Hurstwood marries Carrie under the assumed name Wheeler; it was cut from the film], there is a need for further dramatization. . . . There is a narrative quality in the steady downhill progression of Hurstwood. Also, there is a repetitive quality about these scenes." Wyler was also perceptive in his analysis of Hurstwood's character: "Hurstwood's downfall stems from his own weakness of character, which led him to run off with Carrie as he did. Without the flaw in his make-up, the blows struck at him by fate need not reduce him to the gas jet." He went on to point out that demonstrating Hurstwood's flaw and dramatizing two key moments would ensure that "his total defeat as a human being is more understandable." The first key moment involves "the loss of capital"—Wyler points to the incident in the book where Hurstwood invests in a saloon and loses his money through his partner's duplicity: "The reason this is a good situation is that for a man like Hurstwood, there is no future in a salaried job." The second moment is the loss of Carrie, which occurs in two stages: first, "the loss of the sex relationship," and then, her leaving him. Interestingly, of these suggestions by Wyler, only Carrie's leaving remains in the released film.[17]

Wyler was equally sensitive to one of the central problems with the novel: "But from Carrie's point of view there is a real problem to dramatize. What does a woman do in such a case? . . . Carrie is decent, and feels a certain loyalty to Hurstwood. . . . It is a dreadful thing to do, to leave a man in such circumstances. But then consider her life. What is to become of her?" To clarify her dilemma, Wyler suggested adding the character of Ames—absent from the treatment, but featured in the novel—as someone who is "interested in Carrie and offering her a way out?" Carrie would reject him out of loyalty to Hurstwood, but also, she would recognize that if she went with him, "she would be repeating the near fatal mistakes of her life a third time." This is the key for Wyler—showing that Carrie "has learned something. Just as we show Hurstwood's regression, we want to

show some development in Carrie, her growth from a naïve country girl . . .
to a mature woman, with an emotional greatness."[18] The Goetzes added
Ames in one of their final drafts, only to cut him later, but Wyler's comment on Carrie's evolution remains interesting. Perhaps after depicting the
maturation of Catherine Sloper—who, after acquiring knowledge of the
world, rejects it—Wyler wanted to present a heroine whose education pro-
duces more positive results. However, the end of the film as released raises
questions about his final intentions.

Wyler's film is more compact and streamlined than either the Goetzes'
treatment or their final screenplays. When Wyler began shooting on August
21, the script still retained scenes of Carrie's theatrical debut at the Elks'
Lodge; her marriage to Hurstwood in New York; her visit to Hurstwood at
Slawson's and her perception of the place's shabbiness; Hurstwood's relief
at the loss of the baby and Carrie's disgust with him; the introduction of
Ames, who is now the director of a revue Carrie auditions for; her friendship with Lola, another actress; and Hurstwood's rejection from a series of
jobs, in large part because of his age. Wyler eliminates all this detail to focus almost exclusively on the relationship between Hurstwood and Carrie
and the impact of money on that relationship.

The first part of the film moves rapidly. After bidding farewell to her
parents at the train station in Columbia City, Missouri (a scene that has no
counterpart in the novel), Carrie boards the train and meets Drouet (Eddie
Albert), a traveling salesman who gives her his card. During their conversation, Carrie displays self-confidence when she informs Drouet, "I can be
better than Minnie [her sister]. I went to school." This boast is almost immediately followed by a shot of Carrie sewing in a shoe factory, where she
is one of a long line of workers, laboring at a tedious job. Wyler's cut immediately establishes the economic reality of an America entering the modern
age and undercuts Carrie's bold desire to make something of herself.

She is next seen, her face framed by the opening between the sink and
the dining area in her sister's apartment, complaining about her job and
worrying that she will work for years and have nothing to show for it—
again, Wyler's framing emphasizes the hopelessness of her position. In the
next scene, Carrie is at her sewing machine again, and because of the bad
light, she catches her finger in the machine and screams. She is paid off and
told to come back when she has healed, but Carrie knows she is being fired.

Her replacement stands right behind her and further back in the frame, and Wyler shows the other women bent over their machines, not stopping to watch her go.

Although Dreiser's novel is, in part, a panorama of life in Chicago at the turn of the century, Wyler's is very much an indoor film. Almost all the early scenes are interior shots of the train, the factory, and Minnie's apartment. Wyler is less interested in re-creating an era than in evoking a mood, a state of mind, and a psychological atmosphere. This intention is realized a short time later when Carrie meets Drouet for dinner at Fitzgerald's. The scene outside is standard and uninteresting, but when Carrie walks through the door of the restaurant, Wyler's camera peers over her shoulder as she stares inside. Her view is of a resplendent dining room, not at all like the eating area of her sister's apartment. As Wyler cuts from her face in the doorway to a large buffet table full of gourmet dishes, all the emphasis is on the lure of the luxury that money can buy.

In a deep-focus shot framed by a small dividing wall, we get our first view of Hurstwood. He seems almost incidental in a frame stuffed with well-dressed men eating and laughing. For Dreiser, life had much to do with what he called "chemisms"—invisible material forces, of which the drives for power, sex, and money are primary. This shot exposes Hurstwood's standing as nothing more than an object to be tossed around by these whirling forces and ultimately crushed by them. In this artfully structured image, Wyler captures both the essence of Dreiser's world and one of the focal points of his own.

When Carrie joins Drouet for dinner, Wyler again visually echoes Dreiser's emphasis on money as the central value of American life. Drouet offers Carrie some money and insists that she use it to buy a coat. Ambivalent about his offer, Carrie leaves the money on her plate. Drouet then picks it up and tells her to take it before the waiter does. At that moment, a shrimp cocktail is placed on Carrie's plate, and Drouet stuffs the bills into her purse. Carrie's acceptance of the money signals her acceptance of Drouet as her lover. Wyler's images of food and the splendid décor of the restaurant thus approximate the effect of Dreiser's language, suggesting that the transfer of money and the lure of luxury are bound up with sexual excitement. Ironically, when Carrie abandons Hurstwood at the end of the film, she leaves him a purse filled with money, along with a note. Before reading the note, Hurstwood removes the money from the purse, fingers it, and stuffs it back in. Wyler is visually conveying Hurstwood's painful recognition that money does not bring happiness or excitement.

It is at Fitzgerald's that Carrie meets Hurstwood for the first time. He helps her navigate the restaurant after she mistakenly enters the male-only bar entrance. While she explains her business there to the maitre d', Hurstwood comes to her aid, and as they are talking, Wyler utilizes one of his rare deep-focus compositions, showing Drouet entering in the background while Carrie and Hurstwood occupy the front of the frame. This spatial separation signals Drouet's decreasing importance in Carrie's life. When Hurstwood comes calling on Carrie for the first time and invites her to the theater, Wyler captures her face in the mirror, signaling her entrapment. Within a very short time, Wyler manages to foreshadow the unhappy fates of all three characters.

Carrie's mirrored face transitions to another scene in Fitzgerald's, where Hurstwood is picking up a bottle of champagne after escorting Carrie to a performance of *Camille*. He meets Fitzgerald—the Goetzes' variation on Odets's Moy. (In the film, Dreiser's Fitzgerald and Moy's has become simply Fitzgerald's.) Less sinister but also less generous than Moy, Fitzgerald is a pious old man who suspects Hurstwood of infidelity and warns him, "Count your blessings one by one and then you'll see what the lord has done." Hurstwood undercuts this admonition by showing him the cash box, which he refers to as his boss's real blessing. Fitzgerald, who is also a good friend of Julia Hurstwood's, informs her of her husband's affair and aligns himself with her against Hurstwood. Both Fitzgerald and Julia are examples of the pious, hypocritical morality that Dreiser condemns—people who worship money above all else.

Hurstwood's declaration of his love for Carrie in the carriage is vintage Wyler. Its staging resembles that of the courtship scene between Morris and Catherine in *The Heiress*, in that Carrie is leaning away from Hurstwood as he earnestly declares his affection. Like Catherine, Carrie yields, and Wyler frames the image of their embrace by having his lovers occupy all the interior space. When Carrie exits the carriage, Hurstwood watches her walk toward the stairs of Drouet's home. The deep-focus shot emphasizes that the lovers are safe as long as they occupy a world of their own; beyond it, their passion will be destroyed when it confronts a harsh, pitiless world.

In the following scene, in which Carrie agrees to go away with Hurstwood, Wyler stages one of his few outdoor sequences in Lincoln Park. In the light and out in public, Hurstwood cannot display his affection; he seems hesitant and tentative. Then, at Fitzgerald's, Carrie learns from Drouet that Hurstwood is married, and moments later, Julia confronts Hurstwood about his affair. Hurstwood and Carrie then quarrel over his deception; Wyler stages the scene with Carrie in a carriage while Hurstwood leans in but remains outside—their public and private worlds thus merged after Hurstwood's public image has been shattered. Hurstwood's most passionate moment, when he tells his wife he intends to grab the happiness he desires, comes as he climbs the staircase of his home and enters Julia's room. After this confrontation, he descends the stairs and exits.

In a parallel scene, Hurstwood runs to Carrie, ascending the stairs to her apartment. Now less sure of himself and less aggressive, he lies, telling her that Drouet has been injured so that she will go with him. As she opens the door, Wyler frames Hurstwood in the doorway while, on the left, Carrie is framed in the mirror. Again, the shot reveals that their fate is sealed. Later, on the train, Hurstwood again declares his love, explaining that he is getting a divorce and will marry Carrie in New York. He then gives her the opportunity to get off the train at the next stop if she does not love him. Carrie's moment of decision is staged on the platform outside the door of the train. She is about to step off—half on, half off, like Hurstwood in the second carriage scene—but suddenly decides to stay, and they embrace. As the train begins to move, their faces are alternately lit and then dark as the train picks up speed. Darkness and light fight for dominance as the first half of the film ends.

The second half, which takes place in New York, deals mostly with Hurstwood's decline. Interestingly, Hurstwood becomes a man of few words at this point, speaking softly and rarely raising his voice.[19] Olivier reveals the character mostly through his eyes and gestures, while Wyler utilizes light and shadow effectively here. These techniques become especially telling near the end of the film, after Carrie and Hurstwood separate. She is achieving success, while he is reduced to begging in the street. In one scene, as Hurstwood walks past the theater where Carrie's picture is displayed, Wyler has his shadow practically overwhelm her image.

Olivier himself eventually became so upset by the gloomy, depressing nature of the film that he asked Wyler why they were making it. Wyler's description of his motivation, quoted by Archer Winston of the *New York Post*, perhaps best explains the film's dreary atmosphere: "The thing that intrigued me, the reason I made the picture against so much advice, was because I think a man's mistakes are more interesting than his virtues. Dreiser's people make mistakes"[20]

One problem with the second part of the film is that Wyler, in part to placate the Breen office, turns Carrie into a noble, sacrificing, and understanding wife. Also, the filmmakers cut and economize too much in this section, retaining less of Dreiser's plot and thus softening the emotional impact of Hurstwood's decline. They omit both Ames and the Vances, the couple in Carrie's building who introduce her to the glories of New York City life, and they do away with Hurstwood's investment in a Warren Street saloon. In the novel, Hurstwood keeps enough of the stolen money to buy into a business while he and Carrie live in middle-class comfort for two years, whereas in the film, a detective tracks Hurstwood to a luxurious New York hotel almost as soon as he arrives, taking back most of the money. As the detective is counting the cash, he remarks that Hurstwood still has his health and, nodding toward Carrie, implies that he also has a beautiful young woman. But as Hurstwood realizes at that moment, in a world governed by money, these advantages will not be enough. In the hotel room, Carrie tries on a new hat, her happy face caught in the mirror; Hurstwood is at the door, his face in shadows. He tells Carrie that he is broke, and she embraces him. He pulls away from her—their positions have changed. Carrie assures him that she is his wife and still loves him, and Hurstwood replies that love may not be enough. The couple's fall into poverty is almost instantaneous.

In the film, a series of brief scenes dramatizes Hurstwood's decline. We see him getting fired from a job as a waiter at a working-class saloon, looking for work at an employment agency, and being reduced to tears when his last good pair of pants is splattered with mud. Paralleling these scenes, Wyler shows Carrie's quick rise in the theater world: first, she is seen auditioning for a chorus line; then a montage of sequences shows her getting more prominent roles.

Throughout much of this section, Wyler's Carrie remains devoted to Hurstwood, dealing patiently with his economic setbacks. Emotions come to a head, however, when she becomes pregnant soon after Hurstwood loses his job. Then Julia and her lawyer arrive, insisting that Hurstwood give her permission to sell their house, and Carrie is shocked to learn that Hurstwood is not divorced. Seeking to placate her, Hurstwood bargains away his share of the house, losing his chance to gain some financial stability. Shortly afterward, Carrie loses the baby. In an effort to console her, he promises that they can have another child when times get better, but Carrie attacks him, demanding, "When? When you're rich? . . . When you're eighty?" Later, she tells him that she is "still young" and is "going to live somehow." In the novel, Dreiser chronicles Carrie's growing resentment of Hurstwood's failings and his age; in the film, all her bitterness comes out in this one emotional moment.

When she learns that Hurstwood is going to see his son, who is visiting New York on his honeymoon, Carrie decides to sacrifice herself and leave him, so that he will be free to return to his world. While waiting at the pier, however, Hurstwood is overcome with shame and cannot bring himself to face his son. Ironically, he returns home to find Carrie's farewell note. Dreiser's naturalistic tale of characters at the mercy of forces beyond their control suddenly becomes a story of good intentions gone awry.

The character of Carrie is domesticated enough to be sympathetic to film audiences of the time, yet liberated enough to reflect the new woman emerging in postwar films. She reflects Brandon French's contention that women in 1950s films longed for both a secure, domestic lifestyle and the adventure inherent in an unconventional way of life.[21] The examples of domestic reality in the film—Minnie's life of grinding poverty and the Hurstwoods' marriage, in which the pursuit of social status has destroyed any semblance of happiness—push Carrie to look for fulfillment elsewhere. *Carrie* is uncompromising in viewing marriage as a trap, and it certainly seems to be an attack on the American way of life in the 1950s, grounded in an institution wholly shaped by money.[22]

From the beginning, Wyler's Carrie displays spunk and confidence in the face of this dreary prospect. On the train, she tells Drouet that she will not end up like her sister. When Hurstwood teaches her how to play cards, she exults in beating Drouet. Ignoring Hurstwoood's help, she exclaims, "I won!" Her strength again comes to the fore when, after her miscarriage, she realizes that she can no longer devote herself to an aging husband and declares her intention "to live." That bedside awakening is immediately followed by a scene in which she auditions for the chorus line in a musical revue. This new Carrie is a woman of action. When the director asks for her name, she answers, "Carrie Madenda"—coming up with a new identity on the spot. She will rise and succeed.

Hurstwood initially accepts Carrie's success in the theater. After her opening night, he escorts her home and encourages her dreams. He tells her to buy some good clothes and get a nice place to live, adding, "You can make your way up to that other world that I left." Carrie responds, "You mean alone," to which Hurstwood replies, "You're never alone up there. It's down here where it's lonesome." These lines are telling, for they highlight the contradictions in Hurstwood's mind (and in Dreiser's), indicating that he still worships at the altar of success. Equating happiness with good clothes and a beautiful home, he evidently believes that success functions as a barrier to loneliness and despair. In this context, it is interesting that Wyler lifts an image that Dreiser associates with Carrie and transfers it to Hurstwood: Dreiser uses the rocking chair as an image of Carrie's restlessness, an activity that cannot take her to a satisfying place, whereas Wyler uses it to signify Hurstwood's isolation. He is seen a number of times rocking by a window with a newspaper in his hand, cut off from the world he once navigated successfully. Immediately after Hurstwood's reply to Carrie about the comforts of success, Wyler cuts to Hurstwood in the rocker—the epitome of one who has lost it.

Carrie leaves Hurstwood because she believes he will be happier if he reunites with his son and returns to his former life—the "other world" he left behind. That decision, however, sets him on a downward spiral. Once Carrie becomes more successful, she tries to find him again, but none of her leads proves fruitful. One evening, as she readies herself for a performance, Drouet visits her dressing room. In a scene that parallels the one in the film's first half, when he tells her that Hurstwood is married, he now informs Carrie that Hurstwood stole money before they ran away together. Drouet confesses that despite his current success, he was happier in his old apartment with Carrie. All Wyler's principals—even Drouet—learn something about the nature of success. As Drouet tells Carrie about the theft, she is looking at herself in a full-length mirror—reminiscent of her first moment as Mrs. Hurstwood, admiring her new hat just before Hurstwood is forced to return the stolen money. She has come a long way, but Wyler's camera still imprisons her in the frame, indicating that although she has gained much, she has lost more. Suddenly recognizing her part in Hurstwood's downfall, she exclaims that she has "ruined him."

When next seen, Hurstwood is in a rooming house for derelicts. This scene, which was cut from the film shown in theaters but restored when it was released on DVD, is one of the most haunting sequences in the movie. Wyler's camera, surveying the place from above, looks down on the men, confined in individual cells that look like cages at an animal shelter. Hurstwood is sick and has just come from the hospital; his once impeccable appearance has deteriorated markedly. He is told to leave in the morning and is forced to roam the streets in search of money. Out on the street and starving, he swallows his pride and decides to ask Carrie for a handout.

Hurstwood's meeting with Carrie is filmed in a noirish style. He hides in the shadows, near the brightly lit stage door area. When Carrie emerges, her face is illuminated, while Hurstwood's remains dark. She invites him into her dressing room and orders one of the workers to bring food. When she turns on the light, Hurstwood looks away, devastated and humiliated by his appearance. When Carrie asks, "What happened?" he can only reply, "I've forgotten"—he is unable to articulate what life has done to him, or what he has done to himself. Carrie tells him that she now has security and success and wants to share it with him; she understands what he did for her and wants to reclaim his love. But Hurstwood advises her not to live in the past, telling her (repeating her words to him) she has time to find someone to love and, finally, that "it's a great experience." At the end, he seems to be holding on to one of the reasons for his fall—the romantic notion that there is something greater than the materialism pursued by all the film's characters.

When Carrie leaves to get more money, Hurstwood removes just one coin from her purse and fingers it—this is Wyler's third use of this image—then flicks the bills back inside. The gesture of rejecting money seems to consolidate his epiphany, but as he rises to leave, Hurstwood catches sight of himself in Carrie's mirror. His desolate expression suggests that the lesson has come too late and cannot redeem him. He manipulates the burners on Carrie's stove, and we hear the hissing of the gas as Hurstwood leaves. The image hints at Hurstwood's end, and it is the only indication that re-

294 William Wyler

mains—his actual suicide scene was filmed but removed before the film's release.

In the script version, Hurstwood returns to the dreary shelter, where he uses Carrie's money to rent a room, locks himself in, and stares at the window. The script reads, "An especially hard blast of wind rattles the window and the slip lock falls securely into place. Hurstwood closes his eyes." Both versions—the Goetzes' script and the finished film—thus close on images of death. Wyler, unlike Dreiser, ends with Hurstwood, not Carrie. Indeed, both his independent postwar films conclude with death images: Catherine Sloper locking herself in her home, and Hurstwood exiting Carrie's dressing room to commit suicide.

Wyler completed shooting on November 2, just a few days over schedule and roughly $60,000 over budget. The film did not fare well with the critics—the *New York Times* called it "mawkish."[23] Its failure, however, may have been attributable in large part to the national mood: the House Un-American Activities Committee was preparing a new round of hearings for April 1951, which paralyzed Hollywood; the Cold War was at its height; America was at war with Korea; and Alger Hiss was being tried in front of Senator McCarthy's committee. Sensitive to this rancorous political climate, Paramount panicked about handling a property that was so critical of the American way of life. Wyler delivered his final cut in March 1951, but Paramount sat on it until July 1952, releasing it with no promotion. The studio heads also cut the film without Wyler's input: "I was in Rome preparing *Roman Holiday* when I got a cable from the studio as long as my arm. It said the picture would be shelved unless I agreed to cuts. They were not allowed to make the cuts without my approval, according to my contract. But faced with the prospect of having the picture shelved permanently, I decided to let them do it."[24]

Paramount's handling of the film infuriated David Selznick, who sent lengthy letters to executives Frank Freeman and Barney Balaban with suggestions on how to market it, which theaters it should play in, and what film festivals it should be entered in. In one letter to Freeman he wrote, "Now I am extremely eager about 'Carrie.' I wish I were handling it. With the combination of what I regard as the picture's superb quality, and the prestige names of Theodore Dreiser, William Wyler, Laurence Olivier, and Jennifer Jones, it would have a build-up such as few pictures have had before."[25] Paramount obviously did not share the producer's enthusiasm.

Wyler looked back on the film's failure sardonically: "The picture frightened them because of the shameful McCarthy era. *Carrie* showed American life in an unflattering light. . . . So we had a flop instead of a success, which I suppose was better for America."[26]

14

The House Un-American Activities Committee

Detective Story (1951), *Roman Holiday* (1953),
The Desperate Hours (1955), *The Children's Hour* (1961)

In September 1947, J. Parnell Thomas, a Republican congressman from New Jersey, reconvened the House Un-American Activities Committee (HUAC) to investigate "alleged subversive influence on motion pictures." More than forty people from the film industry received subpoenas to appear before the committee. There were two groups of witnesses. One—termed "friendly" by the committee—was made up of individuals willing to name fellow workers whom they thought to be members of the Communist Party and to identify moments in films that contained communist propaganda. The second group—labeled "unfriendly"—consisted of nineteen actors, writers, producers, and directors who became, in effect, the defendants. Of these nineteen, only eleven were called to testify. One of the eleven, German playwright Bertolt Brecht, denied membership in the Communist Party and promptly left the country. The others, who became known as the "Hollywood Ten," were eventually tried, fined, and imprisoned for contempt of Congress.

Shortly after the announcement that the HUAC would hold its first hearings in October 1947, Wyler and his friends John Huston, Philip Dunne, and Canadian actor Alexander Knox met to form a group in opposition to the hearings. At first, they called their campaign Hollywood Fights Back, but they later changed the name to the Committee for the First Amendment (CFA). The CFA gathered at Ira Gershwin's home—along with a group of Hollywood stars that included Edward G. Robinson, Danny Kaye, Humphrey Bogart, Lauren Bacall, Burt Lancaster, Gregory Peck, Myrna Loy, Ava Gardner, Henry Fonda, and Gene Kelly—and prepared a statement that ran a few days later in newspapers across the country and was also presented to Congress in the form of a petition. An early version of the petition, which was signed by David Selznick, John Ford, Bette Davis, George Stevens, and Frank Capra, among others, read in part:

> The America we love and defend is the traditional America where men of goodwill and of different political faiths assemble in town meeting[s], discuss their political differences, and remain friends. For when the freedom to disagree, the right to dissent, is threatened in America, the whole fabric of our beloved country is endangered. . . .
>
> We are tired of our industry, and our professions, and of our family and friends, eternally being placed in a defensive position by every group seeking notoriety at Hollywood's expense. We have faith that the great majority of the elected Congressional representatives of the American people resent equally with us abuses of powers of the Congress.[1]

The statement that ran in newspapers was much shorter than the original three-page, single-spaced document. It read:

> We, the undersigned, as American citizens who believe in constitutional democratic government, are disgusted and outraged by the continuing attempt of the House Committee on Un-American Activities to smear the Motion Picture Industry.
>
> We hold that these hearings are morally wrong because:
>
> Any investigation into the political beliefs of the individual is contrary to the basic principles of our democracy;
>
> Any attempt to curb freedom of expression and to set arbitrary standards of Americanism is in itself disloyal to both the spirit and the letter of our Constitution.[2]

This statement was signed by all those who had attended the meeting at Gershwin's home.

The CFA also agreed on a steering committee: director Anatole Litvak, screenwriter Julius Epstein, producer Joseph Sistrom (a conservative Republican), and David Hopkins (son of FDR friend and adviser Harry

Hopkins). The CFA next decided to send a delegation to the hearings in Washington as a show of support for the unfriendly witnesses. They chartered a plane from Howard Hughes for $13,000. John Huston told the *Washington Daily News* that Hughes had no interest in politics: "It was strictly a business deal."[3] The stars who attended this rally included many of those who had gathered at Gershwin's home and signed the petition. Wyler wanted to go but was advised against it by his doctors. Dunne and Huston joined the actors in Washington.

The night before the flight, Wyler called a meeting at Chasen's restaurant and reminded the delegates that they would likely be attacked. According to Dunne, Wyler cautioned that "if anyone aboard that plane was in the slightest degree vulnerable, our entire group and its cause could be discredited. If there is anything in any of your pasts that could hurt you or us, don't go. You don't have to tell us about it. Just don't show up at the airport tomorrow morning."[4] Wyler, Dunne, and Huston were also concerned that when the CFA delegation entered the caucus room of the House Office Building, HUAC chairman Thomas might subpoena the delegates and force them to testify under oath. After some discussion, the group agreed on a plan: "If any or all of us were called to the stand and asked the question, we would reply, 'I must respectfully decline to answer that question on the grounds that the information is privileged under the First Amendment to the Constitution.' We would then call a press conference, ask a Supreme Court justice to put us under oath . . . and answer all questions the newspapermen cared to ask us, including the Sixty-Four-Dollar one."[5] Dunne admitted decades later that he did not like that compromise, but he thought Justice Felix Frankfurter (a friend of his father) would swear the group in on the radio, and they "would come out. But it would not be under the direct duress of the committee."[6]

In his autobiography, Dunne wrote that the CFA had two goals: "First, we timed our flight to support the scheduled testimony of Eric Johnston, spokesman for the Producers Association, who had publicly declared that the motion picture companies would never impose a blacklist nor submit to censorship. Second, we intended to confront Richard Nixon, the only congressman on the House Committee from our home state, and request that he either call off the hearings or insist on a reformation of its procedures."[7] The CFA's plan was upended, however, when Thomas decided to bypass

Johnston and call screenwriter John Howard Lawson instead. Lawson was a passionate Marxist who had come to Hollywood after establishing a reputation as a playwright and a theorist of political theater. Considered one of the Hollywood Left's most intellectual and passionate spokesmen, Lawson was aggressively brash, and his appearance set the tone for the testimony by the rest of the Hollywood Ten. Dunne considered Lawson's performance unfortunate—a setback for the cause—and felt that Lawson and others erred in not making the First Amendment the center of their defense: "An examination of what they said on the witness stand will reveal few references to the constitutional issue and an emphasis on the barren tactic that they were refusing to answer the congressmen's questions, but were trying to answer them in their own way."[8] Many members of the CFA were appalled by the hostile and belligerent testimony and the subsequent negative press coverage. By the time the CFA members returned to Hollywood, their movement was riven by dissent, and they faced pressure from their agents and their colleagues to distance themselves from the Hollywood Ten and that group's opposition to the HUAC. The CFA sputtered for a little while longer but would soon dissolve. Wyler told Axel Madsen:

> With our Committee for the First Amendment, we tried to defend the *principle* of the secret ballot. We tried to defend not so much the Ten as a person's right to keep his political beliefs to himself, that no one would have to disclose whether he was a Communist. We tried to stand up and defend political affiliation. I remember we did try to urge some of the Ten to disclose their political beliefs to the press, but not the Un-American Activities Committee before going to jail. I knew we were on the right side of things, but we were not able to fight the whole mood of the McCarthy era.[9]

The CFA's attempt to confront Richard Nixon also ended in failure. Nixon had flown back to California just as the CFA delegation arrived in Washington. As Dunne recalled, "We phoned Willy Wyler . . . and asked him to organize a delegation and present our petition to Nixon in California. But Nixon was not to be found, either at his home or his California office, and nobody seemed to know where he was. Somehow, he had managed to disappear into thin air."[10]

During the first week of the hearings, the HUAC trotted out a horde of friendly witnesses, including Adolphe Menjou, Gary Cooper, Walt Disney, Ayn Rand, and Louis B. Mayer. To counter this opening salvo, the CFA released a radio ad entitled "They Do Not Speak for Us," which concluded, "Listen to the real Hollywood. You will find its voice is like your own. It speaks for decency, tolerance, and democracy. It defends its own point of view and defends your right to express yours." Other radio ads followed. In one, Frank Sinatra asked, "Once they get the movies throttled, how long will it be before the Committee goes to work on freedom of the air? How long will it be before we're told what we can and cannot say into a radio microphone?"[11] In another, Gene Kelly defended Wyler's film: "Did you happen to see *The Best Years of Our Lives*? Did you like it? Were you subverted by it? Did it make you un-American? Did you come out of the movie with a desire to overthrow your government?"[12] Wyler himself took to the radio as well: "I wouldn't be allowed to make *The Best Years of Our Lives* today. That is directly the result of the activities of the Un-American Activities Committee. They are making decent people afraid to express their opinions. . . . They are creating fear in Hollywood. Fear will result in self-censorship. Self-censorship will paralyze the screen. . . . You will be given a diet of pictures which conform to an arbitrary diet of Americanism."[13]

The references to *Best Years* were prompted by a statement from Dr. John R. Leehner, the new director of the right-wing Motion Picture Alliance, declaring that Wyler's film was one of roughly a dozen named in a recent HUAC report as containing communist propaganda. This report provoked a response from Samuel Goldwyn that was covered in the press. It read in part: "There cannot be the slightest excuse for having given any currency whatever to such a fantastic ill-conceived and unworthy statement. . . . You could not knowingly render a greater disservice to American ideals (for whose preservation you purport to stand) and to the motion picture industry than to permit such baseless irresponsibility to be uttered about a picture which has been unanimously acclaimed as exemplifying the very best of America."[14]

Thomas suddenly ended the hearings on October 30, citing the Hollywood Ten for contempt; on November 24 the House of Representatives voted to uphold those contempt citations. On the same day, a group of motion picture executives gathered at the Waldorf-Astoria Hotel in New York;

later, their spokesman Eric Johnston announced that they supported the
HUAC's actions against the Hollywood Ten, who would be fired immediately and not rehired until they either were acquitted or swore under oath
that they were not communists. The executives also declared, "We will not
willingly employ a Communist," but went on to state: "We are frank to
recognize that such a policy involves dangers and risks. There is danger in
hurting innocent people, there is the risk of creating an atmosphere of fear.
We will guard against this danger, this risk, this fear."[15] The Hollywood
blacklist was now officially in place.

Wyler played an active role in this politically charged period—a fact
that would cause him considerable trouble in the mid-1950s. On May 15
he hosted a party at his home for Henry Wallace, a former vice president
under FDR and the Progressive Party's current presidential candidate, who
championed universal health insurance and welcomed the support of the
American Communist Party. The *Los Angeles Examiner* headlined a story
"Wallace Talks to 12,000 after Secret Fund Raising," which breathlessly
reported: "Out of the parlors of rich leftist Hollywood society after closed
door excursions into fat pocket books, Henry A. Wallace stalked back to
the 'common man' last night. Wallace was back 'on the record' at Gilmore
Field before 12,000 cheering admirers. Ended was his sojourn into 'top se-
crecy' at the Beverly-Wilshire Hotel with 400 well-healed [sic] west-enders
and later with a strictly Class A clique at the mansion of film director William Wyler."[16]

In 1948 Wyler attended a benefit at the Beverly-Wilshire Hotel to raise
funds for the defense of the Hollywood Ten, and he was a sponsor of the
conference for world peace held at the Waldorf-Astoria Hotel on March 30,
1949. Later that year, he signed a brief in support of two of the Hollywood
Ten: John Howard Lawson and Dalton Trumbo. In 1950 he agreed to sponsor a petition to the New York City school authorities, calling on them to
lift a ban of the *Nation* from public school libraries. He also contributed to
Helen Gahagan Douglas's campaign for the U.S. Senate and wrote letters to
the Federal Parole Board, asking that body to reconsider the parole applica-
tions of Alvah Bessie, Lester Cole, Ring Lardner Jr., John Howard Lawson,
Albert Maltz, and Samuel Ornitz (all members of the Hollywood Ten). He
also wrote a special letter on behalf of Adrian Scott, stating that he "has
a young son, now aged seven, who is in school but suffers from the fear he

will be abandoned, and needs a parent's love and care."[17] When Dashiell Hammett was arrested for refusing to tell a grand jury what he knew about a bail fund for four communists convicted as subversives, Wyler put up part of his bail.[18]

When the HUAC hearings started in 1947, Bosley Crowther, film critic for the *New York Times*, wrote an essay entitled "Will Film-Making Be Complicated by the 'Un-American' Probers?" Wyler replied to Crowther in a letter—undated, but probably written in 1947—in which he responded to that question:

> I can answer unequivocally that film-making will be, and in fact already is, seriously complicated by the "Un-American" probers. I do not envy you your job of having to sit through the pictures that will be made to conform to Mr. Thomas or Mr. Hearst's standards of entertainment and Americanism. As one who has always regarded motion pictures as an important part of American cultural life, and as one who has constantly advocated and encouraged good films about contemporary life and problems, you must be as outraged as I am by these vicious attacks against the film industry.[19]

It was in response to this national cultural crisis that Wyler undertook the task of filming Sidney Kingsley's play *Detective Story*. Wyler became interested in this project as early as 1948, when Kingsley asked him to invest $1,500 in the Broadway production. Kingsley loved Wyler's film version of his play *Dead End* and looked forward to another successful collaboration. In May 1950, three months before he started filming *Carrie*, Wyler announced that *Detective Story* would be his next project for Paramount.

As he had done with *Dead End*, Wyler asked Kingsley to write the screenplay, but the playwright declined for the same reason he had cited earlier—an unwillingness to go back over the same material he had just finished writing. Wyler then offered the assignment to Dashiell Hammett, who was living in California with Lillian Hellman. Broke and in poor health, Hammett was being hounded by the HUAC, and Wyler wanted to give him a job. Hammett was unable to come up with anything, so Wyler turned the writing duties over to his brother, Robert (who also served as associate producer), and Philip Yordan (whose previous writing credits included *Dillinger, Suspense,* and *Anna Lucasta*).

Detective Story opened on Broadway on March 23, 1949, eventually becoming the second-longest-running play of Kingsley's career at 581 performances—eclipsed only by *Dead End*'s 684 performances. The new play starred Ralph Bellamy and Meg Mundy, and it was directed by Kingsley, who had also staged *Dead End*. Like his earlier successes, *Detective Story* offers a didactic plot, in this case centered on Jim McLeod, a fascistic, intolerant police officer whose marriage and job are both adversely affected by his callous treatment of the suspects he deals with. (Kingsley would return to the subject of fascism in his adaptation of *Darkness at Noon* in 1951.) But this play represents an artistic advance over Kingsley's earlier successes, in that the message does not overwhelm the story. Kingsley's command of dramatic pacing and his attention to the unities of time (the story takes place over a four-hour period), place (limited to the second floor of a police precinct), and action create a vivid portrait of a day in a New York City police station.

Thematically, the play revolves around McLeod's treatment of two criminals. Arthur Kindred, a former navy war hero, is brought in for stealing $480 from his boss. He admits to the crime, explaining that he was driven to it by his love for a woman named Joy and his desire to take her out on an expensive date and buy her things, and he is willing to pay the penalty. There are moments in the play when Arthur discusses his problems adjusting to civilian life—a theme that obviously appealed to Wyler. During his time at the police station, Arthur discovers that Joy's sister, Susan, truly loves him when she arranges to repay the money to Arthur's boss, who then agrees to drop the charges. Despite Arthur's military record and evident good character, McLeod refuses the offer, treating Arthur like any other criminal.

McLeod's second case involves an abortionist named Schneider, whose sloppy practices have killed several young women. McLeod has been after him for some time, and when he learns that his key witness against the man has died—another victim of the doctor's incompetence—he beats Schneider, sending him to the hospital. McLeod then finds out that his own wife, Mary, used Schneider's services years before she met her husband. Mary tries to explain the situation, but McLeod refuses to understand, exclaiming that her affair and subsequent abortion represent "everything I hate" and even calling her a "whore." His unyielding attitude drives Mary away, and he ignores all advice to try to get her back. Following his final confrontation with Mary, a thief who was arrested earlier takes a gun from one of the policemen at the station, and McLeod is shot trying to retrieve it. Before he dies, however, he relents and lets Arthur go, suddenly realizing the cost of his lack of humanity.

In this play, Kingsley tries to move away from agitprop by melding social drama with tragedy. McLeod is a larger-than-life, charismatic figure who is undone by a moral flaw, and in part, the play hinges on an incident, buried in the past, that comes to light and destroys the lives of McLeod and his wife. Kingsley, however, is not a good enough playwright to bring it off. His characters remain stubbornly one-dimensional, lacking the depth and complexity necessary to lift *Detective Story* from the level of effective melodrama to that of compelling theater.

In a preface written for a paperback reprint of his major plays, Kingsley states that his visit to a police precinct house provided the thematic impetus for the play: "I saw that the measure of a free society can be taken right there in the police station in the relation of police activity to constitutional law." He goes on to note, "In writing *Detective Story*, I was influenced by General George C. Marshall's speeches in 1947 in which he used the phrase 'the police state.'"[20] Kingsley also points out a second level to the play:

> I took as my premise "Judge not, but ye be judged" from the Sermon on the Mount. . . . The central figure . . . is a moralist, wanting to bolster a collapsing civilization by turning back the clock. . . .
> . . . He wants to achieve efficiency by taking the law into his own hands, by making people abide by the right as he sees it, or by personally bringing them to account if they do not. Of course, the inefficiency comes from our checks and balances, so that no man can be trusted with absolute power. The answer to McLeod is that the inefficiency of humankind is really a higher efficiency, since it permits the human spirit to breathe.[21]

The parallels between McLeod's authoritarian approach to law enforcement and the unwillingness of the HUAC and its supporters to let America or its artists "breathe" were certainly not lost on Kingsley—and they surely account for the alacrity with which Wyler took on the project and the speed with which he finished it. Wyler completed *Detective Story* in only three months—a record for him.

Having encountered problems with the Breen office over *Carrie*, Wyler again faced difficulties with *Detective Story*, over the subject of abortion. In an interview with the *New York Times*, he lashed out against the Production Code:

> Certain subjects can't even be discussed. It's as if they didn't exist. The play forcefully condemns abortion and it is proper to insist on condemnation of crime in film. But apparently we are not even permitted to condemn. This is ludicrous. The code is old-fashioned. It is fifteen years old, but the company heads won't hear of amendments. Why not discuss reality? I have two daughters who are more important to me than my pictures. There are many things I wouldn't want them to see. It is my responsibility to keep them from seeing such things. But that doesn't mean it is my responsibility to make pictures for children.[22]

The Breen office was unmoved by Wyler's comments, so the screenwriters were forced to come up with a new plot twist. By changing Dr. Schneider's specialty to the delivery of out-of-wedlock babies and implying that he dabbles in illegal adoptions, they managed to leave the language sufficiently vague yet allow the audience to pick up on the illicit nature of his services. In the film, McLeod learns that his wife's delivery was botched and that the baby died at birth, thus suggesting the reason for Mary's current inability to have a child.[23] When he learns about her past, he calls her a "tramp"— the play's "whore" was rejected by Breen's office.

The filmmakers also simplified the role of Feinson, a newspaper reporter who hangs around the police station. In the play, he and McLeod are old friends; he calls McLeod "Seamus," while McLeod calls him "Yussel." Like McLeod's partner Brody, he functions as an adviser and a conscience, at one point warning, "Sometimes you've got to bend with the wind . . . or break! Be a little human. . . . Don't be such a friggin' monument!"[24] In the film, Feinson becomes a minor character, mostly a hanger-on. Otherwise, the film is faithful to the play's plot, characters, and setting.

In casting the film, Wyler retained four actors from the Broadway production: Lee Grant (the shoplifter), Horace McMahon (Lieutenant Monaghan, the precinct chief), and Joseph Wiseman and Michael Strong (a pair of burglars). For McLeod and his wife, he chose Kirk Douglas, who had starred in *Champion* in 1949 and would play another ruthless, destructive character in Billy Wilder's *Ace in the Hole* that same year, and Eleanor Parker, who had received a Best Actress nomination for *Caged* in 1950. He rounded out the cast with Cathy O'Donnell as Susan Carmichael (the woman who loves Arthur) and William Bendix as Joe Brody, McLeod's partner.

Douglas later wrote in his autobiography that he had "misgivings" about doing the film: "I had seen the play in New York with Ralph Bellamy starring. It had problems. The vignettes and characters were wonderful, but the main character had to lug the story line." To ensure a more smoothly integrated ensemble, Douglas suggested that Wyler gather the cast and have them "do it as a play. Then you can watch the whole thing. . . . I put the play together at the Sombrero Playhouse in Phoenix, Arizona. Wyler came to see it several times."[25] Douglas also spent several weeks at a precinct in Midtown Manhattan, where the detectives dressed him in a uniform, had him sit in on investigations, and even let him fingerprint a burglary suspect. In his autobiography, Douglas called Wyler "a strange director: he never directed you. He'd just say, 'Do it again,' until he got what he wanted."[26] In an interview twelve years earlier, however, Douglas had different opinion, ranking Wyler among the five best directors he had ever worked with.[27]

As was his wont, Wyler shot most of the film indoors. Except for a few brief exterior shots of the street outside the station and a paddy-wagon ride with back projection of city streets, the action took place on a single sound stage that housed the squad room, the lieutenant's office, an interrogation room, a file room, and the building's roof. The multilevel set was an illusion, as Wyler had all the rooms built side by side to accommodate cameraman Lee Garmes's traveling camera. Garmes recalled:

I told him to find a stage with smooth floors at Paramount; if there were any holes in them he must fill them up with putty and sandpaper them. I told him I'd use a crab dolly; he'd never used it before and he was delighted with the idea of a camera he could move wherever he wanted it . . . and I told him to rehearse the actors while I rehearsed the camera and lights at the same time; if I made too much noise he was to tell me. And then I suggested to him that stills be made of each final rehearsal with the dialogue attached each time, so as to speed up the actual shots. Willy had a ball with the crab dolly! We came in six days under schedule, a record for him.[28]

Detective Story is similar in style to *Counsellor-at-Law*, which also takes place on a single set (George Simon's law office). But in the film version of Rice's play, Wyler manages to avoid any feeling of confinement through his fast-paced direction and skillful movement of the actors between sets. He repeats this effect in filming Kingsley's play by adding rooms to the precinct house and moving his camera and characters freely between those spaces. In doing so, Wyler provides the illusion of ample space where there is, in fact, very little. Michael Anderegg correctly observes that the film "moves like an efficient, well-lubricated machine."[29]

Conversely, Anderegg faults Wyler—less accurately—for "allowing Kingsley's play to speak for itself with as little interference as possible."[30] In fact, Wyler's introduction of McLeod significantly alters Kingsley's version and immediately complicates the audience's reaction to him. In the film, we meet McLeod outdoors, where he is walking a prisoner to the station house. He is waylaid by his wife; they embrace and talk like newlyweds. He then takes her to a parked taxi, and the cabbie allows them to continue their conversation in the back. When they kiss, Wyler frames the scene much like the one of Hurstwood and Carrie kissing in a carriage, indicating that McLeod's passion for his wife is still strong. He promises that he will be home for dinner and asks about her visit to the doctor. She tells him that things are no different, but McLeod, undeterred, insists that they will confound the medical establishment and have both a boy and a girl. McLeod is thus effectively introduced as a loving husband and popular on the street.[31] After leaving his wife, he ascends the staircase—again, a sign of power in Wyler's films—and enters his work area, where he starts to book Arthur Kindred, treating the prisoner in a friendly, civil manner.

When he is called in to Lieutenant Monaghan's office to meet Schneider's attorney, Sims, the audience sees another side of McLeod. Sims is aware of his client's less than savory past with McLeod and is worried about turning him over. He does not want Schneider's constitutional rights violated and he declares that he does not want McLeod to "degrade [Schneider's] dignity as a human being." After Sims leaves, Monaghan chews out McLeod, objecting to his "moral indignation." The look on McLeod's face during these scenes is disturbing, but the audience is still with him at this point because Schneider has, after all, been charged with murder, and his lawyer, in his buttoned-up black suit, comes across as officious, while the casually dressed McLeod seems more human. But when Monaghan accuses him of being "a one man army against crime," McLeod retorts savagely that he wants to put "criminals in the electric chair and pull the switch myself." Immediately, he realizes he has gone too far and pulls back. Clearly troubled, he walks away from the camera and changes moods.

Wyler amends Kingsley's work again by cutting back to the squad room, where he introduces McLeod's partner, Joe Brody (William Bendix). First shown giving sandwiches and coffee to the criminals being arraigned, Brody takes an interest in Arthur because of his navy record. Brody, we learn, lost his son during a naval battle. Wyler moves this sequence up to this early point in the film not only to contrast Brody with McLeod but also to offer a hint of the latter's humanity. If McLeod can be a partner to a man like Brody, he must have redeeming qualities that were not on display during his confrontation with Sims.

Just as in the film version, Kingsley's play introduces McLeod as he is bringing in Arthur. But in the play, his arrival interrupts Sims's meeting with Brody, who is handling the Schneider case until his partner arrives. Sims refers to McLeod as "a law unto himself"—which plants quite a different image in the mind of the audience. A few moments later, reporter Joe Feinson refers to him as "the mortal God—McLeod! Captain Ahab pursuing the gray Leviathan!" This double-barreled indictment immediately characterizes McLeod as a man who is, like Ahab, fueled by a moral indignation that will ultimately lead to his death. Like Melville's maniacal sea captain, McLeod feels that he has the right to play God, to pass judgment and mete out punishment. Kingsley thus clearly sets up his protagonist as a villain. His McLeod may be charismatic, but the audience is immediately put on notice to be wary of him. In Wyler's hands, by contrast, the character is presented as a troubled but sympathetic figure.

This change of emphasis is reinforced in a scene that follows the film's introductory sequence. As McLeod, Brody, and another officer, Dakis, are questioning the burglar Lewis Abbott, Wyler films the entire procedure in a tight four-shot that establishes the camaraderie of the men as they do their job. During the interrogation, McLeod conducts himself in a manner closely matching that of his colleagues. And later, when McLeod beats up Schneider, Wyler—who rarely opens up a play merely for the sake of variety—films the scene in the back of paddy wagon, where the two men are alone, whereas Kingsley's McLeod beats his victim in the precinct room. In the film, McLeod's psychosis is made less of a public spectacle.

Another important change follows when a witness (who has been bribed) fails to identify Schneider in a lineup. A frustrated McLeod walks into another room, followed by Feinson. There, McLeod reveals that his hatred of criminals is rooted in his disgust for his father, who was a criminal himself, and he complains that "the thieves and murderers could have written the penal code themselves." In the play, he goes on to say, "Your democracy, Yussel, is a Rube Goldberg contraption." Feinson replies, "That's what's great about it. That's what I love. It's so confused, it's wonderful."[32] The latter exchange is excised from the film, as Wyler again sidesteps Kingsley's tendency to preach. The film version is subtler and more suggestive than the play.

Wyler also makes some strategic changes in the scene in which Mary confesses her past to McLeod in Monaghan's office. When McLeod enters the room, Monaghan has already talked with Mary and Tami Giacopetti, a gangster, about their affair and her loss of a baby. (The play makes it clear that Schneider performed an abortion.) Kingsley has McLeod walk into the office, where he is confronted by Mary, meets Giacopetti, threatens him, and verbally abuses his wife about her past. In Wyler's scene, however, McLeod is framed by all three characters as he enters—the audience is allowed to view all four characters at once. McLeod is introduced to Giacopetti, but he merely nods; there are no threats. Instead of abusing Mary, McLeod is solicitous, leading her to a chair and making sure she is comfortable. Here, Wyler reinforces McLeod's humanity and compassion by placing husband and wife on the same visual plane as he kneels by her chair. When the scene begins, the audience is still sympathetic to McLeod, but when Mary admits that she sought Schneider's services in the past—thus acknowledging her pregnancy and the affair that led to it—the framing shifts. McLeod stands, clenches his fist, threatens Giacopetti, and asks to be alone with his wife. When the couple is framed together, Mary remains in her chair, asking McLeod's forgiveness, but he cannot face her. Instead, he is shown standing in the front of the frame, viewed from a modified low angle, his face expressing hatred and disgust while Mary stays seated in the rear. When he asks her what happened to the baby, he is facing a window covered with wire, his face registering pain. The dialogue about the baby is conveyed in a shot–reverse shot, implying that this is the issue separating them. Then, as he gets up and screams, "Everything I hate . . . what's left to understand!" we see only Mary's startled reaction—as if the look on McLeod's face is too much for the camera to bear.

Under Wyler's direction, Kirk Douglas portrays McLeod as a man who is deeply conflicted, at odds with himself. Like his characterization of Chuck Tatum in *Ace in the Hole*, Douglas's McLeod is aware of his irrational tendencies but seems unable to curb them. The inner turmoil that is so clearly reflected in his facial expressions makes him a more tragic character than Kingsley's unbending moralist, while Wyler's subtle changes of emphasis and direction make his story more poignant and dramatic. When Mary returns to the precinct house to say good-bye, she is dressed in black, like Catherine Sloper on the night she is jilted. The couple is about to reconcile when McLeod suddenly protests that he cannot let go of "the dirty pictures" Mary's confession has put in his brain. Then, standing on his level, confronting him face-to-face, she tells him, "You haven't even a drop of ordinary human forgiveness in your whole nature. You're a cruel and vengeful man. You're everything you've always said you hated in your own father." And when she exits, declaring that she will never see him again, Mary wears the same hard, determined expression displayed by Catherine when she takes vengeance on the two men who have betrayed her.

The film ends quickly after Mary walks out. When one of the burglars grabs a gun from a policeman, McLeod, who now has nothing to lose, goes after him and is shot. As he is dying, he realizes that he has sacrificed the only person he ever loved, and in a final act of remorse, he tears up Arthur's report and drops the charges. He dies while saying the Catholic prayer of contrition, which is completed by Monaghan in the play; in the film, this is done, more appropriately, by Brody. During this death scene, in which

Douglas invests the character with real empathy, Wyler cuts to Arthur and Susan, who are watching. As they leave, they momentarily look back in deep focus, as Wyler's camera pulls back to reveal the entire squad room—McLeod's body lies in the front of the frame, the couple exit in the rear, and Brody stands in the middle. Wyler's composition thus brings together the bad cop, the good cop, and the couple they have both united, with Brody—the intermediary—significantly in the center. Brody seems to have loved his partner, and Arthur, who reminds Brody of his dead son, has been given the second chance his boy was denied. McLeod's final act of grace becomes a moment of contrition for both of them.

The film ends with a dissolve from the precinct to Arthur and Susan, who are swiftly walking, hand in hand, down the street. This ending is reminiscent of the final shot in *The Little Foxes*, where Wyler concludes with an image of Xan and David rather than of Regina. In both cases, he ends on a note of hope by focusing on the young couples—the characters who seem best suited to reject the hardhearted ethics represented by Regina and McLeod. It is interesting to note that Wyler, having offered uncompromisingly dark endings in his two most recent films—*The Heiress* and *Carrie*—chose to give this film a more optimistic turn. In all likelihood, he was thinking of the audience's disappointing reception of those earlier works. *Detective Story*, by contrast, was quite successful at the box office, which put Wyler in a better position to negotiate the terms of his next film, *Roman Holiday*. In addition, *Detective Story* netted Wyler another Best Director nomination from the Motion Picture Academy, as well as nominations for Eleanor Parker for Best Actress, Lee Grant for Best Supporting Actress, and the Robert Wyler–Philip Yordan script for Best Screenplay.

Kingsley told the *New York Times* that he liked the film better than his own Broadway production: "On the whole, I'd say the impact of the film is greater than that of the play. . . . It is simply that Wyler and Paramount have been able to get wonderful characterizations out of the cast."[33] The acting was indeed excellent—especially that of Douglas, whose complex performance, coupled with some of the script changes and Wyler's dramatic staging of scenes, made the story more effective. The tragic nature of McLeod's downfall, not fully realized in the play, comes closer to fruition here. Both the play and the film indict the HUAC for violating the principles of due process and the constitutional rights of individuals, which are the backbone of the American justice system. Kingsley warns that if those principles are not upheld and protected, chaos and fascism will follow. By making the protagonist more human and by carefully integrating his story with those of the other characters, Wyler brings these points home more effectively.

He employs the technique of deep focus to make these thematic points as well. This device is particularly revealing in the confrontation between Mr. Pritchett and Arthur. As Pritchett beseeches his employee to explain why he stole from him, Wyler keeps McLeod in the frame; his back is to the others, though still centered, as he talks on the phone. Susan enters the frame to the right of McLeod, her expression drawing the attention of the audience, which is still listening to the dialogue between Pritchett and Arthur and wondering about McLeod's intentions. Then, as she moves to the center of the frame and offers to repay Pritchett, Susan displaces McLeod, who is still in the frame and distracted by her presence. When McLeod turns his attention back to Arthur, he seems to take over the frame, though in the distance, Wyler lets us see another officer who is whispering something into Monaghan's partly opened door. (They need to get McLeod out of the office so they can get Mary in.) Wyler thus keeps the audience engaged in multiple levels of action without cutting or leaving the precinct room. Although *Detective Story* remains, to some degree, essentially a filmed play, Wyler effectively uses space to articulate his themes and sharpen the plot's dramatic focus. In spite of its rather prosaic location and straightforward story line, this film represents one of Wyler's virtuoso performances in the art of transferring theater to the screen and using the camera to improve on the original.

In 1951 the HUAC reopened its hearings, and a second wave of fear gripped Hollywood. Wyler's close friend Lillian Hellman was called before the committee, where she invoked her Fifth Amendment rights. Michael Wilson, who wrote the script for *Friendly Persuasion* for Capra, was also called; he eventually left the country to circumvent the blacklist.

A schism also developed within the Screen Directors' Guild (SDG) over the anticommunist investigations. In the fall of 1950 the guild's board passed a bylaw requiring a loyalty oath by its members. This move was instigated by Cecil B. DeMille, who also proposed that directors keep lists of suspicious personnel—particularly writers and actors—working on their films and share those lists with the SDG. Joseph Mankiewicz, president of the guild, had been out of the country during these discussions and was determined to reopen the issue of loyalty oaths. But when he announced a membership meeting, DeMille moved to block it and initiated a movement to recall Mankiewicz from office. DeMille tried to isolate the "foreigners" in the guild—Wyler, Billy Wilder, and Fred Zinnemann—by accentuating the exotic pronunciations of their names. (He referred to Wyler as "Vy-ler.") Wyler told Axel Madsen, "At one time, DeMille said something to the effect that some of us were traitors and not good Americans. I remember getting up and saying that if anybody doubts my loyalty to my country, I'll punch his nose 'and I don't care how old he is,' looking directly at DeMille as I said it."[34] The members voted to repudiate DeMille and his faction, forcing them to resign.

Considering the political climate, it is not surprising that Wyler looked forward to leaving the country in 1952, headed for Italy to film his next project, *Roman Holiday*. This movie would also be a change of pace—after a series of dark and mostly claustrophobic films, it would allow Wyler to return to comedy for the first time since helming *The Good Fairy* and *The Gay Deception* in 1935. (*The Gay Deception* is a Cinderella story featuring a small-town stenographer who wins a lottery prize and uses her windfall to enjoy the high society life at the Waldorf-Astoria Hotel. There, she meets a bellhop, a European prince in disguise who is working at the Waldorf to learn the hotel business. After a series of complications, they fall in love and live happily ever after.)

Roman Holiday, a reverse Cinderella tale, is the story of a princess (Audrey Hepburn) from an unnamed country who is in Rome on a good-will visit. Bored and frustrated by diplomatic protocol and round-the-clock schedules, she escapes her hotel room to explore the city. There, she sheds her role as a princess—cutting her hair, wearing informal clothes, and reveling in the freedom her position has denied her. She enjoys these simple pleasures in the company of Joe Bradley (Gregory Peck), an American newspaperman, who discovers her asleep on a park bench, takes her back to his apartment, and then shows her the sights. He soon discovers who his guest really is and plans to write an exclusive story about her. Eventually, however, the princess decides to return to her royal obligations and tells Joe, "At midnight I will turn into a pumpkin and ride away in my glass slipper." Joe, behaving like a gentleman and an idealized American, does not write his story.

The script for the film is tinged with the politics of the time, which followed Wyler to Europe. He already had a script by Ben Hecht but was dissatisfied with it, so he worked on revisions while crossing the Atlantic on the *Queen Mary* with his brother Robert and Lester Koenig. According to Ian McLellan Hunter, who received an Oscar for the original story, Dalton Trumbo (one of the Hollywood Ten) actually wrote the story and asked Hunter to front for him when the property was initially sold to Frank Capra. Hunter gave Trumbo the money Paramount paid for the story and then wrote the first screenplay for Capra. He told Jan Herman: "I was given an Academy Award for a story that was clearly not mine. Had it [the award] been for the screenplay, I could have convinced myself that I had done most of it."[35] Hunter had no involvement with the film after Wyler took over, but he told Herman that, unlike Capra, Wyler was not scared off by either his or Trumbo's politics. Hunter ultimately shared credit for the screenplay with John Dighton, a British writer Wyler hired while in Rome in 1952. Trumbo received a posthumous Oscar for his work on the film, and his name was restored to the credits on the DVD version.

Roman Holiday is Wyler's most free-floating film since signing with Goldwyn. From the opening credits, which feature some spectacular shots of Rome, Wyler seems to revel in the world around him. Apparently enjoying his Roman holiday as much as his heroine does, he eschews the closed, restricted constructions of his work since 1936: even Joe's small, one-room studio has a large window that faces a square, filling it with sunlight. It is as if getting out of America allowed Wyler to temporarily release his inhibitions and engage in the spirit of play. Yet, like the princess, Wyler knew he must eventually return to the real world and reengage with the politics of his own country—perhaps hoping that when he did so, America would behave with the decency and integrity Joe Bradley exhibits in refusing to "out" Princess Anne.

Despite the seeming joie de vivre exhibited in his film, Wyler was experiencing political problems of his own while in Rome. Those problems stemmed in part from his insistence on using Lester Koenig, who was blacklisted, as an associate producer on *The Heiress*, *Detective Story*, and *Carrie*. He also insisted on bringing Koenig to Rome to work on *Roman*

Holiday. In December 1952 the right-wing newsletter *Counterattack* reported that Wyler invited two communists to the wrap party for that film. In January 1953 Wyler's close friend Paul Kohner wrote to inform him that "a very careful check [is] being made on all of your activities and associations in Europe," including a meeting Wyler had attended in Switzerland with Irwin Shaw, Lester Koenig, Bernard Vorhaus, Joe Losey, and Bob Parrish. Kohner urged Wyler "not to take this thing lightly" and to talk with John Huston, who had experienced "the same situation with MOULIN ROUGE." Kohner warned his friend of potential difficulties in getting backing for his next film if he did not deal more effectively with this delicate situation, and he recommended that Wyler speak with an attorney, Arthur Jacobs, who had handled things for John Huston and José Ferrer.[36] In fact, Jacobs had written to Kohner the day before, suggesting, "I feel that I can, with Mr. Wyler's cooperation, alleviate any pressure that may be brought upon him now, or any unpleasant action against him that may be contemplated." Jacobs even offered to fly to Europe to meet with Wyler, provided Wyler would cover his expenses.[37]

Three weeks later, Kohner reiterated that the fate of Wyler's film was secondary to "your own personal standing and the sooner you start to get yourself cleared like all the others are doing, the better it will be for you." He told his friend, "Once what Talli [Wyler's wife] calls 'such a clean-up job' is done, if it is done properly and right, it should be good for all time. The very fact that your movements over there are being reported, whether correctly or incorrectly, should indicate to you that this situation is a serious one." Kohner again mentioned John Huston's situation, which he considered analogous to Wyler's: Huston, though aware that he was listed in the "Legion Magazine," had not thought it necessary to do anything about the implications of that listing. Kohner again counseled Wyler to speak with Huston, whom Jacobs had managed to convince of the gravity of his situation. "But the fact is that before he [Huston] met with these people here, he was not aware of the work they were doing and was also not aware of how he was lured into organizations and causes which definitely now have been exposed as communistic fronts."[38]

Wyler soon decided to take the advice he was getting. In 1953 Wyler was also corresponding with Art Arthur, executive secretary of the Motion Picture Industry Council, in an effort to clear his name. In a letter to Wyler, Arthur indicated that he had set up a meeting between the director and labor leader Roy Brewer, a studio-approved right-wing mediator, to discuss clearing his name. A few days later, he wrote to Wyler about the HUAC's list of "all in Hollywood who have been identified under oath as Communists up to the end of 1952," adding that the list did not include "the names of people who might have been innocently or unintentionally associated with the committee." He named John Garfield and José Ferrer as examples of the former and urged Wyler to use the list as a guide in an effort to remember "who might have been named and under what circumstances."[39] The director, however, was not quite out of the woods.

Y. Frank Freeman, production chief at Paramount, had berated Wyler for his careless behavior: "It is hard for anyone to understand how you would have these men as your guests knowing their record. You and I have discussed the Communist problem on several occasions."[40] In February 1954 he drafted a lengthy reply (never sent), making it clear that his political activism had always revolved around two principles: "Up to 1945: to fight Nazism and Facism [sic] abroad. After 1945: to fight for the preservation of civil liberties at home." Wyler was adamant about his opposition to communism: "I was always fundamentally opposed to Communism and all its basic teachings, though not actively engaged in opposing it. . . . I strongly insist that any activity of mine in connection with, or in support of, Communist front organizations has been with the sincere belief that I was furthering one or another of the above two purposes, which I pursued with unvarying consistency." He went on to deny that communists were attempting to gain control of the Screen Directors' Guild and spent considerable time discussing his involvement with the Committee for the First Amendment. His evaluation of the CFA's work and aims was filled with ambivalence, and he admitted having misgivings about the experience: "Many of us who joined sincerely, with the highest motives, have often regretted the whole thing." He also tried to distance himself from the Hollywood Ten. He defended the CFA for standing up for the First Amendment but then backpedaled by writing that the Supreme Court decision rendered that belief "erroneous." He went even further, complimenting the present House committee for acting with "decorum" and admitting that if the Thomas Committee had "conducted itself with dignity," the CFA might have had no reason to oppose it. He remained steadfast in his defense of

those among the Ten who were not communists but "were sacrificing themselves for a principle. It was these men whom I was anxious to defend."[41]

The letter that Wyler finally mailed to Freeman, dated May 3, 1954,
was shorter, less detailed, and less conciliatory. He was still adamant about
his anticommunism, however: "I hate and oppose any form of dictatorship
anywhere in the world. This of course includes the most dangerous of
these: Communism." He maintained that his participation in or support of
certain organizations and activities had been based on "the sincere belief
that I was either fighting Nazism abroad or helping preserve our civil liberties at home." He admitted that some of these causes did not serve their
avowed purpose, and he was wrong to lend his name to them: specifically,
he cited his sponsorship of the Cultural and Scientific Congress for World
Peace and his signing of an amicus curiae brief on behalf of John Howard
Lawson and Dalton Trumbo. He defended his work with the CFA: "Most
of us were motivated by a desire to defend what we believed to be basic
American freedoms. We had no desire or intensions of defending Communists and Communism." Consistent with his earlier draft, he regretted
his support of the Hollywood Ten, asserting that he had not known that
many of them were indeed communists and that if he had known "the
facts that ultimately developed, I am sure, I would have done nothing to
help them."[42] There are no other documents in Wyler's files on this issue.
Whether the meeting with Brewer and the letter to Freeman cleared him
is not completely clear. The attacks on Wyler by anticommunist groups,
however, seem to have ceased.

Although the red-baiting started to ease off in 1954, after the Senate
censured McCarthy, Lester Koenig did lose credit as Wyler's associate producer and screenwriter for *Roman Holiday*. Koenig had taken the Fifth in
an earlier HUAC hearing, and his name had made the blacklist even before
he left for Rome with Wyler to work on the film. Paramount wanted to
fire Koenig, but Wyler interceded, convincing the studio that Koenig was
essential to the production. In a letter written to defend his position after
the film was released, Wyler reminded Freeman that Koenig was the only
person, other than himself, who was familiar with the three script versions,
"as well as much other material, all of which had to be put together into
the final shooting script."[43] Koenig had been allowed to go to Rome with
the understanding that he would testify upon his return. When he refused

to do so, Paramount dropped his name from the released film, over Wyler's objections.

When Wyler returned to Hollywood in 1953, his political problems had soured his mood, and his last film for Paramount, *The Desperate Hours*, reflects that state of mind. Like *Detective Story*, it is an indoor piece, but here, the action is set in a suburban home, only occasionally shifting to scenes outside the house. Unlike *Roman Holiday*, which was filmed on location, *The Desperate Hours* was shot entirely on Paramount's sound stages—the studio even built a seven-room house to Wyler's specifications. This would be Wyler's last black-and-white film for some time, although he utilized Vista-Vision, a widescreen format developed in the 1950s to differentiate Hollywood's products from television.

Joseph Hayes's novel *The Desperate Hours* became one of the hottest literary properties in 1954 (even before it was published). The book was first serialized in *Collier's* magazine; it was then chosen as the main selection of the Literary Guild Book Club and eventually became a best seller. There was a bidding war for the film rights, and one of the most prominent seekers was Humphrey Bogart, who wanted to produce and star in the film for his Santana Productions. Although Bogart did not acquire the rights, he did end up costarring in the film. Wyler, who had read the unpublished manuscript and coveted the property, asked Paramount to top any bid. Hayes signed a deal with Paramount for $50,000 against a percentage of the gross. The studio also agreed to let him write the screenplay, and Hayes was excited at the prospect of working with Wyler. Hayes eventually signed another contract to turn his book into a Broadway play. Due to a strange confluence of events, the play was not written until after the film was completed, but the film was not released until after the play had closed.

Despite the fact that Hayes's theatrical version came after the making of the film, the two adaptations share a similar structure. The story revolves around three escaped convicts who terrorize a suburban family of four, holding them hostage while awaiting the arrival of their getaway money. The film's action takes place primarily in the Hilliard home, although there are a number of scenes in the police station, where both local and federal officers are looking for Glenn Griffin, the mastermind behind the escape. The irony of this variation on the standard sequence of composition is that while the screenplay is not technically an adaptation of a play, its confined setting makes the plot seem stage bound, and Wyler is unable to exploit the drama and excitement inherent in the basic situation.

Wyler never talked much about *The Desperate Hours* because, in all likelihood, he was dissatisfied with it. One problem was that he did not get the cast he wanted. His first choice for the role of Dan Hilliard, the father and protagonist, was Spencer Tracy. When Bogart was cast as Glenn Griffin, however, the two actors could not agree on top billing, and Tracy dropped out. Wyler's backup choices were Gary Cooper and Henry Fonda, but he could not secure their services either. Finally, at the suggestion of Don Hartman, who had recently become Paramount's head of production, Wyler settled for Fredric March, who had won an Oscar for *The Best Years of Our Lives*. Meanwhile, Wyler's first choice for the convict was not Bogart but either Marlon Brando or James Dean—believing that a much younger actor would be more menacing. At Hayes's urging, however, he eventually decided that having a middle-aged convict mirror the father's maturity—allowing the two to play off each other—would add dramatic value and tension to the film.[44] Wyler shot the film in eight weeks, beginning in mid-October 1954 and finishing in mid-December. The play opened in New Haven a month later and premiered on Broadway in February 1955.

Like *Detective Story*, this film reflects the anxieties and paranoia of 1950s America. Michael Anderegg likens *The Desperate Hours* to Donald Siegel's *The Invasion of the Body Snatchers* (1956), which some critics have read as a parable of the incursion of Soviet communism, fueled by the HUAC's investigations of communist infiltration into various aspects of American life. He notes, however, that Wyler's suburban family represents a "far less metaphysical embodiment than Siegel's aliens."[45] Certainly, the HUAC associations implicit in Hayes's plot were not lost on Wyler, but his film has a broader political message. Wyler's concern for America at this time—and the likely message of Siegel's film as well—is his fear of conformity and the resultant loss of individuality. As Wyler indicated in his letter to Freeman, the primary motivation for his political activism was standing up for individual liberty. *The Desperate Hours* is a parable, warning against the use of force as a mechanism of social control.

In his study of 1950s films, Peter Biskind identifies a group of movies that deal with the "enemy within." These, he notes, are realistic films that portray aliens inside society, taking their cue from the headlines of the day. The "troublemakers" in these films are communists, "but also gangsters, juvenile delinquents, and minorities." Biskind discusses various approaches to the threat posed by these "aliens," including the approach of the pluralists, who rejected force as an answer because "it contradicted the permissive, consensual model of society." The pluralists believed that, in America, "power was dispersed among the people," and they rejected force as an instrument of social control because it did not work. "It made things worse, drove dissidents into rebellion, and over the long haul it destabilized society."[46]

The Desperate Hours, with its repudiation of violence, seems to belong in this category. At its climax, as Dan Hilliard faces Griffin with a loaded gun, the criminal taunts him, daring him to shoot. Dan realizes that he cannot do it—he understands that he is not a killer. Ultimately, he triumphs because he is resourceful and summons up the courage to confront a crisis. Instead of shooting his adversary, he slaps Griffin and orders him out of the house. The last line of the play (not included in the film) is spoken by Carson, an FBI agent: "World's full of Hilliards." It is a valedictory to the ordinary American citizen who is resourceful, ethical, and courageous. Hayes goes even further in his novel: "Magnificence. That was the word. You'd never think of applying it to Dan Hilliard and his wife. But it applied. Maybe you didn't think of it normally because the chips weren't down but when the chips were down—."[47] Wyler does not rely on any character to express these thoughts directly, but presumably, his audience is feeling them. And indeed, it may have been reasonable to expect such a clear-cut recognition of everyman's heroism in 1955, when the film was released, although today's audience is likely to react far more ambivalently.

In the 1950s, the rise of suburbia in America was in full swing. As reflected in *Best Years*, countless soldiers had returned from the war and were trying to reintegrate into American life—often by marrying and starting families. In Kantor's novel, Al Stephenson has a home in the suburbs, while Fred and Peggy aspire to live in a similar place. Fred eventually accepts a job building suburban homes; presumably, he and Peggy will move into such a home someday. That promised future is also depicted by Wyler in *The Desperate Hours*, with Frederic March providing a personal link between the two films.

Wyler's suburbs are marked by a lack of individuality. Many of the houses built after the war were identical, prefabricated structures, and the Hilliards' home looks like all the others on the street. Unlike Hayes, who opens his play in the police station, Wyler begins the film by focusing on a suburban street, the sun down on shining on a tranquil, quiet neighborhood. The placid street scene and the Hilliards' tidy home are no different from the environs of the suburban families presented in countless television dramas of the time. This banal setting quickly establishes Wyler's focus on the peaceful conformity of American life and the sanctity of the nuclear family.

The Hilliards, however, possess a gun—a disturbing image that undercuts the seeming serenity of their surroundings. Dan hides this weapon from his son, Ralphie, but its mere presence indicates that the family anticipates trouble. As both the play and the film make clear, however, they are totally unprepared for the reality of such an event. When a band of escaped convicts suddenly takes up residence in their midst, the utility of the suburban lifestyle and the idealized American nuclear family as barriers against the invasion of "others" is revealed to be a sham. The Hilliards become prisoners in their own home, a place where they expect to exert control; the Griffin gang takes that illusion of safety away from them. Wyler's postwar America, clearly, is faced with dangers from within as well as without.

By immediately focusing on the family, Wyler shows that attempting to shield ourselves from political reality by withdrawing into our own private worlds can have disastrous effects. This danger is dramatically represented when Eleanor Hilliard (Martha Scott) begins to straighten up the house after her family has departed for the day's activities. She is listening to the radio, and when news of the escaped convicts is broadcast, she switches to a music station. Eleanor, apparently, feels safe and secure in her home, the dangers of the outside world easily distanced from her. Within moments, however, that threatening reality will intrude on her peaceable kingdom. Her world and, by extension, the suburban community that embodies it will be shattered by the abrupt entrance of the convicts. Likewise, the typical American family of the 1950s tended to ignore the realities of the HUAC and the dangers of nuclear war, preferring to socialize with friends and neighbors—the insular security of their neighborhoods no more than an illusion. In reality, the Hilliards will find that they are protected by no one in their community. The arrival of Ralphie's teacher, of Cindy's boy-friend, and of Mr. Peterson, the garbage collector, will only bring them more trouble—the last resulting in Peterson's death. The Hilliards will fi-nally learn that they are indeed alone.

The suburban family is balanced by the criminal family. The Griffins are also a family: Glenn and Hal are brothers. Glenn looks out for his younger brother, and the play implies that they are together because of their familial tie. In the play, Glenn is described as being in his mid-twenties, with "a rather appealing boyish expression," while Hal is younger, with a "confused, hard but somehow rather sensitive face." The casting of Bo-gart (who was already ill with the cancer that would soon kill him) makes Glenn more of a father figure. He is clearly much older than Dewey Mar-tin, who plays Hal, and he looks even older than Fredric March, whose mature status he now clearly parallels. In addition to being one of Bogart's final roles, Glenn Griffin is one of his more unsavory ones. In his first role for Wyler—as Baby Face Martin in *Dead End*—the character's criminal-ity is placed in the social context of the slum environment where he grew up. Here, he is a social misfit who preys on innocent women and children, motivated by simple envy. The play implies that the Griffins grew up in an abusive home, but the social factors are only hinted at, not developed, and Wyler cut Glenn's final moment of hallucinatory reproach to his father, just before his death. Jesse Bard, the deputy sheriff who is in charge of the inves-tigation and has dealt with Glenn Griffin before, labels him a psychopath, unfit for human society.

Wyler moves the film beyond the scope of the play by making the strug-gle between March and Bogart a battle of authority figures who are men-tors to their children (in the film, Hal is Glenn's surrogate child). Hal rejects Glenn at the end, leaving the Hilliards' house and vowing to strike out on his own. But during his time in the house, Hal has been affected by the lov-ing attachment among the family members, and he has even fallen for the older daughter, Cindy. He recognizes that although Glenn helped him es-cape their father, the life Glenn has provided cannot replace the family life he was deprived of—one of the key ingredients being the female presence that is so clearly lacking in the Griffin brothers' lives. Hal comes to regret his life of crime, but once he is away from the Hilliards, he reverts to his old ways, stealing a car, and soon he is killed.

At the end of the film, the tables are turned, and Hilliard has the gun. When he threatens Glenn and orders him out of the house, the criminal tells him, "You ain't got it in you," to which Hilliard replies, "I've got in me. You put it there!" What has the suburban American patriarch found within himself? Is it a capacity for brutality, for evil? Has he discovered what Young Charlie learns from her uncle in Alfred Hitchcock's *Shadow of a Doubt*, another parable of a sleepy suburb invaded by evil? Wyler's film, like Hitchcock's, removes the veil of innocence from postwar America's view of itself, suggesting, through the doubling of the two older actors, that we have been harboring "it" all along.

Wyler accentuates the connection between the men in the staging of the final sequence. As Hilliard reenters his home, he and Griffin face each other in profile in a two-shot. Later, in Ralphie's room, when Griffin is holding the boy at gunpoint, Wyler shoots them in a shot–reverse shot, accentuating the distance between them. March's face reflects a rediscovered strength that is somewhat undercut by Wyler's filming him in shadow, while Bogart's reveals a weariness that is accentuated by the stubble on his face. After the "You ain't got it in you" exchange, Wyler significantly amends the end of the play. Holding the gun, Hilliard informs Griffin that his brother is dead, shot full of police bullets, adding, "You put them there." Then they square off as father figures—one who has just saved his son, the other culpable in the death of his own—as Wyler returns to a shot, uniting them for a moment in the same frame.

This moment is not in the play. There, when Hilliard slaps Griffin and orders him to "Get out of my house," the gangster reverts to childish whining, as if he is speaking to his father: "You hit me for the last goddamn time. . . . You ain't ever gonna hit Hal again. . . . You can sit here 'n' rot in your stinkin' house." He is still yelling as he runs out of the house: "You ain't gonna beat it into Hal and me. Hal 'n' me's gonna be right on top!" He is shot down by a police officer and dies. In the play, Hayes thus has his gangster figure reenact a scene out of *White Heat*, shot down in a blaze of glory.

Wyler's closing scene, in contrast, avoids such mock heroism. In a Wyleresque gesture, Hilliard does not slap Griffin but pushes him down the stairs. The film's Glenn Griffin then exits the Hilliard home with his hands up. But when he sees a light shining in his face, he throws his empty gun at it and, in a moment that combines resignation and bravado, is shot down in a volley of machine-gun fire. Wyler's Griffin is weary, but still proud. The excessive machine-gun fire is a testament to his audacity, but it seems a bit much for a man who has nothing left.

Wyler's coda also differs from the play, which ends with the FBI agent Carson praising the Hilliards as a counterpoint to Bard's "disgust with the human race." Wyler's ending is mostly devoid of dialogue, as the camera focuses first on photographers taking shots of the dead Griffin and then on Eleanor Hilliard, who watches from across the neighbor's lawn until she sees her husband exit the house. Wyler unites them in a long shot and then, in a scene reminiscent of the reunion of Fredric March and Myrna Loy in *Best Years*, she runs toward him. Here, the couple falls short of an embrace, but the children then run to their father—first Ralphie, then Cindy. The film concludes with the family walking arm in arm into their ravaged, bullet-riddled home. Wyler chooses not to sing the praises of the family's heroism, though he celebrates their decency and integrity. The restrained ending indicates that the Hilliard family may be intact and resilient, but their encounter with the "enemy" has clearly changed them. Wyler is warning that, like the Hilliards, America must turn outward; it must face the world and engage with it. We isolate ourselves at our peril, he seems to say.

The film was not as successful as Wyler or the studio had hoped. Whereas the play won a Tony Award for Best Play, the film did not resonate with either the public or the critics. Although it did return its investment, it was not the smash hit the studio had clearly wished for and predicted. Wyler blamed the lukewarm reaction on "not enough violence." He went on, "I tried to make it on a more intellectual level, and the picture was a disappointment. The people want violence. To try to eliminate that is absolutely ridiculous."[48] Wyler is more specific in his production notes, which outline his aims but also contain the seeds of the film's undoing: "The audience wishes to see—longs to see—the hero or heroine accomplish certain ends. The villains are very clearly defined. They're bad, and the audience wishes to see them get their comeuppance. Everything is based on a single threat to sympathetic people." This bare analysis explains the basic, emotional thrust of the material, but Wyler actually aimed higher, seeking to create some uncertainty in the audience: "Any ambivalence creates tension, almost unbearable tension."[49] This extra layer of heightened tension was the

"Wyler touch"—which separated the film from the novel and the play yet undoubtedly contributed to its disappointing performance at the box office, because it complicated the film's portrayal of good and evil.

In casting Bogart and thus making Glenn an older man who cares deeply for his brother, and in having Hal learn that his life has been ruined by a series of bad choices, Wyler creates some sympathy for the villains. And just as his Griffin gang is not "clearly defined," Wyler's Hilliards are not entirely likable, either. Michael Anderegg perceptively observes that the Hilliards have "few of the saving graces" of the Minivers.[50] No doubt affected by his own precarious political situation, Wyler chastens the Hilliards for their smug self-righteousness and complacent attitudes. If such even-handedness left the audiences of 1955 uncomfortable, Wyler's less than enthusiastic attitude toward the American nuclear family and his evident sympathy for the underdog make the film more interesting today.

The film also failed to resonate because, despite Vista-Vision, it looked too much like a television show. This result was truly ironic, for Wyler's intention was to critique the stereotypical treatment of the American family that was characteristic of 1950s television. By going outside the home too often, Wyler also failed to exploit, as he did so well in *Detective Story* and *The Heiress*, the spatial restrictions of the home that could have made it seem more of a trap. The long takes that served him so well in adaptations such as *The Little Foxes* were not the best visual strategy to exploit "the unbearable tension" he wanted to create. Instead, those extended perspectives merely dissipated the film's emotional energy.

Wyler started out the 1960s with the blacklist still on his mind. At a National Press Club luncheon for *Ben-Hur*, he denied there was ever a communist infiltration of Hollywood, condemned blacklisting policies, and asserted his intention to hire writers without regard to their politics. To illustrate the absurdity of the blacklist, he mentioned that Ian McLellan Hunter had been blacklisted as a communist, yet his original story for *Roman Holiday* was a monarchical fairy tale: "Royalists everywhere loved it."[51]

Wyler made three big-budget color films—*Friendly Persuasion*, *The Big Country*, and *Ben-Hur*—before remaking *The Children's Hour* (1961), his last black-and-white film and a work that belongs with the HUAC-inspired group considered here. He claimed to be unhappy with *These*

Three, his first try at Hellman's play and his first film for Goldwyn. Wyler told Curtis Hanson, "I had been dissatisfied with 'These Three'; it was not the picture I intended. . . . It was emasculated. On the stage it was a tragedy."[52] So he decided to remake *The Children's Hour* and remain faithful to Hellman's original text. The result, as he later told Charles Higham, was "a disaster." This time, he "had adhered too closely to the original play, which had dated badly."[53]

Ironically, as Wyler pointed out, the play's central point was integral to both versions: " I saw the story as a tragedy about the power of a lie—in this case the lie that one of the students spread about two of her teachers. I thought the film a serious study of the evil that a lie can wreak in people's lives."[54] It was for this very reason that Hellman felt she had not damaged her 1936 adaptation by shifting the emphasis from lesbianism to a love triangle. The remake's connection to the Hollywood blacklist gave the newer film a certain resonance, but interestingly, the earlier version was superior, despite the interference of the censors.

In announcing his intention to remake Hellman's play, Wyler sidestepped the issue of lesbianism. He claimed that the story's subject was a moral one and not essentially about lesbianism, which he said did not interest him. (If so, one wonders why he chose to revisit the play.) He went on to say, "We haven't attempted to make a dirty film. We plan to do everything possible to keep [children] away, even to telling them: We don't want your money if you're under sixteen." Producer Walter Mirisch told the press that he was working to get the Production Code revised. Hellman, of course, had never used the word *lesbian* in her play, and in spite of all the posturing, it was not used in the film either.[55]

Once Wyler had settled on the idea of remaking *The Children's Hour*, he contacted Hellman about writing the screenplay. He informed her that he had no deal as yet but hoped to start filming in 1961. Hellman was thrilled at the prospect of working for Wyler again, but when she did not hear from him for two or three months, she accepted a teaching position at Harvard. (After her appearance before the HUAC in 1952, Hellman had been forced to sell her farm, and she needed to work.) Wyler, in the meantime, had persuaded Mirisch to buy the rights from Samuel Goldwyn, and Mirisch had taken out a ten-year lease on the property for $350,000. Learning that Hellman was now committed to Harvard, Wyler implored her to write a draft before starting her teaching assignment, but this proved impossible, as she was going to London for a revival of one of her other plays.

Wyler ultimately persuaded Hellman to work on an outline while sailing to London on the *Queen Elizabeth* in October. (Hellman wanted to introduce Wyler to Peter Schaffer—a young playwright who would later write *Equus* and *Amadeus*—whom she recommended as a screenwriter, but his schedule conflicted with Wyler's.) Once Hellman returned to New York, Mirisch drew up a contract, agreeing to pay her $50,000 to write the screenplay. But the producer was not satisfied with the outline she submitted some months later, and he became concerned about Hellman's working only part-time on the script while teaching at Harvard. He insisted that Wyler send the outline to someone else, and the director decided on Ernest Lehman and John Michael Hayes, both of whom had had recent successes with Hitchcock (Lehman with *North by Northwest*; Hayes with *Rear Window*, *To Catch a Thief*, and *The Man Who Knew Too Much*). After reading Hellman's outline, Lehman passed, but Hayes accepted and was hired.

Wyler was not pleased with the draft Hayes submitted in April—he had changed the title to "The Infamous" (later pared down to "Infamous")—and the director sent it to Hellman for suggestions. She found it "mostly workable" but, interestingly, did not consider it very good "because it borrowed too literally and not always too wisely from the original play." She also felt that everybody in Hayes's version "talks too much."[56] She mailed Wyler some revisions from her home on Martha's Vineyard but declared that an extensive rewrite was necessary, and she could not do that herself unless production was delayed, which was impossible.

Wyler had already cast the principals. Audrey Hepburn had accepted the role of Karen even before Wyler had a screenplay. Shirley MacLaine was cast as Martha, and James Garner would play Joe. The supporting roles went to Fay Bainter (who had won an Oscar for *Jezebel*) as Mrs. Tilford, and Miriam Hopkins (who had played Martha in *These Three*) as Lily Mortar, Martha's aunt. Wyler had a difficult time casting Mary, the student who lies about Martha and Karen. In a rare casting error, he settled for Karen Balkin, who had starred in a regional production of *The Bad Seed*, a dramatization of the popular novel about a murderous child.

The failure of *The Children's Hour* stems from both Wyler's decision to remain too faithful to a thirty-year-old play and Balkin's overacting to such an extreme that her character's accusations lack any credibility. Wyler, inexplicably, only heightens this mischaracterization by filming some of Mary's outbursts in close-ups that are jarring and destroy the narrative flow. In addition, James Garner projects neither depth nor charm as Joe, leaving the audience wondering what Karen sees in him. Even their love scenes seem perfunctory. Nonetheless, the film contains some scenes that are among Wyler's most visually expressive.

The film opens with idyllic, rural images that mirror the feel of some early scenes in *These Three*. We see girls bicycling across a bridge and then playing a game of catch by a lake. The openness and playfulness reflected in these scenes stand in marked contrast to much of the rest of the film, where even the outdoor scenes seem constrained. The camera next tracks through the tree-lined entry to the Wright-Dobie School and goes inside, where a piano concert is being held for the parents. Wyler introduces Karen and Martha on opposite sides of the room in separate frames, as if to accentuate the schism between them even in the midst of a happy occasion.

He then cuts to Martha, Karen, and Aunt Lily, who are in the kitchen washing and drying glasses after the party. In this scene and in many others set in the home/school, Wyler's camera includes the ceiling in the frame, which creates a feeling of confinement. In these rooms, the ceilings seem to bear down on the characters, trapping them even when they are happy and content. Some of the rooms—especially Karen's and the one shared by Mary and Rosalie—and the corridors in the house are at angles. Wyler's camera emphasizes these angles while also employing shadows that seem to lurk everywhere. A constant atmosphere of oppressiveness thus pervades the film, robbing the school, which is also Karen and Martha's home, of any feeling of comfort.

Joe Cardin's introduction matches the oppressive feel. He is framed first by the kitchen door and then by the open space between the kitchen and the classroom behind it. Here, Wyler's use of the frame-within-a-frame structure highlights Martha's antagonistic attitude toward this intruder, who clearly wants in. When he leaves with Karen, they are filmed in a tight shot in a car—a marked divergence from the outdoor stroll and the cake they share in *These Three*. Their conversation is also tense: Joe wants to get married, but Karen wants to put off this commitment until the school is financially stable. In fact, there is hardly a friendly, open, or loving moment in the entire film.

When Joe drives Karen back to the school, Wyler cuts to Martha's sad face framed by her window—an image he will repeat before her suicide. When Karen goes upstairs to announce her wedding plans, Martha is alone, ironing. Wyler again emphasizes the ceiling pushing down on the two women; the beams seem to touch their heads. Then, as she hugs Karen, Martha's face echoes her desolate expression at the window moments earlier.

Wyler's most forceful compositions come at three important moments in the film, offering subtle variations on one another. In the first, after Mary makes her accusations in the backseat of her grandmother's car, Mrs. Tilford decides to stop at the school to confront the women. There she meets Lily Mortar, who is packing to leave after having a fight with her niece. Descending the stairs and dropping her suitcase, Lily notices Mrs. Tilford, who has already entered the house. Lily complains about her niece, and Mrs. Tilford questions her use of the word *unnatural* to describe Martha. As Lily answers, she is seated on a step separated from Mrs. Tilford by the stairway railing and bars, though joined in the frame by Wyler. Their culpability in the crime they are about to commit links them, although they are separated by the degree of their guilt. When Mrs. Tilford leaves to rejoin Mary in the car, Wyler reverts to a tight, enclosed framing. As the sequence ends, Mary looks out the rear window of the car as Wyler tracks away from the school, reversing the camera movement that first introduced the place and the festive concert inside.

Wyler later varies this linking composition when Mrs. Tilford discovers the truth about Mary. Mrs. Tilford is in her living room, her back to the camera. When she hears Mary, she turns toward the camera and calls to the girl, who is near the top of the staircase. At first, they are shown in separate frames. Then, as she calls for Mary to come to her, Mrs. Tilford walks toward the staircase, and they are joined in the same frame but at a distance. Again, the stair railing separates them, and Wyler highlights the verticals and horizontals of the banister to emphasize entrapment. When Mrs. Tilford trips as she is walking toward the stairs, she ends up sitting on the floor, framed by the doorway; Mary is still in the frame, but separated by the stairs, almost approximating the earlier framing of Mrs. Tilford and

Lily Mortar. The double framing of the sitting woman and the girl above her on the stairs diminishes Mrs. Tilford. She then rises and walks silently toward the stairs as Mary, facing her grandmother, backs up. Silent and defeated, she moves to the upper level of the house and is not seen again. As is often the case in Wyler's films, a recognition scene has taken place on a staircase—Mrs. Tilford finally recognizes her granddaughter's villainy, just as Alexandra comes to know her mother's in a similar scene in *The Little Foxes*. Mary's backward progress up the stairs here is not quite the same as Catherine Sloper's ascent at the end of *The Heiress*, but the movement's similarity suggests some ambivalence in Wyler's attitude about Catherine's act of vengeance at the end of that film.

From that recognition scene, Wyler dissolves to Martha entering her house in the evening. She walks toward Karen, who is seated to the side and framed by a doorway, just as Mrs. Tilford was in the earlier scene. When Karen informs Martha that Joe has left, Martha stands again, and though she seems to be on a somewhat higher plane than the seated Karen, the space between them is diminished—in part because their house is so bare, dark, and lifeless. When Martha confesses that she truly loves Karen, she is seated, facing front, not looking at her friend. They are on the same physical plane, but the truth will not set anyone free.

After the confession, Martha retires to her room. When Karen goes upstairs, Wyler places Martha in a corner, with an angled wall behind her, and Karen is framed in the doorway. The low-ceilinged room is again oppressive and shadowed. Martha tells Karen that she would prefer to talk tomorrow, and Karen leaves to take a walk. Martha's face is then framed in the window, and additionally by the curtains, as she watches Karen leave; Karen's image is also framed within the window. The framing of Martha's face here recalls a similar shot of Regina at the end of *The Little Foxes*. In the earlier film, Wyler traps Regina in the vortex of her greed while at the same time freeing Alexandra, who goes off with David to escape her mother and her past. Martha, in contrast, looks down on a scene of desolation.

Inexplicably, Wyler and Hayes altered the ending of Hellman's play, wherein Mrs. Tilford goes to the school after learning the truth and offers to make restitution to Karen. This gesture of reconciliation occurs after Martha has confessed her love to Karen, and it is followed by her suicide. In the film, however, Martha is present for Mrs. Tilford's apology and offer of money, so her suicide after this revelation undercuts its dramatic impact and drains the scene of its irony. Because of this restructuring of events, the film ends not with Mrs. Tilford's visit to an unforgiving Karen but with Martha's funeral.

The film, which opens with children at play, thus ends in a cemetery. Karen is standing at Martha's coffin, fingering a flower. Wyler opens up the scene to reveal the gravestones behind her and then cuts to Mrs. Tilford and Joe. Karen next escorts Lily Mortar to a cab and then walks the same roadway leading out of the cemetery. Wyler follows her in a deep-focus composition, foregrounding Joe and the graves while Karen seems almost lost in the distance. The central players in the drama are thus isolated amid the prevailing images of death. Karen's gait becomes bolder and changes to a stride as the camera shows her walking away. The image is ambivalent: Karen seems resolute but alone as she leaves behind Joe, the school, and her dead friend. Unlike *These Three*, which concludes with Karen and Joe finding each other in Vienna, the new film carries a death-inflected finality that would not have pleased Samuel Goldwyn but suited the mood of William Wyler.

Despite the loosening of the Production Code to allow homosexuality as a subject in 1961, Wyler's film seems tentative, and it was neither a critical nor a commercial success. Two other films dealing with homosexuality and released the same year—*Advise and Consent* and *The Best Man*—fared better. Shirley MacLaine told Jan Herman that Wyler "chickened out" and "gutted scenes in the middle of the picture which showed that Martha was in love with Karen."[57] This faintheartedness seems obvious in Wyler's filming technique, which is full of melodramatic close-ups that overplay either dramatic moments or revelatory ones. Wyler, who rarely reverted to close-ups, was clearly uncomfortable with the material and unsure how to handle it. His usual control over an ensemble of actors broke down, and much of the film is poorly paced and flat. He seems more at home with the two scenes that reflect the blacklist. In the first of these, Joe is fired from his job at the hospital in what is clearly a case of "guilt by association"; in the second, Martha is shown berating her aunt Lily for not coming home sooner to testify in their defense. Lily makes it clear that she did not want to be tainted by her niece's scandal.

Wyler made *The Children's Hour* after living in Italy for more than a year during the filming of *Ben-Hur*. As was the case when he returned from Italy after *Roman Holiday*, Wyler's mood had soured. There is a scene early in *Ben-Hur* in which Judah (Charlton Heston) is speaking to his childhood friend Messala (Stephen Boyd), who has returned to Judea as commandant of the troublesome province. Messala asks Judah to help him weed out pockets of rebellion by revealing the names of rebel leaders. Asking, "Would I retain your friendship if I became an informer?" Judah refuses to help Messala maintain a "stranglehold on his people." In a film that is partly a critique of America's ambitions of empire (recalling Rome's), Wyler effectively pits friend against friend in a political struggle that ends in Messala's death. In choosing to revisit *The Children's Hour*, he wanted to make a smaller, more intimate film, but one that reflected an American tragedy and spoke of his growing mistrust of the government. He stumbled, however, by overestimating the relevance and power of a play that had no tragic dimension, and by failing to confront the play's sexual issues squarely and thus turn them into a compelling symbol of America's ills.

15

The Pacifist Dilemma

Friendly Persuasion (1956), *The Big Country* (1958),
Ben-Hur (1959)

Wyler was ready to leave Paramount after his five-picture deal ended in
1955. The studio had retained veto power over many of his decisions, and
Wyler felt that he was never allowed the artistic control he had been promised. Paramount pressed to keep him, offering profit participation, but Wyler decided, while still shooting *The Desperate Hours*, to move to Allied
Artists. He had been courted for some time by Allied's vice president Harold Mirisch, whom he had met in 1952.

Originally part of Monogram Pictures, a B-picture unit that released *Thunderbolt* after the war, Allied had been restructured in 1953
and was now ready to produce high-quality films. In pursuit of that ambition, Mirisch signed not only Wyler but also Billy Wilder, who would direct *Love in the Afternoon*, starring Gary Cooper and Audrey Hepburn.
Mirisch then completed his "hat trick" in early 1955, signing Wyler's close
friend John Huston, who was planning to reunite with Gregory Peck and
follow up their adaptation of *Moby Dick* with another Herman Melville
project, *Typee*. Huston was also considering filming Stephen Crane's *The
Blue Hotel*. (He had already filmed Crane's *The Red Badge of Courage*, in
1951.) In the end, however, Huston never made a film for Allied, and Wyler
and Wilder completed only one film each—both starred Gary Cooper—in
their short-lived association with the studio.

Wyler decided which film he would make for Allied while still editing
The Desperate Hours. *Friendly Persuasion*, based on Jessamyn West's series of interrelated stories about an Indiana Quaker family during and after
the Civil War, had been published to some acclaim in 1945, and the screen
rights were purchased by Liberty Films for Frank Capra a few months later.
Capra then hired Michael Wilson, who had worked on *It's a Wonderful*

Life, to write the screenplay as a vehicle for Bing Crosby and Jean Arthur. Wilson, having returned from World War II a pacifist, was drawn to West's portrayal of the testing of the Quaker family's nonviolence in wartime. He completed a script for Capra, but the director decided that the political climate in 1946–1947 made the story's antiwar message too dangerous, and he shelved it. When Wyler decided to do the film some ten years later, he inherited Wilson's script.

Wyler's assistant, Stuart Millar, loved Wilson's script. He was impressed that the screenwriter had adhered closely to West's stories, and he called the script "the most incredible job of construction."[1] But Wyler had problems with it: he felt that it lacked dramatic focus and needed extensive revisions. Wilson had paid too much attention to peripheral characters, Wyler thought, and he especially disliked the treatment of the Civil War theme in the second part of the script.

Wilson concentrated his adaptation on West's story "The Battle at Finney's Ford," which centers on the decision of Josh Birdwell, the son of the protagonists, to join his neighbors in battle because he believes that his duty to country and home supersedes his commitment to nonviolence. After focusing on Josh's intense internal conflict as he reaches this decision, West's story ends with the Confederate army bypassing Finney's Ford and Josh going home without being fully tested. In Wilson's script, Josh does join the battle, but when he discovers Confederate soldiers at the river crossing near his land, he cannot fire at them and shoots into the air instead. He then gets into a fight with his brother Labe, who has followed him. (Wyler cut this character from the final script.) Gardner Overby, who is the son of a friend and engaged to the Birdwells' daughter, breaks up the fight, and the boys go home.

At the end of Wilson's script, Josh decides to become a stretcher-bearer —thus serving his country while maintaining his pacifist principles. Wilson, who would be blacklisted in 1951 for refusing to inform on others, wanted to emphasize that in America an individual can remain loyal to his principles. He even included a scene in which a Union major comes to the church to recruit volunteers, only to find himself ignored. The officer angrily shouts that there "appears to be an organized violation of the law." He then backs off, stating, "I am not charging you with treason! President Lincoln himself has taken a sympathetic view of your . . . your pacifist convictions."[2] This episode represents a clear attack on President Truman's intolerance of dissenters.

Wyler felt that Wilson's script, like West's story, evaded the question of what a Quaker would do when confronted with violence. He wanted his film to deal with that issue more directly, insisting that it form the dramatic crux of the story. Unable to use Wilson, who was blacklisted by this time, he asked Millar to compile a list of possible writers to rework Wilson's original script. Initially, Wyler was reluctant to consider West herself for the job because she had ducked the issue in her story, but Millar convinced him that it would be worthwhile to at least speak with the author. When Millar contacted West, however, she told him that she was working on a new novel and was not interested in any movie. She added that she had heard plenty of Hollywood stories about her book over the years, including rumors that her protagonist Jess Birdwell would be played by Bing Crosby or Spencer Tracy. When Millar pressed, telling her that he was William Wyler's assistant, West claimed she had never heard of the noted director. But after Millar reeled off a list of his boss's credits, West admitted that she had seen them all and thought "they were good pictures."[3] She then agreed to meet Wyler at his home.

West recounted her first meeting with him in her book *To See the Dream*: Wyler asked her, "Who have you thought of as the central figure in these stories of yours?"

"Jess, of course," she said, referring to Jess Birdwell, the father of the family. "Jess is the hero from beginning to end."

"Stu tells me you think if a movie were made, it would have to center around the Civil War story."

West explained, "Everything else is either comedy, or has to do with the Birdwells when they're much older, or is very slight."

"Frank Capra had a script written which centers on the Civil War episode," Wyler told her. "The last half of it has to do with the boys. Jess becomes an onlooker."

"In the one story, 'Battle of Finney's Ford,' that's true," West replied. "But it's not true of the book as a whole."

"If you were to center the story on the Civil War episode, how would you get around this?" Wyler asked.

"Invent something."

"What would you think of Gary Cooper as Jess?" Wyler asked.

"Will Cooper play the part?" West countered.

"Not in this script. Coop says if he starts a movie he likes to be in it at the finish."[4]

West and Wyler were charmed with each other, and they agreed to work together. West claimed that during the meeting she actually invented a new character for the film: a close friend of Jess's who is not a Quaker and not a pacifist, "someone as strong in his way as Jess is in his."[5] Wyler was pleased with her suggestions and asked her to write them down. He promised to forward them to Cooper and to have her over for dinner.

Wyler also wanted to impress upon West that he was no Quaker. "He had been in the Navy [he was actually in the air force] during the war—his ear was deafened by gunfire. Evil, in his experience, had to be resisted with violence."[6] Indeed, this need to resist oppression as strongly as possible was a key issue for Wyler; in fact, it was the main reason he was drawn to the novel. He had witnessed the mayhem of the First World War from the basement window of his home and had participated in the next one. To Wyler, placing his protagonist in an extreme position that tested his faith seemed to be the crux of the story. It was also analogous to what so many in the film industry had to face in their dealings with the HUAC. Pauline Kael's observation that Wyler's Quakers are present "only to violate their convictions" was a rather flip reaction to the film's crucial issue, but it hinted at the contemporary relevance of that moral quandary.[7]

When West met Cooper at Wyler's dinner party, the actor told her: "There comes a time when people who see me in a picture expect me to do something."

"You mean pull a trigger?" West asked.

"Deliver a blow. Fist or bullet. Or sword. They expect it. They feel let down without it."[8]

In a subsequent meeting, when Cooper wanted to know what his character would do in the way of action, West replied: "Refrain. You will furnish your public with the refreshing picture of a strong man refraining." But Wyler could not decide how Jess Birdwell would "refrain" until almost a year later, when the film was being edited. John Huston read the script and liked it, but when he saw that Jess was going to pick up a gun near the end of the film, "he had to stop reading," according to Wyler. "He said it was painful for him to watch Jess, a man whose whole life had been given to nonviolence, waver." West, however, was adamant that Jess should at least pick up the gun: "Jess is a good man, but a man with a flaw. He must be tempted to violence; and we must see him tempted. We have promised the audience that. And he must have the means of killing in his hand at the moment of his temptation."[9] In the end, Wyler decided to stretch Jess's temptation to the limit. He put aside Huston's objection and did indeed put the gun in Jess's hand, but he chooses not to pull the trigger.

Wyler eventually offered the screenwriting job to West, whose first draft was titled "Mr. Birdwell Goes to War." Wyler liked her work but did not consider it a shootable script. He then hired another writer, Harry Kleiner, but was so disappointed in Kleiner's script that he discarded it entirely. Wyler next teamed West with his brother Robert, who helped her with construction and dialogue; he also served as associate producer.

Gary Cooper was signed to star in what would be his second Wyler film in the spring of 1956. For the role of Eliza, Jess's religious and opinionated wife, Wyler wanted Katharine Hepburn, but she was not available. The part was subsequently turned down by both Vivien Leigh and Ingrid Bergman. Bergman wanted to work with Wyler but was still unwelcome in Hollywood because of her affair with Roberto Rossellini. Wyler then considered multiple actresses for the role, including Jane Wyman, Teresa Wright, and Maureen O'Hara, before finally choosing Dorothy McGuire.

For the role of Josh, the Birdwells' elder son, Wyler wanted a fresh face, and he sent Millar to New York to find someone. Anthony Perkins was not exactly a newcomer—he was then appearing in the Broadway hit *Tea and Sympathy*, where he had recently replaced John Kerr. Wyler went to see the show, and Perkins sealed the deal when he did a reading for the director. Wyler next recruited two of his actors from *The Desperate Hours* for two other crucial roles—Richard Eyer was cast as Little Jess, and Robert Middleton was given the role of Sam Jordan, which West had created to balance Jess's Quaker beliefs. Phyllis Love played Mattie, the Birdwells' adolescent daughter.

West's *The Friendly Persuasion* consists of a series of stories, set in late-nineteenth-century Indiana, that are integrated less by plot continuity than by a pastoral mood and a cast of characters centered around the Birdwell family. Except for the Civil War story mentioned earlier, the action does not revolve around "big" events, drawing instead on the routines of family life. These everyday happenings are flavored by local color and charm, depicting a vanished bucolic world. In many respects, West's book resembles Jan Struther's *Mrs. Miniver*—another loosely connected series of stories about life's small routines portrayed in idyllic terms, unified by the presence of the Miniver family and the consciousness of the eponymous heroine. In both works, the approach of war threatens to unravel the central families' unity, beliefs, and most deeply held values.

Wyler's film begins, as does his adaptation of Henry James's *Washington Square*, with credits that appear to be stitched onto nineteenth-century needlepoint samplers. This homespun style, as in the earlier film, creates the feel of a vanished world, and Wyler transitions into the film's narrative by dissolving the final needlepoint into the actual setting. Unlike *The Heiress*, however, *Friendly Persuasion* is in color—it is Wyler's first color film. The look is so vibrant and the colors so intense, especially at the beginning, that the Birdwells' farm and the surrounding countryside look like they have emerged from a storybook illustration or a painting.

Friendly Persuasion appealed to Wyler because he saw it as opportunity to deal with the subjects of pacifism and war, which would also figure prominently in his next two films, *The Big Country* and *Ben-Hur*. He later told Axel Madsen that he would have liked to make a film about a child of war:

> Not just a child in war, that's appallingly common, but a child in a place where loyalties are divided. Because it is always the same in all countries, isn't it—patriotism and flag waving. You see them here parade with flags, hundreds of flags, and in the Soviet Union or Nazi Germany all the same. Where I grew up you didn't know. You heard one thing at school and another at home. Some people were on this side and those who were on the other side were not traitors. One neighbor was on this side, one neighbor on the other. It was not simply everybody waving the same flag, right or wrong. I never found the story that would tell that. But it must have been like that in Vietnam.[10]

Wyler was, of course, referring to his own childhood memories of growing up in a region with allegiances to two countries and to parents of different nationalities. He had been educated in schools run by both sides, and at the age of twenty, he had immigrated to another country and eventually participated in a war against one of the countries occupying the borderland of his childhood.

This personal history of mixed allegiances and contradictory experiences made Wyler naturally sympathetic to a project exploring divided loyalties—in this case, pacifist Quakers who are torn between their religious beliefs and the need to protect their homes during wartime. Although Wyler's film has sometimes been described as an homage to pacifism, it is hardly that; his dramatic framings and editing invariably undercut its value as a viable philosophy in today's world. The film's idyllic mood reflects Wyler's fondness for the Birdwells' way of life, but he repeatedly summons that mood in such a way as to emphasize that these scenes function more as a wish-fulfillment dream than a realistic portrait of life.

Just after needlepoint credits transition to the Birdwell home, Wyler introduces a note of discord by showing the house reflected upside down in a stream. The opening scene, narrated by Little Jess, is a comic sequence that introduces the ongoing rivalry between him and Samantha, Eliza's pet goose. Little Jess, who is dressed to go to Sunday meeting, warily watches Samantha, who is waiting for a chance to bite him. When she eventually succeeds, the child threatens to kill the goose but is stopped by his mother, who chides him about his violent tendencies. Little Jess then goes to play with his older brother, Josh, and the boys pretend that they are shooting Confederate soldiers. These two scenes, though played for comedy, immediately introduce the subject of war and the human tendency toward violence, which the Quaker religion preaches against.

Wyler soon injects another discordant note when he pictures the Quakers entering the meetinghouse. He cuts inside to a shot of the congregants walking into a space where the women are seated to the left and the men to the right. As the camera pulls back to show each section outlined by the beams of the building, this frame within a frame suggests that the Quakers are trapped by their beliefs, which will soon be severely tested. The camera then pans around the meetinghouse, finding some of the Quakers deep in meditation; others, like Jess, seem bored. When one of the children looks out a window, Wyler cuts to the inside of a nearby Methodist church, where the spirited congregants are singing a hymn. This lively scene is followed by a cut back to the meetinghouse, where Wyler again utilizes the same beam framing that seems to confine the Quakers in the passivity of their quiet faith. The contrast is striking: the Quakers appear severe and unyielding compared with their more joyful and expressive neighbors.

The silence of the meetinghouse is broken when an elderly woman who recently celebrated her eightieth birthday reads from Proverbs: "Who so hearkeneth to Me, shall dwell safely and shall be quiet from fear of evil." This homily is followed shortly by a long shot of the building's exterior, where a buggy driven by two soldiers is pulling up to the front door. As Major Harvey steps out and enters, Wyler cuts to a medium-long shot of him at the front of the meetinghouse, with the congregants on either side; his very presence seems ominous. After talking about the war and the sacrifices made by thousands of people in the service of the Union, he asks the Quakers to pitch in to fight against slavery. Eliza answers that while her people oppose slavery, they are also against killing men to free others. The officer then asks if they are willing to stand by and let others fight for them. This challenge temporarily silences the congregation.

When Major Harvey asks Josh if he will fight, the young man replies, "I don't know." Purdy, another congregant, berates Josh for wavering in his faith and then announces that nothing, not even a threat to his family, could push him to violence against his fellow man. Jess, in an attempt to diffuse the situation, reveals his own doubts but concludes that if presented with a situation in which his family's safety was at stake, he hoped the Lord would show him the way. Unable to recruit any volunteers, Harvey leaves, and the camera follows him as he limps toward the door past the silent congregation. Wyler's framing of the service—from the elderly woman's reading of Proverbs to the entrance of the soldier, who is passionate about the need to fight, and the ensuing discussion of war as a defensive action—points to the director's ambivalence toward the Quakers' philosophy. While their aims may be laudatory, their ideals are seemingly out of the sync with the world they live in. This perception is hammered home later when Purdy does a complete about-face and becomes a vocal advocate for violent revenge after his farm is plundered and burned.[11]

Much of the film, however, is too lighthearted to be taken seriously as an examination of the moral issue it raises. The screenwriters retain some of the incidents from West's story collection and weave them into more integrated plot elements. The film deals humorously with Jess and Eliza's disagreement over his purchase of an organ, with Jess and Sam's friendly competition in racing their horse and buggies to church, and with Little Jess's confrontations with Samantha the goose. There is also a comic inter-lude—in which Jess and Josh visit the Widow Hudspeth (Marjorie Main) and her three daughters—that is so broad that West detested it. In *To See a Dream*, she writes that she "cannot stomach" it, but "Mr. Wyler loves [it] with the unreasoning infatuation of a Titania for Bottom." She goes on to describe his treatment of the incident, which is depicted much differently in the book, as "Dogpatch exaggeration."[12]

The central failure of *Friendly Persuasion*, however, is that, unlike to *Mrs. Miniver*, it does not effectively integrate the war and its aftermath into the narrative. In the earlier film, the war becomes central to the fam-ily's story: Clem and his motorboat take part in the evacuation of Dunkirk, Mrs. Miniver captures a German pilot, Vin joins the RAF, and his wife (a character invented for the film) is killed during an air raid. Even the Mini-ver home is bombed and partially destroyed. In *Friendly Persuasion*, by contrast, the war remains peripheral—even when the conflict arrives on the Birdwells' doorstep, it has little lasting effect. This distancing is found in the book as well, but the filmmakers explicitly set out to make more of a point of how war affects the Quakers' pacifism.

In light of Wyler's professed interest in the war theme, it seems strange that he eliminated from the film various references to it in the West-Wyler final shooting script—especially those that prepare the audience for Josh's decision to take part in the battle to protect his town. For instance, after hiding from the raiders at the Hudspeths' farm, Josh has to be reassured by his father that he is not a coward. Another scene features Gard, Sam Jordan's son (soon to be engaged to Mattie Birdwell), who returns home wounded from the war: Josh asks Gard if he hates him for not fighting. In a scene with Enoch (a runaway slave who works on the farm), Josh talks about dying. They hear sounds that Enoch thinks might be bushwhackers, and Josh takes a horse to see what is going on. This bold action, in defi-ance of his parents' warning to avoid any potential violence, represents a significant move toward his decision to fight. That scene is followed by another in which Josh encounters some refugees who have been displaced from their homes and others who are wounded. If Wyler wanted to make a strong argument about the compelling realities of war, one wonders why he cut these sequences.

In the film, however, Josh does come into conflict with his mother over his decision to fight. His doubts, as reflected in the Sunday meeting scene described earlier, have now hardened into certainty. West's point—that pacifism is not a rule but a matter of conscience for Quakers—is effectively demonstrated in the scenes between Josh and his parents. While Eliza is firmly opposed to Josh's participation in the war, Jess believes it would be wrong to interfere in his son's decision; as he tells his wife, "I am his father, not his conscience." He also tells Josh that if he has a "sword in his heart," he "should pull it out and use it." As he often does in scenes of family conflict, Wyler presents this discussion in a three-shot around the kitchen table, with Josh in the middle, thus avoiding the impression of prioritizing one position over the other.

When Josh comes down from his bedroom on the morning he is supposed to leave, Wyler utilizes a modified deep focus, showing Jess and Eliza in the kitchen in the rear of the frame, while the staircase dominates the camera's gaze. As Josh descends, only his hand holding a rifle is seen at first, as if that image represents his new identity. Eliza moves near him, her eyes on the gun, and Wyler creates another three-shot, with Jess in the rear. Then, as he bids farewell to his parents, Josh is again placed in the center of a three-shot—Eliza stands with her back to her son, while Jess, his hand on his son's shoulder, says, "God bless thee."

Considering its importance to Wyler's conception, the battle sequence is especially disappointing. West's "The Battle of Finney's Ford" sidesteps the issue of Josh killing anyone in the war by having him fall off a cliff and crack his skull. His battle experience is thus turned into a pratfall, and all the fighting is over by the time he wakes up. In Wyler's version, however, Josh does fight, killing Confederate soldiers, and he is wounded. That scene, in addition to one created for the film to introduce the runaway slave Enoch (Joel Fluellen), embodies Wyler's belief that pacifism is no defense against hatred and racism. Hearing rumors of advancing Confederate troops, Enoch asks Jess for a gun, declaring that he would rather die fighting than return to the South as a slave.

Josh's wounding is not shown. Instead, Wyler cuts from the battle to Josh's riderless horse returning to the Birdwell farm, which motivates Jess to retrieve his rifle from a closet. Wyler's composition is interesting here: As Jess holds his rifle, Eliza enters the house at the left of the screen. The door seems to cut the frame in half, emphasizing the gulf between Eliza's pacifist domesticity (she is in the kitchen) and Jess's decision to take up arms and fight. She begs him not to go, but he persists, and Wyler's camera follows Jess as he takes on the heroic demeanor of Gary Cooper—riding away on his horse, rifle in hand, in a shot that resembles a number of similar images from *The Westerner.*

On his way to find Josh, Jess discovers his friend Sam Jordan, who has been shot; after a few words, Sam dies in Jess's arms. The Confederate soldier who shot Sam then returns to steal his horse and shoots at Jess but misses. Jess wrestles the gun away from him and points it at his stomach. Then, after a poignant moment of decision, Jess tells the soldier to go, assuring him, "I'll not harm thee." With a beatific look on his face and Dmitri Tiomkin's music swelling in full angelic mode, the soldier walks slowly toward the camera and out of the frame as Cooper stands next to a tree in the distance, holding his rifle and looking noble. Wyler would use such sequences more effectively when depicting Christ in *Ben-Hur.* Here, the composition just seems ponderous, and the attempt at grandeur falls flat.

The battle scenes are more protracted and more fully developed in the script. There, a sergeant who is stationed next to Josh is killed immediately after the first battle begins, which motivates Josh to shoot and kill. Another battle scene follows, and in a series of revised pages, the writers have Josh kill a rebel soldier. Another intense battle is detailed, and on another revised page, the screenwriters add, "Josh is a fighter now." In the act of reloading his rifle, he is hit and "badly wounded."[13]

The final shooting script also features a gallant Gary Cooperish scene in which Jess, on horseback, scoops up a wounded rebel soldier, saving him from an oncoming horse. There is another cut to the Confederate camp, where a captain tells the lieutenant in charge that Morgan, the commanding officer, has decided to bypass the town of Vernon and pull out. This announcement signals the end of the conflict—at least in the Quakers' vicinity. The scene of Jess saving the wounded Confederate soldier was important to West, and in July 1955 she explained to Wyler why it was thematically essential: "It will establish what the audience needs to know 1) that Jess is no coward 2) that he is concerned with, involved with the lives of human kind, not just his family—that his decision not to fight is not negative. . . . He not only doesn't want to kill—he wants to save. And [in] addition to all this—the scene will be beautiful and exciting to see."[14] Wyler apparently did not agree, since the scene does not appear in the finished film.

The film ends almost the same way it began, with the Birdwells getting ready for Sunday meeting. The war seems to have had little effect on the idyllic appearance of either the Birdwell home or the surrounding country-side. The notable changes between "then" and "now" are slight: Eliza has allowed Jess to move the organ from the attic to the living area, Josh's arm is in a sling, and Little Jess has made friends with Samantha. Gard Jordan (Mark Richman), who proposed to Mattie earlier, is now escorting her to church. Unlike war's profound effect on the Minivers, it seems to have been only a slight inconvenience in the lives of the Birdwells.

Again, the final shooting script's ending is more poignant and power-ful. There, Josh and his father have an important exchange when Jess finds his son lying wounded on the battlefield:

JOSH: Father, did thee fight?
JESS: No, Josh . . . I didn't fight . . . and thee did. We both lived up to all the Light we had. That's all that's asked of us.[15]

The script's final scene, which follows that moment of reconciliation, finds the Birdwells and Enoch in the Methodist church, where the minister reads off the names of those who have died, including Sam Jordan. Then he asks the congregation to rise, and Jess is shown singing "Praise God from Whom All Blessings Flow." Eliza, who was formerly opposed to all music and ob-jected to having an organ in her house, looks on and smiles. Mattie is seat-ed by Gard, who is in mourning for his father. Showing the Birdwells and Enoch attending a Methodist church to honor Sam's memory offers a pro-found image of the changes not only in one family but also in the country.[16]

Friendly Persuasion's postproduction life proved to be more dramatic and contentious than its story. Because Jessamyn West and Robert Wyler had rewritten much of Michael Wilson's original script, Wyler suggested on February 8, 1956, that the screenplay credit should read, "Screenplay by Jessamyn West and Robert Wyler from the book by Jessamyn West."[17] Wilson protested, and the dispute was submitted to the Writers' Guild.

On March 9 the guild informed Allied Artists that the credits should read: "Screenplay by Michael Wilson from the book by Jessamyn West." However, the guild also informed the studio that, according to its bylaws, if a screenwriter had ever lied about being a member of the Communist Party or invoked the Fifth Amendment—which Wilson had done—Allied did not have to give him screenplay credit. The studio then informed the guild that it had decided against giving screenplay credit to anyone. The dispute went public when Wilson received a Writers' Guild award for best screenplay and an Oscar nomination (the Academy subsequently disqualified him). Wilson then sued Wyler, Allied Artists, and Liberty Films over the denial of credit, asking for $250,000 in damages.

Wyler was angry and disgusted by this controversy. He urged Allied to appeal the guild's decision and offered a compromise that would give all three writers credit. The studio, however, was worried that if Wilson's name appeared onscreen, the film would be picketed by the American Legion, adversely affecting its profit margin. *Friendly Persuasion* thus became the only film in Hollywood history to be released with no screenplay credit at all—although, when the DVD version was released in 2001, Wilson was credited as the sole screenwriter, per the guild's ruling. Wyler, meanwhile, remained frustrated that West and his brother had been deprived of credit and of a potential Oscar nomination. (The script was indeed nominated, but with no names attached.) Wyler complained to Madsen: "If only the Guild had agreed to a three-way credit, Allied wouldn't have objected and perhaps the American Legion would have overlooked it. It was a damn pity because I think all three might have gotten Oscar nominations, because that was the year Dalton Trumbo won under a false name."[18]

As Wilson's lawsuit progressed, Wyler filed a deposition in which he defended his original position on the awarding of screenplay credit. He reiterated that Wilson's narrative emphasis had been wrong "and that in particular the second part of the script entirely avoided the issue by treatment in comedy terms and never bringing the principal character to his ultimate test, which is now the dramatic highlight of the picture." This is an interesting statement in light of the changes Wyler made to the West-Wyler script, which kept the comic emphasis of the film as well as including a test for the hero. He went on to state, "I believe that a viewing of the so-called shooting script . . . would not actually show the proper results, since a good deal

of the material that is in the final version of the picture was actually contributed during the shooting, by Jessamyn West and Robert Wyler."[19] This
is certainly true, because the final film, as discussed earlier, differs markedly from the final shooting script. Stuart Millar seconded Wyler in his deposition, stating that West and Wyler had essentially written the entire second
half of the film, as well as many scenes in the first half.[20]

Wyler has been accused of appeasing the blacklisters by keeping Wilson's name off the screen, and his initial decision to do so is indeed puz-
zling. An examination of Wilson's scripts clearly shows that he contributed
substantially to the finished film.[21] Numerous incidents and the lighthearted tone that dominates the first half of the film are derived from his script.
Wyler is correct in asserting that significant changes were made, especially
in the war sequences, but his refusal to acknowledge Wilson's contributions
does not seem justified.

Wyler may have simply felt intimidated by the government's monitor-
ing of his affairs and the attendant pressure to be more selective about the
organizations he supported and the people he worked with. His correspondence with Y. Frank Freeman at Paramount (discussed in chapter 14) shows
Wyler's more conciliatory mood and indicates a willingness to consider the
consequences of his political actions. A note in Wyler's file on *Friendly Persuasion* indicates that he spoke with Freeman about the Wilson matter on
April 8, 1954, and that the studio chief assured him that "no screen credit
need be given Michael Wilson, even if his script is used."[22] In that same file
is an article clipped from *Variety* detailing how the Motion Picture Alliance for the Preservation of American Ideals had criticized Samuel Goldwyn, Wyler's former boss, for purchasing the rights to *Guys and Dolls*.
That hit musical had been coauthored by Abe Burrows, who was named in
the alliance's publication the *Vigil* for his "vague testimony and for being
identified as a Communist by two admitted former Communists." This episode may have emboldened Wyler to deny credit to Wilson.

When Wilson died in 1978, his obituary in the *Los Angeles Times*
mentioned the dispute, and Wyler wrote a letter, published in the paper,
in which he recounted his revised opinion of the screen credit controversy:

> The fact is that I only objected that Wilson be acknowledged as
> the film's only screenwriter. Wilson's screenplay . . . was written

for another producer-director years before I undertook to make the film. Subsequently, two other writers, namely Jessamyn West and Robert Wyler together rewrote parts of Wilson's screenplay contributing significantly to the final picture and I felt their work should be acknowledged as well as Wilson's. So I proposed that all three names receive credit for the screenplay with Wilson's name in first place, thereby recognizing him as the "principal" screenwriter. When the Writers' Guild awarded Wilson exclusive solo credit, then the film's financiers and distributors—Allied Artists Corp—decided to release the film with no screenplay credit whatsoever, a decision I regretted but had no control over.[23]

Friendly Persuasion opened at Radio City Music Hall on November 1, 1956, and like *Roman Holiday*, it received respectable but not glowing reviews. The film did well at the box office but was not the unqualified hit Allied Artists had expected. In 1957 Wyler took the picture to the Cannes Film Festival, where it won the Palm d'Or as the festival's best film.

The film had a curious afterlife. At the request of the Soviet Union, and with the blessing of the U.S. State Department, Wyler took *Friendly Persuasion* to Moscow in 1960, where it was presented as a symbolic remedy to the Cold War. Then, almost thirty years later—at the advent of glasnost—President Ronald Reagan (whose politics Wyler detested) gave a videocassette of *Friendly Persuasion* to Mikhail Gorbachev. In a toast, Reagan lauded the film for showing not only the horrors and tragedy of war but also "the problems of pacifism, the nobility of patriotism, as well as the love of peace."[24] When the *New York Times* printed the text of Reagan's remarks, it occasioned some letters noting the red-baiting president's hypocrisy in praising a film written by a blacklisted communist sympathizer. The final irony (apparently lost on Wilson's supporters) was, as Jan Herman points out, that Josh's agonizing decision—whether to go to war or stick to his pacifist beliefs—was Wyler's focus, not Wilson's.[25]

Wyler's next film would explore similar issues with the same muddled results, but within the generic conventions of the western. Wyler had not made a film in that genre since 1940's *The Westerner* with Gary Cooper. Now, in the spirit of the times, he would make a "big" western. By the mid-1950s, television had absorbed a substantial portion of the movie audience. In an effort to compete, theatrical films became bigger and more expensive as directors began experimenting with Technicolor, Cinerama, CinemaScope, and Technorama. To shoot *The Big Country*, Wyler hired Franz Planer, and together they decided to make the film in Technorama and Technicolor.

Wanting to retain full artistic control of his projects, Wyler decided to form a partnership with Gregory Peck, who had become a close friend since their work on *Roman Holiday*. Their first venture was supposed to be a comedy, however, not a western. In December 1957 Peck announced that they would make a film about an art heist from the Prado museum in Madrid, and they hired Michael and Fay Kanin (*Woman of the Year*) to write a script. The screenplay proved unsatisfactory, and the project was shelved—though Wyler would later make a similar film, *How to Steal a Million*, with Audrey Hepburn (Peck's *Roman Holiday* costar) in Paris.

While that first project was unraveling, James Webb, a prolific writer of westerns (*Vera Cruz* and *Apache*; he would later write *How the West Was Won* and *Cheyenne Autumn*) brought to Peck's attention a story by Donald Hamilton, "Ambush at Blanco Canyon," which had been serialized in the *Saturday Evening Post* and later expanded into a novel titled *The Big Country*. Peck showed the story to Wyler, noting that it had at least six good parts and was "an anti-macho western."[26] Wyler liked the project, and the two friends divided up their responsibilities and formed two separate production companies—Wyler's was called World Wide Productions, and Peck's was Anthony Productions. Wyler would be in charge of artistic matters, while Peck, in addition to having casting and script approval, would choose the livestock, horses, and riders. Peck, who also had a development deal with United Artists, arranged for that studio to finance and distribute the film.

Again, Wyler had problems with the script. Five writers were listed on the final credits, including Robert Wyler and Jessamyn West; Leon Uris (uncredited) also worked on the script. Ironically, the Writers' Guild of America, successor to the Screen Writers' Guild, would be called on to arbitrate the credits on this film (as the latter had done on *Friendly Persuasion*), although Wyler claimed to have little recollection about who had written what. Donald Hamilton was originally hired to adapt his story, though he warned Wyler and Peck that he had no real screenwriting experience. When this proved to be a problem, the producers turned to Sy Bartlett, who had helped Wyler get into the air force and was now a screenwriter working with Peck. Robert Wilder, whose name is also on the credits, was a novelist (*Flamingo Road*) and a friend of Robert Wyler's.

Wyler assembled a big-time cast to complement the size of the picture. In addition to Peck, he signed Burl Ives, fresh from his stage success as Big Daddy in *Cat on a Hot Tin Roof* (a role he would repeat in the film) to play Rufus Hannassey; Charles Bickford, who had not worked for Wyler since *Hell's Heroes*, to play Henry Terrill, patriarch of the family feuding with the Hannasseys; Carroll Baker as Pat Terrill, who is engaged to Peck's character Jim McKay; and Jean Simmons as Julie Maragon, who owns the water supply the two families are feuding over. The final important role, Steve Leech (McKay'a antagonist), was offered to Charlton Heston. Already a star and a leading man who had just triumphed as Moses in Cecil B. DeMille's *The Ten Commandments*, Heston decided to pass because, in his opinion, at least three parts in the film were better than the one being offered to him. In his autobiography, Heston elaborated:

> I was still very preoccupied with the size and centrality of my part. . . . Is it better to have a good part in an important film, or the best part in an OK film? I know the answer to that now. . . . I didn't then. I called Herman [his agent], "Look I know this is a major movie, and it's a very good script, but my part isn't very good. We're getting a lot of offers now anyway. I'll pass on this one."
>
> "Kid," he said, "you don't know what the fuck you're talking about. You have an offer to work with Gregory Peck and for maybe the best director in film, and you're worrying the *part* isn't good enough for you? Don't you know that actors take parts with Wyler without even reading the damn script? I'm telling you, you *have* to do this picture!"[27]

Heston agreed, and Wyler had his cast.

United Artists agreed to a $2.8 million budget for the film. The shoot, which started in July 1958 and lasted four months, was done on two major locations. At one, near Stockton, California, Wyler built a ramshackle,

minimal town and shot the range scenes. The other, used for the more remote scenes, was in Red Rock Canyon and the Mojave Desert, which he
had used as backdrops for *Hell's Heroes* almost thirty years earlier.

The plot revolves around the feud between the families of two cattle
barons. Both want to take over the Big Muddy, a spread with a bountiful
water supply that is owned by the schoolmarm, Julie Maragon (Simmons).
She inherited the land from her grandfather but lacks the money to work
it. The Hannasseys, headed by Rufus (Ives), and the Terrills, headed by the
Major (Bickford), have hated each other for as long as they can remember. Julie will not sell to either of them because she wants the water to be
shared, not fought over. Within the generic plot structure of the western,
the Terrills seem to be influenced by eastern values: they live in a grand,
manor-like home with imported furniture, chandeliers, and carpets. The
Major's daughter, Patricia (Baker), dresses well and flaunts ladylike airs;
she has been back east, where she met Jim McKay (Peck), the scion of a
family of ship owners. In contrast, the Hannasseys, though considerable
property owners, are of a lower class; they live in a small, run-down home
and dress like westerners. Rufus's son, Buck (Chuck Connors), is a drunken
lout. Both Patricia and Buck are intimidated by their fathers—no mothers
are evident—the difference being that Patricia worships her father to an unhealthy degree, while Buck mostly hates his.

Arriving from the East to marry Patricia, McKay not only becomes
embroiled in the feud but also finds himself at odds with the Major's foreman and surrogate son Steve Leech (Heston), who is also in love with Patricia. Leech hates McKay's eastern, gentlemanly ways, which he considers
effete and unmanly. As if that were not bad enough, McKay compounds
his strangeness by not believing in violence and feeling no need to prove
his courage. This pacifist attitude eventually causes a falling-out with Patricia, who comes to doubt his manhood; she also belittles him for not being like her father. Meanwhile, McKay is having second thoughts about
Patricia and begins to fall in love with Julie. When Patricia and McKay
fight over what she perceives as her fiancé's cowardice and inability to live
up to her father's example, he walks out. The feud ends when Major Terrill
and Rufus Hannassey kill each other during a shoot-out in Blanco Canyon.
McKay and Julie then ride off together.

As he did in *The Westerner*, Wyler breaks with a number of generic conventions. He makes his hero an easterner who wears fancy clothes (including a derby hat) and does not carry a gun. Jim McKay has a seagoing heritage; he has no knowledge of the wilderness or the land—when he goes out on his own, he needs a map and a compass—and he is clearly not a man of the West. In contrast, the traditional western hero has no associations with the East, which is linked with education and culture; in fact, he is considered upright and strong precisely because he is a child of nature, uncontaminated by civilization.

None of the westerners in Wyler's film are strong, pure, or upright—they all make McKay look admirable by comparison. Major Terrill, whose home boasts eastern influences, and Patricia, who dresses like an eastern lady, are revealed to be greedy and selfish, with no discernible redeeming qualities. The viewer is relieved when McKay leaves the Terrill home and moves into town, for he is clearly too good for them. The Hannasseys, however, are no better than their rivals. Unlike the Terrills, they have not been contaminated by eastern ways, but their status as pure westerners does not make them very sympathetic either. Their isolated, all-male lifestyle has deprived them of social graces, and Buck is a boor and a bully who, late in the film, tries to rape Julie. Rufus, though endearingly honest, straightforward, and possessed of an innate sense of proper behavior, is brutally disfigured by his hatred of the Terrills. Despite his defects, Rufus may seem preferable to the Major, but both are presented as single fathers who have not succeeded in raising admirable children.

The other westerner, Steve Leech, is too much of a Terrill to command the sympathy of the audience. He is openly contemptuous of McKay and regularly tries to goad him into fights. In the climactic scene between the two, when McKay finally agrees to a fight, the brawl goes on for some time and concludes in a draw, with both men exhausted. Leech thereupon changes his mind about McKay, and after the fight, when the latter asks him, "Now, what did we prove?" he is unable to reply. He seems to be having second thoughts about the western code of violent behavior.

Wyler's standing the genre on its head might have been interesting, but the script remained a problem throughout the shoot; it offered no compelling dramatic conflict and provided no ending. Since both families are essentially unsympathetic and the central love stories uninteresting, there is no one for the audience to care about. Peck brings little to his rather stiff character beyond his usual presence and dignity. Each of the other central characters has only one dimension, as Wyler no doubt recognized early on, for he shows little interest in the human drama but concentrates most of his attention on the landscape instead. (Perhaps Robert Warshow was right when he wrote that the notion of "the western" is violated when social issues become its central concern.[28])

The idea of a "big country" did seize Wyler's imagination, however, and he turns "bigness" itself into a theme. The film's most recurrent stylistic feature—repeated so often that it becomes annoying—is the contrast between big and small. It is introduced with the opening credit sequence, as a stagecoach makes its way toward town. Between close-ups of the horses' hooves and wheels, Wyler cuts to extreme long shots of the stagecoach, which appears like a speck on a vast landscape. Then, as it approaches the town, Wyler cuts to a different angle, showing the town from the coachman's point of view. It appears remote, and that feeling is magnified by a crane shot looking down on the town, which is small and primitive and located in the middle of nowhere. There is nothing around it but space.

Once it is introduced in this dramatic manner, however, the town—usually a major presence in westerns—is of little interest in this film. Here, the major reason for its existence seems to be that it is the home of Julie, who, significantly, has planted a garden in front of her house. During the party given by the Terrills to introduce McKay to their friends, one of the guests comments to Jim that "it's civilized out here," though the town is obviously isolated, and it is not even clear whether there is a marshal to keep the peace. Indeed, later in the film, this judgment about being civilized seems to be contradicted when Rufus says to McKay that he would consider him a "law abiding man, if there was any law to abide by." The filmmakers appear to be more interested in the grandeur of the land than the issue of bringing civilization to the wilderness. When McKay steps out of the stagecoach in his fancy suit, tie, and derby, accompanied by his elegant leather suitcases, he is clearly out of place. He is immediately derided by Buck and some other cowboys. Leech, who has come to pick him up, advises him to get rid of the derby, or else some cowboy will get rid of it for him. How McKay and his eastern ways will transform the area is introduced as a potential central theme, but it gets lost too often before reemerging at the end of the film.

The contrast between the immensity and grandeur of the land and the insignificant, petty people who inhabit it frames the conflict between pacifism and violence that seems to be the film's central organizing theme. McKay, the easterner, has an aversion to settling disputes with guns or fists. As a gift for his future father-in-law, he brings his father's dueling pistols, noting that they have not been used in ten years. His peaceful ways are clearly in conflict with those of the Terrills, who believe in fighting—as do the Hannasseys. Such dualities extend throughout the film. Like the elegant McKay, the rough, violent Leech is in love with the spoiled and temperamental Patricia, who admires her father's ways and comes to despise her fiancé's views. She, in turn, is contrasted with the schoolteacher Julie, who is calm and sensible and eventually wins the love of McKay but is also pursued by the brutish Buck Hannassey. Finally, Patricia's love for her father is opposed to Buck's hatred for his own, though both relationships are presented as unnatural and problematic.

Early in the film, McKay is taunted, especially by Leech and the Hannasseys, but he refuses to be drawn into fights. His behavior is disapproved of but tolerated by Patricia and the Major. Like the Birdwells, however, McKay has his limits. After an argument with Patricia over his nonviolent philosophy, he decides to move out of the Terrill house. Before leaving, however, he challenges Leech to a fight, which takes place at night, with no witnesses. Again, Wyler pulls his camera away from the combatants to emphasize their puny insignificance against the massive expanse of their natural surroundings. Even the music fades out, leaving only the sounds of insects and pounding fists. The silence and the seeming stillness of the moonlit scene are in stark contrast to the way such a thematically crucial scene of violence would be handled in almost any other western.

The film's other violent scene, Buck's attempted rape of Julie, is handled in a similar manner. Wyler films this sequence inside the Hannassey house, which, unlike the Terrill mansion, is small and confined. As he so often does, Wyler includes in the frame the structure's low ceilings, creating a cramped space that seems to bear down on the inhabitants. Julie has been taken prisoner by Buck at his father's command—the goal being to get her to marry him and thus give them control of the Big Muddy. When Julie refuses, she is confined to a bedroom, and when Rufus leaves, Buck sneaks into the room. It is mostly dark, and the sequence is filmed in close-up, occasionally making the action difficult to follow. In one shot, Wyler films Buck on his knees framed through the legs of the bed. The darkness, the savagery, and Buck's caged-in posture become Wyler's symbols of a family deformed by violence and hate. When Rufus returns, he almost strangles his son, and the elemental hatred of son for father is displayed. This is Wyler's most brutal enactment of human behavior in either of his two pacifist films.

McKay's pacifist philosophy is further tested when he rides to the Hannassey place to demand Julie's release. Rufus admires his gumption, and when Buck tries to assault Julie again, McKay immediately moves to defend her by fighting off her assailant. His impulsive resort to violence parallels that of Eliza Birdwell when she lashes out with a broomstick at a Confederate soldier to defend her pet goose, as well as Josh's need to defend his land. When Buck tries to shoot McKay, Rufus draws on his own son, telling him that he will not tolerate the shooting of an unarmed man. Rufus then insists on an old-fashioned duel, using McKay's father's pistols. Buck violates protocol by shooting before his father says "Fire," but his bullet only grazes McKay, who then fires into the ground rather than shooting the now defenseless Buck. Unlike Leech, who seems to have learned something from McKay, Buck does not. He runs to retrieve a gun from a friend, only to be killed by his father.

The evolving disposition of McKay—who has now twice compromised his code of nonviolence—is paralleled by a change in Leech, who refuses to follow Major Terrill into Blanco Canyon to kill Hannassey and his men. His decision is motivated, in part, by his newfound respect for McKay but also by his realization that he and his men are outnumbered and are likely to be killed. Earlier, when trying to talk Hannassey out of the fight, McKay rhetorically asked him, "How many men know what they are fighting for?"—boiling down this proposed battle to a test of wills between two stubborn old men. Terrill now bears out the truth of this judgment in his own confrontation with Leech. Learning that he has been forsaken by his surrogate son and then by the rest of his men, he resolves to go it alone.

At this point, Wyler's mise-en-scène becomes problematic. As Major Terrill rides alone into the canyon, he is shown from the back and later from the front, looking like a gallant warrior, while marshal music plays. The audience knows Leech is right—the fight will be futile—but the framing of Terrill undercuts this recognition, suggesting, apparently, that his sense of honor trumps his foolish decision (as did Owen Thursday's in John Ford's *Fort Apache*). When Leech sees Terrill riding off alone, he decides to join him, despite his misgivings, and Wyler's shot of the two riding side by side, followed by the rest of the men, undercuts whatever power the pacifist message might have had.

Rufus Hannassey, however, has been influenced by McKay's opinion that he is a selfish old man. Realizing that the feud is indeed between himself and Terrill, he halts the gunfight and challenges his foe to a one-on-one duel. Again, Wyler pulls away his camera as the two old men fire at each other. Both are killed, but that end result is not represented visually. Thus, the final confrontation in Blanco Canyon is undercut by Wyler's ambivalence. He seems to want to distance his audience from the violence, yet some part of him (the former air force officer?) admires the sense of honor and the esprit de corps that motivate Leech and his men at the end.

Wyler's lack of involvement in this project became evident when he decided to leave for Rome to begin work on his next film, *Ben-Hur*, before the final sequence of *The Big Country* was even shot. His assistant Robert Swink, who had worked on Wyler's last five films, was left to craft the ending. So Swink called Peck and Simmons together to shoot what became the final scene. Having ridden to the foot of a mountain overlooking a majestic valley, McKay and Julie rein in their horses, look significantly at each other in separate shots, and then head down toward the Big Muddy together. They will, no doubt, marry and live together in the peaceful country. After seeing the final print, Wyler wrote to Swink, expressing his delight with the scene: "I can't begin to tell you how pleased I am with the new ending. . . . The shots [you] made are complete perfection. Exactly what was needed."[29] Whether Wyler truly meant that or was just happy to be rid of the film is open to question.

Wyler's letter to Swink camouflages the mood on the set, which seems better suited to the feuding Terrills and Hannasseys than to a famed director and his handpicked cast. The set was tense, as ego-driven fights erupted between the assembled stars, and even Wyler's friendship with Peck was affected. In an early scene, McKay and Patricia are seen riding in a buckboard back toward the ranch, when they are accosted by Buck and some Hannassey hands; McKay is tied up, dragged around, and humiliated. Objecting to one of the close-ups, Peck asked Wyler four or five times to retake the scene, and the director finally relented, agreeing to redo it before the company went home. When it became apparent that Wyler had not scheduled the retake, however, Peck left the set. The close-up was never reshot. Heston later defended his costar's reaction, explaining, "To him, I think, it was a question of ethics, not art. I agree—you have to keep your promises."[30] After this incident, Peck and Wyler did not speak to each other for three years.

The film opened to mixed reviews, but in spite of the critics—and the fact that westerns were a television staple and hardly a novelty anymore—business at the box office was brisk. Audiences thrilled to the colorful, widescreen splendor of Wyler's landscape, accompanied by Jerome Moross's Oscar-nominated score (which Heston considered the finest ever composed for a western film). Despite winning one Oscar—for Burl Ives as Best Supporting Actor—and finishing in eleventh place among top-grossing films that year, The Big Country barely broke even. Neither Peck nor Wyler participated in any profit sharing.

Like many westerns made in the 1950s, The Big Country grapples with the notion of negotiating with the enemy rather than engaging in violent confrontation, debated in response to various international conflicts arising during the decade. As in the global political aftermath of World War II, peace on the western frontier would require a spirit of mutual understanding and a desire to forgo violence. This pacifist inclination is clearly reflected in McKay's attempts to avoid violence even in self-defense, as it is in the stubborn Quaker faith of Amy Kane (Grace Kelly) in High Noon and Friendly Persuasion's Eliza Birdwell. In each of these cases, however, the pacifist position is finally undercut. When faced with an implacable and irreconcilable enemy, the nonviolent position proves untenable. Interestingly, The Big Country's most memorable sequences, including Peck and Heston's fight in the moonlight and the final shoot-out in Blanco Canyon, make their own statement about the inevitability of violence in a "pacifist" film.

Wyler would reconsider these questions one more time in what became his most honored film, Ben-Hur (1959). Judah Ben-Hur (Charlton Heston), a Jewish merchant of royal blood, reunites after many years with his close boyhood friend Messala (Stephen Boyd). Messala has returned to Judea, where he and Judah grew up, as the newly appointed Roman tribune. It is Messala's job to put down the locals, who are planning to rebel against the Roman occupation. Messala wants Judah to inform on the rebel leaders and persuade the rest of his countrymen that they should simply accept Roman rule. When Messala insists that "you are either for me or against me," Judah chooses to be "against." Later, during a procession, a tile from the Hur house is dislodged and hits the Roman governor. Although this was an accident, Messala refuses to intervene, condemning Judah to be a galley slave and imprisoning his mother, Miriam (Martha Scott), and his sister, Tirzah (Cathy O'Donnell). Judah, who earlier described himself as being "against violence," vows vengeance against his former friend.

The film presents the story of Judah's determination to survive his ordeals and return to Judea to kill Messala. As the original novel's subtitle suggests, it is also "A Tale of the Christ." Although the latter is only a minor thread of the story, Judah eventually embraces Christ's teaching that "forgiveness is more powerful than hatred." Wyler pays less attention to this aspect of the plot than the novel does, although the film does end with a stirring re-creation of the crucifixion and a miracle.

Sam Zimbalist, who had produced *Tortilla Flat* and *Thirty Seconds over Tokyo* in the 1940s, headed more extravagant productions in the 1950s, including *King Solomon's Mines* (1950) and another Roman/Christ epic, *Quo Vadis* (1951). He had learned that he could make big-budget films for less money in Rome, and he wanted to economize further by utilizing the sets from *Quo Vadis* for another film set in the same era. Zimbalist spoke to Wyler as early as 1957 about directing a remake of *Ben-Hur*, which had been a huge success for MGM as a silent film in 1925, when Wyler worked as an assistant on the chariot race scene. At first, thinking the producer was joking, Wyler suggested that he take his proposal to Cecil B. DeMille, whose reputation had been built on making epic films. Zimbalist, however, was not interested in the spectacle aspect of the movie: "What we want, what we're interested in, is good intimate stuff. Intimacy is the meat of the story and proportionally, the spectacle, is perhaps, one tenth of the whole film."[31] What Zimbalist wanted was the "Wyler touch"—the sophistication and depth Wyler could bring to the central relationships in the story. And, in fact, Wyler had more success bringing his distinctive flair to *Ben-Hur* than he had with *The Big Country*. Perhaps *Ben-Hur*'s more polished style was also due, in part, to his success in getting some better writers to work on Karl Tunberg's original script, including novelist Gore Vidal and playwright Christopher Fry, although neither of them received credit on the released film.[32]

Ultimately, Wyler was attracted to the project because he saw it as a challenge. He had never done an epic film, and he wanted to see if he could make a "DeMille picture." Perhaps more important, he was offered a great deal of money—$350,000, which, at the time, was the largest fee ever paid to a director. This sum was raised by $100,000 when he took over as producer after Zimbalist suddenly died during filming—plus 8 percent of the gross revenues or 3 percent of the net profits, whichever was greater. The film would eventually gross $76 million worldwide, making Wyler financially secure for the rest of his life.

The novel on which the film was based was a cultural phenomenon. Lew Wallace, a Union general, had begun writing the novel in Indiana after the Civil War and completed it eight years later in New Mexico, where he was the territorial governor. Published in 1880, *Ben-Hur* sold poorly for a few years, but by 1885, it was selling 50,000 copies a year; it would go on to become the best-selling American novel of the nineteenth century. Its success on the page was then matched by its triumph on the stage, when it was produced on Broadway in 1899, starring William S. Hart as Messala. Various versions of the original production toured the country for twenty years, and other productions were mounted in London, Paris, Berlin, and as far away as Australia.

In 1907 the Kalem Company brought out the first film version—a fifteen-minute affair featuring a chariot race staged by the Brooklyn Fire Department. MGM released a hugely successful version in 1925 at a cost of $4 million; it starred Ramon Novarro as Ben-Hur and Francis X. Bushman as Messala, and it was directed by Fred Niblo. This, too, was an enormous success, although its run was cut short by the advent of sound. Wyler's version would match its predecessors' success, being nominated for twelve Academy Awards and winning eleven (a record at the time), including Best Picture and Best Director (Wyler's third). Its financial success was so great that it temporarily saved MGM from bankruptcy and revolutionized the industry by spawning countless big-budget films.

Wyler's film alters Wallace's narrative in some important ways. In the novel, the Judah-Messala relationship receives only cursory attention, for Wallace is more interested in Judah's relationship to Christ. Wyler underplays that theme, however, making the relationship between the former friends central to the story, even though they do not interact during a significant portion of the film. In concentrating on this relationship, Wyler elicits some fine acting from Charlton Heston and Stephen Boyd (neither of them known as very expressive actors), vividly evoking their initial affection, which eventually turns to hate. Indeed, the emotional nature of their disagreement and estrangement dominates the opening movements so powerfully that it hangs over the film until the end.

Gore Vidal, who claims to have written much of the first half of the film, suggested to Wyler: "Could it be that the two had some sort of emotional relationship the first time 'round, and now the Roman wants to start up again? Ben-Hur doesn't—and doesn't get the point?"

"Gore," Wyler said, "this is *Ben-Hur*. You can't do that."

"If you don't do something like that you won't even have *Ben-Hur*," he retorted. "You'll have a motiveless mess on your hands."

"Well, you can't be overt," Wyler cautioned.

"I'm not going to be overt. There won't be one line. But I can write it in such a way that the audience is going to feel that there is something emotional between these two, which is not stated and which blows the fuse in Messala. He's spurned, so it's a love scene gone wrong."[33]

In later years, Wyler would claim that he did not remember having that conversation, but the relationship seems too charged, and Messala's reaction to Judah's turning him down too extreme, for a mere political disagreement. Wyler's framing of the reunion scene between the boyhood friends—clearly echoing the postwar reunion of Al and Milly Stephenson in *The Best Years of Our Lives*—confirms that he took Vidal's suggestion seriously, without being "overt." Judah is introduced in deep focus, framed in a doorway with crossbeams above it in the shape of a cross, thus anticipating both Judah's fate at the hands of Messala and his presumed conversion. At first, Judah is barely visible because Messala, his back to the camera, occupies the front of the frame. Once they catch sight of each other, the two men pause, then walk toward each other, meeting roughly in the center of the frame, and embrace. The sequence is filmed without a cut.

The intransigence of their subsequent hostility is similar to that of the

Terrills and the Hannasseys, but in this film, the motivations transcend simple hatred. The psychological complexity of the characters—an element that is sorely missing from *The Big Country*—feeds the intensity of their conflict, which, like the feud in the earlier film, severely tests Judah's antipathy to violence. Indeed, at one point, he prays, "May God grant me vengeance." The famed chariot race—the film's centerpiece—is, in effect, a variation of hand-to-hand combat, an alternative version of the confrontation between the Major and Rufus in Blanco Canyon. As Messala says to Judah before the race, "This is the day. It is between us now." While *The Big Country* ends with the death of the two antagonists, the chariot race ends in Messala's death and Judah's eventual redemption. Both films posit that pacifism is antithetical to human nature or, at least, that it violates masculine codes of conduct.[34]

The conflict between pacifist ideals and active resistance to oppression resonated with Wyler because of the correspondence between Messala's politics and that of the Nazis. As tribune, he announces, "The emperor is displeased. He wants Judea to be made into a more obedient and disciplined province." Then he goes on to counsel his friend: "Be wise, Judah. It's a Roman world; if you want to live in it, you must become part of it. . . . Persuade your people that their resistance to Rome is stupid. It's worse than stupid—futile. For it can end in only one way, extinction for your people." The ideology behind those words is recognizably Nazi, as signaled in the references to providence, obedience, and extinction. The association is made even more explicit in the following exchange:

MESSALA: In the name of the gods, Judah, what do the lives of a few Jews mean to you?
JUDAH: If I cannot persuade them, that does not mean I would help you murder them.
MESSALA: You are a conquered people, you live on dead dreams, you live on myths of the past.

Wyler was an enthusiastic supporter of Israel, and according to Madsen, he donated money to Israeli causes.[35] He certainly knew that in 1956, shortly before he started work on the film, Israel, backed by England and France, had started a war against Egypt in response to its president's nationalizing of the Suez Canal. When President Eisenhower condemned the attack, the troops were withdrawn.

Another dialogue sequence between Messala and Judah obviously resonated with Wyler as well. When the tribune demands that Judah reveal the names of Jewish resistance leaders, he labels them "criminals." Judah counters by calling them "patriots" and asks, "Would I retain your friendship if I became an informer?" This overt reference to the HUAC hearings compares America, in its attempt to subvert civil liberties, to the Roman Empire.

Though Messala's spirit hovers over the second part of the film, the action is dominated by Judah's love for Esther (Haya Harareet). The couple first meets in one of Wyler's signature staircase scenes: she stands at the top and then descends to meet Judah below. Esther functions as the link between the secular story and the more religious one, since she is the person who leads Judah to Christ. Whereas the novel's Judah comes to Christ more actively—he is the one who listens to Christ's Sermon on the Mount—Wyler's Judah, still bitter about the fate of his sister and mother, walks away from the sermon and hears about it from Esther. It is also through Esther that Judah is eventually reunited with his mother and sister.

In his final scene with Pontius Pilate, Judah rejects the governor's offer to become a Roman citizen. Although he was adopted, earlier in the film, by Quintus Arrius (Jack Hawkins), an admiral of the Roman fleet whose life he saved, he now asserts that he is not Young Arrius but Judah Ben-Hur. Declaring himself a Jew and not a Roman, he goes on to blame Rome for destroying Messala and turning him into a monster: "I knew him—well—before the cruelty of Rome spread in his blood. Rome destroyed Messala as surely as Rome is destroying my family." Despite this epiphany, Judah remains consumed with hatred because his mother and sister have become lepers and outcasts. Esther berates him: "Hatred has turned you to stone. It's as though you have become Messala."

Judah and Esther take Miriam and Tirzah to see Jesus, who, unbeknownst to them, is being led to his crucifixion. During a thunderstorm that signals Jesus's death, Esther leads the women to a cave. The darkness of the cave and the tight framing recall the gloomy, cramped room where Buck tries to rape Julie, as well as the catacombs where these women were imprisoned earlier, except that here, Wyler uses the dark enclosure as a forerunner of rebirth. As the water flowing from the storm mingles with Christ's blood, the women are cured of their leprosy, symbolically cleansed by the blood of Christ. (In this film, as in *The Big Country*, water has redemptive associations; this connection is reversed in *The Collector*.)

The final scene finds Judah, who followed Jesus and witnessed the crucifixion, entering his home and meeting Esther there. In another of Wyler's dramatic staircase scenes, he then sees his mother and sister, cured of their leprosy, at the top of the stairs. In a framing that matches the end of *The Heiress*, Judah ascends the stairs, but whereas Catherine's destination is not pictured in the earlier film, here, the camera follows Judah to the top, where he embraces the women amid the swelling of religious music.

Wyler's conversion scene is more indirect and vague than Wallace's or even Niblo's. The film's Judah seems less influenced by the teachings of Jesus—which, unlike his fictional counterpart, he never experiences directly—than by the dedication and love of Esther and the rehabilitation of his mother and sister. It is Esther who teaches him that "blessed are the merciful." Nonetheless, Wyler's Judah has finally embraced a unity with his people and a vision of brotherhood that is seemingly divorced from hatred and touched by the spirit of forgiveness, love, and hope.

The personal journey of Judah Ben-Hur is more dramatically compelling than that of the characters in *The Big Country* because Jim McKay and Julie Maragon never really learn anything. Their attitudes and beliefs are set from the beginning, so the events that unfold do not mold them in any way. One wonders how Steve Leech and Patricia Terrill will evolve after the death of the Major and their association with McKay, but the film does not tell us. Although both Hannasseys are dead, it is unclear whether their blood will cleanse the "big country." The pacifist argument of *Friendly Persuasion* poses similar problems. Jess and especially Eliza are steadfast from the beginning in their rejection of violence and the taking of another's life. Of all the central characters, only Josh is unsure, and he eventually joins his community's volunteers and fights in the war. Still, Wyler never delves deeply into the war's lasting effects on the Birdwells or even on Josh. In *Ben-Hur*, however, he offers a more spiritual journey, in that Judah learns something about the importance of love, and this realization changes his life.

What links the three films is Wyler's rejection, in each case, of the pacifist, nonviolent philosophy. After the war, his view of human nature had darkened, and the change would be even more clearly reflected in the three personal films that rounded out his career: *The Children's Hour*, *The Collector*, and *The Liberation of L. B. Jones*.

16

Final Projects

The Collector (1965), *How to Steal a Million* (1966),
Funny Girl (1968), *The Liberation of L. B. Jones* (1970)

After the enormous success of *Ben-Hur*, Wyler wanted to move away from big, expensive pictures and return to his roots by making a smaller, intimate drama featuring mostly interior sets. Choosing to return to the black-and-white format as well, he first took a second try at Lillian Hellman's *The Children's Hour*. As discussed earlier, that film was not successful, but its failure did not damage Wyler's reputation. He was by then one of the industry's giants and an elder statesman.

Darryl Zanuck, who was about to become president of Twentieth Century–Fox, wanted him on the board of directors, but after serving in that capacity for a short time, Wyler discovered that boardroom politics did not interest him. Zanuck's son Richard, who had been installed as head of production, then asked Wyler to direct the film version of Rodgers and Hammerstein's *The Sound of Music*, which had been running on Broadway for three years and won the Tony Award for Best Musical in 1960. Wyler went to see the play in New York but was not overly enthused about it. He remarked to his friend Bob Swink, "They want me to make this picture and I don't know what to do. The people in this musical are playing a scene and all of a sudden somebody starts to sing. Sometimes they're just walking along and somebody starts to sing. Why the hell do they start singing?"[1] Wyler was obviously aware of the conventions of musicals; he just saw no compelling motivation for many of the songs in the show. Nevertheless, he thought it would be a challenge to direct a musical—something he had never done. Fox had already signed Ernest Lehman (*North by Northwest*, *West Side Story*) to write the screenplay, and he encouraged Wyler to take on the film.

Wyler agreed, and he cast Julie Andrews. "I had seen her play *My Fair*

367

Lady in New York and was very impressed," he recalled. "She was working on *Mary Poppins*. I went over to the studio and Walt Disney showed me some rushes and introduced me to her on the set."[2] Wyler even went to Austria to scout locations and then traveled to Salzburg to meet the mayor and look at settings there as well. While making all these preliminary moves, however, he remained bothered by the idea of making a musical about the Nazis. When Lehman argued that they were really making a film about a heroic family who escaped the Nazis, he seemed at least partially convinced: "I knew it wasn't really a political thing. I had a tendency to want to make it, if not an anti-Nazi movie, at least say a few things. It was true that Nazism was not what the movie was about; I knew it would be a success; although not *that* big."[3] Wyler, however, was never entirely happy during preparation for the film, and when circumstances intervened that offered him a chance to back out, he took it.

Those circumstances involved a script provided by two young former television writers, Jud Kinberg and John Kohn, who had moved to London and were producing movies for Blazer Films. After reading *The Collector*, the first novel by British author John Fowles, they purchased the screen rights and then interested Mike Frankovich, head of Columbia Pictures' overseas division, in the project. Next, they sent the galleys of the novel to their first choice to play the lead, Terence Stamp, who was riding high on his success as Billy Budd in Peter Ustinov's film and his follow-up triumph on stage as Alfie. Kinberg and Kohn also wanted Wyler to direct. When Frankovich was made head of Columbia, he sent the two to visit Wyler at his home. By this time, the producers already had a first-draft script by Stanley Mann (*The Mouse that Roared*), which they left with Wyler, along with a copy of the novel.

Wyler loved the story, telling *Time* magazine, "I found I couldn't put the book down," although he thought Mann's script needed work.[4] He told Frankovich he wanted to do the picture and was even willing to relinquish his producer's hat to Kinberg and Kohn. Fowles's novel, which soon became a best seller, tells the story of Freddie Clegg, a compulsive, neurotic bank clerk who collects butterflies. One day, he wins the football pool and uses his winnings to buy a secluded mansion with a gothic cellar. It is there that he brings his latest specimen—Miranda, the girl of his dreams, an art student he has kidnapped off the street in London.

It is easy to see why Wyler was intrigued by this property. It features a protagonist whose obsessive nature recalls that of many of his earlier characters, including Seth Law of *A House Divided*, Martha Dobie and Mary Tilford of *These Three* and *The Children's Hour*, Julie Marsden of *Jezebel*, Heathcliff of *Wuthering Heights*, Regina Giddens of *The Little Foxes*, Catherine Sloper and Morris Townsend of *The Heiress*, James McLeod of *Detective Story*, and George Hurstwood of *Carrie*—all of whom work out their dramas within a confined space. Filming *The Collector* promised to be a more contemporary project than the remake of *The Children's Hour*, as the main character's seemingly innocent and gentle manner in fact camouflages a sick and damaged personality (much like Alfred Hitchcock's Norman Bates in *Psycho*). Wyler thus agreed with his producers that the role should be played by Stamp, who embodied angelic innocence in *Billy Budd* but was equally convincing as a womanizer in *Alfie*, a role that mimicked his tabloid life.

To cast the part of Miranda Grey, Wyler had screen tests made of young British actresses in London. Eventually, Samantha Eggar won the role, although she had little professional experience. Wyler was afraid she would not be able to handle the part, but Frankovich was taken with her and insisted that she be given a chance. Eggar was fired three weeks into rehearsals, however. As she later recalled, "Terry Stamp's nasty attitude toward me undermined me so much that I just became sort of a squashed balloon and, rightly, I got fired."[5] Wyler then contacted Natalie Wood and offered her the role two weeks before shooting was set to start, but a scheduling conflict prevented her from accepting. Finally, Wyler made a deal with Frankovich: he would rehire Eggar if she had an acting coach with her at all times. For that assignment, he chose veteran character actress Kathleen Freeman, who stayed with Eggar throughout the shoot, helping to mold her characterization.

At first, Wyler wanted to make the film in black and white because of the bleak subject matter, but he changed his mind after seeing Eggar's makeup tests, which were made both in black and white and in color. Cinematographer Robert Surtees was dazzled by Eggar's red hair and fair skin in the color test, which Wyler agreed was better, but he wanted the color to be subdued and muted. He also decided to film *The Collector* in sequence, hoping to help the young actress build her character more effectively.

Like *Ben-Hur*, the film version of *The Collector* departs significantly from the novel on which it is based. Fowles's novel is divided into two narratives, each relating the point of view of one of the protagonists—Freddie Clegg, the clerk who wins a large amount of money, and Miranda Grey, the doctor's daughter, art student, and political radical whom Freddie kidnaps. Her story is told in the form of a diary, which Freddie finds after her death. The film eliminates this dual perspective, effectively omitting Miranda's story; instead, it brings captor and captive together in one narrative presented from a detached, objective viewpoint. As he did in *The Big Country* and *Ben-Hur*, Wyler uses this material to examine themes of power and possessiveness, but this time, the story's more concentrated focus results in a much darker, more brooding and pessimistic film. Wyler was undoubtedly influenced by Hitchcock's *Psycho* and perhaps also by Michael Powell's *Peeping Tom*—both films about obsessive young men whose need for a woman's affection leads to destructive ends.

The film begins with a long shot of an open green meadow. Freddie then enters the frame chasing a butterfly, which he soon captures in his net and puts in a glass jar. He then moves toward a beautiful old Tudor mansion that is for sale. He jumps over the fence, approaches the side of the house, and enters a room that looks like a cellar out of a gothic horror film. The juxtaposition of field, house, and dungeon is jarring in its abrupt progress from freedom to confinement, and the concept of openness effectively disappears from the film after this first movement. We then hear Freddie's narration, which serves as a framing device at the beginning and end of the film. He talks of his decision to buy the house because of its remoteness and isolation but claims he had no idea he would actually go ahead with his plan to bring her (Miranda) there, even though he had made all the preparations. Wyler films Freddie from a low angle, emphasizing his freedom and power and making him seem almost larger than the house.

The dungeon that will be Miranda's prison becomes the film's central locus and metaphor. Wyler's framing evokes the dark, cave-like room where Buck Hannassey attempts to rape Julie Maragon, the dungeons where Tirzah and Miriam are imprisoned and the caves where they are kept as lepers, and the galleys where Judah Ben-Hur is confined. Julie, however, is redeemed by McKay's love, and the Hur family is saved in large part through divine intervention, while Miranda is afforded no such redemption. She will never escape her prison.

Our first view of Miranda is Wyler's. We see her through the window and blinds of Freddie's van as she exits the art school, vibrant and laughing. Wyler does not utilize point-of-view shots during these sequences; instead, the camera shows Freddie watching Miranda. She is then caught in a frame within a frame in the rearview mirror. Throughout these sequences, Wyler films Freddie mostly from behind in a silhouette-like shot. Dark and barely visible, he is associated with the dungeon, while Miranda is smiling and happy, enjoying the only moments of freedom she will have in the film before being captured like the butterfly.

Having subdued Miranda with chloroform and taken her to her "guest quarters," Freddie returns to his house and sticks his head under the sink faucet, wetting his hair and face. He is ecstatic, barely able to contain his joy at accomplishing his goal. When it begins to rain, he runs out, dancing with his hands in the air, and then lies down in the grass to let the rain wash over him. Wyler thus inverts the rain-redemption scene from *Ben-Hur* (when Miriam and Tirzah are cured of their leprosy), here emphasizing its perverse implications by cutting from Freddie's face to that of Miranda, who is just waking up and realizes she is imprisoned in a dungeon. Freddie's antics also mimic the exuberance of Heathcliff, who escapes to the moors to revitalize himself outside the confinement imposed by Earnshaw, who has become his jailer. Freddie, however, is no child of nature, for his love is an aberration, and he himself is the jailer.

When he brings Miranda her breakfast the next morning, Freddie utters his first words in character: "I hope you slept well." He seems solicitous and shy, but he betrays a total lack of understanding of her reaction to the situation she finds herself in. Apparently nonplussed by her demand to know where she is and why she was brought here, he expresses his conviction that, having been provided a room complete with art books and a wardrobe, she should be content to be his "guest."

The thematic center of the film occurs in the scene in which Freddie shows Miranda his butterfly collection. For the first time, he is verbally unrestrained and able to speak with enthusiasm about his hobby—referring to himself as an "ornithologist." Miranda, having been allowed to take a bath, is invited into Freddie's butterfly room, which is filled with framed exhibits. At first, she is dazzled by their variety and beauty, but she soon turns on him and bewails "all the living beauty you've ended." Defensively, Freddie echoes Messala's comment about the Jews when he replies, "What difference does a few specimens make to a whole species?" When Miranda sees her reflection in a butterfly case, she realizes that she, too, is being collected. She cries out that everything in the room is dead: "Is that what you love? Death!" Here, Wyler resorts to shot–reverse shots in a film that is dominated by two-shots. His camera lingers on Freddie's face after Miranda's accusation—he can say nothing, for this perception goes to the heart of his psychosis. Her words force him to recognize, finally, that his obsession with capturing and pinning down objects of beauty is not a matter of class difference (as implied in an earlier retort) but a perverse need to kill what he loves. Wyler then cuts to Miranda, whose look indicates that she knows she will die, like all the beautiful specimens in the room.

Freddie is not really attracted to Miranda as a woman, despite his claims of love. In the novel, Miranda clearly recognizes and articulates this lethal irony: "I am one in a row of specimens. It's when I try to flutter out of line that he hates me. I'm meant to be dead, pinned, always the same, and always beautiful. He knows that part of my beauty is being alive, but it's the dead me he wants." A reverse Pygmalion, Freddie really wants to possess an art object, and in this coldblooded pursuit, he closely resembles the Hitchcockian psychopaths Norman Bates, who also collects dead things, and Scottie Ferguson, who seeks to drain the humanity out of Judy Barton in *Vertigo*. All of them are slightly in love with death. As Miranda realizes that she will never be free—forever frozen, forever the same, forever beautiful, like the figures on Keats's Grecian urn—Wyler significantly cuts from her face to the pinned butterflies, which flutter as she closes the door, then to her drawings of Freddie hanging in her cave, and then to Miranda sketching a self-portrait while looking at her face, framed in a mirror, as Freddie watches her. Wyler, like Hitchcock in *Vertigo*, seems to be associating the preoccupation with art and beauty with an unhealthy, deathlike madness. Miranda, whose name is an ironic reference to the wizard Prospero's daughter, is herself an artist, and she is now fated to become an object like her drawing. When Freddie asks her for the sketch, she rips it half, telling him to put it in the drawer with the butterflies.

Freddie has promised to let Miranda go after a month, and on what is to be their last night together, he gives her a white dress to wear to their "last supper." When he comes to fetch her for the occasion, she looks lovely and virginal in the dress.[6] He has prepared a lovely table with flowers, champagne, and caviar, and he tells her, "I will be lonely here without you." Wyler films this remark in a suggestive three-shot, with Freddie in the foreground and Miranda's framed self-portrait hanging in the rear, while she stands in the middle. Over dinner, he proposes marriage, but when she accepts as a ploy to facilitate her escape, he goes mad. Again, Wyler uses the shot–reverse shot technique, as the camera moves in ever so slowly on Freddie's face. Reacting to his dangerous look, she runs from him. Once more, he chloroforms her—this time in his butterfly room—and carries her up the stairs. The upward movement here is a progress toward death, or death in life. Placing her gently on his bed, he lies down next to her and takes her in his arms. Freddie has now achieved his dream: he has embraced a ghost.

In the next scene, Miranda is seen descending the stairs after a bath and attempting to seduce Freddie. She embraces him, entices him to kiss her, and then undresses. Clearly distressed, Freddie can barely look at her. Instead, he mostly looks away and yells that he could buy what she is offering in London, and he rips her portrait off the wall. She has become flesh and destroyed his ideal. Realizing suddenly that she will never get out of there alive, Miranda runs to the door and escapes into a rainstorm. As they are about to enter her dungeon, she grabs a shovel and hits him over the head, drawing blood. She is horrified by what she has done, and her hesitation allows Freddie to run after her and imprison her again. In this case, however, the rainwater—here mixed with the blood of Freddie Clegg—will not be redemptive, as it is in *Ben-Hur*. When he returns from the hospital, Miranda is suffering from pneumonia and soon dies. Freddie is unrepentant. The final scene shows him in his van, following another woman.

The Collector is Wyler's darkest film, evidently conveying his rebuttal to the quasi-religious, redemptive ending of *Ben-Hur*. He flattens out Fowles's characters, eliminating much of the detail of their lives.[7] The film's Miranda is more likable—and therefore more of a victim—than her counterpart in the novel. Freddie, too, seems more vulnerable in the film, for Stamp gives him a boyish charm (again, like Norman Bates) that is emphasized visually by having Freddie dress in a suit and tie nearly every time he comes calling on Miranda. The diminished complexity of the film's char-

acters allows Wyler to concentrate more intensely on the dynamic of victim and victimizer. And he crystallizes this theme by making a dramatic
change at the end of the film. Whereas Fowles's Miranda is simply not
strong enough to overpower Freddie, Wyler's Miranda, after hitting her
captor with a shovel, is horrified by what she has done, and although she
has the opportunity to deliver a second and potentially fatal blow, she cannot do it. In Wyler's hands, this character's revulsion against violence links
her to the protagonists of his earlier films examining the limits of pacifism.
In this case, Miranda's inability to match her jailer's cruelty seals her fate.

The film received some glowing reviews and some that were more reserved. Stanley Kaufman, in the *New Republic*, found the film version superior to Fowles's novel. Andrew Sarris (Wyler's nemesis) characterized
Wyler's direction as "impersonal," yet he still called it "the most erotic
movie to come out past the production code." He went on to say: "Yet I
can't think of anything more exciting and more cinematic than locking up a
boy and girl in an old house and an intriguing situation. Just as the human
voice is the most sublime musical instrument, the human face and body are
the most sublime visual subjects, and one shot of Samantha Eggar's elon-
gated leg turning on a water faucet is worth every shot of every antelope
that ever roamed."[8]

Wyler took the film to Cannes, where he gave numerous interviews and
conceded that he did not like the film's French title, *L'Obsede*, because it
revealed too much of the story's central theme before it could be developed
onscreen. The Cannes jury awarded its best acting prizes to Stamp and
Eggar—the first time in the festival's history that both awards went to actors from the same film—and *Cahiers du Cinema* called it one of Wyler's
best films. Wyler was also nominated for an Oscar as Best Director for the
twelfth and final time. (Eggar was nominated as well, as was the screenplay.) Ironically, however, the Best Director prize for 1965 went to Robert
Wise for *The Sound of Music*.

After making three bleak films for Paramount between 1949 and 1952, and
weary from the HUAC battles, Wyler had escaped to Rome, where he directed the charming *Roman Holiday* and made Audrey Hepburn a star in
the process. Now, after making three films devoted to examining man's in-
humanity to man, followed by the deeply pessimistic *The Collector*, Wyler

took another break. This time, he flew off to Paris to make another trifle, *How to Steal a Million*, again with Audrey Hepburn. Wyler was especially pleased by the French shooting schedule. He told a reporter, "It's a miserable life in Hollywood. You're up at five or six o'clock in the morning to be ready to start shooting at nine. The working hours aren't arranged to suit the artists and the director; they're for the convenience of the technicians." In Paris, though, "you start at noon. Then you work right through to seven-thirty. It's much less exhausting that way. Anyhow, who can play a love scene at nine o'clock in the morning?"[9]

How to Steal a Million (originally titled *Venus Rising*) would be Wyler's first caper film. The opportunity to explore a new genre, work with Hepburn again, and direct Peter O'Toole, who was a hot young star at the time, made the project irresistible to Wyler. The top supporting role, Hepburn's father, went to Hugh Griffith, who had won an Oscar as Sheik Ilderim in *Ben-Hur*. The plot revolves around Hepburn and O'Toole's attempt to pull off a museum heist. Hepburn's father, a successful creator and purveyor of art forgeries, has loaned a replica of Cellini's *Venus* (made by his own father) to the museum. When they learn that the museum intends to authenticate the statue for insurance purposes, Hepburn hires O'Toole to help her steal the *Venus*. O'Toole turns out to be a private detective who is investigating Hepburn's father. Naturally, they fall in love in a very Wylerian spot—a cramped broom closet, where they are waiting for the museum to close so they can steal the statue. After a variety of complications, all ends well for the two lovers.

When the shoot for *How to Steal a Million* was almost over, Wyler was honored with a retrospective at the Cinémathèque Française. He attended the first film, *The Little Foxes*, but was too busy tending to the final details of his current project to participate in the homage. The program notes, written by Henri Langlois, state that "toward the end of the 1930s [Wyler] created a new style. It is fitting to associate with Wyler the turning point which—by error of judgment now corrected by the passage of time—postwar critics attributed to *Citizen Kane*, when in fact, Welles in this film, was still groping and being influenced by Wyler."[10]

How to Steal a Million, an old-fashioned Hollywood comedy, was quite out of step with many of the films being produced in the 1960s, and it got a less than enthusiastic reception from critics and the public. Nevertheless,

Fox wanted Wyler to remain with the studio. The Zanucks offered him a
four-picture deal that called for Wyler to direct two films at $500,000 each
and to produce two more at $300,000 each; he would also receive a per-
centage of the gross revenues for the four films. His first project was to be
Patton, which Darryl Zanuck would produce (hoping to replicate the success of his recent megahit *The Longest Day*). For Wyler, the subject matter
offered a step back into the past and an opportunity to rethink aspects of
the war. He had never made a studio film dealing directly with World War
II, and as such, the project presented him with some interesting challenges.

Making a film about George S. Patton was a pet project of producer Frank McCarthy, who had first proposed it in 1951. McCarthy, a re-
tired brigadier general, had been a top aide to Army Chief of Staff General
George C. Marshall and had at one point actually worked under Patton.
The film was going to be made in Spain because it had all the necessary
architecture and landscape to duplicate the various battle scenes; in addition, the Spanish army still maintained World War II hardware in working condition. *Patton* was budgeted at more than $10 million, and filming
was set to begin in February 1967. McCarthy had commissioned a script
from a recent film school graduate, Francis Ford Coppola, but there were
some problems with its narrative structure. (Coppola did, however, pen the
film's famous opening speech with the American flag in the background.)
To work out the problems, Wyler wanted James Webb, a World War II veteran who was familiar with Patton and had worked with the director on
The Big Country. Webb's hiring, however, delayed production, for he could
not begin script revisions until March. With no starting date in sight, Wyler
was free to pursue another project in the meantime. So he accepted when
Columbia asked him to replace Sidney Lumet as the director of the big-
budget musical *Funny Girl*, which was to be Barbra Streisand's film debut.

Funny Girl was originally intended to be a film, but it ended up being
a film version of a successful Broadway show. The whole enterprise was the
creation of Ray Stark, an agent turned producer who formed Seven Arts
Productions with Eliot Hyman in 1957. Stark, who was married to Fanny
Brice's daughter, wanted to produce a sanitized, laudatory film biography
that would please the family. He had commissioned a screenplay from Ben
Hecht as early as 1948, but that effort was deemed unsatisfactory by the
family, as was a revision by Phoebe and Henry Ephron three years later.

The project was eventually turned over to Isobel Lennart, who had written the screenplay for *Love Me or Leave Me*, based on the life of singer Ruth Etting. Her working titles for the screenplay were "Fanny" and then "My Man." No studio showed any interest in the project, but when stage director Vincent Donehue read the script, he was convinced it would make a great stage drama. He contacted Mary Martin, who was then enjoying success on Broadway in *The Sound of Music*. She expressed interest, so plans got under way to turn the Fanny Brice story into a big-budget Broadway musical.

It was Barbra Streisand, however, who eventually won the role of Fanny Brice. Mary Martin, citing problems with the book, withdrew early in the process. Stark's wife then wanted Anne Bancroft, while Jerome Robbins, hired to choreograph and direct, wanted Carol Burnett. Jule Styne, who composed the music, wanted a singer—not an actress who could get by as a singer. He had seen Streisand, who had a featured role in the musical *I Can Get It for You Wholesale*, starring her then-husband Elliott Gould and directed by Styne's collaborator on *Gypsy*, Arthur Laurents.[11] Streisand eventually convinced everyone that she was perfect for the part of Fanny Brice. Her performance made Broadway history.

When the show's Broadway run ended, Streisand was signed to reprise the role in London, and Ray Stark announced that she would make her film debut in *Funny Girl*. Columbia wanted to buy the film rights but balked at signing Streisand, whom the studio heads considered too Jewish, too unattractive, and too inexperienced to carry a film. They wanted Shirley MacLaine instead. Stark, however, was adamant. Streisand had signed a four-picture deal with him in 1965, guaranteeing her the movie version of *Funny Girl* for a salary of $250,000, plus a small percentage of the box office. Stark ultimately convinced Columbia president Mike Frankovich to accept both the project and Streisand by agreeing to a modest budget for a musical: $8.5 million. When the Starks threw a party at their home to welcome Streisand to Hollywood in May 1967, she had already been signed to appear in two other highly anticipated big-budget musicals—*Hello, Dolly!* and *On a Clear Day You Can See Forever*—and she had not yet made a single film.

After considering Gene Kelly (who would later direct Streisand in *Hello, Dolly!*) and George Roy Hill, Stark, at Streisand's request, decided to choose a director associated with dramas rather than musicals. Convinced that the weakest element of the stage production had been the development of the relationship between Fanny and Nicky Arnstein, he wanted a director who could effectively handle the personal drama at the heart of the story. In the summer of 1967, Stark announced that he had signed Sidney Lumet (*Twelve Angry Men, Long Day's Journey into Night, The Pawnbroker*) to direct his film. By January, however, Lumet was no longer associated with the project, which led to the hiring of Wyler.

Stark had been interested in hiring Wyler to direct the film as early as the Broadway run. Like Streisand, he appreciated Wyler's flair for dramatic material and his ability to help actors bring nuance to their performances. Indeed, Streisand saw *Funny Girl* as essentially a dramatic film with musical numbers and was "thrilled when Wyler accepted."[12] Wyler, who at first turned the film down because he felt he was too hard of hearing to direct a musical, eventually accepted the assignment, largely because of Streisand's participation: "I wouldn't have made the picture without her. She's an interesting performer and represented a challenge for me because she's never been in films, and she's not the usual glamour girl."[13] Wyler was being a bit disingenuous here, since he had stipulated a number of conditions before agreeing to direct his first musical. He insisted that the film be billed as a "William Wyler–Ray Stark Production," that his work be completed in time for him to shoot *Patton*, and that a first-rate choreographer be found to stage the musical numbers. To satisfy the last condition, Stark hired Herb Ross, who had staged the musical numbers for *I Can Get It for You Wholesale* and had choreographed the dance sequences for *Dr. Doolittle*.

As late as the spring of 1967, no costar for Streisand had been found, and shooting was scheduled to begin in a few weeks. Some big names were bandied about to play Nicky Arnstein, including Sean Connery, Gregory Peck, and Tony Curtis. For a while, it seemed that David Janssen would play the role, but that deal fell through as well. Jule Styne wanted Frank Sinatra, who agreed to take the part only if he were paid $750,000 and received top billing; Stark said no.

Wyler had seen Omar Sharif regularly at the Columbia cafeteria when Sharif was under contract to that studio, and he finally recommended the actor. Sharif was an established male lead (*Doctor Zhivago*), looked great in a tuxedo, and, like Arnstein, was an accomplished gambler and card player. He could even sing well enough. Stark was convinced to sign him when he learned that, under the terms of his studio contract, Sharif could be had for only $20,000.

Funny Girl is not a great American musical. Its book, which narrates the simple story of Fanny Brice and her meteoric rise as a vaudeville star and the leading light of the Ziegfeld Follies, is not dramatically notable. Fanny suffers no setbacks on the road to the top—she even comments at one point that everything has come too easy. She is a hit in her first performance, "Roller Skate Rag," even though she cannot skate, and almost immediately thereafter, she is starring in the Ziegfeld Follies. The second half of her story charts the disintegration of her marriage to gambler Nicky Arnstein. As her career continues to blossom, his life spirals out of control, culminating in his imprisonment for embezzling. The score produced two theater standards—"People" and "Don't Rain on My Parade"—but otherwise is not memorable. Indeed, *Funny Girl*'s main claim to musical theater immortality is that it made Barbra Streisand a star; its status as a Streisand vehicle rather than a substantive work in its own right is confirmed by Stark's conception of the play as no more than a dry run for the film version.

Nonetheless, despite the mediocre material, *Funny Girl* is a better film than the adapted versions of far superior Broadway musicals such as *West Side Story, Guys and Dolls, South Pacific, Kiss Me, Kate,* and *Gypsy.* Indeed, it is one of the best examples of musical adaptation to film in the history of the medium, and it is a testament both to Wyler's ability to present the story effectively and to the intelligent staging of the musical numbers (here, much of the credit goes to Herb Ross). By insisting that Streisand remain front and center, Stark also ensured that the Broadway show's major asset was in place for the film as well. In doing so, he rejected the prevailing wisdom that movie stars have to replace Broadway stars to make a successful film—even though Frank Sinatra and Marlon Brando had not saved *Guys and Dolls,* Rosalind Russell merely undercut *Gypsy,* and Lucille Ball was miscast in *Mame.* Streisand was the raison d'être for *Funny Girl,* and Wyler knew that going in.

The dramatic arc of *Funny Girl* resembles that of *Carrie*: each charts the rise of a young, lower-class woman and the fall of a debonair, sophisticated man. Each film ends with a final meeting in a theater dressing room. In *Carrie*, Hurstwood, unemployed and sick, comes asking for a handout; in *Funny Girl*, Nick, just out of prison, wants a divorce. In each case, the heroine is successful but alone at the end.

Funny Girl opens with a framing device—an enormous theater marquee on which Fanny Brice's name is prominently displayed above the show's title but below "Ziegfeld Follies." As a woman in a leopard coat and hat walks into the camera's view, the lights go bright on the marquee, lighting the names of Fanny, Ziegfeld, and the show's title, "Glorifying the American Girl"—which could well serve as the film's subtitle. The opening is a stylized gesture, announcing that the film will be, in part, an homage to the vanished world of the theater. The well-dressed woman proceeds to walk through an alleyway toward the stage door, followed by the camera. At a certain point, the camera stops moving, and this woman is framed in a long shot by the walls on either side of the alley and a wooden staircase. This elaborate prologue announces that this film is about the theater, about Fanny Brice, and about the catastrophe of success. It is the first of many such compositions in which Wyler imprisons Fanny in the frame.

The alley functions as an important backdrop throughout the film, along with stage doors and Wyler's signature staircases. Fanny continues to walk through the alleyway and is again framed between two brick walls before turning left into a space dominated by props, including a large mirror. As she looks into the mirror and says, "Hello, Gorgeous," her smile is replaced by a glum look—she is not convinced by her own bravado. Next, she walks into a dark, empty theater, Wyler's camera emphasizing both its size and its emptiness. She begins to play "People," the show's signature song, on the piano but then slams down sharply on the keys. At this point, Wyler cuts abruptly to a high-angle shot of the empty theater from above, dwarfing Fanny. As he cuts back to her, she is facing stage right, listening to imagined applause; then she pretends to machine-gun the imaginary audience. Wyler cuts to another high-angle view of the side of the theater, watching as Fanny takes a seat by herself and looks at the stage. After a brief exchange with her assistant, who tells her that Mr. Ziegfeld would like to see her at her convenience, Fanny says, "Did you hear that Mrs. Strakosh, Mr. Ziegfeld is waiting for me." The camera moves in for a medium profile shot of Streisand's face, emphasizing her un-star-like nose,

then moves forward and into the past as a young Fanny is again seen looking into a mirror.[14]

This cinematic tour de force is Wyler's acknowledgment of the opening of *Citizen Kane*, as he utilizes spatial framing, expressive editing,
close-ups, and mirrors to herald his story of an "American Girl" who is
not gorgeous, who achieves great acclaim but does not win the love of the
man she so desperately wants. If "people who need people" are "the luck-
iest people," she is not one of them. In *Sister Carrie*, Dreiser concludes
with an image of his heroine in a rocking chair, where she sits successful
but alone and muses, "shall you dream such happiness as you may never
feel." Wyler did not use this image in his film version of that novel, but in
Funny Girl, he has Fanny sitting alone in the theater thinking much the
same thing.[15]

Wyler's visual strategy throughout the first half of the film, which deals
with Fanny's rise, is intended to emphasize her entrapment. When the plot
flashes back to the past, Wyler repeats the frame within a frame—Fanny
looking into the mirror—seen in the film's opening. He repeats another visual strategy from the opening when Fanny sings her first song, "I'm the
Greatest Star," to an empty theater. Midway through the number, Wyler
again pulls his camera back, isolating Fanny in space.

The number that pushes Fanny toward stardom, "I'd Rather Be Blue
over You" (than be happy with somebody else), is also performed solo onstage, but this time, she is gliding on roller skates. The lyrics, which anticipate the substance of her marriage to Nicky, also prefigure the soaring
stagecraft of the song that closes the first half of the film, "Don't Rain on
My Parade"—only the second of Fanny's numbers not staged in a theater.
Fanny's love for Nicky liberates her, and Wyler takes his cue from the line
"Don't tell me not to fly," showing her as she seems to fly from the train
station to a train to a cab and then to a pier, where she boards a tugboat
that takes her past the Statue of Liberty. Even Wyler's framing shots of
Fanny in the windows of the train and the cab seem dwarfed by the momentum of the song. This moment is the emotional high point of the film
for Fanny. As she concludes her song on the tugboat, she is (as in her first
number) singing to no one in particular. She has, however, been liberated
from the theater and thrust into the world, where the Statue of Liberty signifies that her dream of personal and professional success is finally within

her grasp. The second half of the film charts her loss of the personal aspect of that success.

Nick Arnstein's first two appearances—after Fanny's "I'd Rather Be Blue" performance and after her triumph at the Follies—are also framed within frames, both times by doorways. In *Carrie*, Wyler's heroine sees Hurstwood for the first time through the door of Fitzgerald's, in a deep-focus shot across the room, where he is framed by a partition. The staging of "People" occurs outside in the alleyway behind the Brice saloon. Fanny and Nick are the only two people in the scene. She sings much of the song while standing on the steps of a nearby building and staring in front of her. Nick looks at her from the far left of the frame. Not once during the song do their eyes meet, and at the end of the song, the camera moves in on Fanny's face and then, in a reverse shot, catches Nick. At the end of what is arguably the film's most romantic song, Wyler thus separates them. Nick then announces that he has to go to Kentucky, foretelling that his business ventures and his need for freedom will pull them apart. Later, in his final appearance in Fanny's dressing room, when he decides to finalize their divorce, he is first seen framed in Fanny's mirror.

The second half of the film deals with Fanny's unraveling marriage. There is only one big production number, "The Swan," as Wyler concentrates on narrative rather than musical theater. The first musical number in this section, "Sadie, Sadie," is more typical of Wyler's approach to theatrical material at the start of his career. He keeps the action moving, turning "Sadie, Sadie" into a montage of time passing. The sequence begins with a close-up of Fanny's ring, moves to her first look at her new home (complete with a Wylerian multilevel winding staircase), to the decoration and refurbishment of the house, and to an outdoor champagne party, all culminating in the birth of a daughter. There is even a moment when Nick carries Fanny, in a white dress, up the staircase, reprising a similar moment from *The Collector*, albeit in a much different context.

After "The Swan," Wyler cuts to Fanny, who sits smoking as she waits for Nick to come home from the card game that caused him to miss her premiere and the party that followed. Wyler films her from behind as Nick enters their apartment, the distance between them telling. Here, he repeats the staging of a scene from *The Little Foxes*, when Regina enters the house after Horace has discovered the theft of his bonds: Horace, like Fanny, is seated (though he is seen in profile) as Regina comes through the front door, the stark contrasts of space and movement emphasizing the gulf between them. Wyler repeats this framing when Nick finds out that Fanny has bankrolled his share of a potential business partnership. He turns the offer down and walks the businessman to the door. Wyler then films this movement again from behind Fanny, keeping her in the foreground while the two men stand at the door. The subsequent argument between the couple takes place as they stand in the same positions, far across the large room. Later, after Fanny finds out about Nick's arrest, Wyler reverses her movement from the film's prologue. Now facing the camera, she runs through the alley toward a waiting car; Wyler then cuts to the car driving off, with the Follies marquee lit up at the right side of the screen.

In a musical film, all the songs are usually prerecorded before the actual number is filmed, and *Funny Girl* was no different. Though he did not interfere with Herb Ross's handling of the big Ziegfeld production numbers, Wyler reserved the right to redo Streisand's character songs. Streisand remembers: "The last day of shooting was the song 'My Man.' The next day in the projection room, after watching dailies, everyone started applauding and congratulating each other. Willy turned to me and asked what I thought. I said, 'I think I could do it better.' The room became silent. I thought I really needed to do it live, to be in the moment. How could I feel the emotions if I was trying to lip-synch to a recording made three months before? I'm very bad at lip-synching. So I said, 'Willy, can we do it over?' And he did." Robert Swink recalls that Wyler "got Omar Sharif to stand behind those black curtains—the whole scene was black—and he told him to talk to Streisand between takes. He wanted him around to help build up her sadness. They must've done at least ten takes. Willy shot the thing live and recorded it live. It was pretty emotional for her."[16] He also filmed it in one long take. Pauline Kael called it a "bravura stroke."[17]

The scene's presentation may have been dreamed up by Streisand, but the staging of the song closely resembles that of "Rose's Turn," the finale of *Gypsy*, for which Jule Styne also wrote the music. Fanny's song (by Maurice Yvain) shares some superficial similarities to that musical tour de force, but it lacks the other song's power, dramatic arc, and incisive lyrics.[18] "Rose's Turn" is also performed on an empty stage with the character surrounded mostly by darkness, though it is usually staged with the word

ROSE in lights. Her song is a testament to her own strength as she makes it clear that she is responsible for her daughter's success. Although she realizes her daughter no longer needs her, she declares her worth, proclaiming, "Everything's coming up roses, for me." She repeats the word *me* four times.

At the end of Wyler's film, Fanny declares her love for her man with an increasing sense of desperation: "What's the difference if I say, I'll go away. When I know I'll come back on my knees some day. For whatever my man is, I am his." Fanny refuses to admit that she cannot have the one love she always wanted. Angela Lansbury, who played Rose in an award-winning revival of *Gypsy*, described the show as "a tragedy of good intentions."[19] The same can be said of *Funny Girl*, which presents two characters who want the best for each other but let their insecurities get in the way. Wyler's ending is, appropriately, both poignant and edgy. Fanny seems strong but also desperate, clutching at the happiness she has lost. The stage version, conversely, ends on a high note, with Fanny reprising "Don't Rain on My Parade." Her final declaration—"I simply gotta march, My heart's a drummer. Nobody, no nobody is gonna rain on my parade"—ends the play with a celebration of her strength and endurance, whereas Wyler's ending emphasizes her vulnerability and her loss.

During filming, Streisand had several run-ins on the set with Ray Stark, but Wyler claimed he got along with his star: "What captivated me was, of course, Barbra, and my principal concern was to present her under the best possible conditions as a new star and a new personality. She was terribly eager, like Bette Davis used to be, to do different and new things. She wanted everything to be the very best. The same as I do." He elaborated on that statement: "She fusses over things, she's terribly concerned about how she looks, with the photography, the camera, the makeup, the wardrobe, the way she moves, reads a line. She'd tell the cameraman that one of the lights was out—way up on the scaffold. If the light that was supposed to be on her was out, she saw it. She's not easy, but she's difficult in the best sense of the word—the same way I'm difficult."[20]

Wyler admitted he had trouble with Streisand at first, but he managed to establish that he was in charge: "She was a bit obstreperous in the beginning. But things were ironed out when she discovered some of us knew what we were doing."[21] In fact, he exerted his control on the first day of filming, which began with location shooting in Newark, New Jersey, and

New York City. (Wyler was using Newark's Penn Station as a substitute for the Baltimore train station.) Streisand recalls: "I asked him, 'What if we do a takeoff on Garbo's entrance in *Anna Karenina*, where this beautiful woman appears through a cloud of smoke, except Fanny would come out coughing through the smoke?' He didn't go for that, but he did let me do a version of my cough a bit later. He was always open to suggestions, even from me, who had never done a movie before."[22]

Funny Girl was a huge financial success. It cost about $10 million to make and grossed $66 million, remaining on the list of top moneymaking films for a long time. At the end of his career, Wyler thus showed that he could make an epic film better than DeMille and could more than hold his own with a musical. *Funny Girl* still ranks among the best examples of how to transfer a musical to the screen. In this musical-dramatic project, he succeeded, in part, by paring down the musical numbers and adding some period songs staged in theaters to provide the flavor and look of period pieces. Other songs, such as "People" and "My Man," are presented simply as monologues, without any trappings; as a result, they do not seem so jarring onscreen, as many overblown numbers staged outdoors often do. Most important, Wyler gave *Funny Girl* what he called "the illusion of movement," while retaining the playwright's interest in focusing dramatic scenes within a circumscribed area. Ultimately, it is his effective use of the camera as it moves through space and his characteristic lengthy takes, deep-focus photography, and long shots that make *Funny Girl* such an intelligent adaptation. As in his dramatic adaptations, Wyler allows the audience to observe the relationships between the characters and interpret the action.

When Curtis Hanson interviewed Wyler in 1967 and asked if he was currently working on anything, Wyler replied, "Yes, I'm doing my first musical, *Funny Girl*. After that I will feel like the man who has done everything."[23] Wyler was, indeed, one of the few directors who did everything, and one of fewer still who did it all well. *Funny Girl* received eight Academy Award nominations, including for Best Picture—Wyler's thirteenth film nominated in that category. As the co-winner of the Best Actress Oscar—which she shared with Katharine Hepburn and, like Audrey Hepburn, received for her first starring role—Barbra Streisand became the thirteenth actor to win an Academy Award under Wyler's direction.

While working on *Funny Girl*, Wyler had remained involved with *Pat-*

ton, particularly in reviewing the script revisions by James Webb. He was pleased with the revised script, which he considered superior to Coppola's first draft, and excited about making a war film told from the perspective of feuding generals. He expressed his enthusiasm in a telegram to Zanuck: "I still believe, as I always have, that we have the makings of a most unusual war story, different from most that have been made. It is war as fought by the commanding generals with a conflict of personalities and differing views on the conduct of war rather than battles in the field. While parts of some battles can't be avoided, I should like to see them kept to a minimum."[24]

The film was supposed to be made with Burt Lancaster as Patton, but when production was delayed a second time, he was forced to drop out. After Rod Steiger and Lee Marvin also passed on it, the role was offered to George C. Scott. Despite the fact that Wyler had fired Scott from *How to Steal a Million* because of his unprofessional behavior, he thought the actor would make an ideal Patton.

However, Wyler's health was in decline—he had stomach ulcers and other problems—and his wife felt that an eight-month shoot in Spain would be too much for him, not to mention the aggravation of having to deal with Scott. Wyler reluctantly pulled out of the project. *Patton*, like *The Sound of Music*, went on to win many accolades, including the Oscar for Best Picture and another for its new director, Franklin J. Schaffner.

Before ending his career, Wyler would make one more film. *The Liberation of L. B. Jones* is a harsh, uncompromising study of racism that was too far ahead of its time and failed at the box office. It was a rare financial disaster for Wyler—all the more surprising because it came after *Funny Girl*, which had been a box-office bonanza. Wyler, however, had long been interested in making a film on the subject of racism. Having touched on it briefly in *The Little Foxes*, he, along with Lillian Hellman, started working in 1942 on the documentary *The Negro Soldier*, which was intended to boost the morale of the troops. The film was never made, in part because Wyler feared the army would not allow him to present the material the way he wanted to.

After the war, he wanted to make a film about a black doctor facing white hatred in the South, but Paramount would not allow it. Talking about the genesis of *L. B. Jones*, Wyler told Axel Madsen: "I had always wanted to do something on the racial issue . . . and when Ronald Lubin brought me Jesse Hill Ford's novel, it seemed a good story, very powerful, very blunt, in a way a harsh and shocking story. When the author came to us and I asked him, 'Aren't you putting it on a little thick?' he answered, 'Not at all, it is all based on facts.'"[25] Shortly after *The Liberation of L. B. Jones* was released, Wyler told *Entertainment World*, "I like films that contribute something to the social consciousness of the times and that is what I tried to do with this picture."[26]

The film rights to the novel had been bought by Ronald Lubin (*The Outrage, Billy Budd*) and screenwriter Stirling Silliphant, who won an Oscar in 1967 for his screenplay of *In the Heat of the Night*—a more commercial, entertaining, and compromised film than this one would be. However, the two were unable to interest a studio in the material until Wyler agreed to direct it. Released from his contract with Fox, Wyler then signed a six-picture deal with Columbia, stipulating that he would produce three films and direct three. *The Liberation of L. B. Jones* would be the first. The film was first titled *The Liberation of Lord Byron Jones* (echoing the novel), but the studio shortened it to prevent any possibility of its being confused with a costume drama about the famous poet. (There is also, perhaps, the ironic echo of LBJ.)

Wyler cast the film primarily with unknowns. Seeking an actor who could project some sympathy into what was essentially an unsympathetic role, he wanted Henry Fonda to play lawyer Oman Hedgepath, the most powerful figure in town. Fonda was interested, but he was unable to fit it into his schedule. Wyler then cast Lee J. Cobb, who was a well-known character actor but hardly a star. The two key roles, L. B. Jones and Willie Joe Worth, went to Roscoe Lee Browne, who had just appeared in *The Comedians* opposite Richard Burton and Elizabeth Taylor, and Anthony Zerbe, who had recently debuted in *Cool Hand Luke* starring Paul Newman. Lola Falana was chosen to play Jones's adulterous wife, whose affair ignites the racial tensions in the story; it was her American screen debut, and her sexy image would be prominently displayed in the film's racy ads. Yaphet Kotto, who would later become a television star, was cast as Sonny Boy Mosby, who returns to town to kill a policeman who beat him as a child, while Lee Majors and Barbara Hershey had the nondescript roles of Hedgepath's liberal nephew and his wife.

The film was scheduled for a ten-week shoot. Two weeks were spent on location in and around Humboldt, Tennessee—near where Jesse Hill Ford lived—and the rest of the film was shot at Columbia Studios and other locations around Hollywood. To avoid any racial confrontations while on location in the South, the crew stayed at a Holiday Inn outside of town. Black cast members stayed put at night, although, as Wyler remembered, "There was no place to go anyway."[27]

The Liberation of Lord Byron Jones, published by Atlantic–Little Brown in 1965, established Jesse Hill Ford's reputation as an important American writer. The novel was nominated for a National Book Award, chosen as a Book-of-the-Month-Club selection, and regarded as an important literary property. Set in the small Tennessee town of Somerton (based on Humboldt), it explores the consequences of the decision by a prosperous black undertaker, L. B. Jones, to divorce Emma, his much younger wife, on the grounds that she is having an affair with a white policeman. Jones wants a dignified divorce, so he asks the town's leading white lawyer, Oman Hedgepath, to represent him. Jones seriously complicates matters, however, when he insists on naming the policeman, Willie Joe Worth, as her lover. Hedgepath feels compelled to tell Worth of Jones's intentions, and Willie Joe tries to persuade Emma not to contest the divorce. When she refuses, he beats her; when she is still not persuaded, he murders Jones. The case is hushed up by Hedgepath and the mayor because they do not want to involve a police officer in a scandal and because the lawyer has implicated himself by advising Willie Joe to make sure the case never got to court.

The Liberation of L. B. Jones is the darkest of Wyler's final films, all of which—with the exception of the trifling *How to Steal a Million*—deal with man's propensity for hatred and violence and the uselessness of pacifism or nonviolence as a deterrent. This film also highlights the failure of liberalism, which was Wyler's own political philosophy. Although Steve Mundine, Hedgepath's liberal nephew who comes to town with his new bride to be his uncle's law partner, is central to the thematic development of the novel, he remains a nonpresence in the film. Other than occasionally voicing understated objections to his uncle's actions and once even expressing his disappointment directly, Steve takes no action. At the end, he leaves town, disillusioned yet having accomplished nothing.

What is most remarkable about the film is its consistent refusal to offer its audience any of the hopeful signs Ford presents to his readers. The novel takes place in 1963, against the background of the March on Washington and other civil rights protests, but none of this historical context is mentioned in the film. Also, the film's minimization of the Steve Mundine character is telling. In the novel, both Steve and his wife, Nella, take active steps to intercede in Jones's case, even visiting his home to warn him about the danger he is in. Later, Steve bails out a radical who wanders into town and ends up in jail, along with Benny, who is Jones's best friend. (Hedgepath frees him in the film.) Finally, once he quits his uncle's law practice in disgust and leaves town, Steve joins the NAACP and, at the end of the novel, proclaims, "Never again will I stand aside, defer to age and bigotry. We'll take to the streets."[28]

In the novel, in addition to Steve and his wife being radicalized by their experience in Somerton, Mosby eventually joins the Nation of Islam, as does Emma Jones, who becomes a generous benefactor of the movement after her husband's funeral. In one of the concluding passages of the novel, Oman Hedgepath comments that Willie Joe, who confessed to killing Jones before it was hushed up, was unable to live with his crime—he became a drunk and eventually killed himself by crashing his car into a bridge.

All the standard Hollywood tropes offered in the source novel—the death of the bad guy, the redemption of the man of principle, and the beginnings of redemption for an oppressed people—are eliminated in the film. Little remains there except brutality, cynicism, and hopelessness. Given the time in which the film was made, this bare-bones treatment is more than audacious. In the words of Charles Champlin of the *Los Angeles Times*, "There are no punishments, no deathbed repentances, nothing to suggest that anything has changed or will change tomorrow. . . . The argument of the movie is that we can only be served by the truth, unpalatable as it may be."[29]

The film does not look like a classic Wyler film. In telling the multiple stories entwined in Ford's plot, Wyler cuts extensively from one narrative to the other, some sequences lasting barely a minute. His signature long takes filmed in mid-distance are used sparingly here, replaced by more medium close-ups and close-ups than usual. Wyler's best films concentrate on character dilemmas played out within a social space. As always, he focuses on how inner imperatives affect the social sphere, but in *The Liberation*, the elimination of this social space signifies a breakdown of any communal cohesion. In the savagely alienated environment of this small southern town, communication is minimal and usually meaningless. Wyler's strength in presenting character in context is tested here because he tends to search with his characters for the consummation of integrated and healthy relationships. In *The Collector*, he explores a dead-end of individuals in isolation. In his final film, he presents a society on the brink of collapse, upended by racial hatred.

One would be hard-pressed to name another mainstream American film that looks at racism so unsparingly. The word *nigger* is used often and offhandedly by both upper-class and working-class whites. The subhuman treatment of blacks by whites is an everyday occurrence, regarded casually and indifferently. Wyler's camera presents these actions objectively as well, and this steely objectivity heightens the power of the film. When the two police officers, Worth (Zerbe) and Bumpas (Arch Johnson), return from killing Jones, the desk officer, Mr. Ike (Chill Wills), asks where they've been. When Bumpas replies, "We killed us a nigger," there is barely a reaction. Wyler films the scene in middle distance, as Ike asks about the identity of the victim and Bumpas stands behind him at the filing cabinet. They are soon joined by Worth, who is still visibly shaken by his partner's mutilation of Jones's corpse and asks for a drink. Wyler composes the shot by placing Worth on the left, Ike leaning on the desk on the right, and Bumpass standing behind them, so that they form a triangle—in Wyler's films, this configuration usually signifies that a community cannot be healed or put back together. (A similar pictorial structure is introduced earlier in Hedgepath's office, when Jones announces that despite Emma's determination to contest the divorce, he plans to go through with it. As the lawyer questions the wisdom of naming a white man in court, Jones replies, "To hell with the white man!" In that scene, Wyler places Steve, the new liberal law partner, at the top of the triangle, with Jones and Hedgepath on either side. Jones's bold defiance will cost him his life and accomplish nothing.)

Wyler also alternates between locales that are darkly and brightly lit. Virtually all the scenes in Mamma Lavorn's tavern, the primary place where black people congregate, are done with very little lighting. Throughout, the lives of the black characters are associated with darkness, a kind of life in death, like the leper caves in *Ben-Hur*. Jones is murdered at night; Erleen, a black woman whose husband is in jail, is raped by Willie Joe at night; and Mosby and Benny meet with Jones at night. L. B. Jones, of course, is in the death business himself, and in the two scenes in which he meets with clients to plan their funerals, both women seem to be looking forward to a grand interment, as if dying will grant them the importance they were denied in life. The darkness also emphasizes the violence and brutality of the black characters' lives. Their personal spaces—the bars and dingy homes—are filled with the tension of violence and mystery housed within them, the sense that something is brewing and will soon explode.

The streets of downtown Somerton, however, are invariably bathed in sunlight, as are Oman Hedgepath's office and estate. The gentleman lawyer, who is served by a good-natured black butler and likes to relax in his hammock with a drink at his side, looks like a character out of Wyler's *Jezebel*—indeed, his antebellum house looks like it was lifted off the set of that film. Nonetheless, the darkness that overshadows a good portion of the film threatens to envelop this elegant way of life and what it represents.

The film opens with a visual metaphor: the camera focuses on railroad tracks that eventually crisscross, as the plot strands involving the white and black characters eventually do. On the train heading for Somerton are Steve Mundine and his wife, Nella. Steve is looking forward to joining the law firm of his uncle, who has made him a partner. On the same train but in another car is Sonny Boy Mosby, whose luggage consists of a cigar box containing a gun, which he looks at as the train nears the station. Sonny Boy is coming home to seek revenge on a policeman, Stanley Bumpas, who beat him when he was a boy. The introductory shots of both men are through the train windows, suggesting that both are trapped, though for different reasons. Their initial views of Somerton out those windows distinguish the two characters' social standing—Steve sees an open, verdant country streetscape, while Sonny Boy looks out on a dilapidated, slum-like neighborhood. Although their two stories will intersect during the course of the film, Steve and Sonny Boy never meet. At the end of the film, both are seen on the same train headed out of town, but across the aisle from each other, their lives linked by the events of the story.

The plot is triggered by L. B. Jones's desire for a divorce from his wife, Emma. Jones, a wealthy undertaker, asks Hedgepath to represent him because he is "the best." The lawyer refuses at first but then reluctantly takes the case to please his nephew, who has just arrived in town. Tensions escalate when Emma decides to contest the divorce, which means that her lover, Willie Joe Worth, a white policeman, will be named in open court. Hedgepath then visits Willie Joe at police headquarters and tells him to fix things with Emma. Wyler's framing is suggestive here: the back office at the station is cramped, so cluttered that Hedgepath has trouble closing the door. The scene is conveyed mostly in two-shots, as Wyler emphasizes the dark, constricted area but also keeps his camera focused on the window. The entire locus of the law is thus presented as compromised and corrupt, and Hedgepath, the town's leading citizen, is implicated as well.

Willie Joe first tries to ward off trouble by paying a visit to Emma. As he enters her room, Wyler frames him in the doorway, while at the extreme left, Emma is framed in a full-length mirror. The geometrical patterning of the door molding and the edge of the mirror seem to divide the frame into three sections, creating a triptych effect. The scene's action, presented primarily in two-shots, is one of the most violent in the Wyler canon. Willie Joe slaps Emma around and draws a gun on her, but she is not intimidated. Then she tells him that she is pregnant with his baby, and when she refuses to get an abortion, he beats her and leaves.

Willie Joe, frustrated by Emma's refusal to back down and consent to the divorce, visits Hedgepath at his home, where he is dining with Steve. The lawyer is again implicated by being at the head of another triangular shot that joins him with Steve and Willie Joe. The policeman next tries to intimidate Jones, who, like his wife, refuses to back down. But Jones is lured into the police car (like Erleen), where Willie Joe jumps into the backseat and starts to beat him. Jones jumps from the moving car and flees to a junkyard. Bumpas kills the blind junkyard owner's dog before Willie Joe finally shoots Jones in the back of the head. Bumpas then mutilates Jones's corpse and hangs him from a hook to make it look like a revenge killing. Wyler shoots the hanging body from above, picturing it among the useless motors and auto bodies, the detritus of the modern world—a telling commentary on how little we have progressed since the era of *Jezebel*. Wyler repeats this high-angle shot when shooting Emma and Benny from above, through the bars of the jail, where they have been imprisoned for Jones's death—more human debris.

Hedgepath is appalled to learn that his suggestion to "fix things" may have caused Jones's murder. But when Willie Joe confesses to the crime, Hedgepath nonetheless convinces him that concealing the murder would be best for the community. He then assures his nephew that the incident has been handled "quietly."

Wyler concludes the film with Steve and Nella leaving Somerton. Disgusted by the compromises made by Hedgepath, they have decided that they cannot live in such a racist community. Meanwhile, Jones is being buried in a lavish funeral ceremony with a chorus of singers at his graveside. While the funeral is going on, Mosby visits Bumpas's farm and—in what is surely the grisliest scene in a Wyler film—pushes the policeman into a harvester. The final sequence shows the Mundines and Mosby on a train again, though now Mosby sits opposite Steve and Nella. Wyler's last shot is of Mosby, perhaps indicating that his fury will be the agent that precipitates change, though that interpretation may be a bit too forward-looking for what is, essentially, an angry and despairing film. The Mundines, who represent liberal ideology, are empty, ineffectual people—well-meaning but useless—and Jones's decision to stand up to his oppressors is a meaningless gesture as well. Killed at night with no witnesses, in a junkyard owned by a blind man, he finds his glory in the most expensive funeral his establishment can provide. The killer goes free; the status quo is preserved.

Stirling Silliphant's Oscar-winning *In the Heat of the Night* is a more nuanced film that ultimately celebrates the potential for reconciliation and respect between the races, as Gillespie (Rod Steiger) and Tibbs (Sidney Poitier) become allies and friends. In his *Pictures at a Revolution*, Mark Harris writes that early in the development of that film, director Norman Jewison decided to "strip away scenes in which Tibbs faced the systemic racism of a small southern town."[30] Emphasized instead, in the words of *Time* magazine, is the lesson "that men can join hands out of fear and hatred and shape from base emotions something identifiable as a kind of love."[31] Wyler's film offers no such compromises. Having labeled *In the Heat of the Night* a "fantasy of racial discrimination," Andrew Sarris, never a champion of Wyler, called *The Liberation of L. B. Jones* "the most provocative brief for Black Power ever to come out of a Hollywood studio." He went on to say that "it may be the first American movie, black or white, to dramatize the matter-of-fact exploitation of black women by white supremacists."[32] It was certainly the first mainstream Hollywood film to condone the murder of a white police officer by a black man. Wyler's final film is perhaps his most revolutionary. It is surely among his most powerful.

The Liberation of L. B. Jones was Wyler's first out-and-out financial failure. It was popular with African American audiences, but whites stayed away, in Samuel Goldwyn's immortal words, "in droves." At the time, Wyler tried to downplay the controversial nature of the material, telling Entertainment World that the film was not about the South or black-white relations: "We made a film about one incident that took place and we translated what happened just like in the film In Cold Blood [released in 1967]. It was not about Kansas or farmers. It was about one incident that happened."[33] Three years later, however, he was more forthright, telling Madsen, "I wanted the audience to go out with a sense of guilt, of embarrassment at knowing what was going on and perhaps a feeling that they should do something about it." He added that he was proud of his film and "highly prejudiced in its favor."[34]

Wyler's next film was to be another stage adaptation—Forty Carats, a light comedy that had enjoyed a successful run on Broadway and earned Julie Harris a Tony. It would be a change of pace after L. B. Jones. With a good script in hand, he sent Robert Swink to Mexico to scout locations (for the opening scenes, which the play places in Greece). Wyler's health was in decline, however, and the sudden death of his brother Robert in 1971 made him rethink his priorities. He managed to get out of the remainder of his contract with Columbia, with the help of his childhood friend Paul Kohner, who stated: "I gave him lots of arguments but he insisted that he be freed of all commitments. He quit films right then and there."[35]

On March 9, 1976, Wyler was honored as the fourth recipient of the American Film Institute's Life Achievement Award. The affair, held at the Century Plaza Hotel in Beverly Hills, was attended by First Lady Betty Ford and numerous Hollywood luminaries, including Audrey Hepburn, Gregory Peck, Henry Fonda, James Stewart, Charlton Heston, Greer Garson, Fred Astaire, Barbra Streisand, Frank Capra, and George Cukor. Fonda called Wyler "the most versatile director to ever grace our industry"; Streisand described him as "an American institution." George Stevens Jr., director of the American Film Institute, emphasized Wyler's singular "ability to conceal the brush-strokes—to put the poem on the pedestal, and not the poet."

William Wyler died on July 27, 1981, ten years after his retirement. Shortly after his funeral at Forest Lawn Cemetery, a memorial service held at the old Directors' Guild of America building was attended by more than 500 people. Former guild president George Sydney said, "Willy's films will be enjoyed as long as man wants to see the best." Bette Davis commented, "The entire town should be at half-mast. When the king dies, all the flags are at half-mast." Her comment echoed that of his frequent collaborator Lillian Hellman, who called him "the greatest of all American directors." Biographer Jan Herman noted that of all the eulogies accorded him, Wyler's wife, Talli, was fondest of the remarks made by Philip Dunne: "Talent doesn't care whom it happens to. Sometimes it happens to rather dreadful people. In Willy's case, it happened to the best of us."[36]

Wyler was often associated with "the best"—garnering twelve Oscar nominations as Best Director and winning that award three times, as well as the French Victoire Award and three New York Film Critics Awards as Best Director. His actors were also named "best" by the Motion Picture Academy thirteen times. Few directors could match Wyler's range, his psychological subtlety, his ability to inspire and encourage actors, his poetic sensibility, or his humanism. Whether or not he was "the best," Wyler most certainly belongs in the company of the most accomplished and distinguished of American directors.

Acknowledgments

First, I must thank the Rutgers Research Council, which awarded me several grants that allowed me to travel to Los Angeles to study William Wyler's papers. While in Los Angeles, I benefited from the generosity and expertise of the staff at the Margaret Herrick Library of the Academy of Motion Picture Arts and Sciences; in particular, very special thanks to Kristine Krueger; Barbara Hall, the head of Special Collections; and Jenny Romero. Another special thank you to Lauren Buisson and her staff at the Charles E. Young Research Library, Department of Special Collections at UCLA. I am also indebted to Harry Miller, senior reference archivist at the Wisconsin Historical Society, for his help with the Ruth and Augustus Goetz Papers.

I also extend my gratitude to Catherine Wyler and Pat McGilligan for their encouragement, many acts of kindness, and words of wisdom. A special thank you to Anne Dean Watkins for her enthusiasm and belief in this project.

My deepest appreciation goes out to Merve Fejzula, who translated three essays from the French and, like Wyler, knows how to pronounce *auteur*. She also located numerous essays and interviews and reformatted all the notes and the bibliography.

As always, my wife, Kathy, offered countless suggestions that made this book better. Over the years, Lizzie, Matt, Jessica, and Adam have made me better as well.

Filmography

1920s

Crook Buster (1925)
Universal
Director: William Wyler
Story and scenario: Leigh Jacobson
Cast: Jack Mower
Mustang western, two reels, released December 26, 1925

The Gunless Bad Man (1926)
Universal
Director: William Wyler
Story: John Hall
Cast: Jack Mower
Mustang western, two reels, released March 13, 1926

Ridin' for Love (1926)
Universal
Director: William Wyler
Story: William Wyler
Scenario: Joseph Murray
Cast: Jack Mower
Mustang western, two reels, released April 17, 1926

The Fire Barrier (1926)
Universal
Director: William Wyler
Story: C. D. Lenington
Scenario: William Lester
Cast: Jack Mower
Mustang western, two reels, released June 12, 1926

Don't Shoot (1926)
Universal
Director: William Wyler

Story and scenario: William Lester
Cast: Jack Mower, Fay Wray
Mustang western, two reels, released August 26, 1926

The Pinnacle Rider (1926)
Universal
Director: William Wyler
Story and continuity: William Lester
Cast: Jack Mower
Mustang western, two reels, released October 30, 1926

Martin of the Mounted (1926)
Universal
Director: William Wyler
Story and continuity: George H. Plympton
Cast: Edmund Cobb
Mustang western, two reels, released December 11, 1926

Lazy Lightning (1926)
Universal
Director: William Wyler
Story: Harrison Jacobs
Cinematography: Eddie Linden
Cast: Arthur Acord, Fay Wray, Bobby Gordon, Vin Moore, Arthur
Morrison, George French
Blue streak western, five reels, released December 12, 1926
Length: 4,572 feet

The Stolen Ranch (1926)
Universal
Director: William Wyler
Story: Robert F. Hill
Screenplay: George H. Plympton
Cinematography: Al Jones
Cast: Fred Humes, Louise Lorraine, William Norton Bailey, Ralph
McCullough, Nita Cavalier, Edward Cecil, Howard Truesdale, Slim
Whittaker, Jack Kirk
Blue streak western, five reels, releaed December 26, 1926
Length: 4,587 feet

The Two Fister (1927)
Universal
Director: William Wyler
Story and continuity: George H. Plympton

Cast: Edmund Cobb
Mustang western, two reels, released January 8, 1927

Kelcy Gets His Man (1927)
Universal
Director: William Wyler
Story and scenario: William Lester
Cast: Edmund Cobb, Alice Goodwin
Mustang western, two reels, released February 19, 1927

Tenderfoot Courage (1927)
Universal
Director: William Wyler
Story: F. V. Lautzenhiser
Cast: Fred Gilman, Alma Rayford
Mustang western, two reels, released February 26, 1927

The Silent Partner (1927)
Universal
Director: William Wyler
Story: Basil Dickey
Scenario: George Morgan
Cast: Edmund Cobb, Hazel Keener
Mustang western, two reels, released March 19, 1927

Blazing Days (1927)
Universal
Director: William Wyler
Story: Florence Ryerson
Screenplay: George H. Plympton and R. Hill
Cinematography: Al Jones
Art direction: David S. Garber
Cast: Fred Humes, Ena Gregory, Churchill Ross, Bruce Gordon, Eva
Thatcher, Bernard Siegel, Dick L'Estrange
Blue streak western, five reels, released March 27, 1927
Length: 4,639 feet

Galloping Justice (1927)
Universal
Director: William Wyler
Story and scenario: George H. Plympton
Cast: Edmund Cobb
Mustang western, two reels, released April 9, 1927

Filmography

The Haunted Homestead (1927)
Universal
Director: William Wyler
Story: L. V. Jefferson
Cast: Fred Gilman, Violet La Plante
Mustang western, two reels, released April 16, 1927

Hard Fists (1927)
Universal
Director: William Wyler
Screenplay: William Lester and George H. Plympton, from Charles A. Logue's *The Grappler*
Cinematography: Edwin Linden
Art direction: David Garber
Cast: Art Acord, Louise Lorraine, Lee Holmes, Albert J. Smith
Blue streak western, five reels, released April 24, 1927
Length: 4,387 feet

The Lone Star (1927)
Universal
Director: William Wyler
Story and scenario: William Lester
Cast: Fred Gilman, Barbara Worth
Mustang western, two reels, released May 7, 1927

The Ore Raiders (1927)
Universal
Director: William Wyler
Story and scenario: William Lester
Cast: Fred Gilman, Fred Humes, Barbara Starr
Mustang western, two reels, released May 21, 1927

The Home Trail (1927)
Universal
Director: William Wyler
Story: Rhea Mitchell
Cast: Fred Gilman, Shirley Palmer
Mustang western, two reels, released June 4, 1927

Gun Justice (1927)
Universal
Director: William Wyler
Story and scenario: William Lester

Cast: Fred Gilman
Mustang western, two reels, released July 2, 1927

The Phantom Outlaw (1927)
Universal
Director: William Wyler
Story and scenario: William Lester
Cast: Fred Gilman
Mustang western, two reels, released July 16, 1927

The Square Shooter (1927)
Universal
Director: William Wyler
Story: Kenneth Langley
Cast: Fred Gilman
Mustang western, two reels, released August 13, 1927

Daze of the West (1927)
Universal
Director: William Wyler
Story: Billy Engle
Scenario: William Lester
Cast: Vin Moore, Fred Gilman, Elaine Forest
Mustang western, two reels, copyrighted Library of Congress, Catalog of
Entries, Motion Pictures, August 16, 1927

The Horse Trader (1927)
Universal
Director: William Wyler
Story: Brandt Riley
Cast: Fred Gilman
Mustang western, two reels, released August 20, 1927

The Border Cavalier (1927)
Universal
Director: William Wyler
Screenplay: Basil Dickey
Titles: Gardner Bradford
Cinematography: Al Jones
Art direction: David Garber
Cast: Fred Humes, Evelyn Pierce, Joyce Compton, C. E. "Captain"
Anderson, Gilbert "Peewee" Holmes, "Smilin'" Benny Corbett, Dick
L'Estrange, Scott Mattraw, Boris Bullock

Blue streak western, five reels, released September 18, 1927
Length: 4,427 feet

Straight Shootin' (1927)
Universal
Director: William Wyler
Screenplay: William Lester
Titles: Gardner Bradford
Cinematography: Milton Bridenbecker
Art direction: David Garber
Cast: Ted Wells, Garry O'Dell, Lillian Gilmore, Joe Bennett, Al Ferguson, Wilbur Mack, Buck Connors
Blue streak western, five reels, released October 16, 1927
Length: 4,205 feet

Desert Dust (1927)
Universal
Director: William Wyler
Screenplay: William Lester
Titles: Gardner Bradford
Cinematography: Milton Bridenbecker
Art direction: David Garber
Cast: Ted Wells, Lotus Thompson, Bruce Gordon, Dick L'Estrange, Jimmy Phillips, Charles "Slim" Cole, George Ovey
Released December 18, 1927
Length: 4,349 feet

Thunder Riders (1928)
Universal
Director: William Wyler
Screenplay: Basil Dickey and Carl Krusada
Titles: Gardner Bradford
Cinematography: Milton Bridenbecker
Editor: Harry Marker
Art direction: David Garber
Cast: Ted Wells, Charlotte Stevens, William A. Steele, Gilbert "Peewee" Holmes, Dick L'Estrange, Bill Dyer, Leo White, Julia Griffith, Bob Burns
Released April 8, 1928
Length: 4,363 feet

Anybody Here Seen Kelly? (1928)
Universal
Producer: Robert Wyler

Director: William Wyler
Scenario: John B. Clymer
Titles: Walter Anthony and Albert De Mond
Story: Leigh Jason
Photography: Charles Stumar
Editor: George McGuire
Cast: Bessie Love (Mitzi Lavelle), Tom Moore (Pat Kelly), Kate Price (Mrs. O'Grady), Addie McPhail (Mrs. Hickson), Bruce Gordon (Mr. Hickson), Alfred Allen (Sergeant Malloy), Tom O'Brien (Buck Johnson), Wilson Benge (Butler), Rosa Gore (French Mother), Dorothea Wolbert (Slavey)
Approximately 83 minutes

The Shakedown (1929)
Universal-Jewel
Director: William Wyler
Scenario: Charles A. Logue and Clarence Marks
Titles and dialogue: Albert De Mond
Story: Charles A. Logue
Photography: Charles Stumar and Jerome Ash
Editors: Lloyd Nosler and Richard Cahoon
Musical score: Joseph Cherniavsky
Cast: James Murray (Dave Hall), Barbara Kent (Marjorie), George Kostonaros (Battling Rolf), Wheeler Oakman (Manager), Jack Hanlon (Clem), Harry Gibbon (Bouncer)
Sound: approximately 88 minutes; silent: approximately 90 minutes

The Love Trap (1929)
Universal
Director: William Wyler
Scenario: John B. Clymer and Clarence J. Marks
Story: Edward J. Montagne
Dialogue: Clarence Thompson
Titles: Albert De Mond
Photography: Gilbert Warrenton
Editor: Maurice Pivar
Cast: Laura La Plante (Laura/Evelyn Todd), Neil Hamilton (Peter Cadwaller/Paul Harrington), Robert Ellis (Guy Emory), Jocelyn Lee (Bunny), Norman Trevor (Judge Cadwaller/Harrington), Clarissa Selwynne (Mrs. Cadwaller/Harrington), Rita Le Roy (Mary Cadwaller/Iris Harrington)
Sound: approximately 83 minutes; silent: approximately 85 minutes

1930s

Hell's Heroes (1930)
Universal
Presented by: Carl Laemmle
Director: William Wyler
Screenplay and dialogue: Tom Reed, based on the novel *The Three Godfathers* by Peter Kyne
Photography: George Robinson
Editors: William Boyce and Earl Neville (silent version); Harry Marker (sound version)
Supervising story chief: C. Gardner Sullivan (silent version)
Recording engineer: C. Roy Hunter
Sound technician: William W. Hedgecock
Cast: Charles Bickford (Bob Sangster), Raymond Hatton (Barbwire Gibbons), Fred Kohler (Wild Bill Kearny), Fritzi Ridgeway (Mother), Jose de la Cruz (Jose), Buck Conners (Parson Jones), Walter James (Sheriff)
Sound: approximately 82 minutes; silent: approximately 78 minutes

The Storm (1930)
Universal
Presented by: Carl Laemmle
Director: William Wyler
Screenplay: Wells Root, based on the play *The Storm* by Langdon McCormick
Adaptation: Charles A. Logue
Dialogue: Tom Reed
Photography: Alvin Wyckoff
Recording engineer: Joseph P. Lapis and C. Roy Hunter
Cast: Lupe Velez (Manette Fachard), Paul Cavanagh (Dave Stewart), William Boyd (Burr Winston), Alphonse Ethier (Jacques Fachard), Ernest Adams (Johnny), Tom London, Nick Thompson, Erin La Bissoniere
Distribution: Universal
76 minutes

A House Divided (1931)
Universal
Producer: Carl Laemmle Jr.
Director: William Wyler
Assistant producer: Paul Kohner
Screenplay: John B. Clymer and Dale Van Every, based on the story "Heart and Hand" by Olive Edens
Dialogue: John Huston
Photography: Charles Stumar

Supervising film editor: Maurice Pivar
Editor: Ted Kent
Art direction: John Hughes
Special effects: John Fulton
Cast: Walter Huston (Seth Law), Kent Douglass (Matt Law), Helen
Chandler (Ruth Evans), Vivian Oakland (Bess), Lloyd Ingraham (Doc),
Charles Middleton (Minister), Frank Hagney (Mann), Mary Foy (Mary),
Walter Brennan (Musician)
70 minutes

Tom Brown of Culver (1932)
Universal
Director: William Wyler
Screenplay: George Green and Tom Buckingham, based on a story by
George Green and Dale Van Every
Additional dialogue: Clarence Marks
Photography: Charles Stumar
Editor: Ted Kent
Art direction: John J. Hughes
Cast: Tom Brown (Tom Brown), H. B. Warner (Dr. Brown), Slim
Summerville (Slim), Richard Cromwell (Bob Randolph), Ben Alexander
(Ralph), Sidney Toler (Major Wharton), Russell Hopton (Doctor), Andy
Devine (Call Boy), Willard Robertson (Captain White), Norman Philips
Jr. (Carruthers), Tyrone Power Jr. (John), Kit Wain, Matt Roubert, Dick
Winslow, personnel of the Culver Military Academy
70 minutes

Her First Mate (1933)
Universal
Presented by: Carl Laemmle
Producer: Carl Laemmle Jr.
Director: William Wyler
Screenplay: Earle Snell and Clarence Marks, based on the play *Salt Water*
by Daniel Jarrett, Frank Craven, and John Golden
Photography: George Robinson
Editor: Ted Kent
Art direction: Stanley Fleischer
Cast: Slim Summerville (John Horner), ZaSu Pitts (Mary Horner), Una
Merkel (Hattie Horner), Warren Hymer (Percival Todd), Henry Armetta
(Nick Socrates), Berton Churchill (Harvey Davis), George Marion (Sam),
Jocelyn Lee (Redhead)
66 minutes

Counsellor-at-Law (1933)
Universal
Personally supervised by: Carl Laemmle Jr.
Producer: Henry Henigson
Director: William Wyler
Screenplay: Elmer Rice, adapted from the stage play by Elmer Rice
Photography: Norbert Brodine
Editor: Daniel Mandell
Editorial supervision: Maurice Pivar
Art direction: Charles D. Hall
Cast: John Barrymore (George Simon), Bebe Daniels (Regina Gordon),
Doris Kenyon (Cora Simon), Onslow Stevens (John P. Tedesco), Isabel
Jewell (Bessie Green), Melvyn Douglas (Roy Darwin), Thelma Todd
(Lillian La Rue), Mayo Methot (Zedorah Chapman), Marvin Kline
(Herbert Howard Weinberg), Conway Washburne (Arthur Sandler), John
Qualen (Breitstein), Bobby Gordon (Henry Susskind), John Hammon
Dailey (McFadden), Malka Kornstein (Sarah Becker), Angela Jacobs
(Goldie Rindskopf), Clara Langsner (Lena Simon), T. H. Manning (Peter
J. Malone), Elmer Brown (Francis Clark Baird), Barbara Perry (Dorothy),
Richard Quine (Richard), Victor Adams (David Simon), Frederick Burton
(Crayfield), Vincent Sherman (Harry Becker)
78 minutes

Glamour (1934)
Universal
Director: William Wyler
Adaptation: Doris Anderson, based on the short story by Edna Ferber
Continuity: Gladys Unger
Photography: George Robinson
Editor: Ted Kent
Art direction: Charles D. Hall
Musical score: Howard Jackson and Roy Turk
Cast: Paul Lukas (Victor Banki), Constance Cummings (Linda Faye),
Phillip Reed (Lorenzo Valenti), Joseph Cawthorn (Ibsen), Doris Lloyd
(Nana), Lyman Williams (Forsyth), David Dickinson (Stevie), Peggy
Campbell (Amy), Olaf Hytten (Dobbs), Alice Lake (Secretary), Lita
Chevret (Grassie), Phil Tead (Jimmy)
74 minutes

The Good Fairy (1935)
Universal
Producer: Carl Laemmle Jr.
Director: William Wyler
Associate producer: Henry Henigson

Screenplay: Preston Sturges, based on the play by Ferenc Molnár as
translated by Jane Hinton
Photography: Norbert Brodine
Editorial supervision: Maurice Pivar
Editor: Daniel Mandell
Art direction: Charles D. Hall
Costumes: Vera West
Music director: Heinz Roemheld
Sound supervision: Gilbert Kurland
Cast: Margaret Sullavan (Luisa Ginglebusher), Herbert Marshall (Dr.
Max Sporum), Frank Morgan (Konrad), Reginald Owen (Detlaff), Alan
Hale (Schlapkohl), Beulah Bondi (Dr. Schultz), Cesar Romero (Joe),
Eric Blore (Dr. Metz), Al Bridges (Doorman), June Clayworth (Actress),
George Davis (Chauffeur), Hugh O'Connell (Gas Collector)
98 minutes

The Gay Deception (1935)
Twentieth Century–Fox
Producer: Jesse L. Lasky
Director: William Wyler
Screenplay: Stephen Avery and Don Hartman
Additional dialogue: Arthur Richman (and Sam Raphaelson, uncredited)
Photography: Joseph Valentine
Art direction: Max Parker
Costumes: William Lambert
Music: Louis de Francesco
Sound: A. von Kirbach
Assistant director: A. Schaumer
Cast: Francis Lederer (Sandro), Frances Dee (Mirabel), Benita Hume
(Miss Channing), Alan Mowbray (Lord Clewe), Paul Hurst (Bell Captain),
Ferdinand Gottschalk (Squires), Richard Carle (Spitzer), Lenita Lane (Peg
DeForrest), Lennox Pawel (Consul-General), Adele St. Maur (Lucille, the
Maid), Lionel Stander (Gettel), Akim Tamiroff (Spellek), Barbara Fritchie
(Joan Dennison)
Distribution: United Artists
79 minutes

These Three (1936)
Samuel Goldwyn Production
Producer: Samuel Goldwyn
Director: William Wyler
Screenplay: Lillian Hellman, based on her play *The Children's Hour*
Photography: Gregg Toland
Editor: Daniel Mandell

Art direction: Richard Day
Costumes: Omar Kiam
Music: Alfred Newman
Assistant director: Walter Mayo
Sound recorder: Frank Maher
Cast: Miriam Hopkins (Martha Dobie), Merle Oberon (Karen Wright),
Joel McCrea (Dr. Joseph Cardin), Catherine Doucet (Mrs. Lily Mortar),
Alma Kruger (Mrs. Tilford), Bonita Granville (Mary Tilford), Marcia
Mae Jones (Rosalie Wells), Carmencita Johnson (Evelyn), Margaret
Hamilton (Agatha), Marie Louise Cooper (Helen Burton), Mary Ann
Durkin (Joyce Walton), Walter Brennan (Taxi Driver)
Distribution: United Artists
93 minutes

Dodsworth (1936)
Samuel Goldwyn Production
Producer: Samuel Goldwyn
Director: William Wyler
Associate producer: Merritt Hulburd
Screenplay: Sidney Howard, based on the novel by Sinclair Lewis and on
the play adapted by Sidney Howard as produced for the stage by Max
Gordon
Photography: Rudolph Maté
Editor: Daniel Mandell
Art direction: Richard Day
Costumes: Omar Kiam
Music: Alfred Newman
Assistant director: Eddie Bernoudy
Sound: Oscar Lagerstrom
Location cameraman: Harry Perry
Cast: Walter Huston (Sam Dodsworth), Ruth Chatterton (Fran
Dodsworth), Paul Lukas (Arnold Iselin), Mary Astor (Edith Cortwright),
David Niven (Major Clyde Lockert), Gregory Gaye (Kurt von Obersdorf),
Maria Ouspenskaya (Baroness von Obersdorf), Odette Myrtil (Mme.
Renée de Penable), Kathryn Marlowe (Emily), John Payne (Harry McKee),
Spring Byington (Matey Pearson), Harlan Briggs (Tubby Pearson), Charles
Halton (Hazzard), Beatrice Maud (Mary, the Dodsworths' Maid), Wilson
Benge (Steward), Inez Palange (Teresa)
Distribution: United Artists
101 minutes

Come and Get It (1936)
Samuel Goldwyn Production

Directors: Howard Hawks and William Wyler
Associate producer: Merritt Hulburd
Logging scenes directed by: Richard Rosson
Screenplay: Jules Furthman and Jane Murfin, based on the novel by Edna
Ferber
Photography: Gregg Toland and Rudolph Maté
Editor: Edward Curtiss
Art direction: Richard Day
Set decoration: Julia Heron
Costumes: Omar Kiam
Music: Alfred Newman
Assistant director: Walter Mayo
Sound technician: Frank Maher
Cast: Edward Arnold (Barney Glasgow), Joel McCrea (Richard Glasgow),
Frances Farmer (Lotta Morgan/Lotta Bostrom), Walter Brennan (Swan
Bostrom), Andrea Leeds (Evie Glasgow), Frank Shields (Tony Schwerke),
Mady Christians (Karie), Mary Nash (Emma Louise Glasgow), Clem
Bevans (Gunar Gallagher), Edwin Maxwell (Sid Le Maire), Cecil
Cunningham (Josie), Harry Bradley (Gubbins), Rollo Lloyd (Steward),
Charles Halton (Hewitt), Phillip Cooper (Chore Boy), Al K. Hall
(Goodnow), Robert Lowery (Young Man), Jack Pennick (Foreman),
Stanley Blystone, Constantine Romanoff, Harry Tenbrook, Max Wagner
(Lumberjacks)
Distribution: United Artists
105 minutes

Dead End (1937)
Samuel Goldwyn Production
Producer: Samuel Goldwyn
Director: William Wyler
Associate producer: Merritt Hulburd
Screenplay: Lillian Hellman, based on the play by Sidney Kingsley as
produced by Norman Bel Geddes
Photography: Gregg Toland
Editor: Daniel Mandell
Art direction: Richard Day
Set decoration: Julia Heron
Costumes: Omar Kiam
Music: Alfred Newman
Assistant director: Eddie Bernoudy
Sound recorder: Frank Maher
Dialogue director: Edward P. Goodnow
Cast: Sylvia Sidney (Drina Gordon), Joel McCrea (Dave Connell),

Humphrey Bogart ("Baby Face" Martin), Wendy Barrie (Kay Burton), Claire Trevor (Francey), Allen Jenkins (Hunk), Marjorie Main (Mrs. Martin), Billy Halop (Tommy Gordon), Huntz Hall (Dippy), Bobby Jordan (Angel), Leo Gorcey (Spit), Gabriel Dell (T.B.), Bernard Punsley (Milty), Charles Peck (Philip Griswold), Minor Watson (Mr. Griswold), James Burke (Mulligan), Ward Bond (Doorman), Elisabeth Risdon (Mrs. Connell), Esther Dale (Mrs. Fenner), George Humbert (Mr. Pascalgi), Marcelle Corday (Governess), Charles Halton (Whitey), Donald Barry (Intern)
Distribution: United Artists
93 minutes

Jezebel (1938)
Warner Brothers
Executive producer: Hal B. Wallis
Director: William Wyler
Associate producer: Henry Blanke
Screenplay: Clements Ripley, Abem Finkel, and John Huston, based on the play by Owen Davis Sr.
Script contributor: Robert Buckner
Photography: Ernest Haller
Editor: Warren Low
Art direction: Robert Haas
Costumes: Orry-Kelly
Music: Max Steiner
Musical direction: Leo F. Forbstein
Songs: "Jezebel" by Johnny Mercer and Harry Warren; "Raise a Ruckus" by Harry Warren and Al Dubin
Technical adviser: Dalton S. Reymond
Assistant director: Bob Ross
Sound: Robert B. Lee
Cast: Bette Davis (Julie Marsden), Henry Fonda (Preston Dillard), George Brent (Buck Cantrell), Margaret Lindsay (Amy), Donald Crisp (Dr. Livingston), Fay Bainter (Aunt Belle), Richard Cromwell (Ted Dillard), Henry O'Neill (General Bogardus), Spring Byington (Mrs. Kendrick), John Litel (Jean La Cour), Gordon Oliver (Dick Allen), Janet Shaw (Molly Allen), Theresa Harris (Zette), Margaret Early (Stephanie Kendrick), Irving Pichel (Huger), Eddie Anderson (Gros Bat), Stymie Beard (Ti Bat), Lew Payton (Uncle Cato), George Renevant (De Lautruc), Georgia Caine (Mrs. Petion), Fred Lawrence (Bob), Ann Codee (Madam Pulard, Dressmaker), Daisy Bufford (Flower Girl), Trevor Bardette (Sheriff at Plantation), Jack Norton (Drunk), Jacques Vanaire (Duretta), Alan Bridge (New Orleans Sheriff)

Distribution: Warner Brothers
104 minutes

Wuthering Heights (1939)
Samuel Goldwyn Production
Producer: Samuel Goldwyn
Director: William Wyler
Screenplay: Ben Hecht and Charles MacArthur, from the novel by Emily
Brontë
Photography: Gregg Toland
Editor: Daniel Mandell
Art direction: James Basevi
Set decoration: Julia Heron
Costumes: Omar Kiam
Music: Alfred Newman
Technical adviser: Peter Shaw
Assistant director: Walter Mayo
Sound recorder: Paul Neal
Cast: Merle Oberon (Cathy), Laurence Olivier (Heathcliff), David Niven
(Edgar Linton), Flora Robson (Ellen Dean), Donald Crisp (Dr. Kenneth),
Hugh Williams (Hindley), Geraldine Fitzgerald (Isabella Linton), Leo
G. Carroll (Joseph), Cecil Humphreys (Judge Linton), Miles Mander
(Lockwood), Romaine Callender (Robert, the Butler), Cecil Kellaway
(Earnshaw), Rex Downing (Heathcliff as a Child), Sarita Wooton
(Cathy as a Child), Douglas Scott (Hindley as a Child), Helena Grant
(Miss Hudkins), Susanne Leach (Guest), Tommy Martin and Schuyler
Standish (Little Boys), Diane Williams (Little Girl), Mme. Alice Ahlers
(Harpsichordist), Vernon Downing (Giles)
Distribution: United Artists
103 minutes

1940s

The Westerner (1940)
Samuel Goldwyn Production
Director: William Wyler
Screenplay: Jo Swerling and Niven Busch, based on a story by Stuart N.
Lake
Photography: Gregg Toland
Editor: Daniel Mandell
Art direction: James Basevi
Set decoration: Julia Heron
Costumes: Irene Saltern

Music: composed and conducted by Dmitri Tiomkin (Alfred Newman, uncredited)
Assistant director: Walter Mayo
Cast: Gary Cooper (Cole Hardin), Walter Brennan (Judge Roy Bean), Doris Davenport (Jane-Ellen Mathews), Fred Stone (Caliphet Mathews), Forrest Tucker (Wade Harper), Lilian Bond (Lillie Langtry), Paul Hurst (Chickenfoot), Chill Wills (Southeast), Charles Halton (Mort Borrow), Tom Tyler (King Evans), Arthur Aylsworth (Mr. Dixon), Lupita Toyer (Teresita), Julian Rivero (Juan Gomez), Dana Andrews (Bart Cobble), Roger Gray (Eph Stringer), Trevor Bardette (Shad Wilkins), Jack Pennick (Bantry), Arthur Mix (Seth Tucker), Helen Foster (Janice), Connie Leon (Langtry's Maid), Charles Coleman (Langtry's Manager), Lew Kelly (Ticket Man), Heinie Conklin (Man at Window), Lucien Littlefield (Stranger), Corbet Morris (Orchestra Leader), Stanley Andrews (Sheriff), Henry Roquemore (Stage Manager), Hank Bell (Deputy), Bill Steele (Tex Cole), Blackjack Ward (Buck Harrigan), Jim Corey (Lee Webb), Buck Moulton (Charles Evans), Ted Wells (Joe Lawrence), Joe De La Cruz (Mex), Frank Cordell (Bean Henchman), Philip Connor (John Yancy), Capt. C. E. Anderson (Hezikiah Willever)
Distribution: United Artists
99 minutes

The Letter (1940)
Warner Brothers/First National
In charge of production: Jack L. Warner
Executive producer: Hal B. Wallis
Director: William Wyler
Associate producer: Robert Lord
Screenplay: Howard Koch, based on the play by W. Somerset Maugham
Photography: Tony Gaudio
Editors: George Amy and Warren Low
Art direction: Carl Jules-Weyl
Gowns: Orry-Kelly
Music: Max Steiner
Technical advisers: Louis Vincenot and John Villasin
Assistant director: Sherry Shourds
Sound: Dolph Thomas
Cast: Bette Davis (Leslie Crosbie), Herbert Marshall (Robert Crosbie), James Stephenson (Howard Joyce), Frieda Inescort (Dorothy Joyce), Gale Sondergaard (Mrs. Hammond), Bruce Lester (John Withers), Elizabeth Earl (Adele Ainsworth), Cecil Kellaway (Prescott), Sen Yung (Ong Chi Seng), Doris Lloyd (Mrs. Cooper), Willie Fung (Chung Hi), Tetsu Kornai (Head Boy)

Distribution: Warner Brothers
95 minutes

The Little Foxes (1941)
Samuel Goldwyn Production
Producer: Samuel Goldwyn
Director: William Wyler
Screenplay: Lillian Hellman, based on her stage play as produced by
Herman Shumlin
Additional scenes and dialogue: Arthur Kober, Dorothy Parker, and Alan
Campbell
Photography: Gregg Toland
Editor: Daniel Mandell
Art direction: Stephen Goosson
Set decoration: Howard Bristol
Costumes: Orry-Kelly
Music: Meredith Wilson
Sound recorder: Frank Maher
Assistant director: William Tummel
Cast: Bette Davis (Regina Hubbard Giddens), Herbert Marshall (Horace
Giddens), Teresa Wright (Alexandra Giddens), Richard Carlson (David
Hewitt), Patricia Collinge (Birdie Hubbard), Dan Duryea (Leo Hubbard),
Charles Dingle (Ben Hubbard), Carl Benton Reid (Oscar Hubbard), John
Marriott (Cal), Jessie Grayson (Addie), Russell Hicks (William Marshall),
Lucien Littlefield (Sam Menders), Virginia Brissac (Mrs. Lucy Hewitt),
Terry Nibert (Julia), Charles R. Moore (Simon), Henry "Hot Shot"
Thomas (Harold), Alan Bridge (Hotel Manager), Kenny Washington
(Servant), Hooper Atchley (Guest), Lew Kelly (Train Companion), Henry
Roquemore (Depositor)
Distribution: RKO Pictures
116 minutes

Mrs. Miniver (1942)
Metro-Goldwyn-Mayer
Producer: Sidney Franklin
Director: William Wyler
Screenplay: Arthur Wimperis, George Froeschel, James Hilton, and
Claudine West, based on the novel by Jan Struther
Photography: Joseph Ruttenberg
Editor: Harold F. Kress
Art direction: Cedric Gibbons
Set decoration: Edwin B. Willis
Musical score: Herbert Stothart

Song: "Midsummer's Day" by Gene Lockhart
Cast: Greer Garson (Mrs. Miniver), Walter Pidgeon (Clem Miniver), Teresa Wright (Carol Beldon), Dame May Whitty (Lady Beldon), Reginald Owen (Foley), Henry Travers (Mr. Ballard), Richard Ney (Olin Miniver), Henry Wilcoxon (Vicar), Christopher Severn (Toby Miniver), Brenda Forbes (Gladys), Clare Sandars (Judy Miniver), Marie de Becker (Ada), Helmut Dentine (German Flyer), John Abbott (Fred), Connie Leon (Simpson), Rhys William (Horace), Mary Field (Miss Spriggins), Ben Webster (Ginger), Paul Scardon (Nobby), Aubrey Mather (Innkeeper), Forrester Harvey (Huggins), Billy Sevin (Conductor), Ottola Smith (Saleslady), Gerald Oliver Smith (Car Dealer), Alec Craig (Joe), Clara Reid (Mrs. Huggins), John Burton (Halliday), Leonard Carey (Beldon's Butler), Eric Lonsdale (Marston), Arthur Wimperis (Sir Henry), David Clyde (Carruthers), Colin Campbell (Sickles), Herbert Clifton (Doctor), Thomas Louden (Mr. Verger), Peter Lawford (Pilot), Miles Mander (German Agent's Voice), St. Luke's Choristers
Distribution: Metro-Goldwyn-Mayer
134 minutes

Memphis Belle (1944)
Presented by: War Department
Produced by: U.S. Eighth Air Force Photographic Section, in cooperation with Army Air Forces First Motion Picture Unit
Producer: William Wyler
Director: William Wyler
Script: William Wyler
Photography: William C. Clothier and Harold Tannenbaum (William Wyler, uncredited)
Additional photography: William Wyler
Editor: Lynn Harrison
Music: Gail Kubik
Narration: Lester Koenig
Narrators: Eugene Kern and John Beal
Distribution: Paramount Pictures Inc., under the auspices of the War Activities Committee
41 minutes

Thunderbolt (1945)
Produced by: Carl Krueger Productions and the U.S. Air Force, under the command of Lieutenant Ira C. Eaker
Direction and editing: William Wyler and John Sturges
Script: Lester Koenig
Music: Gail Kubik

Introduced by: James Stewart
Narrated by: Eugene Kern and Lloyd Bridges
Distribution: Monogram Pictures
44 minutes

The Best Years of Our Lives (1946)
Samuel Goldwyn Production
Producer: Samuel Goldwyn
Director: William Wyler
Screenplay: Robert E. Sherwood, based on the verse novel *Glory for Me*
by MacKinlay Kantor
Photography: Gregg Toland
Editor: Daniel Mandell
Art direction: George Jenkins and Perry Ferguson
Set decoration: Julia Heron
Costume design: Irene Sharaff
Musical score: Hugo Friedhofer
Music direction: Emil Newman
Assistant director: Joseph Boyle
Production assistant: Lester Koenig
Cast: Myrna Loy (Milly Stephenson), Fredric March (Al Stephenson),
Dana Andrews (Fred Derry), Teresa Wright (Peggy Stephenson), Virginia
Mayo (Marie Derry), Cathy O'Donnell (Wilma Cameron), Hoagy
Carmichael (Butch Engel), Harold Russell (Homer Parrish), Gladys
George (Hortense Derry), Roman Bohnen (Mr. Derry), Ray Collins (Mr.
Milton), Steve Cochran (Cliff), Minna Gombell (Mrs. Parrish), Walter
Baldwin (Mr. Parrish), Dorothy Adams (Mrs. Cameron), Don Beddoe
(Mr. Cameron), Victor Cutler (Woody), Erskine Sandord (Bullard),
Marlene Aames (Luella Parrish), Michael Hall (Rob Stephenson), Charles
Halton (Prew), Ray Teal (Mr. Mollett), Howland Chamberlin (Thorpe),
Dean White (Novak), Ralph Sanford (George Gibbons)
Distribution: RKO Pictures
172 minutes

The Heiress (1949)
Paramount
Producer: William Wyler
Director: William Wyler
Associate producers: Lester Koenig and Robert Wyler
Screenplay: Ruth and Augustus Goetz, based on their play *The Heiress*,
suggested by the novel *Washington Square* by Henry James
Photography: Leo Tover
Editor: William Hornbeck

Production design: Harry Horner
Art direction: John Meehan
Set decoration: Emile Kuri
Costumes: Edith Head
Makeup supervision: Wally Westmore
Music: Aaron Copland
Special photographic effects: Gordon Jennings
Assistant director: C. C. Coleman Jr.
Cast: Olivia de Havilland (Catherine Sloper), Montgomery Clift (Morris
Townsend), Ralph Richardson (Dr. Austin Sloper), Miriam Hopkins
(Lavinia Penniman), Mona Freeman (Marian Almond), Vanessa Brown
(Maria), Selena Hoyle (Elizabeth Almond), Ray Collins (Jefferson
Almond), Betty Linley (Mrs. Montgomery), Paul Lees (Arthur Townsend),
Harry Antrim (Mr. Abeel), Russ Conway (Quintus), Davis Thursby
(Geier), Donald Kerr (Fish Peddler), Harry Pipe (Mr. Gebhardt), Una
Mortished (Chambermaid), Ralph Sanford (Captain, *Castle Queen*),
Lester Dorr (Groom)
Distribution: Paramount
115 minutes

1950s

Detective Story (1951)
Paramount
Producer: William Wyler
Director: William Wyler
Associate producers: Lester Koenig and Robert Wyler
Screenplay: Philip Yordan and Robert Wyler, based on the play by Sidney
Kingsley
Photography: Lee Garmes
Editor: Robert Swink
Art direction: Hal Pereira and Earl Hedrick
Set decoration: Emile Kuri
Costumes: Edith Head
Cast: Kirk Douglas (Detective James McLeod), Eleanor Parker (Mary
McLeod), William Bendix (Detective Lou Brody), Cathy O'Donnell
(Susan Carmichael), Bert Freed (Detective Dakis), Frank Faylen
(Detective Gallagher), William Phillips (Callahan), Grandon Rhodes
(Detective O'Brien), Luis Van Rooten (Joe Feinson), Craig Hill (Arthur
Kindred), Lee Grant (Shoplifter), Horace McMahon (Lt. Monaghan),
Warner Anderson (Endicott Sims), George Macready (Karl Schneider),
Joseph Wiseman (Charles Gennini), Michael Strong (Lewis Abbott),
Russell Evans (Patrolman Barnes), Howard Joslyn (Patrolman Keogh),

Gladys George (Miss Hatch), Burt Mustin (Willy), Gerald Mohr (Tami Giacopetti), James Maloney (Mr. Pritchett), Edmund F. Cobb (Detective), Mike Mahoney (Coleman), Catherine Doucet (Mrs. Farrigut), Ann Codee (Frenchwoman), Ralph Montgomery (Finney), Pat Flaherty (Desk Sergeant), Bob Scot (Mulvey), Harper Goff (Galents), Donald Kerr (Taxi Driver)
Distribution: Paramount
103 minutes

Carrie (1952)
Paramount
Producer: William Wyler
Director: William Wyler
Associate producer: Lester Koenig
Screenplay: Ruth and Augustus Goetz, based on the novel *Sister Carrie* by Theodore Dresier
Photography: Victor Milner
Editor: Robert Swink
Art direction: Hal Pereira and Roland Anderson
Set decoration: Emile Kuri
Costumes: Edith Head
Musical score: David Raskin
Cast: Laurence Olivier (George Hurstwood), Jennifer Jones (Carrie Meeber), Miriam Hopkins (Julia Hurstwood), Eddie Albert (Charles Drouet), Basil Ruysdael (Mr. Fitzgerald), Ray Teal (Allen), Barry Kelley (Slawson), Sara Berner (Mrs. Oransky), William Reynolds (George Hurstwood Jr.), Mary Murphy (Jessica Hurstwood), Harry Hayden (O'Brien), Charles Halton (Factory Foreman), Walter Baldwin (Carrie's Father), Dorothy Adams (Carrie's Mother), Jacqueline de Wit (Carrie's Sister, Minnie), Harlan Briggs (Joe Brant), Melinda Plowman (Little Girl), Donald Kerr (Slawson's Bartender), Lester Sharpe (Mr. Blum), Don Beddoe (Mr. Goodman), John Alvin (Stage Manager), Judith Adams (Bride), Martin Doric (Maitre d'), Ralph Sanford (Waiter)
Distribution: Paramount
118 minutes

Roman Holiday (1953)
Paramount
Producer: William Wyler
Director: William Wyler
Associate producer: Robert Wyler
Screenplay: Ian McLellan Hunter, John Dighton, and Dalton Trumbo, based on a story by Ian McLellan Hunter
Photography: Frank F. Planer and Henri Alekan

Editor: Robert Swink
Art direction: Hal Pereira and Walter Tyler
Costumes: Edith Head
Musical score: Georges Auric
Assitant directors: Herbert Coleman and Piero Mussetta
Cast: Gregory Peck (Joe Bradley), Audrey Hepburn (Princess Anne),
Eddie Albert (Irving Radovich), Hartley Power (Mr. Hennessy), Harcourt
Williams (Ambassador), Margaret Rawlings (Countess Vereberg), Tullio
Carminati (General Provno), Paolo Carlini (Mario Delani), Claudio
Ermelli (Giovanni), Paolo Borboni (Charwoman), Alfredo Rizzo (Taxicab
Driver), Laura Solari (Hennessy's Secretary), Gorella Gori (Shoe Seller)
Distribution: Paramount
119 minutes

The Desperate Hours (1955)
Paramount
Producer: William Wyler
Director: William Wyler
Associate director: Robert Wyler
Screenplay: Joseph Hayes, based on his novel and play
Photography: Lee Garmes
Editor: Robert Swink
Art direction: Hal Pereira and Joseph MacMillan Johnson
Costumes: Edith Head
Music: Gail Kubik
Second unit director: John Waters
Assistant director: C. C. Coleman Jr.
Sound: Hugo Grenzbach and Winston Leverett
Cast: Humphrey Bogart (Glenn Griffin), Fredric March (Dan Hilliard),
Arthur Kennedy (Jesse Bard), Martha Scott (Eleanor Hilliard), Dewey
Martin (Hal Griffin), Gig Young (Chuck), Mary Murphy (Cindy Hilliard),
Richard Eyer (Ralphie Hilliard), Robert Middleton (Sam Kobish), Alan
Reed (Detective), Bert Freed (Winston), Ray Collins (Masters), Whit
Bissell (Carson), Ray Teal (Fredericks), Michael Moore (Detective), Don
Haggerty (Detective), Ric Roman (Sal), Pat Flaherty (Dutch), Beverly
Garland (Miss Swift), Louis Lettieri (Bucky Walling), Ann Doran (Mrs.
Walling), Walter Baldwin (Patterson)
Distribution: Paramount
112 minutes

Friendly Persuasion (1956)
Allied Artists
Producer: William Wyler

Director: William Wyler
Associate producer: Robert Wyler
Screenplay: Jessamyn West, Michael Wilson, and Robert Wyler
(uncredited), based on the collected stories *The Friendly Persuasion* by
Jessamyn West
Photography: Ellsworth Fredericks
Editors: Robert Swink, Edward A. Biery, and Robert A. Belcher
Art direction: Edward S. Haworth
Costume design: Dorothy Jeakins
Muisc: composed and conducted by Dmitri Tiomkin
Songs: "Friendly Persuasion (Thee I Love)," sung by Pat Boone; "Mocking
Bird in a Willow Tree"; "Marry Me, Marry Me"; "Coax Me a Little";
and "Indiana Holiday," lyrics by Paul Francis Webster, music by Dmitri
Tiomkin
Technical adviser: Jessamyn West
Assistant to the producer: Stuart Millar
Assistant director: Austen Jewell
Cast: Gary Cooper (Jess Birdwell), Dorothy McGuire (Eliza Birdwell),
Marjorie Main (Widow Hudspeth), Anthony Perkins (Josh Birdwell),
Richard Eyer (Little Jess), Robert Middleton (Sam Jordan), Phyllis
Love (Mattie Birdwell), Mark Richman (Gard Jordan), Walter Catlett
(Professor Quigley), Joel Fluellen (Enoch), Richard Hale (Purdy),
Theodore Newton (Major Harvey), John Smith (Caleb), Samantha
(Goose), Mary Carr (Quaker Woman), Edna Skinner, Frances Farwell,
and Marjorie Durant (Hudspeth Daughers), Russell Simpson, Charles
Halton, and Everett Glass (Elders), Richard Garland (Bushwacker), Jean
Inness (Mrs. Purdy), Nelson Leigh (Minister), Helen Kleeb (Old Woman),
John Craven (Leader), Frank Jenks (Shell Game Man), Diane Jergens
(Elizabeth), Ralph Sanford (Businessman), Donald Kerr (Manager)
Distribution: United Artists
119 minutes

The Letter (1956; television)
NBC, Producer's Showcase
Producer: William Wyler
Director: William Wyler
Television director: Kirk Browning
Based on the play by Somerset Maugham
Cast: Siobhan McKenna (Leslie Crosbie), John Mills (Robert Crosbie),
Michael Rennie (Howard Joyce), Anna May Wong (Mrs. Hammond)

The Big Country (1958)
Anthony–World Wide Production

Producers: William Wyler and Gregory Peck
Director: William Wyler
Associate producer: Robert Wyler
Screenplay: James R. Webb, Sy Bartlett, and Robert Wilder
Adaptation: Jessamyn West and Robert Wyler, based on the novel *The Big Country* by Donald Hamilton
Photography: Franz F. Planer
Supervising editor: Robert Swink
Editors: Robert Belcher and John Faure
Art direction: Frank Hotaling
Music: Jerome Moross
Music editor: Lloyd Young
Second unit directors: John Waters and Robert Swink
Director of photography, second unit: Wallace Chewning
Assistant director: Ivan Volkman
Second assistant director: Ray Gosnell
Assistant to William Wyler: Clarence Marks
Title design: Saul Bass
Cast: Gregory Peck (James McKay), Jean Simmons (Julie Maragon), Carroll Baker (Patricia Terrill), Charlton Heston (Steve Leech), Burl Ives (Rufus Hannassey), Charles Bickford (Major Henry Terrill), Alfonso Bedoya (Ramon), Chuck Connors (Buck Hannassey), Chuck Hayward (Rafe), Buff Brady (Dude), Jim Burk (Cracker), Dorothy Adams (Hannassey Woman), Chuck Robertson, Bob Morgan, John McKee, and Jay Slim Talbot (Terrill Cowboys)
Distribution: United Artists
166 minutes

Ben-Hur (1959)
Metro-Goldwyn-Mayer
Producer: Sam Zimbalist
Director: William Wyler
Screenplay: Karl Tunberg (and Christopher Fry, S. N. Behrman, and Gore Vidal, uncredited), based on the novel by Lew Wallace
Photography: Robert L. Surtees
Additional photography: Harold E. Wellman and Pietro Portalupi
Second unit directors: Andrew Marton, Yakima Canutt, and Mario Soldati
Editors: Ralph E. Winters and John D. Dunning
Art direction: William A. Horning and Edward Carfagno
Set decoration: Hugh Hunt
Costume design: Elizabeth Haffenden
Music: Miklosz Rosa
Special effects: A. Arnold Gillespie, Lee LeBlanc, and Robert R. Hoag

Assistant directors: Gus Agosti and Alberto Cardone
Cast: Charlton Heston (Judah Ben-Hur), Jack Hawkins (Quintus Arrius), Stephen Boyd (Messala), Haya Harareet (Esther), Hugh Griffith (Sheik Ilderim), Martha Scott (Miriam), Sam Jaffe (Simonides), Cathy O'Donnell (Tirzah), Finlay Currie (Balthasar), Frank Thring (Pontius Pilate), Terence Longden (Drusus), Andre Morell (Sextus), Marina Berti (Flavia), George Relph (Tiberius), Adi Berber (Malluch), Stella Vitelleschi (Amrah), Jose Greci (Mary), Laurence Payne (Joseph), John Horsley (Spintho), Richard Coleman (Metellus), Duncan Lamont (Marius), Ralph Truman (Aide to Tiberius), Richard Hale (Gaspar), Reginald Lal Singh (Melchior), David Davies (Quaestor), Dervis Ward (Jailer), Claude Heater (The Christ), Mino Doro (Gratus), Robert Brown (Chief of Rowers)
Distribution: Metro-Goldwyn-Mayer
212 minutes

1960s

The Children's Hour (1961)
Mirisch–World Wide Production
Producer: William Wyler
Director: William Wyler
Associate producer: Robert Wyler
Screenplay: John Michael Hayes
Adaptation: Lillian Hellman, based on her stage play
Photography: Franz F. Planer
Editor: Robert Swink
Art direction: Fernando Carrere
Set decoration: Edward G. Boyle
Music: Alex North
Assistant directors: Robert E. Relyea and Jerome M. Siegel
Cast: Audrey Hepburn (Karen Wright), Shirley MacLaine (Martha Dobie), James Garner (Dr. Joe Cardin), Miriam Hopkins (Mrs. Lily Mortar), Fay Bainter (Mrs. Amelia Tilford), Karen Balkin (Mary Tilford), Veronica Cartwright (Rosalie), Jered Barclay (Grocery Boy)
Distribution: United Artists
107 minutes

The Collector (1965)
The Collector Company/William Wyler Production
Producers: Jud Kinberg and John Kohn
Director: William Wyler
Screenplay: Stanley Mann and John Kohn, based on the novel by John Fowles
Art direction: John Stoll

Editor and second unit director: Robert Swink
Music: Maurice Jarre
American staff:
  Photography: Robert Surtees
  Set decoration: Frank Tuttle
  Music editor: Richard Harris
  Assistant director: Sergei Petschnikoff
  Camera operator: Andrew McIntyre
  Sound supervision: Charles J. Rice
  Sound: Jack Solomon
  Script supervisor: Isabel Blodgett
British staff:
  Photography: Robert Krasker
  Editor: David Hawkins
  Assistant director: Roy Baird
  Camera operator: John Harris
  Second unit cameraman: Norman Warwick
  Production manager: Philip Shipway
Cast: Terence Stamp (Freddie Clegg), Samantha Eggar (Miranda Grey),
Mona Washbourne (Aunt Annie), Maurice Dallimore (The Neighbor),
William Beckley (Crutchley), Gordon Barclay and David Haviland
(Clerks)
Distribution: Columbia Pictires
119 minutes

How to Steal a Million (1966)
World Wide/William Wyler Production
Producer: Fred Kohlmar
Director: William Wyler
Screenplay: Harry Kurnitz, based on the story "Venus Rising" by George
Bradshaw
Photography: Charles Lang
Second unit director and editor: Robert Swink
Miss Hepburn's clothes: Givenchy
Makeup: Alberto de Rossi and Frederick Williamson
Music: Johnny Williams
Orchestration: James Harbert
Sound: Joseph de Bretagne and David Dockendorf
Assistant director: Paul Feyder
Unit production manager: William Kaplan
Production assistant: François Moreuil
Main title design: Cinefx, Phill Norman
Cast: Audrey Hepburn (Nichole Bonnet), Peter O'Toole (Simon Dermott),

Eli Wallach (David Leland), Hugh Griffith (Charles Bonnet), Charles
Boyer (De Solnay), Fernand Garvey (Grammont), Marcel Dalio (Señor
Paravideo), Jacques Marin (Chief Guard), Moustache (Guard), Roger
Treville (Auctioneer), Eddie Malin (Insurance Clerk), Bert Bertram
(Marcel)
Distribution: Twentieth Century-Fox
127 minutes

Funny Girl (1968)
William Wyler/Ray Stark Production, presented by Columbia Pictures
and Rastar Productions
Producer: Ray Stark
Director: William Wyler
Screenplay: Isobel Lennart, based on her musical play
Photography: Harry Stradling
Supervising editor: Robert Swink
Editors: Maury Winetrobe and William Sands
Art direction: Robert Luthardt
Set decoration: William Kiernan
Production design: Gene Callahan
Barbra Streisand's costume design: Irene Sharaff
Makeup supervision: Ben Lane
Makeup artist: Frank McCoy
Hairstyles: Vivienne Walker and Virginia Darcy
Musical numbers: directed by Herbert Ross
Music supervisor and conductor: Walter Scharf
Orchestrations: Hack Hayes, Walter Scharf, Leo Shuken, and Herbert
Spencer
Vocal-dance arrangements: Betty Walberg
Music editor: Ted Sebern
Assistant directors: Jack Roe and Ray Gosnell
Sound: Charles J. Rice, Arthur Piantadosi, and Jack Solomon
Cast: Barbra Streisand (Fanny Brice), Omar Sharif (Nick Arnstein), Kay
Medford (Rose Brice), Anne Francis (Georgia James), Walter Pidgeon
(Florenz Ziegfeld), Lee Allen (Eddie Ryan), Mae Questel (Mrs. Strakosh),
Gerald Mohr (Branca), Frank Faylen (Keeney), Mittie Lawrence (Emma),
Gertrude Flynn (Mrs. O'Malley), Penny Santon (Mrs. Meeker), John
Harmon (Company Manager), Thordis Brandt (Bettina Brenna), Virginia
Ann Ford, Alena Johnson, Karen Lee, Mary Jane Mangler, Inga Neilsen,
and Sharon Vaughn (Ziegfeld Girls)
Distribution: Columbia Pictures
151 minutes

1970s

The Liberation of L. B. Jones (1970)
William Wyler–Ronald Lubin Production
Producer: Ronald Lubin
Director: William Wyler
Screenplay: Stirling Silliphant and Jesse Hill Ford, based on the novel by
Jesse Hill Ford
Photography: Robert Surtees
Supervising film editor and second unit director: Robert Swink
Editor: Carl Kress
Production designer: Kenneth A. Reid
Music: Elmer Bernstein
Sound: Jack Solomon and Arthur Piantadosi
Camera operator: William Johnson
Assistant directors: Anthony Ray, M. Frankovich Jr., and Robert M. Jones
Cast: Lee J. Cobb (Oman Hedgepath), Anthony Zerbe (Willie Joe Worth),
Roscoe Lee Browne (Lord Byron Jones), Lola Falana (Emma Jones), Lee
Majors (Steve Mundine), Barbara Hershey (Nella Mundine), Yaphet
Kotto (Sonny Boy Mosby), Arch Johnson (Stanley Bumpas), Chill Wills
(Mr. Ike), Zara Cully (Mama Lavorn), Fayard Nicholas (Benny), Lauren
Jones (Erleen), Dub Taylor (Mayor), Ray Teal (Police Chief), Joseph Attles
(Henry), Brenda Sykes (Jelly), Larry D. Mann (Grocer), Eve McVeagh
(Miss Griggs), Sonora McKeller (Miss Ponsella), Robert Van Meter (Blind
Man), Jack Grinnage (Driver), John S. Jackson (Suspect)
Distribution: Columbia Pictures
102 minutes

Notes

Introduction

1. Roger Leenhardt, "À bas Ford / vive Wyler!" *L'Ecran francais* 146 (April 13, 1948). Merve Fejzula, my research assistant, translated this article.

2. Andrew Sarris, *The American Cinema* (New York: E. P. Dutton, 1968), 167.

3. *Show*, March 1970, 15.

4. Gabriel Miller, *William Wyler: Interviews* (Jackson: University Press of Mississippi, 2010), 129.

5. William Wyler, "No Magic Wand," *Screenwriter* 2, no. 9 (February 1947): 10.

6. Curtis Lee Hanson, "William Wyler," *Cinema* 3, no. 5 (Summer 1967): 24.

7. David Bordwell, The *Classical Hollywood Cinema* (New York: Columbia University Press, 1985), 346.

8. William Wyler, "Escape to Reality," *Liberty* 24, no. 1 (January 4, 1947), 16, reprinted in *Picturegoer*, March 15, 1947, 8.

9. *Directed by William Wyler* (Tatge Productions, 1986; New York: Kino Video, 2002), DVD.

10. Thomas Schatz, *The Genius of the System* (New York: Pantheon Books, 1988), 5–8, 225.

11. Hanson, "William Wyler," 24.

12. Simon Callow, *Charles Laughton: A Difficult Actor* (New York: Grove Press, 1998), 290.

13. *The New Biographical Dictionary of Film* (New York: Knopf, 2004), 975.

14. Wyler, "Escape to Reality," 16.

15. *New York Times*, June 18, 1950.

16. Sarris, *American Cinema*, 167.

17. Schatz, *Genius of the System*, 5.

18. Miller, *William Wyler: Interviews*, 119.

19. A. Scott Berg, *Goldwyn: A Biography* (New York: Ballantine, 1990), 271.

20. Ibid., 273.

21. Quoted in ibid., 272.

22. Ibid., 309.

23. Wyler to Y. Frank Freeman, February 24, 1954, William Wyler Collection, Margaret Herrick Library, Academy of Motion Picture Arts and Sciences, Los Angeles, California.

24. Jan Herman, *A Talent for Trouble: The Life of Hollywood's Most Acclaimed Director, William Wyler* (New York: G. P. Putnam's Sons, 1995), 13.

25. William Wyler, "Flying over Germany," *News Digest* 2, no. 13 (August 15, 1943): 26.

26. André Bazin, *Bazin at Work: Major Essays and Reviews from the Forties and Fifties*, ed. and trans. Bert Cardullo and Alain Piette (New York: Routledge, 1997), 5.

27. Charles Higham, "William Wyler," *Action* 8, no. 5 (September–October 1973): 20.

28. Sidney Kingsley, *Five Prize Winning Plays* (Columbus: Ohio State University Press, 1995), 244.

29. On December 21, 2011, the *New York Times* reported that nearly sixty years after the film's release, the Writers' Guild of America West had restored Dalton Trumbo's writing credit for *Roman Holiday*.

30. Hanson, "William Wyler," 34.

31. *Directed by William Wyler.*

32. Joseph I. Anderson and Donald Ritchie, *The Japanese Film: Art and Industry* (Princeton, N.J.: Princeton University Press, 1983), 382.

33. Herman, *A Talent for Trouble*, 436.

34. Quoted in Louis Giannetti, *Masters of the American Cinema* (Englewood Cliffs, N.J.: Prentice-Hall, 1981), 206.

1. Discovering a Vocation and a Style

1. "William Wyler," *Film Reference*, last modified 2012, http://filmreference.com/Directors-Ve-Y/Wyler-William.html.

2. Dave's boss, for instance, tells him that the people of Boonton have money but don't know how to spend it.

3. Internal reports, November 16, 1928, Wyler Collection.

4. Wyler would revisit a scene like this in *Funny Girl* almost forty years later.

5. Herman, *A Talent for Trouble*, 88.

6. Axel Madsen, *William Wyler: The Authorized Biography* (New York: Crowell, 1973), 68.

7. Herman, *A Talent for Trouble*, 91.

8. Ibid.

9. Wyler rarely resorted to such imagery, but he would do so again in *Dodsworth* (1936), when Arnold Iselin sets fire to a letter that Fran Dods-

worth received from her husband. Iselin wants Fran to leave her husband and forget the past. Wyler's camera follows the burning letter as it wafts across the balcony.

10. Herman, *A Talent for Trouble*, 92.

11. Carl Laemmle Jr. to Wyler, August 29, 1931, Wyler Collection.

12. Laemmle Jr. to Wyler, September 3, 1931, Wyler Collection.

2. Coming into His Own

1. Quoted in Madsen, *William Wyler*, 81.

2. John Huston, *An Open Book* (New York: Knopf, 1980), 59.

3. Wyler to Oliver La Farge, December 16, 1932, William Wyler Papers, 1925–1975, Arts Library Special Collections, Young Research Library, UCLA.

4. Huston, *An Open Book*, 60.

5. Wyler to La Farge, January 30, 1933, Wyler Collection.

6. Huston, *An Open Book*, 60.

7. Ibid. There is a copy of Huston's script in the Wyler Collection.

8. Herman, *A Talent for Trouble*, 108.

9. Wyler to Carl Laemmle, December 29, 1932, Wyler Collection.

10. Madsen, *William Wyler*, 85.

11. Elmer Rice, *Minority Report* (New York: Simon and Schuster, 1963), 164.

12. Ibid., 121.

13. Elmer Rice, *Seven Plays* (New York: Viking Press, 1950), 269.

14. Madsen, *William Wyler*, 90.

15. Telegram from Elmer Rice to Wyler, September 2, 1933, Wyler Collection.

16. Rice, *Minority Report*, 332.

17. Margot Peters, *The House of Barrymore* (New York: Knopf, 1990), 353.

18. Madsen, *William Wyler*, 93.

19. Herman, *A Talent for Trouble*, 114.

20. Wyler to Carl Laemmle, September 9, 1933, Wyler Collection.

21. Peters, *The House of Barrymore*, 354.

22. Ibid., 586.

23. Delays memo, 1933, Wyler Collection.

24. Herman, *A Talent for Trouble*, 117.

25. Ibid., 118.

26. Ibid.

27. Madsen, *William Wyler*, 93.

28. Ibid., 94.

29. Hanson, "William Wyler," 30.

30. Richard H. Pells, *Radical Visions and American Dreams* (New York: Harper and Row, 1973), 79.

31. Pauline Kael, *Kiss Kiss Bang Bang* (New York: Bantam, 1971), 311.

32. Peters, *The House of Barrymore*, 354.

33. James Rorty, *Where Life Is Better* (New York: John Day/Reynal and Hitchcock, 1932), 98.

34. Interoffice communication, November 13, 1933, Wyler Collection.

35. Telegram from Rice to Wyler, November 27, 1933, Wyler Collection.

3. First-Class Pictures

1. Berg, *Goldwyn*, 263.

2. Ibid., 265.

3. Joseph Breen to Samuel Goldwyn, July 31, 1935, Samuel Goldwyn Papers, Margaret Herrick Library, Academy of Motion Picture Arts and Sciences, Los Angeles, California.

4. *Directed by William Wyler.*

5. Berg, *Goldwyn*, 267.

6. Herman, *A Talent for Trouble*, 141.

7. Doris V. Falk, *Lillian Hellman* (New York: Frederick Ungar, 1978), 37.

8. Carl Rollyson, *Lillian Hellman: Her Legend and Her Legacy* (New York: St. Martin's Press, 1988), 65.

9. *New York Times*, November 21, 1934.

10. William Wright, *Lillian Hellman: The Image, the Woman* (New York: Ballantine, 1986), 79.

11. Lillian Hellman, *Four Plays by Lillian Hellman* (New York: Random House, 1972), viii.

12. Rollyson, *Lillian Hellman*, 70.

13. William Wright, *Writers at Work: The Paris Review Interviews*, 3rd ser. (New York: Viking Press, 1967), 126.

14. Hellman's early treatments are in folder 2356, Goldwyn Papers.

15. Berg, *Goldwyn*, 267.

16. *Directed by William Wyler.*

17. Herman, *A Talent for Trouble*, 145.

18. Hanson, "William Wyler," 24.

19. Douglas Slocombe, "The Work of Gregg Toland," *Sequence* 8 (Summer 1949): 68–69.

20. André Bazin, *What Is Cinema?* vol. 1, ed. and trans. Hugh Gray (Berkeley: University of California Press, 1967), 35–36.

21. Hanson, "William Wyler," 24.

22. Mark Schorer, *Sinclair Lewis: An American Life* (New York: Dell, 1961), 616.

23. Rollyson, *Lillian Hellman*, 86.

24. John Baxter, *Hollywood in the Thirties* (New York: A. S. Barnes, 1968), 116; Bernard F. Dick, *Hellman in Hollywood* (Rutherford, N.J.: Fairleigh Dickinson University Press, 1982), 34.

25. Lillian Hellman, *Six Plays by Lillian Hellman* (New York: Vintage, 1979), 58.

26. "Dialogue Continuity: A Version," November 23, 1935, Wyler Papers.

27. Graham Greene, "These Three," *Spectator*, May 1, 1936.

28. Telegram from David Selznick to Wyler, February 25, 1936, Goldwyn Papers.

29. Telegram from Jesse Lasky to Wyler, undated, Wyler Collection.

4. The Wyler Touch

1. Sinclair Lewis, *Dodsworth* (New York: Harcourt, Brace, 1929), 11.

2. Ibid., 142.

3. Ibid., 192–93.

4. Richard Lingeman, *Sinclair Lewis: Rebel from Main Street* (St. Paul, Minn.: Borealis Books, 2002), 333.

5. Ibid., 332.

6. Ibid, 255.

7. Berg, *Goldwyn*, 277.

8. Lawrence Grobel, *The Hustons* (New York: Avon Books, 1990), 169–70.

9. Sidney Howard, *Sinclair Lewis's* Dodsworth (New York: Harcourt, Brace, 1934), xvii.

10. Ibid., xii.

11. Grobel, *The Hustons*, 177.

12. Memo from Wyler to Goldwyn, March 17, 1936, Goldwyn Papers.

13. Madsen, *William Wyler*, 145.

14. Sidney Howard, "Notes for a Treatment," undated, Goldwyn Papers.

15. H. C. Potter, early version of *Dodsworth* script, April 4, 1936, Goldwyn Papers.

16. Herman, *A Talent for Trouble*, 153.

17. Howard, "Notes for a Treatment."

18. Mary Astor, *A Life in Film* (New York: Delacorte Press, 1967), 119.

19. Herman, *A Talent for Trouble*, 153.

20. Ruth Chatterton's agent to Wyler, June 11, 1936, Goldwyn Papers.

21. Astor, *A Life in Film*, 119.

22. David Niven, *The Moon's a Balloon* (New York: G. P. Putnam's Sons, 1972), 216–17.

23. Herman, *A Talent for Trouble*, 154–55.

24. Astor, *A Life in Film*, 118–19.

25. Herman, *A Talent for Trouble*, 155.

26. Ken Doeckel, "William Wyler," *Films in Review* 22, no. 8 (October 1971): 473.

27. Berg, *Goldwyn*, 185.

28. Madsen, *William Wyler*, 147.
29. Howard, *Sinclair Lewis's* Dodsworth, 3.
30. Astor, *A Life in Film*, 121.
31. Berg, *Goldwyn*, 285.
32. Ibid.
33. Herman, *A Talent for Trouble*, 160.

5. A Concoction

1. Sam Goldwyn to Edna Ferber, October 27, 1936, Goldwyn Papers.
2. Joseph McBride, *Hawks on Hawks* (Berkeley: University of California Press, 1982), 85.
3. Ibid.
4. Berg, *Goldwyn*, 282.
5. Ibid., 183.
6. Madsen, *William Wyler*, 153.
7. Berg, *Goldwyn*, 13.
8. William Arnold, *Frances Farmer: Shadowland* (New York: Jove/HBJ Books, 1979), 55–56.
9. Herman, *A Talent for Trouble*, 162.
10. Daniel Mandell transcript, Wyler Papers.
11. Arthur Marx, *Goldwyn: A Biography of the Man behind the Myth* (New York: W. W. Norton, 1976), 225.
12. Todd McCarthy, *Howard Hawks: The Grey Fox of Hollywood* (New York: Grove Press, 1997), 240; Berg, *Goldwyn*, 283.
13. McCarthy, *Howard Hawks*, 241.
14. Telegram from Eddie Curtiss to Wyler, October 29, 1936, Goldwyn Papers.
15. Joseph McBride, ed., *Focus on Howard Hawks* (Englewood Cliffs, N.J.: Prentice-Hall, 1972), 47.
16. Goldwyn to Ferber, October 27, 1936, Goldwyn Papers.
17. Ferber to Goldwyn, October 31, 1936, Goldwyn Papers.
18. Telegram from Ferber to Goldwyn, October 28, 1936, Goldwyn Papers.
19. Edna Ferber, *Come and Get It* (Garden City, N.Y.: Doubleday, Doran, 1935), 39.
20. Ibid., 28.
21. Ibid., 39.
22. Ibid., 296.
23. Ibid., 316.
24. Robin Wood, *Howard Hawks* (Garden City, N.Y.: Doubleday, 1968), 121–22.
25. Ferber, *Come and Get It*, 133.
26. Berg, *Goldwyn*, 282.

27. Wood, *Howard Hawks*, 119–20.
28. *New York Times*, November 12, 1936.
29. Jimmy Townsend to Wyler, October 29, 1936, Goldwyn Papers.

6. The Street Where They Live

1. Wyler to Goldwyn, September 3, 1936, Goldwyn Papers.
2. Quoted in Wendy Smith, *Real Life Drama* (New York: Knopf, 1990), 146.
3. Kingsley, *Five Prize Winning Plays*, 7.
4. In Nicholas Martin's 1997 revival at the Williamstown Theater Festival—the only major revival of the play since its premiere—set designer James Noone replicated Bel Geddes's set but actually did fill the orchestra pit with water.
5. Merritt Hulburd to Goldwyn, November 8, 1935, Goldwyn Papers.
6. Hulburd to Goldwyn, November 22, 1935, Goldwyn Papers.
7. Berg, *Goldwyn*, 278.
8. Goldwyn to Hellman, October 16, 1936, Goldwyn Papers.
9. Kingsley, *Five Prize Winning Plays*, 78–79.
10. Herman, *A Talent for Trouble*, 169.
11. Berg, *Goldwyn*, 193.
12. Ibid., 293.
13. Joseph Breen to Goldwyn, October 28, 1936, Goldwyn Papers.
14. Quoted in Rollyson, *Lillian Hellman*, 102–3.
15. Kingsley, *Five Prize Winning Plays*, 125, 109.
16. Telegram from Kingsley to Goldwyn, undated, Goldwyn Papers.
17. Kingsley, *Five Prize Winning Plays*, 164.
18. Rollyson, *Lillian Hellman*, 104, 105.
19. Franklin D. Roosevelt, "Second Inaugural Address," January 20, 1937, http://www.bartleby.com/124/pres50.html.
20. Robert Sherwood, *The Petrified Forest* (New York: Scribner's, 1935), 158.
21. Robert Wyler, notes, April 23, 1937, Wyler Collection.

7. Gone with the Plague

1. Herman, *A Talent for Trouble*, 174–75.
2. Memo from Walter MacEwen to Hal Wallis, in *Inside Warner Bros.: 1935–1951*, ed. Rudy Behlmer (New York: Viking, 1985), 40–41.
3. Behlmer, *Inside Warner Bros.*, 42–44.
4. Legal file on *Jezebel*, undated, Wyler Collection.
5. Lou Edelman, undated memo, Wyler Collection.
6. Herman, *A Talent for Trouble*, 176.

7. Whitney Stine with Bette Davis, *Mother Goddam* (New York: Berkley Books, 1979), 100.

8. Bette Davis, *The Lonely Life* (New York: G. P. Putnam's Sons, 1962), 176.

9. Owen Davis, manuscript version of *Jezebel*, March 9, 1937, box 17, folder 233, Wyler Collection. Owen Davis (1874–1956) was one of the most prolific writers in the history of the American stage. (Despite the southern setting of *Jezebel*, he was from Portland, Maine.) Davis made his early reputation by turning out dozens of sensational formula melodramas, but when the popularity of that genre began to wane, he decided to write realistic plays for Broadway. An early success was *Detour*, a variation on Eugene O'Neill's *Beyond the Horizon*; Owen's play premiered in 1921, a year after O'Neill's seminal drama. Two years later, Davis won the Pulitzer Prize for *Icebound*. His dramatic adaptation of Edith Wharton's *Ethan Frome* (1936) was also a success. Since much of his early work has been lost, estimates of his dramatic output run from 150 to more than 300 plays. He also wrote some film scripts, notably *They Had to See Paris* (1929) for Will Rogers and an adaptation of Arthur Frederick Goodrich and George M. Cohan's *So This Is London* (1930).

10. Ibid.

11. Robert Buckner, script, April 30, 1937, Wyler Collection.

12. Hal Wallis and Charles Higham, *Starmaker: The Autobiography of Hal Wallis* (New York: Macmillan, 1980), 91.

13. Stine, *Mother Goddam*, 102.

14. Charles Higham, *Bette: The Life of Bette Davis* (New York: Macmillan, 1981), 104.

15. *Directed by William Wyler*.

16. Herman, *A Talent for Trouble*, 182.

17. Barbara Leaming, *Bette Davis: A Biography* (New York: Simon and Schuster, 1992), 141.

18. Charles Higham, "William Wyler Directs Bette Davis in *Jezebel*," Columbia University Oral History Office, *Fathom: The Source for Online Learning*, last modified 2002, http://www.fathom.com/feature/35675/.

19. Quoted in Leaming, *Bette Davis*, 141.

20. Charles Affron, *Star Acting* (New York: E. P. Dutton, 1977), 225.

21. Bazin, *Bazin at Work*, 17.

22. Affron, *Star Acting*, 229.

23. Richard Gilman, *The Making of Modern Drama* (New York: Farrar, Straus & Giroux, 1975), 103.

24. Whitney Stine with Bette Davis, *I'd Love to Kiss You: Conversations with Bette Davis* (New York: Pocket Books, 1990), 14.

25. Herman, *A Talent for Trouble*, 176.

26. Leaming, *Bette Davis,* 144.

27. Production notes, Wyler Collection.

28. Treatment by Clements Ripley, July 14, 1937, Wyler Collection. This collection also contains a revised treatment by Ripley and Abem Finkel dated September 14, 1937.

29. Affron, *Star Acting*, 233.

8. Home on the Moors and the Range

1. See George Bluestone, *Novels into Film* (Berkeley: University of California Press, 1973), and Michael A. Anderegg, *William Wyler* (Boston: Twayne Publishers, 1979). John Harrington's "Wyler as Auteur," in *The English Novel and the Movies*, ed. Michael Klein and Gillian Parker (New York: Frederick Ungar, 1981), focuses more on Wyler's contributions as a director.

2. Anderegg, *William Wyler*, 67.

3. Slocombe, "The Work of Gregg Toland," 71.

4. Richard Griffith, *Samuel Goldwyn: The Producer and His Films* (New York: Museum of Modern Art Film Library, 1956), 34.

5. Anderegg, *William Wyler*; Harrington, "Wyler as Auteur."

6. Harrington, "Wyler as Auteur."

7. John Gassner and Dudley Nichols, *Twenty Best Film Plays I & II* (New York: Garland, 1977), 331.

8. *Variety*, April 13, 1939.

9. Berg, *Goldwyn*, 328.

10. Herman, *A Talent for Trouble*, 198.

11. George N. Fenin and William K. Everson, *The Western* (New York: Penguin, 1977), 247.

12. Herman, *A Talent for Trouble*, 205.

13. Darryl Zanuck to Goldwyn, July 3, 1939, Goldwyn Papers.

14. Stuart Lake to Goldwyn, July 10, 1939, Goldwyn Papers.

15. Goldwyn to Zanuck, August 14, 1939, Goldwyn Papers.

16. Lillian Hellman to Goldwyn, August 9, 1939, Goldwyn Papers.

17. Oliver La Farge, notes on script, August 31, 1939, Goldwyn Papers.

18. Stuart Lake's revised treatment, June 1, 1939, Goldwyn Papers.

19. Niven Busch treatment, October 24, 1939, Goldwyn Papers.

20. Edwin Knopf, memo, September 26, 1939, Goldwyn Papers.

21. Memo from Jock Lawrence to Goldwyn, October 19, 1939, Goldwyn Papers.

22. Jeffrey Meyers, *Gary Cooper: American Hero* (New York: Cooper Square Press, 1998), 139.

23. Goldwyn to Gary Cooper, November 2, 1939, Goldwyn Papers.

24. Cooper to Goldwyn, November 18, 1939, Goldwyn Papers.

25. Goldwyn to Cooper, December 29, 1939, Goldwyn Papers.

26. *Hollywood Reporter*, December 1, 1939.

27. Quoted in Herman, *A Talent for Trouble*, 206.

28. Telegram, January 6, 1940, Goldwyn Papers.

29. Dmitri Tiomkin to Goldwyn, April 25, 1940, Goldwyn Papers.

30. Richard Slotkin, *Gunfighter Nation* (New York: Harper Perennial, 1993), 286.

31. Herman, *A Talent for Trouble*, 206–7.

32. La Farge, notes on script, August 31, 1939.

33. Jock Lawrence, notes on script, October 19, 1939, Goldwyn Papers.

34. One need only compare the conflict between Ryker and Starrett in *Shane*, where both sides are presented sympathetically. Director George Stevens (like Wyler) recognizes the historical necessity of the homesteaders' viewpoint, but the magnitude of the struggle between the two sides is more compelling in the later film.

35. *San Antonio* (1945; directed by David Butler) deals with outlaws' attempts to steal cattle and ruin the Texas economy during the 1870s, a decade before Wyler's film takes place. That film, which opens with shots of large herds of cattle, stars Errol Flynn as Clay Hardin, who will save the cattle industry from the outlaws.

36. Wyler's best friend, John Huston, would revisit the Bean-Langtry story in *The Life and Times of Judge Roy Bean* (1972), with Paul Newman as the judge and Ava Gardner as Lillie.

37. Robert Warshow, *The Immediate Experience* (1962; reprint, New York: Athenaeum, 1970), 138.

38. This relationship can be seen as the prototype for other buddy-rival westerns, such as *Bad Company*, *Butch Cassidy and the Sundance Kid*, *Vera Cruz*, and others.

39. Toland uses a flickering candle again, to far different effect, in *The Grapes of Wrath* (released the same year), when Tom Joad lights a candle in his parents' deserted house and discovers Muley.

40. Herman, *A Talent for Trouble*, 211.

41. Ibid., 212.

42. Affron, *Star Acting*, 239.

43. Davis, *The Lonely Life*, 250–51.

44. Herman, *A Talent for Trouble*, 212.

45. Ibid.

46. Ibid., 215. Another ending was filmed in which the disputed scene between Leslie and Robert is eliminated. We see Leslie put on her glasses and try to knit her lace. She breaks down in frustration and walks out the back door, dropping the lace. The rest of the scene is the same, except that Wyler cuts from the party to the lace on the floor.

47. Ed Sikov, *Dark Victory: The Life of Bette Davis* (New York: Henry Holt, 2007), 162.

48. Herman, *A Talent for Trouble*, 215.

9. Bette Davis and the South Redux

1. Telegram, February 22, 1939, Goldwyn Papers.

2. Berg, *Goldwyn*, 355.

3. Ibid.

4. Philip Dunne, *Take Two* (New York: McGraw-Hill, 1980), 93.

5. Ibid., 94.

6. Ibid.

7. Ibid., 96.

8. Herman, *A Talent for Trouble*, 219.

9. Dunne, *Take Two*, 97.

10. Hellman, *Six Plays*, 156–57.

11. Ibid., 205.

12. Ibid.

13. Hellman to Goldwyn, undated (possibly March 1940), Goldwyn Papers.

14. Reeves Espy, May 3, 1940, Goldwyn Papers.

15. Interoffice memo from Edwin Knopf to Goldwyn, May 3, 1940, Goldwyn Papers.

16. Memo from Jock Lawrence to Goldwyn, undated, Goldwyn Papers.

17. Wyler to Goldwyn, May 6, 1940, Goldwyn Papers.

18. Hellman to Goldwyn, January 27, 1941, Goldwyn Papers.

19. Telegram from Goldwyn to Wyler, March 21, 1941, Goldwyn Papers.

20. Berg, *Goldwyn*, 358.

21. Davis, *The Lonely Life*, 206.

22. Sikov, *Dark Victory*, 179.

23. Berg, *Goldwyn*, 358.

24. Telegram from Wyler to Goldwyn, March 21, 1941, Goldwyn Papers.

25. Madsen, *William Wyler*, 210.

26. Lillian Hellman also saw Regina as more multifaceted: "When I wrote it, I was amused by Regina—I never thought of her as a villainous character—all I meant was a big sexy woman." She also referred to the play as a "dramatic comedy" and to Regina as "kind of funny." Quoted in Peter Feibleman, *Lilly: Reminiscences of Lillian Hellman* (New York: William Morrow, 1989), 261.

27. Leaming, *Bette Davis*, 196.

28. *New York World-Telegram*, September 9, 1941.

29. Leaming, *Bette Davis*, 199.

30. Ibid.

31. Stine, *Mother Goddam*, 151.

32. Hellman to Davis, May 20, 1941, Wyler Collection.

33. Bazin, *What Is Cinema?* 69.

34. Affron, *Star Acting*, 250.

35. Anderegg, *William Wyler*, 106.

36. Most of Hellman's early drafts begin with Oscar shooting at Lionnet. Zan is riding across a bridge as we hear gunshots, which startle her horse; this in turn causes Oscar to miss his shot. He tells Simon to inform Zan not to ride along the road again. Even the final script (April 15, 1941, Goldwyn Papers) opens with Zan and Addie riding through Lionnet as the camera reveals the house's disrepair. Addie is commenting on how fine the place once was when Simon stops them and warns them not to drive through while Oscar is shooting. Then there is a cut to the Hubbards' warehouse and Leo sneaking off the train.

37. The box imagery is also discussed in Affron, *Star Acting*.

38. *Directed by William Wyler*.

39. Charles Higham and Joel Greenberg, *Hollywood in the Forties* (New York: Zwemmer and Barnes, 1968), 116.

40. A similar shot with rain in the background is used in *Dodsworth*, when Fran tells Sam that she has decided to stay in Europe.

41. *Directed by William Wyler*.

42. Quoted in Stine, *Mother Goddam*, 159.

43. Ibid.

44. Rollyson, *Lillian Hellman*, 180.

45. Ibid.

46. Wright, *Lillian Hellman*, 161. Pendleton had played Leo in Mike Nichols's 1967 revival at Lincoln Center, which starred Anne Bancroft as Regina. Nichols, like Wyler, preferred a softer view of the Hubbards; he presented them as decent people who are transformed into monsters by events.

10. War Films

1. Franklin D. Roosevelt, "FDR and the Four Freedoms Speech," January 6, 1941, *Franklin D. Roosevelt Presidential Library and Museum* (accessed January 30, 2012), http://www.fdrlibrary.marist.edu/fourfreedoms.

2. Draft letter from Wyler to Y. Frank Freeman, February 24, 1954, Wyler Collection.

3. *Directed by William Wyler*.

4. This charge was revived seven years later, and the studios were ordered to divorce production from exhibition and distribution.

5. Bernard F. Dick, *The Star Spangled Screen* (Lexington: University Press of Kentucky, 1985), 89.

6. Ibid., 90.

7. Berg, *Goldwyn*, 368.

8. Clayton R. Koppes and Gregory D. Black, *Hollywood Goes to War* (Berkeley: University of California Press, 1990), 224.

9. According to Koppes and Black (*Hollywood Goes to War*, 225), RKO and MGM wanted to re-release *Gunga Din* and *Kim* to increase sympathy for the British. The OWI appealed to the studios to drop their plans, citing the dangers those pictures posed for Allied unity.

10. Wyler to Hedda Hopper, August 2, 1942, Wyler Collection.

11. Michael Troyan, *A Rose for Mrs. Miniver* (Lexington: University Press of Kentucky, 2005), 130.

12. Script dated October 18, 1941, with pink page revisions dated as late as November 7, 1941, Wyler Collection.

13. *Directed by William Wyler.*

14. For the same reason, he would cut the more overtly preachy scenes from *The Best Years of Our Lives* four years later.

15. Script, October 18, 1941, Wyler Collection.

16. Bosley Crowther, *The Lion's Share* (New York: Dutton, 1957).

17. Troyan, *A Rose for Mrs. Miniver*, 126.

18. Ibid., 129.

19. Unidentified clipping, August 2, 1942, Wyler Collection.

20. The first air-raid episode in the film is experienced from the Beldons' point of view. They are forced into their basement along with their servants, and Mrs. Beldon objects to being ordered about by an air-raid warden. But when she hears the planes coming, Wyler isolates her in the frame, dwarfing her beside a large fireplace, and she seems diminished and alone.

21. Script, October 18, 1941, Wyler Collection.

22. Herman *A Talent for Trouble*, 235.

23. Ibid.

24. Letter, March 1942, Wyler Collection.

25. Frank Capra, *The Name above the Title* (New York: Macmillan, 1971), 318.

26. Lillian Hellman, *An Unfinished Woman* (New York: Bantam, 1970), 103.

27. Ibid., 105.

28. Ibid.

29. The Russia film was eventually made as a full-length feature, *The North Star*, with a screenplay by Hellman. It was directed by Lewis Milestone and starred Anne Baxter, Dana Andrews, Walter Huston, and Walter Brennan.

30. Telegram from Frank Capra to Wyler, April 8, 1942, Wyler Collection.

31. Wyler, handwritten note, April 8, 1942, Wyler Collection.

32. Wyler to Capra, April 22, 1942, Wyler Collection.

33. Capra to Wyler, undated, Wyler Collection.

34. May 25, 1942, Wyler Collection.

35. Madsen, *William Wyler*, 225.

36. Wyler's physical, May 25, 1942, Wyler Collection.

37. Wyler's first choice for a writer was Irwin Shaw, who was not eligible

for a commission due to his age (twenty-eight) and his draft status (1-A).
Memo, July 31, 1942, Wyler Collection.

38. Army orders, August 22, 1942, Wyler Collection.

39. Wyler to Commanding General of the Eighth Air Force, April 21,
1943, Wyler Collection.

40. Ibid.

41. Quoted in Herman, *A Talent for Trouble*, 249.

42. Lieutenant Jerome Chodorov, October 6, 1942, Wyler Collection.

43. "Wyler Escapes Injury," *New York Times*, February 4, 1943.

44. Herman, *A Talent for Trouble*, 252.

45. *Los Angeles Herald Express*, February 15, 1943.

46. Herman, *A Talent for Trouble*, 252.

47. Wyler to Mrs. H. J. Tannenbaum, May 5, 1943, Wyler Collection.

48. Wyler, "Flying over Germany," 25.

49. Ibid.

50. Wyler to Robert Lovett, June 28, 1943, Wyler Collection.

51. August 26, 1943, Wyler Collection.

52. Telegram from Wyler to Beirne Lay, July 27, 1943, Wyler Collection.

53. Ibid.

54. Wyler to Tex McCrary, November 6, 1943, Wyler Collection.

55. Ibid.

56. Uncredited, undated script, "Eighth Air Force," August 6, 1943,
Wyler Papers.

57. Uncredited, undated script, Wyler Papers.

58. Lester Koenig, *Memphis Belle* script, December 10, 1943, Wyler
Collection.

59. Ibid.

60. Wyler, "Details of Service M/Sgt Lester H. Koenig," Wyler
Collection.

61. He would return to these bucolic images again and again in his
postwar work—for instance, in the shots of Boone City at the beginning of
The Best Years of Our Lives and particularly in the vast expanses of land,
space, and beauty in *Friendly Persuasion* and *The Big Country*. There is
even a fleeting feel for the countryside in his dark and bitter final films, *The
Collector* and *The Liberation of L. B. Jones*.

62. Karel Reisz, "The Later Films of William Wyler," *Sequence* 13
(1951): 25.

63. Herman, *A Talent for Trouble*, 265.

64. Review by Bosley Crowther, *New York Times*, April 14, 1944.

65. Zanuck to Wyler, April 2 1944, Wyler Collection.

66. Wyler to Moss Hart, February 20, 1944, Wyler Collection.

67. Wyler to Zanuck, February 22, 1944, Wyler Collection.

68. Memo from Edward Munson Jr., May 18, 1944, Wyler Collection.

69. Memo from Wyler, June 19, 1944, Wyler Collection.

70. Herman, *A Talent for Trouble*, 271.

71. Wyler to Tex, October 12, 1944, Wyler Collection.

72. Madsen, *William Wyler*, 256.

73. Lester Koenig, treatment, June 27, 1944, Wyler Collection.

74. Ibid.

75. Lester Koenig, revised treatment, June 17, 1944, Wyler Collection.

76. Wyler to Francis Harmon, November 27, 1945, Wyler Collection.

77. Wyler to Harmon, December 4, 1945, Wyler Collection.

78. Ibid.

11. The Way Home

1. Hermine Rich Isaacs, "William Wyler: Director with a Passion and a Craft," *Theatre Arts* 31 no. 2 (February 1947).

2. Marx, *Goldwyn*, 307.

3. "The Way Home," *Time*, August 7, 1944.

4. Marx, *Goldwyn*, 308.

5. Isaacs, "William Wyler," 22.

6. Pat Duggan to Goldwyn, June 15, 1945, Goldwyn Papers.

7. Robert Sherwood to Goldwyn, August 27, 1945, Goldwyn Papers.

8. Telegram from Goldwyn to Sherwood, September 4, 1945, Goldwyn Papers.

9. Interoffice memo, November 16, 1945, Goldwyn Papers.

10. Berg, *Goldwyn*, 410.

11. *New York Times*, November 17, 1946.

12. Wyler, "No Magic Wand," 6.

13. Ibid.

14. Charles Affron and Jona Mirella Affron, *Best Years: Going to the Movies, 1945–1946* (New Brunswick, N.J.: Rutgers University Press, 2009), 226.

15. Isaacs, "William Wyler," 22–23.

16. James Agee, "What Hollywood Can Do," *Nation*, December 7, 1946, 14.

17. In earlier versions of the script (Goldwyn Papers), the men discuss their families in more detail and even share some pictures. Fred sees Peggy for the first time—in a picture—and is immediately taken with her. Fred also talks about Gadorsky, the pilot he has nightmares about but never discusses in detail in the final film. Homer mentions a book he is reading, *Victory over Fear*, and remarks that "every one of us has got to fight out that battle inside himself." Al later tells Fred, "A kid like Homer is lucky in a way. . . . He's got his scars where you can see them. . . . Maybe it's easier to have them where you can see them, than have them hidden inside." Perhaps Wyler's three-shot framing was influenced by that line, which was eventually cut from the script.

18. Miller, *William Wyler: Interviews*, 136.

19. In Sherwood's earliest drafts, Fred goes right to the drugstore to see Mr. Bullard, who tells him that Marie no longer lives at home. He then calls his parents to get her address.

20. Early script, November 17, 1945, Goldwyn Papers.

21. Arthur Miller, *All My Sons* (New York: Reynal and Hitchcock, 1947), 31–32.

22. Robert Sherwood, script entitled "Glory for Me," December 10, 1945, Goldwyn Papers; additional revised page dated February 20, 1946.

23. Wyler, "No Magic Wand," 6–7.

24. In an earlier version of the script (November 17, 1945, Goldwyn Papers), Peggy's boyfriend (named Payne) is puzzled that she would date a soda jerk. (In earlier versions, it should be remembered, Fred asks Marie for a divorce early in the film.) He says, "What happened to this country while I've been away? Has it turned into a democracy or something?"

25. Wyler, "No Magic Wand," 8.

26. Griffith, *Samuel Goldwyn*, 41.

27. Early script, November 17, 1945, Goldwyn Papers.

28. Later draft of script, December 10, 1945, Goldwyn Papers.

29. In a departure from the novel and from earlier versions of the script, Marie asks Fred for a divorce, claiming that she is sick of having no money and is tired of waiting for him to find a job.

30. Later draft of script, December 10, 1945, Goldwyn Papers.

31. Telegram from Wyler to Sherwood, June 6, 1946, Wyler Collection.

32. Wyler, "No Magic Wand," 9.

33. Ibid., 10.

34. Ibid.

35. Slocombe, "The Work of Gregg Toland," 75.

36. Ibid.

37. André Bazin, *William Wyler ou le janséniste de la mise en scene*, *Revue du Cinema* (1948), reprinted in *Qu'est-ceque le cinema* (1958). Hugh Gray did not translate this essay or include it in the American edition of Bazin's *What Is Cinema?* It was later translated by Bert Cardullo and included in *Bazin at Work*.

38. Anderegg, *William Wyler*, 142.

39. Wyler, "No Magic Wand," 10.

40. Madsen, *William Wyler*, 274.

41. "MacKinlay Kantor's Charges Baffle Him," undated clipping, Goldwyn Papers.

42. Wyler to lawyer, June 6, 1948, Wyler Collection.

12. The American Scene I

1. Joseph McBride, *Frank Capra: The Catastrophe of Success* (New York: Simon and Schuster, 1992), 507.

2. Madsen, *William Wyler*, 280.

3. McBride, *Frank Capra*, 507.

4. *Film Daily*, November, 13 1946.

5. "The Story of Liberty Films," Wyler Collection.

6. Quoted in McBride, *Frank Capra*, 530.

7. Madsen, *William Wyler*, 288.

8. Wyler memo, August 10, 1948, Wyler Collection.

9. Herman, *A Talent for Trouble*, 307.

10. In the casting notes for the play, then titled "Washington Square," a second page of possible actors to play Morris includes Montgomery Clift and Henry Fonda; Gene Barry and John Forsythe also appear on the list. The list for Catherine includes Olivia de Havilland and her sister Joan Fontaine; Wyler's first wife, Margaret Sullavan; and Jane Wyatt, Jessica Tandy, and Mercedes McCambridge. The candidates for Dr. Sloper include Ralph Richardson, Cedric Hardwick, and Wyler favorite Walter Huston, along with Vincent Price, Louis Calhearn, and Ronald Colman.

11. Patricia Bosworth, *Montgomery Clift* (New York: Bantam, 1979), 142.

12. Ibid.

13. Ibid., 142, 143.

14. Herman, *A Talent for Trouble*, 310.

15. Hanson, "William Wyler," 28.

16. In a letter, the Goetzes describe the origins of their play:

> Well, our latest play, "One Man Show," closed after five weeks. . . . We thought it was a very good play. . . . One of us said to the other: "Well, we're better off than Henry James." Mr. James had the experience to stop all experiences. He came out on the stage the opening night of "Guy Donville" to calls of "Author, Author," and then was hooted. Thinking about James, one day we picked up an early novel of his, "Washington Square." . . . As dramatists we saw in it a number of things: First, it was about the father-daughter relationship of which we still had much to say; second, it was told in terms of characters who did what people always do, the worst things for the best reasons; third, there was the real challenge of turning poor, dull "Catherine Sloper" into a true heroine. We could not forget that girl. She kept at us.

Ruth and Augustus Goetz to John Chapman, March 17, 1948, Ruth and Augustus Goetz Papers, Wisconsin Historical Society, Madison.

17. Lee Sabinson pointed out this stark portrait of a world comprising unattractive characters in his evaluation of the play, which he read in manuscript and declined to produce: "I found Washington Square an extremely well-written and interesting character study but unfortunately nowhere in the play did I find a single character I was interested enough to root for one hundred per cent. Catherine . . . I found completely unattract-

ive. . . . Dr. Sloper is psychotic on the subject of his daughter . . . and the final denouement of her inner struggle comes too late in the play for me to care about her." Letter from the Goetzes' agent to Leah Salisbury, July 23, 1946, Goetz Papers.

18. That early script also indicates that the Goetzes wanted to experiment with a narrator whose voice would introduce the characters, but they wisely dispensed with that approach.

19. John Hobart, "Director William Wyler and *The Heiress*," unidentified newspaper clipping, Wyler Papers.

20. Ruth Goetz and Augustus Goetz, *The Heiress* (New York: Dramatists Play Service, 1975), 41, 52.

21. The dialogue for this confrontation was created for the film. In the play, Catherine avoids an encounter with her father by excusing herself, telling him, "I have some letters to write."

22. *New York Times*, October 7, 1949.

23. *Variety*, May 26, 1950, Wyler Collection.

24. Ronald Davis, "Southern Methodist University Oral History Project: William Wyler (1979)," reprinted in Miller, *William Wyler: Interviews*, 101.

13. The American Scene II

1. Theodore Dreiser, *Sister Carrie* (1900; reprint, Boston: Houghton Mifflin, 1959), 55.

2. Herman, *A Talent for Trouble*, 318.

3. Terry Coleman, *Olivier* (New York: Henry Holt, 2005), 220.

4. David O. Selznick to Wyler, June 14, 1950, Wyler Papers.

5. Coleman, *Olivier*, 223.

6. Ibid., 222.

7. Elia Kazan, *A Life* (New York: Knopf, 1988), 144.

8. Coleman, *Olivier*, 222–23.

9. Stephen C. Brennan, "*Sister Carrie* Becomes *Carrie*," in *Nineteenth-Century American Fiction on Screen*, ed. R. Barton Palmer (Cambridge: Cambridge University Press, 2007), 187.

10. *Variety*, October 12, 1949.

11. *San Francisco Chronicle*, November 12, 1949.

12. Madsen, *William Wyler*, 299.

13. Wyler to Goetzes, June 7, 1949, Wyler Collection.

14. In light of the Breen office's objections to the material, it is interesting that RKO commissioned a "story test report" on *Sister Carrie*—which was to star Ingrid Bergman—from Audience Research Inc. That agency concluded that the story "has below average appeal for moviegoers both as to subject matter and as a vehicle for Ingrid Bergman." Audience Research Inc., "Story Test Report," July 21, 1944, Wyler Papers.

15. Goetzes' treatment, May 27, 1949, Goetz Papers.

16. Goetzes to Wyler, May 31, 1949, Goetz Papers.

17. Wyler to Goetzes, June 7, 1949, Goetz Papers.

18. Ibid.

19. Even in one of the later versions of the script, the Goetzes are still portraying Hurstwood as an aggressive man with a quick temper. For example, when Carrie visits him at the restaurant and Slawson catches the couple in an embrace and orders them to "carry that on in the back room," Hurstwood retorts, "Keep your filthy mouth to yourself. You fathead!" He then throws down his coat and walks out. He never exhibits this kind of bravado in the released film.

20. Archer Winston, *New York Post*, February 11, 1952.

21. Brandon French, *On the Verge of Revolt: Women in American Films of the Fifties* (New York: Frederick Ungar, 1978).

22. This is not an unusual view for a Wyler film. A similar pessimism informs *Counsellor-at-Law*, *Dodsworth*, *The Little Foxes*, *The Heiress*, and, to some extent, *The Best Years of Our Lives*, although in all but *The Heiress*, the negativity is balanced by a promise that happiness is possible with the right partner. Dodsworth seems headed for a happier future with Edith Cortwright, Regina's blighted marriage is contrasted by her daughter's love for David Hewitt, and the failure of Fred Derry's marriage is offset by his love for Peggy and the marriage of Homer and Wilma. No such balance is offered here.

23. Bosley Crowther, "'Carrie,' with Laurence Olivier and Jennifer Jones, Is New Feature at the Capitol," *New York Times*, July 17, 1952.

24. Herman, *A Talent for Trouble*, 330.

25. David Selznick to Frank Freeman, August 22, 1951, Wyler Papers.

26. Herman, *A Talent for Trouble*, 330.

14. The House Un-American Activities Committee

1. "Committee to Defend the Motion Picture Industry against Unjust Attacks," undated, Wyler Collection.

2. Quoted in Herman, *A Talent for Trouble*, 299.

3. *Washington Daily News*, November 6, 1947.

4. Dunne, *Take Two*, 194.

5. Ibid., 199.

6. Herman, *A Talent for Trouble*, 301.

7. Dunne, *Take Two*, 197.

8. Ibid., 199.

9. Madsen, *William Wyler*, 286.

10. Dunne, *Take Two*, 198.

11. Gordon Kahn, *Hollywood on Trial* (New York: Boni and Gaer, 1948), 219–20.

12. Ibid., 223.

13. Ibid., 221.

14. *Valley Times*, May 7, 1947. The August 25, 1947, issue of *Newsweek* reported that *Best Years* was on a list, compiled by the HUAC, of films that portray "congressmen as crooks and bankers as stony-hearted villains." Examples of un-Americanism cited in the film include the Dana Andrews character (Fred Derry) being denied a plane reservation on his way home, even though a prosperous fat citizen has no trouble getting one; Fred being turned down for anything better than his former job as a soda jerk by the 4-F personnel manager of an unsympathetic drugstore chain; and the Fredric March character (Al Stephenson) as an ex-sergeant who is unhappy in his postwar job as vice president of a bank, which heartlessly insists on collateral for loans to ex-GIs.

15. Kahn, *Hollywood on Trial*, 184.

16. "Wallace Talks to 12,000 after Secret Fund Raising," *Los Angeles Examiner*, May 17, 1948.

17. Letter from Wyler on behalf of Adrian Scott, November 28, 1950, Wyler Collection.

18. Herman, *A Talent for Trouble*, 339.

19. Wyler to Bosley Crowther, undated, Wyler Collection.

20. Kingsley, *Five Prize Winning Plays*, 241, 242.

21. Ibid., 243–44.

22. *New York Times*, July 23, 1950.

23. The filmmakers inserted a scene at the beginning in which McLeod and Mary meet in a cab and she tells him about a doctor's visit for another failed pregnancy.

24. Kingsley, *Five Prize Winning Plays*, 320.

25. Kirk Douglas, *The Ragman's Son* (New York: Pocket Books, 1989), 163. Wyler's recollection was different: he claimed that he suggested Douglas play the part on stage in Phoenix, "where a troupe was doing a revival of the play. They were delighted to have him. He got a hundred dollars, maybe." Herman, *A Talent for Trouble*, 335.

26. Douglas, *The Ragman's Son*, 165.

27. George Stevens Jr. et al., "The Test of Time: William Wyler," *American Film* 1, no. 6 (April 1976). The others were Howard Hawks, Billy Wilder, Elia Kazan, and Joseph Mankiewicz.

28. Charles Higham, *Hollywood Cameramen* (Bloomington: Indiana University Press, 1970), 51–52.

29. Anderegg, *William Wyler*, 175.

30. Ibid.

31. It is interesting to note that in the second draft of the screenplay, that conversation takes place in a bar called the Hangout, not in the privacy of a cab. When Mary tells McLeod that she cannot have a baby and suggests a trip to Lake Tahoe, he turns her down because of the Schneider case: "I

can't sleep with that killer loose in the city." Clearly, Wyler wants to introduce McLeod sympathetically, as a family man. First draft of *Dead End*, November 11, 1950, Wyler Collection.

32. Kingsley, *Five Prize Winning Plays*, 280.

33. *New York Times*, November 17, 1951.

34. Madsen, *William Wyler*, 304.

35. Herman, *A Talent for Trouble*, 347.

36. Paul Kohner to Wyler, January 22, 1953, Wyler Collection. In his autobiography *An Open Book*, John Huston wrote (135–36):

In 1952 both José Ferrer and I ran head-on into trouble after bringing *Moulin Rouge* back from Paris for its premiere in Los Angeles. Joe had a reputation for being far left but he was in fact no more a Communist than my grandmother. Nevertheless, when we opened in Los Angeles some splinter groups from the American Legion—inspired, no doubt, by Hedda Hopper's constantly raking me over the coals in her column—paraded in front of the theater with placards declaring that José Ferrer and John Huston were Communists. I must say it took the edge off the festivities.

37. Arthur Jacobs to Paul Kohner, January 21, 1953, Wyler Collection.

38. Kohner to Wyler, February 14, 1953, Wyler Collection.

39. Art Arthur to Wyler, April 4 and 8, 1953, Wyler Collection.

40. Y. Frank Freeman to Wyler, January 2, 1954, Wyler Collection.

41. Draft of letter from Wyler to Freeman, February 24, 1954, Wyler Collection.

42. Wyler to Freeman, May 3, 1954, Wyler Collection.

43. Ibid.

44. The Broadway producers would adopt Wyler's original notion and cast Paul Newman, in his first starring stage role, opposite Karl Malden.

45. Anderegg, *William Wyler*, 180.

46. Peter Biskind, *Seeing Is Believing* (New York: Pantheon, 1983), 162, 164.

47. Joseph Hayes, *The Desperate Hours* (New York: Random House, 1954), 245.

48. Bernard Kantor, Irwin R. Blacker, and Anne Kramer, eds., *Directors at Work* (New York: Funk and Wagnalls, 1970), 428.

49. Wyler, "Production Notes," Wyler Collection.

50. Anderegg, *William Wyler*, 182.

51. *Film Daily*, March 16, 1960.

52. Hanson, "William Wyler," 31.

53. Higham, "William Wyler," 18.

54. Gene D. Phillips, "William Wyler," *Focus on Film* 24 (Spring 1976): 7, reprinted in Miller, *William Wyler: Interviews*.

55. *Variety*, March 8, 1961.

56. Hellman to Wyler, April 1961, Wyler Collection.

57. Herman, *A Talent for Trouble*, 417.

15. The Pacifist Dilemma

1. Herman, *A Talent for Trouble*, 367.

2. Michael Wilson, script, February 14, 1947, p. 17, Wyler Papers.

3. Jessamyn West, *To See the Dream* (New York: Harcourt, Brace, 1957), 8.

4. Ibid., 92–93.

5. Ibid., 94.

6. Ibid.

7. Kael, *Kiss Kiss Bang Bang*, 238.

8. West, *To See the Dream*, 101.

9. Ibid., 265–66.

10. Madsen, *William Wyler*, 318.

11. In the final script by West and Robert Wyler, there is more participation by the Quakers. A farmer reads from a letter his daughter received from Abraham Lincoln: "Your people—the Friends—are having a very great trial. On principle and faith opposed to both war and oppression, they can only practically oppose oppression by war. In this hard dilemma, some have chosen one horn and some the other. For your sons and friends appealing to me on conscientious grounds, I have done and shall do the best I could and can, in my own conscience, under my own oath to the law." These sentiments are voiced by Major Harvey in Wilson's script but do not appear in the finished film. Perhaps Wyler felt this presidential tolerance lent more credence to the Quaker position than he wanted to show. The script also has a businessman recommending that instead of giving all they earn "to the meeting," they give that money to the families of those wounded and killed in the war. Jessamyn West and Robert Wyler, "Final Script," August 18, 1955, Museum of Modern Art.

12. West, *To See the Dream*, 286. Interestingly, in the final script, this comic sequence takes a serious turn when, during the Birdwells' visit, the Hudspeths arm themselves and hide in the barn when they hear Confederate raiders near their farm. The raiders eventually leave, but not before taking Red Rover, the horse Jess has just traded to Mrs. Hudspeth. Jess is willing to return Lady, the horse he received in the exchange, but the widow insists that the trade is final.

13. West and R. Wyler, "Final Script," 153A.

14. Jessamyn West to Wyler, July 1955, Wyler Collection.

15. West and R. Wyler, "Final Script."

16. Wilson's script also had a more thematically satisfying ending than that used in the film, since it deals with the consequences of war. Eliza announces that Josh will return with Gard to the battlefront, where the war

is obviously still raging. Josh, who admits that he has "no stomach for killing," wants to contribute to the war effort as a stretcher-bearer. Michael Wilson, script, February 13, 1947, Wyler Papers.

17. Herman, *A Talent for Trouble*, 376.

18. Madsen, *William Wyler*, 326.

19. Wyler affidavit, March 1957, Wyler Papers.

20. Stuart Millar affidavit, March 1957, Wyler Papers.

21. Michael Wilson, versions of *Friendly Persuasion* script, September 20, 1946, and February 13, 1947, Wyler Papers.

22. Memo from Wyler to Freeman, April 8, 1954, Wyler Papers.

23. Letter from Wyler to *Los Angeles Times*, April 16, 1978.

24. "Some Summit Lore from Silver Screen," *New York Times*, May 31, 1988.

25. Herman, *A Talent for Trouble*, 379.

26. Ibid., 382.

27. Charlton Heston, *In the Arena: An Autobiography* (New York: Boulevard Books, 1997), 164.

28. Warshow, *The Immediate Experience*, 147.

29. Wyler to Robert Swink, May 16, 1958, Wyler Collection.

30. Heston, *In the Arena*, 169.

31. Madsen, *William Wyler*, 338.

32. In making *Ben-Hur*, Wyler became embroiled in yet another writing credit controversy, albeit without the political implications involved in *Friendly Persuasion*. Wyler wanted both Christopher Fry and Karl Tunberg to get credit for the screenplay, and according to Wyler, Tunberg initially agreed but changed his mind when the matter came before the Writers' Guild. Gore Vidal claims that Wyler wanted Fry to receive sole credit, but Fry thought Vidal should get co-credit. As with *Friendly Persuasion*, the guild ruled in favor of the original writer (Tunberg) and denied credit to the two other writers who had substantially revised the script. Because Wyler had campaigned against Tunberg's sole credit, the guild eventually blamed him for ruining the writer's chances at the Oscars—of the film's twelve nominations, it won everything except the award for Best Screenplay. While accepting his Best Actor award, Charlton Heston inflamed matters further by thanking Christopher Fry, which prompted the Writers' Guild to send an angry letter to Heston.

33. "Ben-Hur: The Making of an Epic," *Ben-Hur*, directed by William Wyler (1959; Santa Monica, Calif.: MCM/UA Home Video, 1993), VHS.

34. In the novel, Messala is merely wounded in the race, not killed. But he is also bankrupted as a result of his wager with Sheik Ilderim.

35. Madsen, *William Wyler*, 339.

16. Final Projects

1. Herman, *A Talent for Trouble*, 420.
2. Madsen, *William Wyler*, 366.
3. Ibid., 367.
4. "Movies: Wyler's Wiles," *Time*, June 18, 1965.
5. *Directed by William Wyler*.
6. The novel establishes that she is a virgin, despite her relationship with an older man.
7. The screenwriters eliminate Miranda's relationship with G.P. (George Paston), an artist who mistreats women. He tells Miranda that he has seduced many women like her and even married two of them. G.P. collects conquests and, in this regard, is similar to Freddie. The fact that Miranda worships him and admires his values is disquieting. Miranda's politics and class prejudices are also cut from the film's characterization. The screenwriters omit particulars from Freddie's past as well, including the death of his father when he was a child, the abandonment by his mother, and his subsequent rearing by an aunt who disparages his interest in butterfly collecting.
8. *Village Voice*, June 24, 1965.
9. *Saturday Review*, December 25, 1965.
10. Quoted in Herman, *A Talent for Trouble*, 436.
11. Laurents would later write one of Streisand's most famous film roles—Katie Morosky in *The Way We Were*.
12. Barbra Streisand, e-mail message to author, May 10, 2013.
13. Ibid.
14. The opening sequence is a total reimagining of the play, which opens in Fanny's dressing room. She enters the room and says, "Hello, Gorgeous," followed by the stage manager's announcement, "Half hour, Miss Brice."
15. The earlier script versions, which were written for Sidney Lumet by Sidney Buchman, eliminate the framing device: the first opens with Fanny asking Eddie Ryan, "You think beautiful girls are going to stay in style forever?" and ends with her singing "Nicky Arnstein, Nicky Arnstein—I'll never see him again"; the second opens with Mrs. Strakosh singing "If a Girl Isn't Pretty." Sidney Buchman, scripts for *Funny Girl*, September 23 and November 7, 1966, Wyler Papers.
16. Barbra Streisand, e-mail message to author, May 10, 2013. Herman, *A Talent for Trouble*, 447. During the shoot, Streisand and Sharif had a passionate affair, which ended when filming was over. Wyler channeled this emotion in Streisand for the final song.
17. Pauline Kael, *Going Steady* (New York: Bantam, 1971), 165.
18. The film added three songs not written for the show. In addition to "My Man," the writers included "Second Hand Rose" and "I'd Rather Be Blue." Seven songs from the original show were cut.

19. Quoted in Keith Garebian, *The Making of* Gypsy (Oakville, Ont.: Mosaic Press, 1998), 120.

20. Madsen, *William Wyler*, 390, 391.

21. Randall Riese, *Her Name Is Barbra* (New York: St. Martin's Paperbacks, 1994), 282.

22. Barbra Streisand, e-mail message to author, May 10, 2013.

23. Miller, *William Wyler: Interviews*, 34.

24. Telegram from Wyler to Darryl Zanuck, September 19, 1967, Wyler Collection.

25. Madsen, *William Wyler*, 397–98.

26. *Entertainment World*, April 10, 1970.

27. Herman, *A Talent for Trouble*, 452.

28. Jesse Hill Ford, *The Liberation of Lord Byron Jones* (Boston: Atlantic–Little Brown, 1965), 346.

29. Charles Champlin, *Los Angeles Times*, May 15, 1970.

30. Mark Harris, *Pictures at a Revolution* (New York: Penguin, 2008), 335.

31. *Time*, August 11, 1967.

32. Andrew Sarris, "Director of the Month," *Show* 1, no. 6 (June 1970): 14–15.

33. *Entertainment World*, April 10, 1970.

34. Madsen, *William Wyler*, 403.

35. Herman, *A Talent for Trouble*, 455.

36. Ibid., 467.

Selected Bibliography

Books and Articles

Affron, Charles. *Cinema and Sentiment*. Chicago: University of Chicago Press, 1982.

———. "Reading the Fiction of Nonfiction: William Wyler's *Memphis Belle*." *Quarterly Review of Film Studies* 7, no. 1 (Winter 1982): 53–59.

———. *Star Acting*. New York: E. P. Dutton, 1977.

Affron, Charles, and Jona Mirella Affron. *Best Years: Going to the Movies, 1945–1946*. New Brunswick, N.J.: Rutgers University Press, 2009.

Anderegg, Michael A. *William Wyler*. Boston: Twayne Publishers, 1979.

Armstrong, Richard. "*The Best Years of Our Lives*: Planes of Innocence and Experience." *Film International* 5, no. 6 (2007): 83–91.

Arnold, William. *Frances Farmer: Shadowland*. New York: Jove/HBJ Books, 1979.

Astor, Mary. *A Life in Film*. New York: Delacorte Press, 1967.

Baxter, John. *Hollywood in the Thirties*. New York: A. S. Barnes, 1968.

Bazin, André. *Bazin at Work: Major Essays and Reviews from the Forties and Fifties*. Edited and translated by Bert Cardullo and Alain Piette. New York: Routledge, 1997.

———. *What Is Cinema?* Edited and translated by Hugh Gray. Berkeley: University of California Press, 1967.

Behlmer, Rudy, ed. *Inside Warner Bros.: 1935–1951*. New York: Viking, 1985.

Bellour, Raymond, ed. *Le Cinema Américain: Analyses de Films*. Vol. 1. Paris: Flammarion, 1980.

Berg, A. Scott. *Goldwyn: A Biography*. New York: Ballantine, 1990.

Bergstrom, Janet. "Alternation, Segmentation, Hypnosis: Interview with Raymond Bellour." *Camera Obscura* 3–4 (Summer 1979): 71–103.

Biskind, Peter, *Seeing Is Believing*. New York: Pantheon, 1983.

Bluestone, George. *Novels into Film*. Berkeley: University of California Press, 1973.

———. "Word to Image: The Problem of the Filmed Novel." *Quarterly Review of Film, Radio, and Television* 11, no. 2 (Winter 1956): 171–80.

Bosworth, Patricia. *Montgomery Clift*. New York: Bantam, 1979.

Bowman, Barbara. *Master Space: Film Images of Capra, Lubitsch, Sternberg, and Wyler*. Westport, Conn.: Greenwood Press, 1992.

Brennan, Stephen C. "*Sister Carrie* Becomes *Carrie*." In *Nineteenth-Century American Fiction on Screen*, edited by R. Barton Palmer. Cambridge: Cambridge University Press, 2007.

Brownlowe, Kevin. "The Early Days of William Wyler." *Film* 37 (August 1963): 11–13.

Capra, Frank. *The Name above the Title*. New York: Macmillan, 1971.

Carey, Gary. "The Lady and the Director: Bette Davis and William Wyler." *Film Comment* 6, no. 3 (Fall 1970): 18–24.

Cartnal, Alan. "Wyler on Wyler." *Interview* 4 (March 1974): 10–11.

Coleman, Terry. *Olivier*. New York: Henry Holt, 2005.

Coursodon, Jean-Pierre. *American Directors*. Vol. 1. New York: McGraw-Hill, 1983.

Crowther, Bosley. *The Lion's Share*. New York: Dutton, 1957.

Davis, Bette. *The Lonely Life*. New York: G. P. Putnam Sons, 1962.

Dick, Bernard F. *Hellman in Hollywood*. Rutherford, N.J.: Fairleigh Dickinson University Press, 1982.

———. *The Star Spangled Screen*. Lexington: University Press of Kentucky, 1985.

Dixon, Wheeler Winston, ed. *American Cinema of the 1940s*. New Brunswick, N.J.: Rutgers University Press, 2006.

Doeckel, Ken. "William Wyler." *Films in Review* 22, no. 8 (October 1971): 468–84.

Dunne, Philip. *Take Two*. New York: McGraw-Hill, 1980.

Dworkin, Martin. "*The Desperate Hours* and the Violent Screen." *Shenandoah* 11, no. 2 (Winter 1960): 39–48.

Falk, Doris V. *Lillian Hellman*. New York: Frederick Ungar, 1978.

Fenin, George N., and William K. Everson. *The Western*. New York: Penguin, 1977.

Ferber, Edna. *Come and Get It*. Garden City, N.Y.: Doubleday, Doran, 1935.

Ford, Jesse Hill. *The Liberation of Lord Byron Jones*. Boston: Atlantic–Little Brown, 1965.

Fredericks, Ellsworth. "Photographing *The Friendly Persuasion*." *American Cinematographer* 37, no. 4 (April 1956): 216–17, 250–52.

French, Brandon. *On the Verge of Revolt: Women in American Films of the Fifties*. New York: Frederick Ungar, 1978.

Gassner, John, and Dudley Nichols. *Twenty Best Film Plays I & II*. New York: Garland, 1977.

Geist, Kenneth. "*Carrie*." *Film Comment* 6, no. 3 (Fall 1970): 25–27.

Giannetti, Louis. *Masters of the American Cinema*. Englewood Cliffs, N.J.: Prentice-Hall, 1981.

Gilman, Richard. *The Making of Modern Drama*. New York: Farrar, Straus & Giroux, 1975.

Goetz, Ruth, and Augustus Goetz. *The Heiress*. New York: Dramatists Play Service, 1975.

Griffin, Susan M., ed. *Henry James Goes to the Movies*. Lexington: University Press of Kentucky, 2002.

Griffith, Richard. *Samuel Goldwyn: The Producer and His Films*. New York: Museum of Modern Art Film Library, 1956.

———. "Wyler, Wellman, and Huston: Three Directors with a Past and a Future." *Films in Review* 1, no. 1 (February 1950): 1–5.

Grobel, Lawrence. *The Hustons*. New York: Avon Books, 1990.

Hanson, Curtis Lee. "William Wyler." *Cinema* 3, no. 5 (Summer 1967): 22–35.

Harris, Mark. *Pictures at a Revolution*. New York: Penguin, 2008.

Hayes, Richard. "*These Three*: The Influence of William Wyler and Gregg Toland on Lillian Hellman." *Film Literature Quarterly* 37, no. 3 (2009): 176–83.

Hellman, Lillian. *Four Plays by Lillian Hellman*. New York: Random House, 1972.

———. *Six Plays by Lillian Hellman*. New York: Vintage, 1979.

Herman, Jan. *A Talent for Trouble: The Life of Hollywood's Most Acclaimed Director, William Wyler*. New York: G. P. Putnam's Sons, 1995.

Heston, Charlton. *The Actor's Life: Journals 1956–1976*. Edited by Hollis Alpert. New York: E. P. Dutton, 1976.

———. "*Ben-Hur* Diaries." *Cinema* (California) 2, no. 2 (July 1964): 10–13, 29, 34.

———. *In the Arena*. New York: Boulevard Books, 1997.

———. "The Questions No One Asks about Willy." *Films and Filming* 4 no. 11 (August 1958): 9, 32.

———. "William Wyler." *Dialogue on Film* 1 (1972): 6–9.

Heston, Charlton, and Jean-Pierre Isbouts. *Charlton Heston's Hollywood*. New York: GT Publishing, 1998.

Higham, Charles. *Bette: The Life of Bette Davis*. New York: Macmillan, 1981.

———. *Hollywood Cameramen*. Bloomington: Indiana University Press, 1970.

———. "William Wyler." *Action* 8, no. 5 (September–October 1973): 14–22.

Higham, Charles, and Joel Greenberg. *Hollywood in the Forties*. New York: Zwemmer and Barnes, 1968.

Horner, Harry. "Designing *The Heiress*." *Hollywood Quarterly* 5, no. 1 (Fall 1950): 1–7.

Howard, Sidney. *Sinclair Lewis's Dodsworth*. New York: Harcourt, Brace, 1934.

Huston, John. *An Open Book*. New York: Knopf, 1980.

Isaacs, Hermine Rich. "William Wyler: Director with a Passion and a Craft." *Theater Arts* 31, no. 2 (February 1947): 21–24.

Jacobsen, Wolfgang, Helga Belach, and Norbert Grob. *William Wyler.* Berlin: Argon, 1996.

Kael, Pauline. *Going Steady.* New York: Bantam, 1971.

———. *Kiss Kiss Bang Bang.* New York: Bantam, 1971.

Kahn, Gordon. *Hollywood on Trial.* New York: Boni and Gaer, 1948.

Kantor, Bernard, Irwin R. Blacker, and Anne Kramer, eds. *Directors at Work.* New York: Funk and Wagnalls, 1970.

Kantor, MacKinlay. *Glory for Me.* New York: Coward-McCann, 1945.

Kazan, Elia. *A Life.* New York: Knopf, 1988.

Kern, Sharon. *William Wyler: A Guide to References and Resources.* Boston: G. K. Hall, 1984.

Kingsley, Sidney. *Five Prize Winning Plays.* Columbus: Ohio State University Press, 1995.

Klein, Michael, and Gillian Parker, eds. *The English Novel and the Movies.* New York: Frederick Ungar, 1981.

Koenig, Lester. "Gregg Toland Film-Maker." *Screenwriter* 3 (December 1947): 27–33.

Koppes, Clayton R., and Gregory D. Black. *Hollywood Goes to War.* Berkeley: University of California Press, 1990.

Kozloff, Sarah. *The Best Years of Our Lives.* London: Palgrave Macmillan (BFI Book), 2011.

———. "Wyler's Wars." *Film History: An International Journal* 20, no. 4 (2008): 456–73.

Langlois, Henri. *Hommage à William Wyler.* Paris: Cinématheque Française, 1965.

Leaming, Barbara. *Bette Davis: A Biography.* New York: Simon and Schuster, 1992.

Leenhardt, Roger. "À bas Ford / vive Wyler!" *L'Ecran francais* 146 (April 13, 1948).

Lennart, Isobel. *Funny Girl.* New York: Random House, 1964.

Lewis, Sinclair. *Dodsworth.* New York: Harcourt, Brace, 1929.

Lyon, Peter. "The Hollywood Picture." *Hollywood Quarterly* 3, no. 4 (Summer 1948): 341–61.

Madsen, Axel. *William Wyler: The Authorized Biography.* New York: Crowell, 1973.

Marcus, Daniel. "William Wyler's World War II Films and the Bombing of Civilian Populations." *Historical Journal of Film, Radio, and Television* 29, no. 1 (March 2009): 79–90.

Marton, Andrew. "*Ben-Hur*'s Chariot Race." *Films in Review* 11, no. 1 (January 1960): 27–32, 48.

Marx, Arthur. *Goldwyn: A Biography of the Man behind the Myth.* New York: W. W. Norton, 1976.

McBride, Joseph. *Frank Capra: The Catastrophe of Success.* New York: Simon and Schuster, 1992.

———. *Hawks on Hawks.* Berkeley: University of California Press, 1982.

McCarthy, Todd. *Howard Hawks: The Grey Fox of Hollywood.* New York: Grove Press, 1997.

Meyers, Jeffrey. *Gary Cooper: American Hero.* New York: Cooper Square Press, 1998.

Miller, Gabriel. *William Wyler: Interviews.* Jackson: University Press of Mississippi, 2010.

Mills, Pamela. "Wyler's Version of Brontë's Storms in *Wuthering Heights.*" *Literature Film Quarterly* 24, no. 4 (1996): 414–22.

Monroe, Dale. "William Wyler: The Appeal of L. B. Jones." *Entertainment World,* April 10, 1970, 19–20.

Morse, David. "*Carrie.*" *Brighton Film Review* 19 (April 1970): 10–11.

Niven, David. *The Moon's a Balloon.* New York: G. P. Putnam's Sons, 1972.

O'Connor, John E., and Martin A. Jackson. *American History/American Film: Interpreting the Hollywood Image.* New York: Frederick Ungar, 1979.

Orr, Christopher. "Authorship in the Hawks/Wyler Film, *Come and Get It.*" *Wide Angle* 6, no. 1 (1984): 20–26.

Palmer, R. Barton, ed. *Nineteenth-Century American Fiction on Screen.* Cambridge: Cambridge University Press, 2007.

Peary, Gerald, and Roger Shatzkin. *The Classic American Novel and the Movies.* New York: Frederick Ungar, 1977.

Pells, Richard H. *Radical Visions and American Dreams.* New York: Harper and Row, 1973.

Peters, Margot. *The House of Barrymore.* New York: Knopf, 1990.

Phillips, Gene D. *Exiles in Hollywood: Major European Film Directors in America.* Bethlehem, Pa.: Lehigh University Press, 1998.

———. "William Wyler." *Focus on Film* 24 (Spring 1976): 5–10.

Plimpton, George. *Writers at Work: The Paris Review Interviews,* 3rd ser. New York: Viking Press, 1967.

Reid, John Howard. "A Comparison of Size." *Films and Filming* 6, no. 6. (March 1960): 12, 31–32, 35.

———. "A Little Larger than Life." *Films and Filming* 6, no. 5 (February 1960): 9–10, 32.

———. "William Wyler—His Rise and Fall." *Film Guide* (Summer 1950): 4–10.

Reisz, Karel. "The Later Films of William Wyler." *Sequence* 13 (1951): 19–30.

Rice, Elmer. *Minority Report.* New York: Simon and Schuster, 1963.

———. *Seven Plays.* New York: Viking Press, 1950.

Riese, Randall. *Her Name Is Barbra.* New York: St. Martin's Paperbacks, 1994.

Rollyson, Carl. *Lillian Hellman: Her Legend and Her Legacy.* New York: St. Martin's Press, 1988.

Rorty, James. *Where Life Is Better.* New York: John Day/Reynal and Hitchcock, 1936.

Roud, Richard, et al. *William Wyler: An Index.* London: British Film Institute, 1958.

Sarris, Andrew. *The American Cinema.* New York: E. P. Dutton, 1968.

———. "Director of the Month." *Show* 1, no. 6 (June 1970): 14–15.

———. "William Wyler." *Film Culture* 28 (1963): 34.

Schorer, Mark. *Sinclair Lewis: An American Life.* New York: Dell, 1961.

Sherwood, Robert. *The Petrified Forest.* New York: Scribner's, 1935.

Shibuk, Charles. *An Index to the Films of William Wyler.* New York: Theodore Huff Memorial Film Society, 1957.

Sikov, Ed. *Dark Victory: The Life of Bette Davis.* New York: Henry Holt, 2007.

Slocombe, Douglas. "The Work of Gregg Toland." *Sequence* 8 (Summer 1949): 69–76.

Slotkin, Richard. *Gunfighter Nation.* New York: Harper Perennial, 1993.

Smith, Wendy. *Real Life Drama.* New York: Knopf, 1990.

Stevens, George, Jr., et al. "The Test of Time: William Wyler." *American Film* 1, no. 6 (April 1976): 4, 9, 13–14, 20, 22–23, 25, 27.

Stine, Whitney, with Bette Davis. *I'd Love to Kiss You: Conversations with Bette Davis.* New York: Pocket Books, 1990.

———. *Mother Goddam.* New York: Berkley Books, 1979.

The Story of the Making of Ben-Hur. New York: Random House, 1959.

Swindell, Larry. "A Life on Film." *American Film* 1, no. 6 (April 1976): 7–27.

Troyan, Michael. *A Rose for Mrs. Miniver.* Lexington: University Press of Kentucky, 2005.

Tuska, John, ed. *Close-up: The Hollywood Director.* Metuchen, N.J.: Scarecrow Press, 1978.

Wallis, Hal, and Charles Higham. *Starmaker: The Autobiography of Hal Wallis.* New York: Macmillan, 1980.

Warshow, Robert. *The Immediate Experience.* 1962. Reprint, New York: Athenaeum, 1970.

West, Jessamyn. "Hollywood Diary." *Ladies' Home Journal* 73 (November 1956): 70–71, 158–84.

———. *To See the Dream.* New York: Harcourt, Brace, 1957.

Whitcomb, John. "*Ben-Hur* Rides Again." *Cosmopolitan* 147 (December 1959): 26–29.

"William Wyler." *Film Reference.* Last modified 2012. http://filmreference.com/Directors-Ve-Y/Wyler-William.html.

Wood, Robin. *Howard Hawks.* Garden City, N.Y.: Doubleday, 1968.

Wright, William. *Lillian Hellman: The Image, the Woman.* New York: Ballantine, 1986.

Wyler, William. "Censorship through Fear." *Screenwriter* 3, no. 7 (December 1947): 20–21.

———. "Escape to Reality." *Liberty* 24, no. 1 (January 4, 1947): 16. Reprinted in *Picturegoer,* March 15, 1947, 8.

———. "Flying over Germany." *News Digest* 2, no. 13 (August 15, 1943): 25–26.

———. "Hand Tailored Films." *Hollywood Reporter* 132, no. 4 (November 12, 1954): sec. 2.

———. "'Heiress' Director Finds Character Conflicts Exciting." *New York Herald Tribune,* October 2, 1949, sec. 5, p. 3.

———. "A Letter from William Wyler." *Sequence* 8 (Summer 1949): 68–69.

———. "No Magic Wand." *Screenwriter* 2, no. 9 (February 1947): 1–14.

———. "Statement of Principles." *New York Times,* June 18, 1950, sec. 2, p. 5.

Audiovisual Material

Higham, Charles. "William Wyler Directs Bette Davis in *Jezebel.*" Columbia University Oral History Office. *Fathom: The Source for Online Learning.* Last modified 2002. http://www.fathom.com/feature/35675/.

Directed by William Wyler & The Love Trap. Tatge Productions, 1986. New York: Kino Video, 2002. DVD.

Manuscript Collections

Ruth and Augustus Goetz Papers. Wisconsin Historical Society, Madison, Wisconsin.

Samuel Goldwyn Papers. Margaret Herrick Library, Academy of Motion Picture Arts and Sciences, Los Angeles, California.

William Wyler Collection. Margaret Herrick Library, Academy of Motion Picture Arts and Sciences, Los Angeles, California.

William Wyler Papers, 1925–1975. Arts Library Special Collections, Young Research Library, UCLA.

Index

Screen Classics

Screen Classics is a series of critical biographies, film histories, and analytical studies focusing on neglected filmmakers and important screen artists and subjects, from the era of silent cinema to the golden age of Hollywood to the international generation of today. Books in the Screen Classics series are intended for scholars and general readers alike. The contributing authors are established figures in their respective fields. This series also serves the purpose of advancing scholarship on film personalities and themes with ties to Kentucky.

Series Editor

Patrick McGilligan

Books in the Series

Mae Murray: The Girl with the Bee-Stung Lips
Michael G. Ankerich

Hedy Lamarr: The Most Beautiful Woman in Film
Ruth Barton

Von Sternberg
John Baxter

The Marxist and the Movies: A Biography of Paul Jarrico
Larry Ceplair

Warren Oates: A Wild Life
Susan Compo

Jack Nicholson: The Early Years
Robert Crane and Christopher Fryer

Being Hal Ashby: Life of a Hollywood Rebel
Nick Dawson

John Gilbert: The Last of the Silent Film Stars
Eve Golden

Mamoulian: Life on Stage and Screen
David Luhrssen

My Life as a Mankiewicz: An Insider's Journey through Hollywood
Tom Mankiewicz and Robert Crane

William Wyler: The Life and Films of Hollywood's Most Celebrated Director
Gabriel Miller

Raoul Walsh: The True Adventures of Hollywood's Legendary Director
Marilyn Ann Moss

Some Like It Wilder: The Life and Controversial Films of Billy Wilder
Gene D. Phillips

Arthur Penn: American Director
Nat Segaloff

Claude Rains: An Actor's Voice
David J. Skal with Jessica Rains

Buzz: The Life and Art of Busby Berkeley
Jeffrey Spivak

Thomas Ince: Hollywood's Independent Pioneer
Brian Taves

Carl Theodor Dreyer and Ordet: *My Summer with the Danish Filmmaker*
Jan Wahl